THE CORRESPONDENCE OF

W.E.B. DU BOIS

VOLUME I   SELECTIONS, 1877–1934

W. E. B. Du Bois, 1907

THE CORRESPONDENCE OF

W. E. B. DU BOIS

VOLUME I   SELECTIONS, 1877–1934

EDITED BY HERBERT APTHEKER

UNIVERSITY OF MASSACHUSETTS PRESS—Amherst

Copyright © 1973 by the University of Massachusetts Press
Paperback edition with corrections, 1997
All rights reserved

Printed in the United States of America

LC 72-90496

ISBN 0-87023-131-6 (cloth); ISBN 1-55849-103-1 (pbk.)

Library of Congress Cataloging-in-Publication Data

Du Bois, William Edward Burghardt, 1868–1963.
  The correspondence of W. E. B. Du Bois.

  Includes bibliographical references.
  CONTENTS: v. 1. Selections, 1877–1934.—v. 2. Selections, 1934–1944.
—v. 3. Selections, 1944–1963.
  1. Du Bois, William Edward Burghardt, 1868–1963. 2. Afro-Americans—
Correspondence. 3. Intellectuals—United States—Correspondence. I. Aptheker,
Herbert, 1915–   ed,
E185.97.D73A4   1973   301.24'2'0924 [B]   72-90496

British Library Cataloguing in Publication data are available.

∞ The paper used in this publication meets the minimum requirements of the
American National Standard for Information Sciences—Permanence of Paper for
Printed Library Materials, ANSI Z39.48-1984.

GRATEFUL ACKNOWLEDGMENT is extended to the following for permission to print their letters: Nnambi Azikiwe; Arna Bontemps; Sterling A. Brown; Leonard C. Cartwright; John W. Davis; Earl B. Dickerson; Paul H. Douglas; St. Clair Drake; Shirley Graham Du Bois; Buell S. Gallagher; Ernest H. Gruening; Walter Lippmann; Rayford W. Logan; Mildred Scott Olmsted; A. Philip Randolph; George S. Schuyler; Clarence Senior; Louise A. Thompson Patterson; Robert C. Weaver; Roy Wilkins.

Grateful acknowledgment for permission to publish is also extended to John H. Sengstacke for the letter of Robert S. Abbott; Eleanor Anderson the letter of Sherwood Anderson; Newton D. Baker III for the letters of Newton D. Baker; Elizabeth Brandeis Rauschenbush for the letter of Louis D. Brandeis; Kathleen W. Green and Theresa W. Browne for the letter of William M. Brewer; Francis Dwight Buell and the Foreign Policy Association for the letter of Raymond L. Buell; Margo Ann Berdeshivsky for the letter of V. F. Calverton; Fisk University Library for the letters of Charles W. Chesnutt; Hardy C. Dillard for the letter of James H. Dillard; the Historical Society of Pennsylvania for the letter of W. E. B. Du Bois to Jacob C. White and the letters of Ellis P. Oberholtzer; Catherine E. Harris for the letter of Edwin R. Embree; Mrs. Lehr Fess for the letter of Lehr Fess; Wilbur Collection, Guy W. Bailey Library, University of Vermont for the letter of Dorothy Canfield Fisher; Carolina M. Bell for the letter of Joseph B. Foraker; Johns Hopkins University Archives for the letters of Daniel C. Gilman, Frank J. Goodnow, and Francis G. Peabody; Moorland-Spingarn Collection, Howard University for the letters of Francis J. Grimké and Jessie Moorland; the Estate of W. C. Handy for the letter of W. C. Handy; Ellen Knowles Harcourt for the letters of Alfred Harcourt; Encyclopaedia Britannica for the letters of Franklin H. Hooper; John Hope II and Edward S. Hope for the letters of John Hope; the Estate of Langston Hughes for the letter of Langston Hughes; Alexander R. James for the letters of Henry James and William James; Francis C. Jameson for the letter of J. Franklin Jameson; Grace N. Johnson for the letters of James Weldon Johnson; George B. Murphy for the letter of William N. Jones; Helen Hall Kellogg for the letter of Paul U. Kellogg; the Estate of Oliver La Farge for the letter of Oliver La Farge; the State Historical Society of Wisconsin for the letter of Robert M. La Follette; the Estate of Sinclair Lewis for the letters of Sinclair Lewis; William H. Lewis, Jr. for the letters of William H. Lewis; Robert Loeb for the letter of Jacques Loeb; Malcolm MacDonald for the letters of J. Ramsay MacDonald; Hope McKay Virtue for the letters of Claude McKay; the Mercantile Safe Deposit and Trust Company for the letters of H. L. Mencken; Collection of American Literature, Yale University Library for the letter of Eugene O'Neill; Theodore O. Kingsbury for the letters of Mary White Ovington; Arthur W. Page, Jr. for the letter of Walter Hines Page; Arthur B. Perry for the letter of Bliss Perry; William Pickens II for the letter of William Pickens; Paul Robeson, Jr. for the letter of Eslanda Goode Robeson; Raymond S. Rubinow for the letter of Isaac M. Rubinow; Grant Sanger for the letter of Margaret Sanger; Edward M. M. Warburg for the letter of Jacob H. Schiff; Eustace Seligman for the letter of Edwin R. A. Seligman; David Sinclair for the letters of Upton Sinclair; Mildred Coy for the letter of Agnes Smedley; Amy Spingarn for the letters of Mr. and Mrs. Joel E. Spingarn; Arthur M. Storey for the letter of Moorfield Storey; Marjorie Content Toomer for the letter of Jean Toomer; Gerard W. van Loon for the letters of Hendrik Willem van Loon; Donald C. Gallup for the letter of Carl Van Vechten; Henry H. Villard for the letters of Oswald Garrison Villard; Rosamond Walling Tirana for the letters of William E. Walling; James P. Warbasse, Jr. for the letter of James P. Warbasse; Portia Washington Pittman for the letters of Booker T. Washington; George Philip Wells for the letter of H. G. Wells; Alfreda M. Duster for the letter of Ida B. Wells-Barnett; Dwight L. Wilbur for the letter of Ray Lyman Wilbur; Mary V. Wissler for the letter of Clark Wissler; Charles H. Wesley for the letters of Carter G. Woodson.

CONTENTS

	Introduction	xxiii

Student, 1877–1894

1877 March	To Grandmother: First letter	3
1883 July	To Mother: New England journey	3
1886 Feb	To Rev. Scudder: Life at Fisk University	5
1887 Oct	To Harvard University: Admission inquiry	6
1890 Feb	To George W. Cable: Appreciation of Cable speech	7
Spring	To Harvard Academic Council: Scholarship application	7
Nov	From L. A. Bowers: Fisk class letter	8
1891 Feb	From William James: Invitation to supper	10
1890–1892	Correspondence with Rutherford B. Hayes, Francis G. Peabody, Daniel C. Gilman: Slater Fund loan	10
1892 Sept	To Sunday School: Report on Germany	19
1892–1894	Correspondence with D. C. Gilman, Adolph Wagner, G. Schmoller: Slater Fund, reports and recommendations	20

Teacher-Scholar, 1894–1904

1894 Summer	Correspondence with Booker T. Washington and S. T. Mitchell: Job seeking	37
1895 June	To D. C. Gilman: Slater Fund loan repayment	38
Sept	To Booker T. Washington: Atlanta Exposition speech	39
1896 June–Aug	From C. C. Harrison: University of Pennsylvania job	40
1897 May	To Carroll D. Wright: Plan for study of Negro industrial development	41

1898	Oct	To Jacob C. White: *The Philadelphia Negro*	43
1900	March	From Booker T. Washington: Superintendent of Schools, Washington, D.C.	44
	March	To S. T. Hardwick: Segregation on Southern Railway	45
1902	July	From Booker T. Washington: Du Bois's *Outlook* essay	46
	Summer	From Bliss Perry, Horace Bumstead, W. P. Thirkield: "Of the Training of Black Men"	47
	Sept	From William Monroe Trotter: Invitation to speak in Boston	49
1903	Feb	From S. M. Sexton and James A. Cable: Atlanta study of Negro workers	50
	Feb–Nov	Correspondence with Kelly Miller and Booker T. Washington: Carnegie Conference	53
	May	From Ida B. Wells-Barnett: *Souls of Black Folk*	55
	June	From Charles W. Chesnutt: National Negro Journal	56
	July	From Kittredge Wheeler: Industrial education	58
	Oct	From J. Douglas Wetmore: *Souls*	60
	Nov–Feb '04	Correspondence with Ellis Paxson Oberholtzer: Genesis of *John Brown*	61
	Dec	From Jessie Fauset: Student request for assistance	66
1904	Jan	Correspondence with George Foster Peabody and Horace Bumstead: William Monroe Trotter	67
	Jan	Exchange with F. A. McKenzie: Indian unity	71
	Jan–Feb	Correspondence with Richard Lloyd Jones: *Collier's Weekly* article	72
	March	Exchange with Walter Francis Willcox: "The Future of the Negro Race in America"	74
	June	From Casely Hayford: *Souls*	76
	June–Nov	Correspondence with Mary White Ovington: Negro poverty in New York; "Credo"	76
	Nov	Exchange with Samuel H. Comings: *Souls*	79
	Nov	Exchange with Isaac M. Rubinow: Socialism	81
	Dec	Exchange with Geraldine L. Trotter: Reprinting of "Credo"	82

Dec	Exchange with Margaretta Atkinson: *Souls;* advice to a Negro student	83

Organizer-Editor-Author, 1905–1920

1905	Jan	From Francis J. Grimké: "Credo"	91
	Jan	Correspondence with Kelly Miller, Bishop Alexander Walters: Projected meeting with Theodore Roosevelt	92
	Feb	From Jessie Fauset: Thanks	94
	Feb–April	Correspondence with William Hayes Ward, Oswald Garrison Villard, William Monroe Trotter: Booker T. Washington's control of Black press	96
	March	To Archibald H. Grimké and Kelly Miller: Committee of Twelve	105
	March	From Max Weber: *Souls*	106
	April	Exchange with Robert M. La Follette: Invitation to Atlanta University	107
	April	Correspondence with Jacob H. Schiff: National Negro journal	108
	April–Oct	Exchange with Albert Bushnell Hart: Du Bois and Booker T. Washington	110
	May	Exchange with Theodore Roosevelt: Invitation to Atlanta University	111
	Aug	To Archibald H. Grimké and Kelly Miller: Niagara Movement	112
	Nov	Correspondence with Walter Hines Page: Works in progress	113
	Nov	From Clark Wissler: Negro anthropology and ethnology	115
	Dec	From James Weldon Johnson: Niagara Movement	115
1906	Feb–March	Exchange with Horace Curzon Plunkett: *Souls* and Ireland	116
	April	To T. Nelson Baker and the *Congregationalist:* Criticism of an article	117
	May	From Mary White Ovington: News of work in New York City	118

	May	To Andrew Carnegie: Support sought for Atlanta Conferences	121
	Oct	From Edwin R. A. Seligman: "A Litany of Atlanta"	123
1907	Jan	To William P. Pickett: Colonization	123
	Feb	From Hallie E. Queen: *Souls* and Cornell University	125
	March	To M. B. Marston: Women and Negro reformers	127
	March	To Yolande Du Bois: News	127
	March–April	Correspondence with S. S. McClure: *McClure's Magazine* and race issue	128
	April–May	Exchange with Samuel H. Bishop: American Church Institute for Negroes	130
	April	From Mary White Ovington: News	131
	May	Exchange with William James: Projected trip; notes on work	133
	Aug	From Henry James: Plans for visit	134
	Oct	Exchange with Joseph B. Foraker: Niagara and Brownsville incident	135
	Oct	To Alfred Vollum: Federal aid to Negro education	135
	Oct	Exchange with Moorfield Storey and Erving Winslow: "After the Battle of Mt. Dajo"	136
	Dec	Exchange with Samuel May, Jr.: Industrial education and philanthropy	138
1908	Feb	From Carter G. Woodson: Thesis on Negro Church	140
	March	Exchange with William Hayes Ward: Negro voting in Atlanta	141
	Oct	From David R. Wallace: Resignation from Niagara	142
	Nov–Dec	Correspondence with Charles Francis Adams: "The Solid South"	142
1909	March	To Guarantors of the *Horizon:* National Negro journal	144
	April–May	To Edward W. Blyden and Mr. Williams: Encyclopedia Africana	146
	June	From William English Walling: Committee of the National Negro Congress	147
	July	Exchange with J. R. L. Diggs: Studies of Reconstruction	150

	Sept–Oct	Exchange with W. D. Hooper, O. G. Villard: *Souls*	152
	Nov–Dec	Correspondence with Paul Elmer More, O. G. Villard: The *Nation* and *John Brown*	154
1910	Jan	Exchange with John Hope: Friendship and Negro politics	165
	Feb	Exchange with Richard T. Greener: *John Brown*	168
	June	Exchange with William English Walling: Founding of the NAACP	169
	June–July	Correspondence with J. Franklin Jameson: Capitalization of "Negro"	171
1911	Feb	To Dr. Ettie Sayer: English trip and Booker T. Washington	173
1912	Feb	From Edward T. Devine: Commission on Industrial Relations	176
	March	From J. Max Barber: *Voice of the Negro*	176
	March–April	Exchange with William T. Brewster: *The Negro*	177
	April	To Harry Pace: Job on *Crisis*	179
	May	From Edward H. Clement: *Crisis*	180
	Nov	To Carolina M. Dexter: Resignation from the Socialist party	180
1913	March	To O. G. Villard: *Crisis* and the NAACP Board	181
	July	From J. E. Kwegyir Aggrey: Request to study under Du Bois	182
	Oct	From Robert T. Lincoln: Emancipation Proclamation celebration	186
	Dec	From Paul U. Kellogg: "Black Man's Program for 1914"	186
1914	Jan–Feb	Exchange with J. Ramsay MacDonald: Bedales School for Yolande Du Bois	187
	April	Exchange with Mary White Ovington: *Crisis* and the NAACP Board	188
	April	Exchange with C. G. Kidder: Robert C. Ogden	194
	April	From Ernest H. Gruening: "The Philosophy of Mr. Dole"	195
	May	From Jacques Loeb: "Heredity and Racial Inferiority"	195

May–June	Exchange with Pauline Schneider: *Souls*	196
July	From Benjamin R. Tillman: Negroes and Reconstruction	197
Aug–Sept	Correspondence with Upton Sinclair: Negro slave songs	198
Oct	Exchange with Joel E. Spingarn: Race and NAACP leadership	200
Oct	To Yolande Du Bois: Advice in her new school	207
Nov	From Richard H. Pratt: *Crisis*	209
1915 April	Exchange with Harriot Stanton Blatch: Elizabeth Cady Stanton centennial	209
June	From John Hope: Du Bois's work	210
Aug	To Woodrow Wilson: United States intervention in Haiti	211
Dec	From Miner Chipman: *Souls*	213
1916 Jan	From Walter Lippmann: Capitalization of "Negro"	214
April	Exchange with Marcus Garvey: Garvey's first public lecture	214
May–June	Exchange with Paul H. Hanus: Ideals of the Hampton Institute	215
Oct	Correspondence with Woodrow Wilson, Joseph Tumulty, O. G. Villard: Race and 1916 election	217
Nov	To James Weldon Johnson: NAACP job offer	219
Nov	From H. L. Mencken: "Dreiser Protest"	220
1917 Jan	Exchange with Carrie W. Clifford: Du Bois's health	221
June	From Charles Young: Forced retirement from army	222
Aug	Exchange with Garrett Distributing Company: Cigar promotion	223
Dec	Exchange with Newton D. Baker: Negroes in the army	224
1918 Feb	Exchange with Frank A. Hosmer: Du Bois's fiftieth birthday	225
July	To NAACP Board of Directors: Army captaincy	227

	July–Aug	Correspondence with Byron Gunner, L. M. Hershaw: *Crisis* editorial on the war	228
	Oct	From Joel E. Spingarn: Report from the French front	230
	Nov	From Ephraim D. Adams: Negroes at Stanford University	231
	Nov	From Joseph P. Tumulty: Pan-African Congress	232
1919	Jan	F. P. Schoonmaker to Intelligence Officers: Du Bois in France	232
	Feb	From Walter Lippmann: Pan-African Congress	233
	May	From James A. Martin: Negro self-defense in Georgia	233
	Aug	From William A. Hewlett: Black soldier in France	234
	Oct	From Petruchio E. Moore: *Brownies' Book*	235
	Nov	From Novella Clark: Response to a *Crisis* notice	236
1920	May	Exchange with Newton D. Baker: Segregation in the National Guard	236

National and International Leader: The Era of Postwar 'Prosperity,' 1920-1929

1920	July	Exchange with Marcus Garvey: Universal Negro Improvement Association	245
1921	Jan	From Dorothy Canfield Fisher: *The Brimming Cup*	246
	March–April	Exchange with William Pickens: NAACP field work	247
	May–June	Exchange with F. E. DeFrantz: Segregated high schools	249
	June–July	Exchange with Charles Evans Hughes: Pan-African Congress	250
	July	From John H. Owens: Socialism and the American Negro	252
	Dec	To Sidney Hollander: Black soldiers in World War I	254
	Dec	To Yolande Du Bois: News of a party	255
1922	Jan	Exchange with Thomas S. Stribling: *Birthright*	256

	June	From Richard E. Enright: Harlem Fair-Play League	257
	Dec	Exchange with *Saturday Evening Post:* Race chauvinism	258
1923	Jan	To Charles Evans Hughes: Liberia; Garvey movement	260
	Jan	From Robert S. Abbott: Politics and race	262
	Jan	From Charles E. Russell: Book on the Philippines	262
	Jan	Exchange with William A. Domingo: Marcus Garvey	263
	April	To Richard E. Enright: Park improvement	264
	April	Exchange with Franklin C. Lewis: The "larger questions"	265
	June	To Walter White: Reflections on Booker T. Washington	266
	July	Exchange with Frank R. Crosswaith: *Crisis* and the Socialist party	267
	July	Exchange with Ida May Reynolds: Marcus Garvey	271
	July	Exchange with J. A. Walden: Jim Crow schools	272
	July–Aug	Exchange with Annie H. Howe: Tuskegee veterans' hospital	273
	Aug	To Mrs. E. A. Duffield: Defense of Langston Hughes's poetry	276
	Sept–Nov	From J. Ramsay MacDonald, H. G. Wells: Trip to England	276
	Oct	From William H. Lewis: Du Bois's appointment to Liberia	277
1924	Jan–July	Correspondence with Charles D. B. King: Liberia	279
	March	Exchange with Ellen Winsor: *Crisis* and non-resistance	283
	March	From Ernestine Rose: Schomburg Collection	285
	April	Exchange with James Weldon Johnson: NAACP annual conference	286
	July	From James C. Jackson: American Negro in Russia	289
	July	Correspondence with Hendrik Willem van Loon: Story for *Crisis*	290
	July	To Joel E. Spingarn: Note on NAACP affairs	291

	Aug	Exchange with G. Victor Cools: La Follette campaign	293
	Sept	From Eugene O'Neill: *Crisis* contest	294
	Sept–Oct	Exchange with Jean Toomer: Work for *Crisis*	295
	Oct	From Lambert M. Terry: "The Dilemma of the Negro"	296
	Nov	From John Hope: National election; Morehouse College; friendship	297
	Nov	To N. B. Brascher: Fisk University	299
1925	Jan	To Burton J. Hendrick: Walter Hines Page	300
	Feb	Exchange with Margaret Sanger: Statement on birth control	301
	Feb	Exchange with Edwin Seaver: Speech on Philippine independence	302
	Feb	Exchange with Joel E. Spingarn: Troutbeck Leaflets	303
	Feb	Exchange with James P. Warbasse: Cooperatives in Harlem	305
	Feb	From James W. Ford: Experiences at Fisk University	306
	Feb	From Almyra Randall: Du Bois Community High School	308
	Feb–March	Correspondence with Joseph B. Glenn: Catholic Church and Negroes	309
	March	To John Hope: Carter G. Woodson for Spingarn Medal	312
	March–April	Exchange with R. H. Athearn: YMCA and Negroes	312
	April	From W. C. Handy: *Blues: An Anthology*	313
	May	From W. R. Castle, Jr.: Du Bois's appointment to Liberia	313
	June	From Agnes Smedley: Lynching	315
	Aug	From Charles W. Chesnutt: *Crisis* contest	316
	Aug	From P. B. Young: NAACP and Marcus Garvey	317
	Sept	Exchange with A. Philip Randolph: Brotherhood of Sleeping Car Porters	319
	Oct	From Claude McKay: Poems for *Crisis*	320

[xvi] Contents

Oct–Nov	Exchange with Firestone Tire and Rubber Co.: Liberian rubber plantations	320
Oct–Nov	Exchange with Carl Van Vechten: *The Wooings of Jezebel Pettyfer*	324
Nov	Exchange with Frank J. Goodnow: Segregation at Johns Hopkins University	326
Nov–Dec	Exchange with Abram L. Harris, Jr.: New Negro college	327
Nov–Dec	Exchange with Roland Hayes: Carnegie Hall concert	328
Nov–Feb '26	Correspondence with Sinclair Lewis: Negro literature	329
1926 Feb–March	Exchange with Ben N. Azikiwe: Publishing inquiry	331
Feb–March	From David Belasco: *Lulu Belle*	332
March	Exchange with Sydney Strong: 'Souls of All Folks"	333
March	From Kathryn M. Johnson: Visit to Tuskegee Institute	334
March–April	Exchange with Ferdinand Johnson: Residential segregation	335
May	Exchange with Gifford Pinchot: 150th anniversary of the Declaration of Independence	336
June–July	Correspondence with William E. Borah: Negro rights	338
no date	From Sherwood Anderson: Negro art	342
Oct	From Charles W. Chesnutt: *Crisis* contest	343
Oct	From Louis F. Post: European trip	344
Oct	Correspondence with Arna Bontemps: *Crisis* poetry award	344
1927 March–April	Exchange with Sterling A. Brown: Work for *Crisis*	346
April	From Havelock Ellis: Du Bois visit	347
April	Exchange with Fannie Goldstein: George W. Forbes	347
April	From Tillman Jones: Land stealing in Mississippi	349
May	To H. B. Hayden: Reply to racist statements	350
May	Exchange with Jesse E. Moorland: Alain Locke and Howard University	352
May–June	Exchange with Ralph J. Bunche: Job seeking	353

	May	From Clement G. Morgan: George W. Forbes	355
	July	Exchange with Louis A. Carter: *Crisis* "pacifist-bolshevic doctrines"	355
	Aug	From J. Max Barber: Race murder in Mississippi	358
	Aug–Sept	Exchange with James M. Jones: Separate Negro state	358
	Oct	Correspondence with "a loyal Hamptonian" and Louise A. Thompson: Student strike	360
	Nov	Exchange with Bernice E. Brand: Questions on race answered	364
	Nov	Exchange with Rockefeller Foundation: History of Negro in World War I	365
	Dec	Exchange with H. L. Mencken: Voting in the South	368
	Dec	To Mrs. M. V. Boutté: Proposed birthday celebration	369
	Dec	From A. Philip Randolph: Thanks for help	371
1928	Jan	Exchange with Amy Spingarn: Ways to encourage Negro writers	371
	Feb	From Langston Hughes: Poems in *Crisis*	374
	June–Aug	Correspondence with Claude McKay: *Home to Harlem*	374
	Aug	Exchange with Richmond Barthé: Guggenheim Scholarship	376
	Sept	Exchange with Victor F. Calverton: *Anthology of American Negro Literature*	377
	Sept–Oct	Exchange with L. C. Cartwright: *Lantern*	379
	Oct	From George S. Schuyler: *Dark Princess*	382
	Dec	Exchange with Margaret Wade Deland: Negro politicians	383
1929	Jan	Exchange with Robert P. Sims: Nominee for Secretary of Labor	385
	Jan	To the *People:* Lajpat Rai	386
	Jan	From Louis D. Brandeis: Regrets	386
	Jan	Correspondence with Herbert Putnam and O. G. Villard: Discrimination in Library of Congress cafeteria	387

[xviii] Contents

Feb	Exchange with Algernon Lee: Negroes and the Socialist party	388
Feb–March	Correspondence with L. P. Dudley and F. H. Hooper: *Encyclopedia Britannica* article	390
March	Exchange with Quincy Ewing: Article on Southern Negroes	400
April	Correspondence with Alexander M. Bing: Planned residential segregation	401
Feb–May	Exchange with Mahatma Gandhi: Message to American Negroes	402
May	Exchange with Raymond L. Buell: Report on Haiti	403
July	From Amiya C. Chakravartz and Rabindranath Tagore: Message to American Negroes	404
June–Aug	Correspondence with Devere Allen: League for Independent Political Action	405
Oct	From Clarence Darrow: Religion	408
Dec	Correspondence with William J. Cooper, Rufus W. Weaver, Ray Lyman Wilbur, Florence Kelley: Advisory Committee on National Illiteracy	409
Dec	From Anna J. Cooper: Study on Reconstruction needed	411

National and International Leader: The Depression and Resignation from the NAACP, 1930–1934

1930 Jan	To Lillian A. Alexander: People's College	415
Jan	From Ben N. Azikiwe: British atrocity in Africa	415
Feb	To Ferdinand Q. Morton: Discrimination in New York Public Library	416
Feb	Exchange with Edward P. Clarke: *Crisis* and organized labor	418
Feb	Exchange with Paul H. Douglas: League for Independent Political Action	419
March	From Rayford W. Logan: Capitalization of "Negro"	420
March	To Mordecai Johnson: "Education and Work"	420
April–May	Exchange with Kathleen Simon: *Slavery*	422

	May	To New York Telephone Co., Great Atlantic and Pacific Tea Co.: Employment discrimination	423
	May	To Rev. Mdolomba: Movement in South Africa	424
	May	Exchange with William E. King: Negro Gold Star Mothers	425
	June	To Kirby Page: Reflections on the world war	425
	July	From Roy Wilkins: Business managership of *Crisis*	426
	July	Exchange with Eslanda Goode Robeson: News from England	427
	Aug	Exchange with J. G. St. Clair Drake: Student life at Hampton Institute	429
	Dec	Exchange with Mary White Ovington: *Crisis* and NAACP Board	430
	Dec	Exchange with Robert L. Vann: NAACP presidency	431
1931	Jan	From Soren A. Mathiasen: Pocono People's College	433
	Jan–Feb	Exchange with Robert C. Weaver: Thesis on industrial education of Negroes	434
	Jan–Feb	Exchange with Buell G. Gallagher: Advice on interracial work	436
	Feb	Exchange with Oliver La Farge: *Crisis* literary contest	437
	April–May	Exchange with Edwin R. Embree: *Brown America: The Story of a New Race*	438
	May	From Simeon D. Fess, George W. Norris: Future of the Negro in American politics	440
	Sept	Exchange with John W. Davis: Negroes in the depression	441
	Sept–Oct	Correspondence with Alfred Harcourt: *Black Reconstruction*	442
	Oct	Exchange with Albert Einstein: Race prejudice	444
	Oct	Exchange with John D. Marshall: Cleveland Blacks and the depression	445
	Nov–Dec	Exchange with James H. Dillard: Encyclopedia of the Negro	447
1932	Jan–Feb	Exchange with Carter G. Woodson: Encyclopedia of the Negro	448

Jan–March	Correspondence with Mildred Scott Olmsted: Race and reform	449
March	Exchange with Elizabeth Nutting: Segregated education	452
April	From Tom Mooney, Anna Mooney: Lynching article request	454
May	Exchange with S. L. Smith: How to promote knowledge of Negro achievements	456
July–Aug	Exchange with L. F. Strittmater: Tactics for Negro liberation	458
Aug–Sept	Exchange with Clarence Senior: Negroes and socialism	461
Sept	To Henry H. Proctor: Herbert Hoover	463
Oct	From Earl B. Dickerson: Franklin D. Roosevelt	463
Nov	Exchange with Ben N. Azikiwe: Marcus Garvey and Liberia	464
1933 May	To David de Sola Pool: Communists	466
July	Exchange with William L. Hansberry: Notes on work	466
Oct–Dec	Exchange with William N. Jones: Interracial work in Baltimore	467
1934 Jan	Exchange with Abram L. Harris: Negro lecture forum; tactics	470
Jan	Exchange with Harry E. Davis: Du Bois and NAACP	474
Jan	To Walter White: NAACP and segregation	475
Feb	Exchange with George Vaughan: Spiritual "awakening"	477
May–June	To NAACP Board of Directors: Resignations	478
June–July	Exchange with Owen R. Lovejoy: On Du Bois's resignation	481
June	Exchange with Shirley Graham: Tribute and thanks	482
	Index	485

ILLUSTRATIONS

W. E. B. Du Bois, 1907	*frontispiece*
Mary Sylvina Burghardt Du Bois with her infant son, William	30
Du Bois with his high school graduating class, 1884	30
W. E. B. Du Bois, age nineteen	31
Fisk University graduating class of 1888	32
Du Bois with other graduation speakers, Harvard, 1890	33
Du Bois with his University of Berlin classmates, ca. 1894	34
1897 family photograph	86
Final manuscript page of *The Souls of Black Folk*	87
Du Bois spending a quiet half hour, 1905	88
Booker T. Washington	88
The Niagara Movement, 1905	89
Atlanta University faculty and staff, 1906	90
Du Bois at an early Niagara Movement meeting	90
Du Bois and Clement G. Morgan, 1907	160
Mrs. Nina Gomer Du Bois, 1910	161
Mary White Ovington, 1909	162
William English Walling	162
Du Bois in his office at Atlanta University, 1909	163
Crisis office, ca. 1914	163
First Amenia Conference, August 1916	240
1917 NAACP parade protesting lynching and mob violence	240
Oswald Garrison Villard	241
Joel E. Spingarn	242
James Weldon Johnson, 1920	243
Du Bois in 1920 on his annual Maine vacation	244
Yolande Du Bois	394

Tuskegee Institute postcard: portrait of Du Bois   395
Members of the Third Pan-African Congress, May 1923   395
1924 sketch of Du Bois   396
Mr. and Mrs. Du Bois with James Weldon Johnson   396
W. E. B. Du Bois, late 1920s   397

INTRODUCTION

THE FAMILY and friends of William Edward Burghardt Du Bois recognized even in the young boy an extraordinary potential. Du Bois himself, while still in high school, felt that he might make significant contributions toward the advancement of his people. Possibly for this reason he began systematically to preserve his papers and letters before he had reached his twentieth year, a habit he maintained until his death at ninety-five. He saved literally everything—menus, train tickets, tourist cards, leaflets—as well as letters received and copies of letters sent. He was a most conscientious and prompt correspondent; rare are the letters to which he did not reply and rarer still the replies of which he did not retain a copy.

The general scope of Du Bois's public life may indicate the extent of his correspondence. He was a student at Fisk, Harvard, and the University of Berlin for ten years; a faculty member at Wilberforce University, the University of Pennsylvania, and Atlanta University for over twenty-five; the author of nineteen books of history, sociology, anthropology, and fiction and the editor of eighteen additional titles; a contributor of weekly columns to leading Black newspapers for more than twenty years, and of hundreds of articles and reviews to publications throughout the world. Over four decades, he edited five magazines (the *Moon*, the *Horizon*, the *Crisis*, the *Brownies' Book*, and *Phylon*); again over four decades, he was a founder and leader of the Niagara Movement, the National Association for the Advancement of Colored People, and the Pan-African Movement. He was, additionally, a source of inspiration to the Black intelligentsia in the United States; a progenitor and participant in the so-called Harlem Renaissance of the 1920s; a staunch opponent of racism, colonialism, and imperialist war; an advocate of independent political activity for the Afro-American people; and, for over half a century, an adherent of socialism.

Toward the latter part of 1946, Dr. Du Bois indicated to me that he would be pleased if I would undertake the editing of his letters, papers, and published works. By spring 1947, appeals calling for relevant letters were published in such periodicals as the *Crisis* and the *New York Times;* correspondence with and visits to various university and commercial publishers began later that year. A few indicated some interest, but with the Cold War, hostility to the unceasing anti-war and anti-racist leadership of Du Bois (culminating in indictment, trial, and acquittal early in the 1950s), the onset of McCarthyism, and my own notoriety, it became increasingly clear by the end of the 1950s and early 1960s that the project could not then be launched.

[xxiv] Introduction

Even so, work on his papers did not stop. When Dr. and Mrs. Du Bois accepted President Nkrumah's invitation to be the guests of Ghana while Du Bois assumed direction of the Encyclopedia Africana (a project he had conceived back in 1909), he had his correspondence placed in my custody. This transfer was made in the summer of 1961; and for years thereafter my wife and I labored to arrange these tens of thousands of documents and letters in chronological order and to master their contents. Individuals, libraries, and archives supplemented the collection as efforts continued to secure the wherewithal for publication.

There were hints of eventual success before Du Bois's death in August 1963; he had assured me throughout the earlier period that at some point the project would become feasible and had rejected the suggestion that its feasibility might be enhanced if a less "controversial" individual were to be the editor.

Details of efforts with various publishing houses and governmental and private funding institutions need not be given here. What is important is that Du Bois persisted in his advocacy of the project, and that after his death Mrs. Du Bois continued that advocacy; with that encouragement, it was not possible for us to do otherwise than to persevere. Now, a decade after his death, his correspondence and unpublished papers are beginning to appear in published form and—under other auspices—all of his previously published writings will reappear in what is hoped to be a definitive edition.

The letters, after their collation and arrangement, were selected to fit the limitations of two large volumes. The major decision to concentrate upon Du Bois's historical dimensions excluded practically all personal correspondence. Then, in the correspondence having significant historical and public quality, in each case a representative letter was chosen and all correspondence essentially repetitious omitted. These, and, of course, editorial judgment concerning the relative significance of the letters, were the basic principles of selection. Du Bois's own letters did not raise questions of libel or even insult as possible grounds for exclusion. However, he was the recipient from time to time—as a public and militant Black figure in the United States is bound to be—of obscene and disgusting letters, usually unsigned. Such letters, with rare exceptions, have been excluded, as have letters suggesting mental instability that Du Bois filed under the term "curious."

Since neither Dr. nor Mrs. Du Bois ever suggested any form of exclusion, nor asked to examine the manuscript, the faults of this volume in selection, preparation, footnoting, and introductions belong solely to me.

All the letters included are published in full; no substantive change of any kind has been made. They have been grouped in five sections for the convenience of the reader. Misspellings and other slips have usually been corrected, especially in the case of Du Bois's own dictated letters, but idiosyncracies in the spelling of personal names have been retained. The publishers have included Du Bois's name for clarity after each of his letters; his signature reached its characteristic form, "W. E. B. Du Bois," by 20 October 1887. Significant in the choice of signature was his inclusion of the initial "B" or his occasional use of the form W. E. Burghardt Du Bois. These variations were chosen to distinguish him from others with the name W. E. Du Bois, and, since the Burghardts were Black, to distinguish his African and Afro-American derivation.

Of course, all books represent more than one individual's efforts. This is especially true of the present volume. From time to time, within the work itself, acknowledgment is made of courtesy or assistance involving some particular document or question. In addition, I wish to acknowledge with deep appreciation the assistance of Professor Arthur S. Link of Princeton University; Professor Louis R. Harlan of the University of Maryland; Professor Robert G. Weisbord of the University of Rhode Island; Mrs. Louise T. Patterson of New York City; Mrs. Dorothy Swanson of the Tamiment Library of New York University; Mr. L. C. Cartwright of New York City; the late Dr. James M. Warbasse; Mrs. Lillian M. Lewis, in charge of Special Collections, Trevor Arnett Library, Atlanta University; Mrs. Sara B. McCain, Associate Curator of Manuscripts, George Arents Research Library, Syracuse University; Dr. Paul S. Clarkson, Archivist, Robert Hutchins Goddard Library, Clark University. I also gratefully acknowledge help from the State Historical Society in Madison, Wisconsin, and the Historical Society of Pennsylvania; the libraries of Tulane University, Howard University, Western Reserve Historical Society in Cleveland, the University of Michigan, Harvard University, Johns Hopkins University, and Fisk University; the Library of Congress; and the Schomburg Collection, New York Public Library.

The assistance of Malcolm Call, of the University of Massachusetts, has been great indeed. Mrs. Leone Stein, Director of the University of Massachusetts Press, and Mr. Paul Wright, until recently that press's Editor, have been very helpful. Each of the three caught several errors and helped straighten out ambiguities and overcome inadequacies. Professor Sidney Kaplan and Mr. Ernest Kaiser, of the University of Massachusetts and of the Schomburg Collection, respectively, applied their scholarship to the manuscript and significantly improved it.

The support and quiet sustaining confidence of Mrs. W. E. B. Du Bois made everything possible. I hope she does not find the work altogether unworthy of her husband.

Finally, here as in everything I have ever been able to do, the active participation and the consistent and creative encouragement of Fay P. Aptheker have been simply indispensable.

HERBERT APTHEKER

STUDENT 1877–1894

Footnotes to letters are keyed numerically, beginning with 1 each new letter. Footnotes to headnotes are keyed symbolically, † ‡

THE FIRST known letter by Du Bois, probably meant for his maternal grandmother, Sarah Lampman Burghardt, was written on lined paper just after his ninth birthday. Six years later, at age fifteen, he added the note dated 27 August 1883. Apparently the letter was never mailed.

Gt. Barrington, Mass. march, 8. 1877

My dear grandmama.

I thank you for your present, and hope you will be here this summer my schoolhouse stands a little way from Main, St.

This was writen when I was nine years of age.
W E Du Bois

Aug. 27, '83.

At fifteen, Du Bois visited his paternal grandfather, Alexander Du Bois, a boat steward living in New Bedford, Massachusetts. In his *Autobiography*, Du Bois describes the origins and events of this "greatest boyhood trip";* some of the details given there are not quite accurate, as the letter shows. It covers both sides of three lined sheets and is written in ink.

New Bedford July 21, 1883.

Dear Mam,

I arrived here safely friday after noon. It was just noon when I got to Hartford. After eating my lunch & buying my ticket I went up to the capitol which is but a little ways to the depot. The grounds are laid out beautifully and the building is magnificent. It consists of a main part and two wings. The main part is surmounted by a tower & dome, which, by the way, is gilded, & upon this is a bronzed statue. As you go in the main entrance the first thing you see is a very large statue of a woman holding a wreath. On either side in cabinets are the different flags. the floor is of colored marble. The staircases are also of marble. There is a book to write your names there & of course my illustrious name is there. I looked into the chamber of the House of representatives. It is very nice. The chairs & desks are arranged in a semicircle. The chairmans seat is in the

---

* *The Autobiography of W. E. B. Du Bois*, ed. Herbert Aptheker (New York: International Publishers, 1968), pp. 97–99.

middle. In front are seats for the clerks & at the side for reporters. there is an elevator which anybody can go up & down in when they wish to. The whole building is frescoed splendidly. On the outside there are niches for statues. There is a picture gallery in the state library room. I cannot tell you ½ what I saw there. I did not go up in dome fearing that the train would leave me. When I came down to the depot & finding that I had a little time left I took a walk up a street near by. When I got back to the depot the train was *gone*, & news agent told me there was no other to providence that afternoon. imagine my situation! At last however I found out there was another train out on another road. so I had to sell my ticket which I paid $2.70 for, for $1.50 because I had my baggage checked on it & baggage had gone by the other train. At last I was on the way to providence. The railroad runs down parelal with the Connecticut river & the scenery is beautiful. I saw two or three steamers. After we had got to the coast I changed cars & to took the shore line. There the scenery was magnificent the steamers, sailboat, the beautiful seaside resorts &c. I reached providence about 8 pm. & there was no one to meet me, sarah thinking that I would not come because I did not come on the other train I asked a policeman & he directed me to her residence. Providence is a very nice city & I like it very much.

I went around a good deal what little time I was there.

Sarah has a very nice little cottage. I saw the soldiers monument & I will tell you about it when I come. I started on the 8 A.M. train for N.B. & arrive there about 11 A.M. There was no one to meet me & I was mad, very mad. in fact if I could got hold of some one I should have hurt them, but I didn't. by inquiries I found the house which is about half a mile from the depot. The house is white with green blinds & the yard is full of flower gardens. Grandma is about my color & taller than I thought. I like her very much. Grandpa is short & rather thick set. I like him better than I thought I would. He say very little but speaks civily when I say anything to him. Grandma says by and bye he'll talk more I like it *very* much here & am having a nice time.

Last night Grandma & I took a walk up street & visited some of her friends. I have been walking out this afternoon. We are going on a picnic to onset point next week & down to Martha's Vineyard & to hear the Miss Davis the elocutionist &c. I have not been to Mr. Freedom's yet but will go next week. Tell Jennie not to forget the courier. Tell Grace I would like to slap her once I suppose you are very lonesome. I felt a little home sick this afternoon. Will write soon, with love to all, good by

        Your son,
        W E Du Bois.

In June 1884, Du Bois graduated from the Great Barrington high school. His family made plans and began to accumulate funds to assure his going to college. When his mother died later in 1884, the family persisted in the plans for Du

Bois's education, with assistance from members of the community: Frank Hosmer, principal of the high school; Edward Van Lennep, principal of a local private school and active in the Congregational Church attended by the Du Bois family; the Reverend Mr. Scudder, pastor of that church; and another Congregational minister, the Reverend Mr. Painter (whose son had been Du Bois's school-chum). Each of four Protestant churches in Great Barrington agreed to contribute twenty-five dollars a year toward Du Bois's college education; in addition Du Bois worked during much of 1885 as a timekeeper (at the fabulous wage of one dollar per day) for the widow of the railroad tycoon, Mark Hopkins, who was building a mansion in Great Barrington. At the end of that year, when seventeen years old, Du Bois went south to Fisk University in Nashville, Tennessee. From there, he wrote to the Reverend Mr. Scudder.

Fisk, Feb. 3, 1886.

Dear Pastor:

You have no doubt expected to hear of my welfare before this, but nevertheless you must know I am very grateful to you and the Sunday-School for what you have done. In the first place I am glad to tell you that I have united with the Church here and hope that the prayers of my Sunday-school may help guide me in the path of Christian duty. During the revival we had nearly forty conversions. The day of prayer for Colleges was observed hear with two prayer-meetings. The Rev. M. Aitkins, the Scotch revivalist spoke to us a short time ago, and tomorrow Mr. Moody will be present at our chapel exercises.[1]

Our University is very pleasantly situated, overlooking the city, and the family life is very pleasant indeed. Some mornings as I look about upon the two or three hundred of my companions assembled for morning prayers I can hardly realize they are all my people; that this great assembly of youth and intelligence are the representatives of a race which twenty years ago was in bondage. Although this sunny land is very pleasant, notwithstanding its squalor misery and ignorance spread broad-cast; and although it is a bracing thought to know that I stand among those who do not despise me for my color, yet I have not forgotten to love my New England hills, and I often wish I could join some of your pleasant meetings in person as I do in spirit. I remain

Respectfully yours,
William E Du Bois

As a youngster in the Great Barrington high school, Du Bois dreamed of going to Harvard. As he neared graduation from Fisk, he sent an application to the secretary of Harvard University from Nashville.*

1. Dwight L. Moody (1837–1899) was then a world-famous evangelist.

* The letter is in the archives of Harvard and is used with the university's kind assistance.

[6] Correspondence 1877–1894

29 October, 1887

Dear Sir:

I am a Negro, a student of Fisk University. I shall receive the degree of A.B. from this institution next June at the age of 20. I wish to pursue at Harvard a course of study for the degree of Ph.D. in Political Science after graduation. I am poor and if I should enter your college next year would probably not be able to raise more [than] $100 or $150. If I should teach a year and then enter I could earn enough to pay my expenses for a year. I wish your advice as to what I had better do. You can see by the catalogue I shall send herewith what our course of instruction is here. I can furnish satisfactory certificates of character and scholarship from the President and Professors of Fisk, and from Western Massachusetts where I was born, and graduated from the public schools.[1] I am also Editor of the *Fisk Herald, a copy of which I send*.[2] As I said I wish your advice as to whether I had better teach a year or two or come immediately after graduation. I expect to take the special field of Political Economy.

I am, Sir,
Yours,
W. E. B. Du Bois

George Washington Cable (1844–1925), the distinguished Southern writer (*Old Creole Days*, 1879; *The Grandissimes*, 1884) was an impassioned opponent of the oppression of Black people. Having expressed his views in *The Silent South* (1885), he was forced to leave Louisiana. Thereafter he resided in Massachusetts, where he maintained his rejection of Bourbon domination of the South and his insistence that only through an anti-racist democratic order could the South flourish. One of his most influential expressions of that view—uttered in opposition to the "New South" propaganda being brought into the North by men like Henry W. Grady—was his address in Boston before the Massachusetts Club on Washington's Birthday in 1890. The speech was widely reported in the press; young Du Bois, then at Harvard, may possibly have heard it delivered. Certainly

---

1. In April 1888, letters highly recommending Du Bois went to Harvard from Principal Frank A. Hosmer of the Great Barrington high school, from President E. M. Cravath of Fisk, and from Professors Chase, Bennett, Wright, Morgan, and Spence (who wrote in March). On the basis of Du Bois's record and these recommendations, he was awarded a Price Greenleaf grant and entered Harvard.

2. These words are stricken in the original.

he was impressed with it, and the next day—his own birthday—he wrote to Cable a letter made noteworthy by its concluding thought.*

Cambridge, Mass., Feb. 23, 1890

Mr. Geo. W. Cable
Dear Sir:

I cannot refrain from writing you a word to express my deep appreciation for your recent Boston words in behalf of me and my people. In the midst of so much confusion and misapprehension, the clear utterance and moral heroism of one man, is doubly welcome to the young Negro who is building a Nation.

Respectfully yours,
W. E. B. Du Bois

In the spring of 1890, with his Harvard graduation impending, Du Bois sent a letter to the "Academic Council" of Harvard University. Preceding the text given below, he indicated that he was applying for "appointment to a *Lee, Goodwin,* or *Bromfield Rogers* fellowship": he was granted the last. As his 1887 letter clearly affirmed his goal of a Ph.D., which Du Bois was to obtain eight years later, so this letter of 1890 states his desire to attend for some time a "European institution," a goal which he was to realize two years later; the letter also affirms that his aim is the advancement of his people. This letter is not precisely dated, but there is no doubt that it was written in the spring of 1890, probably in April.†

I have devoted most of my college work to Philosophy, Political Economy, and History, and wish after graduation to study in the graduate department for the degree of Ph.D. I wish to take the field of *social science* under *political science* with a view to the ultimate application of its principles to the social and economic advancement of the Negro people. I wish to spend the first year at Harvard and one or more years at some European institution. I propose to take the advice of the proper professors as to the exact method of study, which I have not as yet determined.

Respectfully yours,
W. E. B. Du Bois '90

---

* This letter is in the George W. Cable Collection, Special Collections Department, Tulane University Library. The text of the Cable speech is in Arlin Turner, ed., *The Negro Question . . . Writings of G. W. Cable* (Garden City, New York: Doubleday and Co., 1958), pp. 212-44. See, also, Philip Butcher, *George W. Cable: The Northampton Years* (New York: Columbia University Press, 1959), p. 72.

† Appreciation is expressed to the Archives of Harvard University for making this letter available.

[8] Correspondence 1877–1894

In 1888, Du Bois received a B.A. degree from Fisk and was admitted to Harvard as a junior. In 1890, he graduated *cum laude* from Harvard in a class of three hundred. Du Bois was one of six commencement speakers, with a paper on Jefferson Davis which attracted nation-wide comment. Miss Bowers, author of this letter, refers to his success. The letter is the result of Du Bois's having organized the Fisk class of 1888 into a club, the members of which corresponded regularly with each other for some years.

Galveston, Texas, Nov. 14, 1890

My Dear Classmates:

It affords me much pleasure to write you this letter, but I am anticipating even more pleasure when I can have the class letter and see what each one is doing. When I think of you all in a body I am carried at once back to our Alma Mater where so many happy moments were spent. I can see you all now as we sat in the Science room laughing and discussing something entirely foreign to the lesson, having a pleasant time, or as we sat under our rigid President, sober and quiet, or as we pulled through the long pages of Greek and Latin, and other occurrences, that as I now look back over them seem all joy and happiness. How often do I wish again for those days. I have found that those were our happiest days.

I am working still in the Public Schools of this city. This is my third year in this work, as I have worked here ever since my graduation. The work is pleasant; we have a pleasant set of teachers. I am teaching the Eighth and ninth grades in our High School. My grades study higher Arithmetic and Grammar, Physical Geography, Physiology, History, Philosophy, Geometry, Algebra, Rhetoric, General History and Latin. I enjoy the higher work more than I did the work of the lower grades. The schools are good here, we will have our first graduating class this year. There are five who will finish our High School. We end up with the Eleventh grade. Since Mr. Edmondsom's resignation we are in need of a teacher; in fact we need two teachers. And I am sure it would be very pleasant could I have one of you or two of you to fill these vacancies. Galveston is a pleasant place and I am sure if you would once come here you would like the city. I receive a salary of fifty dollars [per month] now but hope to be promoted this year and receive ten or fifteen dollars more. I do not do a great deal of studying now but I find I am kept busy most of the time. I do not get from school until three o'clock and then I must give several music lessons before dark. I attend church almost as much as I did when at Fisk. I am organist and Ass. Supt. of our Sabbath School and of course must be there every Sunday. I am also organist of the church and must be there to services in the morning, sometimes at night. We have a very intelligent and upright Christian man for our pastor and I rather enjoy the services. I have sometimes had occasion to address our people on certain subjects and have sometimes impressed them, I am told.

I do not take a very active part in society which somewhat surprises even myself. I am more retired than I ever thought I would be. I am interested in my work and give most of my attention to that. I wonder what are the marriage prospects of the class, who is thinking most about marriage and who is nearest to it. For my part I have made up my mind never to enter such a contract. I am in good health, still doing my best to hold up the average weight of the class. I have told you everything that would interest you, so I must stop. I extend a hearty invitation to every member of the class to sometime visit me in my home at Galveston. We are very plain and poor but should any one of you wish to come to our city I will throw my doors open to you and entertain you as long as you wish to stay. I am sure that all of us have been very proud of Mr. DuBois as one of us. He has crowned the University, the class and himself with honor. As I read of his success in the paper I felt proud to be able to tell persons that he was a classmate of mine.

With best wishes for the success of each one of the class, I am
Your loving classmate
L. A. Bowers

I agree with the president's suggestions, and vote for Mr. Edmonson as secretary.

I do not vote for Miss Bowers for president, but am rather willing to keep Mr. DuBois as our president.
L. A. Bowers

During the years Du Bois was at Harvard, an especially distinguished faculty included Charles Eliot Norton, Justin Winsor, Francis Child, Frank Taussig, Nathaniel Shaler, Francis G. Peabody, George Palmer, George Santayana, Josiah Royce, Barrett Wendell, Edward Channing, Albert Bushnell Hart, and William James. The latter two in particular—in United States history and in philosophy—befriended and influenced Du Bois. Du Bois wrote later, "I was repeatedly a guest in the home of William James; he was my friend and guide to clear thinking...."[*] The letter that follows, written in James's own hand, reflects this splendid friendship.

[*] Du Bois, "A Negro Student at Harvard at the End of the Nineteenth Century," in *Black and White in American Culture*, eds. Jules Chametzky and Sidney Kaplan (Amherst: University of Massachusetts Press, 1969), pp. 119-37; the quotation is from p. 128. This essay appeared originally in the *Massachusetts Review* 1, no. 3 (Spring 1960).

[10] Correspondence 1877–1894

Cambr., Feb 9th 1891

Dear Mr Du Bois,
Won't you come to a philosophical supper on Saturday, Feb 14th, at half past seven o'clock?

Yours truly
William James

Du Bois was granted the Henry Bromfield Rogers fellowship to begin graduate study at Harvard in 1890, and the award was renewed for 1891–92. In 1891 Du Bois received his M.A. in history. He delivered a paper at the 1891 meeting of the American Historical Association—the first Afro-American to do so—based on his study of the African slave trade. Though penniless, an orphan, and Black, Du Bois was determined to enhance his education with the essential study abroad, which at that time meant Germany.

At the end of 1890, Du Bois read (in the *Boston Herald*, 2 November) a statement by former President Rutherford B. Hayes, who chaired the Slater Fund for the Education of Negroes, that the fund would be willing to subsidize "any young colored man . . . to send him to Europe or give him an advanced educacation." Du Bois promptly sent a letter of application to Hayes;* a letter of recommendation followed from Francis G. Peabody, one of several Harvard professors who agreed to assist, to the active head of the fund—President Daniel C. Gilman of Johns Hopkins University.†

Cambridge, November 4, 1890

Dear Sir:
The following clipping from the Boston *Herald* of Nov. 2nd, has come to my notice:

NEGROES IN THE SOUTH

Ex-President Hayes Says Their Chief and Almost Only Gift Is Oratory
Baltimore, Md., Nov. 1, 1890. Ex-President Hayes said today to the students of Johns Hopkins University, on the subject of negro education in the South:

If there is any young colored man in the South whom we find to have a talent for art or literature, or any especial aptitude for study, we are willing to

---

* This letter is published in *Teach the Freeman: The Correspondence of R. B. Hayes and the Slater Fund for Negro Education*, ed. Louis D. Rubin, Jr., 2 vols. (Baton Rouge: Louisiana State University Press, 1959), 2:158–61.
† The original letter is in the archives of Johns Hopkins University Library and is printed with its permission. Letters of recommendation from Professors Nathaniel S. Shaler and Albert B. Hart are in Rubin, 2:189–90, 247–48.

give him money from the education funds to send him to Europe or to give him an advanced education, but hitherto their chief and almost only gift has been that of oratory.

What you find as historical students, as to their condition in the South, especially in the black belt, is surely not encouraging. They are seen most favorably in what is called the Virginia land district of Ohio. This tract of land, between the Scioto, Little Miami and Ohio rivers, was granted by the state of Virginia to its officers in the revolutionary war, many of whom settled there with their slaves. Most of these were freed, and have increased rapidly with a corresponding increase in education. A careful examination of that region will show a considerable advance in the good qualities of civilization, and proper appreciation of citizenship.

But I do not despair of the other negroes, but am rather hopeful of their being uplifted in the future.

If this be a true report of your words, I wish to lay my case before you.

I am a Negro, twenty-three years of age next February, (23rd), and a graduate of Fisk University, '88. After leaving there I came to Harvard University and entering the Junior class graduated in 1890. This year I have entered the graduate School and am a candidate for the degrees of A.M. and Ph.D. in Political Science. I have so far gained my education by teaching in the South, giving small lectures in the North, working in Hotels, laundries, &c, and by various scholarships and the charity of friends. I have no money or property myself and am an orphan. My particular field in Political Science is the History of African Slavery from the economic and social stand point. The faculty of Harvard College have seen fit to recognize whatever ability I have by appointing me to Price Greenleaf aid, a Mathews Scholarship and finally for the year 1890–90 [*sic*] to a fellowship. For further information as to my character and fitness for my line of work, I respectfully refer to the following gentlemen with whom you may communicate or whose opinion I can procure and forward you:

President Eliot, of Harvard Univ.
Prof. N. S. Shaler,   "   "
Prof. F. G. Peabody,   "   "
Prof. Wm. James,   "   "
Prof. A. B. Hart,   "   "
Prof. T. W. Taussig,   "   "
Frank Bolles, Esq., Sec. Harvard Coll.
President E. M. Cravath, Fisk Univ.
Prof. F. A. Chase,   "   "
President F. A. Hosmer, Oahu College, Honolulu, H. I. or the Dean of the Graduate School, Harvard Univ.

If it appears to you upon investigation that I show "any especial aptitude for study," I respectfully ask that I be sent to Europe to pursue my work in the continental universities, leaving the details of the work to the recommendations of the appropriate professors in Harvard.

If the extract above is not correct I pray you will pardon my trespassing.

Respectfully Yours,
W. E. B. Du Bois

Cambridge, Mass., April 20, '91

My dear Sir—

Mr. W. E. D. DuBois has been a student with me & has, as in all his work, gained high distinction. The opinion of the University concerning him is proved by his holding a fellowship this year. This is a matter in which his color is in no degree involved. It simply indicates that he is among the most satisfactory students of the last few years.

I commend him as a person of devotion to the higher scholarship & with the practical intention to make his life useful to his race.

Respectfully yours
Francis G. Peabody

Du Bois sent two more letters to Hayes, reflecting the intensity of his effort to win the grant.*

Cambridge, April 19, 1891 [dated 1890]

Dear Sir:

You will have received by the time this reaches you, I think, testimonials from President Eliot, Prof. Shaler, Prof. Hart, and Prof. Peabody, of Harvard.

I will give you a brief statement of my case.

I was born in Great Barrington, Berkshire County, Mass., on the 23rd Feb. 1868. My grandparents, on my mother's side, were slaves among the Dutch in New York, on my father's side, among the French in the West Indies. I was educated in the public schools of the town; I supported my self and partially supported my mother during my course thro' the High school (father having died when I was quite young) graduating there in June 1884. I went South to Fisk University in Nashville Tenn. on the recommendation of Rev. C. C. Painter of the Indian Bureau (to whom I am well known) in September 1885. Here I entered the Sophomore class and graduated in June 1888. I was supported while there by the contribution of my own Sunday-school in Gt. B. & three others, and by teaching summer schools in the country. In the fall of '88 I secured a Price Greenleaf aid at Harvard and entered the junior class. I supported myself by lectures, loans and prizes. The next year I rec'd a Matthews Scholarship and

---

* These letters are published in Rubin, *Teach the Freeman*, 2:194-95, 198.

another prize which with readings delivered during the summer paid my way. I received my degree here in '90 (A.B., *cum laude*), being one of the Commencement speakers. I then entered the Graduate school to study social science, and was appointed to the Bromfield Rogers Memorial Fellowship. I expect to spend next year here at the same work, after which I wish to spend a couple of years in study in Europe on the same subject.

I am in good physical condition as may be ascertained by the records of the Harvard gymnasium.

I hereby respectfully apply to the board for a fellowship which will enable me to study in Europe one or two years.

Respectfully yours,
W. E. B. Du Bois

P.S. I omitted stating that I am, in blood, about one half or more Negro, and the rest French and Dutch.

Cambridge, May 6, 1891

Dear Sir:

In reply to your favor of the 23, ult. let me say that I have inquired of the head of my department, Prof. Hart, and he informs me that the expense of study in Europe will be about six hundred dollars a year. It is of course possible that the second year would be cheaper than the first as one would know better how to economize. I think therefore that one thousand or eleven hundred dollars would suffice.

Respectfully,
W. E. B. Du Bois

Despite such letters, Hayes wrote young Du Bois in a communication that does not seem to have survived, but was summarized by the latter, that the original newspaper report was in error and that Hayes "was sorry the plan had been given up; that he recognized that I was a candidate who might otherwise have been given attenion." Du Bois "sat down and wrote Mr. Hayes a letter that could be described as nothing less than impudent."*

May 25, 1891

Your favor of the 2nd. is at hand. I thank you for your kind wishes. You will pardon me if I add a few words of explanation as to my application. The outcome of the matter is as I expected it would be. The announcement that any agency of the American people was willing to give a Negro a thoroughly liberal

---

* The description was offered by Du Bois in his *Dusk of Dawn*, first published in New York by Harcourt, Brace and Co. in 1940, and republished by Schocken Books (New York, 1968); see p. 44. The letter is printed in the *Autobiography*, pp. 151–52.

education and that it had been looking in vain for men to educate was to say the least rather startling. When the newspaper clipping was handed me in a company of friends, my first impulse was to make in some public way a categorical statement denying that such an offer had ever been made known to colored students. I saw this would be injudicious and fruitless, and I therefore determined on the plan of applying myself. I did so and have been refused along with a number of cases beside mine.

As to my case I personally care little. I am perfectly capable of fighting alone for an education if the trustees do not see fit to help me. On the other hand the injury you have—unwittingly I trust—done the race I represent, and am not ashamed of, is almost irreparable. You went before a number of keenly observant men who looked upon you as an authority in the matter, and told them in substance that the Negroes of the United States either couldn't or wouldn't embrace a most liberal opportunity for advancement. That statement went all over the country. When now finally you receive three or four applications for the fulfillment of that offer, the offer is suddenly withdrawn, while the impression still remains.

If the offer was an experiment, you ought to have had at least one case before withdrawing it; if you have given aid before (and I mean here toward liberal education—not toward training plowmen) then your statement at Johns Hopkins was partial. From the above facts I think you owe an apology to the Negro people. We are ready to furnish competent men for every European scholarship furnished us off paper. But we can't educate ourselves on nothing and we can't have the moral courage to try, if in the midst of our work our friends turn public sentiment against us by making statements which injure us and which they cannot stand by.

That you have been looking for men to liberally educate in the past may be so but it is certainly strange so few have heard it. It was never mentioned during my three years stay at Fisk University. President J. C. Price of Livingstone has told me that he never heard of it,[1] and students from various other Southern schools have expressed great surprise at the offer. The fact is that when I was wanting to come to Harvard, while yet in the South, I wrote to Dr. Haygood for a loan merely, and he never even answered my letter.[2] I find men willing to help me thro' cheap theological schools, I find men willing to help me use my hands before I have got my brains in working order, I have an abundance of good wishes on hand, but I never found a man willing to help me get a Harvard Ph.D.

W. E. B. Du Bois

1. Price was then a leading Negro spokesman.
2. Atticus G. Haygood was a leader of Southern white liberals.

The young Du Bois submitted to the authorities of the Slater Fund an autobiographical statement of great interest. The statement is undated, but was no doubt written early in 1892: a barely visible entry on the original indicates that the fund received the letter in May.

The Honorable Board of Trustees of the John F. Slater Fund
Gentlemen:
In accordance with your directions I send herewith a sketch of my life.

My name is William Edward Burghardt Du Bois; I was born at Great Barrington, Massachusetts, on the 23rd day of February, 1868, being the sole issue of the marriage of Mary S. Burghardt and Alfred Du Bois.

My paternal great-grandfather was a French doctor in the West Indies, and brought my grandfather and his brother to the United States when quite young. My grandfather settled in Connecticut and afterward removed to New Bedford, Mass. He was a boat steward by trade. My father was one of many children, and a barber by trade. He died when I was young.

My mother was a mulatto, the fourth in direct descent from Thomas Burghardt, who when young, was brought from Africa as a slave to the Dutch in New York state, early in the 18th century. He fought in the Revolutionary war. His son Jack Burghardt had several children, among whom was Othello, my grandfather. Othello and his wife, Sally Lampman, were both born slaves, but freed at majority. My mother was the youngest of several children, and received a good common-school education.

Both grandfathers and my father had good common educations. Alexander Du Bois, as my grandfather was named, had accumulated some property, but most of it went to his maintenance in his old age. There was some property in my mother's family but none of it reached me. My father saved nothing, and after his death we were often near pauperism. Nevertheless my mother kept me in school until she was disabled by paralysis, when I managed to keep on by means of work after hours and on vacation. In 1884 I graduated from the Gt. Barrington High School, and in the fall of 1885 I went south on the advice of friends, and entered the sophomore class at Fisk University. My mother died in the spring of 1885.[1]

I remained at Fisk three years, graduating with the degree of A.B., in 1888. My vacations were spent in teaching country schools. I now determined to come to Harvard and pursue a course for the degree of Ph.D. On the strength of my recommendations I was appointed to $250 of Price Greenleaf Aid at Harvard before coming. During the summer of 1888 I worked in a hotel in the northwest, and in the fall entered the Junior class at this place. I managed to pay the ex-

1. In his *Dusk of Dawn* (p. 20) and *Autobiography* (p. 102), Du Bois states that his mother died in the fall of 1884.

penses of the first year by the Aid, lecturing, loan fund, and a prize; the next year I was granted a Matthews Scholarship, which added to a series of summer readings and another prize enabled me to finish that year. For the year '90–'91, I was appointed to the H. B. Rogers Memorial Fellowship in Political Science, and re-appointed to the same for 1891–92.

Of the four years spent at Harvard, the first was spent in general studies (e.g. Chemistry, Geology, Ethics, Economics &c), the second year in Philosophy, and Economics, and the last two in History and Political Science. My doctor's thesis has been written and is on the suppression of the slave trade in the United States, including colonial times. My future study will be in political science with especial reference to the history of social problems.

Respectfully submitted,
W. E. B. Du Bois

It speaks exceedingly well for Rutherford B. Hayes—he may here have performed the greatest service of his career—that he responded gently to Du Bois and even seems to have encouraged him to hope that perhaps in 1892 an application would be successful. As a result, early in that year Hayes was favored with another letter from Du Bois.

Cambridge, 3 April '92

Hon. R. B. Hayes
Sir:

I venture with some diffidence to address you again on the subject of a European scholarship from the Slater fund. You expressed the hope, if I remember rightly, that this year the board might see its way more clearly than last year. I wish, therefore, to bring the question to your mind again, and to state my present situation.

At the close of the last academic year at Harvard, I received the degree of master of arts, and was reappointed to my fellowship for the year 1891–92. As it is the general policy of the college to appoint for only two successive years I can have little chance for a third year. My work this year has been the general study of history, sociology &c., and the preparation of my thesis for the doctor's degree, on the suppression of the African Slave Trade in America. A preliminary paper on this subject, I read before the Annual meeting of the American Historical Association, of which I have been made a member. The paper will be shortly published in their proceedings, and a preliminary report may be found in the *Independent,* 7 Jan., '92 (also *Congregationalist* about same date). The thesis itself is now finished in rough draft, and will be ready for publication May 1.¹

To properly finish the education thus begun, a careful training in a European university for at least a year is, in my mind, and in the minds of my professors, indispensable to my greatest usefulness. I therefore desire to lay three propositions before you:

1. That the board grant me a scholarship from the funds, upon which I may be enabled to spend a year in study at a European university, under the direction [of] those whom they appoint.

2. If this be impracticable, that the board loan me a sum sufficient for such a purpose. I could only give my note of hand as security for this, but I do not think that such a note would be worthless. I could probably repay the sum within two years after finishing.

3. If neither of the above plans are agreed to by the board, could you or they suggest some person interested enough in the "Negro problem," to make such a loan to me?

In case all these suggestions fail, I would like to ask if you would object to returning to me the recommendations forwarded you in regard to my case (except personal notes) in order that I may use them in other directions for the same purpose.

I trust you will pardon my importunity—I can only say by way of excuse, that I do not consider it is a question of merely personal interest.

       Respectfully yours,
       W. E. B. Du Bois

Entries in Hayes's diary reflect the progress of Du Bois's effort: 12 April, 1892: "Du Bois to be recommended." 13 April: "Aid to Du Bois." 15 April: "At breakfast received a card from Du Bois, the colored scholar from Harvard. Pres. Gilman and I arranged to give him seven hundred and fifty dollars—one-half cash donation, one-half on his note—to support him one year in Germany at some university. Very glad to find that he is sensible, sufficiently religious, able, and a fair speaker."* In May 1892, the Slater Fund notified Du Bois that it would help finance his European studies. These two letters provide the details of that understanding.

 1. The thesis was *The Suppression of the African Slave Trade to the United States of America, 1638–1870*, and was published in 1896 by Longmans, Green and Co. (New York) as Harvard Historical Series no. 1. The paper on "The Enforcement of the Slave-Trade Laws" appears in the *Annual Report of the American Historical Association for the Year 1891* (Sen. Misc. Doc. 173, 52nd Cong., 1st Sess., Washington, 1892), pp. 161–74. It was commented upon by Herbert B. Adams in the *Independent*, 7 January 1892, pp. 10–11, and by Edward G. Bourne in the *Congregationalist*, 14 January 1892, p. 2.

 * *Diary and Letters of Rutherford B. Hayes*, ed. P. Williams (Columbus, Ohio: Heer Publishing Co., 1926), 5:74–76.

[18] Correspondence 1877–1894

Baltimore, Md., May 23, 1892

Dear Sir,

I believe that the understanding when we met you in New York was this—that we should loan you $350. on your personal security & give you $350. as a scholarship, in order that you may pursue your studies abroad, with the additional understanding that twice in each year you should write me fully respecting your work. Does this accord with your understanding? If so when would you like to go abroad and in what way would you like payments to be made?
                              D. C. Gilman

Cambridge, 24 May 1892

Pres. D. C. Gilman
Dear Sir:

As I understood the agreement at New York it was that the trustees were to loan me $375, and give me $375 as a scholarship; I was to report to you twice a year with a preliminary report of my life, etc. This is in accord with your statement except as to the sum—I understood it to be $750 instead of $700. The life &c I have already forwarded you. The method of payment I suppose would best be made in two or three installments—one to be paid before starting. I should like to go about the 25th of June, so as to have as much time as possible on the language.
                    Sincerely yours,
                    W. E. B. Du Bois

P.S. There was also I believe a clause in the agreement in which the committee expressed the willingness to consider the case of a second year's appointment.
                    W. E. B. D.

Young Du Bois sailed for Europe in the summer of 1892 aboard the Dutch ship "Amsterdam"; he noted at the time that Holland was "extremely neat" and smelled of clover and was "situated at the confluence of the English, French and German languages."

Soon after getting settled in Germany, he wrote Edward Van Lennep, superintendent of the Sunday school which Du Bois had attended, and enclosed a rather long travelogue for the edification of the students.

Eisenach, 29 Sept. '92.

Dear Mr. Van Lennep:

I send enclosed a letter to the Sunday-school—after having written I have had doubts as to its appropriateness, but I shall send it at any rate—perhaps it would be better for the *Courier*, if so I should like to see a copy. I am well and happy, expecting to enter the University of Berlin soon. I send my best regards to your Mother, Ma and Miss Byrd &c. Also to all friends and to yourself. I send you

herewith a photo of the Wartburg. Thanking you for many kindnesses, I remain
                             Truly yours,
                             W. E. B. Du Bois

                             Eisenach, 29 Sept. 1892
To the Congregational Sunday-School:
   I venture to send you a few words about the German town in which I have been spending the summer, because it is so intimately connected with the life of Martin Luther whom we all reverence. In the middle of Germany, on the northwest edge of the famous Thuringian forest stands the town of Eisenach, one of the most beautiful spots of a beautiful region. I shall not attempt to describe the natural beauty of the place, first because I know I could not do it justice, and secondly because the memory of my own blue Berkshire hills tells me that the task would be an unnecessary one. It is however of the rich legacy of history and legend which belongs to these hills that I wish to speak. It is ever a strange experience for an American to walk for the first time in a land, the natural beauty of which is surrounded and enhanced by the thought, legends, and deeds of a thousand years. Such is the case here, and the deeds are all the more interesting because they furthered that freedom of conscience and deeper religion which is the heritage of Gt. Barrington and of the world. Let us suppose the hills were thrown in somewhat wilder confusion, our shingles turned into red tiles, and our streets crooked a bit; so you could imagine yourselves in Eisenach; now we can take a walk through the old town treading on centuries of footsteps and breathing air full of ancient whispers. Here on the Luther place is the house where Martin Luther, the first Protestant, lived, while he attended school in Eisenach. His father and mother dwelt over the hills yonder to the west, in Möhra—poor ordinary peasants, too poor to keep the boy in school. So Frau Vroula Cotta gave a place at her table and here, in the same decade in which Columbus discovered America, lived the great boy, in this queer old house with its projecting stories and little windows. A little farther on, in the great square market-place, he went to school under the shadow of a huge, unsightly Gothic church, which for half a thousand years has stood there. I attended service here last Sunday: it is a queer place with stiff old pews, great pillars, galleries, ancient gravestones, and an old high gilded pulpit. As I heard the grey-haired preacher in the pulpit, I remembered that 371 years ago, Luther himself had preached in the self-same pulpit, and under the same cherub-bedecked covering. It was on his return from the Diet of Worms in 1521, where, before the Emperor Charles V, and the assembled princes and prelates of Europe he had defended liberty of conscience. Excommunicated by the church and forbidden to preach, he nevertheless defied the edict of the Emperor and preached in this church, and then was spirited away by his friends and for nearly a year hidden from his persecutors—so costly was it to be brave. And where was he hidden? Let us see; imagining still that Gt. Barrington is Eisenach, let us take our stand in the market-place in front

of the Town Hall. Look now upon East Mountain, and in place of East Rock, imagine the height crowned by a rambling old castle with great walls, buildings and towers. It is the castle Wartburg, and is very old; when Washington was President it was old; when your great-great-grandfathers stole my great-great-grandfather and brought him a slave to America, it was old; when Wycliffe translated the Bible, it was old—indeed, it was at the time William the Conqueror invaded England that Ludwig the Springer, a warrior, saw this height and saying: "Wart Berg! Du sollst mir ein Burg sein" (Wait, mountain! You shall be my fortress), he forthwith builded this castle. Thus for 825 years has it guarded the land, and here Luther found asylum in 1521 when the rest of Christendom was closed against him. Protestantism could have had no more significant cradle. Here classic heathen and Christian legend meet and join hands. Here is the scene of Wagner's great opera Tannhauser. The Frankish singer came riding out of the west at the behest of Herman lord of the Wartburg, but when upon the Horselberg, the peak facing the castle, he was turned aside from his journey by the goddess of beauty and perished miserably. So runs the legend. Here too lived that beautiful half-mystic Austrian princess, St. Elizabeth, whom the Germans have made an ideal figure of self-denying charity, and whom they always picture as standing before her hard-hearted lord with the food in her apron which she carried to the hungry, turned, as by a miracle, into roses to deceive his greed. In the midst of such scenes of much more or less true tales, Luther lived for nearly a year, known to the castle as Junker-Jorg, and buried himself in writing polemics and translating the Bible. The chamber where he lived and the table on which he wrote are still shown to visitors. While we may not indeed be certain as to many small details in the life of this great man in Eisenach, we are nevertheless sure that here occurred many important events in which you and I have even more than a personal interest.

Sincerely yours,
W. E. B. Du Bois

The grant from the Slater Fund was renewed in 1893; Du Bois had some hopes of obtaining a doctorate from the University of Berlin by 1895, but the fund decided not to renew his award a third time. As a result Du Bois returned—still penniless, but now with debts to the Slater Fund—in the summer of 1894. Correspondence between Du Bois and Gilman follows, with Du Bois's enclosures, including letters of recommendation from German professors and his own reports of work and plans while in Germany.

Berlin, October 28, 1892.

President D. C. Gilman
Sir:
   In accordance with the terms of my appointment, I have the honor to make to you my first report as Scholar of the John F. Slater Fund.

Arriving in Rotterdam about Aug 1st, I spent some ten days in visiting the chief places of interest in Holland. I then ascended the Rhine, stopping at Düsseldorf, Cologne, Mainz, and Frankfort. From the latter place I went to Eisenach in Sachsen-Weimar, where I boarded for seven weeks with a German family, and spent my time in reviewing my German grammar, conversing and reading in German, and making excursions to interesting points in the neighborhood.

After making a careful examination of the programmes of lectures offered at the various Universities, I decided to go to Berlin for my first semester. Accordingly I left Eisenach on the 8th of October, and, after spending some time in Weimar and Leipsic, I came to Berlin, and matriculated under the Philosophical Faculty, 17 October. I also registered at Harvard University as a non-resident member of the Graduate School.

Here, after the usual preliminary difficulties, I have finally made myself ready for my term's work. I have hired a room about a mile from the University, take my meals at restaurants, and have the following program of work: First I have, fortunately, succeeded in entering a *Seminary of Political Economy*, under Professor Schmoller and Dr. Rathgen; here Professor Schmoller has requested me to prepare a paper on the labor question in the southern United States, which I shall do. In addition, I shall take the following courses:

1. Politics, under *Prof. von Treitschke*
2. Political Economy, under *Prof. Wagner*
3. Prussian Constitutional History, under *Prof. Schmoller*
4. Beginnings of Modern States, under *Prof. Scheffer-Boichoist*
5. Prussian Reforms, under *Prof. von Gneist*
6. Labor question in England and Germany, under *Prof. Sering*.

This will make in all about 20 hours a week of lectures. During spare hours I shall give some attention to local politics, administration, etc., and to music and art.

My address is: Oranienstr. 130 A IV, Berlin, S., Germany. I will cheerfully furnish any omitted particulars. With deepest obligation to you and the Board for these opportunities,

I remain, Sir,

                    Respectfully yours,
                    W. E. B. Du Bois.

                    Berlin, 10 March '93

President Gilman
Dear Sir:

I send herewith my second report and petition to the trustees, and letter from Prof. Schmoller. May I trouble you to write me when convenient as to what you think the fate of my petition will be, and when I can first know definitely? It would be a great favor and enable me to plan accordingly.

May I also ask that the letter of Prof. Schmoller, together with the other letters concerning me be returned to me when convenient, as I wish to keep them.

            Respectfully,
            W. E. B. Du Bois

            March 1893

To the Honorable,
The Trustees of the John F. Slater Fund
Gentlemen:

 I desire to express to you, hereby, my sincerest gratitude for the scholarship which at your last annual meeting you were pleased to grant me. I am especially grateful to the memory of him, your late head, through whose initiative my case was brought before you, and whose tireless energy and singleheartedness for the interests of my Race, God has at last crowned.[1] I shall, believe me, ever strive that these efforts shall not be wholly without result.

 The use to which your grant has been put, I have according to agreement laid in the hands of the Educational committee.

 In addition to this grant, I feel compelled humbly to petition that a similar grant be made to me for the coming year. It is with the greatest diffidence that I make this request, for I am well aware how manifold and worthy the objects are, for which the fund intrusted to your care is spent. Upon maturest consideration however, I feel in duty bound to make the petition: I do not ask for another year of European study merely because it would be pleasant, but because I regard such a period in the highest degree necessary to the completion of my education. I realize, Gentlemen, the great weight of responsibility that rests upon the younger generation of Negroes, and I feel that, handicapped as I must inevitably be to some extent in the race of life, I cannot afford to start with a preparation a bit poorer or cheaper than that deemed best for the best usefulness of my white fellow-students. To the American Negro even more than to the white, is the contact with European culture of inestimable value in giving him a broad view of men and affairs, and enabling him to view the problems of his race in their true perspective.

 I therefore ask that the Honorable Trustees extend their grant to the coming year to enable me to finish my studies at the University of Berlin and the School of Economics at Paris, under whatever conditions they may see fit to impose.

 I am, gentlemen

            Your Obedient Servant,
            W. E. B. Du Bois

1. Rutherford B. Hayes died 17 January 1893.

Berlin, 10 Mch, '93

To the Educational Committee,
of the Honorable Trustees of the
John F. Slater Fund
Gentlemen:

I have the honor to make hereby my second report concerning my study in Europe as a scholar of the honorable Trustees.

During the winter semester, October 16 to March 15, 1892–3, I have been a resident student at the University of Berlin, following the plan of study outlined in my first report. Most of my time was spent in the seminary of Economics under Professor Gustav Schmoller. For this seminary I prepared a thesis on "Der Gross- und Klein Betrieb des Ackerbaus, in der Südstaaten der Vereinigten Staaten, 1840–90."[1] This was prepared from material already in my possession, from the United States census reports, Agriculture and labor reports, etc. Professor Schmoller expressed himself as much pleased with the work, and wishes me to continue it and either publish it as a doctor's thesis or let it appear in his "Jahrbuch für Gesetzgebung, &c."[2]

I have attended two sets of lectures by Professor Wagner. He has expressed himself as interested in my work and will admit me to membership in his seminary next semester. I have also found the lectures of Treitschke and Gneist of especial interest.

Beside my regular work, I have been following the present interesting and important political and social movements in Germany; as e.g., socialism, agrarianism, and anti-Semitism. I have attended meetings, conversed with the students and people, etc. I have lately joined the "Verein für Sozial Politik" which meets here soon, and includes in its membership many well-known economists.[3] I have also put myself to considerable pains to ascertain just the sort of reception a Negro receives in Germany socially, both in public and in private, with curious and instructive results. My chief relaxation has been attending concerts, etc., where I have heard the masterpieces of music for a nominal sum.

My Christmas vacation I spent in making a trip through South Germany, visiting Weimar, Frankfort, Heidelberg, Strassburg, Stuttgart, Ulm, Augsburg, Nuremberg, Munich, Prague, and Dresden. In the Pfalz region we stopped for a week in a small country village where I had the opportunity of studying peasant life and comparing it with the country life in the United States, north and south. We visited perhaps twenty different families, talked and ate with them, went to their assemblies, etc. In the other places we gave our attention to sightseeing, to the art galleries and to the museums. The whole trip cost $80.

1. The German may be translated: "The large- and small-scale management of agriculture in the Southern United States, 1840–1890."
2. "Yearbook for Legislation."
3. "Social-Political Club."

My expenses from July until April 18, are as follows:

Received			Paid	
1892 Cash on hand	$50.	July, 1892	Outfit, clothes, &c	$50.
July Slater Fund		18	Passage to Rotterdam	50.
Scholarship	$750.	Aug 1–15	Travel in Holland & Rhine	75.
		" 15 to Oct, 1892	Pension in Eisenach	125
		Oct. 16–Apr 16,	Expense 1st Semester	270.
		Dec '92,	Christmas Journey	80
		Apr 18.	Cash on Hand,	150
Total	$800			$800

My plans for the future are these:

I shall spend the month of vacation at Cassel where it will be cheap and pleasant. I shall then return to the University of Berlin and commence this course of study, which the professors here have recommended:

Seminary in Economics: Prof. Adolf Wagner
Seminary in Modern History; Prof. Lenz.
General Political Economy, Prof. Schmoller.
History of Philosophy, Prof. Dilthey,
labor question, Prof. Schmoller,
History of 18th Century, Prof. Lenz

and a few other minor lectures in economics. My money on hand will I calculate enable me to stay until July 10th or 15th, when, if I do not receive a reappointment to my scholarship, I shall return to America.

In case the accompanying petition is favorably acted upon, I shall spend the next two semesters, i. e., until March '94, at this University in the study of Economics and History. I have been assured by Professor Dr. Hirschfeld, Dean of the Philosophical Faculty, and by Prof. Dr. Schmoller, that I have a fair possibility of being allowed to take my examination here for the degree of PH.D., at the end of three semesters. This is an unusually short time—the Berlin degree being the most difficult of German degrees for foreigners to obtain— and indeed for Germans. I am very anxious therefore on my own account but especially for the sake of my race, to try to obtain this degree.

After these three semesters, I shall go to the School of Economics at Paris where I shall stay as long as my money purse allows, and then return, *via* London, to America. I estimate my expenses as follows:

Semester at Univ of Berlin, Apr 18–Aug 18, '93	$175.
Vacation, Aug & Sept '93	75.
Semester, Oct. 18 '93 to Mch 18 '94,	200.
cost of doctors examination	100.

" at Paris, Journey &c., Mch 18–Aug. (?), '94,	275
Journey to U.S. *via* London,	75
Total	$900
Apr 18, '93 Cash on hand	150
Scholarship petitioned for =	$750

Just how I shall commence my work after I return to America I cannot of course now say. My plan is something like this: to get a position in one of the Negro universities, and to seek to build up there a department of history and social science, with two objects in view: (a) to study scientifically the Negro question past and present with a view to its best solution. (b) to collect capable young Negro students, and to see how far they are capable of furthering, by independent study and research, the best scientific work of the day.

Such a work to be successful must enlist the services not only of devotion and long patient strife, but also of the ripest and best scholarship—in no other way would it be a fair experiment. I therefore desire, so far as in me lies, to obtain the best results of European scholarship and culture, and to this end, I regard another year here, occupied as I have indicated, absolutely necessary.

I therefore wish humbly to petition for a renewal of my scholarship for the coming year on the same terms as last year. I would even be willing to accept less favorable terms rather than to lose this which I must needs regard as the opportunity of my life.

I have made bold to make this petition (which I address to the trustees and send enclosed) because in my appointment the committee while making "no promise either expressed or implied" nevertheless expressed a willingness to consider the question of a second year.

I send also enclosed a letter from Professor Schmoller, with translation, etc. Professor Hart of Harvard will communicate with you later.

Allow me to express to the Committee my heartfelt thanks for their interest and pains.

I remain, gentlemen,

      Respectfully yours
      W. E. B. Du Bois

      Baltimore. May 5th, 1893.

W. E. B. DuBois
Dear Sir:—

The Trustees of the Slater Fund are willing to renew your appointment for another year on the same terms as last year. I believe you gave your note for $350. and received $350. as a scholarship.

You will need to send your note for the second sum to Mr. M. K. Jesup, Treasurer, #44 Pine St., New York. He will remit as before the amount due you

      [D. C. Gilman]

Berlin, 6 Dec, 1893

To the Honorable,
The Trustees of the John F. Slater Fund
Gentlemen:

I have honor hereby to submit my first report for the year 1893-4, as holder of a scholarship under you.

I spent the spring vacation in the old Hanse cities, and the Harz mountains, and then returned to the University of Berlin, where, in this my second semester, I heard lectures under Professors Schmoller (Economics), Lenz, (modern History), Dilthey (Philosophy); and took part in the Seminar of History (Professor Lenz), and the Seminar of Economics (Prof. Adolf Wagner).

During the summer vacation, August and September, I took a trip to Switzerland, and Italy as far south as Naples. Returning I sought to get a nearer view of certain European race questions by going to Vienna and Budapest, and thence riding and tramping through the Carpathian mountains to Crackow the old capital of Poland; thence by Breslau back to Berlin.

The work of this, my third semester here, I have laid out as follows:

(a) Writing of a doctor's thesis.

(b) General reading in Economics and History.

(c) Seminary work in Economics under Prof. Schmoller, Seminary work in Statistics under Prof. Neitzen, Lectures on history of the Reformation, under Prof. Lenz.

The doctor's thesis, which as already reported was commenced sometime ago, is now finished (Dec. 1). It is entitled: "Der landwirtschaftliche Gross = und Kleinbetrieb in den Vereinigten Staaten." It is a statistical inquiry into the relative economic advantages of the large and small farm. On the evening of 4th December I read a part of it before the Seminary of Economics under Professor Schmoller. I shall now hand it to the ministry, with the request to be allowed to take my doctor's examination at the close of this semester. I do not know what their decision will be. Meantime I shall proceed with my work as laid out.

I have all along enjoyed the best of health.

With great Consideration, I remain, Gentlemen,

Your obliged Servant,
W. E. B. Du Bois.

Berlin, 29 Mch. '94

President Gilman
Sir:

I have the honor hereby to mail my fourth semiannual report to the honorable trustees of the Slater Fund as holder of a travelling scholarship under them.

My study has been carried on here at the University of Berlin on the lines previously indicated, viz., Economics, Economic history, and Modern European history. I have, for now the third semester, taken part in the Seminary of Economics, where I read a paper, Dec 4, '93, on "Die landwirtschaftliche Entwickelung in den Südstaaten der Vereinigten Staaten."¹ The larger part of my time has been spent in making the acquaintance of the important part of the modern German economic and historical literature.

I must with great regret announce that the faculty of the University, in spite of the kind efforts of Professors Wagner and Schmoller and others, have found it impracticable to make so great an exception in my case as to admit me to the doctor's degree with but 3 German semesters. Altho' there had been but one case of the sort, and that years ago, yet, my professors thought it possible, and indeed, as they assure me, the petition would have been granted, had not at the last moment the Professor of Chemistry threatened that if so great an exception was made in my case, he must bring forward ten similar cases from his laboratory. This naturally settled the question.

I still have enough funds at hand to spend a fourth semester but could not of course stay for a fifth, which with graduating expense would cost some $350 extra. I shall next semester go to Tübingen, where I shall study under Professors Neumann and Schönberg, and then return to the United States.

I enclose two letters, one from Professor Adolph Wagner and one from Professor Gustav Schmoller, which they have kindly offered to write for me.

I desire to express my most sincere thanks to the honorable trustees and to yourself for the interest shown and aid afforded me.

I am, Sir

Most Respectfully Yours,
W. E. B. Du Bois.

P.S. Will you kindly return the original letters of Wagner and Schmoller.

My address after April 1, will be Neustadt a/d Haardt, Pfalz, Germany.

Translation [made by Du Bois]

Berlin, 28 March 1894.

Mr. E. B. Du Bois has laid before me his work upon "The Large and Small System of Farming in the [Southern] United States of America"; this careful as well as comprehensive work, resting on a basis of wide study, has impressed me very favorably. The author has succeeded in bringing much material together to prove that American experience offers no ground for the assumption that Agriculture tends to develop toward the large-farming system, as the most advantageous.

The work proves that the author possesses talent and diligence, and that he has made good use of the time spent in study in Germany. It is much to be desired that it should be made possible for him to remain still a short time here and gain the outward completion of his studies through promotion to the Doctor degree. For this the rules of German universities require that he shall have at-

1. That is, "Agricultural Development in the Southern States of the United States."

tended an University here somewhat longer than he has. The before-mentioned thesis would, without doubt, be received as a Doctor's thesis.

Dr. Adolph Wagner
Professor of Political Economy
at the University of Berlin

Translation [made by Du Bois]

5 March 1894

Mr. William Edward Burghardt Du Bois, who has studied now three semesters at the University of Berlin, wished in course of the Winter semester, '93–94, to pass the doctor's examination; for this purpose he prepared a scientific thesis on the large and small systems of farming in the southern parts of the United States. This work would have been sufficient; but the Faculty refused to admit him to the oral examination, because according to their rules only those persons can be admitted to examination who have studied 6 semesters in German universities. Several times one of these semesters has been dispensed with, in the case of those who had studied at foreign universities some time. The philosophical faculty might, indeed, on the recommendation of Professor A. Wagner and myself, have possibly dispensed with 2 semesters, because we were able to express so favorable an opinion in regard to Mr. Du Bois. They could not, however, see their way clearly to dispense with three semesters, especially as a dozen foreign chemical students here had sent in similar petitions.

If it were made possible that Mr. Du Bois could study 5 semesters in Germany, he would certainly be able to stand the Berlin doctor examination.

Prof. Dr. G. Schmoller.
Professor of Political Economy at Berlin,
Member Academy of Sciences, etc.

Berlin 31 Mch '94

President Gilman
Dear Sir,

I mailed you day before yesterday the more formal report of my last half-year's work, together with the letters of my professors. I write you now personally for your advice.

I have been somewhat puzzled as to just what course I ought, under the circumstances, to take with regard to the doctor's degree. My failure to be admitted to examination was of course no fault of mine, but due to purely technical grounds of precedent. Ought I now to seek to stay the extra semester or ought I to give up the attempt and return to work at home? I know that the and other friends and ask your advice.[1] I am, as I say, by no means decided in my own mind as what is best under the circumstances—I do not wish to appear grasping

1. The sentence is incomplete in the original.

on the one hand—I do not, on the other, wish to relinquish a great opportunity without a struggle.

Your kind advice under these circumstances would be greatly appreciated by
Your humble servant,
W. E. B. Du Bois

Address: Neustadt a/d Haardt, 16 Sauter St., Pfalz, Germany.

Balto. April 13, 1894.

Mr. W. E. B. DuBois
Dear Sir,

Your favor of the 31st. of March has reached me this morning. A day or two earlier came your formal report to the Slater Trustees. All the evidence conveyed by the testimonials of your professors should be a great encouragement to you. I am glad to see their letters. The Slater Trustees, at their recent meeting, considered the question of giving aid to advanced students, and reached the conclusion that it was not best to renew your appointment, or to make any other at present.

In regard to the question of the degree, I do not feel capable of giving you advice. But it seems to me you would do well to return to Harvard and offer yourself as a candidate there.

It is probable that the time spent in German Universities, and the acquisitions you have made, would be counted in estimating your qualifications for the Harvard degree of Ph.D., and I think that the Harvard degree would be, in all respects, as advantageous to you as that of Berlin.

The Slater Trustees inquired particularly in respect to your course of study, and some of them expressed, with great earnestness, the hope that, on returning to this country, you will devote your talent and your learning to the good of the colored race.

[D. C. Gilman]

Mary Sylvina Burghardt Du Bois with her infant son, William

Du Bois with his high school graduating class, Great Barrington, Massachusetts, 1884. Du Bois is at the extreme left.

W. E. B. Du Bois, age nineteen

Fisk University graduating class of 1888. Du Bois is seated at left.

Du Bois, seated right, with other graduation speakers, Harvard, 1890

With University of Berlin classmates, 1894.
Du Bois is third from the left in the second to back row.
Courtesy of Mrs. Alice Burghardt Crawford.

TEACHER-SCHOLAR 1894–1904

IN THE spring of 1894, Du Bois started back to the United States. He went first to Paris and remained there briefly, then to London, and finally home, steerage, from Southampton, arriving in New York with enough money to pay his fare to Great Barrington, plus two dollars. Once back in the Berkshires, he lost no time in sending job-application letters to Negro institutions—not, as he wrote in his *Autobiography*, to any "white institution—I knew there were no openings there" (p. 184). One of his letters, written in what he called in his *Autobiography* a "systematic" campaign, was directed to Booker T. Washington at Tuskegee.

Gt. Barrington, Mass., 27 July, 1894

President Washington
Sir!

May I ask if you have a vacancy for a teacher in your institution next year? I am a Fisk and Harvard man (A.B. & A.M.) & have just returned from two years abroad as scholar of the John F. Slater trustees. My specialty is history and social science but I can teach German, philosophy, natural science, classics &c. Your wife knows of me, and I refer by permission to President [Daniel C.] Gilman, Johns Hopkins Univ., Baltimore; Secretary Harvard Univ., 5 University Hall, Cambridge; President Fisk Univ. Nashville; Rev. C. C. Painter of Indian Rights Association; President Calloway of Alcorn[1]

I can procure letters from any and all of these.

Respectfully yours,
W. E. B. Du Bois

Du Bois's job-hunting campaign evoked three positive responses: the first from Wilberforce University in Ohio, the second from Lincoln in Missouri, and the third from Tuskegee. He accepted the first at once and so felt it necessary to reject the others (though the one from Lincoln carried with it $350 more per year

---

1. Booker T. Washington's wife, Margaret Murray, was in the 1888 class of Fisk with Du Bois; the president of Fisk at the time of this letter was Erastus M. Cravath; C. C. Painter was then the Washington agent of the Indian Rights Association and was the author of several studies of Indian peoples in the Southwest; Thomas J. Calloway was president of Alcorn Agricultural and Mechanical College in Mississippi. A copy of this letter was kindly supplied the editor by Professor Louis R. Harlan of the University of Maryland, editor of the Booker T. Washington Papers.

than that from Wilberforce). These three came within a period of eight days; had their order been reversed, as Du Bois later wrote, "It would be interesting to speculate just what would have happened if I had received the offer of Tuskegee first, instead of that of Wilberforce."* Below are the first and the last of these three offers; both came as Western Union telegrams.

Aug 17 1894

Dated   Wilberforce University Ohio
To   Mr. W. E. B. Dubois
          Box 165
Our chair of classics eight hundred dollars salary is yours wire acceptance and come next week

S. T. Mitchell Prest.

8/25- 1894

Dated   Tuskegee Ala
To   W. E. B. Du bois—
          Gt Barrington Mass
Can give mathematics here if terms suit. Will you accept Wire answer

Booker T. Washington

At Wilberforce, Du Bois worked very hard indeed for his eight hundred dollars a year: he taught Latin, Greek, German, English, and some modern history. He wanted also to teach sociology, but could not get permission. The orthodoxy at Wilberforce disturbed him, and evidences of church-college politics appalled him; he made clear his opposition to both, and so his stay lasted but two years.

Further, he was in love with a student named Nina Gomer, from Iowa, and by the spring of 1896 they were married. For all these reasons, another position with some increase in pay was ardently sought by the new doctor. The money problems and the hopes come out in a letter he wrote to President Gilman of Johns Hopkins lamenting his inability to repay the loan from the Slater Fund.

Wilberforce, O., 28 June, '95

President Gilman
Sir:
   I spite of all that I could do, I have been compelled to inform the treasurer of the Slater Fund of my inability to meet my note of $250 this year. I am very sorry. My salary has however been small, and the incidental expenses of a teacher even at a small institution like this unexpectedly large. I have been promised an

* *Autobiography*, p. 185.

increase of salary in the "near future," and thus I hope, in spite of this first failure, to be able to complete payment within the proposed three years. I trust you will pardon this delinquency, which I, too, feel is not an auspicious beginning.

One item of additional expense was that incurred by my taking the degree of Ph.D. at Harvard, which I succeeded in doing this spring. I felt that I could not put this off longer in justice to myself and race.

I shall this year make a systematic endeavor to secure a better position and to this end I would [appreciate receiving] if possible copies of several letters of commendation which are in your possession; if at your convenience you could forward them to me I should be greatly obliged.

Respectfully yours
W. E. B. Du Bois

Great historical interest attaches to the immediate response of the young Du Bois, teaching at Wilberforce, to the speech delivered in Atlanta at the Cotton Exposition by Booker T. Washington on 18 September 1895. While the accommodationist message of that speech drew sharp criticism from segments of the Afro-American leadership and press at the time—and Du Bois soon was to become *the* voice of that opposition—his initial reaction was enthusiastic.*

Wilberforce, 24 September, 1895

My Dear Mr. Washington:

Let me heartily congratulate you upon your phenomenal success at Atlanta—it was a word fitly spoken.

Sincerely yours,
W. E. B. Du Bois

A result of Du Bois's job-hunting was an offer from the University of Pennsylvania to employ him for one year, with payment of nine hundred dollars,† to make a detailed study of the Black ghetto in Pennsylvania. Du Bois's appointment was to be as "assistant instructor." In fact, he was not even included in the faculty list printed in the university's catalogue, and he taught no class, "except once to pilot a pack of idiots through the Negro slums."‡

In the spring of 1896, the provost of the University of Pennsylvania sent him

---

* The original of this letter is in the Booker T. Washington Papers in the Library of Congress; a copy was kindly supplied by Professor Louis R. Harlan. The full text of Washington's 1895 speech is in *A Documentary History of the Negro People in the United States*, ed. Herbert Aptheker (New York: Citadel Press, 1951), pp. 753-57 (hereinafter cited as *Documentary History*).

† In his *Dusk of Dawn* the sum is mistakenly given as six hundred dollars (p. 57).

‡ *Dusk of Dawn*, p. 59.

the telegram given below; after Du Bois had accepted, and he and his bride had moved into the ghetto themselves, Harrison provided the young scholar with the letter of credential also published.

June 8 1896

Dated   Phila Pa
To   Dr WE DuBois
Are ready to appoint you for one year at nine hundred dollars maximum payable monthly from date of services If you wish appointment will write definitely
C C Harrison

Philadelphia, August 15, 1896.
To whom it may concern:

In connection with the College Settlement, the Trustees of the University of Pennsylvania have undertaken the study of the social condition of the Colored People of the Seventh Ward of Philadelphia. The University has entered upon this work as a part of its duty and wishes to make the investigation as thorough and exact as possible. We want to know precisely how this class of people live; what occupations they follow; from what occupations they are excluded; how many of their children go to school; and to ascertain every fact which will throw light upon this social problem; and then having this information and these accurate statistics before us, to see to what extent and in what way, proper remedies may be applied. Dr. W. E. B. Du Bois is the investigator on behalf of the University, and I write to bespeak for him your cordial reception and earnest co-operation.

Very respectfully yours,
C. C. Harrison

Du Bois's study of the actual living conditions of the Black community in Philadelphia—which resulted in his pioneering work *The Philadelphia Negro: A Social Study* (published for the university in 1899)*—was in line with analogous work in social settlement and sociological investigations then just beginning. Significant work in this direction was being done by Carroll Davidson Wright who, from 1885 to 1905, was the (first) commissioner of the United States Bureau of Labor, then within the jurisdiction of the Interior Department. In 1895, Wright had published *The Industrial Evolution of the United States;* his *Outline of Practical Sociology* appeared the same year as Du Bois's *Philadelphia Negro*.

---

* *The Philadelphia Negro: A Social Study, together with A Special Report on Domestic Service* by Isabel Eaton, Series in Political Economy and Public Law, of the University of Pennsylvania (Boston: Ginn and Co. for the University, Philadelphia).

Sometime in the spring of 1897, Mr. Wright inquired of Du Bois—probably in a letter which seems not to have survived—about ways in which the industrial history of Black people might best be studied. The pencilled draft of a letter replying to this request is published below; that it foreshadows much of the future effort of Du Bois is clear. The immediate consequence was the publication in January 1898, as *Bulletin of the Department of Labor,* vol. 3, pp. 1–38, of a study by Du Bois titled "The Negroes of Farmville, Virginia," and in May 1899 (vol. 4 of the same *Bulletin,* pp. 401–17), of another study, "The Negro in the Black Belt: Some Social Sketches." The two men continued this fruitful relationship until Wright left the Bureau of Labor in 1905.

Philadelphia May 5 1897

Carroll D Wright Esq.
Dear Sir:

In accordance with your suggestion I have been for the last month giving considerable thought as to methods of studying certain aspects of the industrial development of the Negro. It seems to me that the difficulties of studying so vast and varied a subject are so large that the first work to be done should be rather of an experimental or preliminary nature calculated to locate & define the difficulties & to indicate lines upon which a larger investigation could be carried to success. At the same time the results of a series of preliminary studies could be published and would by allaying false notions & prejudices prepare the public mind for the larger work.

Both the preliminary and the main work must of course be strictly limited in scope; great care must be taken to avoid giving offence to white or black, to raise no suspicions and at the same time to get definite accurate information. For the preliminary work I propose two plans—the first to my mind preferable, the second feasible:

Plan A

The Industrial Development of the Negro

Preliminary Study: The Economic situation of a typical town containing from 1000–5000 Negro inhabitants situated in Va., or the Carolinas, or Ga.

Study: Occupations
        Wages
        Ownership of Homes
        Hours of labor
        Economic history
        Cost of Living
        Organizations
        Crops

Study to be conducted, visits, schedules, county records &c.
To be carried out in the months of July & August 1897.

Plan B
The Industrial Development of the Negro
Preliminary Study: Condition of Negroes in the   Barber
                                                                          Public Waiter
                                                                          Caterer
                                                                          Building   } trade
                                                                          Mining
                                                                          & c.

in the city of   Richmond
                      or
                      Raleigh
                      or
                      Charleston
                      or
                      Atlanta
                      &c.
   Study: Number
                      Wages
                      Hours of labor
                      Cost of living
                      Economic history
                      Organization
                      General conditions

Other Plans
A Study of Domestic Service in a certain city.[1]
A Study of the N. in the Professions in several cities.
"   "   "   "   " Farm Laborer in a typical agricultural region.
A Study of the Negro Church as a Social Institution in certain cities.
An "Enquête" of the Graduates of Southern schools into their own Economic life & the general industrial situation.[2]
A Study of the Attitude of Organized Labor toward Negroes.
A Study of Negro stevedores.
A bibliography of the Economic condition of the Negro since Emancipation.

    Plan A could be begun immediately. I could spend the summer in some typical village of the South and have the results ready to print in the fall. This plan could be repeated from time to time until these preliminary studies conducted

---

    1. It is to be noted that a (white) Quaker, Miss Isabel Eaton, contributed an appendix to Du Bois's *The Philadelphia Negro*, under the title, "Special Report on Domestic Service"; Miss Eaton and Du Bois remained friends for many years thereafter.
    2. *Enquête* (French), a scientific investigation; a piece of research.

in various districts in various times of year and under various circumstances would give a basis of fact and experience upon which a larger inv[estigation] could be planned with a great sav[ing in] time & expense.³ Or, after one or two experiments the whole inquiry might take the form of a series of simultaneous investigations of this sort in selected typical districts of town & county upon lines indicated by the actual experience of the preliminary studies.

Plan B could also be carried out this summer within certain limitations. The other plans are suggested and if they strike you as preferable to the first two I could work them out more carefully.

Will you kindly look over these plans and let me know which if any best meet your ideas. We can then discuss details further.

I am, Sir,

Respectfully yours
W. E. B. Du Bois
Assistant in Sociology U of P.

Du Bois's habits as author and scholar reflected great conscientiousness. A letter he sent to Jacob C. White, Jr. (1837–1902) while working on the galleys of his pioneering work in sociology, *The Philadelphia Negro,* is characteristic. White retired in 1896 from his position as principal of the Roberts Vaux Consolidated School in Philadelphia, a position he had held for over thirty years; he was acknowledged as a leading Afro-American figure in education. There is no record of any response from White, although he may have indicated suggestions or corrections directly on the galleys. At this time Du Bois had begun his teaching career at Atlanta University.

Atlanta, Ga., 18 October, 1898

My Dear Sir:

The Report of the University of Pennsylvania on the Colored people of Philadelphia is now in press. Some of the proof-sheets are at hand and I take the liberty of send[ing] you the proof-sheets of chapter VIII on Education and Illiteracy. Will you kindly look them over and note any errors of fact or judgement into which I have fallen? Please write out any corrections &c and return them with the proof-sheets to me by the 28th of the month if possible. If there is any one who knows of the subject to whom you would like to show the proofs, very

---

3. The manuscript is torn at two places, but the bracketed additions almost certainly were in the original.

[44]   Correspondence 1894-1904

well; only as the book is soon to appear copyrighted I should not like any publicity given to the matter. Thanking you in advance for your favor, I remain,
                    Very Sincerely Yours,
                    W. E. B. Du Bois[1]

Early in 1900, a vacancy appeared in the position of Superintendent of Negro Schools of the District of Columbia. Responsible officials naturally turned for candidates to Booker T. Washington—the leading dispenser of patronage among Black people. Washington wrote to Du Bois in this connection from the Grand Union Hotel in New York City.*

                    Mar. 11, 1900
Dear Dr. Du Bois:
   Please consider the contents of this letter strictly private. If you have not done so, I think it not best for you to use the letter of recommendation which I have sent you. I have just received a letter direct from one of the Commissioners in the District asking me to recommend someone for the vacancy there and I have recommended you as strongly as I could. Under the circumstances it would make your case stronger for you not to present the letter which I have given you for the reason that it would tend to put you in the position of seeking the position. It is pretty well settled, judging by the Commissioner's letter, that some one outside of the District is going to be appointed.
   This will be my address for the next week.
                    Yours truly,
                    Booker T. Washington

At the conclusion of the year's contract (1896-97) and of his work at the University of Pennsylvania, Du Bois agreed to take a professorship of economics and history at Atlanta University in Georgia. Immediately he immersed himself not

---

   1. This letter is in the Jacob C. White, Jr., Papers, Historical Society of Pennsylvania; the editor is appreciative of the society's assistance. In Harry C. Silcox, "Philadelphia Negro Educator: Jacob C. White, Jr., 1837-1902," *The Pennsylvania Magazine* 97 (January, 1973):75-98, the question in the above letter is quoted (on p. 75), but the word "any" is mis-rendered as "my." Silcox, in quoting this, writes that Du Bois "asked timidly." There is nothing "timid" about this letter and there was never anything timid about Du Bois; Du Bois wrote letters of this nature frequently in connection with his publications. He sent them to people whose opinions he valued and did this until his final years.
   * For an indication of the context in which this letter was written see the editor's book, *Afro-American History: The Modern Era* (New York, 1971), p. 119. When, in 1949, the editor asked Du Bois about this letter, he stated that he remembered two things about the event: he had not sought the appointment, and he did not get it.

only in teaching and in such scientific work as the conducting of the Annual Conference for the Study of Negro Problems, held at the university from 1897 through 1915, but also in agitational and organizational efforts, including battles for suffrage for Black people in Georgia and for the outlawing of jim-crow transportation.*

In connection with the latter, Du Bois personally instituted proceedings against the Southern Railway, commencing with this letter, sent special delivery early in 1900. Discussions and hearings on the matter were protracted, lasting for over four years; finally, as the records of the Interstate Commerce Commission show, at its general session held in Washington on 13 November 1905, in the case of *W. E. B. Du Bois v. Southern Railway Company*, it was *"Ordered,* that this case be and the same is hereby indefinitely postponed."

March 15, 1900

Mr. S. H. Hardwick,
Assistant Gen'l. Pass. Agent, Southern Ry.
Sir:

On the evening of the 19th of February last I had occasion to go from Atlanta to Savannah on business for the Commissioners of the Paris Exposition.[1] I boarded the Brunswick sleeper of the Cincinnati–Jacksonville train, leaving Atlanta at 10:45 P.M. On this train the sleeping car conductor, Mr. E. Davidson, declared that he could not furnish me a berth until the train conductor came through. The train conductor, Mr. J. A. Eikson (?), said that under orders issued by the Southern Railway, he could not give me a berth, as I was a Negro. I thereupon demanded separately both the Pullman conductor and the train Conductor to give me a berth and they both refused in the presence of W. B. Arwood, flagman of the train, and Booker Taylor, the porter of the car. There was plenty of room in the car—only four or five berths being made up, and I doubt if all of those were occupied. I thereupon left the car and was compelled to sit up all night—a matter which interfered with both my health and work, as I was then under the physician's care.

I was absent two weeks or more from Atlanta, but immediately on my return hastened to acquaint you with the facts, but was unable to catch you in your Office. I write to ask that you will state to me plainly the position of the Southern Railway on this matter; has the Railway given orders to its conductors to refuse Negroes sleeping car accommodations? Does the Railway propose to fur-

---

* On the suffrage struggle, see the 1899 petition to the Georgia legislature, written by Du Bois and widely signed, in Aptheker, *Documentary History,* pp. 784–86; and Du Bois's article, "The Suffrage Fight in Georgia," in the *Independent,* 30 November 1899, pp. 3226–28.

1. Du Bois was in charge of assembling what was called "The Negro Section" of the Paris Exposition of 1900, held to celebrate the beginning of the new century. For his work Du Bois was awarded the exposition's Gold Medal.

nish separate sleeping car accommodations for Negroes, or to furnish none at all? What interpretation does the Railway put on the phrase of the law "separate compartments"? How does the law affect inter-state traffic when the journey is begun *in* the state, and when it is begun *out* of the State?

I should like a clear frank statement from the Railroad as to its position in this matter, in order that I may be guided in the further steps which, under the circumstances I shall probably be compelled to take.

Very respectfully yours,
W. E. B. Du Bois

Du Bois was the first Afro-American scholar whose work was widely published not only under the auspices of such universities as Harvard and Pennsylvania, and by departments of the federal government, but also by national periodicals with considerable influence. In the latter, from the late 1890s until his death, Du Bois wrote particularly about the education of Black youngsters and adults. In this connection, a letter from Booker T. Washington at Tuskegee to Du Bois is interesting; it was written just a few months before the differences between the two men would produce public polemics.

Tuskegee, Ala., July 15, 1902.

My dear Dr. Du Bois:—

I have just read the editorial in the last number of The Outlook based upon your investigation of the condition of the public schools in the South, and I want to thank you most heartily and earnestly for the investigation of the subject referred to and also for the work which you are doing, through your conference and through your writings.[1] This editorial shows the value of such investigation. I know it is hard work and you may feel often that you are not very much encouraged in your efforts, but such an editorial ought to prove of great comfort to you. Constantly putting such facts before the public cannot but help our cause greatly in the long run.

Yours truly,
Booker T. Washington

1. The *Outlook*, edited by Lyman Abbott, was at this time perhaps the most powerful weekly in the United States. In 1901, it had published serially the autobiography of Booker T. Washington; by 1906, it was to attack Du Bois scathingly. The reference to "your conference" means the Sixth Annual Conference of Atlanta University, devoted to "The Negro Common School"; its proceedings were published in 1901 in a volume edited by Du Bois. In months preceding Washington's letter, Du Bois had published essays on education in the *Atlantic Monthly* (January 1899); in the *Independent* (18 July 1901); and, in five articles on "The Black North," in the *New York Times Magazine* (successive Sundays from 17 November through 15 December 1901).

It was under the distinguished editorship of Bliss Perry (1860–1954), from the years 1899 to 1909, that essays by Du Bois occasionally graced the *Atlantic Monthly*. Among these was "Of the Training of Black Men," one of the more influential of Du Bois's essays, published in the *Atlantic* in September 1902.

Perry's letter accepting it follows, as do two of the many letters Du Bois received expressing appreciation for its appearance. The essay was reprinted the next year in the first edition of Du Bois's classic work, *The Souls of Black Folk*. The first of the two letters here published came from the Reverend D. Horace Bumstead, president of Atlanta University; it is undated but was written late in the summer of 1902 and was sent from Bumstead's summer home in Intervale, New Hampshire. The second letter was from W. P. Thirkield, one of the two corresponding secretaries of the then-influential Freedman's Aid and Southern Education Society; to it Du Bois responded in a characteristically brief note: "I thank you for appreciative words and hope I deserve them."

Boston, June 28, 1902

Dear Mr. Du Bois,

I have your article, and shall take great pleasure in using it in the September number of the Atlantic. It seems to me one of the strongest and most eloquent pieces of writing that have come from your pen, and I am sure it will accomplish a great deal of good.

Assuring you of the genuine satisfaction I feel in being able to print such [a] notable paper, I am

Cordially yours,
Bliss Perry

Intervale, N. H.

My dear Dr. Du Bois:

I have just finished reading with intense delight your article in the September Atlantic. I cannot rest till I write and thank you for it—thank you with all my heart. It makes me feel about ten years younger, and I shall find in its thoughts and phrases a new source of strength in presenting our cause this winter. The article ought to have a much wider reading than it will get in the Atlantic's pages. I am going to write to Mr. Garrison to see if we cannot have a reprint of it in pamphlet form that we can distribute by the thousand.[1] Perhaps Fisk or the A.M.A. would like to co-operate.[2] Would it be well, or not, to have a cover with

---

1. William Lloyd Garrison, Jr., son of the Abolitionist, was himself deeply involved in anti racist efforts.
2. The AMA is, of course, the American Missionary Association.

opportunity for each school to advertise itself in its own edition? A few things in the article will draw southern if not northern fire. Can you make any other suggestion as to the best way to use the article?

Yours very sincerely,
Horace Bumstead.

Possibly it would appeal most to those who need it most if it were sent out without any reference to a particular organization or school.

Another plan would be to get the Atlantic to permit us to set up and print an abridgement of the article, containing its most salient and effective points.

Cincinnati, Ohio. Oct. 14, 1902

My dear Dr. DuBois:—

I cannot refrain from expressing to you the profound satisfaction and delight I experienced in reading your recent article on "The Education of the Black Man" in the Atlantic Monthly. I want to assure you that in my judgment it is an epochal utterance. It is the highest note yet struck on this great and vital question. It puts the entire question on a higher plane. It must command the attention of thinking men and turn the thought of men interested in this great work, that rests upon our hearts, into new channels. I have thought deeply and read broadly on this problem for many years. I have no hesitation in saying that this is the greatest deliverance, both in thought and expression, on this problem that I have ever read. I can not tell you how it breathes fresh courage and inspiration into my soul.

For several years I have been reading before numerous Conferences of preachers a carefully prepared paper on "The Higher Education of the Negro," and have made a strong effort to convince the people that without trained leaders any race is doomed. You have made all thinking men your debtors in giving to the world this in every way remarkable paper, and I praise God that you had the courage in several paragraphs to state the bald truth that the South needs to hear. In their blindness they fail to see their own peril.

With kindest wishes for Mrs. DuBois and your colleagues in the University, and praying that your life may be long spared for the high and noble service for which you are providentially equipped—for surely you have come into the Kingdom for such an hour as this, I am

Most gratefully and faithfully yours,
W. P. Thirkield

A pioneer Black militant, and an opponent of Booker T. Washington, William Monroe Trotter of Boston was an 1895 graduate of Harvard; in 1901 he, with George Forbes (an Amherst graduate of 1895), had founded the influential

Boston Guardian to give expression to clear-cut anti-racist views and demands. Du Bois deeply admired Trotter, though not fully in accord with all his views—particularly where these concerned tactics. Up to 1903, efforts were being made by both the Washington forces and the Trotter supporters to win over Du Bois. Within this context falls the letter from Trotter; it reflects also the rising concern in the Afro-American world about the campaign to smear the Reconstruction era in Southern history and, especially, the role of the Negro people therein.

Boston, Mass. Sept. 30, 1902.

Dear Dubois,

In regard to the Literary, we feel that you must come to us this year.[1] We want to hear you on the side of reconstruction that deals with the ante-reconstruction period and the black code and the things that the reconstruction governments have to their credit. You will do the people here great good by shedding light on that side of the question for us. Now we are poor, but we will pay your way from Washington, round trip if we have to. We want you to come on Jan. 12th. We can pay your car-fare from Washington to Boston. Some of us will house you while here. As I said we will pay the round-trip car-fare if we have to in order to get you to come. The trouble is that our treasury is nigh empty.

Please let me know what you can do for us. We should like to hear as soon as possible.

Yours truly,
W. M. Trotter

The first serious investigation of Black urban workers was undertaken by the Seventh Conference for the Study of Negro Problems, held at Atlanta University in May 1902 under the direction of Du Bois. The report and proceedings of this conference, edited by Du Bois, were published by the university's press as its publication no. 7(1902).

Du Bois sent a copy of that book to several of the national and international unions in the United States, suggesting its study and asking for commentary. Of the several replies received, two are offered below, the first from S. M. Sexton, editor of the *United Mine Workers' Journal,* and the second from James A. Cable, secretary-treasurer of the Coopers' International Union of North America. Du Bois's undated and pencilled copy of his reply to the latter has survived and is also published below.

1. The Black community of Boston maintained a Literary Society, which gathered each month to hear some authority discuss a matter of concern. Du Bois found it impossible to fulfill Trotter's request.

Indianapolis, Ind., Feb. 22, 1903

Mr. W. E. Burghardt Du Bois
Dear Sir:

I beg leave to acknowledge your pamphlet "The Negro Artisan." I am especially glad to become acquainted with a Negro who is taking an interest in the colored man as a worker. The United Mine Workers have always welcomed the Negro into their union. A Negro, D R Davis, was a member of our first National Executive Board. Many Negroes hold responsible offices both in local and state organizations. I desire to call your attention to the fact that in Ohio, Indiana, Illinois, Iowa, Pennsylvania, Kansas and Missouri and such parts of W Virginia, Tennessee, Kentucky and Alabama where our Union has sway, that the Negro members of our organization are citizens *de facto* as well as *de jure*. He has his vote counted as it is cast; there are no lynchings or any other form of summary deprivation of his civil or natural rights. But we do have to contend against negro editors who basely and falsely accuse us of wronging the colored man. They lend their columns to allure colored men from the agricultural districts to the mines of those operators who refuse to deal fairly with their employes of all colors. We seek to secure for the colored man his pay in lawful money of the United States, just weight for the coal he digs, the same rate of wages and the same conditions that the white man secures. If you will investigate the West Virginia coal fields and those in Hopkins and Christian counties, Kentucky, you will find that the Negro miners, outside of our Union, are in a state of peonage, robbed, underpaid and systematically debauched by the coal operators. They are [a word illegible] and led to believe that the U.M.W. of A. are enemies whereas we would only secure justice for them. To the shame of the negro editors be it said they encourage their brethren to accept the slavish and degraded condition offered by the unfair operators. I impute no motives to any one, but there can be no worthy motive in such a course as pursued by the Negro editors. We gladly accept all races in our Union but the Chinaman—he drew the line for himself. You must have observed that our organization has taken men from the lowest and most ignorant European races and made self respecting American citizens of them. We would gladly do the same for the Negro miner but the Negro editor is a mighty barrier to overcome. I write this at length in order to apprise you of what I believe after years of observation is the true cause of race hatred as far as the miners are concerned. That that hatred is there is due to no other cause I believe than the unwise and despicable course of some Negro editors.

With kind regard and best wishes

I am
Truly Yours
S. M. Sexton

Kansas City, Kans., Feb. 26, 1903.

Mr. W. E. Burghardt DuBois
My dear Sir:—

I am in receipt of your "Negro Artisan" and first of all permit me to congratulate you upon the issuance of same which to say the least is a very neat and interesting book and is a monument to the progress of the negro race since its emancipation from slavery in 1865. Please find postage enclosed amounting to fifty cents in payment of same.

By comparing your tables on pages 87 and 158 I find that we have about 8% of the negro coopers organized. If you will compare our white membership with the census report of 1890 you will find that we have very little if any more than 8% of the white coopers organized. Considering that the trade union movement is a Northern institution and has but recently begun to spread into the South where the negro coopers are located we fail to see upon what grounds you base your claim on page 163 where you say that the Coopers' Union "admits negroes but does not seek them." This is a mistake as we want all the negro coopers in our union as well as all the whites.

We also take exception to the remark as it is put on page 159, fourth line from top, where it says that we "admit that local unions can refuse to admit negroes." It is true we do admit but we now have nine negro locals and are after more, and they in like manner can if they choose, refuse to admit whites and we think you should have made mention of this fact in connection with the report. We also have German locals who may, if they choose, refuse to admit Irishmen and vice versa and from what I know of this movement I am of the opinion that the German and Irish coopers discriminate against each other oftener and with more bitterness than the whites discriminate against the negroes.

The General Office of the Coopers' International Union is doing all it can with the facilities at hand to organize the negro coopers wherever found without discriminating and if you know of any who wish to form a local union I can guarantee you that they will be granted a charter and that they will receive the same consideration and the same benefits from the International Union as the whites receive.

Very respectfully yours,
James A. Cable
Intl Secy Treas.

Enclosure.
P.S. I am sending you some marked copies of our Journal under separate cover and in order to aid you in keeping posted have placed you on our free mailing list.
Cable

[Du Bois's Reply]

I thank you for your contribution & letter of the 26th ult. I recognize the force of your comments & yet I think that you will admit with me that race lines between Germans & Irish are as deplorable from a workingman's stand point as the color line & that simply because a colored cooper has not enough fellows about him to form a union of Negroes exclusively that this is no excuse for barring him from the white union. Let us hope that time & Justice will solve all these difficulties.

In 1902, Du Bois received several invitations to leave Atlanta and teach at Tuskegee with a substantial increase in salary. He was urged to undertake this change by some of the wealthiest backers of Washington's school, including the financier, Jacob Schiff; the president of the Long Island Railroad, William H. Baldwin, Jr., and such other "merchant princes" as Robert C. Ogden, J. G. Phelps Stokes and George Foster Peabody, all of New York. During the same year, Du Bois had at least two interviews with Washington, but Du Bois was never satisfied as to just what he would do in Tuskegee and felt increasingly suspicious.

Early in 1903, Washington proposed to Du Bois that a conference—closed to the public—be held with the purpose, as Washington put it in a letter he sent to fifteen Negro leaders, "of considering quietly all the weighty matters that now confront us as a race." The leaders, meanwhile, were formulating their strategies and readying their forces, as indicated by the letter, marked "Confidential," which Du Bois sent to Professor Kelly Miller (1863–1939) of Howard University in February 1903. Negotiations dragged on; a definite date and place for the meeting—6–8 January 1904, Carnegie Hall in New York City—were not set until October 1903. Washington assured all participants that expenses would be met; though the benevolent donor's name was not made public, there is no doubt he was Andrew Carnegie: in 1903, Carnegie's gift of $600,000 to Tuskegee was announced. Washington's letter to Du Bois in November reflects part of the final preparatory efforts; Du Bois's sharp, undated reply foretells the collapse of the effort at conciliation, though the meeting was held.

In the history of the Afro-American people, this Carnegie meeting was consequential as the last effort at producing a *modus vivendi* between the Washington-Du Bois forces*

---

* Details will be found in the editor's article, "The Washington-Du Bois Conference of 1904," *Science and Society* 13 (1949):345–51. The Du Bois letter to Kelly Miller is published, in part, in that source.

(Confidential)

Atlanta, Ga. February 25, 1903.

Dear Miller:—

I was asked to go to Tuskegee some time ago and at that time the Conference you have been invited [to] was cooked up. A little judicious pressure and insistence lead to your invitation and that of [Clement G.] Morgan of Cambridge. I do not recall all the names but it includes [J. W.] Lyons, Bishop [Abraham] Grant, John Trower of Philadelphia, Rev. [C. T.] Walker of New York, [F. L.] McGhee of St. Paul, etc.

I think this will be a chance for a heart to heart talk with Mr. Washington. I propose to stand on the following platform:

1. Full political rights on the same terms as other Americans.
2. Higher education of selected Negro youth.
3. Industrial education for the masses.
4. Common school training for every Negro child.
5. A stoppage to the campaign of self-depreciation.
6. A careful study of the real condition of the Negro.
7. A National Negro periodical.
8. A thorough and efficient federation of Negro societies and activities.
9. The raising of a defense fund.
10. A judicious fight in the courts for Civil rights.

Finally the general watch word must be, not to put further dependence on the help of the whites but to organize for self help, encouraging "manliness without defiance, conciliation without servility."

This program is hardly thought out—what is your opinion?

By the by, Washington wants to invite [T. Thomas] Fortune to the conference. I wrote him that I thought it would be a very unwise thing. I've not had an answer yet.

Please send me when you write Mrs. Mollie Keelan's address.

Sincerely yours,
W. E. B. DuBois

Tuskegee, Alabama, Nov. 8, 1903.

Dear Dr. DuBois:—

Please be kind enough to let me have your opinion of the following matters just as early as possible as time is pressing: Of course the main object of our New York Conference is to try to agree upon certain fundamental principles and to see in what way we understand or misunderstand each other and correct mistakes as far as possible. I agree with your suggestion that in Chicago, for example, we ought to have as far as possible, all shades of opinion represented. I have no objection to inviting either Dr. [Charles T.] Bentley or Mr. [Edward H.] Morris. Which one do you prefer? Of course we could not invite them both. In this same connection I think that we ought to have W. H. Lewis from Boston as we could only get at both sides of New England thought by having him or some such man, as well as Mr. Morgan. The more I think of it, the more I feel convinced that Dr. J. W. E. Bowen ought to be present He represents a very large constituency and I have found him on all questions a pretty sane man. I have already written you as to your opinion about either Bishop [Henry M.] Turner or Bishop [Lucius H.] Holsey. Of course we must avoid having the conference too large and too expensive. Do you really think that Dr. [F. J.] Grimké would represent some idea or element that would not be represented by somebody else already invited? Please think of this and write me. As to Fortune; we may or may not agree with a great many things that he does, but I think there is no question but that he influences public opinion in a very large degree. We must make an especial effort to drop out of consideration all personal feelings, otherwise the conference will be a failure from the beginning.

So far in making up the conference, I fear it has one especially weak point which should be strengthened if possible. We should bear in mind that the bulk of our people are in the South and that the problems relating to their future very largely surround the Southern colored people, and we should be very sure that there is a large element in the conference who actually know Southern conditions by experience and who can speak with authority, and we should not have to depend too much on mere theory and untried schemes of Northern colored people.

Yours truly,
Booker T. Washington

Dear Mr. Washington:

I do not think it will be profitable for me to give further advice which will not be followed. The conference is yours and you will naturally constitute it as you choose. I must of course reserve the right to see the final list of those invited and to decide then whether my own presence is worth while.

W. E. B. Du Bois

The first edition of Du Bois's *The Souls of Black Folk: Essays and Sketches* appeared in April 1903 under the imprint of a small Chicago firm, A. C. McClurg and Co. Printings were modest, but the book immediately created a sensation; by 1905, it was in its sixth edition, and that year Archibald Constable brought it out in London.

The letter that follows reflects something of the book's immediate and significant impact; it is from Mrs. Ida B. Wells-Barnett, a militant Black woman who had been driven out of Memphis, Tennessee: the newspaper she edited, the *Free Press*, was too forthright in its demand for equality.

Mrs. Wells-Barnett was the chief founder of the national movement to end lynching, and the letter published below was written on the stationery of the Anti-Lynching League she chaired. Her husband, Ferdinand L. Barnett, was the first Black assistant state's attorney of Illinois and a significant force for many years in Black journalism.

Chicago, Ill., May 30th, 1903.

Dear Prof. DuBois:—

Your note of April 23rd did not especially call for a reply so I did not send one. I meant though to write you about a Conference which we had over your book at the home of Mrs. Celia Parker Woolley, a very good friend of the race.[1] She had a company of some of the most literary folks here among white folks, at her home one Sunday evening about three weeks ago, and then she had Dr. and Mrs. Bentley; Mr. Lloyd Wheeler, Prof. [Monroe] Work, Mr. and Mrs. Laing-Williams, your humble servant and her better half, all there to do the discussing.[2]

Mrs. Bentley had a fine review about which she had doubtless told you. Most of the others, save my husband and myself, confined their reviews solely to your criticisms of Booker T. and thought the book was weak because of them. Of course you know our sentiments. There was not much time for the white side of the audience to present its view but they too took the same view. Of one thing I am very certain, the discussion stimulated a curiosity to read the book.

But I feel sure you have heard about all this. My main object for writing now is to tell you that Mrs. Woolley, than whom there is not a truer friend of the race, seemed a little hurt that you had not acknowledged the receipt of a little book of her own which she had sent you. It is called "The Western Slope" and I am quite sure that while you may have overlooked its modest proportions in the press and stress of your own multitudinous work, it would need only a hint to have you duly look it up, and send the donor a cordial note of thanks both for what she has said for our race in it, as well as the work she is trying to do to convert her friends to your view of the subject in your own book.

1. Mrs. Celia Parker Woolley was an ordained minister who had served the Unitarian Chuch in Geneva, Illinois, and later the Independent Liberal Church in Chicago. She had been president of the Chicago Woman's Club and was the author of several books in addition to *The Western Slope* (1903), mentioned here. In 1904, she established the Frederick Douglass center in Chicago's ghetto and lived there until her death in 1918.

2. In her autobiography, Mrs. Wells-Barnett declared that "most of those present, including four of the six colored persons," took positions hostile to that of Du Bois. She added that it was at this moment that Mrs. Woolley "announced her determination to give up her pleasant residence, surrounded by literary friends, and come over to Macedonia to help black folks with their problems." See *Crusade for Justice: The Autobiography of Ida B. Wells*, ed. Alfreda Duster (Chicago: University of Chicago Press, 1970), pp. 280-81. Jenkin Lloyd Jones, then the editor of the Chicago magazine *Unity*, was among those present at this meeting. He wrote about it and *The Souls of Black Folk*, in *Unity*, 7 May 1903, pp. 148-49.

I lunched with Miss Jane Addams at Hull House Wednesday and found that she too was disappointed at not seeing you when she was in Atlanta recently. She said she did not blame you for not making your exhibit before the conference. But she tried to get a personal audience with you herself and failed. She said she wrote asking you to call, and that she telephoned over to the University requesting the same thing but that you did not come nor did she hear from you. I do not need to tell you who Miss Addams is. I assured her there must be some mistake, either you did not get the message or they refused to take your card up if you called at the hotel. I am sure that in your leisure moments you will find time to write her a note, to let her know that the silence was not intentional on your part.

We are still reading your book with the same delighted appreciation. I am arranging myself for a meeting of our best brained, to have a discussion thereon, within the next two weeks. Am only sorry that you cannot be present with us.

Yours truly,
I. B. W.-B.

Charles Waddell Chesnutt (1858–1932), a Cleveland attorney, gained fame as an essayist and novelist. Two collections of his short stories—*The Wife of His Youth* and *The Conjure Woman*—were published in 1899 by Houghton Mifflin of Boston; the same firm brought out two of his novels, *The House Behind the Cedars* (1900), and *The Marrow of Tradition* (1901), while Doubleday, Page and Co. of New York issued *The Colonel's Dream* in 1905.

Chesnutt's consistent support of Du Bois in the Washington-Du Bois struggle is reflected in a 1903 letter.

Cleveland, June 27, 1903.

My dear Doctor DuBois:—

I beg to acknowledge receipt of the clipping which you return to me; it was not important but I thank you just the same.

Potts have accepted my article on the disfranchisement of the Negro.[1] I take a firm stand for manhood suffrage and the enforcement of the constitutional amendments. I take no stock whatever in these disfranchisement constitutions. The South is suffering a great deal more from malignity of the whites than the ignorance of the Negro. I have wondered whether your book on the "Souls of Black Folk" had any direct effect in stirring up the peonage investigation in Alabama; it might well have done so.

I have not forgotten what you say about a national Negro journal. It is a matter

---

1. James Pott Company, a New York publishing house, brought out a collection of essays by leading Afro-Americans in 1903; in addition to Chesnutt's article, the book also contained a contribution from Washington and Du Bois's celebrated essay "The Talented Tenth."

concerning which one would like to think and consult before committing himself. There are already many "colored" papers; how they support themselves may be guessed at from the contents—most of them are mediums for hair straightening advertisements and the personal laudation of "self-made men," most of whom are not so well made that they really ought to brag much about it. The question of support would be the vital one for such a journal. What the Negro needs more than anything else is a medium through which he can present his case to thinking white people, who after all are the arbiters of our destiny. How helpless the Negro is in the South your own writings give ample proof; while in the North he is so vastly in the minority in numbers, to say nothing of his average humble condition, that his influence alone would be inconsiderable. I fear few white people except the occasional exchange editors, read the present newspapers published by colored people. Whether you could reach that class of readers and at the same time get a sufficient subscription list from all sources to support the paper is the thing which I would advise you to consider carefully before you risk much money. The editing of a newspaper is the next vital consideration. To do it properly would require all the time of a good man—he ought to be as good a man as yourself.[2] I wish I could talk with you. Where will you spend the summer? Let me know your movements and it is possible that I might find it convenient to be at the same place some time before the fall.

I presume what you have written concerning me has not yet appeared, but have no doubt it will be just and complimentary, and I thank you for it in advance.[3]

                    Sincerely yours,
                    Chas. W. Chesnutt.

In his *Dusk of Dawn,* Du Bois remarked that in the early years of the twentieth century, the Tuskegee machine was arousing "increasing opposition among Negroes and especially among the younger classes of educated Negroes, who were beginning to emerge here and there" (p. 72). A letter of 1903 notably illustrates the opposition and the kind of thinking it produced.

    2. As certain of the letters appearing on previous pages have indicated, Du Bois hoped for such a magazine from his youth. In 1906, he launched a weekly, the *Moon* (published in Memphis), which lasted one year; in 1907, he was decisive in bringing out the *Horizon,* a monthly published in Washington, which lasted until 1910, and gave way then to the *Crisis.*
    3. He refers to an essay, "Possibilities of the Negro: The Advance Guard of the Race," published in *Booklover's Magazine* 2 (July 1903):2–15; here Du Bois wrote of Washington, Granville T. Woods, Edward H. Morris, Henry O. Tanner, Daniel H. Williams, Kelly Miller, and Chesnutt.

Chicago, Ill., July 20, 1903.

Prof. W. E. Burghardt Du Bois
Dear Sir:

I am very greatly interested in everything of a public character which concerns the Negro race. My father belonged to the Underground Railway in an early day, when to be a black abolitionist took nerve and courage and conscience. Some five or six years ago, at my own charges and as a private individual, I visited our schools in the South, including schools at Jackson, Miss., Selma, Montgomery, New Orleans, Nashville, Tuskegee, Atlanta and others. Now to commit myself, and not to commit you, without your knowledge, while I believe in Mr. Washington and Tuskegee, so far as it goes, yet I believe most emphatically that the battle-cry "Manual training for the Negro" is fundamentally false, and harmful, and pernicious.

The South and the North both like it. Why? Because they are willing to meet the negro on the fairest, broadest and unrestricted ground before God and man, or because on its very face, it assumes and asserts a limitation in connection with the negro, and is a discrimination against him. I deplore this fact more than I can tell you; and I know, perhaps better than you, if you have been living some time in the South, how this catchword is eagerly, gladly, selfishly, accepted here. It relieves us in the North of any great responsibility! The education of the hands is easy, simple, a short cut, and if neglected well, what of it? The body perishes—dust to dust. The education of the heart and mind, and soul, the lifting up of a man—this is difficult and long and painstaking. This means—in a word—the giving of one's self to that man who is to be lifted, or to be helped! This is the way of Calvary! Not an easy road.

This catch-word has filled the minds of the people—North and South! It is misleading! It has done incalculable harm, it will take a generation and more to dislodge it. Now, the only reason why I mention Mr. Washington's name here is this: he, more than any other one man is responsible for this idea, and because he is the confessed representative of it. "Booker Washington says so: he knows. He is the foremost man of his race." And this is an answer to every objection. This is the only reply the people of the North deem it necessary to make. Indeed this is such a finality in the consideration of this race problem (I do not like this expression) that few men here in the North stop to give it a careful consideration. Now if Mr. Washington would say "I believe in Education for all men alike, but manual training, or industrial education for the Negro of the South seems for the present, to be most needed, or expedient," I would not have anything to say.

Or, if Mr. Washington would say: "There are many schools of higher education in the South for the negro, and my work in Tuskegee I am best adapted to give manual training." Very good! But you know that is not his attitude; not his position before the public; Mr. Washington of course says in public that Tuskegee gives academic training, and is engaged in fitting many of the students there, to become *School teachers;* but that is kept in the background, that is not his message to the people.

His name, his work, his school, all are used here in the North, even as an argument against the education of the Negro. Why is it that the ignorant, illiterate, low, profane white man of the north catches at the word—"Industrial education; Manual training for the Negro." He is not interested in any moral or educational question under heaven. How is it that such a man is so sure and clear on the best and only thing, for the Negro. I wish Mr. Washington might be persuaded to define his position more sharply; and if he believes in the *education* of the negro, without limitations or discriminations, or differentiations, that he would speedily say so. The sentiment "Industrial Education for the Negro" is the shackle—not removed from his hands but in addition, put upon head and heart—upon the whole man—the whole race. Let us fear him, who casts body and soul into hell! Jesus said.

This sentiment inculcated, re-enslaves the negro race. When the iron manacle was on the slave's limbs, that iron visibly marked the degree or extent of his abject condition. Physical slavery had not yet dared to invade the realm of the soul. And the implication of his subjection or inferiority did not go beyond the iron band, or the physical body.

But now this sentiment is a manacle upon the intellectual, moral, spiritual, upon the higher, nature: upon the whole man.

I think someone should endeavor to make Mr. Washinton see his position; or if it be not his position, then for the sake of the Negro, and the Caucasian, the North and the South, that he should come out publicly and clear the air of this damaging and damnable misrepresentation on his part, and misapprehension on the part of the country. The position is untenable. If he do not hold it, he should say; If he does hold it, he should be driven from it.

Are you to be in Chicago within the next six weeks or in the East later? I wish very much to see you. I would be pleased to hear from you. I have no controversial spirit in this matter. It goes far deeper than that.

May I ask if any of your relatives of the preceding generation lived with Wheelers in New Brunswick in the vicinity of Fredericton?

I have been pastor of the Fourth Baptist Church here in the city for nine years.

Very fraternally,
Kittredge Wheeler

A letter from an attorney in Jacksonville, Florida, reflects, again, the deep impact of Du Bois's writings and the kind of thinking which would eventuate, in 1905, in the creation of the militant Niagara Movement.

[60] Correspondence 1894–1904

Jacksonville, Fla., Oct. 20, 1903

My Dear Doctor:

I have just finished reading "Souls of Black Folk" for the second time, and am so much impressed with it, I feel compelled to write you, and thank you in the name of the Race, for writing so able a book on the Negro's condition in this country, and especially in the South. I believe that you are the only Negro we have, who is in any way worthy to be classed with the lamented Douglas, as an advocate of equal rights and justice for our Race. I want also to express my appreciation of the very excellent article which you wrote for the Book-lovers Magazine in July.

There is to be a Carnival held here the week of November 2nd, which will be very similar to Mardi Gras, which is held annually in New Orleans, and there will be cheap rates from Atlanta to this City during that week, and I should like very much to have you visit me at that time, as my guest, if you can make it convenient. This is a beautiful little southern City, and the Negroes are treated better here, I think, than in any other City in the South, and I believe you would enjoy a visit here very much. If you come, I will see that you are not bored socially, any more than you wish to be. As you know, I am fair enough to be taken for a white man, and therefore I have had great opportunities for studying the Negro question, under different circumstances and conditions, from the rest of my race. I am deeply interested in the problem which surrounds us, and would like so much to have an opportunity to be with you two or three days, and talk to you about a great many things which concern our people and to get your advice on some matters, which are of vital interest to me individually. I am fortunate enough to have a large practice, and am therefore very busy nearly all the time, and when I take the time away from business for a vacation, I always go North, where I can breathe free air, and be treated as a man. I seldom visit southern Cities, unless compelled to do so on business; and I really hate Atlanta, for I think it is one of the meanest places in the United States. As you are a sociological student, I think you would be benefitted by a visit to this City, as the conditions here are so different from most southern communities.

Trusting that you will see your way clear to visit here next month, or some time during the winter, any way, I am

Yours very truly.
J. Douglas Wetmore.

The details of how Du Bois came to write the biography of John Brown (published in Philadelphia in 1909 by George W. Jacobs and Co.) are told in the correspondence published below. The volume was one in the series entitled "The American Crisis Biographies," edited by Ellis Paxson Oberholtzer. The latter, born the same year as Du Bois, had his doctorate from the University of Pennsylvania. At the time of this correspondence, he was already fairly well known in the historical profession because of his *Referendum in America* (1893), and his biography of Robert Morris, the American Revolutionary figure (1902). His life of Jay Cooke (1907), the four-volume work on Philadelphia's history (1912), and especially his five-volume *History of the United States Since the Civil War* (1917–37) were to place him—along with Beard, Rhodes, McMaster, and Channing—among the "standard" historians of the era between the two World Wars.

Here published are Oberholtzer's original letter of 11 November, suggesting that Du Bois write a life of Frederick Douglass; Du Bois's tentative acceptance, dated 18 November; Oberholtzer's rather definite offer of 21 November; and his embarrassed letter of 25 January 1904 where, because of Booker T. Washington's interest, the suggestion that Du Bois write on Douglass had to be withdrawn. Five days later, Du Bois answered, rather graciously under the circumstances, and suggested a book on Nat Turner. Some sparring followed, as subsequent letters show, and finally agreement was reached that Du Bois write not about the Black slave rebel but rather about John Brown, the white leader of a Black-white blow against slavery. Throughout, Oberholtzer misspells the name of John Bach McMaster, the distinguished historian.

Philadelphia, November 11, 1903.

Prof. W. E. Burghardt Dubois
Dear Sir:

I have projected with Mr. Jacobs, the publisher of this city, a series of biographies which we shall call "The American Crisis Biographies." It is our object in this Series to give an impartial view of the causes, the course, and the consequences of the Civil War. We shall begin with the appearance of the issue in American politics and follow it until it fades out of American history. There will be twenty-five volumes, almost uniform in size, each to contain about 300 pages, 12mo, or say about 75000 words. It is designed that each phase of the movement shall be covered by a life of the character most prominently identified with that particular feature of the struggle. It seems to me and to Professor MacMaster, who has promised to assist in the work, that this is a service which now needs to be performed. We have arrived at a period in our history when we can look calmly and dispassionately at the issue and see both sides without the prejudices of the War Time. Having the perspective of a half a century, and having authors who are not survivors of the struggle, but who instead have come forward since the War, we hope that all these requirements shall be fulfilled.

Of the twenty-five volumes about ten will be of Southern men, including Calhoun, Jefferson Davis, Alexander Stephens, Robert Toombs, General Lee, "Stonewall" Jackson, and perhaps one or two others yet to be chosen. It is intended that the lives of the Southern men shall be written by Southern writers as a guaranty of greater impartiality.

In a recent conversation with Professor MacMaster it was suggested that you, if you were willing, might give us a life of Frederick Douglass. With that would be included the history of the Fugitive Slave Law, some account of the African Slave Trade, and a description of the operations of the underground railroad. I have never seen anything in print which could be considered for a moment as an adequate history of the underground railroad to Canada.

Hoping to hear from you, I am,

Very truly yours,
Ellis P. Oberholtzer.

Atlanta, Ga., Nov. 18, 1903

My Dear Sir:

I think I should like to write a life of Douglass on the lines laid down in your favor of November eleventh. Something would depend of course on the time when you would want the Ms. and the general terms. There are as you know I presume several lives of Douglass—his autobiographies, one in the American Reformer series & one in the Beacon Biographies.[1] I presume too you know of [W. H.] Siebert's Underground Railroad. I shall be glad to hear from you further on the subject.

Very Respectfully,
W. E. B. Du Bois

Philadelphia November 21, 1903.

Professor W. E. B. DuBois
My dear Sir:

I was pleased to have your letter of the 18th inst. with its expression of willingness to contribute a life of Frederick Douglass to our "American Crisis Series." I know that Mr. Douglass has had several biographies, but I do not think that anyone has done the work quite as you and I would have it done. Certainly in such a series as the one we have projected it would be necessary to bring out other phases of his life, that it might form a chapter in the general history of the struggle between the northern and southern states. While Siebert's "Underground Railroad" is a work indicating a great deal of research it has always seemed to me as a descendant of one of the principal Pennsylvania Station keepers on this railroad, that much which is most interesting in regard to this remains to be told. There is a mass of anecdote and romantic incident which it might be impossible to bring into such a volume as we project on account of its narrow compass, but which nevertheless could be hinted at, and suggested with great advantage. As we shall not in all probability publish more than five vol-

---

1. Douglass's autobiographies were published during his lifetime, in 1845, 1855, and 1882, with revisions and additions in each case; the two biographies mentioned by Du Bois were: Frederick M. Holland, *Frederick Douglass; The Colored Orator*, in the "American Reformer" series published in 1891 by Funk and Wagnalls; and Charles W. Chesnutt's *Frederick Douglass*, forming part of the "Beacon Biographies" published in Boston in 1899 by Small, Maynard and Co.

umes a year, and as the whole work contemplates twenty-five volumes, I do not think that you need be in any particular haste in sending us the manuscript if it does not suit you to do so. Of course, other things being equal, the manuscript first ready will be first published, although it is our design to bring out a few of the earlier figures before we reach Douglass.

For this work we are allowing the authors 10% upon the retail selling price, the same as is received by the authors of "The Great Commanders Series" and others. Later there will be a subscription edition, upon which we shall allow 10% upon one half of the retail price. This provision is necessary on account of the much larger commissions which must be paid to agents on subscription books. In addition to this, I am allowed to make an advance on account of royalty of one hundred dollars ($100.00) to be paid upon the delivery of the manuscript. These are the same terms upon which I am contributing to the Series, and I know that under this firm's auspices, returns to the author under the royalty system are assured.

I know of your own good work in the historical field from the time when you were in Philadelphia, and I shall be very glad if I can arrange to have your cooperation in an enterprise which interests me personally very much.

Very truly yours,
Ellis Paxson Oberholtzer

Philadelphia January 25, 1904.

Dr. W. E. Burghardt Dubois
My dear Sir:

I have delayed forwarding you the contract for the life of Frederick Douglass for our *American Crisis Series* because of a letter received from Booker T. Washington, concerning the same subject. I had written him first, but not having heard from him for a considerable time and desiring, personally, that you should do the volume because of your superior historical training, I had rather too eagerly sought to secure your cooperation for this volume. I regret to tell you that I must give it to him. The publishers are very desirous of adding Mr. Washington's name to the list of authors for the Series, and it was in vain that I endeavored to have him take an assignment to some character illustrating a later period in the negro's development, some freedman, a period he knows very well, and one that calls for less historical learning.[1] I had from the first planned to have two volumes on colored men.

Now can you suggest any other name which you would be willing to take instead of Douglass? The name while it must be worthy of a place beside the others in the series of twenty-five, will be only a rallying point for a great deal of historical knowledge of the time which I know you can glean, and for a point of view which I know you will give the reader in any study that you undertake.

1. In 1907, the Jacobs firm brought out Washington's biography of Douglass.

[64] Correspondence 1894–1904

I hope that you will understand this matter as it is, and can suggest a way by which I can bring you into the Series, as I particularly desire your aid, and that in any case you will forgive me for what is apparently a very great discourtesy. Believe me,

Very truly yours,
Ellis P. Oberholtzer

Atlanta, Ga., Jan. 30, 1904

My dear Sir:

I have your favor of the 25th. If it falls within your scheme the best subject for me would be Nat Turner—around him would center the slave trade, foreign & internal, Negro insurrections from Toussaint down to John Brown, the beginnings of the Underground railroad, the beginning of abolitionism, the movements of the free Negroes of the North & the whole plantation economy which was changing critically in the thirties, and the general subjective Negro point of view of the system of slavery. Another suggestion would be B. K. Bruce & reconstruction but this does not attract me as much.

W. E. B. Du Bois

Philadelphia February 3, 1904.

Prof. W. E. B. Dubois
Dear Sir:

I am very much obliged to you for your favor of January 30th, and the suggestion which it contains. Perhaps it might be possible to make Nat Turner the central point for a description of the conditions prevailing in the South in the early part of the Century. I confess, however, that I am a little ignorant about the life of Turner and the importance of the movement which he led. If his insurrection had any permanent influence upon the development of the American Crisis, as for instance, in making the Black Laws more stringent, and in altering relations between masters and slaves, as I presume it may have done, I think there would be a good deal of propriety in a biography of the man. Is there sufficient material for such a purpose, and could he be made to appear as anything more than a deluded prophet who led a little band of men armed with scythes and broad axes?

I know your studies will enable you to answer these questions satisfactorily, and awaiting your early reply, I am

Very truly yours,
Ellis P. Oberholtzer

[undated]

Dear Sir:

In my opinion no single man before 1850 had a greater influence on Southern legislation & feeling than Nat Turner and in the North it disfranchised the Negroes of Penn. & strengthened the black laws. There is abundant material for his life & times. I should however not be satisfied to have you depend entirely on my opinion in this matter, but would be glad to have you to get the opinion of men like Professor McMaster & Professor Hart.

W. E. B. Du Bois

Philadelphia, February 16, 1904

Dear Dr. Du Bois:

I am very much interested in what you have told me in regard to Nat Turner and his times. I had already spoken to Professor MacMaster regarding the subject, and have had another talk with him since receiving your note. He is very anxious that someone should make a study of the condition of the free negro before the War, although I scarcely see how a name can be found as a rallying point for such an investigation as important as it must be considered to be. I fear you will think me very hard to suit, but I should prefer, if you can see your way clear to do it, that you should make John Brown the centre for your volume. That, I think, will enable you to give such an account as you outline of the Southampton and other insurrections, and the changing economic system in the South which may have been the result of that affair. It will also give us an opportunity for a chapter or two about the troubles in Kansas, which I am fearful may not elsewhere find a place in the Series. Although Brown has been done by Professor Von Holtz,[1] F. B. Sanborn, and others, your view of him, and the events which led up to the Harpers Ferry Movement would entertain me very much, and I am certain many others too.

I enclose a partial list of authors already assigned to subjects in the Series, and I hope that the arrangement herein indicated may be satisfactory to you. I do not think that of necessity it will greatly change the subject matter of the study, while at the same time giving us a central figure which can be placed beside the other figures we have selected for this Series.

Hoping to hear from you, I am

Sincerely yours,
Ellis P. Oberholtzer

In May 1903, Walter F. Willcox, then dean of the College of Arts and Sciences at Cornell University, wrote to Du Bois requesting his assistance in obtaining a teaching position for Jessie Fauset (1885–1961), one of the very few Negro students then at that university. Du Bois responded quickly and favorably; this 1903 exchange marked the beginnings of very long relationships between Du Bois and Willcox, who was for many years connected with the United States Census Bureau and with the National Association for the Advancement of Colored

---

1. Again, Oberholtzer misspells a leading historian—Hermann Eduard Von Holst—who died in Germany one month before this letter was written.

People (NAACP), and between Du Bois and Miss Fauset, who assisted him for several years when he was editing the *Crisis* and who, in the 1920s, was the author of significant novels.

Toward the end of 1903, Miss Fauset wrote to Du Bois; again he responded helpfully, and Miss Fauset began teaching the following summer.

Ithaca, N. Y., December 26, 1903.

My dear Professor DuBois,

Last year Professor Willcox wrote to you about my desire to do summer-school work. In your answer you were kind enough to say that my name was not unfamiliar to you (it is Jessie Fauset of Philadelphia, Pa.) and you also gave me permission to use your name in making application. Let me thank you now for that kindness.

I am going to draw further on your generosity by asking you if you will tell me of some means whereby I could teach school this coming summer of 1904. I am writing thus early because last year my applications were all too late.

Perhaps if I tell you a little about my work you will understand the matter more clearly. This is my Junior year at Cornell. My work thus far has been chiefly classical, though I have of course done a good deal of English and this year am taking American History. I have had German, French and Psychology— of course I am by no means prepared to teach this last. I would rather teach Latin and rudimentary English—I mean actual English Grammar—than anything else. I want especially to teach this summer because it is the last before I graduate, and I should like to have some experience before going to work for good. I should have no difficulty, my professors kindly tell me, in securing necessary recommendations. I want to work in the South—I know only one class of my people well, and I want to become acquainted with the rest.

Professor Du Bois I am going to thank you, as though it had been a personal favor, for your book "The Souls of the Black Folk." I am glad, glad you wrote it—we have needed someone to voice the intricacies of the blind maze of thought and action along which the modern, educated colored man or woman struggles. It hurt you to write that book, didn't it? The man of fine sensibilities has to suffer exquisitely, just simply because his feeling is so fine.

Will you let Dean Willcox's name serve to introduce me to you? And will you advise me on the school-matter? I hope I shall hear from you very soon.

Most sincerely,
Jessie Fauset.

George Foster Peabody (1853–1938) was born in Georgia but moved north, where his banking and investment successes accumulated. By 1906, he retired from business to devote himself entirely to various philanthropic, political, and educational interests. He was a trustee of Tuskegee and prominent in the financial affairs of many other Black (and white) colleges; he also had political influence, being treasurer of the Democratic National Committee (1904–5) and a close friend of Woodrow Wilson, Alfred E. Smith, and Franklin Delano Roosevelt.

Horace Bumstead (1841–1919) was the second president of Atlanta University (1886–1907); he had been a major with Negro troops in the Civil War and later became a Congregational minister, before going to Atlanta to teach Latin and moving up to the university presidency. He spent much of his time while president in the North raising money for the university; in this connection, Du Bois's militancy tended to be an embarrassment and helped hasten Du Bois's departure from Atlanta in 1910. The following three letters are to be read in this context.

December 28, [1903][1]

My dear Mr. Peabody:—

Some time ago Mr. [Edward T.] Ware, our Chaplain, spoke to me of a letter received from you in which you spoke of certain rumors as to my connection with the disturbances over Mr. Washington in Boston last summer. Later Dr. Bumstead wrote me of a similar letter not mentioning from whom he had received it, but I took it that it was probably from you.

I want therefore to write you frankly of my position in this matter that there may be no misapprehension, and I want you to feel at liberty to use the letter as you may wish.

Mrs. Trotter the wife of the editor of the Guardian is an old friend of mine of school days. Mr. Trotter I have not known so long or so well but met him in college. I had then and afterward disagreed with him rather sharply over many questions of policy and particularly over Mr. Washington. But nevertheless both then and now I saw in him a clean-hearted utterly unselfish man whom I admired despite his dogged and unreasoning prejudices. Last summer while Mrs. Du Bois and I were looking for a boarding place, Mrs. Trotter offered to share her home with us and we gladly accepted. I went first to Tuskegee and then made a trip on a coast steamer. I did not arrive in Boston until after the Zion Church disturbance.[2] Before seeing the account in the morning papers, I had had no inkling or suspicion in any way of the matter. I did not know Mr. Washington was in Boston or intending to go there as I had just left him at Tuskegee. I had had no correspondence with Mr. Trotter for six months save in regard to a boarding

1. This letter is published, not quite in full, in the editor's *Documentary History*, pp. 881–83. There, however, it is incorrectly dated as 1905, partially because the date in the original is indistinct and partially because Du Bois mistakenly placed the "riot" mentioned here in the summer of 1905, when it actually occurred in 1903. (See *Dusk of Dawn*, p. 87.)

2. The Zion Church meeting in August 1903 was addressed by Booker T. Washington but disrupted by the protests of Trotter, George Forbes, and others. Trotter was arrested for his part in this disturbance and actually served a brief term in prison.

place. When I arrived in Boston and heard of the meeting I told Mr. Trotter and Mr. Forbes in plain terms my decided disapproval of the unfortunate occurrence and my conviction that it would do harm. Although I was unable at that time to defend Mr. Washington's position as I once had, I nevertheless took occasion to address a meeting of men at Mr. Trotter's home and remind them of the vast difference between criticizing Mr. Washington's policy and attacking him personally.

Nevertheless, brought into close contact with Mr. Trotter for the first time my admiration for his unselfishness, pureness of heart and indomitable energy even when misguided, grew. And, too, I saw how local jealousies were working to make mountains out of mole hills. So far as I could learn had it not been for Mr. Lewis, the chairman of the Washington meeting, there would have been no riot[3]—the disturbance could have easily and quickly [been] quelled and the dignity of the occasion saved. This same Mr. Lewis a few years ago was a rabid anti-Washington man and wanted to "burn down Tuskegee." I labored with him and Trotter and Forbes in past years was instrumental in getting Mr. Washington and Mr. Lewis together at a small luncheon so that they might understand each other. They evidently came to understand each other so well that Mr. Lewis got a political appointment and turning around proceeded to abuse his former comrades—a conversion in which I had as little faith as I had in his former radical stand.

There were a great many other things not generally known that made me pity and admire Mr. Trotter as well as condemn his lack of judgment and there were also things that made me have less and less faith in Mr. Washington. Nevertheless, I steadfastly condemned Mr. Trotter's action from that day to this—a fact which he will frankly testify to. When the matter was pushed to the extent of actual imprisonment I felt this was too much in view of all the facts and still feel so and I wrote an open letter to the "Guardian" expressing my disagreement on many points with him but my admiration for his honesty of purpose.

While then I had absolutely no knowledge of the Washington meeting before hand and no part, active or passive, in the disturbance and while I did then and do now condemn the disturbance, I nevertheless admire Mr. Trotter as a man and agree with him in his main contentions. When I think him in the right I shall help him, when his methods or opinions go beyond law and right, I shall condemn them.

As between him and Mr. Washington I unhesitatingly believe Mr. Trotter to be far nearer the right in his contentions and I only pray for such restraint and judgment on Mr. Trotter's part as will save to our cause his sincerity and unpurchasable soul in these days when every energy is being used to put black men back into slavery and when Mr. Washington is leading the way backward.

3. William Henry Lewis was the first Black United States assistant attorney-general, appointed by President Taft at the urging of Booker T. Washington.

I am sorry that I was not at the University when you called to welcome your party.

Very sincerely yours,
W. E. B. Du Bois

Brooklyn, New York, Jan 9th 1904

My Dear Doctor DuBois

I am sorry that several relatives present at my house today (I have no family but myself) have prevented my going to Manhattan and also have been unable to make a time when I could ask you to be here with certainty that I could see you—I wanted to have a chance for a careful and frank talk with you—expressing my sympathy with your feeling as shown in many of your remarkable writings and as well asking you to let me tell you of how I thought you were leading people to false views of yourself and so injuring your work and your future reputation that you leave to your family and to your people—I also wanted to tell you of the many strong expressions of sympathy with your position as taken in your book on many points from prominent and pronounced Southerners—Especially on my recent visit South—I was grateful for the frank expressions in your letter but I was deeply sorry to note the unfrank and vague words of depreciation of others and think you too largely endowed and in too important a relation to your race to indulge them—When you are next to be out I should be glad to know in advance if you would care for a frank talk with sympathy even where I may not agree.

Very Truly Yours
George Foster Peabody

New York, Jan. 26, 1904.

My dear Dr. Du Bois:

Your letter to me and the copy of Mr. Peabody's letter to you were very interesting and brought me much encouragement. You seem to have had remarkable success in securing from the conference some of the things that we most desire.[1] Yesterday I saw Dr. [William Hayes] Ward and he gave me some of the results in detail as he had learned them from Bishop [Alexander] Walters. I congratulate you most heartily. It seems to me that, whatever doubts we may have as to the sincerity of what has been done, or as to the backing which the action may receive from the white leaders here in New York, we should credit all hands with entire sincerity and proceed as if we had not the slightest doubt on that point.

Especially important does it seem to me that we should do everything in our

---

1. He refers to the just-concluded New York City conference among Washington–Du Bois forces, paid for by Carnegie. The "three schools" mentioned by Bumstead are Tuskegee, Atlanta, and Hampton. All these plans somehow to overcome the real Du Bois–Washington differences failed.

power to conciliate Mr. Peabody and make a good friend of him. This last letter of his is certainly admirable in tone and shows a spirit of conciliation that ought to be met at least half way. From what I had heard indirectly, I had supposed that he was very much displeased with your letter to him, and so this reply of his is all the more of a surprise to me, especially the extent to which he gives voice to the sympathy of himself and other southern men with some, at least, of the phases of your book. I think he is a man who is willing to work with us and with whom we can work amicably without necessarily holding the same views, if we only can avoid giving him needless irritation. And just here I am going to be frank and say that I think your letter to him would have been very much more effective if you had left out some of the last sentences referring to Mr. Washington. I do not think that they were "unfrank," as Mr. Peabody called them, because you could not well go into details in such a letter, and you were doubtless ready to substantiate your statements if requested to do so. But the legitimate purpose of this letter was accomplished, it seems to me, when you had cleared yourself of any complicity with the Trotter disturbance and expressed your attitude toward him as a man and toward his principles. If you had stopped there, I do not see how anybody could take any exception to the letter. I read the letter the other day to a meeting of our Executive and Finance Committees, all the members being present and also Dr. Hall of New York, and Mr. Twichell of Hartford. When I had finished, there was quite an outburst of dissent from fully half of those present—all based, I judged, on the closing portion. I think I added considerably to their horror by then telling them that I had written to you that I thought it a frank and manly letter and that I was glad that you had written it. I did not think it best just then to qualify my endorsement of the letter by any dissent from the last part of it, as I have expressed it above to you, but I went on to explain your position and to justify your liberty of opinion and utterance on matters of vital interest to your race, especially as you were one of the very few men of your race who were able to defend its rights with ability, dignity, and courtesy. I do not know how much effect my words may have had. But I came away from the meeting with a fresh sense of the difficulty of being honest with ourselves and at the same time being judicious in dealing with those who do not agree with us. Sometime I will talk this over with you more fully.

You will doubtless reply to Mr. Peabody in the spirit in which he has written you. As to proposing a joint meeting of the three schools next year, I think I would not suggest anything very definite just yet. We shall want to think it over and see what other developments may appear as a result of the conference.

Yours very sincerely,
Horace Bumstead.

Early in 1904, Du Bois received a letter from F. A. McKenzie, a teacher at the Shoshoni Agency in Wyoming. It is illuminating in its own right—though nothing seems to have come of his specific suggestion—and the pencilled reply by Du Bois, dated 16 January 1904, summarizes a potent element in his thinking at the time.

The coincidences of history are marvelous; it was this same McKenzie who was president of Fisk in 1924, when Du Bois launched the slashing attack upon that university's administration that resulted in McKenzie's resignation in 1925.

January 9, 1904.

Professor W. E. B. DuBois
Dear Sir:—

May I presume upon your time for a few minutes? I should like to ask your opinion concerning an idea of mine looking toward the advancement of the Indian.

Among all the varying and reciprocally hostile comments upon the many theories for civilizing the Indian, I am more and more impressed with the overpowering and degrading influences which operate to neutralize years of training, when the Indian returns to his comparative isolation among his own people. Stripped of every support, why should he not go back to the life of those around him? All red influences are against a higher life, and white influences, for most, are but foreign, if not inimical forces. This is, in brief, why I make a novel proposition. I do not suggest any panacea, but a brake for the wheels of progress.

If we could persuade 50 or 100 or 200 Indians to combine for the good of their race into an association which stood for the unity and solidity, the intelligence and progress, the encouragement and mutual support of their people, I feel that a great step forward would be made. Such an association would strengthen the hearts of its members scattered widely over the country, would create an ideal and spur on the ambition of those not members, and tend to the creation of a set of leaders to guide the whole race to a higher civilization. Its power and initiative would ensure "the speed of independent thought, the expanding consciousness of manhood" among the red people.

Should this idea prove a popular one, perhaps a convention could be held at St. Louis, which, while directly furthering the objects of the association, would also prove the most interesting and the most convincing "exhibit" in the Indian department.

I shall appreciate a reply, and shall welcome any criticisms or suggestions relative to the general plan or the accompanying tentative (or provisional) pledge.

Very respectfully,
F. A. McKenzie,
(Teacher)

(If you care to know something about me, before you answer, you may address Dr. M. G. Brumbaugh and Dr. Simon N. Patten, of the University of Pennsylvania, and Dr. J. Paul Goode, of the University of Chicago.)

FRATERNITY OF AMERICAN INDIANS.

Membership open to all Indians who can speak English, who are recommended by some reputable school, who will take the following

Pledge

I believe that the Indian has certain inalienable rights, among which is that of freeing himself from the bondage of ignorance, superstitution, and poverty, by education, religion, and self-support.

I believe that by United efforts he can become an independent American citizen, and free himself from all injustice, which ignorance or cupidity has imposed upon him. I, therefore, pledge myself to further all efforts for the advancement of my race in education, morality, and civic rights, to discourage and oppose all backward tendencies, all immorality, and all crime, and to work for the time when all red men shall be brothers in love and purpose, proud of their people, and influential among the united tribes and races of America.

Jan. 16, 1904

Dear Sir:

I think your plan most excellent & would be glad to aid it in any way. The uplift must always come from the top & the training & unification of leaders is the great thing.

W. E. B. Du Bois

From the editorial department of the young *Collier's Weekly* (its chief editor was Robert T. Collier), early in 1904, came the letter published below. Du Bois responded—in a letter that has not been located—with both an editorial statement and a comment critical of the manner in which *Collier's* was dealing with the question of race. This brought from *Collier's* the reply dated 18 January also published. On 30 January, Du Bois replied with a suggestion for a column, which was not to be realized until he was editing his own magazines. *Collier's* expressed interest in one brief article; sent and accepted at the end of May, it was termed "very splendid" by the *Collier's* editor. It was published, as an editorial with the title "The Color Line Belts the World," in the issue dated 18 June 1904.

New York, January 7, 1904.

Prof. W. E. B. Du Bois
My dear sir:

I wish very much you could find it possible to appropriate from your busy time five or ten minutes in which to write for me an editorial comment or opinion of not more than 500 words in length, on what you may conceive to be the most direct solution of the negro problem. This of course is a subject on which volumes have been written, and might still be written, but if I am not mistaken, your views and those of my friend, Mr. Washington, are diametrically opposed, or at least in that you feel that his program in all particulars is not in harmony with the modern spirit.

I would appreciate it very much if you would state your own thought in this short editorial fashion, with directness and frankness, for our use and send it to me at this time.

Very truly yours,
Richard Lloyd Jones

New York, January 18, 1904.

My dear sir:

I am very much obliged to you for the very excellent editorial statement which you have sent to me. I shall be glad to receive at all times your editorial thought on the race problem, or anything else that appeals to you and upon which you would like to address the American public.

I am sorry to note that you seem to feel that Collier's Weekly has treated the negro with injustice. We certainly have no editorial policy of this kind, and I do not know just what particular article or statement has appeared in our paper to cause this offense.

At all times believe me to be

Very heartily yours,
Richard Lloyd Jones

Atlanta, Ga., Jan. 30, 1904

Dear Mr. Jones:

I have been thinking over the invitation you gave in your letter to me of the 18 of Jan. to send you my "editorial thought." Have you ever thought of this: the color line is belting the world today; about it world interests are centering. Would it not be an interesting experiment to start in Colliers a column—or half a column—called "Along the Color Line" or the "Voice of the Darker Millions" and put therein from week to week or month to month note & comment on the darker races in America, Africa, Asia &c., from their standpoint & the standpoint of the serious student & observer—the spirit of it being rather informing & interpretive than controversial. Would it pay? Would the public stand it? I think I could edit such a column.

W. E. B. Du Bois

New York, February 3, 1904

Dear Dr. Du Bois:

I appreciate very much the courtesy of your letter of January 30th. I am afraid it will not be possible, with the wide demands that press for space in our pages, to conduct a regular column or half column on "Along the Color Line," or

"Voices of the Darker Millions." I wish very much indeed, however, that you would try to make it possible to give me an editorial thought of about 500 words in length on the idea you suggest—the color line belting the world today and the growing interests that are centering therein.

Believe me, with all good wishes,

Very cordially yours,
Richard Lloyd Jones

Walter Francis Willcox (1861–1964) was a professor of economics and statistics at Cornell University from 1891 until his retirement in 1931. Beginning in the 1890s, he often lectured and wrote on the "Negro Problem"; in 1904, the United States Census Bureau published his 333-page statistical study, *Negroes in the United States.* In 1903, he sent Du Bois the letter introducing Jessie Fauset, one of the few Afro-American students at Cornell. Undoubtedly, these facts help explain why Du Bois sent him the essay on which Willcox comments in his letter. Despite the sharpness of Du Bois's reply, also published here, the relationship between Willcox and Du Bois continued.

Ithaca, New York, March 13, 1904

Dear Mr. DuBois:

I have received through your courtesy a copy of the "East and West" for January, 1904, containing your article on the Future of the Negro Race in America.[1] I have read the article with much interest and thank you for sending me the pamphlet.

The fundamental difficulty I feel in accepting your position is that it is impossible for me to judge how far the present economic condition of the American Negro is due to persistent characteristics of the people and how far it is due to the heavy economic and social pressure upon them, resulting from drawing the color line in society, in politics and in industry. You seem inclined to attribute almost all of it to the latter. I confess that I do not see that the evidence warrants one in holding either opinion with confidence and therefore for the present I am an agnostic on the subject. Nor do I see any way in which convincing evidence on the question can be derived from an analysis of social processes now in progress in this country. If either factor could be isolated from the other we might derive important evidence, but I do not see how it can be.

Nor can I agree with the bitter condemnation of present social processes which characterizes your view of them. The gradual displacement of one social class by another can only by figure of speech be called murder, since murder in-

---

1. Du Bois, "The Future of the Negro Race in America," *East and the West* 2 (January 1904): 4–19.

volves deliberate intent upon the part of the individual actors. Such a process I take it works itself out much more through the reduction of the birth rate than it does through an increase of the death rate, and to prevent individuals from being conceived or born seems to me even less entitled to the name of murder than the phase of the process you apparently have especially in mind, namely, the maintenance or increase of the death rate.

Yours sincerely,
W. F. Willcox

March 29, 1904

My Dear Mr. Willcox:

The fundamental difficulty in your position is that you are trying to spin a solution of the Negro problem out of the inside of your office. It can never be done. You have simply no adequate conception of the Negro problem in the south & of Negro character & capacity. When you have sat as I have ten years in intimate soul contact with all kinds & conditions of black men you will be less agnostic. I have my prejudices but they are backed by knowledge if not supported. How on earth any fair-minded student of the situation could have stood sponsor for a book like Tillinghast's & actually praised it is simply beyond my comprehension.[1] If you insist on writing about & pronouncing judgment on this problem why not study it? Not from a car-window & associated press despatches as in your pamphlet on crime[2] but get down here & really study it at first hand. Is it a sufficient answer to a problem to say the data are not sufficient when they lie all about us? There is enough easily obtainable data to take you off the fence if you will study it first hand & not thro' prejudiced eyes—my eyes, or those of others.

Pardon this frankness but your letter invited it.

W. E. B. Du Bois

Casely Hayford (1866–1930), a West African lawyer and author, was a significant figure in the development of African national independence movements. The origins of the fruitful connection between Hayford and Du Bois appear in

---

1. Joseph A. Tillinghast, *The Negro in Africa and America* (New York: Macmillan Co. for The American Economic Association, 1902). Willcox contributed a two-page laudatory preface. Tillinghast, as Willcox wrote, was "a southern white man, the son of a slaveholder"; his book is intensely racist, arguing the decay of the "Negro race" to the extent that, as the book concludes, its very survival is in doubt (p. 228).

2. He refers to an address, "Negro Criminality," delivered by Willcox before the American Social Science Association, 6 September 1899. It was reprinted without change as an appendix to Alfred H. Stone, *Studies in the American Race Problem* (New York: Doubleday, Page, 1908), which also has an introduction by Willcox.

[76]   Correspondence 1894-1904

a letter addressed to Du Bois, in care of A. C. McClurg and Co., the Chicago publishers of *The Souls of Black Folk*.

                                    Asain, Gold Coast, 8th June 1904
Dear Prof DuBois
   I have recently had the pleasure of reading your great work "The Souls of Black Folk," and it occurred to me that if leading thinkers of the African race in America had the opportunity of exchanging thoughts with thinkers of the race in West Africa, this century would be likely to see the race problem solved.
   For this reason I venture to forward to you herewith a copy of my recent book "Gold Coast Native Institutions" and "Africa and the Africans" with an introduction by myself, both of which contain points of view which may be new and interesting to you.[1]
   Hoping to have the pleasure of exchanging thoughts with you,
                                    Yours faithfully,
                                    Casely Hayford
P.S. I am of course an African. C.H.

The beginning of a momentous association which was to last for half a century is reflected in a letter from Mary White Ovington (1865-1951), a socialist and social worker, later among the chief founders of the National Association for the Advancement of Colored People (NAACP). This letter is to be placed within the context of efforts, beginning late in 1902, to develop some systematic approach to the question of "philanthropy" for the Black poor in New York City—efforts in which Felix Adler, William H. Baldwin, Jr., George Foster Peabody, and Robert Ogden were interested, and in which they had tried—unsuccessfully—to enlist Du Bois.

                                    Brooklyn, N.Y., June 10, 1904.
My dear Dr. Du Bois,
   I am to attend the Summer School of Philanthropy in New York this year, and have chosen for my bit of research work the economic opportunities for young Negro men and women in New York. I have read your article published some

---

1. *Gold Coast Native Institutions, with Thoughts upon a Healthy Imperial Policy for the Gold Coast and Ashanti* (London: Sweet and Maxwell, 1903); *Africa and the Africans, Proceedings on the Occasion of a Banquet, given at the Holborn Restaurant, Aug. 15, 1903, to Edward W. Blyden, by West Africans in London* (London: C. M. Phillips, 1903). The "address" by Hayford is on pages 23-32. Two later books by Hayford, both published by Phillips in London, attracted wide attention: *Ethiopia Unbound: Studies in Race Emancipation* (1911); and *The Truth about the West African Land Question* (1913). A collection of his speeches, edited by M. J. Sampson, was published in 1951 by Stockwell in North Devon. A biographical notice of Hayford, unsigned but written by Du Bois, appeared in the *Crisis* (May 1921): 22.

years ago in the New York Times on the Negroes in New York,[1] and felt that you might be able to direct me to data on the subject or might tell me to whom to go. I should not feel that I ought to trouble you if I were only to do this little piece of work, but I have a fellowship of a year from the Cooperative Settlement Society of N.Y. to investigate conditions among the New York Negroes and what I do for the Summer School will be only a beginning. If you are in the east now or will be any time this summer can I possibly see you? I shall be in New York until August, and I have hoped that you might be in the near neighborhood. It is difficult to talk of one's personal plans, but it is almost impossible to write of them. If I could see you and tell you what I hope to do next year and learn whether it seems to you wise it would be a great help to me. I was for seven years head worker at the Greenpoint Settlement Brooklyn, and am especially interested in the idea of the opening of a Settlement in the Negro quarter in New York—an idea in which I know you have been interested. I am not planning to go into an investigation simply for the sake of adding a few more facts to what is known of conditions among the Negroes in poverty in New York, but with the hope of helping to start social work among them. I want very much to talk with you. You see, you have talked to me through your writings for many years and have lately made me want to work as I never wanted to work before, but I need now to ask directly for advice.

Very sincerely,
Mary White Ovington.

In the summer of 1904, Mary White Ovington received from the Committee on Social Investigations, connected with Greenwich House, a fellowship for one year's study of conditions among New York Black people. The committee's chairman was the professor of economics at Columbia, Edwin R. A. Seligman; its secretary was another Columbia professor, Vladimir G. Simkhovitch; the remaining board members were Franz Boas, Edward T. Devine, Livingston Farrand, Franklin H. Giddings, and Henry R. Seager. All were at Columbia but Devine, at that time director of the New York School of Philanthropy. Mrs. Mary Kingsbury Simkhovitch, director of Greenwich House from its founding in 1902 until her retirement in 1946, was a close friend of Miss Ovington. When Miss Ovington received this appointment, her correspondence with Du Bois became rather voluminous. An exchange of letters late in 1904 is given here.

1. Late in 1901, Du Bois published five articles in the *New York Times Magazine* on "The Black North"; the first two dealt with New York City and were published 17 and 24 November 1901. The studies begun by Miss White in 1904 resulted in her 1911 book, *Half A Man: The Status of the Negro in New York* (New York: Longmans, Green and Co.), with a foreword by the distinguished anthropologist Franz Boas.

Brooklyn, N.Y. Nov. 4, 1904.

Dear Dr. Du Bois,

I have received the Atlanta publications, Nos. 1,2,5,7 & 8.[1] Thank you for seeing that they were sent to me. From reading in one of them I find that there is a way in which I can ally myself to the economic department of the university—by contribution to the publication of these reports. So will you please see that the enclosed check is used for this purpose. I owe $2.25 on it for the publications sent me.

I have read your Credo.[2] It makes me ache with anger at one's own impotence. Is it as hard, I wonder, when one is alone, away from the outside world, to be of a despised race as of a race that does despicable deeds—I believe not—But thinking of my own problem, it isn't the Negro only who suffers from the greed and the scramble for social precedence here in New York. I am glad I have done many years of work among the laboring people before taking up a special race problem. I know how fierce the fight is for everyone.

It is a delicious sight to-day to see on lower Broadway, in the midst of the greatest crowds of business men rushing to and from their work, boys hawking Chas. Wagner's The Simple Life, for ten cents.[3]

Very sincerely,
Mary W. Ovington.

Nov. 8, 1904

My dear Miss Ovington:

I rec'd your letter of the fourth with a tinge of disappointment. Have I then been entertaining a Millionaire unawares—a mere millionare? Still the university is very thankful and will say so in a day or two. I discovered a little leaflet on N.Y. Negroes written at the time of the conference.[1] I have sent you a copy. Do you want other copies? I am glad you read my *Credo*—I am sorry you ached over it, for after all there are wonderful compensations in all this thing.

W. E. B. Du Bois

Samuel Huntington Comings (1839–1907), a white Southerner attracted to the ideas of Henry George and dissatisfied with traditional educational methods,

1. The Atlanta publications to which Miss Ovington refers were the reports of the university's conferences, directed by Du Bois.
2. The "Credo" was a brief essay published in the *Independent*, 6 October 1904, p. 787; it had a great impact upon both the white and the Afro-American worlds.
3. Charles Wagner (1852–1918) was a French Protestant clergyman and author of moralistic essays. His *La Vie simple* (1895) was translated into English as *The Simple Life* (1901) and widely sold in the United States for several years.
1. The "little leaflet" was *Some Notes on the Negroes in New York City, compiled from the Reports of the U.S. Census and Other Sources,* published in Atlanta in 1903 by the Atlanta University Press.

was, by the early post-Civil War period, propounding concepts of industrial education not too dissimilar from those later associated with the name of Booker T. Washington.

Comings was the author of *Pagan Versus Christian Civilizations,* which first appeared in 1904; there he criticized what he incorrectly took to be Du Bois's insistence, in *Souls of Black Folk,* that thinkers must think and workers must work, and that neither has need of the other's ability. This criticism, in the name of an intense democratic advocacy, was vitiated, however, by a clear racism.*

The exchange afforded Du Bois an opportunity for stating some of his views of that date.

                            Fairhope Ala. Nov'5th, 1904

Prof' DuBoies
My dear Sir,

I am quite disappointed in getting the letter I sent you back with no word of comment from you. I sincerely hope you will not be personally offended at what you may feel is very severe criticism of your words in your able book. I have taken pains to heartily thank all the severest critics I have had and quote one who widely differs with me.

The study of this problem for both races is of too much importance to us all to warrant any personal feeling to blind our anxious eyes, if we can possibly avoid it. It seems to me you ought to see in my severe criticism of our own arrogant and silly race pride, that I am trying to be fair and even in my criticisms, and that I am as much alarmed for the future of all the Anglo Saxon civilization, as you can be for your own race.

In your book I noted with intense interest and pain your able description of the pathetic situation of so many of the "renters" on the old plantation and your picture is well and correctly drawn; but do you know that in Mo' Kansas, Arkansas, Ill, and all the So'West, the white "renters" are almost if not quite as badly off, and drifting into a "Serf class" and a serf condition, as pitiable, and undemocratic, as your picture of your own people in the cotton belts. Single men coming to own whole counties, or towns and their "Rack-rents" eating all the products except the barest subsistence for their tenants, of their own race.

However we may differ now as to details, let us work together for the one common end and aim, the uplift of a true *Democracy,* a higher idea of *Human Brotherhood.* We may be either of us mistaken as to details, but let us agree on

---

* A second edition, revised by Comings's wife, was entitled *Industrial and Vocational Education: Universal and Self-Sustaining* (Boston: Christopher Publishing Co., 1915). The critical references to Du Bois (without mentioning his name) are in this edition, with no correction in accordance with Du Bois's letter (see p. 145). After Comings's death in 1907, his ideas gained influence; money was contributed by Joseph Fels, and John Dewey expressed support. A Society of Organic Education resulted, with some influence in North and South until the first World War.

the general effort at the same end, and we will come to unity as to means in time in essentials.

                    Cordially Yours
                    S. H. Comings.

              Nov. 18, 1904

My Dear Mr. Comings:

Do not for a moment think that I was offended by your criticism. I am quite used to being differed with as all thinking beings must be. I confess however that some of your errors seem to be so obvious that they make me impatient of even attempting reply. The chief of these are:
1. Your assumption that educated Negroes are idle & vicious
2. Your assumption that industrial schools can be made self supporting
3. Your assumption that present methods of study are simply memorizing
4. Your assumption that mental labor is not creative work
5. Your failure to see that the making of good "hands" out of Negroes, with little mental culture & no enlightened leaders will but educate a docile mass of workmen who can be used as [a] club to beat union white labor into submission.

I cannot argue these points at length but will simply assert that (1) is absolutely false—not that no educated Negro is idle or vicious but that certainly the overwhelming majority of those educated by present methods are good & useful citizens. As proof of this in the case of a single institution I enclose a leaflet on the work of our graduates. Similar data is available from nearly every Negro college. If you want to test these facts write to the towns where these people work & find out. That the history of Hampton, Tuskegee, Talladega & some dozen other industrial schools has long since proven the falsity of; in proof of this I enclose a paper. (2) That every modern course of study recognizes the value of manual training & laboratory methods. Certainly we also at A.U. [believe that] of all creative labor that of the mind is the highest & best; and the mass of men who preach exclusive industrial education for Negroes are simply welding new shackles for workingmen white & black.

On the other hand I agree with you on the following points:
1. The importance of well-trained handicraftsmen
2. The value of physical labor for brain workers
3. The value of manual training for children
4. The danger of despising manual toil.

I trust this will make my position clearer. I still stick to the thesis "Teach workers to work & thinkers to think" but I do not mean by this that workers should not think, nor that thinkers should despise manual toil. I mean merely that in the limited time given us to live we must specialize and that with all his thinking the mason must bend his chief energy to laying bricks & that with all his chopping trees, Gladstone must first of all guide empires.

With all this I still agree with you that there is far too much thoughtless toil & far too little knowledge of the material world among thinkers.
W. E. B. Du Bois

Isaac Max Rubinow (1875–1936), an outstanding economist and statistician, and a Socialist, was a pioneer in developing health and social security insurance plans backed by state and federal governments. After service with the United States government as an economist, he served during the First World War as Director of the Bureau of Social Statistics for the Department of Public Charities in New York City. Du Bois's growing emphasis on the economics of racism was clearly indicated in the Seventh Annual Atlanta Conference (1902), which dealt with "The Negro Artisan"; the specific remarks to which Rubinow refers are reflected, for example, in Du Bois's article "The Parting of the Ways," published in the *World Today* (April 1904), where he notes the relationship between the intensified repression of Black people in the South and the fact that "the nation has begun to swagger about the world in its useless battleships looking for helpless people whom it can force to buy its goods at high prices."

Washington Nov 10 1904

Dear Professor DuBois,

Some time ago I came across an item in the Washington Post quoting your address before an Iowa meeting, as saying that you considered the Negro question a part of the general social problem of distribution of wealth. There were other things ascribed to you which I am quite sure you could not have said—as for instance that the colored student was a menace to the white race—and similar things characteristic of the careless writing of our newspapers. I am sorry that I have lost the clipping—you would probably find it amusing. But your main point of view—as to the identity in the final analysis of the race problem with the whole social or labor problem—if you have been quoted correctly—is what made me write to you. It is a point of view that I have always held and that you will find widespread among the more educated socialists of this country—that the actual foundation of the race prejudice is the desire of the stronger to exploit the weaker, though of course historical causes have contributed to the survival of these prejudices—and that the present tendencies in regard to the treatment of the Negro are also largely explained by the same desire of exploitation—that only through emancipation of the whole working class can the emancipation of the negro be brought about. Now this is no desire to instruct you, but merely an effort to find whether there are any points of contact between your point of view and the Socialist doctrine, to which I adhere. With the same end of view I send you a short article (a very rough sketch, which I hope you will not judge too severely) where my point of view is indicated. In later issues of the same publication the Race problem was discussed—and if you should wish, I will gladly send you those issues. I must say that even among certain groups of socialists the Negro problem is not fully understood, and the new Southern members of the movement have not altogether succeeded in freeing themselves from the prejudices that arose in chattel slavery, and persist in wage slavery. But I imagine you will agree that the Socialist party is the only organization in the country that moves in the right direction. It always appeared to me extremely naive to point to acquisition of private capital and bank accounts as a solution of the problem—for the mass of negroes can no more expect to become all capitalists, than the mass of white men can. Mr. B. Washington's is a remedy for the *few*, while what is necessary is relief for the *many*.

I should be happy to have the oportunity to discuss that matter with you. If I am not mistaken you visit Washington occasionally. Would it be asking too much—to favor us with a visit when you are in Washington, or drop me a line informing me of your presence in the city. I take this liberty of writing to you mainly because I had the pleasure to meet you in St. Louis, as you will possibly remember.

Sincerely yours,
I. M. Rubinow

Nov. 17 [1904]

Dear Mr. Rubinow:

While I would scarcely describe myself as a socialist still I have much sympathy with the movement & I have many socialistic beliefs. I was correctly quoted in the main in the article in question except of course the "menace" part. I believe the Negro problem is partly the American Caste problem & that caste is arising because of unjust & dangerous economic conditions. I thank you for the article & when I'm in Washington I'll look you up. I should be glad of other articles on the subject.

W. E. B. Du Bois

The Literary Digest of 15 October 1904 reprinted (from *The Independent*, 6 October 1904) Du Bois's "Credo." He received several letters, from sources as varied as the registrar at Tuskegee Institute in Alabama and the offices of the *Guardian* in Boston, suggesting its republication in card and poster form. The latter was, in fact, done, and throughout the nation "The Credo" hung for years on many a wall in homes "behind the Veil."

On *Guardian* stationery, Mrs. Trotter wrote to suggest such reprinting.

Boston, Dec. 1 1904

Dear Dr. DuBois;

Some of us Boston women, who are very proud of you and very much interested in the welfare of our Race are anxious to print your creed and sell it, the money to go to a work which we are aiding.

I have promised to write and ask you for the privilege. Will you kindly let me hear from you?

Hope you will take good care of yourself this year and not work so hard that you will faint in the Spring and frighten all your friends nearly to death.[1]

With kindest regards I am

> Very sincerely
> Geraldine L. Trotter.

Dec. 6 [1904]

Dear Mrs. Trotter

Reprint the Credo as you will only attach to it "From the New York Independent." Thank you, I'm caring for my health & weight more than even before. Regards to all.

> W. E. B. Du Bois

The impact of Du Bois's *Souls of Black Folk* was immediate, intense, international, and enduring. A letter from a white high school teacher in a Philadelphia suburb illustrates this impact; Du Bois responded to her specific questions and sent along a letter for the troubled youngster.

Berwyn, Pa., Dec. 13, 1904.

My dear Professor DuBois,

Lately I have read and have been greatly interested in your book, "The Souls of Black Folk."

I have thought that perhaps you would pardon the liberty I take in writing and would be willing to aid me in the solution of a difficult problem in my school work.

In our high school we have a colored girl, seemingly bright and capable who is doing practically nothing with her work because she is out of school so much of the time.

In talking with her the other day I found that she is in a hopeless frame of mind—feeling that her effort at gaining an education is useless. To use her own words—"I shall never have a chance to use my knowledge."

I feel that something must be done to make the girl realize that she has work to do in this world, and some effort made to inspire her—to give her an ideal to work for.

Will you be so very kind as to send me a catalog of your University and to tell me what chance there is for a poor girl to be educated in any of your institutions?

If Atlanta offers no scholarships—do you know of any in any other institution for your people?

---

1. Du Bois had been overtaken by sudden illness while visiting Boston in 1903.

I know that your time must be fully occupied and I hesitate to ask for your consideration of this matter, but I feel that it is useless to talk to this girl in general terms. I must have something to show her of what others of her people are doing.

Thanking you for the view your book has given me, I am

Sincerely yours—
Margaretta Atkinson

[Enclosed for the youngster was the following.]

January 7, 1905

I wonder if you will let a stranger say a word to you about yourself? I have heard that you are a young woman of some ability but that you are neglecting your school work because you have become hopeless of trying to do anything in the world. I am very sorry for this. How any human being whose wonderful fortune it is to live in the 20th century should under ordinarily fair advantages despair of life is almost unbelievable. And if in addition to this that person is, as I am, of Negro lineage with all the hopes and yearnings of hundreds of millions of human souls dependent in some degree on her striving, then her bitterness amounts to crime.

There are in the U. S. today tens of thousands of colored girls who would be happy beyond measure to have the chance of educating themselves that you are neglecting. If you train yourself as you easily can, there are wonderful chances of usefulness before you: you can join in the ranks of 15,000 Negro women teachers, of hundreds of nurses and physicians, of the growing number of clerks and stenographers, and above all of the host of homemakers. Ignorance is a cure for nothing. Get the very best training possible & the doors of opportunity will fly open before you as they are flying before thousands of your fellows. On the other hand every time a colored person neglects an opportunity, it makes it more difficult for others of the race to get such an opportunity. Do you want to cut off the chances of the boys and girls of tomorrow?

W. E. B. Du Bois

ORGANIZER-EDITOR-AUTHOR

1905–1920

1897 family photograph: Du Bois with his wife, Nina Gomer Du Bois, and son, Burghardt

The final page of Du Bois's handwritten manuscript of *The Souls of Black Folk: Essays and Sketches*, which was published in 1903

Du Bois spending a quiet half hour.
Sketch by John Henry Adams, 1905.

Booker T. Washington

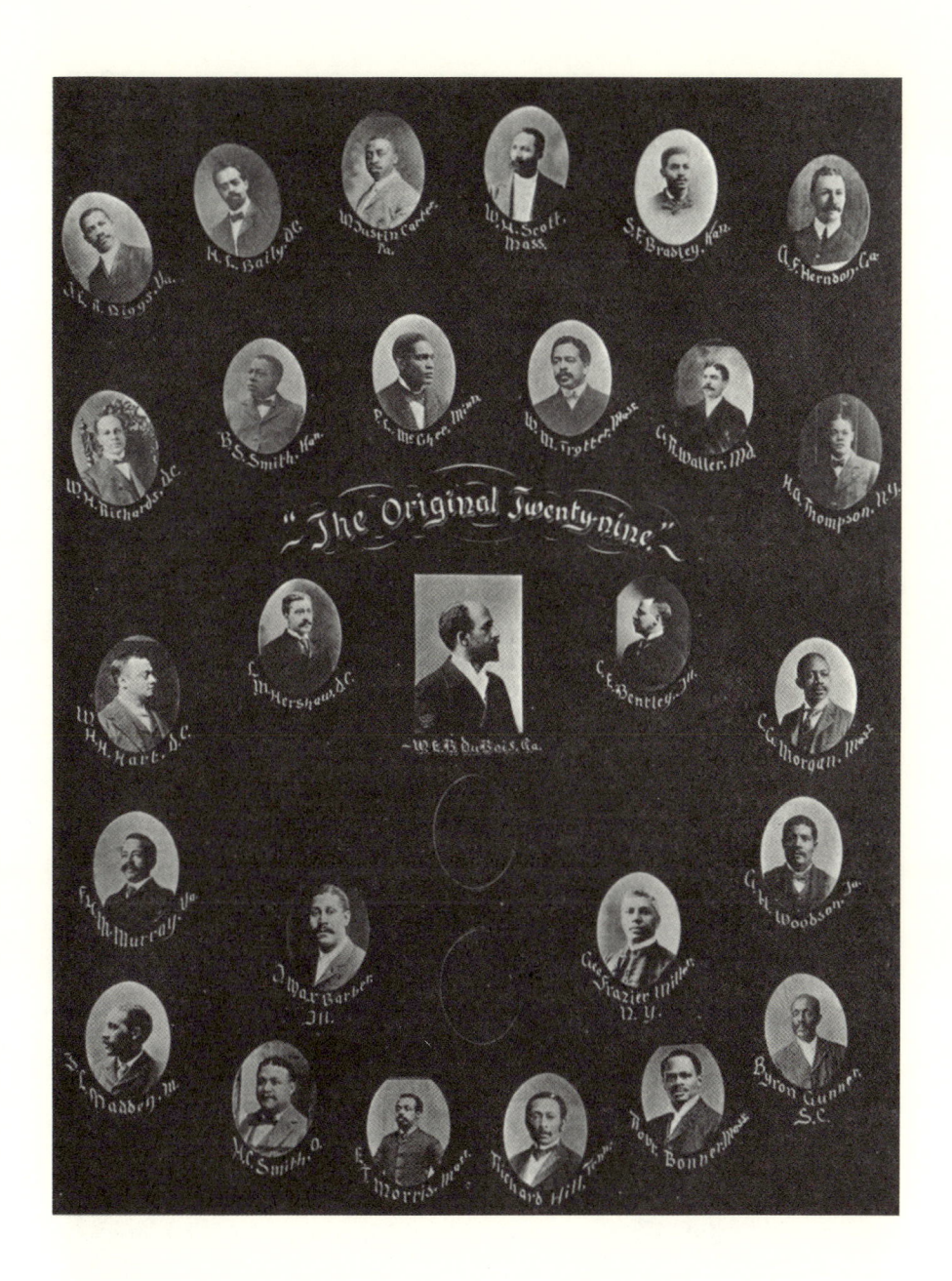

The Niagara Movement, 1905. Missing from "The Original Twenty-nine" who attended the founding meeting are George W. Mitchell, Pa., and E. B. Jourdain, Mass.

Faculty and staff of all-Black Atlanta University, 1906, with their families. Du Bois is at the far right of the back row; Mrs. Du Bois is in the center of the fourth row; Yolande, age five, in the front row.

Du Bois at an early Niagara Movement meeting (ca. 1906) with, left to right, F. H. M. Murray, L. M. Hershaw, and W. M. Trotter

AMONG THE most distinguished Black men of the post-Reconstruction decades were the Reverend Francis J. Grimké (1850–1937) and his elder brother, the attorney Archibald Henry Grimké. They were the nephews of the renowned abolitionists and women's rights advocates, Angelina Grimké (who married Theodore Weld) and her sister Sarah. Francis J. was a Presbyterian minister first in Washington, then in Florida, and then again in Washington; he was a trustee of Howard University. His brother edited a Boston paper in the 1880s, wrote biographies of Garrison and Sumner and an early account of the Vesey slave insurrection, and was appointed United States consul in Santo Domingo (1894–98) by President Cleveland.

Both men were militant and were early leaders in such organizations as the American Negro Academy and the NAACP; from the latter Archibald received the Spingarn Medal in 1919. Devotion and dedication are both evident in a letter to Du Bois from the Reverend Mr. Grimké.

Washington, D.C., January 7th, 1905.
Dear Dr. Du Bois

Many thinks for a copy of your noble Confession of Faith, "Credo," which reached me yesterday morning. I read it, of course, when it first appeared in The Independent, and was delighted with it, as I am with all of your strong manly utterances on the race question. I am glad it has been put in this form for general circulation, and where it can be hung in the homes of the people. I had some correspondence a short while ago with Miss Laney of Augusta, and in the course of it, she expressed a very strong wish that it might take some such form as this. It ought to receive the widest circulation; it ought to be hung in all of our homes, and in all of our school houses. God has gifted you, in a remarkable degree, with vision and power of statement. Your utterances are always clear, leaving no one in doubt as to your meaning, or as to the side upon which you are fighting. And that is what we need to-day more than anything else—the assertion of the truth, clearly, forcibly, never mind who it offends, who is pleased or who is not. There are too many who are over cautious, or sensitive lest we give offense. Sometimes I feel as Mr. Garrison once expressed himself, "These are men of 'caution' and 'prudence,' and 'judiciousness.' Sir, I have learned to hate those words. Whenever we attempt to imitate our great Exemplar, and press the truth of God, in all its plainness, upon the conscience, why, we are very imprudent; because forsooth, a great excitement will ensue! Sir, slavery will not be overthrown without excitement, a most tremendous excitement." And so I say to you, Go on with your plainness of speech; continue to cry aloud and spare not. It is the only way to get permanent and satisfactory results; it is the only way to win in the struggle which we are waging for our rights in this country. I was reading only the other day Lincoln's noble words, "Let us have faith to believe that right makes might, and in that faith, let us have the courage to do our duty as we understand it." And faith and courage, faith in the right, and courage to follow the right, all along the line, never mind how seemingly the odds may be against us, are what we need. It never can be to our interest to compromise with evil. It is very comforting to us to know, that in you, we have a race leader who believes firmly in this doctrine, and who preaches it fearlessly. I for one have no use for time-servers, for trimmers, for men who are willing to sacrifice principle to expediency, simply for some temporary gain or profit. I am with the men, like yourself, who stand up squarely and uncompromisingly for every right that belongs to us. Mrs. Grimké, my brother, and Nana all join in kindest regards to Mrs. Du Bois, Yolande, and yourself.[1] My brother leaves for Atlanta next week to be the guest of Pres. [W. H.] Crogman, and to speak at Clark University on Friday evening.

With best wishes,

> I am yours truly,
> Francis J. Grimké.

A proposal for a meeting between a delegation of leading anti-Tuskegee Afro-Americans and President Theodore Roosevelt was projected early in 1905; it never took place, perhaps because Roosevelt's own position was decidely favorable toward Booker T. Washington. Alexander Walters was a leading bishop of the African Methodist Episcopal Zion (A.M.E.Z.) Church and had been presiding officer of the first Pan-African Conference held in London in 1900, of which Du Bois was secretary; Kelly Miller (1863–1939) was a dean and professor of mathematics at Howard University and an effective and widely published polemicist, and was generally sympathetic—though critically so—toward Du Bois. Most of the men named here were to be associated with the Niagara Movement launched later in 1905 under Du Bois's leadership, and the demands indicated in this letter were to be among those basic to that movement.

Boston, January 13, 1905.

Prof. W. E. B. DuBois
Dear Sir:

At conference held at Mr. Trotter's office today it was agreed that a committee of representative men should visit the President and present broad lines

---

1. Yolande was the infant daughter of the Du Boises.

of policy which we desire him to pursue concerning the colored race.

Three definite propositions have been suggested:

First: That the facilities of the Attorney General's office be utilized to uphold the Fifteenth Amendment in connection with cases that may be brought in the Supreme Court, testing the constitutionality of the revised Constitutions of the South.

Second: To wield the influence of the administration to carry out the Interstate Commerce Clause of the Constitution affecting Interstate traffic including the passenger service.

Third: To encourage national aid to education in the most needy States.

We have decided to invite about fifteen or twenty men to make up the conference, of which the following compose the list:

Prof. DuBois	Bishop Abraham Grant	John A. Hagan, Esq.
" Kelly Miller	" Alexander Walters	George H. Jackson, Esq.
" J. W. E. Bowen	Rev. O. M. Waller	J. R. Clifford, "
" S. G. Atkins	" H. T. Johnson	W. Ashbie Hawkins, "
Hon. D. A. Straker	" C. H. Parish	J. D. Wetmore, "
" H. C. Smith	" Matthew Anderson	William Trotter, "
" J. T. Seattle	" R. D. Boyd	Prof. N. G. Grisham
	" Byron Gunner	Whitfield McKinley, Esq.

It is thought best not to include any known office seeker or office holder on the Committee. Whatever names or suggestions you may have to offer please communicate to Bishop Alexander Walters, 1124 Madison Street, Jacksonville, Fla., until February 15th.

If you approve of this will you serve with the following gentlemen as a committee on arrangements:

Prof. DuBois
" Miller
" Bowen
" Alexander Walters
Bishop Grant

Yours truly,
A. Walters
Kelly Miller

[undated]

Dear Bishop Walters:

I shall be glad to act with the committee suggested in your letter of the 13th. I suggest as additional members to the committee:

W. M. Morris of Minneapolis, Minn.

A. H. Grimké of Boston, Mass.

C. E. Bentley of Chicago

W. E. B. Du Bois

[94] Correspondence 1905-1920

From time to time, Du Bois received the kind of letter published below that must have made all the "arduous labors" to which Miss Jessie Fauset refers seem worthwhile.

Ithaca, N.Y., February 16, 1905.

My dear Mr. Du Bois

Perhaps you would be interested to know that I actually succeeded in getting some summer-school work this past year, and that the thing I desire i.e. a personal touch and intercourse with the south (tho' very brief) fell to my willing lot.

I went to Fisk University in Nashville Tenn.—your own Alma Mater is it not? There I stayed for five happy, interesting, *new* weeks, getting acquainted, getting experience and growing. I taught English branches—English Grammar, American Literature and the Interpretation of three or four of the longer standard poems—notably Hiawatha and the Vision of Sir Launfal. Perhaps it would be fairer for me to say I *undertook* to teach these things.

I liked the work—frankly I suppose no work will ever have about it again for me the glamor which this summer's work wore. It was my first attempt at being useful you see—that is a wonderful feeling is it not? The circumstances under which I went were a little peculiar. The summer-school being poor, could offer only "board and keep" and travelling expenses for the teachers. Well, I, you see, was on the outlook for experience, and so the two correlated well. I was, "not to put too fine a point on it," scared—badly, knowing only too well my lack of experience. That was my point of view. But behold the pupils looked at it in a different light, and saw only the college-trained teacher who was offering her wares for the asking. Don't you see how beautifully it worked out? Oh I was so happy—and I owe it to you in large part you know, for it was you who told me to whom I should apply.

I am looking forward to my teaching days with much pleasure. This is my last term of my last year here, and tho' I do not know as yet what I am to be doing, or even where I am to be this time next year, I *hope* I shall be at my chosen task.

By the way I have had the pleasure of looking over some specimens of the work at your University. Professor Chase sent some translations of the "De Senectute"[1] up here to Professor Durham last month, and Prof. Durham has let me read them. (I have been doing special work in Latin here, that is why.) I was very much pleased with them, and both Professor Durham and I thought they compared very well with translations which we have both heard undergraduates make. My own criticism would be that the pupils need to read more English than they have been reading (I should judge) and that they should not permit themselves to be bound so closely by the original. Professor Durham is going to

1. Cicero's "On Old Age."

write to Professor Chase later. Meanwhile will you let him know for me that I was glad to see his work, and congratulate him upon it.

I saw your article "Credo" sometime ago in either the Outlook or the Independent—I have forgotten which. At that time I meant to write you to tell you how glad I was to realise that that was your belief, and to ask you if you did not believe it to be worthwhile to teach our colored men and woman *race* pride, *self*-pride, self-sufficiency (the right kind) and the necessity of living our lives as nearly as possible, *absolutely*, instead of comparing them always with white standards. Don't you believe that we should lead them to understand that the reason we adopt such and such criteria which are also adopted by the Anglo Saxon, is because these criteria are the *best*, and not essentially because they are white? This kind of distinction would in the end breed self-dependence and self-respect, and subjective respect means always sooner or later an outcome of objective respect. You, I should say, are in an excellent position to inculcate this doctrine, and to illustrate it by your own splendid example. I am so proud, you know, to claim you on our side. Living as I have nearly all my life in a distinctly white neighborhood, and for the past four years as the only colored girl in a college community of over 3000 students, I have *had* to let people know that we too possess some of the best, or else allow my own personality to be submerged. It has been with much pleasure that I have pointed to you as an example of the heights to which it is possible for some of us to climb. It is with the same pleasure and sincerity that I tell you of this now—in the desire that in the hour when your work—always arduous—grows irksome thro' apparent lack of appreciation, you may take heart by remembering that somewhere afar off, some one or other is "rendering unto Caesar the things which are Caesar's."

Very sincerely yours,
Jessie R. Fauset.

A radical publication, the *Voice of the Negro*, was begun in Atlanta in 1904 by Du Bois's friend, Jesse Max Barber. In the first number of the second volume (January 1905, p. 677), under the heading "Debit and Credit," Du Bois condemned segments of the Afro-American press for having sold its integrity for money supplied by the Tuskegee machine (the latter term was not used but was universally understood).* The condemnation produced a wave of excitement and Du Bois was deluged with letters. One came from William Hayes Ward (1835–1916), a clergyman and famed Orientalist, best known as the editor, from 1896 to 1913, of the excellent and influential magazine the *Independent*, to which Du Bois frequently contributed. Du Bois's reply is characteristically unequivocal.

* In his *Autobiography* (p. 247), Du Bois incorrectly states that this article was published in the *Boston Guardian*.

New York, Feb. 18, 1905.

My dear Professor DuBois:—

I see a number of the colored papers are taking up your statement pretty vigorously about the five newspapers that sold out so cheap, and are asking you to give their names. Have you anything to say on the subject? What is the meaning of it? I am a little concerned in the matter. It is unpleasant to find that one whom we so heartily respect as you should be losing the sympathy of the colored people, as if you had been guilty of a slander. It is not at all incredible that what you said was true.

Very truly yours,
William Hayes Ward

(Personal & Confidential)

March 10, 1905

My Dear Dr. Ward:

The only Negro papers that are taking vigorous exception to my plain statement are the ones who have sold out to the "Syndicate," viz: the N. Y. Age, the Chicago Conservator, the Boston Citizen, the Washington Colored American, the Colored American Magazine, & the Indianapolis Freeman. Two of these papers have recently died & one is sick seriously. Of course I do not propose to wash our dirty linen in public & consequently I shall say nothing further in print on the subject until I think a further warning necessary. What I have already said is absolutely true & is well known to leading colored men & provable by documentary evidence: viz that in order to forestall criticism of certain persons & measures money has been freely furnished a set of Negro newspapers in the principal cities; partly this has come as a direct bonus, part in advertising & all of it has been given on condition that these papers print certain matter & refrain from other matter. This movement has been going on now for 3 or 4 years until it is notorious among well-informed Negroes & a subject of frequent comment. You must not be at all worried at my losing the confidence of Negroes—I never had the confidence of those who are aroused over my declaration and never expect it.

W. E. B. Du Bois

Oswald Garrison Villard (1872–1949) was the grandson of the abolitionist William Lloyd Garrison and the son of Henry Villard, a railroad owner, founding president of General Electric, and owner (beginning in 1881) of the *New York Evening Post*. In 1897, that paper became the property of Oswald Garrison Villard, who held control of it until 1918. Villard also owned the *Nation* until 1932. His philanthropies included considerable help to Tuskegee, since he was intensely pro-Washington until about 1910. Finally, breaking with Tuskegee— in part because of Du Bois's work—Villard became a leading founder of the

NAACP. As these letters indicate, the relationship between Villard and Du Bois began with a tinge of unpleasantness that was to remain throughout the four decades of their friendship.

New York City, February 7, 1905.

Professor W. E. B. Du Bois
My dear Sir:—

I notice in a recent publication over your name a statement that $3,000. was used in the year 1904 to purchase the influence of the colored press. As I take it for granted that you have not made so grave a charge without positive proof I write to ask you to kindly let us have the facts for publication in the Even Post.

Yours truly,
Oswald Garrison Villard

March 9 [1905]

My Dear Mr. Villard:

I thank you for your kind offer of the 7th inst. but beg leave to say that I have at present no further matter to publish on the subject.

You are quite right in taking it for granted that the grave charge was not made without positive proof and I should be glad, if you should wish, to furnish for your personal information the nature of the proof.

W. E. B. Du Bois

New York, March 13, 1905.

Dear Dr. Du Bois,

In reply to your letter of the 9th, if you cannot submit your proof for publication I shall be glad to have it for my personal information. I cannot understand, however, your making such a charge without having proofs which you are willing to put into print. If we were to run our newspaper on this basis we should not get very far.

Your very truly,
Oswald Garrison Villard.

In connection with the Villard letter, correspondence ensued between Du Bois and William Monroe Trotter, in Boston.

Atlanta, Ga., March 15 1905

Dear Trotter:

Please send me by return mail every scrap of evidence you have going to prove Washington's bribery of newspapers. Send me as many documents as possible, references to documents, illustrative facts & sources for further knowledge & information. I want this for the private conversion of an influential man and you can assure contributors that there will be no public use of their names without their consent. Give me *facts* & hurry them to me. Send a part at a time if necessary.

W. E. B. Du Bois

Boston, Mass. March. 18. '05

Dear Du Bois

I have sent one or two things more to-night. To-morrow I shall send you all the evidence I can find. It is necessarily of a circumstantial nature. Much depends upon the reasonableness of your prospective convert. Would to God I had the direct evidence. But we may get that yet. [E. E.] Cooper has it and I have written a man at D.C. to see him. [D. R.] Wilkins has the thing and I have written him to divulge to you. Please return to me everything I send you.

Yours for the cause,
W. M. Trotter

On the basis of his own knowledge and material sent him by Trotter and others, Du Bois wrote Villard a long letter; included were exhibits, which came to thirteen typed pages, not reprinted here. There is no question as to the accuracy of Du Bois's general charges concerning the corruption of significant sections of the Negro press by the Tuskegee machine.*

(Confidential)
Atlanta, Ga., March 24, 1905.

My dear Mr. Villard:—

In reply to your letter of the 13th inst, I am going to burden you with considerable matter. I do this reluctantly because it seems like imposing on a busy man. At the same time I want to say frankly that I have been sorry to feel in your two letters a note of impatience and disbelief which seems to me unfortunate and calling for a clear, even if long, statement.

In the *Voice of the Negro* for January, I made the charge that $3000 of hush money had been used to subsidize the Negro press in five leading cities. The bases upon which that charge was made were in part as follows:

The offer of $3000 to the editor of the Chicago *Conservator* on 2 separate occasions to change its editorial policy, and the final ousting of the editor by the board of management, and the installing of an editor with the required policy; with the understanding that financial benefit would result (Exhibit A.) The statement of the former editor of the Washington *Record* that he was given to understand that the *Record* received $40 a month from the outside to main-

---

* See the editor's *Documentary History*, pp. 849–51; and August Meier, "Booker T. Washington and the Negro Press," *Journal of Negro History* 38 (January 1953):67–90.

tain its policy (Exhibit B.) The statement of one of the assistant editors of the Washington *Colored American* that it was worth to them $500 a year to maintain its policy. (Exhibit C) There is similar testimony in regard to papers in other cities, particularly the *Freeman* of Indianapolis, the *Age* of New York and the *Citizen* of Boston. All these papers follow the same editorial policy, print the same syndicated news, praise the same persons and attack the same persons. Besides the more definite testimony there is a mass (Exhibit D) of corroborative circumstantial evidence, and all this leads me to estimate that $3000 is certainly the lowest possible estimate of the sums given these 6 papers in the year 1904; I firmly believe that the real sum expended was nearer $5000 and perhaps more than that.

The object of this distribution of money and other favors was, I believe, to stop the attacks being made on the policy of Mr. B. T. Washington. The reason for this belief is as follows:

1. The fact that these papers praise all that Mr. Washington does with suspicious unanimity.

2. The existence of a literary bureau at Tuskegee under Mr. Washington's private secretary, Emmett Scott. (cf. Exhibit B and F. No. 2.)

3. The sending out of syndicated matter from the bureau to appear simultaneously in the above mentioned papers and several others. This appears often in the form of editorials. (Exhibit E.)

4. The creation of new papers and buying up of old papers by Mr. Washington's friends or former employes. (Exhibit F.)

5. The rewarding of favorable newspapers by Mr. Washington (Exhibit G.)

6. The abuse and warning of enemies through the syndicated papers, sending out of cartoons, etc. (Exhibit H.)

7. The use of political patronage to reward and punish.

Finally I was not the first to make this charge. It was common property among colored people, spoken and laughed about and repeatedly charged in the newspapers (Exhibit J.)

What now ought to be the attitude of thinking Negroes toward this situation, assuming the facts alleged to be substantially true? Two things seem certain:

1. There was some time ago a strong opposition to Mr. Washington's policy developed among Negroes. In many cases this opposition became violent and abusive and in one case even riotous.

2. Since that time by the methods above described and also as the result of conference and statements by Mr. Washington, this opposition has been partially stopped. Now personally I strongly oppose Mr. Washington's positions: those positions have been considerably modified for the better since the time of my first public dissent from them; but they are still in my mind dangerous and unsatisfactory in many particulars.

At the same time I have been very sorry to see the extremes to which criticism has gone. I anticipated this mud-slinging in my book and deprecated it, although

I knew it would come. My rule of criticism has been (a) to impute no bad motives (b) to make no purely personal attack. This has I think been adhered to in every single public utterance of mine on the subject hitherto. And when others have not adhered to it I have not hesitated to criticise them.

Moreover most of the criticism of Mr. Washington by Negro papers has not been violent. The *Conservator* was insistent but courteous; the *Record* under [J. W.] Cromwell was always moderate and saw things both to praise and condemn; the *Freeman* and *American* were open to the highest bidder on either side; the *Guardian* was at times violent although more moderate now than formerly, and has gained in standing as it has become less bitter. All this was a good sign. The air was clearing itself, the demand of the people known, and a healthy democratic out-come of the controversy seemed possible. It seemed at one time indeed possible that even the *Guardian* would see the situation in a better light. Then gradually a change came in. Criticism suddenly stopped in many quarters and fulsome adulation succeeded. Violent attacks on all opposers were printed in a certain set of papers. National organizations of Negroes were "captured" by indefensible methods. (Exhibit K.)

It thus became clearer and clearer to me and to others that the methods of Mr. Washington and his friends to stop violent attack had become a policy for wholesale hushing of all criticism and the crushing out of men who dared to criticize in any way. I felt it time to speak at least a word of warning.

I could not however make this warning as definite as I would have liked for three reasons.

1st. I did not want to drag Atlanta University into the controversy since the proceeding was altogether of my own initiative.

2nd. I did not want to ask those who privately gave me information to do so publicly. They are poor men and if, for instance, Mr. Cromwell, a teacher in Washington Colored schools, were to testify as to the facts in public he might lose his position.

3rd. I uttered the warning to a Negro audience and it was addressed particularly to them; so far as possible I want to keep the internal struggles of the race in its own ranks. Our dirty linen ought not be exhibited too much in public.

For this latter reason many of my friends do not agree with me in the policy of speaking out. Kelly Miller, A. H. Grimké and others have repeatedly expressed to me that they are perfectly satisfied that Mr. Washington is furnishing money to Negro newspapers in return for their [the Newspapers'] support. But they say: What are you going to do about it? He has the support of the nation, he has the political patronage of the administration, he has apparently unlimited cash, he has the ear of the white press and he is following exactly the methods of that press; and moreover his attitude on the race question is changing for the better. These are powerful arguments, but they do not satisfy me. I am however constrained by such representatives to take up the matter cautiously and to see what warnings and aroused conscience in the race will do toward stopping this shameful condition of affairs.

On the other hand when I am convinced that the time has come, that bribery is still going on and gag law manifest, and political bossism saddled on a people advised to let politics alone, I will speak again in no uncertain words and I will prove every statement I make.

I regret to say that honest endeavors on my part in the past to understand and cooperate with Mr. Washington have not been successful. 'I recognize as clearly as anyone the necessity of race unity against a common enemy—but it must be unity against the enemy and not veiled surrender to them.' My attitude is not actuated by sympathy with Mr. Trotter, editor of the Guardian. There was once a rumor that I was acting jointly with him. My reply to that was made in a letter to George F. Peabody, which I venture to enclose as Exhibit L.[1] I went into conference last winter with Mr. Washington and his friends. Mr. Washington selected the personnel of the conference and it did not altogether please me but I attended and urged such of my friends as were invited to come also. In that conference I did not beat around the bush but told Mr. Washington plainly and frankly the causes of our differences of opinion with him.

Mr. Washington replied in a very satisfactory speech and his friends asked me to draw up a plan of a central committee of 12. This I did. The resulting committee which I helped select was good save in two cases where I was overruled by Mr. Washington and his friend. I was taken ill during the summer and the meeting of the committee was postponed; finally the committee was organized at a meeting to which I was not invited, and of which I knew nothing till 2 weeks afterward. Whether this was by accident or design I do not know. At any rate the committee was so organized as to put the whole power virtually in the hands of an executive committee and the appointment of that committee was left to Mr. Washington. Upon hearing this some two weeks after, I resigned my membership. I could not conscientiously deliver my freedom of thought and action into the hands of Mr. Washington and his special abettors like [T. Thomas] Fortune.

I am still uncertain as to how Mr. Washington himself ought to be judged in the bribery matter. I especially condemn the bribe-takers and despise men like Fortune, Cooper, Alexander Manly and [George L.] Knox who are selling their papers. If they agree with Mr. Washington and he wishes to help them, the contributions ought to be open and above board; and if the contrary is the case and it is, to my unwavering belief, in 3 or 4 of the above instances, these men are scamps. Mr. Washington probably would defend himself by saying that he is unifying the Negro press, that his contributions are investments not bribes, and that the Tuskegee press bureau is a sort of Associated Negro Press. The reply

1. This letter, dated 28 December 1903, is printed on pp. 67–69.

to this is that the transactions do not appear to be thus honorable, that the character of the matter sent out is fulsome in praise of every deed of Mr. Washington's and abusive toward every critic, and that the men who are conducting the enterprises are not the better type of Negroes but in many cases the worst, as in the case of Fortune, Cooper, Knox and [Richard W.] Thompson (Exhibit M.)

In the trying situation in which we Negroes find ourselves today we especially need the aid and countenance of men like you. This may look to outsiders as a petty squabble of thoughtless self-seekers. It is in fact the life and death struggle of nine million men. It is easy of course to dismiss my contentions as the result of petty jealousy or short-sighted criticism—but the ease of the charge does not prove its truth. I know something of the Negro race and its conditions and dangers, and while I am sure, and am glad to say, that Mr. Washington has done and is doing much to help the Negro, I just as firmly believe that he represents today in much of his work and policy the greatest of the hindering forces in the line of our true development and uplift.

I beg to remain

Very respectfully yours,
W. E. B. Du Bois.

[Enclosures] Exhibits A,B,C,D,E,F,G,H,J,K,L,M. *Please return.*

Nota Bene: No attempt is made in the following exhibits to present all the evidence obtainable—I am simply giving typical examples of the sort of proof upon which I rely. W. E. B. D.

Two more letters concluded this phase of the Villard–Du Bois exchanges.

April 18th, 1905.

Dear Dr. DuBois

I found your long letter with its enclosures on my return from the South. I must say frankly that it will take a great deal more than the evidence you have presented to shake my faith in Mr. Washington's purity of purpose, and absolute freedom from selfishness and personal ambition. At the same time, the evidence would seem to show that the literary bureau at Tuskegee under Mr. Scott has been extremely injudicious. It also looks as if money aid had been given; but you have failed to substantiate your positive statement in the Voice of the Negro that three thousand dollars was the sum used, since you say the testimony "leads me to estimate." Several of your counts I do not think you substantiate at all, notably the use of political patronage. So far as your witnesses are concerned, I am unable to judge of their reliability. Your "Exhibit C.," for instance, contains the statement of an assistant editor heard by Mr. Ferris, and repeated by Mr. Ferris to a friend who in turn repeated it to you. This sort of thing would have no weight in court. I cite this merely as an instance.

I shall certainly speak to Mr. Washington about Scott's ac——[1] and I think it would be a very good thing if you would let me submit the whole correspondence the next time he comes to New York. I want particularly to take him to task for your connection with the council, and ask him whether the apparent slight to you was not really due to accident. I think you made a great mistake in resigning from it.

I hold no brief for Mr. Washington. As my writings show, I am a sincere believer in the higher education of the negro, and I am doing what I can to help Atlanta and similar institutions. I may also lay claim to being a devoted friend to the race, to whose interests I am giving a very large share of my time. You will perhaps permit me therefore to say frankly that I greatly regret your position and your attitude towards Mr. Washington. I do not think that there are any essential differences between your positions. I do believe that for the masses of the negro race industrialism is the all-important question of the hour. It goes without saying that to have proper industrial schools we must have such institutions as Atlanta and Fisk to furnish proper instructors.

As for Trotter, he was under me at Harvard, and his father was a sergeant in my uncle's company in the 55th Massachusetts. I consider young Trotter a very dangerous, almost irresponsible young man, whose conduct at the Boston riot should make it impossible for anyone to consider seriously his opinions upon any subject relating to his race.

In the hope that you will grant me the permission I desire,

Yours very truly,
[Oswald Garrison Villard]

Atlanta, Ga., April 20, 1905.

Confidential
Mr. O. G. Villard
My dear Sir:—

Good faith to my correspondents will not allow the proposed use of the matter sent to you.

I trust you will not misinterpret my position: your attitude toward the Negro has been commendable; I am not seeking to change your opinions, I am merely showing you, at your own request, the reasons why my faith in Mr. Washington has been shaken.

It happens in the same mail with your letter are two other letters. One is from a man who has edited a Negro newspaper 22 years; he says: "But for the assistance Booker T. Washington has and is rendering the Cleveland O. *Journal* it would have been dead many weeks ago. The same is true of the Boston *Colored Citizen*. That he has subsidized the New York *Age* and Indianapolis *Freeman*,

1. The manuscript is torn; the word is probably "activities."

and owns the *Colored American Magazine* as well as assisting other alleged race papers, you are doubtless aware."

Another is from one of the most intelligent young Negro physicians in New England, who serves some of the best white families:

"He told me a story which firmly convinces me that Mr. Washington heads an organization in every large city whose purpose it is to ruin any man who openly criticises his methods in any particular. And I am now of the opinion that it is time that the decent element of the race take a stand for the things which are necessary for our further progress."

Such actions are not "injudicious," Mr. Villard, they are *wrong*. I do not believe you can make Mr. Scott the scape goat for them—it is scarcely conceivable that he has acted without Mr. Washington's full knowledge and consent.

As I have intimated, I am not submitting to you all the evidence obtainable, nor am I submitting it to a court of law. I am merely showing you the sort of testimony that has moved me to speak and act, and naturally its weight with me depends on the character of the witnesses whom I know and you do not.

Contrary to your opinion there was to my mind no alternative left me but to resign from Mr. Washington's committee: I thoroughly believed that by means of downright bribery and intimidation he was influencing men to do his will and had obtained a majority of such men on his committee; that he was seeking not the welfare of the Negro race but personal power; under such circumstances with the additional slight of not being invited to the most important meeting of the committee, could I continue to co-operate with him?

You have attacked Mr. Roosevelt harshly. Does that mean that he is a rascal? No, but it does mean that you think he loans himself to indefensible deeds and measures, and that the general tendency of his policies is dangerous; if you believe this you have a right to proclaim it and act accordingly, and people must respect your intentions even if they doubt your judgment. So in this case: I am convinced of Mr. Washington's wrong course. You are not. Very well, I only ask for my convictions the same charity that you ask for yours.

Respectfully yours,
W. E. B. Du Bois.

Earlier reference has been made to the "secret conference" held in New York City in 1904 between the Washington and the Du Bois forces. For reasons explained in the letters above and below, Du Bois resigned from a Committee of Twelve, appointed as a result of the 1904 meeting;* the resignation seemed to Kelly Miller and to Archibald H. Grimké precipitous and tending to strain the

---

* For details on the 1904 meeting and the Committee of Twelve, see the editor's book, *Afro-American History*, pp. 118–26.

relationship between them and Du Bois. It is within this context that Du Bois's letter of early 1905 may be understood.†

Atlanta, Ga., March 21, 1905

My dear Messrs. Grimké and Miller:

You will remember that at the first suggestions of a meeting with Mr. Washington my determination communicated to both of you was to enter into no organization controlled by Mr. Washington where he would have me at his mercy by simply having his men outvote me. This position I have always maintained. There was at the New York meeting no obligation expressed or implied that I intended to enter into any permanent organization. I was asked to make some suggestion to keep the meeting from being an utter failure and I suggested the committee of 12. Moreover I went further than this and outlined the possible work and organization of such a committee. This plan I sent to Mr. Washington and Mr. Browne[1] and it was essentially ignored. It was my unalterable decision from the first that unless the committee was so organized as to allow real work by individual members that I would not be a member of it. I was going to St. Louis with the ultimatum: if this committee is to be delivered into the power of Mr. Washington and his followers, I will not serve.

Meantime I was taken ill and cancelled all engagements. The next thing I heard, about the middle of July [1904], was that a meeting had been called in New York "to meet my convenience" and that the meeting had done precisely what I had expected: namely, turned the whole organization into Mr. Washington's hands. I had received absolutely no intimation that the meeting was to be held in New York. I was at the time in Des Moines, Iowa and could not have attended if I had received notice, as I was still unwell.

There was one course left to me and that was to resign. That I did and that resignation stands today. Under no circumstances will I withdraw it.

I am of course sorry to lose the cooperation of you two gentlemen. I count it a great misfortune to the Negro race when two clear headed and honest men like you can see their way to put themselves under the dictation of a man with the record of Mr. Washington. I am sorry, very sorry to see it. Yet it will not alter my determination one jot or tittle. I refuse to wear Mr. Washington's livery, or to put on his collar. I have worked this long without having my work countersigned by Booker Washington or laid out by Robert Ogden, and I think I'll peg along to the end in the same way.

I beg however that neither of you feel at any time or under any circumstances obliged to defend the sincerity of my beliefs or the good faith of my actions.

† The original of this letter is in the Moorland-Spingarn Collection of the Howard University Library in Washington.
1. Hugh M. Browne of Cheyney, Pennsylvania, was a Washington man.

That I trust future history will attend to, and if not it is a small thing anyhow and so let it go. At present I propose to fight the battle to the last ditch if I fight it stark alone.

Very respectfully yours,
W. E. B. Du Bois

Duplicate sent to Mr. Miller.

Max Weber (1864–1920), the distinguished German social scientist, visited the United States in 1904; among those with whom he met was Du Bois. A result was the publication of the article by Du Bois mentioned in this letter—"Die Negerfrage in den Vereiningten Staaten" (The Negro Question in the United States)— in a journal Weber edited, *Archiv für Sozialwissenschaft und Sozialpolitik* 22 (1906):31–79. The translation into German of Du Bois's *Souls*, proposed by Weber, was not to be realized for another twenty years. A note indicates that Du Bois answered Weber's letter on 11 April 1905, but the reply seems not to have survived.

Heidelberg 30/III 05

Dear Sir,

I was glad to receive your kind letter. When, at the 15th, your article was not yet at hand, I supposed you might perhaps be prevented of writing the same now, and so we had to dispose about the space of the next number of the "Archiv." So, your article will be published at the head of the number to be edited November 1st of this year—it would be hardly possible at any earlier time.

Your splendid work: "The Souls of Black Folk" ought *to be translated in German*. I do not know whether anybody has already undertaken to make a translation. *If not* I am authorized to beg you for your authorization to Mrs. Elizabeth Jaffé-von Richthofen here, a scholar and friend of mine, late factory inspector of Karlsruhe, now wife of my fellow-teacher and fellow-editor, Dr. [Albert] Jaffé. I should like to write a short introduction about Negro question and literature and should be much obliged to you for some information about your life, viz: age, birthplace, descent, positions held by you—of course only *if you give* your authorization.

I think Mrs. Jaffé would be very able translator, which will be of some importance, your vocabulary and style being very peculiar: it reminds me sometimes of Gladstone's idioms although the spirit is a different one.

I should like to give in one of the next numbers of the "Archiv" a short review of the recent publications about the race problem in America. Beside your own work and the "Character-building" of Mr. Booker Washington, I got only the book of Mr. Page ("The Negro, the Southerners Problem"—very superficial me thinks) the Occasional Papers of your academy and the article of Mr. Willcox in the Yale Review.[1] If there is anything else to be reviewed, I should be much obliged to you for any information (of course I saw the article of Viereck in the official publication).

Please excuse my bad English—I seldom here had the opportunity to speak it, and realize a language in speaking and writing it is very different.

Yours very respectfully,
Professor Max Weber

When Robert M. La Follette (1855–1925) was in the midst of his second term as governor of Wisconsin—and had won national attention with the reforms called the "Wisconsin Idea"—an exchange occurred between him and Du Bois. Mutual regard between the two men persisted so long as La Follette lived; in 1924, the NAACP officially endorsed La Follette for president.

April 3 [1905]

Hon R La Follette
Sir:

You possibly know something of A.U. Each year we hold here a Negro conference to study the problems of the South. These studies are known throughout the U.S. & somewhat in Europe. This year we hold our tenth annual meeting on Tuesday May 30 & I am extremely anxious to make it a success. To this end I write to invite you to be present & say a few words to us. I know that it is almost presumptuous to ask this of so busy a man & yet I trust you will not refuse this request without some consideration. Of the need which the South & the Negro race has of hearing men like you I need not speak—you [the manuscript breaks off at this point].

Madison, Wis., April 7, 1905

Mr. W. E. B. Du Bois
My dear Sir:

I am in receipt of your letter of invitation to be present and participate in the University Annual on May 30th next. I regret that it is not possible for me to accept. My time will be fully occupied at home for many weeks to come in consideration of legislative matters. The Wisconsin legislature is at present in session, and the probability is will not adjourn until the first part of June. While that body is here, it is imperative that the executive of the state remain constantly at the capital city. The most important measures before the legislature are still pending, and I must be at the call of committees and individual members

---

1. Thomas Nelson Page, *The Negro: The Southerner's Problem* (New York: Charles Scribner's Sons, 1904); Walter F. Willcox, "Census Statistics of the Negro," *Yale Review* 13 (May 1904):274–86. The italics are in the original.

[108]   Correspondence 1905–1920

for conference, and ready to act when any measure is presented for executive consideration. Under our constitution no bill can be held by the executive for approval or veto longer than three days; hence I am obliged to decline all invitations to leave the capitol during the balance of the session.

Again assuring you of my regret, and thanking you for your invitation, I am,
          Very sincerely yours,
          Robert M La Follette

Du Bois's plans and efforts to establish some base and organ better to promulgate his ideas are illustrated in an exchange of letters early in 1905 with Jacob Henry Schiff (1847–1920), then head of the banking firm of Kuhn, Loeb and Company. The printing plant to which Du Bois refers was the one which later, from 1906 to 1907, issued a magazine he edited, the *Moon;* E. L. Simon was the printer and H. H. Pace the business manager. Du Bois was to note of his approach to Schiff that "Nothing ever came of this, because, as I might have known, most of Mr. Schiff's friends were strong and sincere advocates of Tuskegee."* It is nevertheless true that Jacob Schiff contributed generously to the NAACP from its founding until his death, and that his widow continued the gifts for many years.

(Confidential)
                                April 14 [1905]
Mr. Jacob Schiff
Sir:

You will probably remember having met me at Bar Harbor in 1903. I spoke at an Atlanta Univ. meeting then, was at your home & you were kind enough to ask me to call on you in N. Y. which I have not yet had the opportunity to do.

I want to lay before you a plan which I have and ask you if it is of sufficient interest to you for you to be willing to hear more of it & possibly to assist in its realization.

The Negro race in America is today in a critical condition. Only united concerted effort will save us from being crushed. This union must come as a matter of education & long continued effort. To this end there is needed a high class journal to circulate among the intelligent Negroes, tell them of the deeds of themselves & their neighbors, interpret the news of the world to them & inspire them toward definite ideals.

Now we have many small weekly papers & one or two monthlies but none of them fill the great need I have outlined. I want to establish therefore for the 9 million American Negroes & eventually for the whole Negro world a Monthly Journal.

* *Dusk of Dawn*, p. 83. The Schiff–Du Bois letters of 1905 are published, in part, in that source.

To this end I have already in Memphis a printing establishment which has been running successfully at job work a year under a competent printer—a self sacrificing educated young man. Together we shall have about $2000 invested in this plant by April 15.

I expect to have as business manager an honest efficient man, graduate of Brown University & with some actual business experience. I propose myself to do the editing.

I need for the floating of this enterprise a capital of $10,000. I believe that such a capital would be well invested & yield returns, but I cannot of course be absolutely certain of this. There are in the U. S. a million Negro families who can read & write at least 100,000 families of well educated persons. They demand better reading matter about themselves & their ideals, than they are getting. I want to give it to them. I believe I can & I believe that they will pay for it well in time.

If you are in the slightest degree interested in this project may I call on you & explain it further? I shall be North from June to October & also next winter for a month or so. I am Sir,

      Very Respectfully Yours
      W. E. B. Du Bois

      Hot Springs, Va. April 9th, 1905.

Professor W. E. B. DuBois
My dear Sir:—

I well remember our meeting in Bar Harbor in the summer of 1903 and I am glad you have written me. Your plan to establish a high class journal to circulate among the intelligent Negroes, is in itself interesting and on its face has my sympathy. But before I could decide whether I can become of advantage in carrying your plans into effect, I would wish to advise with men, whose opinion in such a matter I consider of much value, but since your communication is marked "confidential" I shall not feel at liberty to take counsel upon your proposition, until you authorize me to do so.

Will you therefore not write me again (to my New York address) and believe me, meantime,

      Yours truly,
      Jacob H. Schiff.

      April 13 [1905]

My dear Sir:

It is very kind of you to take the time to look into my proposal. I am quite willing that you should show my letter of the 4th inst. to your friends. Meantime I am sending you certain notes on the matter you may find of some help in enlightening you on some points. More careful and accurate estimates can be had a little later if you should wish.

I beg to remain,

>Very Respectfully Yours,
>W. E. B. Du Bois

As previously noted, one of the influential teachers in Du Bois's life was the outstanding historian Albert Bushnell Hart (1854–1943), who was at Harvard from 1883 until his retirement in 1926. The letters that follow sharply etch the Washington–Du Bois circumstances.

>Cambridge, Mass., April 24, 1905.

My dear Du Bois:—

I have your letter relative to one of your students, Gibson,* and I will at once communicate with the authorities; a really good man who comes with your endorsement will probably get the Price Greenleaf aid.[1]

As you probably know, I have been writing on the Southern question for the *Boston Transcript* and the *Independent* and I enclose a copy of the two letters to the *Transcript*. I shall be obliged to ask you to return them as my files are very short. You have very likely seen the article in *Independent* for March 23, and another is to follow. I am going to write a third letter to the *Transcript* on the economic condition of the South. Can you commend anything on that subject that does not appear in your own writings and the Census Reports? My thesis is the constant backwardness of the South in the agricultural regions.

Of course in the heat of the discussion I hear of you everywhere. I am rather troubled to find that a great many people suppose that you head a kind of opposition to Booker Washington's ideas; so far as I understand, there is no innate lack of harmony between your purpose in life and his. You take a certain thing which must be done, viz. the higher education of those who can profit by it; he takes another end of the same problem; naturally each of you thinks that his interest is the more important; if you did not, you would exchange activities. But I do not see how either excludes the other. Our bumptious friend Trotter has made a great deal of unnecessary trouble by his assaults on Mr. Washington, in season and out of season, and I have actually found people who seemed to suppose that you and Trotter were working together.

>Sincerely yours,
>Albert Bushnell Hart

1. This is Truman K. Gibson, who graduated from Atlanta University in 1905, was admitted to Harvard and there received his A.B. (cum laude) in 1908. He went on to become president of the Supreme Liberty Life Insurance Company in Chicago. (Mrs. Silba M. Lewis of the Atlanta University Library helped make this identification.)

October 9, 1905

Dear Professor Hart

Thank you for the opportunity of seeing the clippings. On the whole I agree with them & am very glad you wrote them. As to Mr. Washington, the people who think that I am one of those who oppose many of his ideas are perfectly correct. I have no personal opposition to him—I honor much of his work. But his platform has done the race infinite harm & I'm working against it with all my might. Mr. W. is today chief instrument in the hands of a N.Y. clique who are seeking to syndicate the Negro & settle the problem on the trust basis. They have bought & bribed newspapers & men.

W. E. B. Du Bois

There was little love lost between Theodore Roosevelt and Du Bois; the latter, however, did not permit subjective considerations to interfere with the struggle. Du Bois's letter to President Roosevelt is quite pointed; the reply from the president's secretary, quite bland. In fact, Roosevelt did not visit Atlanta University.

May 22, 1905

Mr. Theodore Roosevelt
Sir:

I learn that you are expecting to visit Atlanta this fall and I want to ask you to visit Atlanta University. This is asking a good deal, but I am not making the request lightly. Atlanta University has stood for nearly forty years as an institution peculiarly devoted to the high aspirations of the American Negro. We have suffered for this—we are suffering for it but we are sticking to our ideals. At the same time we think we deserve something of the American people and therefore of you as their Chief representative. We were glad to have President McKinley come to Atlanta even though he did not visit us, and we were glad when he visited a sister institution where many of our graduates teach.[1] Yet when we face the prospect of your doing the same thing we feel differently. You are yourself a college man and have enunciated the highest ideals fearlessly. This institution is the child of Harvard & Yale. It has sent into the world 500 black men & women who mean something. You are coming to our very threshhold—will you not step in a moment and tell us and the world that you have the same faith in the right sort of college-bred black men that you have in the right sort of artisans and workingmen? I sincerely hope you can. A. U. is right in the city—

---

1. President McKinley attended a Peace Jubilee in Atlanta in 1899 to celebrate the victory over Spain; in December of that year he, together with several cabinet members, paid a visit to Tuskegee, where appropriate speeches were exchanged. This visit is described at some length in Booker T. Washington's *Up From Slavery: An Autobiography* (New York: Doubleday, Page and Co., 1907), pp. 302-10.

a mile from the post office so that a call will take but a little time. I beg to remain, Sir,

W. E. B. Du Bois

Washington, May 25, 1905

My dear Sir:

Your letter of the 22nd instant has been received and the President thanks you for the kind invitation extended to him to visit Atlanta University on the occasion of his proposed trip through the South. Your wishes will be borne in mind and given consideration when the details of the trip are taken up.

Very truly yours,
Wm. Loeb Jr.
Secretary to the President.

The Niagara Movement (1905–1909) gave organized expression to positions and personalities rejecting the stance of the Tuskegee Machine; it formed a main stream producing the National Association for the Advancement of the Colored People. The original gathering which eventuated in the movement was held at the Canadian side of the falls in July 1905. Fresh from that meeting, Du Bois went to New England on matters pertinent to the new organization as well as to Atlanta University; there he wrote to two leading Black figures who had been absent from the July meeting and who were to decide, despite Du Bois's letter, not to join Niagara. In reading the letter,* it is well to bear in mind the earlier communication to Grimké and Miller—dated 21 March 1905—which appears on pages 105–6 of this book.

Williamstown, Mass., August 13, 1905

Messrs Archibald Grimké
and Kelly Miller
Gentlemen:

Sometime ago you urged me to a step which I declined to take. As it seemed to me at the time the strongest argument you put forward was the fact that Mr. Washington's committee was practically the only efficient active force in the field, so that it was that or nothing. I determined that this should not long be the case and the result has been the successful launching of the Niagara Movement. I did not ask you two gentlemen to join me in this movement, first because you both belonged to Mr. Washington's committee & membership in both

---

* The original of this letter is in the Moorland-Spingarn Collection, Howard University Library. On the history of the Niagara Movement, see the editor's *Afro-American History*, pp. 157–78; for the relevant documents, see his *Documentary History*, 1:900–915.

organizations seemed to me inconsistent; and secondly I was not sure that I would find 50 men who had not bowed the knee to Baal.

Today we have a growing enthusiastic organization of nearly 75 members, educated, determined & unpurchasable men. I am writing to ask you men to join us as charter members. The platform is I am sure essentially agreeable to you. The members want you & regretted your absence at Buffalo. We are invited for active work, not against persons but for principles. Will you not join us? I shall send you a copy of the constitution & declaration if you desire them. Meantime I await your decision with interest.

Very sincerely yours,
W. E. B. Du Bois

A significant interchange occurred late in 1905 between Du Bois and Walter Hines Page (1855–1918). Page, originally from North Carolina, was a newspaperman in New York and in Raleigh; in the 1880s, his unconventional views obliged him to leave the latter city and the South. He became editor of, in turn, *Forum*, the *Atlantic Monthly*, and *World's Work*, and was a founding partner in 1899 of the publishing house of Doubleday and Page. He served as ambassador to Great Britain from 1913 until 1918.

New York, November 22, 1905

Dear Professor DuBois:

I wonder if you are not at work on material that will in the course of time take book form? I hope so, and if you will permit me to say, surely you ought to be. If you are, may I remind you without prejudice, of course, to any other publishers, that my partners and I are sure to be very deeply interested in anything that you write.

With all good wishes,

Sincerely yours,
Walter H. Page

Nov. 24, 1905

Dear Mr. Page,

I am working on three books—a novel, virtually finished, which is promised to McClurg.[1] I am beginning a life of John Brown, promised to Jacobs of Phil.[2] I have long been collecting for a "Sociology of the Negro America"—a sort of text book, reader's guide & manual of the Negro in America—designed to be a popular presentation of the matter in literary form & small compass with such

---

1. Though Du Bois then thought the novel was "virtually finished," he had second thoughts; *The Quest of the Silver Fleece* was actually not published until 1911.
2. The life of Brown appeared in 1909.

diluted science and history as the mass can stand.[3] This is unpromised and unwritten. At the same time will you let me say frankly that when it is written I cannot help but hesitate to offer it to the exploiters of Tom Dixon?[4]

W. E. B. Du Bois

New York, Nov. 27, 1905.

Dear Dr. DuBois:

I thank you for your letter and it is a pleasure to know that you have so much interesting literary work ahead, because I am interested in what you do not only from a publishing point of view but from a reader's point of view.

I am glad, too, that my little note gave you occasion to make the criticism that you have of our publishing Dixon—although I confess I am a little surprised that you should write as you did about it.

When a publishing house becomes a machine for a propaganda, it immediately ceases to have economic virility, as of course you know. When, years ago, I was fighting my way for and to freedom of opinion in the South, the one thing that those whom I may call the enemies of freedom of opinion granted me was perfect freedom to say what I chose, and in the little circle of my own influence I have used that one weapon to their dismay. That is to say, a democracy can rest absolutely on one principle, perfect freedom of expression, and it cannot rest on any other basis. When, therefore, Mr. Dixon came along—who stands for what I regard as my enemies' doctrine—I should have felt ashamed of myself if I had hesitated, as a director of a publishing house, to give him the same freedom of its use that I have always asked of his side with their machinery of publication.

Of course, you understand this principle as well as I, and it is for this reason that I am a little surprised that you should speak of us as "exploiters" of Dixon. We are simply his publishers.

With all good wishes,

Sincerely yours,
Walter H. Page[1]

Clark Wissler (1870–1947) was, with Franz Boas, one of the outstanding American anthropologists of the first half of the twentieth century. He was a professor

---

3. The nearest of his works to the kind of brief text Du Bois here describes was *The Negro*, published by Henry Holt and Co. in New York in 1915.

4. Thomas Dixon (1864–1946) was the author of such best-selling and viciously racist novels as *The Leopard's Spots* (New York: Grosset and Dunlap, 1902) and *The Clansman: An Historical Romance of the Ku Klux Klan* (New York: Doubleday, Page and Co., 1905). The latter novel was the basis for the film glorifying the Klan, *Birth of a Nation*, first released in 1915.

1. Du Bois wrote a large "F"—his symbol meaning "file"—at the top of this letter; it appears that he did not reply.

at Yale for almost twenty years and was associated for nearly forty with the American Museum of Natural History. His letter to Du Bois reflects the latter's persistent search for data and is also of intrinsic interest.

New York City Nov. 31, 1905

My dear sir:

Upon my return I find a letter from you, asking for a list of the best works on Negro anthropology and ethnology. The fact is that the literature upon this subject is very incomplete and unsatisfactory. The best brief article with which I am acquainted will be found in the History of Mankind, by Ratzel.[1] There is a small book by Deniker on the Races of Man, Scribners.[2] In the foot notes to the discussion of Africa, you will find references to all the important literature of the subject, and while this book is brief, it is in some respects a digest of our present knowledge. I am sure that if I gave you a list of titles it would be a reproduction of the bibliography in this work.

Hoping you may find this satisfactory, I am,

Very truly yours,
Clark Wissler
Acting Curator

James Weldon Johnson (1871–1938) was among the most distinguished and versatile figures in the United States until his sudden and accidental death. He was born in Florida, educated at Atlanta and Columbia universities, and was the first Black man admitted to the Florida bar. He served from 1903 to 1912 in Venezuela and Nicaragua as United States Consul; one of the founders of the NAACP, he served as its secretary from 1916 to 1930. In the first decade of the twentieth century, he was best known as part of the song-writing and performing team of Cole and Johnson, together with Bob Cole and his own brother Rosamond. Johnson's works include *Autobiography of an ex-Colored Man* (1912), *God's Trombones* (1927), *Black Manhattan* (1930), and *Along This Way* (1933). His association with Du Bois was prolonged, fruitful, and affectionate. Among their earliest letters is the one below; the reference to the Niagara Movement suggests Johnson's lifelong commitment to the struggle for justice.

Dec. 16, 1905

Dear Dr. DuBois,

Both my brother and my partner are at present on their western tour; when they return I shall talk with them over your suggestion of the organization of

---

1. Friedrich Ratzel, *The History of Mankind*, trans. A. J. Butler, 3 vols. (London: Macmillan and Co., 1896–98).

2. Joseph Deniker, *The Races of Man* (New York: Charles Scribner's Sons, 1900). Du Bois purchased the Deniker volume as a result of this recommendation.

the colored musical and theatrical talent in New York, in connection with the Niagara Movement, and shall write you.

I hope that you are in very good health. I have not yet received that promised photograph.[1]

> Yours very truly,
> James W. Johnson

Sir Horace Curzon Plunkett (1854–1932) was a leading Irish statesman and agricultural reformer. In 1894, he founded the Irish Agricultural Organization Society, and in Parliament, from 1892 to 1900, he fought hard for reform in Irish land laws. He was chairman in 1917–18 of the Irish convention which brought peace between England and Ireland. He made two rather prolonged visits to the United States, working as a cattle rancher in Wyoming from 1879 to 1889 and returning to visit again in 1905.

Du Bois always maintained a vivid interest in the Irish, seeing a kinship between Irish subjection and Black oppression in the United States. The book mentioned in these letters, issued in 1904, was *Ireland in the New Century*. Plunkett's letter was written on the stationery of the Irish Department of Agriculture, of which he was vice-president from 1900 to 1907.

> Dublin, 5th February, 1906.

My dear Sir,

I have been reading your "Souls of Black Folk." It has moved me to send you, as a slight recognition of the interest, pleasure and profit I derived from its perusal, a copy of a book upon problems more or less analogous to those you treat. I know that I should have been helped when I was writing this book if I had seen yours, which, unfortunately, was not published at the time. This makes me think that, in spite of its inferiority from a literary point of view, you may find in my book some thoughts which will interest you. Dutton & Co. have published the book in New York, but its sale has been almost exclusively on this side of the Atlantic.

I am

> Yours faithfully,
> Horace Plunkett

> March 1, 1906

Dear Mr. Plunkett:

I am reading your "Ireland" with very great interest & thank you heartily for it. I was sorry not to see you when you were in America. I am a little afraid that

---

1. Du Bois penciled a note on this letter: "Order large photo from Purdy for Johnson."

you fell into the hands of the Philistines & did not get that full view of our great problem here that we want sympathetic visitors to get. I hope we may welcome you to Atlanta when you come again. Thank you for your kind words.

        W. E. B. Du Bois

Du Bois was angered when Black people attacked, in white publications, efforts to end racism, but he was infuriated when they simultaneously slandered their own folk, and especially their own women. In one such article, "Not Pity But Respect: A Negro's View of the Color Line," by the Reverend T. Nelson Baker, the author assailed young Black people for opposing segregated seating arrangements at a Student Volunteer Movement Convention in Nashville; he suggested that jim-crow resulted from the defects of Black people, that " a chronic state of whining and pouting" was harmful, and that "the degradation of Negro women" displayed itself in their "perverted aesthetical taste" for white men.*

 Du Bois wrote to both the author and the editor of the periodical in which the essay appeared. His letter to the editor was not published and there is no record of any reply from the Reverend Mr. Baker.

        April 14, 1906.

Mr. T. N. Baker
Sir:—

 Hitherto as your writings have from time to time come to my notice, I have read them with interest and considerable sympathy. I have not agreed with you always but I thought I recognized a fellow soul striving for the light and have hoped that sometime we might see alike and work together, more especially as you were working in a section where my family has lived for more than two centuries.

 The article therefore in the Congregationalist of April 7 has come to me as a sad surprise. I think that the vicious and wanton attack which you have made on educated Negro womanhood—the nasty slur on the chastity of that class of Negro women to which my wife belongs and the young women whom I teach every day—is the most cowardly and shameless thing I have recently read. And while I am sure that my opinion will have no influence upon you, I can not refrain from thus expressing to you my indignation and my righteous contempt for a man who thus publicly maligns that very class of women to which his own wife and mother belong.

        Respectfully yours,
        W. E. B. Du Bois

---

 * *Congregationalist and Christian World*, 91 (7 April 1906): 508.

April 14, 1906.

The Editor of the Congregationalist
Sir:—

I have seldom been more surprised than I was at finding you giving publicity to certain parts of the article by Baker entitled "Not Pity but Respect." Mr. Baker has of course a perfect right to his opinions and you have a right to publish them so long as they are not indecent. But the intimation in this article that educated Christian Negro women such as were delegates to the Nashville convention are little better than public prostitutes is too dirty to be allowed in any paper which calls itself religious. You owe a published apology to my wife, to the young women of Fisk and Atlanta and to that whole class of colored delegates to the Student Volunteer Movement who in every single case are as chaste and decent as the wives, sisters and daughters of the editors of the Congregationalist.

It is a burning shame for men like you to give currency to such slurs simply because we are helpless before you. Nor is it any excuse for you in publishing the words that a colored man was found willing to write them.

Respectfully yours,
W. E. B. Du Bois

Great interest attaches to a long letter written by Mary White Ovington to Du Bois in May 1906. When she refers to "this committee," she has in mind the Committee for Improving Industrial Conditions of Negroes in New York City, founded in 1905 primarily by Dr. William L. Bulkley (then the only Negro principal of a largely white elementary school in New York City), and by the business man William J. Schieffelin; Villard was also on this committee. In 1911, the committee, merging with the National League for the Protection of Colored Women and the Committee on Urban Conditions Among Negroes, became the National Urban League.

Brooklyn, N. Y., May 20, 1906.
Dear Dr. DuBois,

It seems to me it is about time that this committee reported at least "progress" to you, for I shall always feel that you started me on my work, and will want to know how matters proceed.

The Phipps tenement is a tenement as yet only in name. There is a hole in the ground, and that is all. The plans are held up, as the cost of building has increased so the committee is trying to cut down where they can, and I am afraid the most attractive features will be cut out. However, I don't know anything about it, and perhaps the bath rooms, those seem to me the most attractive features, will stay. It is provoking not to have the building, for the kindergarten that was to be housed there is living along in the difficult position of tenant in a Baptist church where the number of meetings is so great we can't get an evening a month regularly for our mothers' meeting, and where the revival seems to occupy all possible afternoons that might be used for clubs. Goodness, how those people go to church! I wish for their health's sake they would go in for camp meetings instead, and get religion in the summer.

But quite a little has been happening though the settlement is postponed. Two committees are now underway in which you will be interested. In April the New York Association of Neighborhood Workers appointed a committee to undertake any immediate work that might seem advisable for the colored people. It is not a permanent committee, the thought being that after it gets underway it will be too large for such an association as the Neighborhood Workers, a delegated body of the city's settlements and church houses, but it is to work for a while under that body. I was made chairman of it, and have started fresh air work among the colored people for the summer. The committee is made up of representatives from the settlements on the west side that are in neighborhoods near the Negroes, and of representatives from Negro philanthropies. (I have confined it to the west side because that doesn't involve any difficulty with Mrs. Matthews. We shall, doubtless, help the east side folk.) Dr. [William L.] Bulkley is also on the committee and Dr. [the Reverend W. H.] Brooks. We are now trying to find out all the places to which we can send colored children and mothers, and to investigate as fully as we are able. The first of July our salaried worker will come to us. We have engaged Miss Mary Cromwell of Washington. I have met her, and seen something of her work, and like her very much. She is a University of Michigan graduate, and has done playground work at Washington. She is a teacher in the Armstrong school, but I know sometime would like to do settlement work. I thought this experience would be excellent for her, and that if I work with her, I shall be in the city until August. I could see whether she was fitted for settlement work, and if she was, be able to recommend her if any position should turn up. I believe that the profession of settlement worker will be one that Negro men and women will find increasingly important the next few years.

Another committee that is under way is one Dr. Bulkley has been the prime mover in getting up. He appealed to the Charity Organization Society two months ago for help or advice in regard to the getting of work for Negro mechanics. They referred him to the research committee, and it decided that an investigation should be made as to the number of such mechanics in the city. Mr. [Francis B.] Kellogg grew considerably interested in the matter, and the next thing a meeting was called of prominent colored folk and a few white people to see if anything definite could be done to improve the economic condition of the Negro in New York. Just at this time the Armstrong Association had been talking about doing something in New York, it felt it ought to help the colored folk at home as well as abroad, and here was surely an opportunity to get them interested. Mr. [William J.] Schieffelin came to the meeting, and was interested at once, and the upshot is a committee has been formed with Mr. Schieffelin as chairman and Dr. Bulkley as secretary to improve the industrial condition of the Negro in New York. Two committees are to go at once to work, one on crafts, and one on small business enterprises. I am especially delighted to have the committee definitely committed to work on the industrial question. (We put it first "economic" question, but Mr. [Isaac] Seligman, the banker, for some reason changed it to industrial which we may have to stretch a little.) It would be easy for the Armstrong folk to give money to a philanthropy and there have the matter end, but this commits them to work on the most difficult of all the Negro problems in New York, and they are just the men to be of help if they are ready to meet the issue. Mr. Schieffelin is genuine in his interest, and he has been a firm friend of the colored woman in the Manhattan Trade School for Girls, seeing that every effort is made to get work for its colored graduates. The best colored men on the committee seem to me to be Dr. Bulkley, a Mr. Scott of Brooklyn who is a mechanic, Mr. [Samuel R.] Scottron, Dr. [Verina] Morton-Jones (she isn't a man!)[1] and Mr. Webster of Brooklyn. I don't know Mr. Webster, but he seems to know a good deal concerning the economic situation. I am tremendously tickled myself to have the industrial education men turned to this practical problem of how the Negro can use an industrial education in New York, and also to the study of occupations in which he is successful, and where he can best be encouraged. But we must wait a couple of years before we know what they will do.

These are the two most important new ventures, indeed they are all I can think of that I did not tell you of at Atlanta.

I have lately been to Hampton and saw the Ogden party there. How I should like to say what I think of the South from a car window, with introductions at the stations to prominent *white* people always, but I won't. Mr. [Robert C.] Ogden is a kindly old man, who has surely done great good with his money, and some of the Hampton trustees are splendid, genuine men. I enjoyed meeting Mr. Jones, and found him growing all the time. Then I called on Mrs. Barrett. She and Mrs. Fernandis graduated from Hampton at the same time, and one has a settlement work at Hampton and the other at Washington. They are two beautiful women, the finest product of Hampton in the old days. Perhaps the graduates are just as fine now, certainly some of the graduates spoke beautifully at commencement exercises, but they are too young yet for one to be able to tell.

I noticed your clipping in the Moon concerning a new settlement on W. 23rd St. I am sorry to say Miss Sabine has had to give it up and go home to take care of her father. I do not think anyone will continue with it. It did little work among the Negroes.

1. Verina Morton-Jones, M.D., was head of Lincoln Settlement in Brooklyn; she was active in the women's rights movement, was a pioneer woman (Black) physician, and, in 1913, was elected to the NAACP board.

Of course you saw Royce's article in the Ethical Review on Race Prejudice.[2] It is the best word said yet.

Please remember me to Mrs. Du Bois and Yolande. I wish I might see them when they come north, but I suppose they don't stop in New York.

Most sincerely,
Mary W. Ovington.

Du Bois tried everything and everyone in an effort to get adequate funding for the scientific work he envisioned, but he never really succeeded. The letter below was sent to Tuskegee's chief benefactor, Andrew Carnegie; there is no record of any reply.

May 22, 1906

Mr. Andrew Carnegie
Sir:

You will possibly remember me as being presented to you and Mr. Carl Schurz at Carnegie Hall some years ago.

I beg leave to bring to your attention the work of the Atlanta Conference with a view to securing if possible your financial support for this work.

I enclose herewith a report on Negro Crime, which is the ninth annual report published by the Conference. The object of this Conference is the systematic and exhaustive study of the American Negro, in order that in the future philanthropists and others who seek to solve this serious set of problems may have before them a carefully gathered body of scientifically arranged facts to guide them.

With this in view we began our work ten years ago and have made the following studies:

    1896 The Mortality of Negroes.
    1897 The Negroes in Cities.
    1898 Efforts of Negroes for Social Betterment
    1899 The Negroes in Business
    1900 The College Bred Negro
    1901 The Negro Common School
    1902 The Negro Artisan
    1903 The Negro Church
    1904 Negro Crime
    1905 Methods & Results of 10 years Study.

---

2. Josiah Royce, "Race Questions and Prejudices," *International Journal of Ethics* 16 (1905–6):265–88. This paper was originally delivered in 1905 to the Chicago Ethical Society; it is reprinted as the first chapter in Royce's *Race Questions, Provincialism and Other American Problems* (New York: Macmillan Co., 1908).

In addition to the above studies the Conference has cooperated in the following additional work:

1. Economic Studies of the Negro made by the U. S. Department of Labor under Carroll D Wright (See Bulletin of the U. S. Dep't of Labor No 10, 14, 22 & 35)

2. Twelfth Census of the United States (Bulletin No 8, "Negroes in the United States.")

3. Investigation of the American Economic Association.

4. The following publications: Philadelphia Negro, Ginn & Co., 1899; Souls of Black Folk, McClurg, 1903.

The studies mentioned above have been widely used; they are in all the large libraries of the world including the British Museum, the Library of Congress, Harvard Univ. &c. They have been commended by periodicals like the *Outlook*, the *Nation*, the London *Times*, the *Spectator*, & the Manchester *Guardian;* they have been favorably spoken of by men like G. Stanley Hall, Walter F. Willcox, Talcott Williams, and most of the teachers of economics & sociology in American Colleges.

So far this work has been carried on by small voluntary contributions. As it begins its second decade it finds a growing field of investigation before it, and it needs to enlarge its scope and improve its methods of research. This work is of such a nature that it cannot be carried on by ordinary scientific agencies—it would naturally be hampered by strong local feelings and prejudices, if, for instance, its work was essayed by the Carnegie Institution.

I have made bold therefore to appeal directly to you and to ask if you would be enough interested to look into the merits & needs of this work. If you are I should be glad to lay before you (a) a complete set of our publications (b) our programs of future study & (c) Press notices & commendations of our work. Moreover I should be glad to secure from men like Carroll D Wright, Walter F Willcox & other prominent sociologists statements as to the value of our efforts in the past.

I am well aware that you are overwhelmed with communications of this sort, but I know of no other way by which to bring to your attention a work which seems to me one of the worthiest and neediest in the land.

I beg to remain, Sir,

                        Very Respectfully Yours,
                        W. E. B. Du Bois

Edwin R. A. Seligman (1861–1939) was professor of economics at Columbia University from 1885 to 1931, editor of the *Political Science Quarterly*, chief editor of the *Encyclopedia of the Social Sciences,* and a president of the American Economic Association. He was also president of the Society for Ethical Culture, from 1908 to 1921, and a founder of the NAACP. "The fire of affliction" he mentions is the recent death of his wife; the immediate cause of his letter was the pogrom against the Black population of Atlanta that resulted in many deaths in the summer of 1906. Du Bois was himself in Alabama at the time, but hastened home and stood guard, shotgun in hand, at his porch; his wife and young daughter had been terrified, but not physically assailed.

New York, Oct. 28, 1906

My dear Professor Du Bois,

Like so many other of your well wishers, I was amazed & disgusted at the happenings in Atlanta. But perhaps I did not realize the horror of it all, until I read your beautiful poem in the Outlook.[1] It must indeed be a tragedy for men like you—a tragedy all the greater because of the seeming impasse. But perhaps you will learn—as I have learned after going thro' the fire of affliction—that there are really only two things worth living for in this world—the one is the love of those most nearly related to you, or thrown into close contact with you, and the other is work, the chance to express oneself in some form of activity however humble. Those things are open to every human being, & at bottom there is nothing else which is comparable with them—wealth, reputation, ambition or what not. Let us hold to the things that are eternally true, & let us seek within ourselves the compensation for the things that are withheld by an unthinking and uncivilized world.

If you ever come to New York, kindly let me know in advance, so that I may have a chance to greet you.

Yours sincerely
Edwin R. A. Seligman

It is apparent from this Du Bois letter that a white man, William P. Pickett of Brooklyn, had written him asking about his publications and also indicating a belief that removing Black people from the United States would solve the "problem." The latter concept dates from the beginnings of the nineteenth century and was institutionalized with the founding, in 1816, of the American Colonization Society. Du Bois's views concerning it, expressed here at some length, are of great significance.

Atlanta, Georgia, January 16, 1907.

Mr. Wm. P. Pickett
My dear Sir:—

In reply to your letter of January 9, 1907 let me say that my works are: The Philadelphia Negro (Ginn & Co., 1899), Suppression of the Slave Trade (Long-

---

1. He refers to "A Litany of Atlanta," published not in *Outlook*, but in the *Independent*, 11 October 1906, pp. 856–58; this great poem has been reprinted scores of times since.

man's 1896), The Souls of Black Folk (McClurg 1903). With regard [to] your study of deportation of the American Negro let me say that the arguments against it are these:

First, as to the number of people to be transported. In the whole slave trade between Africa and America, probably not more slaves were brought over than it is now, according to your plan, proposed to deport. That is, the whole slave trade occupying a century and more and costing a tremendous amount in treasure and blood only transported from Africa something like ten or twelve million human beings. Would it be possible to re-transport such a number of people without practically the same amount of human suffering? People who propose transportation on such a large scale do not realize what it means. Think what it means in effort and suffering and economic ability to bring one million immigrants to the United States inside of a year—it is simply tremendous; to take ten million out—unthinkable.

Secondly, the mere passage would be the small part of it. Not only would the passage have to be paid but the property of Negroes would have to be bought up and more than that capital would have to be furnished for them to start a new place—and capital on a considerable scale too.

In the third place, where could they go? It is usually assumed that there are a plenty of places and yet when one looks at the matter there are very, very few. In Africa would you seriously advise the American Negro to go to the Congo, [or] Liberia, where the American Negroes die like sheep? In South Africa the Negro would be exceedingly unwelcome. They probably would not be allowed to come there under any circumstances. There is practically no place in Africa where there would be a reasonable set of ten million Negroes started. In South America what is wanted today is not strong, common, every day labor but capital. So with the West Indies and Mexico. There is not on the face of the earth a place where the American Negroes with the training that they have had would today have a reasonable chance for success.

Fourth, even if there were a place found, what would be the result? Just as soon as the Negroes had made anything of themselves or had discovered anything worth having, the United States or England or some other European country would gobble it up and it would be ruled by superior strength as colonies, that is they would be ruled under the same caste system as they are ruled in the United States and would be, as I have said in another place, further from the ear of the sovereign.

In the fifth place, it would be impossible to gain the consent of this country to let the Negroes go, particularly in the South. In Georgia today, an [agent] for the immigration of Negroes is charged a fee which is really a fine of $500 a year and not only that, he is liable to be mobbed. It would be practically impossible to take the laboring force out of the South today and have the South recover within a generation or two.

Then sixthly and in the last place, the Negro would not consent to go. What right have you to ask me to leave this country? My ancestors have been in this country for two or three hundred years. They have fought in every single war the United States has waged, except, thank God, the last.[1] They have been citizens. I have just as much right to stay here as you, possibly better. It is usually assumed by people who think of the forcible exportation of the Negro that it wouldn't make much difference whether he wanted to go or not. Let me assure you that it would. In the past all efforts to help the Negro, have been efforts to help him out of the place where he is to a higher plane. When you speak of the disfranchisement of the Negro it is really a misnomer. He has never been enfranchised. The law was put on the statute book but practically never enforced. But when it comes to a matter of migration the Negro of the South is at home and sending him to a foreign land, to which he would be just as foreign as you would be, that is an entirely different question and the Negro would resist it to the last ditch.

Under these circumstances I can seldom argue calmly with anybody who undertakes to champion any such proposition as that which you have in mind.

I beg to remain,

Very sincerely yours,
W. E. B. Du Bois

Du Bois clubs began to appear in the first decade of the twentieth century, among, for example, Negro women in Baltimore and students at the University of Pennsylvania. Reflecting this development is a letter from one of the very few Black students then at Cornell; again, it emphasizes the decisive impact of *The Souls of Black Folk*.

Ithaca, N.Y., Feb. 11, 1907.

My dear Mr. Du Bois,

I know that I am taking an unpardonable license in addressing you but I thought that you would be glad to know of a movement which has been started at Cornell and which concerns you in a peculiarly intimate manner. Let me say at the beginning that I am one of two colored girl students at Cornell, being now a Junior. Some weeks ago a movement was started to make a study of your works. From what I can understand, it originated in the mind of a Philadelphia white girl who had heard you speak before the Ethical Culture Society. At any rate, I was asked to be a member of the Club, as yet unnamed. Altho your works have been so widespread I am sure that you will be pleased at this new departure on the part of a set of young persons at a University which is hardly noted for its broadness of view.

1. Du Bois apparently refers to the war with Spain, or, possibly, the "pacification" of the Philippines; in either case, he is in error in stating that Negroes did not participate.

The Co-Operative Society, the Students' Store, immediately received a large order for your "Souls of Black Folk," with which we began our work. A copy of the book was sent to the wife of Ambassador Andrew D. White (who lives on the Campus) and others were sent to other persons whom we wish to be prepared when we call upon them to help us in any way.

Up to date we have read and discussed three essays—The "Passing of the First Born," "The Coming of John" and "Our Spiritual Strivings." Because of my peculiar connection with the literary department of Cornell I was chosen critic of the Club. May I tell you just a few things that have been said? One of the girls, a Senior from Massachusetts said that the paragraph on page 217 was the most beautiful picture of maternity that she had ever seen. Another said that "Our Spiritual Strivings" reminded her of the One hundred and thirty seventh Psalm—"By the rivers of Babylon"—comparisons of "The Passing of the First Born" with the work of the two Van Dykes and others seldom gave the other writers cause for pride. It was a significant thing that the papers were not actuated by any fanatical sympathy as they generally were kept apart from any racial suggestions.

Your book is in our Library presented by Henry W. Sage and constantly referred to by Dean Walter Willcox of the College of Arts and Sciences.

When we came to study the "Coming of John," things took a different turn. Then all of the pent up sympathy was expressed and I am glad to tell you, Mr. Du Bois, that I believe that the discussion of that one essay has done much toward broadening the racial spirit at Cornell, that is, the best kind of racial spirit.

Now, Mr. Du Bois, will you pardon me for thus occupying your time? I was so full of it—it has meant so much to me that I wanted to tell you. We have thirty one people at Cornell—we have over thirty thousand American white students. As soon as our Club, of which I am at present the only Negro member, becomes incorporated and named, we will want you to know more about it, and all of these peoples will know. Surely the "Veil" is lifting; surely the day is not so far off. The horizon is broadening here—somewhere the Sun is already high.

Again hoping you will pardon me, and thanking you in the name of the Club, for your book, I am

                Very respectfully yours
                (Miss) Hallie E. Queen

The letter which Du Bois is answering here seems to have been lost, although much of its content may be deduced from the reply. The latter is highly suggestive, and within a few years, Du Bois was speaking and writing publicly in favor of enhancing the rights of women.

Atlanta, Ga., March 11, 1907.

Miss M. B. Marston
My dear Madam:—

I thank you for your letter without date. I have given a wrong impression in my book if I have led people to believe that I want the colored people to have simply equality with other people—what I have tried to ask for is justice, treatment according to desert and I have tried to put especial emphasis upon this. I want the colored people to have the right to develop according to their capacity and I certainly would be disappointed if they did not develop much higher things than the white race has developed to. I sympathize too with the women in their struggle for emancipation. I believe in full rights for human beings without distinction of race or sex. At the same time I hesitate to say anything concerning women's rights because most women in the United States are so narrow that anything I should say would be misinterpreted. The Negro race has suffered more from the antipathy and narrowness of women both South and North than from any other single source. While then I should be very glad to say any word which I was sure would help, I do not at present see that there is much chance for me to help in your cause. I wish it however, the greatest success.

Very sincerely yours,
W. E. B. Du Bois

Du Bois was a doting father. When he and his wife lost their first-born, Burghardt, the devotion of the two shaken parents was lavished entirely upon Yolande. Du Bois's work and the precarious health of Mrs. Du Bois tended to produce frequent and rather prolonged separations. Early in 1907, Mrs. Du Bois and Yolande spent much time in Massachusetts; Du Bois wrote to his daughter there.

Atlanta, Ga., March 13, 1907.

Dear little Yolande:—

This is Sunday night and papa has talked all his letters into the graphophone and he has half of one of the records left, so he is going to talk a little while to you. I wonder what you are doing—I suppose you must be in bed. How do you like sliding down hill? Papa used to slide down hills when he was a little boy and used to think that it was great fun. We are having nice sunny weather here now, the grass is green, little buds are coming out on the trees, while you up there are all ice and snow. Everybody asks about you. Miss Ware wants to know how you are getting on and Miss Thomas wants you to write to her and Miss Clifford thinks of you and Mrs. Herndon speaks of you and Miss Pingree, especially misses you. But most of all I think papa misses you when he comes in and has nobody to disturb him and nobody to interrupt his work. He'd be very glad to have you interrupt his work a little while now. I suppose you are being a very good girl and helping mama to get well. You must hurry up and write me a nice letter. Now good-night.

Papa

The muckrakers tended to ignore the oppression of the Black people, while writing reams about bad meat; where they did offer attention, it was almost always either patronizing or openly bigoted. That Du Bois fought against this kind of attention is apparent from an exchange between him and S. S. McClure (1857-1949), publisher of the magazine named for him which was perhaps the most influential of the muckraking publications. Du Bois sent *McClure's Magazine* an article in response to the invitation in McClure's letter of 6 April 1907, but the article was rejected.

Atlanta, Ga., March 21, 1907.

My dear Mr. McClure:

It does seem to me that a magazine which has stood so clearly for the problem as McClure's has hitherto ought not to lower itself to the small narrow anti-Negro propaganda of Thomas Nelson Page and his [kind?].[1] It does not seem to me that even the demand from your southern circulation calls for all that.[2] At any rate, will you not permit the other side to be heard? Will you not let me write you an article on Social Equality from the Negro point of view—a perfectly frank article? I do not expect that you will promise absolutely to publish it before you see it but I should like to know if you would consider such an article favorably.

Very sincerely yours,
W. E. B. Du Bois

New York, March 25, 1907.

W. E. B. DuBois, Esq.
Dear Sir:

I am sorry that the Page article did not come near meeting with your approval. We regard Mr. Page as a well-known southern writer and believe that

---

1. Thomas Nelson Page, who later served as Wilson's ambassador to Italy, published three racist articles in *McClure's* in March, April, and May 1904 (similar to his pieces that same year in *Scribner's* and *Atlantic*), and a particularly odious apologia for Dixiecratism, entitled "The Great American Question," in the March 1907 *McClure's* (28:565–72).

2. Du Bois's remark about "southern circulation" recalls the statement made in 1907 to Ray Stannard Baker by an editor of the *American Magazine*—"For the sake of effect we must keep the interest and friendliness of Southern readers"—quoted in the introduction to the 1964 edition of Baker's *Following the Color Line*, ed. Bernard Wishy and W. E. Leuchtenberg (New York: Harper and Row), p. viii.

his views are of interest to most of our readers as voicing the intelligent opinion of a large section of the country. We have had a good many requests to print replies to his article, but have uniformly refused because we do not wish to open our pages to a controversy. Therefore, I am very much afraid that we cannot promise to bring out a reply if you should submit one. We are extremely sorry that your feeling in the matter is so strong and trust that you will find nothing else in the magazine to which you take such exception.

Sincerely yours,
S. S. McClure

[undated]

I have your favor of the 25th inst. The case would not be so bad if you showed some elementary justice toward us. But here have come 5 successive vicious attacks on us from one pen as if to atone for one article from Schurz.[1] Surely your public has no such extraordinary appetite for injustice—surely you are not called upon to traduce continually & repeatedly helpless or rather dollar-less black men when nearly every other decent cause has your sympathy. I am not asking controversy nor confession of editorial weakness but for God's sake give the underdog one chance in five, don't hammer & pound & sling mud against a gagged people simply because it costs nothing & tickles the white south.

W. E. B. Du Bois

New York, April 6, 1907.

Dear Mr. Du Bois:—

The letter sent you March 25th was a general letter which was sent to people who wished to reply to Mr. Page's article. It was signed by a young associate in the office who did not know who you were. I do not wonder the letter angered you. I would be very glad to have you write an article on the lines you suggest, and on the conditions you suggest. And I would be very glad if I should be able to use it.

There will be several articles by Mr. Schurz, in the series I am now publishing, on reconstruction, which I am sure will please you.

Very sincerely yours,
S. S. McClure[2]

1. The reference is to Carl Schurz (1829–1906), a leading newspaper editor, onetime United States minister to Spain, Civil War general, United States senator from Missouri, and Hayes's secretary of the interior. Articles of his appeared posthumously in *McClure's* in July and September 1907, on Civil War battles, and from April through July 1908, on aspects of the Reconstruction era.

2. The letter of 25 March and this one of 6 April were both signed in ink, "S. S. McClure." They do, however, differ markedly.

[130] Correspondence 1905-1920

The American Church Institute for Negroes, for educational work among the Negroes of the South, was founded in 1906 by the Board of Missions of the Protestant Episcopal Church; among the schools established were: Saint Augustine's College in Raleigh, North Carolina; Voorhees Normal and Industrial School in Denmark, South Carolina; Fort Valley High and Industrial School in Fort Valley, Georgia; and Saint Paul Normal and Industrial School in Lawrenceville, Virginia. The board's treasurer was the George Foster Peabody we have already encountered; its president was the Right Reverend David H. Greer, bishop of New York; and among its trustees were the writer, naval Capt. A. T. Mahan, and the president of Columbia University, Nicholas Murray Butler.

The Reverend Samuel H. Bishop (1863-1914), general agent of the institute,* wrote to Du Bois on 6 April 1907, requesting information about Negro folk songs; on 9 April Du Bois replied, offering the names of people who were specialists in that area. Two letters followed.

New York, 16 April 1907.

My dear Dr. DuBois:—

May I thank you for your letter of 9th of April and its good suggestions? I had already written to Mr. [Monroe] Work, but of Miss [Emily] Hallowell I did not know. I agree with you that it would be a fine thing if we could use money to get at the real Negro music, and I am going to do what I can with the help promised me by at least one competent student of folk music.

I heard some time ago that you are an Episcopalian, which was unknown to me. I want the American Church Institute for Negroes to stand for ideas. As I just wrote Bishop Greer with reference to a little matter which came up at our board meeting, the church must not be behind science in recognizing the manhood of the Negro. It is a very curious and striking fact to my mind that within the past five or ten years the collective voices of anthropologists and ethnologists have declared not only the manhood but the somewhat exceptional manhood of the Negro, and have given assent to the religious proposition that God made of one blood all nations of men for to dwell upon the face of the whole earth. As I see things one of the most important ways to help in the problem of the adjustment of races is to "clear" the contributions the Negro has to make to human civilization, and music is one of them.

I thank you for your assurance of a disposition to help, and I wish you would be on the watch for any intellectual or moral contribution you can make to our work. Of course I speak a little *ex parte*, but I believe the American Church Institute for Negroes is the most significant venture being made today for settle-

* After Bishop's death, Du Bois published a sympathetic account of his career in the *Crisis*, 8 (July 1914):127.

ment of the problem along those lines which lead up to the heart of God, and I shall be glad of your sympathy and help.

Faithfully yours,
Samuel H. Bishop

Atlanta, Ga., May 1, 1907.

My dear Mr. Bishop:—

Replying to your letter of April 16, let me say that my family represents five generations in the Episcopal Church including my little girl and perhaps other generations if I chose to count certain parts of my family which I do not count. I have however no particular affection for the Church. I think its record on the Negro problem has been simply shameful and while I am looking with interest to the work which the Church Institute proposes to do yet I confess I have many misgivings. The fact of the matter is that so far as the Negro problem is concerned the southern branch of the Church is a moral dead weight and the northern branch of the Church never has had the moral courage to stand against it and I doubt if it has now. So far as your statement is concerned, it is certain that the Church always has been behind science and the fact of the matter is, they have been behind most everything else, certainly behind other churches in recognizing human manhood and Christian equality. I am however in hopes that perhaps something will be done.

Very sincerely yours,
W. E. B. Du Bois

A letter from Mary White Ovington in the spring of 1907, while rather short, is full of information and important allusions. Franz Boas was active in many efforts towards overcoming racist practices and, on Du Bois's invitations, participated in the Atlanta Conferences. Like many scientists, however, he wrote infrequently. Hence Miss Ovington's joy that a rare popular essay by him had appeared. Du Bois himself published almost exclusively in the new magazine that he, L. M. Hershaw, and Freeman Murray launched in Washington as successor to the suspended *Moon:* the *Horizon,* the first number of which appeared in January 1907. Du Bois published in no other magazine after his appearance in *Collier's,* 20 October 1906, until an article in the *American Journal of Sociology* in May 1908, and in no popularly circulated national magazine until *World's Work* in May 1909. This background explains the point of one of Miss Ovington's questions.

Brooklyn, N.Y., April 13, 1907.

My dear Dr. Du Bois:—

I have heard of your visiting New York, and I know that you did splendid work here.

Isn't it good that Dr. Boas is writing at last? I have not yet read his article in

Van Norden's, but I know it must be an excellent antidote to much of the nonsense that is about today.[1]

I have to leave New York April 24th to go abroad, and I do not know when I shall return. It is hard to go away at just this time when there is an indefinite amount to do; but my father and mother are both ill, and I must give some time to them.

I called on Mrs. Du Bois at Arlington, and found her living on the top of a hill where the wind that day was blowing a mile a minute. She looked, I thought, much better than when in Atlanta. Yolande was gloriously well. The Boston Literary Association were very good to me, and I had a happy time visiting with them and staying in Cambridge with Mrs. [Clement G.] Morgan.

I saw Mr. Daniels again, and I am sure that he is doing good work, though he may have gone about it stupidly.[2] His thesis will have some valuable stuff in it.

When are we going to see you in print in some of these magazines that are deep in the Negro question? I hope you are going to popularize the Lowndes County material.[3] Don't you think Baker has done fairly well in the April American?[4] There is nothing new in the article, but it seemed to me reasonable and worth the while.

The Constitution League is interesting [William T.] Stead in its work. Mr. [John E.] Milholland is certainly in this matter for all time, and he understands conditions remarkably well.[5]

Remember me to Miss Ware and Miss Pingree, won't you?

       Always sincerely,
       Mary W. Ovington

1. "The Anthropological Position of the Negro," *Van Norden Magazine* 2 (April 1907):40–47. In the same issue appeared Benjamin R. Tillman, "The Race Question"; the editor declared he was "balancing it off" with the essay by Boas!

2. Undoubtedly this is John Daniels, whose book *In Freedom's Birthplace: A Study of the Boston Negro* was published in 1914 (Boston: Houghton Mifflin Co.; reprint ed., New York: Arno Press, 1968).

3. Du Bois's Lowndes County, Alabama, studies appeared as "The Negro Farmer," *Special Reports: Supplementary Analysis and Derivate Tables* (Washington: United States Twelfth Census, 1906), pp. 511–79.

4. This is Ray Stannard Baker, whose series "Following the Color Line" ran in the *American Magazine* from April 1907 to August 1907, and was issued as a book by Doubleday, Page and Co. in 1908. On Baker's series and on what he represented in general at this time, see Herbert Shapiro, "The Muckrakers and the Negro," *Phylon* 29 (1970):76–88.

5. John E. Milholland (1860–1925) was a well-to-do businessman and an anti-imperialist Republican, and was active in prison reform, in various educational reform movements, and in the women's rights movement. He was the founder in 1903 of the Constitution League of the United States, which fought for civil rights. A firm friend of Du Bois, he was among the founders of the NAACP. Miss Ovington was correct when she wrote that he was "in this matter for all time." There is great need for a biography of this extraordinary man (and, one should add, of his daughter, Inez Milholland Boissevain).

Mr. Alexander Irvine, a socialist & preacher who went South for three months disguised as a laborer and worked in turpentine fields & coal mines besides visiting convict camps will write on peonage for Appleton.[6] I met him the other night & he said: "I started South full of admiration for Washington, but after I had been in Alabama among the laborers for a time I could not go to Tuskegee. I knew that he was wrong." Then he spoke in highest praise of you. I wish he might be invited to speak on Socialism at next Summer's Niagara Meetings. Get him to tell of the Socialist party in the South.

As already noted, the relationship between Du Bois and William James was always cordial. While planning a trip to Europe in the summer of 1907, Du Bois asked James for an introduction to his brother Henry in England.

Cambridge, May 23, 1907

Dear Du Bois,

I am right glad to hear that you are going to have a good vacation in a country not as vexed as Georgia is by the "race question." I gladly send you a note to my brother, who lives at Rye, 2 hours from London, on the Coast. I have just ordered my publisher to send you a new little book of mine.[1] Wishing you every refreshment, I am always truly yours,

Wm. James

I have just looked through the last instalment of your studies on the American negro.[2] I wish the portraits might have been better printed. But it is splendid scientific work.

Atlanta, Ga., May 27, 1907.

Dear Professor James:—

I thank you so much for your kind letter. I wish that the pictures in our study could have been made better. It was the old trouble of money even as it was. I spent more in getting these poor reproductions than we really could afford. I wish we could do better. We are trying to get some money from the Sage Foundation but I do not suppose that we can. However it is something to be

6. The Reverend Alexander Irvine (1863–1941) was part of the Social Christianity movement. He published a series, "From the Bottom Up," in *World's Work*, July through December 1909, which reflected some of the experiences mentioned in this letter.

1. James refers to his seminal work *Pragmatism*, published in 1907.

2. *The Health and Physique of the Negro American* was the eleventh Conference for the Study of Negro Problems, held at Atlanta University, 29 May 1906; it was edited by Du Bois and printed late in 1906 by the Atlanta University Press. In the twelve pages of illustrations, the portraits of various Black men and women are rather faded.

doing something. I shall hope to see your brother while I am in England. Thank you for your good word.

       Very sincerely yours,
       W. E. B. Du Bois

Upon arriving in England, Du Bois wrote to Henry James. The two men did not meet at this time, nor, so far as is known, during Du Bois's subsequent visit to England in 1911. In 1907, the year Henry James penned this note to Du Bois, there appeared his book *The American Scene*, based on a 1904–5 tour which took him from New Hampshire to Florida and then to Chicago and California. James wrote in his book, "How can everything so have gone that the only 'Southern' book of any distinction published for many a year is *The Souls of Black Folk* by that most accomplished of members of the negro race, Mr. W. E. B. Du Bois."*

       Rye, Sussex. August 9th, 1907.

Dear Mr. Du Bois

 It is a great pleasure to me to hear from you, but that pleasure is qualified by the fact that I am not in London just now & am seldom there at this time of the year & that as this place is indeed too far from town to be called in any degree suburban I can't propose to you any brief or convenient form of visit that might suit your hours & occupations. (Getting down here by any good morning train, for instance is practically a matter of nearly three hours.) But I do hope to be in London about the 22nd–23rd &c for a couple of days. On the chance that you may be still there I shall immediately inquire for you at your hotel, & if you have (as I indeed fear,) by that time departed, it will be a great regret to Yours very truly

       Henry James

Joseph B. Foraker (1846–1917) was governor of Ohio from 1885 to 1889 and United States senator (R., Ohio) from 1896 to 1908. While friendly to McKinley, he was hostile toward Theodore Roosevelt and particularly denounced the latter for his summary action in dismissing an entire company of Black soldiers for implication in an outbreak in 1906 in Brownsville, Texas. On the latter question, Foraker kept up a steady barrage of condemnation and demands for reopening the investigations; for this action the Niagara Movement, at its third annual meeting in 1907, voted him its thanks. An exchange of letters ensued.

 * The book was republished in 1960 by Indiana University Press (Bloomington); the quotation is from page 418.

Atlanta, Ga., February 6, 1907.

The Honorable J. B. Foraker
Sir:—

On my own behalf and in the name of the *Niagara Movement,* I wish to thank you very heartily for the work which you have done in behalf of the colored soldiers. I trust that you will realize that the colored people of the United States appreciate this service and will always look upon your efforts with the greatest gratitude. If there is anything that I can do or my friends to help you in your work, we should be only too glad to know.

Very sincerely yours,
W. E. B. Du Bois

Cincinnati, Oct. 16, 1907.

Dr. W. E. Debois,
Dear Sir:

I write to acknowledge the receipt of your letter of October 11th advising me of the action of the Third National Meeting of the Niagara Movement in directing you to communicate with me as you have. Be assured of my high appreciation for the same.

With kindest regards, and with thanks in return for your many kind utterances which, under all the circumstaances, have been cheering and encouraging far beyond what you probably realize, I remain

Very truly yours, etc.,
J. B. Foraker.

Late in 1907, Alfred Vollum of Albert Lea, Minnesota, wrote Du Bois for his views on certain aspects of education; the reply is of interest.

Atlanta, Oct. 24, 1907

My Dear Sir:—

Answering your letter of October 17 I beg to say, that I believe thoroughly that the United States Government should give aid to the education of Negroes in the South. I should not call it a "subsidy," and should not care whether the Southern Whites objected or not. This latter seems to me to be rather a curious proviso; it is as though we should say that Child Labor should be stopped in factories providing all the stockholders agreed. Or that labor should be granted decent wages on request of capitalists. The reasons for giving aid to the Negro education in the South are these: First that the Negro is poor because the Nation kept him in slavery, secondly, because the South is poor on account of the war, and thirdly, because it would be a fair requital to the South to give money toward education as an offset to the money which has been spent on pensions for northerners; and fourth but chiefly, because the South is not today settling its educational problem. And it is to the interest of the whole Nation to have that question settled as soon as possible, and get rid of at least the ignorance in the race problem. Publication number six of the Atlanta University would help you in your research.[1] These are out of print or I should send you one.

Very sincerely yours,
W. E. B. Du Bois

The relationship between Moorfield Storey (1845–1929) and Du Bois was among the most significant in United States history. Storey was secretary to Sen. Charles Sumner and was thereafter one of the leading attorneys in the country and a president of the American Bar Association. He was also a potent force in various reform efforts, president of the Anti-Imperialist League, and the first president of the National Association for the Advancement of Colored People, a position he held until his death.[*]

It was through his anti-imperialist work that Du Bois was first attracted to Storey, and the opening of their relationship is recorded in two letters they exchanged in 1907. Printed here also is a letter from Erving Winslow (1839–1922), translator of Maurice Maeterlinck, and the indefatigable secretary of the Anti-Imperialist League.

Atlanta, Oct. 21, 1907.

Mr. Moorfield Storey
My Dear Sir:—

I have your pamphlet on the Philippine Policy and the accompanying picture entitled "After the Battle of Mt. Dajo."[1] I think that picture is the most illuminating thing I have ever seen. I want especially to have it framed and put upon the walls of my recitation room to impress upon the students what wars and especially Wars of Conquest really mean. It has occurred to me, however that this picture is little too small for framing. Would it not be possible to have a reproduction made considerably larger than this? And would it not be a splendid thing to distribute them throughout the United States? If there is any

---

1. Number six, *The Negro Artisan*, was issued in 1902; from the context it is likely that Du Bois meant to refer to number five, issued in 1901, *The Negro Common School*.

* William B. Hixson, Jr., *Moorfield Storey and the Abolitionist Tradition* (New York: Oxford University Press, 1972).

1. He refers to Storey's *Philippine Policy of Secretary Taft* (Boston: New England Anti-Imperialist League). No date is given, but internal evidence establishes that it was published in 1904, sometime after April. The illustration to which Du Bois referred showed a veritable mountain of corpses and skulls—one of the trophies of United States "pacification." The Taft of the title was of course William Howard Taft, then Roosevelt's secretary of war.

possibility of getting a larger print, I wish you would kindly let me know. It is needless to say how much I sympathize with you in your work, and I only [wish] that I could help the matter more.

Very sincerely yours,
W. E. B. Du Bois

Boston 24th October 1907.

W. E. DuBois, Esq.
Dear Sir:

I have your letter of the 21st and as I am about leaving the city I will turn your letter over to Mr. Erving Winslow who will tell you what the chances are of having the picture enlarged. It is certainly a terrible argument. I have long been anxious to meet you, and hope I may have the opportunity before long for I am familiar with what you have written and am in very cordial sympathy with your views. I am glad to find that you feel the same sympathy in the work I have been engaged in.

Yours truly,
M. Storey

Boston Oct. 25, 1907

W. E. Du Bois, Esq.
Dear Sir:

Mr. Storey has referred your letter to me. It is impossible to enlarge the Mt. Dajo picture without destroying its clearness. It may interest you to know that General [Leonard] Wood saw that the photographer had taken a picture of this awful scene and asked to see the negative which, strangely enough, (!) he dropped and let break while handing it back to the photographer who fortunately had, unknown to General Wood, another negative from which this picture was taken.

I am your obedient servant,
Erving Winslow
Secretary.

Some idea of what faced Du Bois and such movements as the Niagara may be gained from examining a late-1907 exchange with the Boston attorney Samuel May, Jr., son of the staunch Garrisonian abolitionist, the Reverend Samuel J. May. The circular to which Du Bois refers was a printed, one-page leaflet signed by Samuel May, Jr., and appealing for funds for the Robert Hungerford Industrial School in Eatonville, Florida, "where," as the leaflet stated, "the population is composed entirely of blacks." The circular affirmed: "The best form of education for the negro—and the only one worthy of consideration at the present time—is industrial education"; it also urged "segregation of the races," so that "the eternal discord, arising from sectional differences over the negro, can be forever settled and silenced." With such "friends," of course, no group needed enemies.

Atlanta, Ga., Dec. 10, 1907.

Mr. Samuel May, Jr.
My Dear Sir:—

I am very sorry to see in your circular, with regard to the school at Eatonville, Fla., two propositions made which are extremely dangerous, and unnecessary to your cause. The first is: that segregation of the black is a good thing. Segregation of any set of human beings, be they black, white or of any color or race is a bad thing, since human contact is the thing that makes for civilization, and human contact is a thing for which all of us are striving to-day. Of course, some segregation must come, but we do not advocate it; we do not advertise it, and we do not think it is in its self a good thing. The second thing is the peculiar idea expressed that industrial education is the only education worthy of consideration for the Negro to-day. How are your Industrial schools going to be taught? Can they teach themselves? From whence are the teachers coming? Is it a good thing to dry up the very sources, which make Industrial schools, and common schools possible? Can you have teachers of Industrial and Common schools without having higher schools? It seems to me that people who argue in this way, surely have forgotten that the College is the foundation of every system of education. And that in this respect the black men are no exception to the universal rule. I have so much sympathy with Industrial education and with common school education that I am sorry to see the foundation of their success ignored or attacked.

Very sincerely yours,
W. E. B. Du Bois

Boston, Dec. 14, 1907

Prof. W. E. B. DuBois
Dear Sir,

I am in receipt of your favor of Dec 10th. It seems to me that you cannot be familiar with the feelings of our Northern folk who contribute most largely to the education of the colored people in the South. I think that the feeling quite generally is that it is best to bring to the front more prominently the industrial side of negro education and make the so-called higher education the next step forward.

Of course there must be opportunities provided for the education of teachers; but it is impolitic to ask contributions for courses of education which are in advance of those which are open to the poor whites of the South, or even of the North. Our Northern citizens are contributing large amounts of money each year for colored schools, and they certainly have a right to express an opinion of the manner in which it shall be used. As the lowest classes of men must be civilized before they can be Christianized, so the next grades must be taught the use of their hands before their brains receive a higher polish.

There has been, I think, too much discussion of the subject of higher education; it has certainly turned away a good many from giving on the theory that good artisans are being sacrificed to make way for preachers, lawyers, physicians &c. &c.

I am very busy or I would go into the matter more fully with you, but let me quote from a letter which I have received this month from a prominent lady of this City. She writes as follows:

"In reply to yours I must tell you that I no longer give to the *blacks* of the South. I think great trouble is in store for the "*poor whites*" from overdoing the education of negros. They treat the poor whites so badly that *in a few* years the matter *will* have to be taken up. I give when I can to the education of the White Mountain boys and other whites. It is absolutely necessary to keep them up to the blacks. And the material is better to work on—they do not come to be so indolent as the colored. I therefore decline to send to your appeal."

We are laboring in a good cause and little differences must be put aside to make the cause successful; and in order to make it successful we must get money; and those who give the money are they who believe in advertising more eminently the industrial side of education. Referring to your remarks about segregation of the blacks, I would ask you if you have seen any of the reports of speeches recently made in various places by friends of the blacks; I cannot lay my hand on any at the moment else I would send you copies.

Yours, very truly (in haste)
Saml May Jr.

Atlanta, Ga., Dec. 24, 1907.

Mr. Samuel May, Jr.
My Dear Sir:—

I thank you for your letter of December 14th, but I am still convinced that you do not realize the full import of what your appeal means. It is not a matter of offering exceptional opportunities for colored boys when the whites have no such opportunities. It is matter of *present necessity* for *present* common and Industrial schools. Schools like Tuskegee and hundreds of other schools of the Industrial type, together with thousands of the public schools, would have to close their doors today, if it were not for Institutions like Atlanta University. It is utterly impossible to carry on the work of the common schools and the Industrial schools unless teachers are properly taught. Moreover, teachers can not be taught except by those who have had some higher training. Therefore in the teaching of teachers, and in the teaching of those who are to prepare teachers, there must be, not by and by, but *now*, higher institutions of learning. This has been proven again and again in the history of civilization. When those beneath are to be civilized it is not a matter of gradually raising them from beneath; it is a matter of putting *ahead of them* a group who can lift them up. The college is the foundation stone of the school system and not its cap-stone.

Very sincerely yours,
W. E. B. Du Bois

Carter Godwin Woodson (1875–1950) was the father of the organized effort to collect and disseminate Afro-American history; he founded the Association for the Study of Negro Life and History in 1915 and was the editor of its *Journal of Negro History* until his death. There were some strains in the long friendship between Woodson and Du Bois, but these never eroded the great respect each had for the other. The first of their letters was written early in 1908, when Woodson was a graduate student at the University of Chicago. While there seems to have been no formal reply from Du Bois, Woodson's letter is marked with a note from Du Bois indicating that he had sent, with a bill, a copy of the Atlanta University Conference Report number seven, *The Negro Church*.

Chicago, Ill. Feb. 18, 1908.

Prof. W. B. DuBois, Ph.D.
Dear Sir:

I have the honor to say that I am a Negro student of the University of Chicago where I hope to appear in June for examination as a candidate for the degree of Master of Arts. The subject of my thesis is the *Negro Church*.[1] Knowing that for a long time you have studied the different institutions of the race, I believe that you can give me much information on this subject. Surely you are in a position to tell me where such information may be found. Whatever you may be able to do to help me will be most gratefully acknowledged; and any expense incurred in so doing will be borne by him who reluctantly asks for so much of your valuable time.

It should be stated, also, that I am anxious to get statistics as to the number of churches in each state, their wealth, membership, intellectual status, and general aspects; in short all such facts as will show what the Church has contributed to the *progress* or *regress* of the race.

Begging your indulgence for this bold request I subscribe myself

Yours very respectfully,
C. G. Woodson,

The question posed to Du Bois early in 1908 by the editor of the *Independent*, and the answers offered by Du Bois, are of interest.

1. Woodson's thesis eventuated in *The History of the Negro Church* (Washington: Associated Publishers, 1921).

New York, March 18th, 1908.

Professor W. E. D. DuBois
My Dear Sir:—

May I ask you a personal question? Do the negroes of intelligence and position about Atlanta, and so far as you know in Georgia, pay taxes and vote? Do you pay taxes and vote? I have heard it said that you do not, and that would certainly surprise me. I have been hoping that gradually the negroes would not claim but be allowed the right to vote, and it would seem to me to be the only right policy.

Pardon me for asking the question if it seems to you impertinent.

Very truly yours,
William Hayes Ward

Atlanta, Mar. 27, 1908.

My Dear Dr. Ward:—

Replying to your letter of March 18th, let me say that practically all the Negroes of intelligence and position about Atlanta and in most of the cities of Georgia, and to a large extent in the country districts, pay taxes. A smaller percent of them vote. I, myself, pay taxes but do not vote in the minor elections; in the more important elections, I do vote.[1] The reason for this is there are a good many of the smaller elections, and it is absolutely useless on account of the white primary system to try and vote, and it takes a great deal of valuable time. What is needed here of course is concerted effort on the part of the Negroes to have them all vote. On account of my position in the school and the attitude in the North, I cannot however take active part in increasing the interest; and therefore put my whole time practically upon my school work. I believe with you that gradually the Negro is going to get the right to vote in the South, and that one of the ways to get [it] is persistently to vote. But unless we can have the enlightened public opinion of the North back of us, we labor under very great handicap.

May I add that I was a little surprised to see my book, Souls of Black Folk, transformed into the Heart of the Black man.

Very sincerely yours,
W. E. B. Du Bois

Some sense of the realities of the struggle Du Bois was leading is reflected in a letter from a rank and file member of the Niagara Movement.

---

1. Presumably, it is a mere coincidence, but in 1906, 1908, and 1910, Booker T. Washington employed agents, secretly, to search out the tax records in Atlanta in order to discover, as he wrote in 1910, "Whether or not Dr. D. is actually a registered voter in Atlanta." Louis R. Harlan, "The Secret Life of Booker T. Washington," *Journal of Southern History* 37 (August 1971):409.

[142]   Correspondence 1905–1920

Chicago, Oct. 16, 1908.
Dear Dr. DuBois:—

I regret to say that I must resign from membership in the Niagara Movement for the reason that I am about to begin work in Chattanooga, Tenn. I should be glad to send you a secret subscription to the able periodical with which you are connected, but I have not the money. Speaking of secret subscriptions, let me say that they are absolutely necessary to the cause. There are many who dare not, for good reasons, speak or contribute openly who ought to know of that method of rendering substantial aid to a cause which, I am sure, lies close to really all Negroes' and many white men's hearts. All praise to those who dare speak and act openly but let us be considerate of those who would speak & act openly if they dared. The thing to insist on is that no man say he believes something he does not believe and contribute to a cause he disbelieves in. Let there be silence & inaction in such matters.

I may later find it possible to be associated with you openly but for the present my resignation is final. You shall have a secret comrade in me. My private prayers shall go up for you who dare, and when opportunity affords I shall be a secret subscriber to our common cause.

Yours for the Cause,
David R. Wallace

From about 1895 to about 1910—coincident with Big Business's take-over of the South and with the legalization of jim-crow and disfranchisement there—major publications in the North and leading Northern figures, including those identified with the Republican party, adopted a line not only of acquiescence in the resubjugation of the Afro-American people, but also of gratification over this "solution." A prominent representative of this group was Charles Francis Adams (1835–1915), grandson of John Quincy and great-grandson of John Adams. This Charles Francis (his father was of the same name and had been Lincoln's ambassador to Great Britain) was a brigadier-general during the Civil War and then became a railroad executive, a member of Harvard's board of overseers, and president of the Massachusetts Historical Society. He wrote frequently for leading national journals; two of his best-known books were *Chapters of Erie* (1871) and a biography of Richard Dana (1890). The correspondence between Adams and Du Bois occurred late in 1908.

Atlanta, Ga., November 23, 1908
Mr. Charles Francis Adams
Sir:—

I have your pamphlet on the "Solid South" [1] and beg to say: One of the most

1. *"The Solid South" and the Afro-American Race Problem. Speech of Charles Francis Adams at Academy of Music, Richmond, Va., Oct. 24, 1908* (Boston, 1908).

unfortunate things about the Negro problem is that persons who "do not for a moment profess to be informed on the subject" insist on informing others. This, for a person who apparently boasts of advanced scientific knowledge is most deplorable and I trust that before publishing further matter on the race problem, you will study it. To this end I am sending you some literature.

                      Very sincerely yours,
                      W. E. B. Du Bois

                      Boston, Nov. 28, 1908

My dear Sir:

I have to acknowledge the receipt of your memorandum of the 23rd inst.

From its wording, I infer that your purpose is to administer me a rebuke in that, while professing to be uninformed, I should also "insist on informing others."

As respects the problem under consideration, my purpose has been carefully to abstain from any word or act which might tend to aggravate an existing situation which I regard as very serious and most unfortunate. If anything I said in the speech, of which a copy was sent you, seems to have tended to this result, I should be under deep obligation if you would point it out to me. I, accordingly, send you herewith another copy, which I beg you to return with your points of criticism indicated thereon.

I am sincerely desirous of studying the "race problem," with a view to its possible satisfactory solution, and have done so to the extent of my ability and the means at my disposal. It is very far from me to boast of "advanced scientific knowledge" on the subject. I have given it, I am aware, a certain degree of superficial attention only. I shall read the three publications you have sent me with close attention, as I have already read the publications of Prof. Kelly Miller, and other more thoroly[1] informed students of the subject. Meanwhile, I am forced to say that by all odds, and to an incomparable degree, the most illuminating book in relation to the problem I have come across, is that of Mr. Stone, entitled, *Studies in the American Race Problem*, to which, in the form of a quotation from Booker T. Washington, I made allusion in my speech at Richmond.[2] It may be ignorance on my part—and, I presume, it is—but I do not know any direction in which to go for safer guides than to Mr. Washington and Mr. Stone. But perhaps you can instruct me better.

                      I remain, etc,
                      Charles F. Adams

    1. This kind of "reformed" spelling was a vogue at the time—one especially advocated by Theodore Roosevelt.
    2. Alfred Holt Stone's *Studies in the American Race Problem* was published by Doubleday, Page and Co., in 1908. Stone was a Mississippi cotton planter, whose "enlightened" views made him a frequent lecturer at Northern gatherings during this period.

Atlanta, Ga., Dec. 15, 1908.

Mr. Charles F. Adams
My Dear Sir:—

I have your letter of November 28th and beg to say that in my humble opinion you have not abstained "from any word or act which might tend to aggravate an existing situation, which I regard as very serious and most unfortunate." I think your article in the Century Magazine was not only ill-considered and wrong but distinctly sensational in the worst sense of that term.[1] I am unable to point out to you "safe-guides" in the matter of social reform; I take it that guides are for directing people toward the truth and not simply toward their individual ease and safety. That a man of the twentieth century would stand up and indiscriminately vilify one hundred and fifty million or more human beings, and then to ask gently for guidance in a study of these matters in which he has already posed as a guide, is to me astounding.

I shall be very glad to return to you in a week or so your pamphlet with comments.

Very sincerely yours,
W. E. B. Du Bois

In the months immediately preceding the establishment of the National Association for the Advancement of Colored People (NAACP) and its organ, the *Crisis* (whose first number was dated November 1910), many efforts were converging toward that goal. Of central importance were the Niagara Movement and its organ, the *Horizon*. A letter from Du Bois early in 1909 reflects something of the process;* in fact, instead of a *New Horizon* as here suggested, the *Crisis* appeared and took over the subscription list of the old *Horizon*. It was, however, a monthly, rather than the hoped-for weekly.

Atlanta, Ga., March 12, 1909

To the Guarantors of the Horizon.
Dear Colleagues:—

In pursuance of your votes the following board of directors were selected: F. H. M. Murray, L. M. Hershaw, J. Milton Waldron, W. A. Hawkins, H. L. Bailey and W. E. B. Du Bois. The board of Control met and organized as follows: J. Milton Waldron, chairman, H. L. Bailey, secretary-treasurer and W. E. B. Du Bois, editor-in-chief.

As you know just as the New Horizon was about to issue the business manager-elect fell and broke his arm. This postponed matters. Meantime, I heard

---

1. "Reflex Light from Africa," *Century* 72 (May 1906):101–11.

* The original of this letter is in the State Historical Society of Wisconsin, to which the editor is grateful for a copy.

that Mr. John E. Milholland, a New York capitalist and Founder of the Constitutional League together with J. Max Barber, late editor of the "Voice of the Negro," proposed issuing a periodical on much the same lines as ours. I, therefore, wrote them both hurriedly saying that it seemed to me that we ought to have no further divided efforts, but all united in one strong periodical. This proposition met the favor both of our board of Control and of Mr. Milholland and Mr. Barber. Considerable negotiations was entered into but the following things have been finally decided upon: to publish in New York a weekly paper with an enlarged edition—I to be editor-in-chief and Mr. Barber to be managing editor. The paper is to be controlled by a board [of] directors consisting of white and colored persons of which board I am to be chairman. The paper is to be a Literary digest of all things concerning the Negro race, and to be made strong by contributions from the best writers of both races.

The financial side of the paper is to be supported by raising a capital of $25,000. Mr. Milholland undertakes to push and aid the raising of this fund, and to this fund I want your authority to subscribe in the name of the board of Control the $1,000 which you promised in sums of $25 each toward the aid of the Horizon this year. This $1,000 worth of stock will be placed in the hands of the secretary-treasurer of the board of Control. If any or all of you should now or subsequently wish to hold stock individually or to invest further the stock will be transferred to you individually. Will you kindly, therefore, write me by return mail whether or not you consent to this proposition? The name of the new paper has not yet been settled. Offices have however been hired at #500 Fifth Ave., New York where the managing editor may be addressed, and the editor-in-chief may be addressed to Atlanta University. We are planning the new periodical to appear before April 15th.

Very sincerely yours,
W. E. B. Du Bois

Edward Wilmot Blyden (1832–1912) was born in the West Indian island of Saint Thomas (then Dutch) and died in Sierra Leone, West Africa. His career shows ambiguous attitudes toward colonization and imperialism, but, together with Hayford and Du Bois, he stands as one of the great forces for the realization of African self-determination. Although trained as a Presbyterian minister, his greatest work was in government service in Liberia; he served that country as minister to Great Britain and also as secretary of interior and secretary of state. Biographies by Edith Holden (1966) and Hollis R. Lynch (1967) have recently been published.

A letter from Du Bois to Blyden, written early in 1909, is of interest because of the men involved, and is of added consequence as an early enunciation of Du Bois's dream of an Encyclopedia Africana. No reply to the letter seems to have survived.

[146]   Correspondence 1905–1920

Atlanta, Ga., April 5, 1909.

My Dear Dr. Blyden:—

I know you by reputation, and I am venturing to address you on the subject of a Negro Encyclopedia. In celebration of the 50th anniversary of the Emancipation of the American Negro, I am proposing to bring out an Encyclopedia Africana covering the chief points in the history and condition of the Negro race. I am asking a number of the leading scholars of the race to be on the editorial board, and I should very much like you to have a place and should like your advice as to what other Negro scholars I could invite. I am trying also to form an advisory board consisting of eminent white scholars who shall give advice and guidance, but the real work I want done by Negroes. If you can give me any names of men who will do to go on the white board I shall be very glad of it, and I shall be very glad of your good will and counsel on all matters. The plan is still in embryo but I think it can be put through.

I beg to remain, Sir,

Very sincerely yours,
W. E. B. Du Bois

Soon after the preceding letter was written, Du Bois had stationery prepared with a letterhead reading: "[Personal and Confidential] Encyclopedia Africana Commemorating the Jubilee of Emancipation in America and the Tercentenary of the Landing of the Negro—Edited by W. E. Burghardt Du Bois, Ph.D. Assisted by a Board of One Hundred Negro American, African and West Indian Scholars, with the co-operation and advice of eminent Specialists in Europe and America—To be published on the co-operative plan, in not less than five octavo volumes, beginning in 1913."

A letter on such stationery, mailed early in the spring of 1909, has survived.*

Atlanta, Ga., May 20, 1909

My Dear Mr. Williams:

In accordance with the heading of this letter, I am proposing to edit an Encyclopedia of knowledge concerning the black race in the world and those descended from it. I very much want you to consent to act on the board of editors. This will involve the selection of a single line of investigation to be pursued by

---

* The editor has not certainly established the identity of the addressee, but it is probably W. T. B. Williams of Hampton Institute in Virginia. Williams delivered a paper on "Reasons for a Systematic Study of the Negro" at the Tenth Atlanta Conference (1905) held at Atlanta University under the direction of Du Bois.

The original of this letter is in the Joel E. Spingarn Collection, Howard University Library; the editor expresses his gratitude to Mrs. Dorothy B. Porter of that library for sending him a copy.

you in consultation with certain selected specialists. The study can be undertaken at once and must be finished between 1913 and 1919, as the exigencies of publication demand.

The scheme is, in other words, a co-operative and exhaustive scientific study of Negro history and sociology with publication of results. If you are interested and willing to join us in the work will you kindly write me, and will you send me the names and addresses of all Colored persons in your State who have had thorough University training or its equivalent, and who would, in your opinion, be capable of joining in this work. I prefer to keep this matter confidential until the editorial board is formed and other details settled.

Very sincerely yours,
W. E. B. Du Bois

Writing in the *Horizon* in November 1909, Du Bois called "The National Negro Conference," held in New York City on 31 May and 1 June, the most significant event of the year. Hindsight would agree, for that conference marked the founding of the National Association for the Advancement of Colored People. Among the decisive figures in this effort were Du Bois, Oswald Garrison Villard, Ovington, and William English Walling. The last, like Ovington a socialist, was a nationally known writer whose account of the 1908 assault upon Blacks in Springfield, Illinois, published in the *Independent,* had been the spark for the events culminating in the 1909 conference; when the NAACP was officially launched in May 1910, Moorfield Storey was named its president and Walling the chairman of its executive committee.

Disagreements from Right and Left, the significant distrust of whites by the more militant Afro-Americans (like Trotter and Mrs. Wells-Barnett), and manifestations of chauvinism from even the most enlightened among the whites, made the original organizational efforts (and later efforts) exceedingly difficult. Some of the difficulties are indicated in a letter from Walling to Du Bois, written one week after the adjournment of the 1909 founding conference. Though Walling does not mention the "Project for the Enlargement of the Committee" published here, it is clear that the document formed an appendix to his original letter. No record of a response from Du Bois has been found.

21 West 38th Street, June 8th, 1909.
My dear Prof. DuBois:—

Mrs. McLane tells me that I may have made an error in addressing my letter and telegram to Wilberforce.[1]

Fortunately, there were four vacancies on the Committee. Mr. Russell has

1. Mary Dunlop Maclean was a socialist, a staff writer on the *New York Times,* and later, briefly, managing editor of the *Crisis.*

appointed Mr. Sinclair and Mrs. [Ida B. Wells-] Barnett without my urgence.[2] I then called on him and urged the appointment of Kelly Miller and Waldron.[3] The former he opposed but Mrs. Wooley called this morning urging his appointment.[4] Also Mr. Bulkley has consented to this and the Rev. Brooks and Dr. Waller have urged it.[5]

Mr. Russell was disposed favorably to the appointment of Waldron until he consulted with Mr. Villard who is opposed to this. But as I had obtained the consent of Sinclair, Brooks, Bulkley, Waller, Mrs. Wooley and Miss Ovington to this appointment, I have written both Mr. Waldron and Mrs. Trotter that I expected Mr. Russell to make the appointment and that if he did not, I would name Mr. Waldron for the first vacancy that occurs on the Committee. It will be much better if you urge Mr. Russell by telegram to make the appointment though indeed he may make it of his own accord.

I have already written Mr. Villard to go ahead with his plans of organization. I shall be glad to resign from the chairmanship in favor of Russell as soon as Waldron is appointed.

Mrs. McLane, who is with me now, urges me to repeat what I have just been talking over with her at length. I did not attend the sub-committee because I had complete confidence that none of those present would make any very important changes in the list of thirty names which Mr. Villard had so carefully drawn up. You had agreed with me that perhaps several colored members should be *added*. Mr. Milholland had the same feeling of confidence, as did several others who had seen the list. Here is what happened: Only three or four new colored names were added to the Committee, as I had urged; but I was no less than shocked to find that where three or four had been added six or seven had been taken off.

This stupendous error, as Mr. Milholland has called it in a letter to me, we cannot now wholly correct; but already, a slight improvement is brought about by the appointment of Mrs. Barnett and Mr. Sinclair.

In no case shall I be satisfied with the Committee, even as re-organized. But the appointment of Waldron and Kelly Miller is the very minimum correction that can be made. If this is done, I shall resign quietly and leave the Committee entirely in the hands of yourself and Mr. Villard, as it will be by its very consti-

---

2. Charles Edward Russell, a leader of the Socialist party, was a prominent writer who in 1927 was to win a Pulitzer Prize. Russell served as chairman of the 1909 National Negro Conference. William A. Sinclair, from Philadelphia, was a very active member of the Constitution League and of the Niagara Movement.

3. The Reverend J. M. Waldron had been a minister in Jacksonville, Florida, but at this time was serving in Washington, D.C., where he was president of the National Negro Political League; he was also in the Niagara Movement.

4. Mary E. Wooley was president of Mount Holyoke College in Massachusetts.

5. The Reverend William Henry Brooks was the Black pastor of Saint Mark's Episcopal Church in New York City.

tution. If these men are not named I shall remain as Chairman of the Committee with the expectation of naming them for the first vacancies, and until they are named I shall try to see that the Committee does not become the mere tool of any faction.

Yours sincerely,
Wm. English Walling

Project for the Enlargement of the Committee From Forty to Fifty.

General Grounds for such an Enlargement.

The proposed addition of ten members would certainly not make the committee of a less practicable size, adding as it does only 25% to the present membership.

The additional ten names could include those of all persons who would have had any good claim to expect to find their names on the Committee; and it would also make possible a thorough representation of the colored element as cannot be carried out now by a list of twelve names. The proposed addition would carry the colored names to twenty and the white names to thirty.

There is, of course, *extreme* dissatisfaction in several quarters. This dissatisfaction is on a high plane and does not take the form of personal grievances or of threats to leave the organization. On that account it is all the more dignified and deserving of consideration.

First, I suggest the names of two persons who have been most active in our meetings and against whom I believe there is no breath of criticism of any kind; both indeed were included on the first suggestion for the proposed committee. These names are Mrs. Ida Wells Barnett and Mr. William A. Sinclair.

The very first call for a Lincoln's Conference was signed by the names of three colored men; DuBois, Waldron, and Walters.

Mr. Waldron represents an extreme view. He is also avowedly a very aggressive Man, but in a large committee like ours this will create no difficulty and on the other hand, add greatly to our strength. As he is an advanced radical, however, I would suggest that the name of Prof. Kelly Miller of Washington be added. He is a conservative but has expressed himself in the fullest sympathy with our movement, and has signed our Call. He is the author of a book which is certainly one of the most interesting and valuable of all those bearing on the situation.

I also suggest the two following names of very important persons, who, while known as radicals, are by no means extremists and are in each case independent and trusted by their communities. These names are those of Rev. E. W. Moore of Philadelphia, and Mr. Archibald Grimké of Boston. The former has been one of the mainstays of the Constitution League. The latter has been active in the Negro American Political League.

I also suggest as the only possible means of giving a full and fair recognition to the Constitution League the names of Mr. Humphrey and Mr. Joseph C. Manning, both of whom I imagine had rather expected to be named as members of the Committee.[6]

This leaves vacant the names of two more colored persons whom I hope will be recommended to me in the near future. They should be selected with reference to the names already mentioned. In case any faction or point of view seems to have been unduly emphasized in these additional names, the last two could be chosen to balance off any such undue preponderance.

It would be a great pity that such strong and energetic personalities as those above mentioned, ready to co-operate with us in any way, and most unlikely to create for us any difficulties inside or outside of the Committee, should not be immediately added to it to correct a number of very wrong impressions that are already afloat. I do not refer to any mere gossip but to the well-based belief that no effort is made to secure a broad or in any sense full representation of the various colored elements. It is impossible that twelve colored members could thoroughly represent all the ideas, sentiments, standpoints, and organizations which ought to receive a constant hearing inside of our Committee.

J. R. L. Diggs, president of the Virginia Theological Seminary and College in Lynchburg, Virginia, was among the founders of the Niagara Movement and served as its state secretary for Virginia throughout its life.

His letter to Du Bois in the summer of 1909 represents a response among Black people to the Bourbon historiography which, at Columbia University under the aegis of William A. Dunning, was producing monograph after monograph detailing the "horrors" of Reconstruction and the grandeur with which the rulers of the South had managed to restore "civilization." In December 1909, Du Bois presented a paper, "Reconstruction and Its Benefits," at the annual meeting of the American Historical Association.* The Association for the Study of Negro Life and History, rather early in its career, began publishing volumes on Reconstruction; in 1935, Du Bois's magnum opus, *Black Reconstruction*, would appear.

Lynchburg, Va. July 12, 1909

Dear Dr. Du Bois:

For some time I have been thinking of a work that ought to be done by the

---

6. A. B. Humphreys was a member of the Constitution League. Joseph C. Manning had been a leader of the Populist-Republican Fusion movement in his native Alabama, a member of the state legislature, and the organizer of the Southern Ballot Rights League in 1895; later, during the 1919 "red scare," he was to attack the NAACP as "Bolshevik."

* The paper was published in the *American Historical Review* 15 (July 1910):781–99.

men who are of our way of thinking. The educated Negro owes the world a history of reconstruction. No subject has been treated in a way more harmful to our race than this one subject.

We have the men. We ought to have a series of ten volumes or more covering the reconstruction periods in Virginia, North Carolina, South Carolina, Georgia, Florida, Alabama, Mississippi, Louisiana, Texas and Arkansas. I have mentioned the matter to Mr. J. W. Cromwell of Washington, D.C., and he thinks it is the supreme need of the day.

We must get our views of that period before the public. The series of works by southern writers present our white brothers' side of the question but I do not find the proper credit given our people for what of good they really did in those trying days.

Now it has occurred to me that Hon. John R. Lynch, who is now retired on a good salary, Dr. Theophilus G. Steward, Gen. Robert Smalls, and others might give the facts from which a good case might be made for our cause.[1] Mr. Cromwell was active in the Virginia Constitutional Convention, was an editor and knows the men. Now would this work, if done say within the next three years, not form a splendid array of facts for the larger work you are planning? Should we not have both sides of reconstruction?

I am willing to write up either State if no one who lived during those days and who for such reasons can do it better than I, can be found. Perhaps if Cromwell will take North Carolina I will work out Virginia. If you will take the lead, we will follow. If not, perhaps Cromwell might be Editor-in-Chief.

Any plan you suggest will suit me. I simply want the work done.

                        Yours truly,
                        James R. L. Diggs

I shall meet the Niagara men in August by all means.

---

1. John R. Lynch (1847–1939) was born a slave in Louisiana but moved to Mississippi during Civil War; thereafter he was a photographer, was elected to the state house in 1869, was Speaker of the House in Mississippi from 1871 to 1873, served in Congress from 1873 to 1877, was auditor in the Treasury Department from 1889 to 1893, served as a major in the Spanish-American War, and was a lawyer and the partner of Judge Robert H. Terrell in Washington. He later made his home in Chicago. Lynch published two books relevant to the Reconstruction: *Facts of Reconstruction* (New York: Neale, 1913); and *The Historical Errors of James Ford Rhodes* (Boston: Cornhill Publishing Co., 1922). Theophilus G. Steward (1843–1924) was a minister and served as a chaplain in the Spanish-American War; he published an account of the Haitian revolution (1914) and an autobiography (1922). Robert Smalls (1839–1915), born a slave in South Carolina, brought the Confederate ship the *Planter* over to the blockading Union fleet; later he captained it through the war. He served in the state house and the senate from 1868 to 1874, and, from 1875 to 1887 (except 1880–81), sat in Congress. He rose to the rank of major-general in the South Carolina state militia, and was collector of the port of Beaufort in his last years.

Wilberforce, O., July 24, 1909.

My dear Mr. Diggs:

Your scheme for the set of histories of reconstruction from the Negro point of view is excellent, and will fit into my encyclopedia project perfectly.

I shall take it up in the fall.

Very sincerely yours,
W. E. B. Du Bois

This letter from a Southern white liberal of the early twentieth century, William Davis Hooper (1868-1945), is a classic. Its author was a professor of Latin at the University of Georgia in Athens. The letter speaks, too, of the impact of Du Bois's *Souls of Black Folk*. Oswald Garrison Villard knew Hooper, and Du Bois sent Villard a copy of the Hooper letter with his reply; Villard's comment to Du Bois is also published below.

Athens, Ga., September 2nd, 1909.

Prof W. E. B. DuBois
Dear Sir:—

I have just read the tragedy which you call "The Souls of Black Folk," and I cannot refrain from writing to tell you how profoundly it has affected me. It is faint praise—but even the pure English was very refreshing in this day of slovenliness.

The pathetic part of the whole thing is what you stress repeatedly—that the control of the South is not in the hands of its best people. The problem is the problem of the lower class whites, and the more enlightened are utterly powerless. I have long grieved over your own position, and wished that there could be some alleviation, and known that there could be none. I have, however, wanted you to know that my skirts at least are clean. I have never wittingly wronged one of your race in any way. I have never defrauded one of them of money, I have never insulted one of them, I have never given even a slight to one of them. I have been careful to train my children to respect their feelings in every way, and have punished them for offenses in this respect which I should else have passed over. And I have been able to be of service to many of them in more ways than in the matter of money. The Principal of the city schools here has had regular teaching from me in both Latin and German, and I have been able also to help others. Of course I voted against disfranchisement.

This is a small thing, but your book has put me on the defensive. These things I have done and left undone, and yet my whole training and environment have been such that I cannot break away from the other things of which you complain—I should not use the word, because the book is notably free from complaint. You, in turn, must look as leniently as you can on feelings which have been made part of us, and we must labor together, in all ways to lighten the gloom. And with it all rest assured that many of us feel most deeply the pathos of your own position.

Yours very truly,
W. D. Hooper

Atlanta, Ga., October 11, 1909

Mr. W. D. Hooper
My dear Sir:

I have read your very kind letter of Sept. 2nd again and again with increasing interest and sympathy. I have taken the liberty to read it to some of my friends and they have been both moved and encouraged. I thank you for your frank words and I want to say two things in answer to them which I will trust will not sound ungracious. First, whenever an aristocracy allows the mob to rule the fault is not with the mob; and secondly, Comrade, you and I can never be satisfied with sitting down before a great human problem and saying nothing can be done. We must do something. That is the reason we are on Earth.

Again thanking you for your kind words, I beg to remain

Very sincerely yours,
W. E. B. Du Bois

New York, October 27, 1909.

Dear Dr. DuBois:

I return with thanks the letter from Prof. Hooper and your reply. It is one of the most encouraging things I have seen. If you could know what a revolution has taken place in him you would be prouder than ever to be the author of your great book.

With kind regards,

Sincerely yours,
Oswald Garrison Villard.

The sources of an ever-present strain in the relationship between Villard and Du Bois have already been indicated. In addition, one of history's quirks did not help matters: Villard worked for years on his very full life of John Brown, but the book did not appear until 1910, while Du Bois's biography of Brown was published in 1909. The latter is marred by factual slips but has yet to be surpassed in terms of analysis and portrayal; it was also, among all his own books, Du Bois's favorite.

Under these circumstances, and as Villard was the owner of the *Nation*, it was natural that he would review Du Bois's effort there;* perhaps it was also natural that the review should be rather carping and ungenerous.

* 89 (30 September 1909):302.

In those days, reviews in the *Nation* were unsigned, but Du Bois knew, of course, who the reviewer was. There followed the correspondence here published between Du Bois and the editor of the *Nation*, Paul Elmer More†—whose efforts to instruct Du Bois in historical methodology were gratuitous, to say the least—and then between DuBois and Villard himself. It may be added that the *Nation* never did publish Du Bois's complaint.

Atlanta, Ga., November 6, 1909

The Editor of the Evening Post and the Nation
My dear Sir:
 I think courtesy calls for the insertion of the enclosed letter in your columns.
Very sincerely yours,
W. E. B. Du Bois

Atlanta, Ga., November 6, 1909

To the Editor of the *Nation*
 I thank the reviewer of my "John Brown" for correcting certain errors: my making Leary slave-born and Gill a Canadian were unfortunate slips of the pen for I knew better. Two other statements of mine as to Leary's middle name and the challenging of the Brown Jury are possible errors although I am not sure.
 There are in the review, however, seven misstatements presumably unintentional, of my words; I am made to say:
 1. That Babb betrayed Brown.
 I said "It was probably Babb." (p. 302) following Hinton's circumstantial account, and not having seen Gue's later declaration.
 2. That "there was wholesale assaulting of women" in Kansas.
 I said that there was "stealing of property, *raping of women*, and murder of men" (p. 140) a statement well within the truth.
 3. That Jeremiah Anderson was a Negro.
 My words are: "The seventh man of possible Negro blood was Jeremiah Anderson. He is listed with the Negroes in all the original reports of the Chatham Convention and was, as a white Virginian who saw him says, 'of middle stature, very black hair and swarthy complexion. He was supposed by some to be a Canadian mulatto.' He was descended from Virginia slave-holders who had moved north and was born in Indiana."
 4. That seventeen slaves were probably killed at Harper's Ferry.
 My words are: "Seventeen Negroes, reported as probably killed, are wholly unknown, and those slaves who helped and escaped are also unknown." (p. 279)

† More (1864–1937) was once literary editor of the *Independent* and of the *Evening Post* in New York, and then, from 1909 through 1914, editor of the *Nation*. Afterward, he taught at Princeton until retiring in 1933 and became a renowned authority on Greek philosophy, especially with the publication of his five-volume work, *The Greek Tradition* (1921–31).

5. That John Anderson was at Harper's Ferry.

I asserted on the testimony of Lewis Hayden (*Atlantic Monthly*, Dec. 1875) that Anderson started for the Ferry. I expressly said it was not clear that he ever arrived. (p. 282)

6. That those killed by Brown at Pottawatomie had a "trial."

I said there was a meeting of the "intended victims" but it is perfectly clear from the context that I meant the intended free-state victims of the border-ruffians. (p. 155)

7. That I believed that Thompson, Brown's messenger, did not reach the rear guard.

I expressly say: "It was at this time that William Thompson came up from the Ferry and reported that everything was all right." (p. 315) I add to this that it is likely that Thompson did not see *Tidd* at all, and I came to this conclusion from a close study of Bryne's testimony, of which the reviewer kindly reminds me. I call attention too, to the fact that John Brown blamed only himself: "It was this inexcusable delay on the part of Tidd and Cook, and possibly, William Thompson, that undoubtedly made the raid a failure. To be sure, John Brown never said so—never hinted that any one was to blame but himself. But that was John Brown's way." (p. 316)

There are two questions of fact mentioned, on which persons may differ as to the evidence:

1. Was John Brown descended from Peter Brown of the *Mayflower*? I have assumed that he was chiefly, I confess, because he himself said so (Sanborn, p. 511).

2. Was John Brown in Iowa in August 1856?

He certainly started for Iowa with his sick son-in-law and was in Nebraska City, just across the river from that state (Kansas Historical Collection. VI, 267) in August. I agree with Sanborn that he undoubtedly entered the state, left his sick son-in-law and then returned with Lane.

Finally, there is the general question as to the worth of the work of Sanborn, Hinton, Redpath, Anderson, and others. I have, I admit, relied strongly on these writers who were largely eyewitnesses of what they wrote. Except where recent research has undoubtedly contradicted them I have regarded their work as source material.

I am, Sir,

Very sincerely yours,
W. E. Burghardt Du Bois

November 12, 1909.

Dr. W. E. B. DuBois
My dear Sir:

We have carefully considered your letter of the 6th of November in regard to the review of John Brown. We do not feel, however, that we can print it for two reasons. First, that it does not convict our reviewer of any substantial injustice, and secondly, it would be of no service to you to print your reply. A difficulty seems to be that you do not understand what is really source material and what is not. The works of your predecessors are source material only in so far as they give original documents. Since they were printed there have been established large collections of original John Brown material not yet printed, in New York, Boston, Philadelphia and Topeka. Again, the fact that the writer of a biography was concerned in John Brown's movements does not, ipso facto, make him a man to be relied upon; indeed, since he thereupon becomes a defendant in the way of his own actions it is all the more necessary for a historian to test his work with the utmost carefulness. Dr. Thomas Featherstonhaugh, of Washington, informs us that he agrees heartily with our review and attributes some of your difficulties in regard to the raid to too great a reliance upon Anderson and Barry.[1] It is precisely the duty of the historian to take such narratives as these and test them carefully by the mass of material existing elsewhere.

Again, it does not excuse a historian that he used the words "possibly," "probably" or "perhaps" when the facts are available, as in the matter of Gue's letter. We submit that our reviewer was justified in saying that you spoke of wholesale assaulting of women in Kansas, in view of your own phrase, "There were pitched battles ... raping of women and murder of men, until the scared Governor signed a truce ..." etc. This could only be taken to indicate the extreme degree of the crimes alleged. It may be in your opinion that such a statement is well within the truth, but that could only be proved by producing many instances of the crime alleged. In regard to your error in regard to Jeremiah Anderson and John Brown's entering Iowa in 1856, if you had communicated with the surviving members of the Brown family these errors would have been impossible. Why not ask John Brown's "sick son-in-law" as to what happened in August 1855? He is still alive. It is true that you expressly said it was not clear that John Anderson arrived at Harper's Ferry, but elsewhere you say that six or seven of the twenty-two raiders were negroes. The only way that you can arrive at that figure, if you except John Anderson, is by putting Jeremiah, a white man, as a negro. I would cite only one more instance of the lack of clarity and thoroughness in your work. On page 315 you harshly blame Cook for delaying at Byrne's and at the schoolhouse, yet Cook was there expressly under orders, and in censuring Tidd, Cook and the others you overlook Owen Brown at the Kennedy Farm who was in charge of the moving of arms, and a man of the greatest physical courage and vigor. Finally, had our reviewer so chosen he could have dwelt upon your treating Shields Green as a brave man, when the

---

1. Citing Thomas Featherstonhaugh probably did nothing to calm Du Bois; Featherstonhaugh's essay "John Brown's Men: The Lives of Those Killed at Harpers Ferry" appeared in *Publications of The Southern History Association* 3 (1899):281–306.

testimony as to his cowardice is so overwhelming;[2] he might also have dwelt upon the injustice of your characterization in the attitude of Lee, Wise and others at the famous interview with John Brown after the raid, in view of the extreme courtesy with which Lee treated his prisoner and his offering to exclude from Brown's presence everybody there if any questioning at all were unpleasant to him. We note that you decline to take our reviewer's word for the fact that you are in error in regard to the challenging of the Brown jury. You will find the minutes of the trial in Charlestown, which will give you the names of the men challenged, the whole proceeding signed by the judge in charge. And if you will refer to Frederick Trevor Hill's recent article in Harper's on the John Brown trial you will find the fact of the challenging also established, if we remember correctly.

        Very truly yours,
        P. E. More.

      Atlanta, Ga., November 15, 1909

Mr. Paul E. More
My dear Sir:

I am very sorry to receive your letter of the 12th inst. I had hoped that after a review of my book which I and others (Mr. Featherstonhaugh and Mrs. Sanborn among them) regard as peculiarly unfair, you would at least have the courtesy to allow me a word in self-defense—a word not directed to you but to the public whom you have misled. Instead of this I receive a letter little short of insulting. I may not be, as you say, a judge of original historical material but I certainly should not think of seating myself at the feet of Mr. Villard for instruction either in History or English. That the book I have written is in the main outline an accurate historical picture I am convinced, and others share the conviction. That it is possible in it, and indeed in most books, to pick numberless immaterial flaws in absolute accuracy is true, but savagely to emphasize these so as to give an impression of total falsity is a contemptible thing to do. The very least reparation which can be made and a thing which courtesy among gentlemen has a right to demand is the printing of the reply of the attacked party, if it is decently couched. Whether it answers the attack or not or will "help" me or not is my business and the public's and not yours.

I sincerely hope therefore, that both you and Mr. Villard will on second thought have the grace to grant me this slight reparation after your peculiarly wanton assault.

 I am, Sir,

        Very sincerely yours,
        W. E. B. Du Bois

 2. Shields Green was the young slave who had escaped from South Carolina, who accompanied Douglass when he discussed Brown's plans shortly before the raid, and who decided to remain with Brown; he did, and was hanged with him.

New York, November 17, 1909.

Prof. W. E. Burghardt DuBois
Dear Sir:—

For reasons which you will understand, we have to make it a rule not to print replies to our reviews unless we have committed some error in fact or have misrepresented an author. I cannot see that either of these reasons holds good in the present case. We admit that your volume is "readable," and we take pains to add a commendation of your sociological studies; but we feel bound to point out the carelessness of your present work in its treatment of facts—"numberless flaws" of this kind do not seem to us "immaterial." I cannot, however, close the incident without expressing my sincere regret that you should feel the Nation has dealt with you unjustly or discourteously. Certainly we had no such intention.

Very truly yours,
Paul E. More

Atlanta, Ga., 11/20/09

Mr. Paul E. More
Dear Sir:

Answering your letter of November 17th, let me say you *have* committed errors of fact in reviewing my book and you *have* misrepresented me. Anyone who asserts that saying a man is "possibly of Negro Blood," that another man "probably" wrote a certain letter, and that there was "raping" of women, is the same as asserting that the man was a Negro, did write the letter and that there was "wholesale" raping of women has a good deal less knowledge of English than you have. Moreover, your reviewer has stated at length his opinion as to whether or not the flaws are immaterial, while at the same time deliberately (as it seems now) falsifying those flaws. Then he emphasizes his judicial attitude by refusing to let me point out to a deceived public just how far those flaws are material. As to your intentions in this matter I am, of course, no judge, but I certainly must conclude and the public will also conclude, that when an author about to publish a book sneaks behind anonymity to give a supposedly rival book an unfair drubbing, it certainly does not improve the appearance of his "intentions" nor of his "sincere regret" in not allowing a courteous reply.

Very sincerely yours,
W. E. B. Du Bois

November 26, 1909.

Dear Dr. DuBois

Mr. More has shown me your letter of November 20th with its amazing charge that a review of your John Brown in The Nation was written with the intent of giving an unfair drubbing to a supposedly rival book of mine. The whole character and standing of The Evening Post and The Nation, maintained through many years, in themselves belie such a charge, but since you have drawn me into this discussion in this way, I want you to have from me an absolute refutation of that statement. My deep interest in you, my appreciation of your usefulness in the community, the way I have praised and widely circulated your "Souls of Black Folk," my asking you to come to my uncle's Memorial, my desire to have you occupy an important position in connection with the proposed National Negro Board, ought in themselves to convince you, after further reflection, of the injustice that you have done. You may rest absolutely assured that if your work had been in any way on a par with "The Souls of Black Folk," nothing could have gratified me more. So far from being jealous of your book, I should have been happy if it had been even superior to your other work—without an error or a flaw or a misinterpretation. I believe that the appearance of your book, so far from injuring the chances of my own—about which I confess myself to be quite indifferent—improves them, and would have improved them still more if it had reached the standard we have a right to expect from you.

As to the review in The Nation, I do not think it was unfair or unjust to you. The book contains other errors than those we pointed out. It is simply putting on record The Nation's belief that no book can be a sound historical work when the author has disregarded many well-established facts, either through oversight or for some other reason. If, for instance, in the matter of Jeremiah Anderson, you had looked up Redpath's story of him and his family in the Liberator for 1860, you would have found so complete and full a history of the Anderson family, their nativity, their holdings, their life, that you could have had no doubt whatever as to the man's race. As so in the matter of the challenging of the jurors, etc. Whether the review was absolutely accurate in its language or not is a matter of opinion. That there are serious errors of fact in your book admits of no possible question.

I sincerely hope, and have no doubt, that such errors as have crept into my book, either of interpretation or fact, will, if it finds a publisher, meet with the treatment they deserve. In the matter of style I believe it must be inferior to yours; but whether it is or is not is, after all, as I see the writing of history, the unimportant point. The only question is how near to the historic truths I may be able to arrive. Finally, I do not think that there can be too many books about the John Brown period.

As always, with best wishes,

Very truly yours,
OGV.

Harvard classmates W. E. B. Du Bois and Clement G. Morgan at a 1907 Niagara Movement meeting

1910 signed portrait of Mrs. Nina Gomer Du Bois

Mary White Ovington, 1909.
Photograph courtesy of
Mr. & Mrs. Theodore O. Kingsbury.   William English Walling

Du Bois at his desk in his office at Atlanta University, 1909. From the collection of Milton Meltzer.

The *Crisis* office, ca. 1914. Du Bois is at right. From the collection of Milton Meltzer.

November 29, 1909.

Dear Dr. DuBois:

I did not, of course, mark my letter to you of the 26th personal and confidential, but that is the spirit in which it was written, and I know that you will accept it as such.

Faithfully yours,
[Oswald Garrison Villard]

Atlanta, Ga., December 1, 1909

My dear Mr. Villard:

The subject in dispute between us is not a matter of praise or blame, appreciation or condemnation, but simply a question of Justice. The very fact that the *Nation* and the *Post* have an enviable reputation for fairness and accuracy makes it the more inexplicable that their editors to-day should stoop to an unworthy and unjust deed. I do not complain of the original review. I complain of your fear to publish a courteous answer to its ridiculous misstatements. And when that astounding refusal came I said, and I repeat, that it could only arise from motives of which most men would be thoroughly ashamed. I would willingly and eagerly believe you guiltless of such motives as you protest at such length and you have it in your power still to give absolute proof thereof by publishing my letter. Will you do it?

Very sincerely yours,
W. E. B. Du Bois

Atlanta, Ga.
December 6, 1909

My dear Mr. Villard:

I neglected to enclose in my last letter another copy of my original letter which I am again asking you and Mr. More to publish.

Very sincerely yours,
W. E. B. Du Bois

Early in 1910, Du Bois received a quite remarkable letter from John Hope, who was visiting friends in Providence, Rhode Island. Written in pencil and covering almost nineteen pages, it reflects not only an intensity of feeling for Du Bois, but also the complex character of the battle for liberation. Hope (1868–1936), born in Georgia in the same year as Du Bois, was until his death one of Du Bois's dearest friends. Although extremely fair in complexion, he always identified himself with the Negro people. He was president of Morehouse College, Atlanta, during Du Bois's first service at the university, and, in the early 1930s, Hope (then president of the university) succeeded in persuading Du Bois to return there as chairman of the sociology department. Du Bois wrote a moving tribute to Hope in his column in the *Pittsburgh Courier* of 28 March 1936, and there is an excellent biography of Hope by Ridgely Torrence (New York: Macmillan Co., 1948).

Providence, R.I., January 17, 1910

My dear Du Bois:

I must ask you to pardon this use of pencil, though it must be confessed I am half glad that I cannot find a pen as I can write better with pencil. Since I left you last Tuesday this is the first leisure that I have had to write. I have been very tediously busy and much on the go. Now that I have an hour, will you listen patiently while I talk about one thing that I want you to hear from me.

I frankly confess that you people at Matthews' home some nights ago let me down much more easily than I could have expected, much more easily than I probably would have let another down, if I had had quite so good a joke with so much fact behind the joke as you folks had on me. I have often taken and given "roasts" and felt, therefore, as I say, quite cheerful that it was so light for me—not a scorching, just a comfortable warm brown.

However, as I thought afterwards of what had been said, as I knew the attitude of many, if not all, there, it occurred to me wherein the ideas of any might be erroneous it would still not be worth my while to clear up anything. Moreover, I have been misunderstood, seriously misinterpreted, even in public print several times in my life and have never made an explanation. Nor should I now depart from my course. And yet I did know that their ideas about me were erroneous, and there was one to whom I possibly owed an explanation, though I regretted even to imagine that he might believe some things that his perfectly pleasant joking implied. Du Bois was the one man to whom I thought I might owe an explanation. Why Du Bois? Because I have followed him; believed in him; tried even, where he was not understood, to interpret him and show that he is right; because I have been loyal to him and his propaganda—not blatantly so, but, I think, really loyal; and because, in spite of appearances, I am just as truly as ever a disciple of the teachings of Du Bois regarding Negro freedom.

It is also true that through the kindness of Mr. Booker Washington I was enabled to secure a conditional offer of ten thousand dollars from Mr. Andrew Carnegie. I may here say that I have credit for more good scheming than I deserve. Without any effort on my part a friend of the school first approached Mr. Washington and pointed a way to me which seemed, and still seems, to me perfectly honorable and so generous as to have called for selfishness on my part not to accept on behalf of a school that needed the assistance and ought to be helped rather than hampered by its president. All of this I carefully thought over and—*naive* as it may appear to you—prayed over. Then without any persuasion or pressure from any one I went frankly to Mr. Washington; told of what I heard; told him my purpose for the school and that larger facilities would mean better opportunity for carrying on the work of this school as it now is without any change of its educational policy and ideals. After hearing this, he was quite as willing to help and did so.

Now Du Bois, I expect to be criticized, perhaps publicly; would be surprised if so great a flop, flop as it *seems*, should go unnoticed and unknocked. I should not wonder that from your position you would have to knock quite savagely. All this and more I expect, would be surprised if I did not get, but would not lift my finger to avert.

Then why write you all this? My impression is that *friendship*—not acquaintanceship or perfunctory intercourse but real friendship—is based not so much on agreement in opinion and policies and methods but upon downright confidence, upon simple faith, no matter what the view or appearances. You and I for nearly ten years have been friends, at least I have fancied so. I write to ask, no matter whether you doubt the wisdom of or resent my action, are we friends?

You may remember that in the early and bitterly misunderstood efforts of the Niagara Movement, I was the only college president that ventured to attend the Harper's Ferry meeting to take part in its deliberations. You may remember too, that while some may have answered the call to that seemingly radical meeting in New York last May, I was the only president, colored or white, of our colleges that took part in the deliberations of that meeting. I cite this to show that I have dared to live up to my views even when they threw me in the midst of the most radical. Furthermore, every man on our faculty does the same and will as long as I am head of the institution. But, Du Bois, may there not be a *tyranny* of views? Have we not required such severe alignments that it has been sometimes as much a lack of courage as a mark of courage to stand either with Du Bois or Washington to the absolute exclusion of one or the other in any sort of intercourse? I confess that it is unpleasant to be charged with apostasy even in joke when one is not truly apostate. But the unpleasant feature in my case finds full compensation in the certainty of my courage to do what I regard as right. There is a feeling of emancipation that a man of genius cannot quite know or appreciate. You go unfalteringly, almost unthinkingly, to a conclusion that has back of it indisputable logic. The opposing views of other men do not so much concern you in your thinking because you have hardly needed them in your equation. That is genius. I am a plodder. My even petty thinking calls for great travail of mind and spirit; and, in the process, I carry along most hospitably all opposing views with which I am acquainted. I am plodding, canny—you go on the wings, and are daring. Yet we can both follow truth and be loyal to it and to each other.

Now, I have not known Washington long, but what I know of him in my personal relations is perfectly pleasant and generous. If I should find out later otherwise, I suppose I would express it as simply and with as little vehemence as I am now writing. I am glad that as a man interested in education I can associate properly with another man who is interested in education yet from a different angle as Washington is. I am primarily interested in education. Quite as heartily as ever I shall disagree with Washington's views where they do not accord with mine, and I would not yield a *principle* for the benefit of myself or my school, obviously for such could not really benefit.

I write to ask you whether you have me in your heart—not on your calling list or your mailing list but in your heart—on your list of friends. I am asking this question fearlessly as a strong man would ask his chieftain. I will receive the answer just as fearlessly. And however it may be, I shall be loyal to my chieftain still. This letter is absolutely personal and I should feel hurt ever to have it mentioned or quoted except between you and me. It comes too much out of my heart. It is no apology to anybody. It is an explanation carrying a question to you. It is a letter from a man to a man between whom a friendship has developed based on mutual interests in a race that we love and are working for. I want that friendship to last. If it does, we shall do even more than we have ever done. Why should it not last?

Your very dear friend,
John Hope

Atlanta, Ga., January 22, 1910

My dear Hope:

You must not think that I have not known and appreciated your friendship for me or that I ever have doubted or doubt now your loyalty to the principles which we both so sincerely believe. If I thought even that you were going back on those principles, my friendship is not of so slight a texture that I would easily give you up. Of course I am sorry to see you or anyone in Washington's net. It's a dangerous place, old man, and you must keep your eyes open. At the same time under the circumstances I must say frankly I do not see any other course of action before you but the one you took. In your position of responsibility your institution must stand foremost in your thought. One thing alone you must not, however, forget: Washington stands for Negro submission and slavery. Representing that, with unlimited funds, he can afford to be broad and generous and most of us must accept the generosity or starve. Having accepted it we are peculiarly placed and in a sense tongue-tied and bound. I may have to place myself in that position yet, but, by God, I'll fight hard before I do it.

I know, however, that you, my friend, are going to do the right as you see it, and I'm too sensible of my own short comings and mistakes to undertake to guide you. As I have said, so far, you have done what you had to do under the circumstances. I only trust that the pound of flesh demanded in return will not be vital.

I thank you with greater feeling than I dare express for your kind letter.

Yours,
W. E. B. Du Bois

[168] Correspondence 1905–1920

Richard T. Greener (1844–1922), born in Philadelphia, was the first Afro-American to receive a degree from Harvard (1870). He taught in Philadelphia and Washington briefly and was an editor, with Frederick Douglass, of the *New National Era* in Washington in 1873. In that year he accepted a teaching post at the University of South Carolina, where he remained until reaction in 1877 closed that university to all but whites. In 1876, Greener received the law degree from the University of South Carolina and was admitted to the bar. He left for Washington in 1877, practiced law there, and became dean in 1880 of Howard University's law school. From 1885 to 1890, he was chief examiner for New York City's civil service. From 1898 to 1906, he served as United States consul in Bombay and in Vladivostok; he then retired from the foreign service and lived his remaining years in Chicago.

One may contrast the response of Greener to Du Bois's *John Brown* to that of Villard.

Chicago, Feb. 4, 1910.

My dear Mr. DuBois:

I have just finished reading your "John Brown" and cry out *Macte Virtute!*[1] To me it is in conception and treatment, easily the best of your many good things. I met O. P. Anderson just before the publication of his pamphlet.[2] I have often heard Douglass eulogize Shields Green, fit to ascend to martyrdom, "wid de'ole man." It was conjectured, what could you say new of the Martyr Brown! Perhaps, little of new: but you have taken up the John Brown bugle and have blown a new inspiring strain, bravely, courageously, and well. "The Legacy of John Brown" surpasses all you have done, and states the ignominy not of the U.S.A. alone; but the commercial barbarity, and heartlessness, of the so-called superior races. Chapter XIII should be spread abroad, and read by the rising generation. I have little hope of the mature sycophants of today, who are apologizing for their existence; still asking hat in hand for largesse and getting ready to celebrate in 1913, *what they have not yet received*.[3] Pariahs! [one word illegible] claiming to be emancipated! The White American is not yet freed from his prejudices, cruelties, meanness, hypocrisy! I had hoped the Conference of last summer, might have freed you from the professor's tread mill: but have no faith in it.[4] At any rate thanks for the telling blows you have struck. Long

1. "Bravo!"
2. Osborne Perry Anderson was a free Canadian Black man, a printer by trade, who participated in the attack upon Harpers Ferry and escaped. His pamphlet entitled *A Voice from Harper's Ferry* was published in Boston in 1861 and reissued in 1873.
3. The 1913 celebration was in commemoration of the fiftieth anniversary of the Emancipation Proclamation; ceremonies were held in many areas.
4. The "conference of last summer" refers to the May-June 1909 National Negro Conference, noted earlier; it did indeed free Du Bois for some time "from the professor's tread mill."

may you be able to wield so trenchant a blade.
                            Yours
                            R. T. G.
Per Contra: I did not like your comment on General [Oliver O.] Howard. I think without intention you did him scant justice. In fact, I did write something to that effect but tore it up.

                        Atlanta, Feb. 10, 1910
My dear Mr. Greener:
    I thank you very much for your kind letter about my book. I am glad that you found so much in it to commend. The fight is an uphill one but somebody is going to win sometime.
                        Very sincerely yours,
                        W. E. B. Du Bois

Symbolic of the nature and purpose of the projected NAACP was Du Bois's relationship to it. A struggle ensued among the sponsors of the 1909 meeting as to whether or not Du Bois was to be a permanent and full-time officer of the association, especially in the function he demanded—namely, the direction of research and propaganda. By June 1910, agreement had been reached and Du Bois was asked to leave Atlanta for work with the association, headquartered at 20 Vesey Street, the address of the *New York Evening Post* (owned by Villard).* The June 1910 correspondence between Walling and Du Bois concerning this step was decisive.

                        New York, June 8, 1910.
My dear Mr. DuBois:
    If I have not written before, it has simply been because there has been nothing definite to say. Nor is there anything definite now. I can reassure you that the whole effort and hope of our Committee is built almost exclusively on obtaining you as director of its investigations. You do not need to be told that we are taking up our time almost wholly with this matter; but the following delays have occurred: The wealthy people of New York and of Boston have nearly

---

* Helpful in elucidating the details of these negotiations and decisions is Charles F. Kellogg, *NAACP: A History of the National Association for the Advancement of Colored People*, vol. 1, *1909-1920* (Baltimore: Johns Hopkins University Press, 1967), although the opinions expressed about the motivations of Du Bois are quite dubious (p. 49).

By June 1910, there existed stationery for the NAACP; it had a general committee of sixty members, of whom twenty-one were Black. Among the sixty were John Dewey, Lillian D. Wald, Stephen S. Wise, Jane Addams, Clarence Darrow, and many others noted in earlier pages. Sixteen of the sixty were women.

all left those cities, and it is utterly impossible to raise money in this way, or to secure any guarantees until October.

This leaves us to rely exclusively on our own resources, pledges from our Committee of One Hundred and such membership as we may obtain during the summer. We have not yet secured any further answers from our own Committee, owing to many necessary delays in getting the organization started and moving our headquarters to 20 Vesey Street; but we shall expect to have the bulk of these replies in within another week or two, and if three-fourths of our members will reassure us that they can raise on the average, $100. each, we shall be able to make you a definite offer before the end of this month.

Our Committee meets again on June 28th, for the especial purpose of considering this question.

I have no doubt you realize that we are offering you work and an opportunity, rather than a financially promising or steady position. Of course we shall be able to pay you what is right and proper during the first year—$2500. plus your expenses—and shall fully hope to employ you in after years, perhaps even at an increasing salary; but you are aware, of course, that the most we can expect to do will be to guarantee your salary and expenses for the first year.

None of our members feels that there is much danger but that we shall be able to make you a definite offer before the end of the month; but we all feel that no matter how many difficulties we may have in raising the necessary money, the main sacrifice will be yours, in leaving a position which you have filled with such credit, and probably with such satisfaction to yourself, for so many years.

On the other hand, if I were an old and intimate friend of yours, I should certainly urge you to take the risk. If I am not mistaken, the moment is a critical one for your work and public activities; but such moments come in the lives of all, and there are certain risks which ought to be taken, both from our own personal standpoints and for the sake of the cause.

Let me know if you are still feeling that you will be willing to take this great move, notwithstanding the uncertainties it involves.

Very sincerely yours,
Wm. English Walling.

Atlanta, Ga., June 13, 1910

My dear Mr. Walling:

I have your kind letter of June 9th. I appreciate very much the efforts and good will of the Committee. I shall be only too glad to second their endeavors in any way I can, and I am willing to accept any reasonable risk for the privilege of engaging in a work which, I agree with you, is of paramount and critical importance. I shall, therefore, await your further communication with great interest.

In looking over your budget it occurs to me that no provision is made for research work, unless something is included under postage. This is a matter which ought to be thought over.

> Very sincerely yours,
> W. E. B. Du Bois

J. Franklin Jameson (1859–1937) was of major consequence in his influence upon the historical profession in the United States. He taught for many years at Johns Hopkins, Brown, and the University of Chicago; was director of the historical research department of the Carnegie Institution in Washington (1905–28), and, from 1928 until his death, headed the manuscript division of the Library of Congress. He was managing editor of the *American Historical Review* (1895–1901; 1905–28) and edited such key works as the *Dictionary of American Biography* and *Original Narratives of Early American History*.

The correspondence published here between Jameson and Du Bois concerns Du Bois's paper "Reconstruction and its Benefits," which appeared in the *American Historical Review* after Du Bois had cut, at Jameson's request, about fifteen hundred words.* It was published with the word in question spelled "negro."

One component of this exchange—expressing Jameson's surprise that Du Bois suggested an intention of "personal insult," followed by a reference to Jameson's own abolitionist family background, and concluding with arguments against capitalizing "Negro"—has been published elsewhere† and thus is not inserted here. It is in answer to that Jameson letter, dated 22 June 1910, that Du Bois replied on 5 July.

Atlanta, Ga., June 2, 1910

My dear Professor Jameson:

I am returning proof herewith. I always ask editors, as a matter of courtesy to allow me to capitalize the word Negro. They usually do so and I trust you will do the same.

> Very sincerely yours,
> W. E. B. Du Bois

Washington, D.C., June 10, 1910.

My dear Mr. Du Bois:

I thank you for the return of the proof. I should be glad to do anything that might seem to you a proper courtesy; but I really do not feel able to make, for

---

* 15 (July 1910):781–99.

† Elizabeth Donnan and Leo Stock, eds., *An Historian's World: Selections from the Correspondence of John Franklin Jameson* (Philadelphia: American Philosophical Society, 1956), p. 133.

one article alone, an exception to the practice which we have maintained from the beginning of the existence of this journal, and expect to continue to maintain in subsequent issues, of printing "negro," which we have not looked upon as a proper name, without a capital.

Hoping that you will not be disappointed in the action which I take only in deference to the uniform office practice, and with many thanks for the article.

I am,

Very truly yours,
[J. Franklin Jameson]

Atlanta, Ga., June 13, 1910

My dear Professor Jameson:

I do not think that mere uniformity in office practice is sufficient excuse for inflicting upon a contributor to your Review that which he (foolishly perhaps, but sincerely) regards as a personal insult, and I sincerely hope that you will find it possible to respect my wish and let the word Negro be capitalized in my article.

Very sincerely yours,
W. E. B. Du Bois

New York, July 5, 1910

My dear Professor Jameson:

I did not mean to imply that the "personal insult" was from you, but that I felt that the usage to which you subscribe was an insult. You are mistaken about the authority of that usage. The word Negro is almost universally capitalized on the Continent and in England (*vide* Sir Harry Johnston's article in the current 19th Century[1]) & it used to be in this country down until about 1840 when "negroes" became definitely cattle for all time. Even now periodicals like the *Outlook* capitalize the word & many books. I am therefore exceedingly sorry to see you range yourself with the least authoritative & more insulting usage.

Very truly yours,
W. E. B. Du Bois

One of the first questions facing the new NAACP was its attitude toward Booker T. Washington, and, reciprocally, his attitude toward it. The latter was rather overtly hostile, while the former tried to avoid hostility or confrontation. In

---

1. Actually, Du Bois had in mind an article not by Sir Harry H. Johnston—who often did contribute to the magazine *Nineteenth Century* and who wrote very extensively on Africa—but by Henry Halco Johnston. The article was entitled "The Negro and Religion," and appeared in *Nineteenth Century and After*, 67 (June 1910): 995–1007.

1910, however, Washington was in England, and there made several speeches affirming that the "Negro problem" was well on its way to being resolved in the United States. John E. Milholland, one of the founders of the NAACP, was in England at the time and wrote Du Bois that he felt Washington had to be answered. Du Bois agreed and drafted a statement "To the People of Great Britain and Europe," issued in printed form on 26 October 1910, with the title *Race Relations in the United States*, and signed by twenty-three Negro leaders acting as a National Negro Committee.* Meanwhile, plans were going forward to hold in London in July 1911 the First Universal Races Congress.† This meeting grew largely out of the plans of the Ethical Culture Society, under the leadership of Felix Adler and its secretary for England, Dr. Gustav Spiller. Du Bois was the American secretary for this congress and, with the aid of Mr. Milholland, was able to attend; he sailed for England on 1 June.

In connection with his arrival, and at Milholland's initiative, efforts were made for Du Bois to match the lecture tour recently given by Washington. But Du Bois did not want this kind of "competition," and there were objections from conservative elements in England to Du Bois's speaking at all. The whole matter finally resulted in a dinner in Du Bois's honor, given by the powerful Lyceum Club on 26 June 1911, and called a "Races Education Dinner." Princesses, bishops, lords, and ladies attended, and appropriate speeches were exchanged.

Difficulties in arranging the dinner were so great, however, that in a letter dated 28 February 1911, to Dr. Ettie Sayer, president of the Lyceum Club, Du Bois suggested dropping the whole matter; the letter is published here. The dinner was held, however, and the visit provided Du Bois the chance to meet H. G. Wells, Mrs. Havelock Ellis, Sir Roger Casement, and J. Ramsay MacDonald.

[Atlanta, Feb. 28, 1911]

Dr. E. Sayer
My dear Madame:

I have been considerably distressed over the developments in London in regard to my visit. I had planned to come to the Races Congress in July, and then it was proposed that I come earlier in order to counteract in some degree Mr. Washington's utterances. This has of course led to much discussion as to my attitude toward Mr. W., which has been very annoying. I am not an "enemy" of Mr. W., neither do I "attack" him, nor stand for everything which he does not.

---

* The text of this statement is in Aptheker, *Documentary History*, 1:884–86.
† The proceedings of this congress, edited by G. Spiller, were issued in French and English in Boston, London, and Paris in 1911; this volume has been republished with an introduction by Herbert Aptheker (New York: Citadel Press, 1970).

I do not agree with much that Mr. Washington does and says, and that which I do not agree with I criticize frankly—but also, I trust, courteously. My object in coming to England was not to talk about or against Mr. W., but to discuss the race problem in the U.S.

When now it was proposed that I make a lecture trip in England two objections immediately arose in my mind:

1. My coming at the time would look like an attempt at personal rivalry with Mr. W., a thing furthest from my mind or wish.

2. I did not see how I could arrange to leave my work here. Nevertheless the duty of telling the world the plain unexaggerated truth about the race problem here, seemed to me of grave importance provided I could reach sympathetic ears, or at least persons willing to listen and weigh.

As your kind letters came to Mr. Milholland I began to fear more & more that if I came I would come as an agitator almost forcing his way among a people who were with difficulty restraining their dislike.

I shrink from such a situation and for that reason was hesitating over going when the demands of my work here settled the question for me peremptorily. We are just getting into working shape the N.A.A.C.P. It has been far more successful than we dreamed but not successful enough to stand at the moment my prolonged absence. Especially does the rapid increase in circulation of our little magazine, the Crisis, make it imperative that I remain here for several months more.[1]

I should rather welcome this necessity were it not for the awkward position in which this decision places you. I shudder when I see a new convert to the righteousness of this great cause, for I know as few others know, what that convert must endure in humiliation & disappointment. When I realize what you have tried to do for a stranger & a strange cause I feel like a deserter from the forefront of battle. I do not pretend that I would have enjoyed the Lyceum luncheon under the circumstances, but I do vividly realize the opportunity it gives for reaching a great public.

I write therefore to express profound regret at my inability to accept the hospitality offered. I shall arrive in London about June 1, but I venture to suggest that it would be asking too much to have the luncheon postponed to that busy season. I should not want you to go through so mad a battle again and I think the whole thing would best be quietly dropped.

Meantime I shall be in England at least during June, July & August—probably in September. If during that time it is possible in any way for me quietly to present the cause of my people to any group of people I should be most happy to do so.

---

1. Volume 1, number 1 of the *Crisis* was dated November 1910; it was issued in one thousand copies.

I am venturing to send you some copies of the Crisis, some of the publications of Atlanta U. & others of my writing.

Believe me, Madame,

Very Respectfully yours,
W. E. B. Du Bois

Edward T. Devine (1867–1948) was one of the outstanding figures in the early history of social work in the United States. He was administrator of the Charity Organization Society of New York City (1896–1918), director of the New York School of Philanthropy for several years prior to the First World War, and the editor of *Survey* (1897–1912). He published in 1904 a standard text, *Principles of Relief,* and in 1939 an autobiographical account, *When Social Work Was Young.*

He served as informal secretary of the Committee on Industrial Relations, based at Columbia University, whose purpose was to secure the congressional appointment of a federal Commission on Industrial Relations. The committee members represented a roster of leaders in reform efforts and social work— Jane Addams, Louis D. Brandeis, John Collier, Henry W. Farnum, Ernst Freund, Franklin H. Giddings, Washington Gladden, John Haynes Holmes, Alvin S. Johnson, Florence Kelley, John A. Kingsbury, John Howard Melish, Henry Morgenthau, George F. Peabody, Lillian Wald, Walter F. Willcox, and Stephen S. Wise. Beginning its work in 1911, this committee helped produce the 23 August 1912 act of Congress that created a Commission on Industrial Relations; its purpose, according to the language of the act, was to "inquire into the general condition of labor in the principal industries of the United States, including agriculture, and especially in those which are carried on in corporate forms."*

It is noteworthy and illuminating that all the members of Devine's committee were white, and that in pushing for the inquiry described above, this committee "forgot" the millions of Afro-American people. Du Bois called that fact to Devine's attention in a missing letter written in February 1912; Devine's reply is published below.

---

* The investigations and reports by the commission (1912–16) exposed the awful conditions existing for masses of agricultural and industrial workers, the ruthless suppression of organizational efforts, and the need for significant change. Du Bois testified before the commission in 1915. The commission was fiercely attacked by dominant media and its work interrupted by the war. There is a good account in *The American Labor Year Book, 1916,* ed. A. Trachtenberg (New York: Rand School, 1916):269–74.

                                New York, February 21, 1912
Dear Dr. DuBois:—
I confess until your letter of February 16th was received, the race question had not occurred to me in connection with the proposed Commission on Industrial Relations. I think that I can speak for every member of the committee in saying that so far as we have any influence in the matter, no industry would be neglected merely because the wage earners were chiefly negroes. We have fixed our attention, it is true, mainly on industries which are carried on in corporate forms and those, I suppose, for the most part are not the industries in which negroes are largely employed, with perhaps some exceptions, such as the Steel Corporation in the South.

I should be exceedingly glad to have your views on this subject for the benefit of the committee. Without giving the subject undue prominence or raising it prematurely, we would desire to guard effectively against any decision which would exclude the industries in which negroes are employed. On the contrary, it would be our desire to make certain that they are included. Of course, the decision rests with Congress.

                                Sincerely yours,
                                Edward T. Devine

Jesse Max Barber was a leading figure in the militant Negro struggle during the first two decades of the twentieth century. He was founder and editor of the *Voice of the Negro*, established in Atlanta in 1904, but was forced to leave after the pogrom of 1906. Barber then published the *Voice* in Chicago until 1907. A founding member of the Niagara Movement and of the NAACP, he was an editorial board member of the *Crisis*—along with Villard, Charles E. Russell, Kelly Miller, William S. Braithwaite, and Mary D. Maclean—when it was established in 1910. He left Chicago in 1911, studied dentistry, and from 1912 until his death, was a dentist in Philadelphia, tending more and more to remove himself from political activity.

Du Bois, as *Crisis* editor, was constantly seeking data and suggestions for its improvement. Barber's 1912 reply to an inquiry from Du Bois offers firsthand information on what was, until the *Crisis*, the leading Negro magazine.

                                Philadelphia, March 2, 1912.
Dear Dr. Du Bois:
Complying with your request of February 28 I beg to state that the largest number of copies of The Voice ever printed was 17000. That was in the month of May of the third year of our existence. 15000 copies of that issue approximately represented subscriptions and copies sold. The rest were used as sample copies to boost the circulation. During the month of November of that year we were in Chicago and some money came to us that would not ordinarily have

come. That month we took in $850.00. The average income however was between $400 and $500 per month when we were at high tide. Our largest circulation was 15000. Between 9000 and 10000 were annual or semi-annual subscribers. The rest were sold by agents.

If this information is of any value to you, I am pleased. I am glad to note the rapid rise of The Crisis.[1]

                    Sincerely yours
                    J. Max Barber.

Just as Du Bois pioneered in Afro-American historiography with his *Suppression of the African Slave Trade* and in urban sociology with his *Philadelphia Negro*, so did he pioneer in producing the first overall examination of the history of African and African-derived peoples, with the 1915 publication of *The Negro*. This book was number ninety-one in the Home University Library of Modern Knowledge, whose English editors were Herbert Fisher, Gilbert Murray, and J. Arthur Thomson, and whose American editor was a Columbia University professor, William T. Brewster.

Brewster wrote Du Bois in March 1912 suggesting such a volume; that letter and Du Bois's positive reply sent in April are published here. On 30 September 1912, young Alfred Harcourt, whose career in publishing was to be so distinguished, wrote on behalf of Henry Holt and enclosed a contract. The preface to the finished volume is dated 1 February 1915; the work was published in London by Williams and Norgate, and in New York by Henry Holt.

                    Luxor, Egypt.
                    March 7, 1912

Professor W. E. B. DuBois
Dear Sir,–

I am writing to ask if you would care to consider the contributing to "Home University Library" of a book entitled *The Negro*. Like other books in the series it should contain about 50,000 words, and should aim to present the facts or wise and sound generalizations on the facts in as broad and interesting a way as possible for the more intelligent readers. The English editor, with whom I have talked the matter over, would like to see a book treating the Negroes in British possessions as well as in America, but at the same time we should welcome any more ideas or interpretative treatment.

The sale of this series are considerable in America and very large in England, so that the series is really one of the best means at present of circulating sound

    1. The Du Bois papers show that the first issue of the *Crisis*, November 1910, totalled 1,000 copies; by December 1911, the run came to 16,000 and by April 1912, 22,500 copies were printed.

ideas. I am asking Messrs. Holt and Co., to send you descriptive circulars and also certain volumes of the series, that you may examine the series more carefully.

Since I shall not return to America until mid-summer, may I ask you, in case you wish to make any immediate inquiries, to write to Mr. Alfred Harcourt, c/o Henry Holt and Co., 34 West 33rd St., New York City. My own address is in the care of Messrs. Brown, Shipley and Co., 123 Pall Mall, London.

I am

Very truly yours,
William T. Brewster

New York, April 4, 1912

Mr. William T. Brewster
My dear Sir:

I have your letter of March 7th. I should be glad to see descriptive circulars and volumes of the series. I think I already have one volume by Sir Harry Johnston if that is the same series.[1] It happens that I was planning this summer to give a series of twenty-five lectures at a summer school on the History of the Negro Race. My idea was out of this material to evolve what I was going to call a preliminary essay on the history of the black race. My plan was to treat

1. Definition of the Negro Race and distribution.
2. History of the Negro Race.
3. The present condition of the Negro race in its various places of residence throughout the world.

I think perhaps this would coincide with your idea. The only difficulty about it would be that an essay of fifty thousand words on so general a subject would have to be rather sketchy.[2] On the other hand a study of the Negro in America simply would be rather narrow, [the manuscript breaks here].

Harry Pace was the young man who served with Du Bois as business manager of his venture in producing the *Moon*, published in Memphis. Although the publication failed, the relationship between Pace and Du Bois persisted and remained firm for many years. A letter sent by Du Bois to Pace in Memphis early in 1912 not only offers details on the financial progress of the *Crisis*, but also illuminates Du Bois's plans and hopes. Pace did not accept this proposal; Augustus Dill became the new business manager in 1913.

1. This was Johnston's *Opening Up Of Africa*, number eighteen in the series.
2. The actual published volume contains about seventy-five thousand words.

New York, April 3, 1912

My dear Mr. Pace:

I am delighted to know that you are considering coming to us. It will mean hard work, but I believe that it will in the end be an enterprise of gigantic proportions. The income of the Crisis since I wrote you has been

November	1911	$803.44
December	1911	924.93
January	1912	961.29
February	1912	918.94
March	1912	1305.61
Surplus April 1st,		825.43

We have not assumed full financial responsibility yet, but we shall May 1st with the single exception of my salary. That will be assumed sometime in the summer. Our regular expense will then be about as follows per month:

Printer	$560
Salaries (including mine)	305
Other expenses	200
	$1065

Our income is, I think, permanently past the $1,000 monthly mark. I calculate by August we can count on $1,200.

My plan would then be that you should plan to come to us September 1st, rather than July 1st, since the July and August are off months while the rise begins in September. I should propose that on September 1st, you join our staff as either "Business Manager" or "Travelling Representative." That your salary be $100 a month and travelling expenses. That your job for the first one or two years be to raise the circulation of the Crisis from 20,000 to 100,000 by travelling over the country. Your method should be to hold mass meetings and meet prominent citizens, we paving the way by correspondence and literature from the office. Then you could appoint general and sub-agents. In some cases I could help by lectures. The information gathered by you could be used in various ways—letters to the Crisis, material for a biographical dictionary, material for future organization of the whole race into a really great effective body. Then there are sidelines in books, mail-order business, etc., to be gradually developed.

After this preliminary two years' work in the field, then you might come into the office and take general charge of the business thus relieving myself and Holsey and letting Holsey go out a year after the big advertisers. This is my present plan. What do you think of it? Criticize it freely.

Very sincerely yours,
W. E. B. Du Bois

Edward Henry Clement (1843–1920) was a leading journalist who served on newspapers in Georgia, New Jersey, and New York, but whose main work was in his native Massachusetts. He became associate editor of the then-powerful *Boston Transcript* in 1875, and was its editor-in-chief from 1881 through 1906. After his retirement, he maintained a nationally-known column, the "Listener," until his death; it is to this column that he refers in his letter. Clement was also a playwright and poet, and was active in anti-racist and anti-imperialist movements.

Boston, May 28, 1912

Dear Dr. DuBois:

Having been away I have just had my first good reading of "The Crisis," since you kindly placed my name on your exchange list. It is evidently going to be one of the best journals that I read through from cover to cover. It is magnificent in its value, strength and clearness of purpose, high, unswerving, uncompromising. "Without haste, without rest," it will surely wear away the rock, indeed grind it to powder, exceeding fine, as the mills of the Gods ever do.

I shall have something to say about it in my side compartment of the Transcript before many days, I hope.

With congratulations (and gratitude as an American citizen who feels keenly, every hour, his country's shame and peril "along the color line")

Most sincerely yours,
E. H. Clement.

Despite his membership in the Socialist party, Du Bois felt it would be tactically best if the Negro people voted for Wilson in the 1912 election. This view brought criticism from many, including fellow-members of the party. Late in 1912, Du Bois received a form letter from Carolina M. Dexter, recording secretary of the executive committee of the Manhattan local of the Socialist party, requesting payment of his dues; his reply is given here.*

New York, Nov. 6, 1912

My dear Madame:

My recent attitude in the political campaign has been called in question and as I do not feel that I ought to change it, I hereby offer my resignation as a member of the Socialist Party.

I beg to remain, Madame,

Very sincerely yours,
W. E. B. Du Bois

---

* This letter is located in the Tamiment Library of New York University. The editor is grateful to its librarian, Mrs. Dorothy Swanson, for making it available and offering helpful information.

As soon as Du Bois reported for work at the NAACP in August 1910, difficulties began to develop between him and others of the executive board. One of the problems arose from the fact that Du Bois was, uniquely, both a member of the board and, in his position as director of research and publications, also its employee. Part of the problem was the chauvinism of several of the white board members, which was exacerbated because Du Bois tended from the first to be politically Left of many of the NAACP leaders.

Particularly difficult in the early years was his relationship with Villard, whose Southern wife refused to have Negro—or Jewish—guests at their home; Villard, himself, tended to be rather imperious, and Du Bois was the last man in the world to take slights—real or apparent.

As chairman of the board, moreover, Villard (himself an author and editor) was anxious to share and perhaps usurp Du Bois's editorship of the *Crisis*. A monumental clash between the two men occurred at a board meeting in March 1913, resulting in this letter from Du Bois to Villard; soon after, in January 1914, Joel Spingarn replaced Villard as chairman of the board, though the latter remained a member.

March 18, 1913

Memorandum for Mr. Villard

I am told that since the passage of words between us in the board meeting you do not think further co-operation between us in the work of the association is possible. It does not seem to me that this conclusion is at all necessary. So far as I am concerned the incident will make no difference in my continued endeavor to give my best service to a great cause and to act harmoniously with all my fellow workers.

All I ask (and that was the essence of what I sought to say) is reasonable initiative and independence in carrying out my part of the work. I count myself not as your subordinate but as a fellow officer. Any suggestions made to me by you will always receive careful attention, but I decline to receive orders from anyone but the board. That any member of the board has a right to criticize my work or suggest amendment goes without saying, but the chairman of the board has, in my opinion, no right to imply in his criticism that my independence of action is a breach of discipline or a personal discourtesy to him.

This is what I meant to say and what I still insist upon. If in the heat of the argument I said or implied anything beyond this, I most cheerfully withdraw it.

W. E. B. Du Bois
Director of Publicity and Research

Among the leading figures in the modern African liberation movement was J. E. Kwegyir Aggrey (1875–1927), who was of great importance in tying together that movement and the Afro-American struggle. Born in what is today Ghana, he was educated in a Methodist missionary school and served as a teacher in the 1890s. Early in the new century, he came to the United States, where he graduated from Livingstone College in North Carolina. He taught at that college and wrote occasionally for such newspapers as the *Charlotte Observer*; by 1912, he was registrar and financial secretary of Livingstone. Later he studied at Columbia University and served on Phelps Stokes Educational Commissions visiting both West and East Africa. In 1924, he was appointed to the staff of the projected Achimoto College in present Ghana, and three years later was named vice principal at that college. He sailed for the United States in the spring of 1927, intending further study at Columbia, but he died suddenly in New York City in July of that year.

In 1913, he sent Du Bois a ten-page handwritten letter; no response survives, but the two men did know and respect each other.

Salisbury, N.C., July 1, 1913

My dear Sir:

Please pardon this intrusion upon your already overcrowded time. Now, I imagine you say, "well, what do you want?" I want three or four things:

1st I would like to know you more than I know now. 2nd I would be pleased for you to know me. 3rd I would like for you to make it possible for me to come up to New York City to study under you this summer. 4th I want to identify myself with the N.A.A.C.P.

To return: I would like to know you more than I do at present. I know you already but only through your books, your other literary work and sociological researches. I use your "Souls of Black Folk" every year in my literature classes. There seems to me a consciousness of kind between us, hence I would like to know you more. I am a student and you a master. You can be of very much help to me, and through me to a thousand others.

I would be pleased for you to know me. I am a native West African born on the Gold Coast and partly educated there. I am a graduate of the above-named school—Livingstone College. I was prepared for the Cambridge Higher Local while in Africa—taught there nine years, became a schoolmaster with five Teacher's Certificates from Her Majesty Queen Victoria. Taught my native language Fanti and did special work in the Akan language spoken by the Fantis and Ashanti. I don't want to say so much about myself. I was obliged to do this much of the disagreeable job just to introduce myself to you. I helped to translate the New Testament into my language, and wrote in it. I did some other translation work.

I want to come up to New York City this summer to study under you. I should be delighted to be there by the end of next week. I have done some systematic studying about my people, our customs, manners and laws. I have had some very good opportunities to do such studying. I have been to Kumasi the capital of Ashanti, and also have had access to the high councils of native Kings.

I have walked through many of the forts or castles built by the Dutch, Russian, Portuguese to house the slaves before they shipped them over here or to the islands. I have stood at the grave of the celebrated L. E. L. whose remains now lie in Cape Coast where I was educated and whose memory I hope some day to enshrine in song and story.[1]

I append hereto a list of a few of the books I have read on Africa and the Africans. I have read more, but I am quoting partly from memory. I have notes on several of the books. A. B. Ellis is very good but fails in places because he could not speak the native language and his interpreters were some of them uneducated, for example he confuses sāman (Sahman, sic) meaning "ghost" with sraman (srahman) lightning and upon such a mistaken or wrong premise builds arguments. He calls us the *Tshi* (should be spelt Twi) speaking Peoples. We don't call ourselves Tshi. We call Twi "Potokan"— meaning Corrupt Akan. I have traversed most of the places mentioned in Cruikshank's 18 years on the Gold Coast. His books are among the most faithful—he stayed there.

I too went "to Kumasi with Scott," and can expose many of the falsehoods and fabrics of diseased imagination he weaves within the covers of his book. There are no cannibals among the Akans—The Fantis and Ashantis. I know Dennis Kemp personally—was on the Gold Coast before he came there, and was there when he left for England. He knows me too.

George McDonald was for years Her Majesty's Inspector of Schools on the Gold Coast. He spent about three or four months a year on the Gold Coast. He came from London, started from the East and worked Westward from Accra to Appolonia. I knew him—my school having about 468 students made 100% in all studies under him.

Miss Mary Kingsley and I sat at the same table and slept under the same roof when she visited Cape Coast.

Sarbah and I are related. He was Knighted by King George V. He is dead now. I have several letters from him. He and I belonged to the court of King Amonoo V. I can prove this, but not necessary.

I knew Casely Hayford, knew him before he left for England to study Law. Was there when he returned.

When the native Kings, chiefs and people of the Gold Coast were fighting Jos Chamberlain in the nineties about the Lands' Bill, I as secretary of the

---

1. "The celebrated L.E.L." was Letitia Elizabeth Landon (1802–38), in her time a very well-known poet, who signed her work with her initials. She was the wife of a Captain George Maclea, governor of the Gold Coast, and died at the Cape Coast Castle in obscure circumstances. There is sympathetic reference to her in Michael Dei-Arrang's *Ghana Resurgent*, published in Accra in 1964. Brodie Cruikshank devotes a chapter to her in *Eighteen Years on the Gold Coast of Africa* (London, 1853), a book mentioned by Aggrey in the appendix to his letter. A study of her writings by Lionel Stevens appears in *Modern Language Quarterly* 8 (1947):355–63; her death is discussed in O. E. Enfield, *L.E.L., A Mystery of the Thirties* (London, 1928).

Gold Coast Aborigines Rights Protection Society with the assistance of Sarbah of Cape Coast, and Bertram & Co of London, retained Asquith, then Q. C., now Premier, as our Counsel. We won our case. This will give you some idea about me, and why I should like to study under you, the Moses of us along this line. I am teaching English Language and Literature, also Latin and New Testament Greek here. I crowded Economics, Geology & Zoology lectures in this past year as we fell short a teacher. Mrs. Morton-Jones of Brooklyn and her son Franklin Wheeler Morton, also Mr. & Mrs. [W. A.] Hunton know me. Mr. J. E. Moorland of Washington and Mr. [John W.] Cromwell had me elected member of the American Negro Academy some six or seven years ago.

I want to be of some special service to my people—hence I am in this country.

I want also especially to be connected if only temporarily with your office in New York this summer to study the ins and outs of the National Association for the Advancement of the Colored People. They have asked me to be a member of the Southern Sociological Congress. I want to learn, to know, and to start branches of the N.A.A.C.P. in Livingstone this Fall and try to introduce in others.

I think I have already taken too much of your time. I hope I have said something of interest. This and I am through. A young woman—my dearest friend, heard you lecture on Africa last summer in Durham and returned to tell me that you corroborated many of the things I had told her.

I should like to see you and have a long talk with you. I want to come up this summer, next week to start work. I write for newspapers sometimes. If I can make enough to defray my expenses and also study I will push ahead.

Kindly let me hear from you at once, and believe me to remain

Yours very respectfully,
J. E. Kwegyir Aggrey

APPENDIX

Some of the Books on Africa I have read:
Dennis Kemp's "Nine Years on The Gold Coast."
A. B. Ellis's The Tshi-Speaking Peoples of the Gold Coast
" " " History of the Gold Coast of West Africa
Livingstone's Travels and Researches
Blyden's Christianity, Islam and The Negro Race.
Horton's Climate and Meteorology of West Africa
Miss Tucker's Abbeokuta
Cruickshank's Gold Coast (18 years on the)
Wells Brown's Three Years in Europe
Cooper's The Lost Continent
Hay's Ashanti and The Gold Coast
Sarbah's Fanti Customary Laws

"   Fanti National Constitution
Casely Hayford's Works on Gold Coast
Tillinghast's The Negro in Africa and America
McDonald's The Gold Coast Past and Present
Miss Kingsley's Works.
Dowd's The Negro Races
Musgrave's To Kumasi With Scott[2]

Robert Todd Lincoln (1843–1926) was the eldest son and only surviving child of President Lincoln. He was a corporation attorney most of his life, but also served as secretary of war under Presidents Garfield and Arthur, and was President Benjamin Harrison's ambassador to Great Britain. In the last two decades of his life, he lived in semi-seclusion, spending his summers at Manchester, Vermont. From there he answered Du Bois's invitation to participate in the celebration in New York of the fiftieth anniversary of the Emancipation Proclamation.

2. The full titles of the works cited by Aggrey follow: Denis Kemp, *Nine Years at the Gold Coast* (London: Macmillan and Co., 1898); Alfred B. Ellis, *The Tshi-Speaking Peoples of the Gold Coast of West Africa*, 3 vols. (1887; reprint eds., Chicago, 1964, The Netherlands, 1966), and *A History of the Gold Coast of West Africa* (1893; reprint ed., New York, 1969); David Livingstone, *Missionary Travels and Researches in South Africa* (London: J. Murray, 1857; New York: Harper, 1858); Edward Wilmot Blyden, *Christianity, Islam and the Negro Race* (London: Wittingham, 1888); James Africanus B. Horton, *Physical and Medical Climate and Meteorology of the West Coast of Africa* (London: J. and A. Churchill, 1867); Charlotte Maria Tucker, *Abbeokuta; or, Sunrise within the Tropics: An Outline of the Origin and Progress of the Yoruba Mission* (New York: Carter, 1857); Brodie Cruikshank, *Eighteen Years on the Gold Coast of Africa, including an account of the Native Tribes, and their intercourse with Europeans*, 2 vols. (London: Hurst and Blackett, 1853); William Wells Brown, *Three Years in Europe; or, Places I Have Seen and People I Have Met* (London: Gilpin, 1852)—the author was the famous American fugitive slave; Joseph Cooper, *The Lost Continent; or, Slavery and the Slave-Trade in Africa, 1875 . . .* (London: Longmans, Green and Co., 1875); John C. D. Hay, *Ashanti and the Gold Coast* (London, 1874); John Mensah Sarbah, *Fanti Customary Laws* (London: Clowes, 1897), and *Fanti National Constitution* (London, 1898; reprint ed., London: Frank Cass and Co., 1968); Casely Hayford, *Gold Coast Native Institutions* (London: Sweet and Maxwell, 1903), and *Gold Coast Land Tenure and the Forest Bill* (London: C. M. Phillips, 1911); Joseph A. Tillinghast, *The Negro in Africa and America* (New York: Macmillan Co., 1902; reprint ed., New York, 1968); George MacDonald, *The Gold Coast: Past and Present* (London: Longmans, Green and Co., 1898); Mary Henrietta Kingsley, *Travels in West Africa* (London: Macmillan and Co., 1897; reprint ed., New York, 1965), and *West African Studies* (London: Macmillan and Co., 1901; reprint ed., New York, 1964); Jerome Dowd, *The Negro Races*, 2 vols. (New York: Macmillan Co., 1907–14); George C. Musgrave, *To Kumasi with Scott* (London: Wightman, 1896).

Manchester, Vermont, October 2, 1913

Professor W. E. B. DuBois
My dear Sir:

I greatly appreciate your invitation to attend the Emancipation Proclamation Exhibition in New York at the end of this month but I am not able to accept it. I am sure that it will be very interesting but I have for some time refrained from being present at any public gatherings.

> Very sincerely yours,
> Robert T. Lincoln

Paul U. Kellogg (1879–1958) was the editor of the *Survey*, with associate editors Jane Addams, Graham Taylor, and Edward T. Devine; the *Survey*'s National Council included William Guggenheim, Charles M. Cabot of Boston, Julius Rosenwald of Chicago, and Paul M. Warburg of New York. For the Charities Publication Committee, with grants from the Russell Sage Foundation, Kellogg edited the six-volume *Pittsburgh Survey* (1909–14), an early and careful study of working men and women in the Pittsburgh area.*

A letter from Kellogg to Du Bois, late in 1913, concerned another of the significant quarrels between Du Bois and some members (again, especially Villard) of the NAACP's board.

New York, December 17, 1913.

My dear Dr. Du Bois:

Confirming our conversation over the telephone: we are publishing in our issue of December 27th a symposium of some twenty people, "pointing out the definite advance which should be striven for in 1914," in various fields which come within the purview of The Survey. In many cases these proposals are put forward by the executive officers of national organizations operating in this field —informally rather than officially, of course; or are of a sort which the organizations so operating would subscribe to and back up as the next stage.

Members of the staff who read your "Black Man's Program for 1914" felt as a matter of tactics the clause "to marry any sane grown person who wants to marry him" would be regarded as the semi-official utterance of the Association for the Advancement of Colored People, and would be misconstrued and prove a boomerang; and as friends to you and the Association we raised the question of its advisability with you from the organization standpoint.

We are not pretending to edit or underwrite the pronouncements in these different fields, so that the attitude of The Survey in the matter is not involved.

---

* See Clarke A. Chambers, *Paul U. Kellogg and the "Survey"* (Minneapolis: University of Minnesota Press, 1971).

You suggested that the last three lines be struck out, with their reference to the National Association—so that the program would stand as your own, rather than as seemingly committing them to your positions. You very properly took the ground that you did not want personally to put out any program which did not include what was to you a vital principle.

At the same time the scheme of the symposium is in the direction of organization proposals rather than individual proposals; just as it is in the direction of immediate practical steps rather than ultimate.

Therefore a statement which sets forth the program which the National Association will be working for in 1914 is being prepared by Miss Nerney, as a substitute for your program as an individual, with your knowledge and acquiescence.

While this change robs us of your contribution to this particular symposium, please understand that our columns are open to you as an individual should you wish to bring out the points in Section BI or other points in your program.

                Sincerely,
                Paul U. Kellogg
                Editor

Among the English public figures Du Bois met in 1911 was J. Ramsay MacDonald, then a young Labour M.P. Their relationship continued for some twenty years.

Another result of Du Bois's 1911 visit was his attraction to the internationally known Bedales School in England, where pre-college training was offered.[*] After investigation, Du Bois decided to try to enroll his daughter, Yolande; he and MacDonald corresponded in this context. Yolande was admitted and did attend the school during part of the First World War, with Mrs. Du Bois accompanying her.

                [New York] January 10, 1914

Personal
Mr. Ramsay MacDonald
Sir:

I am applying at Bedales School for entrance for my daughter of fourteen next

---

[*] Bedales, founded in 1893 by J. H. Badley, was the parent of the progressive school movement in England. To prepare its pupils to play positive roles in society, Bedales was structured, as far as possible, as an ideal model of the outside world. In contrast to the established English preparatory schools at the turn of the century, it was (and is) coeducational and cosmopolitan, encouraging friendship and equality between pupils and teachers and work with the hands as well as the minds.

[188] Correspondence 1905-1920

year, and I have taken the liberty to refer to you as to my character. I trust I have not presumed.

I am, sir,

Very respectfully yours,
W. E. B. Du Bois

London, W. C., February 6th, 1914.

Dear Professor Du Bois,

Your letter of the 10th ult. came to me in the midst of a very heavy Conference of the Labour Party, but I answered Mr Badley's enquiries at once.

I have two boys at Bedales and I am quite satisfied with the school. I hope your daughter will be admitted. I have heard, however, that the lists are very full and that Mr Badley has just decided to limit his numbers. I am sure he would like to take your girl.

Yours sincerely,
J. Ramsay MacDonald

With the growth in the membership of the NAACP and in the circulation of the *Crisis*, problems multiplied which were reflected in the organization's leadership. An exchange between Du Bois and Miss Ovington in April 1914 is among the most remarkable extant between a Black man and a white woman in the United States; at the same time it illuminates many facets, not only of history, but also of the realities and nuances of collective work seeking significant social change.

New York City, April 9th 1914.

My dear Miss Ovington:

I have received from Miss Nerney an invitation to attend a caucus of "a few friends" at 55 Liberty Street, on Monday April thirteenth.[1] I shall be out of town on that date but even if I were here I do not think I should attend.

I feel that I recognize the meaning of the meeting and I am sure that its objects will be best attained if I am not there and I can then be frankly discussed and criticized.

The Association has come to the parting of the ways. I have used every endeavor to stave off this day as long as possible so that we might face it with a sense of responsibility and with a body of work done. It is perhaps on the whole well to fight the matter out now.

The question is whether this organization is to stand on its original radical

1. Miss May Childs Nerney, a white woman, had served as librarian in the state library in Albany and in the Newark, New Jersey, Public Library; she was hired as NAACP secretary and served as such from June 1912 to January 1916.

platform or is to go that way of conservative compromise which turned the Ogden movement, the Southern Education Board and the General Education Board so completely from their original purpose.[2]

What this Association should stand for I have endeavored for three and a half years to set forth clearly and unmistakably in the Crisis. I do not mean that the exposition has been perfect or that mistakes have not been made but on the whole *Crisis* principles have been those which I conceive should be the principles of the National Association for the Advancement of Colored People.

The question now is does the Association agree with this? I do not mean complete and absolute agreement in all details but substantial agreement. If the Association agrees then the proper action would be to arrange in the plan of reorganization for me to continue as the responsible editor under the same general supervision as is provided for other officers.

In the proposed measures which you are to discuss on the thirteenth the Crisis and its editor are put under the "immediate" charge of the executive committee and absolutely barred from all real initiative. No other executive officer is thus humiliated. The secretary is put under "general supervision" only and in addition the power of the office would be astonishingly increased by putting our greatest public functions, our annual conferences and meetings, "in the charge of the secretary"—a power hitherto always discharged by a committee of the Board of Directors with the secretary as executive.

It therefore goes without saying that I should regard the adoption of the proposed provision a vote of lack of confidence and I should immediately resign my position. Meantime, while the matter is under discussion I shall oppose the adoption of the measure before the board, before the membership and before the colored people. I shall do this, however, by honorable means. I shall stoop to no secret cabals or caucuses or seek to force snap judgment at the last moment. And I shall oppose this, I hope you will believe, for no merely personal reasons or mere stubbornness of opinion. I am sorry that the impression is widespread that I do not receive or desire any advice. It is not true. I have not, of course, haunted Mr. Villard's office, or kept Mr. Spingarn on the 'phone or poured out my heart to Mr. Studin, and I shall not do this.[3] But whenever at properly

2. The "Ogden Movement" refers to efforts to enhance Southern education in the post-Reconstruction era; its direction became increasingly conservative and pro-Tuskegee. Its name marked the great influence of Robert C. Ogden (1836–1913)—a Wanamaker partner and trustee of Hampton and Tuskegee (and of Union Theological Seminary in New York)—on the boards mentioned by Du Bois. Helpful on this subject is L. R. Harlan, "The Southern Education Board and the Race Issue in Public Education," *Journal of Southern History* 23 (May 1957):189–202.

3. It is likely that Du Bois had in mind Joel Spingarn (1875–1939), who replaced Villard as chairman of the NAACP board and served in that capacity from 1914 to early 1919. He was professor of literature at Columbia from 1899 to 1911 and author of works in literary criticism; in 1913, there was established the Spingarn Medal, given

appointed times and places, I can arrange to consult with anyone interested in my work I do so gladly. I think you can all understand that the insults which I receive in my life may have made me reticent but it is unfair to assume that therefore I deem my thought or way self sufficient.

I realize the forces opposed to my platform and to me personally in this organization: Mr. Villard has been frank from the beginning. He opposed my coming to the position in the first place and has systematically opposed every step I have taken since. He has told me plainly that he should not rest until I and the Crisis were "absolutely" under his control or entirely outside the organization. On the other hand, there are not in the organization two persons in closer intellectual agreement on the Negro problem than Mr. Villard and myself. It is in matters of personal relation that we disagree. Mr. Villard is not democratic. He is used to advising colored men and giving them orders and he simply cannot bring himself to work with one as an equal.

This same subtle difficulty (which is one of the curious and almost unconscious developments of the race problem) has come in the Association in other ways. In most organizations of this kind the problem has frankly been given up as insoluble and usually an entire force of one race is hired. It has been my dream to make this organization an exception and I have tried desperately and have failed. Every conceivable effort, conscious, half-conscious, unconscious, has been made in the last three and a half years to force me into a position of subordination to some other official. I have resisted not out of a stubborn desire to dominate, as some think, but because I knew that there was no argument on experience or efficiency that ought in reason to force me to be the secretary's assistant or the chairman's secretary. I have therefore, at no little cost in pride, discomfort and chagrin insisted and kept insisting (usually quietly—once in unfortunate anger): "I am an executive officer of this Association, coordinate in power with other officers and not their subordinates; and I am responsible with them to the Board of Directors." This struggle has been all the more unpleasant because my associates have all the time been working so wholeheartedly and effectively for the very things which lie so near my heart. It is an enormously complicated situation and the temptation to submit to the seemingly inevitable is,

---

annually by the NAACP after 1915 to an outstanding Black man or woman. Du Bois dedicated his *Dusk of Dawn* to "Joel Spingarn: Scholar and Knight." From 1919 to 1932, he was connected with the Harcourt, Brace publishing company, which published Du Bois's *Darkwater* (1920), his *Black Reconstruction* (1935), and the *Dusk* volume (1940). It is possible, however, that Du Bois in this instance meant Joel's younger brother, Arthur B. Spingarn, a distinguished attorney who handled much of the law work of the NAACP for several years. See B. Joyce Ross, *J. E. Spingarn and the Rise of the NAACP* (New York: Atheneum Publishers, 1972).

Charles H. Studin was the law partner of Arthur Spingarn and often assisted the NAACP in its early years.

I confess, strong. And yet, that very submission stands in my mind as so fundamental a part of the absolutely essential problem of the Negro in the modern world that I cannot bring myself to acquiese. If in this Association white and black folk cannot work together as equals; if this Association is unable to treat its black officials with the same lease of power as white, can we fight a successful battle against race prejudice in the world?

I have watched recent tendencies in the board with something like dismay. We have at last fully developed the art of compromise and retreat. Just the moment a question of principle evolves we can now depend on strong and well argued speeches councilling the "easier way." We have the persons who are eager for the "popularity" of our cause and who are looking for large sums of money from reactionary sources. To these The Crisis is a source of acute unrest and they want it changed into a periodical which will say nothing that any person, or at least many persons can disagree with. They propose, therefore, to stifle all initiative of thought or action on my part and yet to use my name as editor. This, of course, cannot be. If my position is not to be a position of real dignity and power then a fifty dollar clerk could do the work as well as I and I could not only save my self-respect but keep faith with ten million people who do not expect always to agree with me, but do expect always to hear the truth as I conceive it.

I am writing you quite frankly, Miss Ovington, because you are one of the few persons whom I call Friend. I wish you to read this entire letter to the caucus, unless, of course, you deem it quite unnecessary.

I am,

> Very sincerely yours,
> W. E. B. Du Bois

Brooklyn, N. Y., April 11, 1914.

My dear Dr Du Bois,

Your letter comes on the morning of my birthday and makes me feel like voicing the praise in Ecclesiastes; Better than the dead or living "is he which hath not yet been": which surely is much finer than saying, "I wish I had never been born."

I want to write you before Monday—and I am more sorry than I can express that you will not be at the meeting, as you are the one person needed there above all others—what I am likely to say at the meeting. I had hoped to have a talk with you last week, for I always like to talk over anything I have in my mind first with you; but as we didn't have the talk I will try to write it.

I have thought for some time that there was something the matter with the Crisis from the viewpoint of its white readers. It seemed to me monotonous, and I proposed to you some rather foolish little things that might be introduced that would have made little difference. But while I was away, and in a country where two races of such different traditions lived together,[1] I thought the Crisis matter out—it seemed to me somewhat more clearly. This is my conclusion: *The magazine is the organ of two races, but its psychology is the psychology of the colored race.*

Now perhaps you will get at my point more clearly if you think of the magazine as edited solely by a white man, and a man who has stood always for the things for which our Association has stood since it printed its first platform. Don't you think that such a man might sometimes offend his colored readers, and be wholly unconscious of it? He might, for instance, patronize a little, he might dictate too much, he might rub his readers the wrong way, and yet he would feel that he was only speaking the truth, and that if he said anything else he would be compromising with his conscience. He would be absolutely honorable and yet he would offend.

Now no colored man who stood squarely and unswervingly on our platform can come to the Crisis and edit it and not sometimes make what I should call psychological failures with our white readers. I believe you have made comparatively few, and I think we have usually passed them by as comparatively unimportant; but as our organization grows in power and authority, it must have increasingly careful oversight of its publications and of its speakers. And just as Mr Villard, let us say, in his writing sometimes offends the colored people by giving them orders; so sometimes you offend the white people by calling them hogs, by saying that they are reactionary heathen, by giving them the feeling that they are insulting you, when they have no insult in their heart.

I have thought about this a great deal; and wondered what made you write as you sometimes did, and I came to the conclusion that it was because you had before you a colored audience. Now no one can be more persuasive than you before a white audience, or can write more persuasively to white people. But when you edit the Crisis that white audience is sometimes forgotten and its feelings are badly hurt, or feelings of resentment are aroused. And the white audience to which I allude is the white audience which stands just as squarely on our platform as your colored audience does—sometimes, I think, more squarely.

Now what is the wisest thing for us to do?

Don't we need first to face the issue squarely? Is this a work for colored and white people to do together, or is it a work of revolution for the colored people only? Should we preach race consciousness just as the socialist preaches class consciousness, and should we teach the black man to regard every white man as his enemy except he who repudiates his race? This is a question for each one to answer personally, but unquestionably the Association, through its very organization, has answered it negatively. And if our work, then, is for white and colored, you must work out how we are to get common representation on the Crisis. After reading your letter I think it is something for you to tackle. You

1. France.

think the resolutions we are to discuss Monday are unfair to you, and perhaps they are. I am sure they were not meant to be, but no one of us will be hung for his diplomacy. But we are all willing to listen to one another, and we all want you, *genuinely* want you, and would like to have this thing reasoned out together. Perhaps we can get light from examining into the management of other publications of radical organizations.

As to our being reactionary—I don't think we are nearly as reactionary as when we started. Why, think, we had to fight to keep B. T. W. off the committee in those days! We may have grown to believe that as an organization we must say the right word at the right time, that we cannot each one be a voice in the wilderness crying out what ever comes into our head without regard to what is happening. Anarchism is jolly, and we are all anarchists at heart, but when we get into an organization, whether it is a State or an N.A.A.C.P., we have to consider each the other's work. But it's nonsense for me to talk this to you, who wholly agree to it. Probably you have disagreed with some of the Board on special issues, matters of which I know nothing. But the *work* of the organization, which is what I can judge by, has been aggressive as it should be.

It's always been difficult for me to see why you didn't want a Crisis committee that should take much of the detail off your shoulders. I am angered whenever I think of it—that the one man of genius in our company should deliberately tie himself down to a mass of detail, and from a poet become a preacher—and that most awful type of preacher, an *editor*, laying down the law every month! I have just been with Reinhold von Warlich (the singer) in Paris. The first time I met him he told me that America had no artists, we were all preachers. We spoiled everything we did by preaching. This second meeting he made an exception—raving over the genius of the Negro. What ever he did was good, it was direct and simple. Whether he wrote a song, or painted a picture, or cracked a joke, he never was an amateur. He was an artist, he spoke out directly what was in him. Oh, you should have heard him! But I am reaching the end of my paper. When the typewriting is bad it is mine! Thank you for your word of friendship. No finer gift could come to me to-day. And it is just because we are friends that we can disagree sometimes and enjoy one another all the more for it.

Yours,
Mary W. Ovington.

Can you sup with me the 21st?

In August 1913, Robert C. Ogden died; his career has been noted above. Du Bois wrote of him, critically, but with some sympathy, in his "Men of the Month" department in the *Crisis* 7 (April 1914):274-75, under the title "A Well Wisher." This comment brought an illuminating exchange between a New Jersey reader and Du Bois.

Orange, New Jersey, April 9, 1914.

Dear Sir:

If your engagements permit, will you not kindly tell me in what respect Robert C. Ogden fell short with regard to the colored race, as the "Crisis" article intimates.

I did not know him personally, but somehow had an entirely different notion.

Yours very truly
C. G. Kidder

New York April 20, 1914.

My dear Sir:

As I said in my notice of Mr. Ogden, it is difficult to write of him and not give a false impression.

He was a good man and did good. At the same time he was a man without broad vision and without a deep knowledge of human nature. When therefore, he was almost accidentally set to the unravelling of one of the most difficult of human problems it is small wonder that he fell short, and yet he made the same mistake that most Americans make. They have made up their minds that it is impossible for colored people to be human and free in the same sense as the citizens of modern white countries. If this were simply a belief no great harm would be done, but immediately such people start out to make their belief come true. They seek to educate colored children as inferiors, they lay out inferior careers for colored men, they open up limited opportunity for colored youth and when colored folk chafe under these limitations they regard them as fighting against fate. This, in my opinion, was Mr. Ogden's essential attitude.

I knew him personally and have been treated with great kindness by him, but I have learned that he was much put out and intensely dissatisfied by my general attitude of insistence of equality of opportunity for American Negroes.

As a result of his general attitude the southern point of view on the Negro problem has become widely popular in the North and persons can at once regard themselves as friends of the Negro and yet defend laws which degrade Negro women, defend the "Jim-Crow" car laws, defend disfranchisement and caste.

I regard all this as exceedingly unfortunate and I regard Mr. Ogden as in part to blame for it.

Very sincerely yours,
W. E. B. Du Bois

Du Bois's relationship with Ernest H. Gruening—and, to an even greater degree, with his sister Martha—was long and cordial. Gruening, who was to be editor of the *Nation* and United States senator from Alaska, wrote this letter early in his career, when he was the assistant editor of the *Boston Herald*.

[Boston] April 28, 1914

Dear Dr. Du Bois:—

Will you accept my hearty congratulations on your answer to the Rev. Charles Fletcher Dole.[1] It is bully and right to the point. Much as I esteem the Crisis I think it quite outdid itself on this occasion. Keep it up.

Sincerely yours,
Ernest H. Gruening

Jacques Loeb (1859–1924) came to the United States from Germany in 1891 and soon established himself as one of the leading physiologists in the world. He taught at Bryn Mawr and at the universities of Chicago and California and, from 1910 to his death, was connected with the Rockefeller Institute for Medical Research in New York City. His paper decrying mythologies about "racial inferiorities" was read at the 1914 annual meeting of the NAACP. A letter in this connection is given here.

New York, May 14, 1914.

My dear Dr. Du Bois:—

I am somewhat puzzled in regard to a short statement I sent to Mr. Villard to be read at the meeting in Baltimore. I had intended to go to Baltimore, up to the last minute, providing that an attack of lumbago from which I had been suffering would permit me to do so. But this was not the case. I had prepared to write a long address but found that I was not sufficiently familiar with the negro question in this country to speak with any authority, and for that reason in the last minute tore up the address and wrote instead a short article containing the main results concerning heredity and the so-called racial inferiority. I left this statement in the evening at the house of Mr. Villard and took it for granted that the paper would be read at the meeting, and would under the circumstances at least fill to some extent the gap left by my necessary absence.

I have not heard a word either from Mr. Villard or from any body else whether he received my paper or whether it was considered unsatisfactory which I might well understand, and I only write to you to avoid any possible further misunderstandings. I do not need to assure you of my deep interest in the

---

1. The Reverend Mr. Dole had written to Du Bois, in a letter published in the May 1914 *Crisis* (8:23–24), under the title "A Question of Policy," decrying the agitational quality of his writing in the *Crisis*. In a reply entitled "The Philosophy of Mr. Dole" (pp. 24–26), Du Bois defended the work of radicals and agitators in biblical terms: "They spew out the lukewarm fence straddlers out of their mouths ... they cry aloud and spare not ... and they make this world so damned uncomfortable with its nasty burden of evil that it tries to get good and does get better." As already noted, this position and language provoked not only some readers of the *Crisis* but also certain members of the NAACP board.

problem and my best intentions to help your cause, but under the circumstances it was impossible for me to come. I had taken it for granted that Mr. Villard would explain the matter, otherwise I should have written at once, but since I have not heard from Mr. Villard I have decided not to wait any longer and to write to you.[1]

I remain, with kindest regards,

Yours very sincerely,
Jacques Loeb

An exchange between Miss Pauline Schneider and Du Bois contains much of intrinsic interest.

St. Louis, May 23, 1914

Dear Prof. Du Bois,

I have just read Souls of Black Folks and across the color line I extend to you a hand of sympathy and profound appreciation.

It must be that hundreds of white people have been moved by this book even as I am, and feel the same heavy, despairing pain over our individual inability to contribute even a mite toward the removal of ignorance, injustice and folly. It would ease my impotent pain to know that in my race I am not suffering alone. Assure me if you can. And tell me whether the outlook has not brightened since the book was written.

By what amounts almost to divination, Negroes must learn to recognize their friends in the white race, for friends they must have, though my limited experience has hardly revealed any to me—friends of the Negro's cause. Assuming that such friends exist, they cannot, like you, give open voice to their beliefs. Yet much were gained by a tacit recognition of interest and good will.

What more have you written? What has Kelley Miller published? Kindly let me know where "The Present Crisis" is published.

Pardon the seeming intrusion. Know that not all of the anguish and the despair is on your side of the color line.

Sincerely yours,
(Miss) Pauline Schneider.

New York, June 2, 1914.

Mr dear Miss Schneider:

I appreciate your letter of May twenty-third.

Since the publication of "The Souls of Black Folk," the National Association

---

1. Loeb's article "Heredity and Racial Inferiority" appeared in the *Crisis* in June 1914 (8:83–84); his "Science and Race" was published in the December 1914 issue (9:92–93).

for the Advancement of Colored People has been formed and I regard this as a great step forward. There are also signs in the South of persons like you who will not consent to keep silent longer. At the same time, there is no doubt but that race prejudice against Negroes has steadily increased in the last twenty years and is increasing. The internal development of the colored people has been extraordinary, thus we have two movements which have in them elements of future danger.

I am sending you herewith some sample copies of The Crisis, of which I am editor. The other works which I have written and which you might be interested in are "John Brown," published by Jacobs, Philadelphia, and a novel, "The Quest of the Silver Fleece," published by McClurg.

Kelly Miller has published two books of essays by the Neale Co., of New York; one "Race Adjustment," and the other, "Out of the House of Bondage."

Again thanking you for your interest and kind words, I beg to remain,
Very sincerely yours,
W. E. B. Du Bois

Benjamin R. Tillman (1847–1918) was governor of South Carolina from 1890 to 1894; in the latter year, he was elected to the United States Senate, where he served until his death. His background was Populist and then, devoured by racism, Democratic; in this respect he was much like Thomas Watson of Georgia. Upon Tillman's death, Du Bois wrote a searching analysis in the *Crisis* 16 (August 1918):165, which closes: "Some day a greater than Tillman, Blease and Vardaman will rise in the South to lead the white laborers and small farmers, and he will greet the Negro as a friend and helper and build with him and not on him."

This letter from Tillman to Du Bois was written in response to an inquiry from Du Bois regarding Tillman's views on Reconstruction in South Carolina; it was written on the stationery of the Committee on Naval Affairs, of which Tillman was then chairman.

[Washington], July 23, 1914.
The Editor,
The Crisis
Dear Sir:

I have your letter of July 18th, and am sending under separate cover a copy of the "ringed, streaked and striped legislature of 1868." It is a striking example of what happens when a great mass of ignorant voters are controlled by a handful of scoundrels. If you reproduce the photograph in your magazine, I would like

[198] Correspondence 1905–1920

for you to send me a copy of the issue.[1] You are welcome to the picture without charge.

> Yours very sincerely,
> B. R. Tillman

P.S. The negroes were dupes of course and should never have received the ballot at all, but the fanatical abolitionists under the leadership of Thad Stevens and Chas. Sumner concocted the whole program to wreak vengeance on the Southern white people.

Several letters were exchanged between Upton Sinclair and Du Bois in the latter part of 1914. It is of some interest that Sinclair did not read *Souls of Black Folk* until that year. Though Du Bois formally resigned from the Socialist party in 1912 when he chose to support Wilson, he considered himself a socialist and was so considered by those who knew him; hence one observes the "Comrade" and the "Fraternally" in Sinclair's letters.

In Sinclair's *Cry For Justice; An Anthology of the Literature of Protest*, with an introduction by Jack London (New York and Pasadena: Sinclair, 1915), there are included on page 512 twenty lines from *Souls of Black Folk* and on page 470 the six lines from "Oh, Freedom" that Du Bois recommended.

> Croton-on-Hudson, N.Y.
> August 8, 1914

Dear Comrade:

Permit me to ask your attention to the enclosed statement.[2] Anything you can do in the way of advising me will be greatly appreciated.

> Fraternally,
> U. Sinclair

> Croton-on-Hudson, N.Y.
> Sept. 8, 1914

Dr. W. E. Burghardt Du Bois
Dear Comrade:

Clement Wood tells me that he wrote you about a poem of yours for my an-

---

1. The photograph pictured the members of the radical Reconstruction legislature of South Carolina, Black and white. In the case of South Carolina, an actual majority were Black. The photo is reproduced in *A Pictorial History of the Negro in America*, eds. Langston Hughes and Milton Meltzer, 3rd. ed. rev. with participation of C. Eric Lincoln (New York: Crown Publishers: 1968), p. 204. There is a pencilled note on Tillman's letter—not in Du Bois's hand—reading, "Has this picture been rec'd?" Apparently it was not, and was therefore not reproduced in the *Crisis*.

2. The statement was a printed sheet headed "A Collection of the Literature of Socialism," dated July 1914, and signed by Sinclair. It explained that Sinclair's anthology hoped to reflect "the word Socialism . . . *in the broadest possible sense* . . . the spirit of social protest, the hunger for economic righteousness. . . ."

thology.[3] I hope you will send a copy of it to him or me. I enclose announcement of the anthology, in which you may be interested.

I have just read the "Souls of Black Folk" for the first time, with great interest and admiration. I have taken a couple of passages from it. I wish you would help me by sending me suggestions about your own work other than this.

My purpose in writing this, however, is to ask if you can be of assistance to me in getting together a few passages from genuine negro slave songs, which embody protest against social injustice. I am trying to get specimens from all ancient and primitive writings. I do not mean necessarily things that are definitely socialistic, but things that have an economic implication.

                        Fraternally,
                        U. Sinclair

                    Croton-on-Hudson, N.Y., Oct. 2, 1914

Dear Comrade Du Bois:

I forgot to mention to you the other night a matter about which I wrote you, but I am not sure if you got the letter, as you did not speak of it. I want to get for my anthology one or two genuine slave songs, which contain the note of protest against social injustice. I am sure that you are the man to help me to do this. Or if you are too busy, will you give me the name of some one who can spare the time.

                        Fraternally,
                        U. Sinclair

                      New York, October 19, 1914.

My dear Mr. Sinclair:

I hope you will pardon my long delay in answering your request.

The slave song that best expresses the revolt of the Negro slave is "Oh! Freedom," the words being:

> "Oh! Freedom, Oh! Freedom,
> Oh! Freedom, Over me,
> And before I'll be a slave,
> I'll be buried in my grave,
> And go home to my God
> And be free."

Another is "Fighting On" with these words:

> "Fighting on, hallelujah,
> We're almost down to the shore,
> Fighting on, fighting on,
> We're almost down to the shore."

---

3. Clement Wood (1888–1950), born in Alabama, was a well-known poet, novelist, and critic; perhaps his outstanding work is the collection of his poems, *The Glory Road*, published in 1936. The letter mentioned does not seem to have survived.

A third is "We'll Die in the Field."

>"Oh what do you say seekers,
>Oh what do you say seekers,
>Oh what do you say seekers
>About the gospel war?
>And I will die in the field
>I will die in the field,
>Will die in the field,
>I'm on my journey home."

Another:

>"Oh stand the storm,
>It won't be long,
>We'll anchor bye and bye,
>My ship is on the ocean,
>We'll anchor bye and bye."

>Very sincerely yours,
>W. E. B. Du Bois

There is a prolonged and fascinating correspondence in 1914 between Du Bois and the newly elected chairman of the NAACP board, Joel E. Spingarn. It throws light upon the personalities of both men and upon the continuing problems within the NAACP. It also illuminates the particular difficulties of a man of genius— a Black man in the United States—who knows the grandeur of his task and the capacities within him, and wishes from his fellow-workers a free hand, if not aid, in using those capacities to realize his goal. The letters here published begin in the middle of this correspondence, but are quite able to stand alone.

Amenia, N.Y., October 24, 1914

Dear Dr. Du Bois:

I am glad that you have written this letter. I am glad to know your feelings; I am glad to have an opportunity of frankly telling you mine. I shall be so frank that I may wound your feelings deeply, but at this critical juncture I cannot waive a friend's right to the frankest criticism.

You have mistaken the meaning of the "outward appearance" which you interpret as mistrust of your sincerity. I have never doubted your absolute honesty; or rather, never except once, and then, finding myself mistaken, I apologized to you; and that, I hope, closed the incident for both of us, as it certainly closed the doubt for me. I do think, however, that, like Roosevelt and other men I know and admire, you have an extraordinary unwillingness to acknowledge that you have made a mistake, even in trifles, and if accused of one, your mind will find or even invent reasons and quibbles of any kind to prove that you were never mistaken. The rent of the Crisis office is a case in point. When I said that the Crisis had incurred an additional obligation of over $50 a month by moving from Vesey Street to Fifth Avenue, you wrote me, not that the additional expense was absolutely needed, as perhaps it was, but that there was virtually no additional expense, that the difference was, as I think you put it, "an illusion." But it turns out to be a fact and not an illusion that it costs about $700 a year more to run the new offices than the old ones, and you now merely insist that the expense is justified. I do not doubt that the additional room and convenience may have seemed very desirable; but the question now before us is whether you were right in assuming the additional expense before the Crisis was wholly self-supporting, and whether the present emergency will not require us to sacrifice the room and the convenience, however desirable both may seem to be.

This, however, is only a trifle. It would take a longer letter than this (and I am afraid this is to be a long one) to explain the "outward appearance" which you mistake for distrust. Surrounding you always, I may say frankly, I have found an atmosphere of antagonism. It is not merely Mr. Villard and Miss Nerney and the Board generally; it is in the whole colored world, and even some of your most intimate friends feel toward you a mingled affection and resentment. I realized from the outset that this was in part due to a devotion to principle, and the sacrifice that such devotion must always entail. I at least, I think you will understand, could not doubt that such a sacrifice might be called for, indeed wooed, by devotion to truth. I realized too (it was your boast) that you could never accept even the appearance of "inferiority" or "subserviency" without treason to the race ideals for which you fight, although in this matter it may be weakness rather than manliness to protest too much. On the other hand, I found on the part of others, even those who sympathized with your ideals as much as I did, a conviction that the ideals which they shared with you had nothing to do with the cause of their disagreement with your actions and your methods. These men have come to feel that you mistake obstinacy for strength of character or at least strength of conviction, although it is indeed a very poor substitute for the art of managing men. They have come to feel that you prefer to have your own way rather than accept another way, even when no sacrifice of principle is involved. They have come to feel that you are in fact ready to erect a personal difference into a question of principle, and to assume that wounding your own sensitive nerves is one and the same thing as compounding with injustice and error. They have come to feel that you refused the alternative of co-operation or subordination, the only alternatives when men are working together, and preferred the wreck of a cause to the losing of some preferred point; in a word, that you would not "play the game," at least with others. Perhaps you may have imagined that your victory in many cases of dispute was due to successful argument or strength of character, but these men yielded to you for the reason that parents yield to spoilt children in company, for fear of creating a scene: they were less willing than you to wreck our cause before the colored world.

I do not assume that all this is true, but my own experience at least in part confirms it. Because of the friendliness of our relations, and my constant championship of you, I have been thrust foward by your friends and enemies as intermediary and arbiter in their disputes with you. Whenever I have come to talk over such matters with you, and to effect some form of co-operation by which all of us could fight for the truth together, I found that I could not act toward you as I would toward other co-operators in a great cause. You had to be approached with care and diplomacy, and made to do things by wheedling and questioning, as children are induced to do them. If your obstinacy was aroused I could assume in advance that however just the cause you would antagonize it; however important the issue you would counsel opposition or delay. I might almost assume at the outset that nothing could be done for the most important or immediate cause, if it affected someone you personally dislike, until this personality was first eliminated or its presence disguised. The distrust then, as you will see, was not distrust of your character but distrust of your temperament, if distrust is indeed not too strong a word to use at all.

Now I shall not hide from you the fact that many people whose devotion to this cause is as deep as yours or mine feel that the time has come to put an end to this tragic trifling. They are at last willing, indeed anxious, to "create a scene." They think you are the chief if not the only source of the disorder and lack of unity in our organization. They think that the whole Association cannot work together effectively and without friction unless you are eliminated. I do not agree with them. It is not merely because of our friendship (though I regard that as very real), but because I feel that you are needed in this work as much as any man in the world; because I feel that all that has been urged against you affects your temperament and not your character or your talent; because I feel that you come to this cause with a high purpose and a noble mind. And yet I agree with your critics that we cannot go on unless your talents are subordinated to the general welfare of the whole organization, and the rift between the various departments of the Association is closed once and for all. There can be no Crisis and no non-Crisis; that way of dividing our work has failed; both must be one. You must co-operate with us, as we are all anxious to co-operate with you; the time has come when we must "hang together or be hanged together." If you are not willing to espouse our cause whole-heartedly as one with your own, I am afraid that the Association is doomed. And I may say also that there are people who would not regret its doom, now that they cannot completely control its destinies. I say nothing of your own career, in which I have a deeper interest than you perhaps realize, because I know that it would be unjust to you to present this problem on any but its highest and most impersonal plane.

If this letter gives you great offence, please restrain your resentment until we can talk over the whole matter face to face. I expect to move to town for the winter the first or second week in November.

Faithfully yours,
J. E. Spingarn.

New York City, October 28, 1914.

My dear Mr. Spingarn:

I thank you for your letter of October twenty-fourth. Some of the criticism, I think, is fair. Some I am sure is not. But the spirit of the letter is right and that, after all, is the chief thing. This letter is inexcusably long. I shall not blame you if you do not read it carefully.

I want to take up one or two points. The first is personal to yourself and you will, I am sure, pardon the frankness. You have a very disconcerting and puzzling way of changing your attitude and point of approach on a given matter and forgetting quite completely your previous stand. This is illustrated on the matter of rent. Your first approach to that matter was not: Do you not pay more at 70 Fifth Avenue than you did at 26 Vesey Street? Of course, the *Crisis* pays the difference between $49.75 and $108 a month. I never dreamed of denying that. I assumed, of course, that you knew this. What you did ask as a matter of fact was: (I quote from your letter of Sept. 28) "There is one item in the expense of running The *Crisis*, however, that you have apparently ignored, and that is the item of rent. I have always felt that The *Crisis* was rather extravagant in this matters." I immediately began to argue that as The *Crisis* is *now* no substantial saving can be made by renting a place like 26 Vesey Street. Of course, here lay my mistake, and it is a mistake I often make, of not emphasizing facts that are so clear to me that I wrongly assume they are clear to others. In this case I should have said: The *Crisis* occupied three-fourths or more of the space at 26 Vesey Street when we were there. Now we would have to have all the space and this because of additions of help and machinery that increase our income, and therefore, cannot be given up without loss. (e.g., the multigraph which saves us $25 to $50 a month in printing and requires space, light and electric motor; the larger safe; the book-keeper, whose whole time is needed by The *Crisis*; when we shared Mr. Turner he did not have enough time for us and less for the N.A.A.C.P., the imperative need of more storing space, etc.) I ought then to have said first in my argument as to the rent: we cannot save much because we would have to occupy the whole of a place the size of 26 Vesey Street. I do not think this evidence of quibbling but rather of your forgetting your original question and my failure to emphasize an important fact.

I do not doubt in the least but that my temperament is a difficult one to endure. In my peculiar education and experiences it would be miraculous if I came through normal and unwarped. At the same time you are quite mistaken to think me obstinate and acting from personal likes and dislikes. I do want a chance to do a big piece of work. I hate to see my plans spoiled in detail when I know that those who are spoiling them would be enthusiastic if they understood thoroughly my aim. Always in the past I have been hampered and stopped so many times because good friends not seeing the big ideal thought me petty and opinionated. This would have made me doubt my own conceptions had it not been that once or twice I've gotten a chance to work unhindered. At Atlanta I got a chance to carry on the sociological studies because they were so unimportant that nobody was interested. I had, therefore, a free hand and in the end everybody applauded the result. There was nothing petty or small about it.

So in the matter of The *Crisis:* I got a free hand to establish it because so many were certain that I would fail. What I ask now is not obstinate independence but a reasonable chance to finish the big thing which is now scarcely begun; and what I fear is that little criticisms and annoyances and interferences will spoil the big result simply because people lose faith in my ability and integrity. The *Crisis* has not begun its career. It can be one of the great journals of the world. It can be a center of enterprise and co-operation such as black folk have not themselves dreamed. But for heaven's sakes let me do the work. Do not hamper and bind and criticize in little matters. Of course, there are imperfections, mistakes, shortcomings. But the whole big plan which is developing slowly and surely is not imperfect and is not a mistake.

What I am working for with The *Crisis* is to make the N.A.A.C.P. *possible.* To-day it is *not* possible. We can piddle on, we can beat time, we can do a few small obvious things: but the great blow—the freeing of ten million—and of other millions whom they pull down—that means power and organization on a tremendous scale. The men who will fight in these ranks must be educated and The *Crisis* can train them: not simply in its words, but in its manner, its pictures, its conception of life, its subsidiary enterprises. With a circulation of a hundred thousand we shall have begun work. Then the real machinery of the N.A.A.C.P. can be perfected. Is this a plan of disorganization, of hindrance, of lack of cooperation?

"Tragic trifling" as a judgment of my work for the Association is perhaps the most astonishing of your opinions and the one which I most resent. There never has been an association with our objects or similar objects that has gone on with less friction than ours. Compared with the Anti-Slavery Society ours is a heaven of peace and concord. Moreover, to charge the "friction" to my account is certainly overstating the case. Take our main rows:

In the case of Villard's proposal to publish all Negro crime: the scheme was unwise as everybody said; my reception of it was indiscreet and I apologized. But back of the indiscretion was the piled up slights and unkindnesses of two weary years of heart-breaking work and a physical weariness that put my nerves on edge. This did not excuse but it explained the bitter rejoinder. But surely here is neither trifling nor obstinacy. The second quarrel over Mr. Dill was not at all my fault.[1] Had I been in office it would not have happened. As it was I

1. Augustus G. Dill became business manager of the *Crisis* in September 1913. He was born in 1881 in Portsmouth, Ohio, taught there, graduated from Atlanta University in 1906, and received a bachelor's degree at Harvard in 1908 and a master's at Atlanta in 1909. In 1910, he joined Atlanta's faculty and served thereafter, with Du Bois, as an editor of the Atlanta University Studies. After some years with the *Crisis,* personal difficulties and problems ended a promising career.

was in the library on *Crisis* work. When I came all was over and the question was the healing of the wounds. You suggested an apology by Mr. Dill. Perhaps you do not know that I wrote out such a suggested apology for Mr. Dill to transmit. He did not feel that he should apologize. What was I to do? Can this be charged against me? There have been numberless little disagreements between Miss Nerney and me over office regulations, N.A.A.C.P. notes in The *Crisis*, financial arrangements in subscriptions and loans. In all cases I have done my best to avoid friction, but Miss Nerney, while of excellent spirit and indefatigable energy, has a violent temper and is depressingly suspicious of motives. If I have come under her violent condemnation and suspicion, believe me, neither you, nor Mr. Villard nor Miss Ovington have escaped. It has been no easy matter to keep the peace especially when my unfortunate tendency is to withdraw confidence under fire while hers is to gossip endlessly. Yet I am convinced that in most points of difference between us you or any unprejudiced judge would have at least acknowledged the reasonableness of my stand. I have yielded to Miss Nerney in far more cases than I have insisted. In everything connected with the portion of the N.A.A.C.P. under her control I have yielded with scarcely a word. Slowly but surely I have been elbowed out of all real connection with the general work. I know nothing about it and I am consulted only in the last resort and then for small specific matters like names and addresses, etc. I have not complained of this and do not complain. These matters are in Miss Nerney's charge and her judgment must rule. But I have insisted strenuously that in my realm equal respect be given my judgment. You have no idea of the shape and circumstances in which the N.A.A.C.P. notes come to me. Certainly on matters of presenting facts with clearness and cogency I claim some ability and it is for this reason that I am editor of The *Crisis*. But Miss Nerney again and again seeks to override my judgment or to get you committed before you know all the facts. Take the political enquête.[2] It is in many ways the biggest thing we have done. In the presentation of such work I have had fourteen years of experience and the results have been commended all over the world. The results in this case were to be published in the paper I am editing; yet to this day I have not seen a single answer or been consulted as to its manner of presentation. At the very last available minute I am confronted with a settled manner of presentation which involves every possible difficulty. I acquiesce and rush it through, but the method was an unfair infringement of my prerogative and the presentation could have been done much more effectively. (Miss Nerney has just offered to send me the material for the next *Crisis*.) It is possible that I was wrong in the Survey matter but even that is a fair matter of difference of judgment. I was asked to write an article and was not asked for an official statement. I made a statement which only excessive niceness could say was different from

2. Inquiry. It is likely that Du Bois is here referring to an examination of congressional conduct on bills and proposals, published in the *Crisis* 8 (June 1914):77–79.

our official declaration and official acts. Certainly it was not intended to go beyond it. Miss Nerney and Mr. Villard discredited me behind my back and without my knowledge. Not knowing their action I published my statement with the remark that the Survey had refused it.[3] I am then accused of double-dealing and cannot answer without accusing my fellow officers in public which I would not do. I do, however, take a last fling at the Survey. I do not think this undeserved but it would have been fairer to say nothing or to accuse all parties and not one. But in that I fail to see obstinacy, trifling, and a very serious mistake on my part.

I may in many of these matters have been wrong, but my point is that I was not trifling and obstructing, and that where I exercised my judgment I did it within the realm where I do and ought to have the right to exercise judgment. Take this away and you can get from no man the full measure of manly accomplishment. Given the problems that I have faced do you honestly think that you would have made fewer mistakes? Given a different decision on most of the points alluded to would the Association have been better off?

But deeper than all this, the pathos of an organization like ours has not begun to strike you. I sometimes listen to you quite speechless, when you urge easily co-operation and understanding. You do not begin to realize where the *real* rift in the lute comes. No organization like ours ever succeeded in America; either it became a group of white philanthropists "helping" the Negro like the Anti-Slavery societies; or it became a group of colored folk freezing out their white co-workers by insolence and distrust. Everything tends to this break along the color line. You do not realize this because there is no shadow of the thing in your soul. But you are not "American." The same is true of Miss Ovington because she has lived the life of colored people intimately. She knows "the line" when she sees it. Miss Nerney is quite different. She hasn't an ounce of conscious prejudice. But her every step is unconsciously along the color line. If she consults you as an authority on some points on which you are learned, she accepts your judgment without question. If she consults me on a point where I have knowledge she feels quite at liberty to oppose her judgment to mine because none of my type ever spoke to her or her friends with authority. It is quite unconscious, quite innocent but none the less exasperating. Mr. Villard is the same way, only more so. Now what I have been trying to do is to try to work out a plan in this organization for colored and white people to work together on the same level of authority and co-operation. It is difficult. But if it fails the failure will not be due to my obstinacy or intractability—it will be due to the color line.

Our problem, therefore, is to front this fact squarely and set our teeth. First, it is plain that in America colored and white people cannot work in the same

3. For the incident relative to the *Survey*, see the earlier letter to Du Bois from its editor, Paul U. Kellogg, dated 17 December 1913.

office and at the same tasks except one is in authority over the other. Since there must be some center of authority that center must be white or colored. If the head is colored, the whites gradually leave. I have seen the experiment made a dozen times. If the head is white, the colored people gradually drop out of the inner circle of authority and initiative and become clerks—mere helpers of white philanthropists working "for your people." To avoid this dilemma I've tried to see if we could not have two branches of the same work, one with a white head and one with a colored; working in harmony and sympathy for one end. You say the experiment has failed. Has it? Is it necessary that it should fail? Have we not magnified little differences and chafed at a peculiar organization because few beside myself and Miss Ovington recognize the real underlying difficulty?

I am quite ready to acknowledge that the connecting and unifying power between the two branches has not been found. Perhaps it must eventually be one man rather than, as I had hoped, a committee.

At any rate, we must, first, recognize the inevitable American rift of the color line. You do not realize this. Perhaps I realize it over-much. But remember I've lived beside it nearly half a century. Secondly, I demand a full man's chance to complete a work without chains and petty hampering.

In the white world this has come to be the rule of effective work. Give the man of ability and integrity the right to make mistakes if the final result is big enough to justify his effort.

The colored man gets no such chance. He is seldom given authority or freedom; when he gets these things he gets them accidentally as in my case. Even when his ability is patent it is "inexpedient" to trust him. So far has this gone that even in the black world such authority is feared and given over to white folk. How can this be changed? By changing it. By trusting black men with power.

Finally, when the time comes that the Association or any considerable part of it think that I am in the way it will not take any "scene" to get rid of me.

                Very sincerely yours,
                W. E. B. Du Bois

With Yolande in England, entered at Bedales School, a steady correspondence developed between father and daughter. Its opening is the letter of late-October 1914; his suggestions, advice, and directions were to continue on into her adulthood and through her first and second marriages.

                New York, October 29, 1914

Dear Little Daughter:

I have waited for you to get well settled before writing. By this time I hope some of the strangeness has worn off and that my little girl is working hard and regularly.

Of course, everything is new and unusual. You miss the newness and smartness of America. Gradually, however, you are going to sense the beauty of the old world: its calm and eternity and you will grow to love it.

Above all remember, dear, that you have a great opportunity. You are in one of the world's best schools, in one of the world's greatest modern empires. Millions of boys and girls all over this world would give almost anything they possess to be where you are. You are there by no desert or merit of yours, but only by lucky chance.

Deserve it, then. Study, do your work. Be honest, frank and fearless and get some grasp of the real values of life. You will meet, of course, curious little annoyances. People will wonder at your dear brown and the sweet crinkley hair. But that simply is of no importance and will be soon forgotten. Remember that most folk laugh at anything unusual whether it is beautiful, fine or not.[1] You, however, must not laugh at yourself. You must know that brown is as pretty as white or prettier and crinkley hair as straight even though it is harder to comb. The main thing is the YOU beneath the clothes and skin—the ability to do, the will to conquer, the determination to understand and know this great, wonderful, curious world. Don't shrink from new experiences and custom. Take the cold bath bravely. Enter into the spirit of your big bed-room. Enjoy what is and not pine for what is not. Read some good, heavy, serious books just for discipline: Take yourself in hand and master yourself. Make yourself do unpleasant things, so as to gain the upper hand of your soul.

Above all remember: your father loves you and believes in you and expects you to be a wonderful woman.

I shall write each week and expect a weekly letter from you.

        Lovingly yours,
        Papa

Richard Henry Pratt (1840–1924) advanced from private to captain during the Civil War; in 1867, he re-entered the regular army as a second lieutenant of cavalry and was assigned to the Tenth Cavalry—the famous Black regiment. He was a rather unusual "Indian fighter," for he developed a genuine feeling for the "enemy" and became more interested in education than in genocide. For a time he served at Hampton, but in 1879, he requested from the government the use of the Carlisle Barracks in Pennsylvania for an experimental school; this request marked the beginning of the later-renowned Indian School at Carlisle, formally authorized by Congress in 1882. Pratt regularly battled entrenched bureaucracy and plain racism; he was finally removed from Carlisle in 1904 and retired as a brigadier-general, seeing no service during the world war. He died in the army

1. The manuscript is damaged at this point but it is believed that this is a correct reading.

hospital in San Francisco. His letter to Du Bois reflects something of the quality of this unusual general.

Washington, D.C., Nov. 3, 1914

Dear Sir:

Your November number was so intensely edifying I must drop you a line to say so. I especially and emphatically agree with your stand against segregation. It is repugnant to Christian principles, to American principles, to true manhood and breeds war.

I was delighted to see the honest manly faces of the three sergts, of the 10th Cavy of which I was an officer for thirty years.[1]

Sincerely yours,
R. H. Pratt, Brig-Gen. Ret.

Harriot Stanton Blatch was a daughter of Elizabeth Cady Stanton and very actively carried on her mother's struggle for women's rights. She was president for many years of the Women's Political Union, one of the forces effective in bringing about women's suffrage. Mrs. Blatch and Du Bois corresponded in April 1915.

New York City, April 5, 1915.

My dear Dr. Dubois:

In the autumn of this year falls the one hundreth anniversary of my mother's birth. We are arranging to hold a centennial celebration and in connection with that celebration are forming a centennial committee. I would very much like to have your name as one of the members of that committee.

You of course know how active my mother was in the anti-slavery movement and in the ways of the emancipation and enfranchisement of the negro race. Both because I feel strongly that the battle that you still have to wage for freedom is one and the same with the battle which women are waging for freedom, and also because I know that my mother would be pleased to have you on the centennial committee, I hope that you will feel that you can give your name.

We are planning to hold three meetings: one in Seneca Falls, in honor of the 1848 convention, where my mother presented a resolution demanding Votes for Women; a second meeting at Johnstown, my mother's birthplace, and the third here in New York to be held just before Election Day.

---

1. The pictures of Sergeants E. P. Frierson, W. W. Thompson, and William Payne are in the November 1914 *Crisis* 9:13–14. The issue also carries an essay by Du Bois, "World War and the Color Line" (pp. 28–30), showing the connection between the two and adding that, while all the combatant governments were guilty, the German government absolutely exulted in its racism.

It is an interesting coincidence, is it not, that the very year and month in which the women of New York will for the first time vote upon the question of conferring on women the ballot, is the very year and month in which, one hundred years ago, the woman was born who first at a public convention urged in a resolution the question of the enfranchisement of women?[1]

Very cordially yours,
Harriet Stanton Blatch

New York, April 6, 1915.

My dear Mrs. Blatch:

I should be very glad indeed to be on the Centennial Committee to celebrate the one hundreth anniversary of your mother's birth. I should regard it as an honor.

Very sincerely yours,
W. E. B. Du Bois

John Hope, president of Morehouse College in Atlanta, wrote Du Bois a very perceptive letter in mid-1915. His mention of Du Bois's "History of the Negro" refers to *The Negro*, published in 1915.

Atlanta, Ga., June 5, 1915

My Dear Du Bois:

I received a few days ago a complimentary copy of your "History of the Negro" and wish to thank you very much for remembering me with that tidy book. I have been very busy since Commencement squaring up the year's business and only last night, for the first time, I had the chance to read your book. The first chapter starts off well and I am sure that I will enjoy the book. I like your modest preface and hope that the Public will call on you for the larger history.[2]

A few days ago I invested in a copy of the Atlantic Monthly and read aloud to my wife and a guest of ours your article on the "Roots of the Present War."[3]

---

1. Mrs. Stanton was born 12 November 1815; she introduced and, with assistance from Frederick Douglass, succeeded in getting adopted the resolution demanding votes for women at the Seneca Falls Convention of July 1848. New York failed to grant women the suffrage in 1915, but the goal was accomplished in 1917. On the effective work of Mrs. Blatch, see Eleanor Flexner, *Century of Struggle: The Woman's Rights Movement in the United States* (Cambridge: Harvard University Press, 1959), pp. 249–53.

2. Du Bois's preface to *The Negro* closes with this sentence: "Possibly, if the Public will, a later and larger book may be more satisfactory on these points." In fact, such an enlarged work was published, again by Holt: *Black Folk: Then and Now: An Essay in the History and Sociology of the Negro Race* (1939, 401 pp.).

3. "The African Roots of War," *Atlantic Monthly* 115 (May 1915):707–14.

When I read aloud from your writings, I often think of Mrs. [Mary D.] Maclean's comment on you the first night she ever heard you speak.

I was talking a few weeks ago with a friend of ours about your power as a writer, and he said that you ought to be the best among us because you had the greatest advantages. I asked him to cite those advantages and he did so. I then showed him how, after all, they were not so much greater than the advantages of some other colored men, as for instance of themselves, to make you the most powerful writer we have. After I forced him good and hard he finally said this: "And then too, Du Bois has believed certain things and he has doggedly refused to recede from his position." I replied, "Is not that rather the reason why he is the most powerful writer than that he was at Cambridge, Berlin or Philadelphia?" You can stand this from me as I do not believe that I ever appear to you as spreading it on. You are able because you are honest. I hope nothing will ever come to you so tempting as to make you swerve in the least. Intellectual honesty and moral courage, not Massachusetts or Germany, account for your getting a hearing from foes as well as friends.

Sincerely yours,
John Hope.

Intervention by the government of the United States in Latin America has been notorious: financial, economic, diplomatic, and strategic considerations have been basic, and racism has been characteristic. An example is the case of the Black republic of Haiti. From 1905 to 1941, the United States maintained a customs receivership over Haiti; interventions by the United States Marines were frequent. Among these, that of July 1915 was especially glaring. With marines standing by, the Haitian Congress approved a Washington-selected president for Haiti, who signed a treaty in September 1915 under which United States citizens, appointed by the president of the United States, controlled the nation's finances, police, public works, etc. After dissolution of the Haitian Congress by United States military forces, a new constitution allowing foreign landownership was "approved." (This constitution was written by Wilson's assistant secretary of the Navy, Franklin Delano Roosevelt.)

It is within this context that one should consider the letter sent by Du Bois in August 1915 to President Wilson; there is no record of a reply, nor, as the editor has been informed by Professor Arthur S. Link, of its receipt by Wilson.

New York City, August 3rd, 1915.
To the President of the United States
Sir:

I am so deeply disturbed over the situation in Hayti and the action of the United States that I venture to address you.

It seems to me that the United States in this case, even more than in the case of Mexico, owes it to herself and humanity to make her position absolutely clear. Hayti is not all bad. She has contributed something to human uplift and if she has a chance she can do more. She is almost the sole modern representative of a great race of men among the nations. It is not only our privilege as a nation to rescue her from her worst self, but this would be in a sense a solemn act of reparation on our part for the great wrongs inflicted by this land on the Negro race.

We cannot, however, help most effectively unless we have the cordial support of the Haytian people, nor unless ten million American citizens of Negro descent are made to feel that we have no designs on the political independence of the island and no desire to exploit it ruthlessly for the sake of selfish business interests here.

To make, therefore, our attitude perfectly clear to Hayti, the world and our own citizens, I beg you to consider the appointment of a Haytian Commission with the following objects:

1. To assure the people of Hayti that the United States does not wish to infringe in any way upon their integrity as a nation.

2. To co-operate with a Commission of Haytians in the discussion of plans for the establishment of permanent peace and order, and for hastening the industrial development of the island.

3. To establish closer and more cordial relation and understanding between the United States and Hayti.

The proposed Commission could have proper weight and influence only if composed of men of high standing. It should have among its members representatives of the white North and the white South, citizens of Negro descent and representatives of business interests. Possibly South America might also co-operate.

I believe, Sir, that a frank, high-minded move like this following upon a policy of honesty in Cuba and patience in Mexico would have incalculable effect in establishing the moral hegemony of the United States in the Western hemisphere.[1]

Especially would it be effective in this case because we are dealing with Negroes. The United States has throughout the world a reputation for studied unfairness toward black folk. The political party whose nominee you are is historically the party of Negro slavery. Is this not a peculiarly opportune occa-

---

1. There were repeated United States interventions in Cuba after the first one of 1898 to 1902. One occurred from 1906–9, and early in Wilson's second administration, another was threatened; it finally materialized in 1917 and lasted until 1923. In April 1914, United States troops invaded Mexico, the fleet bombarded Vera Cruz, and, in July, Mexico's president was forced to flee to Jamaica. From March 1916 to February 1917, United States troops under Pershing made war in Mexico, penetrating as much as four hundred miles south of the border, all in the name of "punishing" Villa.

sion to attack both these assumptions by doing, in the words of your letter of October sixteenth, 1912, to Bishop Alexander Walters, "not mere grudging justice, but justice executed with liberality and cordial good feeling" [2] to the only independent Negro government in the World?

I am, Sir,

Most respectfully yours,
W. E. B. Du Bois

An author never knows who will read his books—or what they will mean to those who do read them. A letter to Du Bois from Miner Chipman, who conducted a "Problems of [Business] Management" enterprise in Cambridge, Massachusetts, is illustrative. This letter was written from a New York office; there is no record of a reply from Du Bois, though perhaps he did telephone and dine with Mr. Chipman, as the postscript suggested.

Woodbridge N. Ferris, mentioned in the letter, was governor of Michigan from 1913 through 1916, and United States senator from 1922 until his death. As an educator, Ferris was the founder, in 1884, of the Ferris Institute in Big Rapids, Michigan, today Ferris State College, with an enrollment of some nine thousand students.

New York, December 14, 1915.

Dear Mr. DuBois:

In 1903, Woodbridge N. Ferris, now Governor of Michigan, read to his school at Big Rapids, "The Meaning of Progress" from the Souls of Blackfolk. During these dozen years there has been ringing in my ears "How shall we measure progress there where the dark faced Josie lies?" I have had a great desire to meet the man who wrote that masterpiece, and the poem "The Passing of the First Born." Gods how I love those pieces.

I note you are to attend a dinner at The West End Hotel next Saturday evening. I hope to be there. I am very desirous of meeting you.

Your "Meaning of Progress" has a great lesson in it for we efficiency men. It seems to me that you faced life as it is squarely, and I would change the question you ask as follows: "How shall we measure efficiency, there where the dark faced Josie lies?" And how many Josie's there are in this world of ours, how many Hickman's with a hump on their shoulders, how many Doc Burkes. I have always kept The Souls of Black Folk on my library shelf together with all my other books on "Scientific Management." It belongs there. If every em-

2. The letter from candidate Wilson to Bishop Walters is published in its entirety in Alexander Walters, *My Life and Work* (New York: Fleming H. Revell & Co., 1917), p. 126.

[214] Correspondence 1905–1920

ployer of labor could read that book, and read it right, we would be well on our way toward a real solution of the problem of Human efficiency.

Yours very truly,
Miner Chipman

P. S. If you find it convenient, I would like to have you lunch with me some day this week. Telephone Murray Hill 8860.

Du Bois's effort to capitalize the spelling of Negro covered many years. There is a reflection of this effort in a letter from the young editor of the recently established *New Republic*.

New York City, January 17, 1916.

Dear Dr. Du Bois:

Following our conversation the other night I took up the matter at an editorial meeting, and we all agreed that your point was entirely well taken, and it is now a rule in our office that Negro should be spelled with a capital N. Personally I am sorry that the matter ever had to be discussed because your position is so obviously correct.

With best wishes, I am,

Sincerely yours,
Walter Lippmann

Marcus Garvey, who was born in 1887 in Jamaica and died in 1940 in London, first visited the United States late in March 1916; a year earlier he had been in correspondence with Booker T. Washington, who urged him to come to the United States. When Garvey did arrive, Washington was dead.

One of Garvey's first efforts in the United States was to hold a meeting, with a lecture by himself and musical entertainment, at Saint Mark's Hall at West 138th Street in Harlem. The lecture was on Jamaica and the meeting's purpose, according to the printed announcement, was "helping the Universal Negro Improvement Association of Jamaica to establish industrial farms."

On 25 April 1916, Garvey visited the offices of Du Bois's *Crisis;* Du Bois was out of town, so Garvey wrote a note.

New York City,[1] April 25, 1916.

Dear Dr. DuBois—

I called in order to have asked you if you could be so good as to take the "chair" at my first public lecture to be delivered at the St. Mark's Hall, 57 W.

1. This was the United States headquarters of the UNIA of Jamaica.

138th St—City on Tuesday evening 9th May at 8 o'clock. My subject will be "Jamaica"—a general talk on the phases of Negro life. I also beg to hand you tickets for same and to submit to you a circular in general circulation among prospective patrons.

I shall be pleased to hear from you immediately. Trusting you will be able to help by taking the chair

With [two words illegible]

Yours
Marcus Garvey

The reply came from Du Bois's office.

April 29, 1916

Mr. dear Mr. Garvey:

Doctor Du Bois begs me to thank you for your note of April twenty-fifth and express his regret at not being able to be on hand on account of his being out of town.

Very sincerely yours,
[signature illegible]

Paul H. Hanus (1855–1941) was one of the six faculty members who comprised Harvard University's Division of Education in 1916.* In the spring of that year, he wrote Du Bois; particular interest attaches to the characteristically frank reply.

Cambridge, Mass., May 15, 1916.

My dear Mr. Dubois:

I have been asked by the General Education Board to make a study of Hampton Institute. In preparation for that work I am trying to get all the information I can about the education of negroes, and first of all I would like to clarify my own mind on the aims of education for negroes, and particularly on the aims of such a school as Hampton Institute. I should greatly value a statement on these points from you—a statement as detailed as time and inclination will permit. I shall be grateful for whatever you find it possible to send me.

Very truly yours,
Paul H. Hanus

* At this time, Professor Hanus was president of the American Association for the Advancement of Science; he was a prolific author in educational theory and administration.

New York, June 19, 1916.

My dear Professor Hanus:

I regret the delay in answering your letter of May 15. I tried to lay it aside until I could answer more at length than I felt able to at first, but I think I had better say what I had in mind without further delay.

I am sending herewith two studies of mine on the Negro Common School and the College Bred Negro. These may show my own point of view in general.

As to Hampton Institute I have very strong feelings, and at the same time I have hesitated to express these feelings because it is a great institution with powerful friends and because I am convinced that it is doing more good than harm. At the same time I think that the harm it is doing is very great.

The chief difficulty with Hampton is that its ideals are low. It is, as it seems to me, deliberately educating a servile class for a servile place. It is substituting the worship of philanthropists like Samuel Armstrong (excellent man though he was) for worship of Manhood. It is continually trying to clip the wings of persons who of all folk in the world are not in need of clipped wings. The result is that menial servants [remainder illegible]. At the same time unless the average age of man is going to be seven hundred years instead of seventy years every sensible educator knows that there are serious limits to this method of education, and that book instruction must occupy a large part of all education.

At Hampton the waste of time incurred by the various laboratory methods is great and serious, and it cannot be adequately checked up because Hampton is held to no standards by higher educational institutions and is not compelled to show the real efficiency of its work by the requirements of these institutions. If she was educating white boys and girls parents would quickly bring her to task [and] make her prove the efficiency of her methods. But since she is educating Negroes everybody is willing that she should experiment as long and as freely as she pleases.

The fact of the matter is, that if the Negro race survives in America and in modern civilization it will be because it assimilates that civilization and develops leaders of large intelligent calibre.

The people back of Hampton do not propose that any such thing take place. Consciously or unconsciously they propose to develop the Negro race as a caste of efficient workers, do not expect them to be co-workers in a modern cultured state. It is that underlying falsehood and heresy, the refusing to recognize Negroes as men, which is the real basic criticism of Hampton.

I have written to you frankly and plainly in answer to your question. I would not wish unnecessarily to have my words used so as to hurt the feelings of many excellent persons connected with Hampton. At the same time I do not hold you to keeping this letter private and you are quite at liberty in such ways as you think best to use it.

Very sincerely yours,
W. E. B. Du Bois

In 1916, the board members of the NAACP—especially Villard and Du Bois—actively sought to commit both major political parties to a positive stand on the question of the rights of the Negro people. A joint letter signed by Villard, Du Bois, Joel E. Spingarn, and Archibald H. Grimké went off in the fall to Charles Evans Hughes, the Republican presidential candidate; beyond a formal acknowledgement, Hughes made no reply. At approximately the same time, Du Bois himself, in the name of the NAACP, sent to Wilson a long letter here published in full.* Wilson's directions to his secretary, Joseph Tumulty, about a reply, and Tumulty's actual letter to Du Bois are given below. Du Bois showed Villard Tumulty's letter, which drew from Villard the response also published here.

It may be added that, just before election day, Du Bois let it be known that he favored Hughes over Wilson; Villard's *New York Evening Post*, on the other hand, announced at the same point that it favored Wilson.

New York, October 10, 1916.

To the President of the United States
Sir:

As an organization representing the Negro race and thousands of their friends we are deeply interested in the presidential election.

During the last campaign, believing firmly that the Republican Party and its leaders had systematically betrayed the interests of colored people, many of our members did what they could to turn the colored vote toward you. We received from you a promise of justice and sincere endeavor to forward their interests. We need scarcely to say that you have grievously disappointed us.

We find ourselves again facing a presidential campaign with but indifferent choice. We have waited for some time to gather from your writings and speeches something of your present attitude toward the colored people. We have thought that perhaps you had some statement or explanation which would account for the dismissal of colored public officials, segregation in the civil service, and other things which have taken place during your administration. You must surely realize that if Negroes were Americans—if they had a reasonable degree of rights and privileges, they need ask for no especial statement from a candidate for the high office of President; but being as they are, members of a segregated class and struggling against tremendous prejudices, disabilities and odds, we must for their own salvation and the salvation of our country ask for more than such treatment as is today fair for other races. We must continually demand such positive action as will do away with their disabilities. Lynching is a national evil of which Negroes are the chief victims. It is perhaps the greatest disgrace

---

* The original of this letter and of Wilson's statement to Tumulty are in the Woodrow Wilson Papers in the Library of Congress. Copies were kindly sent to me by Professor Arthur S. Link of Princeton University, the editor of the Wilson Papers; his aid is deeply appreciated.

from which this country suffers, and yet we find you and other men of influence silent in the matter. A republic must be based upon universal suffrage or it is not a republic; and yet, while you seem anxious to do justice toward women, we hear scarcely a word concerning those disfranchised masses of the South whose stolen votes are used to make Rotten Boroughs of a third of the nation and thus distort and ruin the just distribution of political power. Caste restrictions, fatal to Christian civilization and modern conceptions of decency, are slowly but forcibly entering this land and making black folk the chief victims. There should be outspoken protest against segregation by race in the civil service, caste in public travel and in other public accommodations.

As Negroes and as their friends; as Americans; as persons whose fathers have striven for the good of this land and who ourselves have tried unselfishly to make America the land of just ideals, we write to ask if you do not think it possible to make to the colored and white people of America some further statement of your attitude toward this grievous problem such as will allow us at least to vote with intelligence.

We trust, Sir, that you will not regard this statement and request as beyond the courtesy due you or as adding too much to the burdens of a public man.

We beg to remain, Sir,

     Very respectfully yours,
     National Association for the
     Advancement of Colored People
     W. E. Burghardt Du Bois
     Director of Publications and Research

     [no date]

Dear Tumulty:

I would be very much obliged if you would answer this letter for me and say that I stand by my original assurances and can say with a clear conscience that I have tried to live up to them, though in some cases my endeavors have been defeated.

     The President.
     C. L. S.[1]

     Asbury Park, N.J., October 17, 1916

Personal

My dear Dr. DuBois:

The President asks me to acknowledge the receipt of your letter of October 10th, and to say that he stands by his original assurances. He can say with a

---

* C. L. Swem was Wilson's confidential stenographer.

clear conscience that he has tried to live up to them, though in some cases his endeavors have been defeated.

>Sincerely yours,
> J. Tumulty
> Secretary to the President

New York, November 10, 1916

My dear Dr. Du Bois:

I congratulate you most heartily upon getting The Crisis out of debt and being on the high road to still better conditions.[1] I am also much interested in the correspondence from Mr. Tumulty. It is an amazing statement that the President makes through Tumulty & a false one.[2]

>Sincerely yours,
>Oswald Garrison Villard

The first non-white secretary of the NAACP was James Weldon Johnson; he replaced Royal F. Nash and served as acting secretary from May 1917 to January 1918. After a short interval of service by John R. Shillady, Johnson became secretary again in September 1920, retaining that position until January 1931. A letter from Du Bois late in 1916 urged Johnson to accept the position; the letter contains an intriguing and unidentified reference to a "secret organization" that had been previously discussed by the two men.

New York, November 1, 1916.

My dear Johnson:

I think you ought to consider very favorably the proposal of Spingarn that you be candidate for organizer.

At first I was rather afraid that this would not be in accordance with your real life work of literature; but I am inclined to think that contact with human beings will be an incentive rather than a drawback to your literary work. Then, too, you will remember the secret organization that you and I talked of sometime ago. There is no telling what your wide acquaintance as organizer, etc.,

---

1. By the end of 1912, *Crisis* circulation reached twenty-four thousand; by mid-1916, it stood at thirty-seven thousand, and by September 1917, it had reached forty-three thousand.

2. The last four words in this letter were added in ink, in Villard's handwriting. For the realities of Wilson's administrations and Black people, see: Kathleen Wolgemuth, "Wilson and Federal Segregation," *Journal of Negro History* 44 (April 1959): 158-73; Charles F. Kellogg, *NAACP* (Baltimore: Johns Hopkins University Press, 1967), pp. 155-82; Nancy J. Weiss, "The Negro and the New Freedom," *Political Science Quarterly* 84 (March 1968): 61-79.

might not lead to. We might be able to tie a durable knot to insure the permanency of the main organization. Finally, I would expect your field correspondence to be an interesting feature of the *Crisis*.

I think that if you do become candidate, we can land you.

Very sincerely yours,
W. E. B. Du Bois

H. L. Mencken, for many years a friend of Du Bois, was early among the distinguished men of letters to hail the work of Theodore Dreiser. The sharp realism and the intense social criticism in that work induced serious efforts at its suppression, from *Sister Carrie* (1900) and *Jennie Gerhardt* (1911), through *The Financier* (1912), *The Titan* (1914), and, especially, *The "Genius"* (1915). After the appearance of the latter, an international campaign against efforts to suppress Dreiser's work was undertaken; Mencken, then editor of the *Smart Set*, sought and obtained Du Bois's aid in this effort.

New York, Nov. 29, 1916.

Dear Mr. Du Bois:

I surely hope that you will not overlook signing the Dreiser Protest. The list of signatures is already formidable, and such men as H. G. Wells and Arnold Bennett have cabled offers of support from England. There is a great difference of opinion as to the merit of Dreiser's work, but there can be little difference regarding the dangers of an arbitrary and ignorant censorship of letters by persons who boast that they have no regard for artistic values whatever.

If you will return the Protest to me or to Mr. Hersey, whose address appears upon the back, your name will be properly entered. If you are in doubt about signing, I shall be glad to give you any information that you may desire.

Sincerely yours,
H. L. Mencken

Carrie W. Clifford (Mrs. W. H. Clifford), of Ohio and Washington, was long a friend of Du Bois. She was in charge of appeals to women for the Niagara Movement, was later among the Committee of One Hundred which founded the NAACP, and was a president of the National Association of Colored Women.

Du Bois's health and physical vigor were extraordinary (as attested by his longevity); until his last years he was seriously ill only twice—once with typhoid as a lad of seventeen and again with a kidney disorder which required two operations early in 1917. The latter was the occasion for an interchange between Du Bois and Mrs. Clifford.

[Washington] Jan. 20, 1917

Dear Dr. Du Bois:

This is an attempt to express, however, imperfectly, my great sympathy and concern in your present illness.

I want to cheer you with the thought that your friends are thinking of you and earnestly praying that you may soon be restored to perfect health.

Your illness has made us realize how much we owe to you, and that to lose you would mean a greater calamity to the race than we can express.

I but express the sentiments of a host of your friends when I say I look upon you as a leader without a peer! Staunch, faithful, true under the most trying conditions, absolutely fearless in whatever position you may have found yourself, loyal even when repaid by gross ingratitude—these are the steadfast virtues which have endeared you so wonderfully to our hearts. In short, we consider you indispensable to the race, and therefore warn you against over-working as you have done. We beg you to be very careful of yourself in the future.

Please accept these halting words as an indication of my affection and esteem.

With all good wishes for a Happy New Year, I remain,

Yours truly,
Carrie W. Clifford

New York, January 29, 1917.

Dear Mrs. Clifford:

I thank you very much for your letter of January 20.

I was discharged from the hospital January 22 and am rapidly regaining health. I am glad to learn how important I am.

With best regards,

Very sincerely yours,
W. E. B. Du Bois

Charles Young, one of very few Black West Point graduates, was a friend of Du Bois from the 1890s, when both were teachers at Wilberforce. During twenty-eight years of active duty, Young had served the United States Army in the West, in Haiti, in Liberia, and, with Pershing, in Mexico; for the Mexican duty he was particularly cited by Pershing. When, after much agitation, the War Department established in 1917 a center for the training of Negro officers in Des Moines, Young, by then a lieutenant-colonel in the regular army, was universally expected to be the officer in charge. But, that spring, Young was subjected to a medical examination which discovered "high blood pressure" in the forty-nine-year-old officer. Despite protests from the entire Black press and strong efforts by Young himself (he rode horseback from Ohio to Washington,

D.C., to show his physical fitness), he was retired as a colonel in 1917. Within this context may be read a letter from Colonel Young, written from Letterman General Hospital in the Presidio in San Francisco.

San Francisco, June 20, 1917.

My dear Du Bois:

Ada[1] informs me that you have been asking of my whereabouts. I went up for my examination for promotion to Colonelcy. The surgeons claimed that as result of their finding "high blood-pressure" and "Albumen in urine" that they could not recommend that I be continued in active service with troops as it was "liable to endanger my life."

I disclaimed any ailment; not having any aches or pains of any kind and no medical history or sick record whatever, except the Black Water Fever in Africa over four years ago. I protested the finding and as a result, after a month's duty with the regiment in charge of the Training School, was ordered here without ever having been placed on the sick report at the Post. I am not considered sick by these surgeons. Have had the "observation" but no "treatment," since I'm not feeling in the least unwell. These surgeons found the same "high-blood-pressure" and I am informed, have made the same finding as the original board. Not being sick, I have officially asked the Adj't. General to have their finding waived, and to allow me to continue actively with the troops during the war. I have offered to take any and all risks arising from this continued service. No one in the regiment, either officer or man, believes me sick and no one save the doctors here at this hospital; not even the nurses. Indeed one nurse said yesterday evening, when I was preparing to go into the city; "Col. Young, this case of yours seems a joke." I replied, "It is a joke and would be a comical one, if we were not playing in this country the tragedy of War." Without an ache or pain, here I sit twirling my thumbs, when other officers are over-worked, and when I should this minute be at Des Moines helping to beat those colored officers into shape, and later to get my whole heart and soul into the work of organization of the drafted Negro troops.

If some one could let the President and Secretary of War know the bad mental and moral effect this seemingly enforced retirement will have upon our people, rather than permit me to be shelved, they would sacrifice me body and soul for the country's good.

Pardon me for this lengthy letter all about myself; you know I'm not usually given to such self-consideration, but I wanted our people in general, and you in particular, to know that I'm not sick, never felt more in condition than at this minute, and that I am not slacking nor trying to run to cover. To work with my own in this war is all I want for the good we can do our country.

Again I want them to know that the surgeons are honest in finding their

1. Mrs. Young.

facts; which indicate possibilities but not probabilities, seeing that I have a constitution of iron and sense enough to quit when I have enough and feel it.

I hope you are quite restored in health, as I know you are by the tone of the Crisis.[2]

With love to you and family,

Always your devoted,
Young.

Mt. Sterling, Ky., August 20th, 1917

Mr. W. E. B. Du Bois
Dear Sir:

Kindly permit us to use your name as one of our private brands of cigars, also your photograph on our box labels and cigar bands.[1] You will find enclosed an agreement between us and we hope you will sign it and return to us. Thanking you in advance for same, we are,

Very truly,
Garrett Distributing Co.,

New York, August 29, 1917

Gentlemen:

I have no objection to your using my name on one of your brands of cigars providing the cigar is not too bad.

Very sincerely yours,
W. E. B. Du Bois

Newton D. Baker (1871–1937), protégé of the fairly radical Tom L. Johnson, succeeded him as mayor of Cleveland from 1912 to 1916. In 1916, Wilson appointed Baker secretary of war, a position he held until 1921; thereafter, as a corporation attorney, he became increasingly conservative. Du Bois wrote in his *Dusk of Dawn* that Baker "tried to be fair and just"; in any case, serving the racist United States during World War I, such a goal was quite impossible to achieve. With the backing of the NAACP, Du Bois presented to Baker in Washington on 1 October 1917 a lengthy list of grievances; the secretary told Du Bois: "We are not trying by this war to settle the Negro problem." Du Bois acknowledged that fact, but indicated that the government should "settle as much of it as interferes with winning the war."

2. Du Bois devoted editorial comment to Colonel Young in the *Crisis* 14 (October 1917):286 and 15 (February 1918):165; Young himself contributed an article to the *Crisis* 16 (June 1918):59–60. After the war, Colonel Young served as military attaché to the Liberian government. He died in January 1922 and was interred in June 1923 in Arlington National Cemetery.

1. A sample of the label and the band was enclosed; but no cigar.

It is in this connection that the following interchange between Du Bois and the secretary of war, later in 1917, is to be read.

New York, December 6, 1917.

Mr. Newton D. Baker
Sir:

Your special letter on the Negro soldiers who have been drafted has received from some of my friends an interpretation which, as it seems to me is not warranted, and yet I cannot absolutely deny it.

Their interpretation is, of 83,000 drafted Negroes 30,000 are to be used as soldiers and 53,600 as laborers. I cannot think that this is true. My own interpretation is that 30,000 are to be used as soldiers in a special division and that the others are to be used as soldiers in additional divisions along with the white soldiers, and that some are to be voluntarily drafted as laborers.

Will you kindly tell me if my interpretation is correct?

Very sincerely yours,
W. E. B. Du Bois

Washington, December 13, 1917.

My dear Professor Du Bois:

The organization of our military forces in France required two kinds of troops; one—technically combatant troops whose sole training and business is along traditionally military lines, the other—line of communication troops whose principal business is in the transport supply service, and generally in the maintenance of the Army at the front.

Already there has been authorized a fighting unit of 30,000 colored men, including practically every branch of military service, who will constitute the 92d Division, to be detailed for duty in France under General Pershing. These men are being trained along traditional military lines.

Of the additional 53,400 colored draftees, some will be identified with Service Battalions, and a large number of others will be identified with the various Depot Brigades. This latter class receive military training with rifles the same as regular troops, and must be able, whenever occasion demands, to lay down their working utensils and pick up their rifles—as our Engineer troops have recently done in France when they went to the assistance of General Byng at the time of the German counter-attack.

Many of the Depot Brigade men, after they are trained, and as the need arises, will likely be assigned to those branches of the service where they can be of the greatest military value.

The line of communication troops are made up of both white and colored contingents. Men have been enlisted by the volunteer system for such regiments, and drafted men, both white and colored, have been asked to enlist in these regiments, and where were not enough enlistments they have been so assigned.

The situation with regard to the colored man, as with white men, is that they are being formed into both combatant and line of communication troops. So far as I know, no complaints are being made by either white or colored draftees on the subject, and I do not see how there could be.

At Camp Lee, Petersburg, Va., a few days ago, I saw about eight thousand (8,000) of them in a review with perhaps twenty-two thousand (22,000) white men. It may be of interest for me to state that, of the eight thousand colored men referred to, only two thousand of them are at this time identified with the Service Battalion, the other six thousand constituting a part of the Depot Brigade Division. It was a very impressive exhibition that I saw at Camp Lee, and the colored soldiers of both classes were the only men in the line of march who received applause, and I happened to notice that it was started by white officers, and joined in by white citizens who were witnessing the review. I made the subject one of particular inquiry and find that at Camp Lee there is not, at this time, any sort of discontent or dissatisfaction growing out of this subject among either white or colored men, and I believe that a similar condition prevails at all of the other cantonments.

      Cordially yours,
      Newton D. Baker
      Secretary of War.

Frank A. Hosmer (1855–1918) was the principal of the high school Du Bois attended in Great Barrington, Massachusetts. He became a member of the Massachusetts legislature and, thereafter, served for ten years as president of Oahu College in Honolulu. He was an inspiration to the young Du Bois, who would later, in his posthumously published *Autobiography*, several times speak kindly of Hosmer.

      Amherst, Mass., Feb. 8, 1918.
Dear Friend:

I congratulate you on reaching your fiftieth birthday; that is mere form. But I congratulate you more in what you have accomplished both for the colored race as for the white race. I always dislike to use those terms. To me there is no such distinction. I do not remember that there ever was. I had as much pleasure in introducing you to the expeditions of Caesar, to the speeches of Cicero, & the great poems of Vergil as any one but more in your case as I found response. "The Shadow of Years" I read aloud to Mrs. Hosmer & it impressed us both.[1] And she sits here beside me as I write & we both join in our congratulations to you & your wife.

1. This essay by Du Bois—evoked by his having reached the age of fifty in February 1918—appeared in the *Crisis* 15 (February 1918):216–17.

As you know, I went to Honolulu as president of Oahu College. The faculty was complete & there were no vacancies. I made up my mind I should send for you—not because you were of the "colored" race for the students of the college were mostly white—American, English, Spanish, German, Russian, Italian—& my Hawaiians. I found no race prejudices, except toward the Chinese coolies. It took years to eliminate that. At last I got my Chinese boys into the college & they won their way by sheer merit.

I had always wished to tell you I was proud of you when you gave a strong address on Wendell Phillips,[2] when from the president of Atlanta at the Lake Mohawk Conference [I heard] how successful you had been at that college, & when I presided at College Hall in Amherst when you lectured, but most of all of what you have taught the people of my country.

Principal Hosmer had a faint vision of what we [see] in you.

Sincerely,
Frank A. Hosmer

Please ask your Mr. Dill to send me The Crisis. If the price is higher, he will inform me.

New York, February 16, 1918.

Mr dear Mr. Hosmer:

I appreciate your kind greeting of February 8.

I am sure that I owe to you more than to any single person, the fact that I got started toward the higher training in my youth.

Give my best regards to Mrs. Hosmer. I trust I may see you sometime in the near future.[1]

Very sincerely yours,
W. E. B. Du Bois

Du Bois's feelings about World War I and about the proper role and activity of the Afro-American people in connection with it were ambiguous. He and the NAACP maintained pressure against second-class citizenship and all overt expressions of racism. Generally, the conduct of the Wilson administrations very much disappointed Du Bois. Yet there were moments of hope and, as he later called it, of illusion: when seven hundred Black men were commissioned as officers, when Negroes were given high appointments in the Departments of War and Labor, when the Red Cross promised to employ Black women as nurses (a promise not kept), and when Wilson finally said a mumbling word decrying lynch-

---

2. When Du Bois graduated from the high school in Great Barrington, Massachusetts, in June 1884, he delivered a talk on Phillips at the ceremonies.

1. Hosmer died in May 1918; hence his letter to Du Bois may have been one of the last he wrote.

ing. Influencing Du Bois was the pro-Allied attitude of Joel E. Spingarn, who joined the army and was commissioned as a major.

In June 1917, Du Bois was asked by representatives of the general staff if he would accept a captaincy and serve in a projected special bureau in military intelligence whose purpose would be to undertake a "far-reaching constructive effort to satisfy the pressing grievances of colored Americans." With Spingarn urging him on and the War Department asserting that he might still retain oversight of the *Crisis*, Du Bois, after consulting the board of the NAACP and getting a favorable response, accepted. Almost at the same time, he prepared for publication in the July 1917 *Crisis* an editorial, "Close Ranks," which contained the sentence: "Let us, while this war lasts, forget our special grievances and close our ranks shoulder to shoulder with our own white fellow citizens and the allied nations that are fighting for democracy."

The editorial and the suggested captaincy provoked intense controversy. As it turned out, the offer to Du Bois was withdrawn and the captaincy never materialized. By the end of the 1930s, Du Bois was to express keen doubts about the wisdom of his opinion and his course during this episode; by the end of the 1940s, he was to affirm that both were grievously in error. The correspondence that is here published includes Du Bois's letter to the NAACP board on the War Department's offer and letters, pro and con, from two comrades-in-arms in the battle against racism.

July 2, 1918

TO THE BOARD OF DIRECTORS

I have been called into consultation with the General Staff of the Army at Washington with a view to my accepting a commission and joining the Military Intelligence Bureau for service during the war. If the plan should be carried through, I would be associated with Major Spingarn in a constructive attempt to guide Negro public opinion by removing pressing grievances of colored folk which hinder the prosecution of the war.

Both for the Association and myself Major Spingarn and Miss Ovington agree with me that it would be wise to accept this offer if it is finally made; but, of course, I cannot do this if the acceptance involves the giving up of what I regard as my life work—*The Crisis*, or if it reduces my present income. The military authorities are willing that I should retain control of *The Crisis* and receive from it an income supplementary to that which the Government would pay.

I, therefore, ask the Board to consider this action:

Voted that the commission with the General Staff which may be offered to the Director of Publications and Research for the duration of the war be considered work for this Association and that Dr. Du Bois retain his present relation to *The Crisis* and that in view of past services his income from the Government be supplemented by such part of his present salary as is not necessarily expended for extra editorial help.

W. E. B. Du Bois

Hillburn, N. Y. July 25, 1918.

My dear Dr. DuBois:—

I am finding it very difficult, in my mind, to credit to your pen the advice; "Let us, while the war lasts, forget our special grievances."

I've said to myself, and to interested members of my family; "Surely Dr. Du Bois did not write those words *himself;* possibly he's away on his vacation and some other person has written the editorials for the July issue of the Crisis." &c.

As I have known you during the past twenty years, as I recall the addresses I've heard you give, as I remember your wise utterances when sitting in council with you in the Niagara Movement at Buffalo and Harper's Ferry, I simply find myself unable to conceive that said advice comes from you. It seems to me that the impossible has happened and I'm amazed beyond expression.

I believe that we should do just the reverse of what you advise. Now, "while the war lasts," is the most opportune time for us to push and keep our "special grievances" to the fore. This we should do for the very best interest of the democracy for which the war is being waged.

With sincerest wishes for your continued prosperity, I remain,

Yours very truly,
Byron Gunner[1]

New York, August 10, 1918.

My dear Mr. Gunner:

I wrote the editorial which you mention in your letter of July 25. It expresses my exact thought and is in my opinion entirely consistent with my well-known attitude.

Very sincerely yours,
W. E. B. Du Bois

Washington, D. C., July 30, 1918.

My dear DuBois:

I have been hesitating about writing to you concerning the storm now raging over the editorial in the July Crisis, and the captaincy, for the reason that I am so little informed as to all antecedent circumstances. On all hands there has been a degree of reticence and subtilty as to the matters that has left me without

---

1. Gunner was among the original founders of the Niagara Movement. At the time this letter was written, he was the president of the National Equal Rights League, of which William Monroe Trotter was corresponding secretary.

adequate information. At the meeting of the local branch, I endeavored on the spur of the moment to defend you as best I could from what appeared to me, and now appears to me, as being unjust aspersions and innuendoes. I can not understand how anybody who subscribed to the conclusions of the War Department conference, can consistently take issue with the editorial; nor can I see how anybody in his senses can criticize the appointment to the captaincy, unless he is prepared to meet a charge of discouraging persons from joining the military forces of the country. I have been thinking of writing something with these two ideas in mind for our local papers, but am not decided as to whether it would help matters. These attacks on you have a sinister aspect as I view them.

I want to assure you of my sincere confidence and support.

Very sincerely yours,
L. M. Hershaw[1]

New York, August 5, 1918.

My dear Hershaw:

I want to thank you very much for your kind defence of me in that extraordinary meeting. As you have surmised, there is absolutely nothing to argue about. Two weeks after the July *Crisis* was in print I was summoned to Washington and to my great surprise asked if I would accept a captaincy in a new bureau to work among colored people. I replied that I would, provided I could keep general control of *The Crisis* and would not have my salary reduced, the captain salary being one thousand dollars less than I now receive. This was assented to.

I have consulted Grimké, Storey, and a half-dozen other members of the board. They all consented. Even Grimké, although now he denies this and says that he asked for time for consideration. Subsequently at a small meeting of the board which happened to be dominated by pacifists, the scheme was voted down, leaving me in a very difficult dilemma. I should probably have accepted the commission anyway but the General Staff finally decided not to establish the bureau. The offer had, as you may be sure, absolutely nothing to do with the editorial utterances in *The Crisis*. You are quite at liberty to use these facts, only it would be better not to start any controversy over the Grimké matter.

I always depend upon your good-will and friendship and I am sure you know that I appreciate it.

Very sincerely yours,
W. E. B. Du Bois

When the plans for Du Bois to join army Intelligence fell through, Spingarn also changed his course; as a major attached to the Sixth Army Corps, he saw combat

1. Lafayette M. Hershaw (1863–1945) had been associated with Du Bois in the Niagara Movement and in the publication of the *Horizon;* at the time of this letter he was working in the Department of the Interior and was also a member of the District of Columbia bar.

in France with the Allied Expeditionary Force. No other white person was as close to Du Bois as Spingarn (to whom Du Bois dedicated his 1940 autobiography), and the attachment was mutual. Published here is a moving letter written from the front to Du Bois a month before the Armistice.

France, October 9, 1918.

Dear Dr. Du Bois:

    The ties of home assume a new meaning to us here in France, and when the guns rumble, as they do continuously not far off, *The Crisis* and the many friends whom it brings to mind seem very near and dear. I am now commanding officer of a detached battalion in the zone of the advance, with all the responsibilities of a quasi independent command. My overlord is miles away, and in this lonely camp in the woods, where there is no "life" outside of work, I am monarch of all I survey. My old regiment is not far off, and it seems hard to believe that many of my old comrades in it will never see America again. Men from the colored regiments come within my orbit, too, every now and then, and everywhere I hear splendid reports of their labors and fine deeds.

    The other day I made Sunday afternoon a holiday, and paid my first visit to the largest city in this section. The ride there through country not unlike my own Dutchess [County, New York] was most interesting, and from the top of the last hill I could see the sorely tried city in a semi-circle of the hills which it in part climbed. It has been bombed and bombarded for years, and a large part of the civil population was evacuated last winter. Everywhere I saw signs of its sufferings. I sought out the Faculty of Letters (it is a University city) in the hope of finding some scholar I might know. But I found only the old concierge, who told me that there had been no professors, students, or studies since the city was evacuated. She showed me the great hall of the University, and I mounted the rostrum and made my first address in French. My only audience was the concierge, who complimented me on my eloquence and assured me that I spoke excellent French. But though the French was really very bad, and the audience limited, I delivered my message in my most resonant voice, which echoed through the empty chamber, sad in its shattered ceiling and its debris covered floor. I began with the thought that one could love France very dearly without speaking perfect French, just as one could love God without speaking the language of the angels. I ended by tipping my audience and leaving the University. At the corner I bought a paper, and this startling headline stared me in the face: *L'Ennemi demande l'armistice.* When I reached home (most of the way in the dark without lights) and stood outside my quarters, the guns seemed as loud as ever, even louder, and I asked myself the oft asked question, "Peace? Peace?"

    You may say for me to all my friends that colored America has more than justified the hopes of those who have always believed in it, and more than earned all that we have demanded for it. I take off my hat to the courage and devoted patriotism of black men in this war.

                                      Faithfully yours,
                                      J. E. Spingarn

As the Great War moved toward a conclusion, Du Bois conceived of a detailed history of Black people in the war; although he accumulated enough material for several stout volumes, he could never get the work published. As part of his preparation, he instituted a search for young Black people trained in history, and in this connection wrote Ephraim Douglass Adams (1865-1930) of Stanford's history department, asking for suggestions.* The latter's reply is interesting for its rather extraordinary naiveté.

                                  Stanford, Calif., November 21, 1918
Dear Sir:

Replying to your note of November 15th, I regret to state that no colored man or woman has ever received training in the History Department of Stanford University, and that therefore I cannot make such recommendations as you suggest.

This is a remarkable fact and I do not know the reason for it; yet it is true so far as I know, in my fourteen years in the History Department of this University, that we have had no colored students in this department.

                                      Very truly yours,
                                      E. D. Adams

Toward the close of 1918, as an Allied victory became clear, Du Bois undertook to press two projects: first, a full record of the role and participation of Black peoples around the world in the First World War; and second, the assembly of a Pan-African Congress at which the needs and demands of those peoples would be voiced while the peace was being arranged. In connection with the second aim, he wrote many letters to leading figures in the Afro-American world and in United States, British, and French governing circles, both to organize such a congress and to obtain the necessary facilities. In this connection, he wrote to President Wilson late in November 1918, enclosing material relative to the proposed Pan-African Congress and asking to see the President. On the stationery of the White House came the reply.

---

* Adams had already published studies on British diplomacy in pre-statehood Texas and *The Power of Ideals in American History* (New Haven: Yale University Press, 1913). He is best known for his *Great Britain and the American Civil War* (1925) and for joint authorship of some widely used textbooks.

November 29, 1918

My dear Sir:

Your letter of November 27th and enclosed memoranda have been received and will be brought to the President's attention.

I regret that it will not be possible to make the appointment you request, as the President finds it absolutely necessary from this time until he leaves for Europe to reserve all his time for what must be done, and done carefully, by way of preparing for his absence.

Sincerely yours,
J. P. Tumulty
Secretary to the President.

At the end of the war, Du Bois undertook two new missions. The board of the NAACP asked him to go to France to investigate treatment of the United States Black troops and to collect material for a history of their activities; at the same time, Du Bois, active in reviving the idea of a Pan-African movement, planned to call a congress to realize such a movement. Since Wilson was sending to France Robert R. Moton, Washington's successor as head of Tuskegee, aboard George Creel's official press boat, *Orizaba*, and since Du Bois was the editor of the *Crisis*, it was not possible to refuse Du Bois similar passage.

Reflecting the official opinion about Du Bois was the secret order issued on the first day of 1919 at the command of General Erwin, of the Black ninety-second Division. This order, carrying the official stamp of the headquarters of the division, fell into Du Bois's possession.

A. P. O. 766, 1 January, 1919.

SECRET
MEMO:

To Intelligence Officers—

1. A man by name of *Dubois*, with visitor's pass, reported on his way to visit this Division. His presence at station of any unit will be immediately reported in secret enclosure to Assist Chief of Staff, G-2, these headquarters. Likewise prompt report will be made to G-2 of all his moves and actions while at station of any unit.

2. The fact of this inquiry as to *Dubois* and his moves will not be disclosed to any person outside the Intelligence Service.

By command of Brigadier General *Erwin:*

F. P. Schoonmaker,
Major, General Staff.

One of the few prominent white people in the United States, apart from those directly connected with the NAACP, who showed any awareness of Du Bois's work was Walter Lippmann. Lippmann sent to Du Bois a characteristic note on the stationery of the *New Republic*, of which he was then editor.

Feb. 20, 1919

Dear Dr. Du Bois:

I am very much interested in your organization of the Pan-African Conference, and glad that Clemenceau has made it possible.

Will you send me whatever reports you may have on the work.

Sincerely yours,
Walter Lippmann

During and immediately after World War I, violence directed against Black people in the United States was especially prevalent: pogroms took the lives of hundreds; and lynchings, of hundreds more. At the same time, the militancy and resistance of the assaulted intensified, as is reflected by a letter from the Reverend Dr. James Arthur Martin. Born in Georgia in 1878 and educated at Paine College in Augusta, he was a practicing minister from 1906 to 1926, an editor for publications by the Colored Methodist Episcopal Church, an active worker for NAACP in the South, and a Georgia agent of the Rosenwald Fund for several years beginning in 1919.

Macon, Ga., May 30, 1919.

Dear Dr. DuBois:—

I am sending you clippings from the Macon Telegraph. They speak for self. I am also sending you some first hand information. I witnessed it myself. On Tuesday, May 27 I went to Milledgeville to fill engagement of delivering the principal address at the closing of Eddie High School. Upon my arrival I found the town stirred up. The blacks had sent their young men to Macon, a distance of 35 miles, for arms and cartridges. They had sworn to protect the school closing exercises to which I had to speak. Not less than 100 men were armed with rifles, pistols and shot guns while the exercises were going on inside of the First Baptist Church. The occasion for arming themselves grew out of a dispute over Class Colors. It happened that the Georgia Normal (White) School and the Eddie High (Colored) School had chosen the same colors. The white boys met a colored boy and took his colors off of him. The affair was reported to authorities. It failed to bring results. The white students met another colored student on succeeding day and tore from him the colors. One version is: The Negroes went to the authorities and stated that "We are going to protect ourselves." Another is; the mayor said to them, "I cannot stop these white boys. You Negroes will just have to protect yourselves." The latter version is probably the correct one. At any rate the Negroes were well armed. The beauty about it is, they were not at all nervous. The mothers and sons, sweethearts, husbands and wives all walked home together. The males carrying their guns with as much calmness as if they were going to shoot a rabbit in a hunt, or getting ready to shoot the Kaiser's soldiers. They were absolutely calm both males and females.

The atmosphere was full of courage. The servant spoke on "Citizenship after the war." He urged that, "Each man register and vote." He expressed that, "one man had no more right to vote for another than he has to pay another's taxes; house rent or buy him clothes. The Negro has earned every right and must contend for them in Georgia with as much zeal as he fought in Germany. Each local community must cope with every emergency when it arises, caring more for what is right than life itself. Too many principles are too dear to be shunned by running or compromised by grinning. Personal courage in local communities is going a long way in breaking up mischievous people and mobs who impose on what they consider the weak. Do not expect the other race, as such, to correct every personal wrong committed by one of them against the black boy, any more than you may expect them to buy your necessities for life."

"Indeed, the wrongs against all weaker people have their origin of correction among the people who are injured. However wrong or strange this is in the light of Christianity, it is a solemn truth in history and in the face of present evils is very suggestive. Many things we must do for selves in breaking up mobs or would be mobs." This is an abstract of my remarks on this occasion. Milledgeville is still calm and the race relation is very cordial at this writing.

Yours truly,
J. A. Martin.

Characteristic of the mood of resistance—given classical expression in 1919 in Claude McKay's great poem "If We Must Die"—is this letter from William A. Hewlett, one of the hundreds of thousands of Afro-Americans who went to Europe "to make the world safe for democracy."

Le Havre, France, Aug. 26, 1919

Dear Dr. Du Bois:

We are enjoying the blessing of true democracy for which 400,000 of our best young negro men fought on the battle-fields of France.

We regret that on and about October 10th, 1919, we will sail for our home in Petersburg Va—United States of America, where true democracy is enjoyed only by white people—There is an air of liberty; equality; and fraternity here which does not blow in the black man's face—in liberty loving, democratic America there the negro has fought in every war that United States have had from 1776, to present time—for liberty, freedom and justice. After carefully reading the August issue of your valuable Crisis I am forced to write this brief letter to express my hearty approval of the contents therein, and to further state that the United States is not democratic when dealing with her colored people: but almost entirely autocratic: We would to the Almighty that the race had 10,000 Crisis' in America; to write of the 10,000 wrongs perpetrated upon our race: in a land that we have helped to make great among the nations of the earth. If democracy in United States means—disfranchisement; jimcrowism; lynch-law; biased judges; and juries; segregation; taxation without representation; and no representatives in any of the law making bodies of the United States; if that is the White American idea of true democracy—Then why did we fight Germany; why did we frown [on] her autocracy; why did black men die here in France 3300 miles from their homes—Was it to make democracy safe for white people in America—with the black race left out; if we have fought to make safe democracy for the white races, we will soon fight to make it safe for ourselves and our posterity.

Sincerely yours for the race—
Wm. A. Hewlett, of Virginia.

Du Bois's concern for the youngsters among his people was deep and lasting; for years he had dreamed of a magazine created for them. In the October 1919 *Crisis* (18:285–86), he was able to describe in some detail such a magazine, which he there called "The True Brownies." The first number of the *Brownies' Book* appeared in January 1920; the last, December 1921.* The October announcement brought this letter addressed to "Messrs. Du Bois & [Augustus] Dill."

Cleveland, 10.23.19

Gentlemen: I want to be one of the first subscribers for your Junior Crissis, known as the brownies, edition, my age is 7 and I think this is a propper time for me to begin to learn something about my own race, which is not taught in the public schools. Inclosed $1.00 One dollar for one years subscription beginning Nov. 1, 1919.

Resp. Yours,
Petruchio E Moore

There were few services that Du Bois's *Crisis* did not perform. From time to time, for example, the magazine helped arrange for the adoption of a child. In the October 1919 issue (18:287), a baby named Ophelia was so offered; the Novem-

---

* See Elinor D. Sinnette, "The Brownies' Book," *Freedomways* 5 (Winter 1965): 133–42.

ber issue (18:337) indicated that a suitable home had been found. The original notice brought a considerable response; one of the letters is given here.

11-1-19, Hartshorne, Okla.

The Crisis Magazine
Dear Sirs. I am a little girl eleven years old and my name is Novella and I seen in you magazine a little Baby named Ophelia she has no parrents to take care of her. Will you please rite and tell me what she will cost me to get her I will pay her expences and take her if you will rite to me at wonce for I needs her
    Nothing more till I here from you

                      Very truly yors
                      Novella Clark

In establishing the National Guard, after the war, the United States government instituted a policy of discrimination and segregation which has persisted in that service—with some modifications—into the present. A letter from Du Bois to War Secretary Baker drew from the latter an elaborate explanation and an assurance that discrimination was not intended. Despite "intent," the fact of discrimination continued.

New York, May 12, 1920.

My dear Mr. Baker:
    I have read recently several reports of a decision by the War Department with regard to organizing Negroes in the militia. Before publishing anything about this policy, I would like to be sure of my facts. Will you kindly let me know just what the decision was with regard to the regiments of colored troops in the Massachusetts militia and how far that effects such colored regiments as the 8th Illinois and 15th New York National Guard?
    I shall be under great obligations.

                      Very sincerely yours,
                      W. E. B. Du Bois

Washington, May 17, 1920.

Mr. W. E. B. Du Bois
Dear Sir:
    Replying to the request for information contained in your letter of May 12th, I take pleasure in placing before you the reasons on which the War Department bases its policy in dealing with colored units of the National Guard.
    In brief, this policy is to assign National Guard units recruited from colored men to duty that will not incorporate them in a division composed of white organizations. This has led to the decision that colored troops in National Guard service be organized into pioneer infantry units that, in accordance with our

tables of organization, can be assigned to duty under the command of Corps Headquarters. The Corps is the next larger tactical unit above the Division, and it consists normally of four divisions, and, in addition, several other organizations under direct control of the Corps commander to be used to supplement the work of the divisions. These additional organizations include units of various branches such as Engineers and Air Service as well as Pioneer Infantry.

The War Department's decision to maintain separate divisional organizations for white and colored troops is well founded. The division, as you know, is the smallest unit of our Army in which all branches of our military service are represented. It operates as a small Army of 27,000 men, and for it to be successful, it is imperative that sources of internal dissensions be reduced to an absolute minimum. On this account, the War Department has always avoided mixing the races within a division.

Whenever it is necessary and feasible to do so the War Department plans to organize complete divisions of colored troops, but at the present time it appears that this measure should be resorted to only in time of war. The components of such a division, even if its recruitment would be practicable at all during peace time, would necessarily be dispersed over all sections of our country and consequently efficient training for it would be an impossibility.

It is believed that dispassionate thought will indicate the wisdom of the War Department's present policy affecting colored units of the National Guard. Certain members of the colored race have made the mistake of assuming that the Pioneer regiments assigned to Corps headquarters are the same as the Labor battalions or the Stevedore regiments of colored personnel which were organized during the World War. The men making this mistake should be assured that their assumptions are altogether erroneous, since the mission of Corps is not the same as that of troops organized solely for labor purposes. The doubters that are open to reason should also be assured that the avenues now open to colored men volunteering for the National Guard lead to service that is as honorable as any to be had. The training to be given colored infantry units will be the standardized infantry training that is given to all infantry organizations.

Finally, I hope you will see fit to assure our colored citizens through the columns of your periodical that the War Department fully appreciates the very creditable quality of service rendered by our colored organizations during the World War, and that in arriving at our decision concerning the future employment of colored National Guard units, we were guided by considerations bearing on military efficiency, and with no intention whatever of discriminating between the races that go to make up our country's population.

Sincerely yours,
Newton D. Baker[1]

1. Baker's letter was printed in the *Crisis* 20 (July 1920):137; a critical editorial note appeared on page 120 of the same issue.

NATIONAL AND

INTERNATIONAL LEADER

THE ERA OF POSTWAR 'PROSPERITY'

1920–1929

The First Amenia Conference, August 1916. Du Bois is standing, fifth from left; Joel E. Spingarn is seated far right.

1917 NAACP parade in New York protesting lynching and mob violence. Du Bois is at right, with umbrella.

Oswald Garrison Villard

Joel E. Spingarn

James Weldon Johnson, 1920

Du Bois in 1920 on his annual Maine vacation, Camp Idlewild

WITH THE betrayal of the "New Freedom," the widespread repression, and the special terror directed against Black people, nationalistic and separatist concepts and movements developed. Outstanding in this regard was the Universal Negro Improvement Association and African Communities League (to give it its full name at that time) led by Marcus Garvey. An exchange of letters between Garvey and Du Bois in the summer of 1920 is of consequence; Garvey did not respond to the questions proposed by Du Bois. Du Bois wrote occasionally of Garvey and his movement,* and in this early period with general sympathy, calling Garvey "an extraordinary leader of men" and one who had "with singular success capitalized and made vocal the great and long-suffering grievances and spirit of protest of the West Indian peasantry."

New York, July 16th, 1920

Dear Dr. Dubois:

At the International Convention of Negroes to be held in New York during the month of August, the Negro people of America will elect a leader by the popular vote of the delegates from the forty-eight States of the Union. This leader as elected, will be the accredited spokesman of the American Negro people. You are hereby asked to be good enough to allow us to place your name in nomination for the post.

Hoping to hear from you immediately, and with best wishes,

Yours very truly,
Parent Body—Universal Negro
   Improvement Asso.
Marcus Garvey
President General.

New York, July 22, 1920.

Personal
Mr. Marcus Garvey
Dear Sir:

Answering your letter of July 16, I beg to say that I thank you for the suggestion but under no circumstances can I allow my name to be presented.

* See the *Crisis* 21 (December 1920):58, 60; and 21 (January 1921):112–15.

However, I desire to publish in *The Crisis* some account of you and your movement.

For some time *The Crisis* has been in receipt of inquiries concerning you and your organization. To these we have simply answered that we had no reliable information at hand.

It seems, however, increasingly important as your movement grows that we should present to our readers a critical estimate of it.

We wish, however, to be sure to have all the essential facts in hand and I therefore write to ask the following questions. I expect, of course, only such answers as you are willing to divulge and to have the public know.

I trust I may have as early a reply as your convenience permits.

Very sincerely yours,
W. E. B. Du Bois

P.S. Will you please also send a recent photograph and an account of your life?

QUESTIONS

Name of the organization? and of all subsidiary companies, if any.
History: When and where founded, when and where incorporated; address of principle office.
Officers: Names and duties of officers and directors.
Finances: Source and amount of income; chief items of expenditure, amount of capital stock authorized and amount issued, classes of stock and per value of shares, salaries of officers, balance sheet for last fiscal year. Are the books audited annually and by whom?
Members: Number and conditions of membership, distribution.
Property: Kind and location, and liens, if any, on same.
Activities and Accomplishments:
Publications: Sample copies of such as you distribute free and price list of others. Such further general information as you may care to give.

Dorothy Canfield Fisher (1879–1958) was one of the best-known American novelists in her time; especially noted were her books *The Deepening Stream* (1930) and *Seasoned Timber* (1939). Her short stories appeared for decades in leading journals, and a collection, *Foursquare*, was published in 1949.

Arlington, Vermont, January 3rd 1921

Dear Dr. Dubois:

I have today returned from a ten-days absence from home, with no mail forwarded, and find your kind letter of the 22 waiting for me. Thanks very much for the check sent to the Fort Valley School [in Georgia]. I appreciate entirely the difficulties of editing such a paper as the Crisis, and would not have thought of asking for any return for my story,[1] if I had not incautiously promised it to Mr. [H. A.] Hunt, whose school needs help very much. Don't think of ever adding to it in the future. You have plenty of other responsibilities!

I have just finished a new novel, laid in Vermont, concerned with an intimate personal problem in the life of a Vermont woman and her husband. But I wish never to lose a chance to remind Americans of what their relations to the Negro race are, and might be, and so into this story of Northern life and white people, I have managed to weave a strand of remembrance of the dark question. It is a sort of indirect, side-approach, a backing-up of your campaign from someone not vitally concerned in it personally, except as every American must be, which I hope may be of use exactly because it is not a straight-on attack, but one of a slightly different manner.[2]

With best wishes, I am

Cordially and sincerely yours
Dorothy Canfield Fisher

William Pickens (1881–1954), originally from South Carolina, was an influential educator and organizer, and was one of the first participants in the NAACP. During the First World War, he served as dean at Wiley College in Texas and at Morgan College for Negroes (now Morgan State College, Baltimore); he thereafter joined the NAACP as one of its field secretaries. It is in connection with his latter work that he and Du Bois exchanged letters early in 1921.

March 28, 1921.

My dear Mr. Pickens:

I returned to find you already started upon your trip. I had planned to have a long and confidential talk with you about the general situation in the N.A.A.C.P. This I shall do when I see you next. Meantime just let me say this: The work which we executives have got to put over for the Negro race is bigger than any personalities. In an organization like ours injustice is bound to be done from time to time by all of us in relation to others. The greater duty calls us to bear it. Believe me, I have had my share. Meantime, while you are on the field, will you not let me especially ask you to be tactful and careful? Talk up the general organization in private as well as in public and be loyal to every fellow worker.

---

1. The story, entitled "An American Citizen," was published in two installments in the *Crisis* during April and May 1920.
2. The reference is undoubtedly to *The Brimming Cup*, published by Harcourt, Brace and Co. in 1921. There is a brief favorable notice of the book—unsigned, but by Du Bois—in the *Crisis* 22 (August 1921):168, with commentary on Mrs. Fisher on page 266 of the October issue.

Do not let anybody get the impression that there are any differences within the organization. Furthermore, will you not try to be especially tactful in the matter of taking sides in local branch difficulties. In some way you "got in wrong" in three different places where I have lectured. How far it was your fault and how far it was the fault of others, I am, of course, unable to say but we will talk it over sometime. Finally, one warning which I hope you will take in good part, don't talk so much. Listen, get in the habit of listening to other people. Get out of the habit of talking, cut your subjects short.

I know all this may seem, at first sight, like unnecessary interference in your business but I somehow feel that you will take it in the spirit in which it is intended.

With best regards.

Very sincerely yours,
W. E. B. Du Bois

On train, April 12, 1921

Personal to Dr. W. E. B. DuBois
My dear Dr. DuBois:—

Out of consideration for the difficulties under which this letter is written, I am sure you will overlook the more minor of its faults. I am acknowledging your confidential letter of March 28th last, which I have just received from Dr. C. E. Bentley's office [in Chicago]. I am speaking in the same confidential-personal manner, and I believe in the same spirit and purpose.

I do not know how many places you visited on your rather extended tour, but I realize that since I have been working with the Association as a field secretary, I have visited upward of 200 places and delivered addresses. I am therefore interested in the fact that you found three places where I got in wrong—with the branch officers, I suppose. For even in Cincinnati, where I got in wrongest with the then officiating heads, I did not get in wrong with the branch members. And do you know that the very reason why I got in wrong with the officers, was because I insisted upon doing just exactly what you advise me to do in one paragraph of your letter: *not taking sides* in local disputes. I was ordered in plain words to take sides and refused. I acted toward all parties as if there was no local trouble (for me there was none), and I displeased the officers. You have not mentioned Cincinnati or any definite place, but I happen to know of that. The other two places, I could not possibly guess.

I never discuss my personal difficulties to branches. I have much more said to me about my co-laborers that I ever would or could say, but I know that men will differ. Men knock you to me. They make very little impression upon me. It would be embarrassing in many cases if they could know *how* little impression. The chief benefit they have conferred upon me, is to make me reflect that I am not a better nor wiser man than you, that I am no better and far less wise, and that I must therefore not be too discouraged if some men should dislike me or say things against me.

As to talking, I may be more talkative than other men I know—by nature. That is, more physically and temperamentally inclined to talk—to express my thoughts, not to gossip or to meddle [in] other people's business. In twenty years of very active work among men, I have never acquired the reputation for meddling or for speaking ill of men or women.

But I have some enemies, and you have. I have heard of men without enemies and I have often wondered what they could be doing.

I have certainly never gotten in bad with the Chicago branch, for I have never spoken for them in my life that I can recollect, and certainly not since I have been an officer of the N.A.A.C.P.

I will not be unjust or ungenerous to any of the people with whom I have to deal. I shall appreciate your confidence at all times. I trust I shall not have greater faults than to talk readily the truth. I know you realize the difficulty of replying to a general charge of unspecified difficulties.

Sincerely yours,
Wm. Pickens

One of the reflections of the post-war repression was an increase of overt racism in the North. Indiana was a center of such racism: while the KKK grew everywhere in the 1920s, it actually controlled the politics of Indiana in that decade. A letter to Du Bois, written in the spring of 1921 by the executive secretary of the Colored Men's Branch of the Indianapolis YMCA, brought a noteworthy reply.

Indianapolis, Ind., May 25, 1921

Dear Sir:

We anticipate agitation looking towards the establishment of separate High Schools in Indianapolis. In order to discuss the matter intelligently we are asking you to be so kind as to give us the benefit of your observation, experience and judgment.

Would you favor or oppose such a movement? Reasons?

What, if any, is the situation in your own city?

Your answer, let me assure you, will be strictly confidential.

Very faithfully yours,
F. E. DeFrantz

New York, June 16, 1921.

My dear Mr. DeFrantz:

The theory of the public school is that it should be the foundation of the democracy of the land. To separate children usually means their virtual separation through life. This means misunderstanding, friction, group, class and racial hatred. So far then as possible we should strive in every way to keep the public schools open to all citizens, white and black, Jew and Gentile, rich and poor, native and foreign.

In some parts of the land, however, and in some cases, racial feeling is so strong that it would be impossible to carry on schools of this sort. But the community suffers from this and must if it will keep down riot and race hatred substitute bonds of social sympathy to take the place of public school common training.

In a few cities it has been found possible while maintaining separate graded schools to have common high schools.

In these cities above all others in the United States there is the greatest opportunity for real national service. If it is impossible for children of high school age to work together for common knowledge and human training for four years then it is impossible for white and colored people to live together in the United States and for different races to live together in the world. The test of the possibility of democracy is in a certain very real sense the mixed high schools of Indianapolis.

Very sincerely yours,
W. E. B. Du Bois

One of the decisions of the 1919 Pan-African Congress was that similar meetings were to be convened every two years. Consequently, late in 1920 and early in 1921, Du Bois, as secretary, was preparing for the second congress; it was scheduled for the summer of 1921, with sessions in London (the Labour party participating), in Brussels, and in Paris. In this connection, Du Bois corresponded with Charles Evans Hughes (1862–1948), previously governor of New York, then secretary of state, and later chief justice of the United States Supreme Court. Note is to be taken of the rather stark reply from Hughes.

June 23, 1921.

Honorable Charles Hughes
Sir:

In 1919 there was held in Paris the first Pan-African Congress. I am enclosing the resolutions which were passed by that Congress. These resolutions were brought to the attention of Colonel House of the American Peace Commission and received his general approval.

A second Pan-African Congress will be held in August and September at the time and places indicated by the bulletins enclosed.[1] I am writing to appraise

---

1. The second congress met from 29 August to 6 September 1921. There were 113 delegates from 26 groups; 39 were from Africa, 35 from the United States, and the remainder from Latin America and Europe. The congress attracted very wide attention in the European press. While in Europe for the session, Du Bois visited the League of Nations and the International Labor Office.

you of these facts because of some public misapprehension of our aims and purposes. The Pan-African Congress is for conference, acquaintanceship and general organization. It has nothing to do with the so called Garvey movement and contemplates neither force nor revolution in its program. We have had the cordial cooperation of the French, Belgian and Portuguese governments and we hope to get the attention and sympathy of all colonial powers.[2]

If there is any further information as to our objects and plans which you would wish to have I will be very glad to write further or to come to Washington and confer with any official whom you might designate. I am, sir, with great respect

Very sincerely yours,
W. E. B. Du Bois

Washington, July 8, 1921.

Mr. W. E. Burghardt DuBois
Sir:

I beg to acknowledge the receipt of your letter of June 23 communicating the resolutions passed by the Pan-African Congress of 1919, and informing me that a second Pan-African Congress will be held in August and September at the time and place indicated by the bulletins you enclosed.

I wish to thank you for your kindness in informing me of the aims and purposes of the proposed conference, and we shall be glad to have any further information which from time to time you may have at your command.

I am, Sir,

Your obedient servant,
Charles E. Hughes

For the greater part of his life, Du Bois considered himself a socialist; his views changed through the years, however, about what socialism was, what was its connection with the question of racism, and how capitalism was to be superseded. Soon after World War I and especially with the Bolshevik revolution, interest in socialism, Marxism, and communism grew among Black people, and such younger figures as A. Philip Randolph, Claude McKay, and Cyril Briggs helped articulate a positive evaluation.

Responding to these developments, Du Bois published an essay, "The Negro and Radical Thought," in the *Crisis* for July 1921 (22:102-4); this essay brought

---

2. Du Bois sent a somewhat similar letter, on 16 June 1921, to Sir Auckland Geddes, Britain's ambassador in Washington. He added that he wished for Britain's co-operation and hoped that some representative of the Colonial Office might attend the Pan-African Congress. The British refused the latter suggestion. This letter, in the Public Record Office in London, was kindly called to my attention by Professor Robert G. Weisbord of the University of Rhode Island.

in reply a critical letter from John H. Owens, a young Black man serving as an assistant to the Committee for Consideration of a National Budget of the United States Senate. No reply from Du Bois to Owens seems to have survived (if one was written), but two essays by Du Bois, taking a quite positive view toward socialism, were soon published in the *Crisis:* "The Spread of Socialism," 22 (September 1921):199-200 and "Socialism and the Negro," 22 (October 1921):245-47. Owens's own letter was published, in part, in the October issue.

Washington, July 31, 1921.

My dear Dr. DuBois:

In answer to Mr. Claude McKay, in the issue of July, 1921, you state among other things: "that we have one chief cause—the emancipation of the Negro, and to this all else must be subordinated—not because other questions are not important but to our mind the most important social question of the day is the recognition of the darker races." Is there not just a bare possibility that some of the issues which you consider subordinate to your central idea, might possess the nucleus of a tangible and definite solution? Is one to infer that it is your hope to bring about a set of altruistic relationships between dominant and subjugated races; a set of dealings based upon mutual respect and tolerance, in place of cold, calculating exploitation of the weak by the strong? To what extent do you hope to bring about a recognition of the darker races? Those darker races which have the power to enforce the world's respect, already enjoy it.

After all, it would certainly appear that "international solidarity of the proletariat" means much more to the dark races in general, and to the Negroes in particular, than any schemes of a nationalistic character. They may hope to occupy a better niche under the former than the latter. The Negro group is almost a pure proletarian group—this fact admits of no denial. Above 90 per cent of the Negroes are unskilled, untrained workers, and unorganized. Thus it would seem that the race as a whole has less reason to be suspicious of any movement of a proletarian nature than of some scheme which offers a questionable solution for the ills of the talented minority. And thus far, this is about all the relief that local movements have offered.

Even universal political enfranchisement would offer no positive relief. This the Northern Negro already enjoys, yet he suffers under the burden of social, political, and economic injustices. His condition is little more to be envied than that of his Southern brother. Is it not unreasonable to suppose that the universality of the ballot would emancipate the Negro when it has failed to emancipate the white proletariat who have had the use of this weapon of offence and defense for generations? A people can vote and legislate themselves into slavery as easily as into freedom. When the mass of whites vote contrary to the wishes of the master class, they, too, are disfranchised as quickly as the Negro. Were not the white voters of New York disfranchised when they elected five assemblymen from the ranks of the Socialists? Were not the white voters of the fifth Wisconsin Congressional district disfranchised when they legally elected Victor Berger to represent them in congress? Upon what tangible background of fact should the Negro base his premise that the ballot will do more for him?

You state further: "The editor of The Crisis considers himself a Socialist but he does not believe that German State Socialism or the dictatorship of the proletariat are perfect panaceas." Even dogmatic Socialists or Communists hardly have the temerity to hold forth a perfect panacea. Does the editor offer the N.A.A.C.P. as a perfect panacea in place of the former? Even this writer is not going to attempt a perfect panacea. However, does not the editor think that State Socialism, Communism, or even the dread dictatorship of the proletariat offers a better solution to the problems of the proletariat than any scheme suggested by the exploiting classes—those who profit by the present system? And since the Negro is over 90 per cent proletarian, is it not almost logical to assume that this would also offer a better solution to his problem than anything heretofore proposed?

We are both of the opinion that the present method of control and distribution of wealth is desperately wrong. We are en rapport on the conclusion that a form of social control is inevitable. We hold this particular truth to be self-evident—that a change must come about. But How? I think that we both may be safe in assuming that any initiative in bringing about a better distribution of wealth must be taken by those who benefit least by the present system. Surely it is an extreme Utopian fantasy, which would shame a chauvinist, to hope that such a condition will come about through a change of heart on the part of the possessing classes which will cause them to voluntarily share with the non-possessing masses, black or white. Even the conservative Socialist and Opportunists are beginning to admit that it is only by "direct attempts" can we hope for a better distribution, and in due subordination thereunto, a better production of wealth than now prevails.

You ask the question: "How far can the colored people of the world, and the Negroes of the United States in particular, trust the working classes?" This is a good question, and easier asked than answered. But I would like to ask further: "How far can the Negroes and other dark peoples trust the exploiting Nationalists and Imperialists? Is it the English working classes that are exploiting India, sucking the very life-blood from a starving population, and grinding the natives down into the desert dust in order to support English 'gentlemen' in idleness and luxury? Are the English, French, and Belgian working classes raping Africa, taking ill-gotten gains from a trusting population? Are the working classes of America attempting to fasten the yoke of subjugation upon the neck of Santo Domingo, and stifle liberty and freedom of speech and press in Haiti? If we have cause to distrust the working classes, by what precept or example should we put faith in the specious promises of the masters?"

Although this writer is a member of the N.A.A.C.P., and has been since its be-

[254] Correspondence 1920–1929

ginning, he is as hopeful of a "mirage in Africa" as he is of any "emancipation programme" which the N.A.A.C.P. can think out.

       Very truly,
       John H. Owens

Du Bois put in years of labor compiling a history of the American Negro in World War I. His exposure of the racism characterizing United States official conduct in that war caused the Post Office Department to ban temporarily the May 1919 *Crisis;* the fullest single published piece by Du Bois on the subject was "An Essay Toward A History of the Black Man in the Great War," in the June 1919 *Crisis* (28:63–87). A letter reaching the NAACP, from Sidney Hollander of Baltimore, referred to slanders against the Black man's role in the war and asked for information; it was referred to Du Bois for reply.

       December 27, 1921.

Mr. Sidney Hollander
My dear Sir:

 Answering your letter of December 19, to the National Association for the Advancement of Colored People, I beg to say that I am compiling the history of the Negroes in the late war. I hope to have the manuscript ready for publication sometime during the year 1922.

 It is untrue that the Negro made a reputation for cowardice in the war. On the other hand, his bravery and ability have been conspicuously proven. First the Eighth Illinois Negro Regiment with almost entirely Negro officers was brigaded with the French and made a conspicuous record of bravery and efficiency. It was known as the 370th Regiment, A.E.F. In a similar way the Fifteenth New York Regiment, known as the 369th was also brigaded with the French and made a splendid record.

 These regiments, together with the 372nd and 373rd who also had excellent records formed the 93rd Division. This division was never completed and did not function as a division. It fought almost entirely with the French and is usually overlooked or purposely neglected by persons studying the Negro war record. Yet they were the only American Negro troops who really got into the war.

 The 93rd Division,[1] composed also of Negro troops, was poorly organized with white field officers who spent most of their time trying to get rid of the Negro line officers. It did not get into the fighting line until the very last of the war. Then it was in support at the Argonne Battle and in the front line at the final movement on Metz the day of the Armistice.

 In both these cases it made an excellent record except in the disputed matter

1. This is a slip; Ninety Second Division is meant.

of the 368th Regiment. The 368th was a raw regiment which had never been in the front line and was brought up in support of the front line at the Argonne Battle. Then suddenly for reasons never fully explained this regiment without artillery support, without wire cutters, without signals and without proper instructions was rushed into the front line to keep liaison between the French and the Americans.

They advanced under great difficulties and finally occupied their objective but during these three days fighting under extraordinary difficulties two of the battalions twice retreated under orders from their line officers. The white field officers declared that the colored line officers ordered the retreat through cowardice. The colored officers declared that they had received the order which they gave. The result was that a number of the colored line officers were court martialed and sentenced to death, but the sentences and the circumstances were reviewed by the War Department and the officers were entirely exonerated.[2]

I shall be glad to furnish you any other information on this which you may wish.

Very sincerely yours,
W. E. B. Du Bois

Du Bois's life—as a Black man in the United States, a poet, and a fighter—was not an easy one and often had its very grim side; but with his humor and with the devotion he found at home, it had, too, its lighter and lovelier moments. To his daughter, Yolande, then a student at Fisk, Du Bois described one splendid evening.

New York, December 31, 1921.

My dear Yolande:

Guess what happened! Two weeks ago Miss [Jessie] Fauset asked your mother and me to meet some Cornell teachers of hers at the Civic Club and dine and was very insistent that we be dressed up. Then Mrs. Young came and she wanted your mother to buy a new white dress, whereupon your mother declared she would not, she was going to buy a black dress. But somehow Mrs. Young persuaded her and she got a white silk dress with lace overthings and your bunch of violets on one side. Then Thursday the 29th, after we had both attended a reception at Dr. Robert's, we started down in the car. I tried to persuade Miss Fauset that dress suit was too elaborate but she declared that her professors always wore dress suits and then I tried to persuade your mother that her white dress was going it pretty strong, but she said she had promised Mrs. Young.

2. For a good brief account, see John P. Davis, "The Negro in the Armed Forces of America," in *The American Negro Reference Book*, ed. J. P. Davis (Englewood Cliffs, New Jersey: Prentice-Hall, 1966), 2:esp. pp. 590–96.

It was very cold and the car did not want to go. At last we got started and arrived a half hour late, half past seven instead of seven. Miss Fauset let us in the hall very much dressed up and I asked her if she had reserved a table in the dining room. She said she had. Then she started up stairs with us and I supposed she had her guests in the front parlor. Instead she opened the doors to the back parlor and there we stood completely flabbergasted by the sight of a hundred or more people seated at the tables all dressed up to celebrate our silver wedding.

So when we got up courage we went in and sat down and ate and had lots of speeches wherein various people said extraordinary things about us and finally they gave us three magnificent pieces of solid silver plate consisting of a platter and two vegetable dishes. Then we danced until midnight and by this time, the car having been left out in the freezing weather for four hours, absolutely refused to budge and we came home on the street car very happy bringing the silver and big bunches of flowers.

I was sure you would want to know of this extraordinary happening, so I am hastening to write.

Lovingly yours,
Papa

Of the many Southern white novelists after World War I, Thomas S. Stribling (1881–1965) was outstanding. Most of his books dealt with his own region, as did *Teeftallow* (1926) and, especially, the trilogy of *The Forge* (1931), *The Store* (1932, winner of a Pulitzer Prize), and *Unfinished Cathedral* (1934). The letter he sent to Du Bois reveals plans for a novel that Stribling was writing, having as its central character a Negro couple; the man was to graduate from Harvard and begin his teaching career in Tennessee—as Du Bois did. It was published as *Birthright* (New York: Century Co., 1922).

Clifton, Tennessee, January 3, 1922

Dear Dr. Du Bois:

I am engaged in writing a book on the Negro in the north. I am in correspondence with Dr. J. E. Moorland of the New York Y.M.C.A. Col. Dept., and he suggested that I write you for a bibliography of Negro publications.

I am interested in any and every phase of Negro life in Northern cities, industrial, social, artistic.

I would like to understand the problems of the northern Negro, the color line as it is drawn up there. Also I would like to know the real root of the race riots in northern cities. Do they spring out of economic or social friction, or both?

What attitude do the labor unions take toward the Negro up there?

Are Negroes as a rule kept out of administrative positions in the north on account of their color, and when they succeed in gaining one of these places does their color undermine their effectiveness?

It is my intention to make a tour of all the larger northern cities this Spring and Summer studying the Negro populations. In which of these cities will I find colored life most highly developed socially and industrially? Which will best repay a long and careful study?

My object in this is fiction, and I know you understand how myriad-sided is the curiosity of a fiction writer, and how he must be a great deal more careful of his facts than the usual hit-or-miss journalist.

I thank you very much for your kindness if you will give me some idea about these matters.

Yours very truly,
T. S. Stribling

January 11, 1922.

Mr. T. S. Stribling
My dear Sir:

It seems to me it would be a great deal better if you would study one or two northern cities this summer instead of trying to undertake a large number. The Negro life in northern cities is very complicated and highly organized. The most interesting cities would be St. Louis, Chicago, Detroit, Cleveland, Indianapolis, Pittsburgh, New York, Philadelphia, Baltimore and Washington. No one of your questions could be answered in the same way for all these different cities. Everything would depend upon the particular city you were talking about.

Very sincerely yours,
W. E. B. Du Bois

Du Bois was a man concerned not only with the world at large, but also with his own immediate community. While living in Harlem, he and other intellectual, political, and religious leaders there frequently protested inferior public services and, especially, discriminatory and brutal police practices. One result of that protest appears in a letter to Du Bois from Richard E. Enright (1871–1953), the first man to rise through the ranks and serve as police commissioner of New York City (1918–25). Enright was a president of the Policeman's Benevolent Association, an assemblyman, and a city magistrate; in his last years, he was director of the United States Detective Service Bureau.

New York, June 2, 1922

Dr. W. E. B. DuBois
Dear Sir:

In accordance with an agreement reached at the conference recently held at the office of the Police Commissioner, at which were present a number of representative gentlemen from the colored district in Harlem and the West Side, I have appointed the following Committee to cooperate with this Department for the mutual interest of all concerned:

 Hon. Charles W. Anderson, Chairman

Rev. W. H. Hayes	Mr. James F. Adair
Rev. W. H. Brooks	Mr. Ferdinand Q. Morton
Rev. H. Arthur Booker	Lieut. Thomas E. Taylor
Rev. H. C. Bishop	Dr. W. E. B. DuBois
Rev. John Johnson	Mr. John W. Robinson
Rev. W. W. Brown	Mr. John E. Bruce
Mr. F. G. Snelson	Mr. H. J. Edwards

This Committee will be known as the Fair-Play League, and it will be their privilege to visit the station houses in the localities referred to and see for themselves how colored prisoners are treated.

I have directed the Commanding Officers of the districts and precincts covering the territories referred to to accord to this Committee every courtesy. Later on, I shall provide some insignia to be carried or worn by members of this Committee, but, in the meantime, this letter will serve to properly introduce the members thereof.

        Very truly yours,
        R. E. Enright
        Police Commissioner.

George H. Lorimer (1867–1937), originally from Kentucky, became editor-in-chief of the *Saturday Evening Post* in 1899 and held that position until the year prior to his death. He was also president, from 1932 to 1934, of the Curtis Publishing Company. In the 1920s and 1930s, Lorimer's magazine was among the most widely circulated in the United States. Du Bois's letter below, complaining about the fantastically chauvinistic stories printed while Lorimer was in charge, may be contrasted with the remark of Lorimer's biographer that there existed "unqualified acceptance by Negroes and whites alike" of the Octavus Roy Cohen travesties—described by the same biographer as "hilarious pieces about the city Negro." * Lorimer's reply to Du Bois, written from the *Post*'s offices, is signed "The Editors"; there is no personal signature.

---

 * John Tebbel, *George Horace Lorimer and the Saturday Evening Post* (Garden City, New York: Doubleday and Co., 1948), pp. 43, 69. Du Bois publicly attacked the magazine in an editorial in the *Crisis* 25 (April 1923):247–48, but apparently Mr. Tebbel did not know of that.

December 22nd, 1922.

Mr. George H. Lorimer
My dear Sir:—

We are continually receiving by word of mouth and by letter, protests against the treatment of the colored people in the *Saturday Evening Post.*

Especially have colored people objected to some of Irvin Cobb's stories, to nearly all of Roy Cohen's stories and lately to the story "Nick Pride" by Dingle.[1]

I know that under the race conditions in the United States, colored people are apt to be supersensitive, and to want in art and fiction, only those things that paint them at their very best. As a writer myself, I have the strongest belief in the freedom and truth of art and, therefore, while I sympathize with much of the criticism of the sort of thing you continually publish in the *Post* about Negroes, my chief criticism is not on what you *do* publish, but rather on what you *do not* publish.

While it is possible that Cohen's caricatures may have some artistic merit, surely no editor can think that this is the whole of the truth. And I am puzzled to know why it is, that only that type of Negro is allowed to put his foot within your pages.

I am aware that you can expect comparatively little revenue from Negro readers or advertisers, and yet it seems to me that the larger duties and ideals of an editor in your influential place, ought to induce you to look for, or at least to be willing to consider, other conceptions and portraits of Negroes, from those which you have in the past so persistently published.

I should be glad to know, if you are willing to express it, your attitude in this matter.

Very sincerely yours,
W. E. B. Du Bois

Philadelphia, December 29, 1922

Mr. W. E. B. DuBois

Dear Sir:

Many thanks for your letter of the twenty-second. We are always glad to hear from our readers and to receive their comment and criticism on the contents of the magazine. There is not the slightest intention or wish on our part to be unfair in our treatment of the colored people. When Paul Lawrence Dunbar was alive he was a regular contributor to our columns and we would welcome to our pages another colored writer with his ability. As a matter of fact we are inclined to think the critics to which you refer are just a little over sensitive. We do not remember ever having printed an ill-natured story about

---

1. The story "Nick Pride," by A. E. Dingle, appeared in the issue of December 1922 (195:16–17).

colored people and we print a great many more stories about whites a la Cohen than we do about colored. We think that our critics really want not equality of treatment but preferential treatment. As we have already said, we would welcome a colored writer of verse or fiction of Mr. Dunbar's ability to our columns.

Yours very truly,
The Editors

Great interest attaches to the following letter from Du Bois to Secretary of State Hughes, written early in 1923 when Liberia stood at the crossroads of considerable diplomatic and financial activity among the governments and leaders of the United States, France, and Britain. There appears to be no record of a response from the State Department. Du Bois's suggestion of a commercial connection between the United States—and especially its Black citizens—and Africa was not new with him; he had participated in an abortive African Development Company twenty years earlier. In the months just before this letter to Hughes, Du Bois had written several pieces on Africa for the *Crisis* (December 1920, August 1920, February 1922, April 1922) and for other magazines (*Nation*, 25 September 1920; *New Republic*, 7 December 1921; *Century*, February 1923).

January 5th, 1923.

Hon. Charles Hughes
Sir:—

As an American citizen of Negro descent, and a member of the Executive Board of the Pan-African Congress, I am very much alarmed at the failure of Congress to confirm the Liberian Loan.

I believe it is an open secret that the British and French Governments have only been held back in their aggression on Liberian territory, by the interest of the United States and by the prospect of her active aid. If this aid finally fails, I understand that British banking interests, in particular, have secured such financial hold upon Liberia that without the loan, Liberia will practically become a British protectorate with complete absorption looming in the future.

I am writing to ask what the colored people of the United States could do to avoid this contingency? I am convinced that the chance of Congress approving a loan to Liberia is now very small. On the other hand, I am sure if the commercial interests in this country had any adequate idea of the tremendous resources of Liberia, that private capital could help re-establish the country.

Moreover, among these private interests are the resources of Negro Americans. If the matter were properly presented to black America, and if the colored people were safe-guarded from the exploitations which might arise in such a project, they could loan considerable money to Liberia.

One of the best methods of bringing this about, would be to establish a direct commercial intercourse between America and Liberia under a small company in which colored people had representation. This company could do three things: 1st, it could begin direct commerce; 2nd, it could carry a few passengers backwards and forwards, not so much immigrants as observers, men of education and of technical training, who could report and investigate and guide the commerce; 3rd, it could establish in America a museum of Liberian resources, letting both colored and white people realize what tropical Africa means for future industrial development.

If this experiment could be made successful on a small scale, there is no telling what tremendous results both for Africa and America, might not eventually ensue.

There has been, as doubtless you have heard, a plan, looking somewhat toward such a start, in the now Bankrupt Black Star Line. The difficulty with this was that its leader, Marcus Garvey, was not a business man and turned out to be a thoroughly impractical visionary, if not a criminal, with grandiose schemes of conquest. The result was that he wasted some eight or nine hundred thousand dollars of the hard-earned pennies of Negro laborers. However, two things are clear; nearly a million dollars of Black Star Line stock of the Garvey movement is now distributed among colored people and is absolutely without value. On the other hand, the United States owns thousands of vessels, any one or two of which might be used to initiate the plan I have spoken of.

I write, therefore, to ask if there is any feasible and legal way by which the United States Government could aid or guide a plan of furnishing at least two ships for the tentative beginning of direct commercial intercourse between Liberia and America.

If a legal way for such an enterprise could be found, could this be also linked up with an attempt to restore the confidence of the mass of American Negroes in commercial enterprise with Africa, possibly by having a private company headed by men of highest integrity, both white and colored, to take up and hold in trust, the Black Star Line certificates?

It is quite possible that these matters are quite outside the purview and power of the State Department, but I have ventured to address you, Sir, because of the pressing importance of the matter. I am, Sir,

Very respectfully yours,
W. E. B. Du Bois

Robert S. Abbott (1870–1940) began his career as an attorney, but in 1905 he founded the weekly paper, the *Chicago Defender*. This paper gained its position as one of the most potent voices of Black America during and just after World War I; Abbott, who maintained a militant stance, remained in charge of it until his death. Du Bois's response to his letter seems not to have survived.

Chicago, January Fifth 1923.

Dr. W. E. B. DuBois
My dear sir:

Since the Race is robbed of political rights in the south, I believe that the most effective protest against the defeat [in the United States Senate] of the Dyer [anti-lynching] Bill must be economic. Every reputable leader and organization ought to urge our people to leave the south and settle in the west and northwestern states where they can fight for their rights with an even chance. Y.M.C.A., Y.W.C.A., the Urban League and N.A.A.C.P. must not only see to it that these people are guided to freedom but take steps to adjust them to northern environment and conditions.

Once settled in the north and west, civic organizations must teach them the value of the ballot and how to use it. Race voters in the north must vote for the man and issues rather than the party. Political freedom must be used to show Congress that our interests are as important as those of any other group. We can show them by voting against those men who are not with us in our fight for justice and American rights.

Sincerely yours,
Robert S. Abbott

The prolific Charles Edward Russell had two books published in 1922; it is to these that he refers in a 1923 letter. The first was *Railroad Melons, Rates and Wages* (Chicago: Charles H. Kerr, 1922); the second, *The Outlook for the Philippines* (New York: Century Co., 1922).

Washington, D.C., January 7, 1923.

Dear Dr. DuBois:

I hope you will like my railroad book, but the thing I most wanted you to see is my book on the Philippines. I wanted to bring to your attention a slight variation in the Anglo-Saxon attitude toward peoples of a darker complexion. Here at home we exclude them from the operation of the constitution and laws that secure all the rest of us and lately have gone to the length of declaring in effect that the security of their lives against mob violence is no concern of government. In the Philippines we make with them a solemn covenant to which they adhere with meticulous care and when the time comes for us to fulfill our part of the agreement we side-step and lie and fake to avoid our obligations. Taking altogether what I have seen of the Anglo-Saxon in India, the South Seas, the Philippines, the West Indies and the United States the enthusiasm with which some quaint thing called "Anglo-Saxon civilization" is vaunted seems to me a grotesque joke. I thought possibly your notice might not have been drawn to the Philippine trick and I wanted to have your judgment on it.

With best wishes for the new year

Yours very truly
Charles Edward Russell

For about half a century, one of the most effective and radical members of the West Indian community in the United States was William A. Domingo (1889–1968), who made his home in New York City. Although one of the leaders in the early years of the Garvey movement, he left it when it became more and more conservative in its politics and nationalistic in its outlook. Indicative is the exchange between him and Du Bois.

New York City, January 17, '23.

Dr. W. E. B. DuBois
Dear Sir:

I enclose herewith a copy of an open letter that I have sent to the editor of the Messenger Magazine in which I have referred to you and the Crisis favorably.

As I am a stickler for accuracy of statement I would be only too glad if you will advise me if I have correctly interpreted your attitude on the Garvey question in so far as his nativity is concerned.

Thanking you for your mention of my analysis of the U.N.I.A.[1]

Yours for racial unity
W. A. Domingo

January 18th, 1923.

My dear Mr. Domingo:

I thoroughly agree with your thesis that in the attack on Garvey, the object should be the opinions of the man and not the man himself or his birthplace.

American Negroes, to a much larger extent that they realize, are not only blood relatives to the West Indians but under deep obligations to them for many things. For instance without the Haitian Revolt, there would have been no emancipation in America as early as 1863. I, myself am of West Indian descent and am proud of the fact.

My attitude toward Garvey has been, I think, consistent. First, I want him and all people to have freedom of speech and I mean by this, real freedom. But the freedom that he takes must be granted to those who do not agree with him. Secondly, I think his propaganda for the most part is absolutely wrong and to

1. The reference is to Du Bois's essay on the Universal Negro Improvement Association in the *Crisis* 25 (January 1923):120–22.

some extent criminal. So far as he is wrong, I want to expose it; and so far as it is criminal, he ought to be punished by the courts. I do not, however, believe in deportation for him or anybody else; and I do not believe that a man's birthplace, or his race or his color furnishes any ground for attack.

Very sincerely yours,
W. E. B. Du Bois

Reflective of Du Bois's constant effort to improve the quality of living was his concern and activity about his own neighborhood. There is published here one letter of several on this matter; it brought little reform and only a formal response from the police commissioner.

April 3, 1923

Mr. R. E. Enright, Police Commissioner
Sir:

I am a resident of Harlem and one of the persons whom you appointed in June 1922 as a member of the Fair Play League. I am especially interested in the condition of the park known as St. Nicholas Park and on St. Nicholas Avenue between 131st and 130th Streets. I have before complained both to the Police Department and the Park Department of the utter neglect and lack of supervision which is turning one of the most beautiful spots in New York City into a waste.

Last year, a playground was placed there but it is without supervision and almost without apparatus and the children are not confined to the limits of the playground but roam all over the park doing untold damage to trees, shrubbery and grass. I live directly opposite the park and it is seldom if ever that I see a policeman anywhere around. One officer with a tin whistle in these six or eight blocks could easily preserve the looks and decency of the park.

When I complained to the Police Department about the park they blamed the Park Department. When I complained to the Park Department they blamed the police. But whosever fault it is, it is nothing less than a crying shame and it is due as it seems to me, simply to the fact that colored people have moved into the neighborhood and that the city government with rare unanimity is proceeding to make the whole neighborhood as ugly and unpleasant as possible. I am writing to you to ask your good offices in some effort to save this park.

I am, Sir,

Very respectfully yours,
W. E. B. Du Bois

Franklin C. Lewis (1877–1930), born in Massachusetts and a graduate of Dartmouth and Harvard, taught for some years at Dartmouth. In 1906, he became superintendent of the Ethical Culture School located at West Sixty-Third Street in New York City; his letter to Du Bois produced a succinct and significant reply.

New York, April 18, 1923

My dear Mr. Du Bois:

We are planning a course under the auspices of our History Department, the object of which shall be to acquaint our young people with the larger problems they are likely to face when they assume the responsibilities of adult citizenship. Our object is to cultivate an interest in the problems and an open-minded, serious attitude towards them. We desire also to accustom our young people to test such problems by the standards of right human relations.

Will you help by stating for us what, in your judgment, are the larger questions in politics, international relations, industry, etc., that are likely to face the citizens of tomorrow?

We shall greatly appreciate your interest and help.

Sincerely yours,
F. C. Lewis

April 24, 1923.

Mr. F. C. Lewis
My dear Sir:

Answering your letter of April 18th I beg to say that I think the great questions which face the citizens of tomorrow are:

1—"Racial Contact and Intermingling";
2—"The Distribution of Work and Income";
3—"The Education of Children";
4—"The Abolition of War."

Very sincerely yours,
W. E. B. Du Bois

Walter Francis White (1893–1955) was a 1916 graduate of Atlanta University whose family was well-known to Du Bois when he lived in Georgia. At Du Bois's recommendation and with his urging, White as a young man served as James Weldon Johnson's assistant secretary for the NAACP, succeeding him in 1931 as secretary, a position he then held until his death. In addition to such leadership, White was the author of many articles and several books of both fiction and non-fiction.*

In an inter-office memo, dated 12 June 1923, White informed Du Bois that he had promised to prepare an article treating the changes in concepts of solving the

---

* His autobiography is *A Man Called White* (New York: The Viking Press, 1948).

so-called Negro question that had marked the preceding twenty years. Most dramatic among these, he thought, were the conflicting views and policies projected by Booker T. Washington and Du Bois. In light of this, White asked Du Bois several specific questions; their nature will appear in Du Bois' reply:†

June 12th, 1923.

Memo to Mr. White:—

1. The weakness of the Booker Washington philosophy was the assumption that economic power can be won and maintained without political power. The strength of the Washington philosophy was its insistence upon the necessity of manual labor, and its inculcation of thrift and saving.

2. The past twenty years have shown that Mr. Washington was right in his encouragement of industry, saving and business enterprise among Negroes. That he was wrong in his assumption that this increase of Negro wealth, efficiency and intelligence was going to decrease the prejudice of the whites, without any further action or power on the part of the Negroes.

3. The favorable effect of Mr. Washington's propaganda was to make the white people think about Negro problems, and make the colored people have faith in white people. The unfavorable effect was to lead the white people to mistake a temporary makeshift for an eternal solution; and on the part of the colored people it made them dream that they could get their rights by individual working and saving; and that group organization and sturdy resistance to aggression was unnecessary.

There is no reason for retaining much of Mr. Washington's philosophy except as an interesting historical fact. No Negro dreams to-day that he can protect himself in industry and business without a vote and without a fighting aggressive organization. No intelligent white man believes that the Negro is going to accept caste and peonage without a struggle; he knows that the day when white people can choose Negro leaders to tell the colored people what they want the colored people told has not passed to be sure, but is rapidly passing.

P.S. I might add that on the educational side of Mr. Washington's philosophy, he undoubtedly over-emphasized the place and value of manual training and industry as a means of education; and did not appreciate the history and meaning of college training. This was natural because of his own difficult and limited education. Moreover, this philosophy was valuable to the white world, which having already well-established colleges and universities, was undoubtedly neglecting manual training. On the other hand, for the Negro schooled in the hard experience of industrial life and almost without facilities for higher train-

---

† Mrs. Walter F. White has declined to give permission to publish her late husband's correspondence with Du Bois; hence, here and elsewhere in this volume, his letters are summarized.

ing, Mr. Washington's educational plans were almost fatal and are being rapidly overturned to-day. Already Hampton has added a college department and is trying to cut off her lower grades; while Tuskegee has become a high school and will eventually become a college.

W. E. B. Du Bois

Frank R. Crosswaith (1893-1965), born in the Virgin Islands, studied at the Rand School in New York City, served as an organizer for both the International Ladies' Garment Workers' Union and the Brotherhood of Sleeping Car Porters, and was a lecturer for the Socialist party and the League for Industrial Democracy. On different occasions, especially during the 1920s, he ran for public office on the Socialist party ticket. Intensely anti-Communist, in 1941 he was a leader of the right wing in the American Labor party. During World War II, he served as a member of the Housing Authority of New York City.

His letter to Du Bois in the summer of 1923 was written as a commentary on an article, "Political Straws," in the *Crisis* 26 (July 1923):124-26, prepared by Morris Lewis of Charlestown, South Carolina, and R. McCants Andrews of Durham, North Carolina. The article concentrated on moods in the Black communities in Baltimore and Chicago and concluded that their political strategy seemed to be to defeat known enemies, even if that meant voting Democratic, and increasingly to split the Black vote. Closing comments in the essay suggested that both the Farmer-Labor and the Socialist parties were ignoring Black people and their needs.

New York City, July 2, 1923.

Editor "The Crisis"

Since the recent National Convention of the Socialist Party in this city, the air has been thickened with many "poison-gas" lies spread by those recognized enemies of the Party, until now, even those who should know better have become affected and are repeating these falsehoods.

It has been charged by these wreckers that the Socialist Party is prejudiced against the Negro, to the extent that it openly refuses to "fraternize" with Negroes; in other words, the attitude of the Socialist Party toward the Negro is questioned. I do not think it worthwhile to waste any time in answering the Communists who make these charges, for their reputation as "aliens to truth" is a matter of universal knowledge. But, when these falsehoods, for some reason or other, are taken up and repeated by people who should know better, it is time then for us to call a spade by its right name.

In the July number of the Crisis Magazine, considerable space is devoted to a discussion of the probable attitude of the Negro voter in the Presidential campaign of 1924. It is significant to note that in dealing with this question, the writer very carefully avoids mentioning any other political organization but the two old parties of Wall Street. He also, very subtly and conveniently, steered clear of even a reference to those Negroes who were candidates on tickets other than the Republican and Democratic parties. As a matter of fact, any unprejudiced reader, before proceeding very far into the body of [the] article, would become convinced that this "Negro Political Prophet" was making "goo-goo eyes" at the Democratic Party. That however, is not the chief offense. The crime occurs when in closing the article, he mentions, for the first and only time, the Farmer-Labor and Socialist Parties in these words. *"Is it not unfortunate that at this critical period in the history of the Negro voter the Farmer-Labor Party is ducking all of the issues in which Black men are primarily interested, while the Socialists are openly refusing to fraternize with Negroes"?*

It seems indeed a strange performance for any honest person to so charge the Socialist Party, or to question in any way its attitude in regard to the rights —*all the rights*—of the Negro; for history shows no record so persistently spotless in its stand on the Negro question, as that of the Socialist movement, from the formation of the First International under the direct guidance of Karl Marx, until today. Every unprejudiced man and woman who reads and thinks, knows that the Socialist Party has always taken the right stand in regards [to] the Negro. In the dark and barbarous Southland, the Socialist movement has made but little progress, due, in large part, to the fact that it must first break down barriers of prejudice, ignorance and hate, erected chiefly against the Negro. Most Southerners are bitterly opposed to Socialism and the Socialist Party for no other reason than it has taken the right attitude on the Negro question.

The "Searchlight," official organ of the Ku Klux Klan in its campaign against radicalism, pointed out in its issue of September 30, 1923 as one of the greatest crimes of the Socialists the fact that they were appealing to Negroes to join with them on the plane of common equality.

But since the Crisis carries at its mast-head the proud boast of being *"a record of the darker races,"* it might be well that this record be a clear one; and, in order to assist in making it clear, I desire to ask some pointed questions.

In 1918, in the midst of the world's-slaughter, at a time when countless numbers of black and white workingmen were being offered up on the bloody altar of war and profit, a stalwart and fearless champion of the Negro race, George Frazier Miller, was nominated by the Socialist Party to represent the 21st District in the U. S. House of Representatives.[1] The Socialist Party nominated

1. The Reverend George Frazier Miller (1864–1943), a friend of Du Bois, was born in South Carolina and educated at Howard, the General Theological Seminary, and New York University. He served in churches in the Carolinas, but, from 1896 until his death, was the rector of Saint Augustine's Church in Brooklyn, New York. Early in the twentieth century, he was a president of the National Equal Rights League, and he remained a militant—and a socialist—his entire life.

Comrade Miller and presented him to the Negro voters of Harlem, primarily because he stood staunchly for the economic freedom of all men regardless of race, color, religion or nationality; and, to give Negroes the opportunity, denied them by Republicans and Democrats, to have one of their race in a position to voice the race's claims for social justice before the tribunal of the nation, during and after the period of the war.

May I not be bold enough to ask, *Why did not the Crisis and the* N.A.A.C.P. *have something, no matter how little, to say in behalf of this Negro candidate who at the time was an officer of the association?*

Again in 1920, the Socialist Party nominated for Comptroller of the State of New York a Negro, a scholar, one of the most eloquent and dauntless fighters for Negro rights, in the person of A. Philip Randolph. Certainly, that was a distinct advance in the political life of Negro-Americans, but again the "Record of the darker races" had nothing to say of this giant young Negro. *Why*, I ask?

In the election of 1922, the Socialist Party again gave a place on its State ticket, as Secretary of State, to Comrade Randolph. This was indeed a mile-stone in the political journey of the Negro race. What could be nobler, what could lend greater courage and prestige to the claims of the coming generations of black Americans than the fact that one of their race was actually nominated by one of the major parties for the high office of Secretary of State, of the greatest State, in the very land in which his fathers had been slaves. Yet the N.A.A.C.P. and the "Record of the darker races" completely ignored this historic fact. *Again, I ask why?*

I have noticed the Crisis going out of its way to record the nomination and election of Negroes on the tickets of the Republican and Democratic Parties; while persistently ignoring candidates on any other party's ticket. There must be a reason for this strange procedure, *and I boldly ask the Crisis and the* N.A.A.C.P. *to state the reason.*

Surely, at this crucial hour in the life of the American Negro, no one who essays to lead can afford to withhold from the masses truths which will enable them to find a way out of their present chaotic condition. Great questions are being answered in the world of men today; mighty and far-reaching decisions are being made; the human race is again girding its loins in an effort to move forward in its never-ending march of progress. The Negro's destiny is fatally and indissolubly united with the fate of all mankind in this dark hour. Never before has the need been so manifest as now for sound leadership, well-informed and open-minded leadership, and above all, for honest leadership. Never again must the entire Negro race be handed over body and soul to their oppressors; never again must it be recorded that all Negroes are of one political faith. The time has come, when the light of reason and self-interest, "not custom"—intelligence, "not prejudice"—should be the guiding stars to illuminate the Negro's path to freedom.

And, prompted by no other motive but a sincere desire to contribute something, no matter how insignificant, to the enlightenment of my race, hoping in turn to be enlightened by those in the position to enlighten me, I boldly, but respectfully ask: *Is it, or is it not, to the best interest of the race to espouse the cause of Socialism and the social revolution; or, will the best interest of the race be served by further aligning ourselves with the Republican and Democratic parties?*

With a very high regard for the Crisis and the N.A.A.C.P. of which I am a member; and, with a polite request for a reply through the columns of the next issue of the former, I remain

Yours, for all the rights of all men,
Frank R. Crosswaith

July 10, 1923.

Mr. Frank R. Crosswaith
My dear Sir:—

I have your letter of July 2nd. I have been trying in vain to get the facts concerning the resolution of the Negro offered in the last Socialist Convention.

The American Press gave an account saying, "The Convention was divided by a resolution which, in its original state, called for 'fraternization' between Negro and white members of the Socialist Party." It then said that the word "fraternization" was stricken out and the word "cooperation" substituted.

I immediately wrote a long and sharp editorial. Then it occurred to me that this might be an untrue statement. I therefore sent for copies of "The Call" covering the meeting. There I was faced by this statement: "Another resolution was passed highly commending the work of the organization of Negro workers in the Socialist party, the text of which was not quite ready when the convention adjourned." This is manifestly a suspiciously incomplete statement. I therefore published the little article to which you object.[1]

Both the tone of your letter and the tone of "The Call" editorials is again not reassuring. What I am after is facts concerning this resolution. I know the record of the Socialist party toward the Negro very well.[2] On the whole it has been exceptionally good as I have said from time to time. But for the most part its theoretical attitude has never been put to a practical test. Even the nominations which you speak of were of very little importance since there was not the

---

1. The *Call*, in its issue of 29 June 1923, printed a lead editorial, "Some Negro 'Leadership,'" denouncing the *Crisis* for publishing this article. The same issue also published a long letter by George S. Schuyler, then a socialist, attacking the magazine and Du Bois.

2. Du Bois had written on this subject very early: he devoted two articles to it— "A Field for Socialists" and "Socialism and the Negro Problem"—in the radical journal, the *New Review* 1 (11 January 1913):54–57 and 1 (1 February 1913):138–41. For a recent good account, see R. L. Moore, "Flawed Fraternity—American Socialist Response to the Negro, 1901–1912," *Historian* 32, no. 1 (November 1969):1–18.

slightest chance for any of these gentlemen and the Socialist [party] knew this quite well.

On the other hand, the question of segregated Locals in the South is of tremendous practical importance and it is here that the Party is wavering and, I am afraid, failing to stand up to its ideals.

Very sincerely yours,
W. E. B. Du Bois

Marcus Garvey's most ambitious commercial plan was the creation of the Black Star Line; hundreds of thousands of dollars were raised and four ships finally obtained, but no business was ever actually conducted. In January 1922, Garvey was arrested by federal authorities and charged with using the mails to defraud; he was tried in May 1923 before Federal Circuit Judge Julian W. Mack, a contributor to the NAACP. Earlier, eight prominent Black individuals—including John E. Nail, in real estate; Robert S. Abbott, the Chicago publisher; and William Pickens and Robert W. Bagnall, of the NAACP—had petitioned the United States Attorney General to "push the government's case against Marcus Garvey."

Garvey was convicted in 1923 and sentenced to five years in jail, although three co-defendants were acquitted. Coolidge commuted the sentence in 1927 and in December of that year Garvey was deported to Jamaica. During Du Bois's lifetime and since, even distinguished historians have characterized him as Garvey's "arch-enemy";* that description, however, is inaccurate. Deep disagreement did exist but, on the whole, the quality of Garvey's opposition to Du Bois was more bitter, more deep, and his expressions of it more vituperative, than were Du Bois's toward Garvey. Some of the positions of both sides appear in an interchange between a Black woman living in Harlem and Du Bois, soon after Garvey was convicted.

New York, July 5, 1923

Dr. Du Bois
Dear Sir:—

It is the concensus of opinion by quite a large number of the readers of your magazine that if as much effort had been made to arouse interest in the membership of the association of the city as has been given by you and your organization in sending Mr Garvey to jail and trying to wreck the universal negro improvement association especially as to the cowardly way in which it was done while writing letters to the District Attorney, Judge Mack and to others who were in authority.

---

* These are the words, for example, of the Nigerian scholar E. U. Essien-Udom, in his introduction to the second edition of *Philosophy and Opinions of Marcus Garvey*, ed. Amy Jacques Garvey (London: Frank Cass and Co., 1967), p. xxvi.

This has been considered by a great many who have looked into the case as unmanly and cowardly. You must know that while you may destroy the individual you cannot destroy an organization or a principle which has been so deeply imbedded in the minds of the people as the work of Mr Garvey.

While the most of us are not interested in him at all, personally, we feel that the methods used by you and your organization were not only uncalled for and cowardly but will always reflect to the discredit of you and your associates and cause everlasting enmity between the West Indian and the American negroes which feeling will take a long time to eradicate.

Very truly yours,
Ira May Reynolds

July 10, 1923

My dear Madam:

Answering your letter of July 5th, I beg to say I have never written any letters to the District Attorney or Judge Mack or anyone else in authority with regard to Marcus Garvey, nor have I had anything whatsoever to do with the prosecution of the case against him.

Very sincerely yours,
W. E. B. Du Bois

Du Bois consistently fought against forced segregation and discrimination. At the same time, and without any contradiction in his own mind, he insisted that where separate Black institutions or organizations existed, it was necessary and proper to bring these to as high a point of efficiency and service as possible. Some disagreed with this proposition, holding that under all circumstances segregation must be attacked and that nothing else was required; others seem not to have understood Du Bois's position, and frequently garbled reportage of that stance did not help. Inaccurate reporting of one such address delivered in Philadelphia in 1923 resulted in correspondence between a Black Baptist minister of Chicago, the Reverend J. A. Walden, and Du Bois.

Chicago, July 18th 1923.

Dr. W. E. B. Du Bois
Dear Sir;

The Baptist ministers' conference of Chicago appointed me and instructed me to write you concerning your Phila. address inst, that is, whether you are for Jim Crow schools or against them. Will you kindly write us on this matter as we do not like to form an opinion without first hand information when such can be had? Thank you previously for an early reply,

I remain yours truly,
J. A. Walden

July 25th, 1923.

Rev. J. A. Walden
My dear Sir:—

I am enclosing a statement of what I said in Philadelphia.[1]

In addition to this I may say that I believe that a "Jim Crow" school system is the greatest possible menace to democracy and the greatest single hindrance to our advance in the United States. At the same time, we have separate schools in the South and in some cases in the North and these schools have done [and] are doing excellent work. The teachers in them in most cases have been capable, self-sacrificing persons. I believe in these schools in the sense that without them we could not have gotten our present education. I should be sorry and alarmed to see their number increased and I look forward to the time when all separate institutions based simply upon race will disappear.

I trust this will answer your question.

Very sincerely yours,
W. E. B. Du Bois

A letter from Annie H. Howe was precipitated by a Du Bois editorial, "The Tuskegee Hospital," *Crisis* 26 (July 1923):106–7. The editorial noted that, while there had been planned a hospital at Tuskegee Institute for Negro veterans of World War I, to be staffed by Black people, and while Dr. Moton, the head of Tuskegee, was appointed chief of personnel by President Harding, there also was appointed—suddenly and with no consultation of the Black community —Col. Robert H. Stanley, white, as superintendent. The immediately ensuing events are covered in Du Bois's reply to Mrs. Howe, and Du Bois returned to the question with an editorial, "Tuskegee and Moton," in the September 1924 *Crisis* (28:200–201). An excellent modern account of the episode, by Pete Daniel, can be found in the *Journal of Southern History* 36 (August 1970):368–88.

Alstead Center, N.H., July 27th 1923

My dear Mr. Du Bois,

I receive the "Crisis" monthly and have been giving my copy to the janitor in the apartment house in which I live in Springfield, but sometimes I wonder if something that excites you and which seems unjust and vindictive, cannot be explained in other ways.

I enclose a clipping from the "Outlook,"[2] a paper I am sure that can be trusted

1. See "The Negro and the Northern Public Schools," a two-part article by Du Bois in the *Crisis* in March and April 1923 (25:205–8; 25:262–65); and "The Segregated Negro World," *World Tomorrow* (May 1923), pp. 136–38.

2. Reference is to an editorial, "Why Negro Veterans Lack Negro Doctors," in the *Outlook* 134 (18 July 1923):396–98; its content is summarized in Du Bois's reply to Mrs. Howe. The *Outlook*'s editorial closes by citing the paucity of Black physicians and dentists, giving illustrative statistics.

to write what is true, and I wonder why the "Crisis" does not mention some of the good, as well as all the bad reasons imaginable for the Hospital being equipped as it has been with white doctors. I give my copy of the "Crisis" to our janitor because I feel that much in it is calculated to inspire ambition and gratify the pride of any Negro man but I do not wish to arouse bitterness in him over any supposed indignities to his race. I realize there is much real injustice shown both by blacks and whites in this world, but dwelling on it or over-emphasizing it seems to me harmful, not helpful.

I wonder why the "Crisis" does not print some of the statistics which are in this enclosed slip? White people suffer just as much when unjustly accused as colored people do.

Yours sincerely
Annie H. Howe
(Mrs. John K. Howe)

August 1, 1923.

Mrs. John K. Howe
My dear Madam:

I have your letter of July 27th with the clipping from The Outlook. I regret to say that so far as the American Negro is concerned The Outlook cannot be trusted. A decade or more ago The Outlook started to increase its southern white circulation and in order to make sure of this circulation it engaged southern writers to write its editorials concerning the Negro. These writers not only do not represent the best conscience of the white south but they deliberately express the attitude of the men who believe in race segregation, in the subordination of black folk and they have excused at times mob law and even lynching.

Nothing better illustrates the attitude of The Outlook than the editorial which you send me. It would be a fair inference from this editorial to assume that the following were facts in the Tuskegee muddle:

1. That the original plan was to have the hospital under white control.

2. That the government was unable to get a sufficient number of trained Negro physicians.

3. That the Negroes demanded the juggling of the Civil Service rules to their favor.

4. That the hostility at Tuskegee was "incited by the N.A.A.C.P." which asked for the Federal troops to protect Negroes at Tuskegee.

These so-called facts are each separately untrue and the total effect of them is that of a deliberate lie. The original plan was not "to have white nurses and white head nurses, the other nurses to be Negroes." The original plan as stated by the President of the United States and the head of the Veteran's Bureau was to have Negro personnel throughout.

The Tuskegee whites did not ask for white "head nurses." They asked for a complete set of white nurses and each nurse was to have a nurse maid attached to her presumably to carry her train.

The government had no difficulty in finding a complete staff of Negro physicians except in one respect and that was to insure them adequate protection at Tuskegee against the Ku Klux Klan and the people who believe in The Outlook.

The N.A.A.C.P. never asked for Federal troops "for the protection of Negroes at Tuskegee." The N.A.A.C.P. simply asked that the Federal government protect its own property at Tuskegee and its own employees. The N.A.A.C.P. knew then and the Veterans Bureau at Washington knows that the demonstration of the Ku Klux Klan at Tuskegee took place with the aid and consent of the white physician who is now at the head of the Tuskegee hospital, that the Klan was furnished sheets for its mummery and entertained at the Hospital and that as a head government official has recently said the whole present fight is being engineered in the Tuskegee hospital by a white man fighting for his job. If the United States government cannot protect its own property, what in the name of God can it do? If a set of hoodlums in New York or Alabama deliberately, openly and with malice overthrow the authority of the United States Government on its own property no series of lies on the part of The Outlook or anybody else can persuade thinking men that the N.A.A.C.P. is inciting lawlessness at Tuskegee.

The statistics which you and The Outlook triumphantly bring forward to prove the need of physicians among black folk is but additional proof of the righteousness of our stand. Why have we not more physicians and dentists? Because of the present discrimination and discouragement hemming in colored students and the lack of facilities in our own schools.

The Crisis continually has to combat the smug indifference of those people who are so afraid that mention of the evil of the world is going to induce bitterness and discontent. We are not afraid of bitterness and discontent, we are afraid of evil and we have neither patience nor respect for those people who would let the evil of the world go swaggering on because they fear lest some poor victim may raise his shackled hands to Heaven and shake with his righteous anger the foundations of hell. I am, Madam

Very sincerely yours,
W. E. B. Du Bois

Mrs. E. A. Duffield of Washington, D.C., wrote to Du Bois in July 1923 telling him that she generally found the *Crisis* an excellent and valuable magazine. But, she added, the poetry of Langston Hughes, which she thought approached the vulgar, repelled her as unfit for her daughter. Mrs. Duffield no doubt had in mind the August 1923 issue—which reached subscribers the latter part of the preceding month—in which eight poems by Langston Hughes appeared; two, entitled "The Cabaret" and "Young Prostitute," surely perturbed Mrs. Duffield.

August 1, 1923.

Mrs. E. A. Duffield
My dear Madam:

I think your attitude toward Mr. Hughes' poems is absolutely wrong. I too have a daughter, but I am absolutely convinced that the last way to conquer evil is to hide the evil from youth. The poet depicts life as it is and he can be justly condemned only if he makes evil seem more beautiful and good. This Mr. Hughes in his strikingly beautiful poems has never done. He talks about prostitutes frankly and if you think that your children do not know that there are prostitutes in the world you are deceiving yourself.

On the other hand Mr. Hughes does not for a moment make the cabarets of Harlem beautiful and desirable. He paints them with their sobs and tawdry evil and he paints evil as evil and that makes him a great poet and only great poets and prophets like Hughes can teach children where blind parents are simply trying to keep them from seeing.

I thank you very much for your kind words concerning The Crisis.

Very sincerely yours,
W. E. B. Du Bois

By the summer of 1923, plans for the third meeting of the Pan-African Congress were well advanced. The congress met in November of that year, with sittings in London, Paris, and Lisbon. In England, Du Bois met with leaders of the Labour party and stressed the importance of Black-white unity if democracy on a world scale were to be furthered. Three letters in this connection follow. Two are from the then-prominent Labour M.P. and soon-to-be prime minister J. Ramsay MacDonald; the last is from the author H. G. Wells. The first letter from MacDonald was written to Du Bois shortly before he left for Europe; the second and the third were replies to notes from Du Bois while he was in England.

[London] September 24th 1923

Dear Professor du Bois:

I am very glad indeed to hear from you and to know that there is a chance of meeting you again. I am not sure, however, about my movements at the beginning of November. I am just leaving for Constantinople and will certainly be away the whole of next month. If I am in town when you are meeting, it would give me the greatest pleasure to attend one of your Sessions and say a few words.

Yours very sincerely,
J. Ramsay MacDonald.

[London] Nov. 6, 1923

My dear Dr. DuBois,

I am so sorry, but tomorrow (Wednesday) morning I am off to my constituency and I shall not be back until Friday. I shall, therefore, be unable to look in at your Conference.

You know how much I am with every movement that aims at justice being done to your people to open out the world for them and to make them co-operators with all the other races.

With kindest regards,

> Yours very sincerely,
> J. Ramsay MacDonald.

[London] 6 . XI . 23

Dear Mr. du Bois

I've long wanted to meet you. I can't come to the conference on Wednesday & I can't speak on either day because I don't quite know your drift but I may be able to come in on Thursday morning about 12.[1] If I do may I carry you off to the Reform Club for lunch & a talk?

> Very sincerely yours
> H. G. Wells

In 1923, Du Bois was appointed by Coolidge to serve as envoy extraordinary and minister plenipotentiary and to be the president's personal representative at the inauguration of president Charles D. B. King of Liberia on New Year's Day in 1924. The letters here published—one from William H. Lewis (1869–1949) to Du Bois and the second, enclosed with the first, from Lewis to Coolidge—give something of the background to this appointment.[*]

Lewis, born in Virginia of former slaves, had his early education there before moving with his family to New England. He was the first or one of the first of the Negro page boys appointed to the floor of Congress. In Amherst, he made a remarkable record as class orator and athlete. He then graduated from Harvard Law School, and served on the city council in Cambridge (1899) and in the state legislature of Massachusetts (1902). Under Theodore Roosevelt, he served as an assistant United States attorney in the Boston area; under Taft, he was assistant attorney general. In 1913, he returned permanently to private practice; nevertheless, he retained considerable political influence.

Boston, October 4, 1923

My dear Dr. Du Bois:

I have just returned from Washington, where I took up the matter of your

---

1. According to DuBois, Wells did address the congress, as did Harold J. Laski (*Dusk of Dawn*, p. 279).

* For Du Bois's description of this experience, see his *Dusk of Dawn*, pp. 122–25. See also the letter from W. R. Castle, Jr., to Du Bois, 28 May 1925, and its enclosures, pp. 313–14 below.

appointment with secretary Slemp.[1] He seemed to think very favorably of it.

Before going to the White House, I also had the approval of Dr. Emmett J. Scott and Perry W. Howard.[2] I wanted to make sure that there would be no knocks in the machine when it got started. I was able to say to Secretary Slemp, that all the different elements of our people were united in your appointment to this mission.

I am enclosing for your information, a letter which I received from Dr. Scott this morning, and am sending you also a copy of the letter which I am sending to President Coolidge.

I hope that I have not made any great blunder in the matter. I thought that I had better have our forces united, and have the thing move from the White House to the Department of State, rather than from the Department of State to the White House.

I shall be able to talk to either Cassell, or Phillips concerning the matter as soon as it gets into the State Department.[3]

With best wishes for success, I am

Sincerely yours,
William H. Lewis

[Boston] October 4, 1923.

My dear Mr. President:—

It has come to my attention that Dr. William E. Burghardt Du Bois, the distinguished publisher and scholar of the colored race, and indeed of America, intends to make a visit to the Republic of Liberia in the near future, and will probably attend the inauguration of the new President of the Republic, the Honorable C. B. D. King, who recently visited this country as a member of the Liberian Commission.

I am sure you must know that Dr. Du Bois has been for many years connected with the National Association for the Advancement of Colored People, and is editor of the Crisis, a very influential publication among our people.

It occurs to me that it would be a very graceful thing if our government could make Dr. Du Bois its special representative at the inauguration of Presi-

1. Campbell B. Slemp (1870–1943) of Virginia taught at the state's Military Institute and also practiced law there. He was in Congress from 1907 to 1923 and was Coolidge's secretary and right-hand man from 1923 to 1925. Du Bois wrote a blistering denunciation of Slemp's appointment by Coolidge—see the *Crisis* 26 (October 1923):248–49.

2. Emmett J. Scott, a protégé of Booker T. Washington, was one of three commissioners sent as an investigating team to Liberia in 1909 by President Taft; he served as an assistant to War Secretary Baker during World War I. Perry W. Howard, a Fisk graduate and an attorney, practiced from 1905 to his death in 1961; he also served for over forty years as Republican national committeeman representing Mississippi (though he lived in Washington).

3. William R. Castle, Jr., was at this time assistant secretary of state. William Phillips was then undersecretary of state and later ambassador to Belgium.

dent King, which takes place, I think, about the first of January next. It would be a splendid opportunity to show to the Liberian Republic, that notwithstanding the failure of the five million dollar loan in the Congress, yet the Government of the United States still continues to maintain a kindly and friendly interest in that Republic.

At the same time, I feel certain that our Government would make no mistake in honoring such as man as Du Bois as its special representative upon such an occasion.

I have gone over with Secretary Slemp more in detail additional reasons for this appointment.

I very earnestly recommend to your early and favorable consideration the appointment of Dr. Du Bois to be the special representative of the United States at the inauguration of President King.

I have the honor to be,

Very respectfully yours,
William H. Lewis

As a result of Du Bois's service as envoy to Liberia, a friendship marked by fairly regular exchanges of views developed between him and the Liberian president, Charles D. B. King (1878-1961). Three of their letters, written during the winter and summer of 1924, are here published.

Monrovia, Liberia, January 21, 1924

The Honorable C. D. B. King
Your Excellency:

On leaving Liberia I want to lay before you certain considerations of mine, as to the economic development of Liberia.

First: I believe that Liberia must have immediately at least fifty and preferably one hundred miles of railway from Monrovia up the St. Paul as far as the plateau. Eventually, a branch should run southwest to Cape Palmas.

Secondly: I believe Liberia should have a sound Bank and that this must be under Negro control.

Thirdly: I believe Liberia needs the aid of American Negro capital and of colored technical experts to help Liberians in the development of agriculture, industry and commerce.

To attain these things, I suggest, first, that Liberia approach New York Bankers with a definite proposition of railroad building, and that the suggestion be made that these Bankers finance the building of the railroad, on condition that the revenues of such a road, over and above the necessary expenses of economical upkeep, be used to repay the expense of building and the necessary interest.

Secondly: Liberia should approach the soundest of the various colored Bankers of America, with a proposal that they form under the strict laws of the New York State, and in the city of New York, a strong financial institution, to act as a National Banking and Trust Company. That this institution establish in Liberia under such conditions as seem equitable a branch which should become the fiscal agent of the Government and the depository of its funds.

Thirdly: That there should be formed in Liberia and in America an International Corporation of colored men for handling Liberian products, and for furnishing Liberia a regular stream of technically trained colored farmers, mechanics and merchants of high character and efficiency, covering a period of twenty-five years or more, with periodic recruiting, sanitary aids, industrial surveys and systematic study of resources and markets.

I would be glad to have from you Sir, either before or after I leave Liberia, your own opinion and the opinion of your advisers on these matters, and any official communication with which you would care to intrust me. I am now expecting to leave Monrovia, Tuesday January 22, and shall do myself the honor of calling upon you before embarkation.

I am, Sir, with great respect,

Very sincerely yours,
W. E. B. Du Bois

Monrovia, Liberia, 30th June 1924.

My dear Doctor Du Bois,

I beg to acknowledge, with extreme thankfulness and appreciation, your much esteemed letted dated April 4, 1924, with enclosed copy of the most illuminating and interesting report made by you to the American Secretary of State upon the special diplomatic mission you were sent to Liberia on by your Government. This report I read to the Cabinet who were all very much pleased with it and profoundly impressed with its sympathetic and friendly character.

Your wonderful grasp of our past as well as present international problems, during your brief sojourn in Liberia is indeed remarkable. Our needs, for our continued progress, as enumerated in your report, you have correctly visualized. That it remains for Liberia to solve her problems of industry and popular education is a view with which I am in full accord; in fact the future prosperity and greatness of Liberia must be achieved by Liberia itself, of course with a measure of foreign aid and assistance. As to Liberia's ability to accomplish this task I have not the least doubts, if she will only be given a fair and honest chance by her detractors; and with the United States giving assistance, along the lines suggested and recommended in your most valuable report, Liberia's future material and political stability will be forever secured.

With regard to the nature of the expert advice which the United States should offer to Liberia, here, again you have very correctly interpreted our views, when you say that "this system of advice should not be a more or less concealed attempt to take the functions of Government out of the hands of the Liberians: but it should be real advice of the highest order given by men of *training* and *understanding* and offered to Liberia with the idea that America wishes her progress and is pointing out the way. If Liberia will follow the path indicated, she can count on the continued interest and help of the American Government. If she does not see fit to follow the general trend of the advice tendered, America has the right to conclude that she does not wish further assistance."

I have underscored the words *"training"* and *"understanding"* in the above excerpt from your report, because Liberia has in the past suffered no little embarrassments and inconveniences through the mistakes and blunders of foreign officials in our public service posing as "Experts."

Your observations upon our needs for foreign capital and upon the failure of the proposed American five million dollar loan are quite correct. In discussing, in my last inaugural address, the question of foreign loans to Liberia, I endeavored to point out that past experience whispers to our ears a cautious tread along these lines. Foreign loans carry with them too many political entanglements; but rather we should bend all of our energies to the building up of such a healthy revenue that will assure to us financial stability and international credit on equitable basis. In the meantime the economic development of the country should be left, for the present moment, to private foreign enterprise under safe and reasonable terms of operations. To these views I still adhere. With this object in view has the Liberian Government lately come to a most liberal understanding with the personal representative of Mr. Firestone of the "Firestone Rubber Tire Company" of Akron, Ohio, U. S. A. for rubber cultivation in Liberia on extensive plans.

I must also thank you for the article appearing in the April number of the "Crisis" entitled "Sensitive Liberia." [1] Copies of this article were immediately printed in hand bills and freely circulated throughout the country and which, I am happy to say, were read with much delight and appreciation by every true Liberian. Your promise to publish from time to time in the "Crisis" and elsewhere articles concerning Liberia, in order to counter act the propaganda of which Liberia has been the unhappy victim is highly appreciated, and shall, I am sure, be productive of much good to Liberia.

I am glad to know that you arrived in the United States in good health and spirit and with very pleasant memories of Liberia.

In my letter to you, dated September 7, 1923, when you were in Portugal, and which you unfortunately did not receive, I said, in referring to your then proposed visit to Liberia, that, "visits to Liberia by leaders of our racial group in the United States, will undoubtedly lead to a better and clearer understanding of Liberia and the Liberians, and also serve to draw both you and ourselves in a ban of closer union for the political, financial, social and economic advancement

1. Actually, this article appeared in the May 1924 *Crisis* (28:9–11).

of our common race." The impressions of your visit to Liberia I think have to some extent justified my statement above quoted.

I am trying to procure the various specimens of Liberian wood, as requested, and shall forward same on to you as soon as possible for the purpose of exhibition to those of your friends and others who may be interested in African hard woods.

We shall always cherish the most pleasant recollection of your visit to Liberia, and shall look forward, with the greatest pleasure, to its repetition.

In wishing you God's blessings of long life, success, happiness and prosperity, I am voicing not only my sincerest sentiments, but also those of the members of the Cabinet, Mrs. King and the large circle of friends and admirers you left on this side.

With best wishes and kind regards, believe me,

Very sincerely yours,
C. D. B. King

July 29, 1924

My dear President King:

I have your kind letter of June 30 which I beg to acknowledge and thank you for.

May I take this opportunity of emphasizing your stand on the matter of rubber cultivation. Liberia must have capital for her development. If she borrows from the great white nations she will be at the mercy of the lending country. If the capital is invested by private corporations in the great white countries then these corporations are going to exercise power and bring pressure upon Liberia.

The fairness of this exercise of power will, in the case of England, depend entirely upon white Englishmen since the colored people of the British Empire have no influence on imperial politics. If Frenchmen invest in Liberia their actions will be guided by predominant white French opinion. Colored people in France occupy positions of influence but they have not yet learned to use their positions for the benefit of the colored race. They are so thoroughly French in their thought and action and they know so little about their own race and believe so slightly in it that they cannot yet be depended on to make France act fairly toward colored countries.

On the other hand if white Americans invest in Liberia and if they do not treat Liberia fairly and they try and get the United States Government to back up their demands, the Negroes of America have enough political power to make the government go slowly. American Negroes are also beginning to understand and sympathize with Liberia. It seems to me, therefore, that as between these three great countries, Liberia should apprehend least danger from American capital and should proceed to encourage its investment under proper restrictions.

I trust you will extend to your colleagues in government and to Mrs. King my very best regards. I am, dear President King,

> Very sincerely yours,
> W. E. B. Du Bois

P.S. I am venturing to enclose some correspondence concerning Starr's History of Liberia.[1] I should like to have your opinion about these matters. Will you kindly return these letters to me when you are finished?

Ellen Winsor, a Quaker who supported the NAACP, sharply raised the persistent question of attitudes toward violence, especially problematic in the case of palpable social injustice. She wrote to the *Crisis* in response to an article on the subject by E. Franklin Frazier in the March 1924 issue. Though in the postscript Miss Winsor suggested publication of her letter, Du Bois decided against it. In the June 1924 issue of the *Crisis* (28:58), he wrote that he had "received one or two letters protesting" Frazier's article and that he had asked Frazier to reply. Frazier did, and his reply was published by Du Bois as an editorial in that same issue (pp. 58–59). The reply in no way moderated the demand for self-defense by any means necessary, including force.

> Haverford, Pa., March 2, 1924

The Editor, The Crisis
Sir:

It was a shock to read in *The Crisis* for March the article entitled "The Negro and Non-Resistance" by Mr. E. Franklin Frazier. Not that I am one of those who desire to keep the Negro happy and contented in his present lot to which it hath pleased the white over-lord to call him, but because the evidence is so strong that a spirit of rebellion fostered on personal hatred will lead black and white alike into a pit as wide and deep as gaping hell.

In Mr. Frazier's article there is a subtle touch suggesting to his race the use of force and violence, welded together with hate. Has not the Negro learnt to his sorrow that violent methods never win the desired goal? The Civil War but transferred the Negro from one form of slavery to another. The world has had enough of death, hatred and destruction since 1914. Where has Mr. Frazier hidden himself that he has not breathed the poison of disease, poverty, famine and bitterness sown broadcast over the nations of the earth by the makers of war? Is he willing to offer the same cup again to his people? In this direction does his teaching lead them.

Economic justice can be brought about only through education. When it

---

1. The reference is to Frederick Starr (1858–1933); his work *Liberia: Description, History, Problems* was issued in Chicago in 1913; it was published by the author.

comes, it will not recognize sex, creed, nor color. Happiness and freedom will be shared alike by all.

Let me recommend to your readers a little book by a great man who has not one drop of white blood in his veins. It is "The Sermon on the Sea" by Mahatma Gandhi, published [in 1924] by the Universal Publishing Company of Chicago. Gandhi says: "One who is free from hatred requires no sword," and "only fair means can produce fair results."

Who knows but that a Gandhi will arise in this country to lead the people out of their misery and ignorance, not by the old way of brute force which breeds sorrow and wrong, but by the new methods of education based on economic justice leading straight to Freedom.

Ellen Winsor

The Editor:
Sir:
If the above is published in The Crisis please do not omit or change any part of it. E. W.

April 12, 1924

My dear Madam:
I have your letter concerning Mr. Frazier's article. On the whole I like his conclusions. I hate war but there are certain circumstances under which I should fight and I am, I must say, compelled to smile at the unanimity with which the great leader, Mr. Gandhi, is received by those peoples and races who have spilled the most blood.

Very sincerely yours,
W. E. B. Du Bois

Miss Ernestine Rose (1880–1961), a white woman, was the librarian of the 135th Street Branch of the New York Public Library from 1920 to 1942. As Harlem became, especially after the First World War, the home of an ever-increasing number of Black people (including migrants from the South and the West Indies), the demand grew for this branch in particular to gear itself to their needs and interests. A result was the creation of a community committee—including Du Bois—to further this end. This background explains the letter, and its enclosure, sent by Miss Rose to Du Bois early in 1924. In 1926, the Carnegie Foundation purchased and presented to the New York Public Library an extraordinary collection of books, prints, and manuscripts dealing with African and African-derived peoples, assembled by Arthur Schomburg (1874–1938), himself originally from Puerto Rico.

Correspondence 1920–1929 [285]

New York, March 25, 1924

My dear Dr. Du Bois:

Enclosed please find a brief outline of a plan discussed in a meeting called Tuesday, March 11th at the Library,

Will you kindly look this over with a view to criticism and suggestions?

A meeting will be held at the Library next Tuesday, April 1 at 8:30 for the purpose of deciding upon a definite plan.

I hope you will make a special effort to be present.

Very truly yours,
Ernestine Rose

A plan for establishing a Department of Negro History, literature and art in the 135th Street Branch of the New York Public Library.
Purpose:
The purpose is to make easily available for permanent public use a large and representative body of material expressive of Negro culture in the past and the present.
A Society or Foundation:
In order to secure permanency and active public support it is suggested that a group of people interested in the project form themselves into a Foundation with the object of supporting and controlling such a collection of material.
Place:
This collection shall be housed in the 135th Street Branch of the N.Y. Public Library until such time as it has attained sufficient size and financial support as to require and deserve an independent building.[1] It shall be administered by a properly equipped colored person, under the supervision of the N. Y. Public Library.

The question of salary and of financial support, as well as the details of securing provision for permanency and constant availability shall be settled by joint conference between the members of the Foundation and the officials of the N. Y. Public Library.
Study Classes:
It is suggested that classes or clubs might be formed for the study of Negro history and culture in connection with this collection, and that school classes be given the opportunity to receive instruction in these subjects at the library.

Du Bois's great sensitivity to anything which he thought a personal affront is evident in this remarkable letter to James Weldon Johnson; the latter's reply is in-

---

1. After almost half a century and despite frequent appeals, the Schomburg Collection remains confined to part of one branch library.

dicative of the strength and forthrightness that made Johnson's service to the NAACP so consequential.

April 15, 1924.

My dear Mr. Johnson:

I have decided not to attend the Philadelphia conference, and that decision is unalterable.[1] I had thought at first to say that I had another engagement. But that would simply be a subterfuge and I am going to be frank.

From 1909 to 1922 I do not think I have missed a single N.A.A.C.P. annual conference or failed to take part on its program. I have deemed this service to the N.A.A.C.P. as one of my chief duties to the Association. In the last two or three years I seemed to sense on the part of you, Miss Ovington and Mr. White a feeling that I was not needed longer in this capacity and that my gradual elimination as a speaker on the platform of the N.A.A.C.P. was desirable. Last year matters came to a head. Nothing was said of my participation on the Kansas City program until at the last moment I, myself, suggested that my presence was not necessary. The reply made from the executive office was prompt and agreed with me except that the reason was based on possible lack of funds, a contingency which, in fact, never arose.

I was, I confess, surprised and hurt, but I took my medicine as a gentleman should. I did not complain. I did not appeal. I did not explain. Casually I mentioned the matter to Arthur Spingarn in order that he would know why I was not present. But I think the best comment on my attitude is that scarcely a soul in the United States has suspected my real chagrin unto this day.

I did not for a moment then and do not now, question your judgment in this matter. On the contrary the notable success of the Kansas City meeting rather proves its soundness. But I do maintain that that judgment once expressed must be maintained and lived up to. If my services were unnecessary at Kansas City, no amount of argument can make me believe they are indispensable at Philadelphia. Moreover your judgment relieves me of responsibility. I was dispensed with last year and this gives me the right to use my own judgment as to my services as a speaker in the future.

If I should see a time when I was convinced that only my presence would save an N.A.A.C.P. meeting from harm I should, of course, come. I do not anticipate any such contingency in any future annual conference—certainly not in Philadelphia. You are going to have a great meeting there, a meeting which will not need me and will not have me. On the other hand anything else I do to aid this meeting or other meetings I shall do with sincerity and enthusiasm; and I shall always hope in the future as in the past to make the good of the

---

1. Du Bois was mistaken; he did alter his decision and did speak at the NAACP convention in Philadelphia; he comments on this matter in a letter to Joel Spingarn published in this volume (p. 292).

association the highest aim of my work. At the same time you will agree that every man owes a certain respect to his own soul. If he is kicked once that is not necessarily his fault. But to offer himself for repeated kicking is spiritual suicide.

Very sincerely yours,
W. E. B. Du Bois

New York, April 17, 1924

My dear Dr. Du Bois:

I have your letter of the 15th in which you state your reasons for not accepting a place on the program of the Philadelphia Conference. These reasons, as I gather them, are: that you have sensed on the part of Miss Ovington, Mr. White and myself a feeling that you were no longer needed at the conferences and that your gradual elimination as a speaker on the platform of the N.A.A.C.P. was desirable; and that you were not taken to the Kansas City Conference.

I can see no good grounds for either of these reasons. You have been assigned a prominent part of the program of every annual conference, with the exception of Kansas City, since I have been with the Association. Since I have been Secretary, at Detroit and Newark, you were asked to take what we considered the choice spot on the program. At both these conferences you were placed on the most important committee, the Committee on Resolutions, because it was felt with you on the committee the organization and the race would, without any doubt, be properly voiced. The question with us here in the National Office has been that you appeared unwilling to allow us to make fuller use at the conference of your abilities and prestige.

Without knowing that your feelings were such as they are, we placed you on the program of the Philadelphia Conference, with no thought that you would not serve. When you sent a memo to Mr. White stating that you regretted to find yourself unable to be in Philadelphia during the Conference, I, thinking the matter of lecture dates you might have made was in the way, went to your office to urge you to make it possible to be present and speak. If there was any desire to eliminate you, and if the invitation to go to Philadelphia had been merely perfunctory, we would have quickly seized upon your declination, and certainly I would not have gone to you personally to urge you to reconsider and make it possible to be present. At the same time, I made no argument to convince you that your services would be "indispensable at Philadelphia." I do not believe the services of any single individual are now indispensable to the N.A.A.C.P.

As to a desire to eliminate you from the platform of the N.A.A.C.P., may I recall to you that last spring when we learned that you were making a lecture tour to the Pacific Coast, I went to you and asked if we could not arrange to take advantage of your being in the West and have you address, or at least meet with, as many of the branches as possible. Arrangements were made, and we wrote the branches advising them of your visit to the Coast and urging them to do all in their power to make your meetings a success.

As to the Kansas City Conference: On June 29, 1923, you sent a memo as follows to Miss Ovington:

> I would like to have as early as possible some information as to whether my presence is needed at the annual conference at Kansas City. Personally I do not think that the presence of all of the executive officers is necessary each year on acount of the great expense but on the other hand I realize that anyone who is absent might be criticized.

Ten days later (on July 9, 1923) Miss Ovington replied as follows:

> I have just read your memorandum asking me to let you know as soon as possible whether your presence is needed at the annual conference. Of course, it would be a great disappointment to us all if you were not able to be present. We had decided that we could not pay the expenses of as many of our own force as formerly, so that criticism may fall upon us.
> I hope you will feel that it is of sufficient value to *The Crisis* to meet your expenses and that we may have you with us.
> I cannot decide any more than you can as to the amount of criticism that might come if you were not with us.

You question the reason, lack of funds, given by Miss Ovington for not bearing your expenses to Kansas City, and say that such a contingency never arose; nevertheless, up to within a few days before the Conference opened we were justified by the financial outlook in making every possible retrenchment. In fact, the only officer of the Association whose total expenses were borne by the National Office was Mr. White, who had the arrangements in charge. The expenses of Mr. Bagnall and myself were partly borne by branches which we addressed either on the way out or back; all of Mr. Pickens' expenses were so borne, except his living expenses while in Kansas City; Mrs. Hunton bore all of her expenses out of her own pocket except her living expenses while in Kansas City.

I must say I cannot follow you when you state that you regard not being taken to the Kansas City Conference as a "kick," and being invited and urged to go to the Philadelphia Conference as another kick.

I regret very much your determination, because of your absence from the Kansas City Conference, to take part in no other N.A.A.C.P. conference; yet, I presume, it is a matter upon which if there is anything to be said, it should be said between you and the Board of Directors.

Now, Dr. Du Bois, I have written you in reply at such great length both because I consider seriously the things you have said, and because of my regard for you. Perhaps I ought to confess myself surprised and hurt. It may be that I ought to resent the implication that I have conspired against your prestige in the Association. I do not, and perhaps because I could so easily produce proof beyond question that such implications are not only groundless but contrary to the facts.

                      Yours very sincerely,
                      James W. Johnson

P.S. I judged you intended me to show your letter to Miss Ovington and to Mr. White.

Through the years since the Bolshevik revolution, Afro-Americans have regularly visited the USSR; among the earliest was Claude McKay. James C. Jackson, who was there in 1924, wrote to Du Bois before the latter's first visit in 1926—an event that made a lasting impression upon him.

                      Oodelnarya, Russia, July 15, 1924

Dear Sir:

This letter comes from a village deep in the heart of Russia. I am an American-Negro, a native of the South, here in Russia making a study of social conditions. The above named village is the seat of the summer colony of the University for Eastern Peoples, located at Moscow. I have been invited from Moscow to this colony as its guest.

One must visit Russia to understand and appreciate the many beautiful social developments which are taking place in this strange land! Here at this colony are students from all the darker races—all except that of the Negro. And I am daily asked why no Negroes have come. There is a perfect spirit of internationalism here. Women from the various Circassian republics and Siberia, men from China, Japan, Korea, India, etc. all live as one large family, look upon one another simply as human beings. There are a number of little open-air theatres here and there in the forests where at nights plays representative of all lands are organized by the students and presented. Here life is poetry itself! It is the Bolshevik idea of social relation, and a miniature of the world of tomorrow.

Here in Russia the desire for information concerning the Negro is fervent. There is no race of which knowledge is sought with such eagerness as of the Negro. I am kept busy writing articles for newspapers and magazines both in Russia and Ukrainia and giving lectures on the Negro social situation in America. Under the old regime Russia was burdened with many race problems, but today under the Soviet System there are no race problems. I shall visit the Caucasus with its many distinct races, living in the closest juxtaposition. For it is there that one is best able to see the System in operation as it affects racial relations. Stanislav Pestovsky, former president of the Kirghiz Soviet Republic, and I spend many leisure hours together, and he never tires of telling me how Russia alone of all countries has solved her racial problems. And certainly no country had as many, and as intricate as old czarist Russia!

I have been much pleased to know that your little book, "The Negro" and Maran's novel, "Batoula" [1] have been much read in student circles here. The latter book is rendered in the Russian language. But there is such a scarcity of matter pertaining to the Negro here! It is the desire of many to create a department of books, and other matter regarding the Negro Race in general in one of the leading libraries in Moscow.

Thanking you for any bit of assistance, I remain

Very truly yours,
James C. Jackson

Hendrik Willem van Loon (1882–1944), born in Rotterdam, migrated at an early age to the United States, where he attended Harvard and Cornell; he served in Europe as an Associated Press correspondent before and during the First World War. He taught thereafter at various colleges, and also served as an editor with the *Baltimore Sun* and the *Nation*. His *Story of Mankind*, illustrated in his own inimitable style and published in 1921, was a best seller; he published several other books, including biographies of Rembrandt (1931) and Bolívar (1943).*

An interchange between van Loon and Du Bois resulted in the publication of a van Loon story in the *Crisis* for October 1924 (28:252–58).

July 8, 1924

My dear Mr. van Loon:

Thank you so much for letting me see "The Ways of War." We shall be glad to use it and thank you so much for sending it. I shall be glad to return it to you for "polishing" as soon as we determine when it can be used.

My unconscionable delay in answering arises from the fact that the manuscript caught me in Africa.

Very sincerely yours,
W. E. B. Du Bois

New York, 20 July 1924

My dear Mr. Du Bois,

I have read the story which I wrote five years ago and which you have kindly accepted but if you do not mind my saying so it seems pretty poor work and suppose that we suppress it and I give you something else of a more philosophical nature?

1. René Maran, *Batoula; Véritable Roman Nêgre* (Paris: A. Michel, 1921), winner of the Prix Goncourt; in 1922, T. Seltzer published the work in translation in New York.

* There is a recent biography: Gerard Willem van Loon, *The Story of Hendrik Willem van Loon* (Philadelphia: J. B. Lippincott Co., 1972).

Truth to tell I am a rotten short-story writer and I know it but I could give you something along the line of historico-philosophico-sociologico-pedagogico endeavor and that would be better.

What do you think about it?

Sincerely,
Hendrik Willem van Loon

July 24, 1924

My dear Mr. van Loon:

I bow to your judgment. I shall be glad to have the essay which you suggest. I hope to have it very soon, say around the first of August or would we have to wait longer than that? I thank you very much for your offer.

Very sincerely yours,
W. E. B. Du Bois

27 July 1924

My dear Mr. Du Bois,

I read my story again and it did not strike me as quite so terrible. Neither is it very wonderful but it was written years and years and years ago.... and so I asked Van Wyck Brooks to read it and tell me whether it was what I thought it was and he read it and said "Well this wont set the literary ocean on fire but it is perfectly allright and as the date when you wrote it is on it they wont think that you have gone in for short-story writing as a sequel to the history business" and as Brooks knows more about that sort of thing than anyone else I am sending you the revised copy with my pontifical blessing but please keep the date-line at the end and accept my polite bow.[1]

Hendrik Willem van Loon

Joel Spingarn's health was severely impaired as a result of his war service and he retired as chairman of the board of the NAACP in January 1919, to be succeeded by Mary White Ovington. The relationship between him and Du Bois remained very close thereafter; an informative letter to Spingarn from Du Bois, after his return from Africa, is published below. The extensive journey through much of the United States, to which Du Bois refers, was habitual for him and was a source of his firsthand knowledge and sense of reality.

July 16, 1924

My dear Mr. Spingarn:

I have not heard from you in so long that I suspect you are getting lazy in

---

1. In signing this letter, van Loon began his "h" in the form of a bowing figure.

your beautiful home. At any rate I write to know just how you are and what you are doing with yourself.

I returned from Africa March 19th and on May 1st began a trip that took me through Delaware, Virginia, South Carolina, Georgia, Tennessee, Ohio, Michigan, Illinois, Missouri and then down to Alabama and back to Tennessee. It was a most interesting trip. At Nashville I stopped for double duty, first to see my daughter get her A.B., which she did with reasonable credit, and secondly to make a speech to the Alumni of Fisk University in which I took occasion to tell them that the new endowment of a million dollars which Fisk had almost finished was the least of the things which she needed to make her a university, that she lacked the spirit of freedom, that she was giving the students no chance at self expression and that she was choking the truth by propaganda for the benefit of southern whites, and I insisted that the alumni must have a voice in the running of the institution. It was a hard speech to make but I think I did a good job.[1]

I then returned home with the determination of going to work for the summer and fall and not attending the Philadelphia conference of the N.A.A.C.P. My thesis was that if I was not needed at Kansas City I would not be needed at Philadelphia, but when your brother and a few of the other Directors got through expostulating I went to Philadelphia and made a speech. The meetings there were very excellent and the Association is in good condition.

I am doing some writing, but I am in the condition now of having a good deal more to say than I have the physical ability to express which makes me feel mentally stuffed.

I hope this will find you improving in health and reasonably happy. Mrs. Du Bois joins me in best regards to you and Mrs. Spingarn.

Very sincerely yours,
W. E. B. Du Bois

G. Victor Cools (1892–1952) was the national manager of the Negro Bureau, La Follette-for-President Committee. He had been on the faculties of Prairie View (Texas) State College, Saint Augustine College (Raleigh, North Carolina), and Wilberforce, and had contributed to various periodicals, including the *American Mercury*. In the 1930s, he served on the staff of the Agricultural Adjustment Administration, and in the 1940s, edited a monthly magazine in New York, *Vanguard*.

1. Du Bois entitled this speech *Diuturni Silenti* (Prolonged Silence), after one of Cicero's orations; the speech broke that silence and created a sensation. It was a basic element in the rebellion at Fisk against a racist president (Fayette McKenzie) and board of trustees. Du Bois wrote of this event in the *Crisis*, October 1924 and April and June 1925, and in the *Nation*, 3 March 1926.

In his letter to Du Bois, Cools makes reference to a Du Bois editorial, "La Follette," in the August 1924 *Crisis* (28:154). There Du Bois spelled out the fourteen points in the La Follette program, beginning with an anti-monopoly position and concluding with a call for "the outlawing of war," and commended all of them. But Du Bois went on to criticize the absence of any reference to "two tremendous issues—the Ku Klux Klan and the Negro." "This," he wrote, "is inexcusable."

Chicago, August 6, 1924.

My dear Dr. DuBois:

I am taking this opportunity to thank you, in behalf of the Third Party, for your editorial expression in the August number of the Crisis. I am heartily in accord with your reaction on the present political situation. The time has come when we must show those who are responsible for the formulation of the policies of the two old parties that the Negro voters can think. As you know it is impossible to enslave the thinking man.

The editorial on Senator LaFollette I have read with great care. I agree with you in every respect. I feel, however, Senator LaFollette's attitude on the Ku Klux Klan is generally misunderstood. I am in a position to say that the Senator is no more friendly to that organization than we are. The man's record—the position which he has taken on all matters affecting the individual freedom, his determination to fight against tyranny by the few and privileged class—attests that.

May I take you in our confidence a moment? Here is the position which we have taken in order to put over the comprehensive program of the Third Party. In order to concentrate our attention on our objective we have decided to eliminate as far as possible the moral issues. This decision was made after very careful deliberations. It was felt that our strength in an open fight with factions of the Klan and Prohibition would be playing into the hands of the enemy. Our strength must not be diffused. We remember too well what happened at Madison Square Garden.

Our fight will be made along economic lines. We are fighting the battles of economic slaves—the battles of millions of people who have no voice in the government of this country. We are fighting the battle which you have been fighting for years, but on a more extensive front line. We are not fighting the battle of the white earners. There is no difference between the white earner and the black wage earner. When we strike a blow for the freedom of the white wage earners we strike, as well, a blow for the freedom of the black wage earners. We are fighting for the oppressed people of this country and, incidently, for the oppressed people of the world. This is the creed of the Third Party.

I would like to get from you at your earliest convenience a frank expression of your attitude on the candidacy of Senator LaFollette. To be perfectly frank with you, Dr. DuBois, I would like for you to give us not only your support, but

[294] Correspondence 1920-1929

to accept a place on our advisory council. I may say, in connection with this, that I am ready to co-operate with you on any constructive plan you may have in mind for a more equitable representation by our people in the affairs of the government.

Your attention is invited to the enclosed statement released to the press by Congressman John M. Nelson, National Manager of LaFollette's Campaign.

Thanking you for your kindness, I am

Yours for the absolute freedom
of the black people,
G. Victor Cools
National Manager
Negro Bureau LaFollette for President

August 14, 1924.

My dear Mr. Cools:

I thank you very much for your letter of August Sixth. Personally I am going to vote for Senator LaFollette and I have great faith in him and admiration for him. At the same time as Editor of The Crisis and as Director of the National Association for the Advancement of Colored People I am going to insist that Mr. LaFollette must say something concerning the Negro problem if he expects the support of Negroes, and for this reason I think it would not be wise for me to have any official connection with the campaign such as would be assumed if I became a member of your Advisory Council.

I congratulate you upon your appointment and shall note it in The Crisis.

Very sincerely yours,
W. E. B. Du Bois

Eugene O'Neill (1888-1953) was already an outstanding figure when, in 1924, he responded positively to Du Bois's request that he serve as one of the judges of the best plays published in the *Crisis*. He won the Pulitzer Prize in 1920 for *Beyond the Horizon* and two years later won it again for *Anna Christie*. In 1920, his *Emperor Jones* was first produced with Paul Robeson in the title role; *The Hairy Ape* followed in 1922 and *Desire under the Elms* in 1924. Cordiality marked the long relationship between O'Neill and Du Bois, with the playwright expressing the highest estimation of Du Bois's literary skill.

Provincetown, Mass., September 24, 1924

My dear Dr. Du Bois:

I feel guilty at not having answered your letter before this—but I found it here on my return from Nantucket, where I have been visiting. I can't understand why it was not forwarded.

I would feel it an honor to help you out with the prize plays, and am hoping that my plans will make it possible to do so. We expect to go abroad immediately after the opening of "Desire Under The Elms." But I think it is likely that I will be back before February first, and in that case you can count on my reading them.

We were so sorry about missing you at Ridgefield—we had come up to Provincetown just a couple of weeks before. I had had an idea, from what Miss Fawcett[1] said, that you would be out earlier. It was a great disappointment to me not to meet you.

With all best wishes,

Sincerely,
Eugene O'Neill.

One of the finest products of the Harlem Renaissance of the 1920s was also one of the earliest—Jean Toomer's *Cane*, published in 1923 by Boni and Liveright. Du Bois, the *Crisis*, and the magazine's assistant editor, Jessie Fauset, were of decisive importance in the movement. Letters from Toomer and Du Bois are characteristic of the way in which Du Bois personally encouraged that flowering.

September 12, 1924

My dear Mr. Toomer:

I wish very much you would send something to us for publication in the *Crisis*. I think that with the splendid beginning you have made, the *Crisis* readers ought to be kept in touch with you. We cannot pay much but we can pay a little.

I had been hoping that I might see you sometime. I trust you will let me hear from you very soon.

Very sincerely yours,
W. E. B. Du Bois

Paris, 18 Oct 24.

Dear Dr. DuBois,

Your kind letter of the 12th. reached me in Paris, delayed somewhat owing to the uncertainty of my movements.

I too feel that I should like to touch Crisis readers, and have them keep in touch in me. And I thank you for this opportunity. Though I have written practically nothing for almost a year, that is, nothing available for immediate publication, yet I feel that the time may soon come when I will. It will surely

1. Jessie Fauset.

be sent you. And I hope to see you personally when I return to America, which I expect to do within a month.[1]

                         Sincerely,
                         J. Toomer.

A fascinating and illuminating letter from, as its author says, a young "Anglo-Saxon" is published below. Du Bois did see the young man, probably on 11 October, and supplied him with notes of introduction to James Weldon Johnson, Augustus G. Dill, and Walter White.

                         New York, Oct. 23, 1924

My dear Doctor:

You will, I hope, pardon the liberty I take in writing you in this rather unconventional manner.

The fact is, I have just finished reading your able article in the current "American Mercury" and am still somewhat under the spell of your forceful, close knit English.[2]

I am white, American born, college educated young chap of 25—a nobody. I have no axe to grind; no oil stock to sell and no favors to ask. So please understand that this letter is just a spontaneous outburst of appreciation on my part; a positive reaction to the test you made. In my case, at least, the steel of your message has met flint and the resultant spark will smoulder into the flame of complete understanding.

But, I would know more! I'd like to spend an evening in the company of some Negro intellectual who could give me thrust and parry. Ye gods Doctor! I didn't even *know* there were such men as yourself. It must seem a stupid thing to you, I have no doubt, but to me Negros have always been just Negros. I've always loved them in a way—but they were just Negros. I've listened, nerves atingle, to their music. I've sworn by them as cooks. But—I am utterly ashamed to admit it—they were always "just Negros."

All the while these "just Negros" were pining for my sympathy and my understanding and my companionship.

Oh, I knew in a vague way that there were such institutions as Fisk; such men as Washington; such publications as "The Crisis," but I hadn't given it much thought. And can you blame me? How could I be expected to know anything about or interest myself in the advancement of the colored people?

And then I read your article—Gad! It was like finding a diamond in the street.

1. Du Bois published part of Toomer's letter in the January 1925 *Crisis* (29:118). Toomer did not thereafter write for the *Crisis*, but Du Bois reprinted in November 1931 (38:381) a poem of his that had appeared originally in the *Crisis* in 1922.
2. "The Dilemma of the Negro," *American Mercury* 3 (October 1924):179–85.

What blind, bigoted nit wits we Anglo-Saxons are. It never occurs to us that for every one hateful characteristic we *pretend* to see in the Negro, the colored man can point to a dozen worse ones in us.

Our inferiors! Ha! The horrible jest of it all—

Listen, Doctor:

Immediately after reading your article, I became possessed of a desire to see a copy of The Crisis. Finding your address in the telephone book, I hastened to satisfy that desire. Was I met at the door by some gum-chewing "chippy"? I was not. A lady directed me to your office and I'm sure no white man's stenographer was ever as courteous. The mere act of buying a 15¢ magazine was rendered graceful by a gentleman of culture and refinement. The very atmosphere of your office is one of order, efficiency and refinement.

I realize, of course, that this letter is an incoherent jumble of words—Please remember that I have just awakened from a sound sleep, however.

May I have the pleasure of a 15 minutes' talk with you some day next week? I appreciate the fact that you must of necessity be a very busy man. . . . But, I think you will be doing a lot of good by answering a few questions that are bubbling to the top of my mind.

I am, my dear Doctor, yours with genuine admiration and respect,

                        Lambert Maxim Terry.

In July 1924, Du Bois wrote to several leading Negro figures soliciting their views on the pending presidential elections. A very belated reply, written after Coolidge's election, came from the president of Morehouse College in Atlanta.* Here, as often when he wrote to Du Bois, John Hope really unburdened his soul.

                    Atlanta, Ga., November 15, 1924

Dear Du Bois:

I have come across your letter of July 21st which I did not answer. Any answer now is quite out of the question. Coolidge is elected. I myself intended to vote for him and did do so. On the other hand, I had no complaint to make about colored people who saw and voted differently. I furthermore think it hardly worthwhile to talk as much as we used to about the Negroes' vote being divided, because the Negroes' vote is already divided. We are not by any means voting solidly Republican. Some Negroes even in the South voted for La Follette. But this letter is not written for publication or anything else except as an acknowledgment.

Now, to something else. I read in the American Mercury some weeks ago your kind words about Morehouse College and me. I have gone along here

---

* About half of this letter is published in Ridgely Torrence's *Story of John Hope* (New York: Macmillan Co., 1948), pp. 243–44.

for many years about the best I could. Here and there I might have done better. Here and there I might have done worse. But on the whole with all the agencies, circumstances, conveniences and inconveniences, I suppose I have done about the best *I* could. During these years I have often wondered what some of my dearest friends were thinking about my work, and how they were valuing it. But I suppose I would allow myself to burst wide open before asking them what they thought about it. That is the way with many of us. Few of us tell our closest friends those things which lie deepest in us, which distress us most, or which thrill us most with joy. Those things are ever beneath the surface. They are with us. Now you come to me at the beginning of my 19th year as President of this school, at the beginning of my 31st year as a teacher of colored boys and men, and tell me that I have not made altogether a miserable failure, but on the contrary have done something worthwhile. I am grateful to you for this quite beyond words.

Two nights ago I was at Tuskegee and talked with Dr. Moton about several matters. One of these was the Fisk situation. Moton told me that he was coming to New York sometime next week to talk with you and Boutté.[1] It is my impression that not only is he in a position to render valuable assistance, but he wishes to do this—he is ready to take very strong ground if what he regards as the facts warrant it. I am sure that you and Boutté will let him help you in every way that he can. I would suggest that you sort of mark time until after this conference. The chances are, you men can work things out much more easily than it may now appear. As you work on this question of Fisk University, bear in mind that I along with many other people desire the best things for Fisk, and it is my wish that these best things will come to pass, with the least commotion possible and with as little embarrassment as possible to Fisk University, because an institution of learning is such a delicate organism, it is almost human. It *is* human. The slightest touch sometimes disturbs its healthy function. If I can be of any service, you know well from our conversation last summer that I am willing.

When I come to New York again I believe I will look you up and ask you to spend the evening with me. I come to New York frequently, but we get together less frequently than we used to. Years ago it was one of the thrills that I got out of a trip to New York, to spend an evening with you, but you are so busy now with so many demands upon your time that I rather hesitate to take you for a whole night.

After all, the most and the best that I have got out of life has been beautiful comradeships, and the memories of these will probably cling with me out of

1. M. V. Boutté, born in Louisiana in 1884, was a long-time friend of Du Bois, his fraternity brother, and fellow-Fisk alumnus. He received a degree in pharmacy from the University of Illinois, taught chemistry at Meharry College before the war, and served as a captain with the Ninety-second Division; thereafter he practiced as a pharmacist in New York City.

this difficult, unsatisfactory world into some abode where I may feast and think with fewer interruptions and no clangor of alarm. Courage, the necessity of the enterprise, and a certain amount of pugnacity, along with a modicum of self-respect, make me continue rather ceaselessly in the fight; but I am bound to tell you, my dear friend, that blowing one's brains out is a great sight easier than some of the things we have to do and stand.

This is a much longer letter than I expected to write.

Affectionately yours,
John Hope

Du Bois led a historic and successful fight against the racism and corruption that marked the administration of Fisk University, particularly during, and for some years after, World War I. One of many letters that Du Bois wrote in connection with this struggle was addressed to the president of the Associated Negro Press, N. B. Brascher of Chicago.

November 17, 1924

My dear Mr. Brascher:

I want the Press Association to get into this Fisk fight on the right side and from time to time I am willing to send you inside information for the accuracy of which I will personally stand responsible.

I wish you would send out this week this information: Lillian E. Cashin is a colored woman, a graduate of Fisk and assistant professor of English. All of the seven students who are making English their major subject must write a thesis of 5000 words for Miss Cashin. This year and a few weeks ago Miss Cashin announced that the subject would be "Reasons Why Dr. McKenzie Should Be Retained at Fisk University." Not one of these seven students, as I am reliably assured, believes that this is true. That is, they think that McKenzie is not fit for the presidency. But imagine the predicament in which they are. If they do not write the essay they cannot graduate. If they do not write a strong and convincing essay they cannot graduate. If they do write strong and convincing essays to show why Dr. McKenzie should stay at Fisk University, those essays or the best of them will immediately be published in the Fisk News as evidence that the students of Fisk University want McKenzie retained.

This shows the depths to which the present administration of Fisk is going in order to hold power. The school has been in an uproar this fall with protests and meetings from the students and with white Southerners invited repeatedly to the platform to tell them that they should not criticize and what their duty is. They are celebrating this week the million dollar endowment but, in inviting the alumni to the celebration, no alumnus who has joined in protest against these conditions, has received an invitation to be present.

I wish also you would make these facts clear as given directly from me: I have no personal animus against Fayette McKenzie. He has always treated me with courtesy. My daughter, while a student at Fisk, was treated just as other students, no better and no worse. There is absolutely nothing that Fisk University could give me. The statement that I want the presidency of the institution is too ridiculous to consider. I wouldn't accept it under any possible circumstances. The only question in which I am interested is whether or not colored students are being treated decently at Fisk University and I do not think they are.

I hope you can send out some of these facts and let me know if I can give you any further information. Enclosed I am sending extracts from two students' letters.

Very sincerely yours,
W. E. B. Du Bois

Burton J. Hendrick (1871–1949), a well-known journalist and three-time Pulitzer Prize winner, was finishing his two-volume *Life and Letters of Walter Hines Page*, published by Doubleday late in 1925, when he wrote Du Bois asking for his memories of the man. Du Bois's reply is highly interesting. Page was editor of the *Atlantic Monthly* (1896–1900); the article to which Du Bois refers in the following letter, "Strivings of the Negro People," appeared in the August 1897 issue (80:194–98). Page was later Wilson's ambassador to Britain and in this capacity was of help to Du Bois.

January 2, 1925

Mr. Burton J. Hendrick
My dear Sir:

If I mistake not, the late Walter H. Page was the first magazine editor who ever accepted an article of mine. This article formed the first chapter in my book, "The Souls of Black Folk."

I afterwards went to Boston and met Mr. Page in his office. We had a simple talk together but that talk meant a great deal to me. He intimated that he would be glad to see more of my work and expressed a great deal of sympathy with my point of view which was unexpected to me at that time because I knew him to be a Southerner.

I remember particularly, he impressed it upon me for the first time that there was great difference of opinion among Southern whites as to their attitude toward Negroes. Among other things he told me this story: While he was in one Southern city (I think it was Charleston), he was astonished and pained by the virulence of both of the leading newspapers toward the Negro. One day the editor of one of these papers called on him and told him that he wanted employment in the North; that he was sick and tired of the situation in the

South and especially at being compelled to take the stand which he did on the Negro problem. He said that the things that he wrote were not at all in accordance with his belief but that he had to say them because the other paper would take him to task if he did not. Mr. Page said that he laughed at the man and told him that the other editor had been to him with the same story.

Just at the outbreak of the war, my wife and daughter were going to England where my daughter was to enter school. All preparations had been made, the school authorities urged her to come, and in spite of the war I sent her. At the last moment the passports did not arrive but I let them go and cabled to Mr. Page. I shall not forget the great courtesy which he showed toward my family, sending down a special representative to meet them and see that they were landed, and helping in other ways. I did not know Mr. Page intimately but my few contacts with him have left me with a peculiarly fine impression of his personality and of his great breadth of sympathy.

I may have some of his letters in my old files. I will look and see and forward them to you if I can find them.

Very sincerely yours,
W. E. B. Du Bois

Du Bois was a very early supporter of birth control propaganda and activity, though he early warned as to the racist perversions that such a movement might suffer. Pioneering the movement was the single-minded and dauntless Margaret Sanger (1883–1966); an exchange between Mrs. Sanger and Du Bois occurred early in 1925.*

[New York] February 7, 1925

My dear Dr. Du Bois:

Would you be willing to write a short message, say of two or three hundred words, to be read at our International Conference?

This is the Sixth International Neo-Malthusian and Birth Control Conference and is to be held at the Hotel McAlpin [in New York City] March 25–31, 1925.

We would greatly appreciate a message from you to either encourage us to continue our work, or to express your frank opinion of what we should do and how to do it, if possible.

Thanking you,

Cordially yours,
Margaret Sanger
President.

* See Virginia Coigney, *Margaret Sanger: Rebel With A Cause* (Garden City, New York: Doubleday and Co., 1969), esp. chapter 17.

[302]   Correspondence 1920–1929

February 14, 1925

My dear Mrs. Sanger:

Enclosed is a short statement which may be of some use to you in accordance with your letter of February 7.

Very sincerely yours,
W. E. B. Du Bois

STATEMENT
by W. E. B. Du Bois

Next to the abolition of war in modern civilization comes the regulation of birth by reason and common sense instead of by chance and ignorance. The solution for both of these problems of human advance is so perfectly clear and easily accomplished that it is only kept back by the stupidity of mankind, the utter refusal of even educated persons to face the problem frankly. While this is, in the highest degree, discouraging, it is on the other hand, encouraging to know that only "light, more light" is needed and here as elsewhere we have simply to keep everlastingly at it to bring ultimate triumph.

An enclosure in a letter by Du Bois early in 1925 is quite indicative of his developing thought on the central problems of the world. Du Bois was replying to a request from Edwin Seaver (b. 1900), then publicity director for the Fellowship of Reconciliation and an editor of *A Magazine of the Arts*. Seaver was well known as a novelist, poet, and editor in the 1930s and 1940s. The fellowship, founded in England in 1914 and established in the United States the next year, began as a Christian-pacifist effort; in this period, it was supported by such men and women as Jane Addams, A. J. Muste, Norman Thomas, Rufus Jones, Oswald Garrison Villard, and John Haynes Holmes.

New York, February 13, 1925

My dear Dr. Du Bois:

In reference to your speech for the Philippine Independence Demonstration in Cooper Union, February 23, could you send us beforehand about four or five hundred words covering some of the points you may make or things you will say so that we could send it to the papers to use in conjunction with their own stories? I should appreciate it very much.

Very sincerely yours,
Edwin Seaver

February 19, 1925

My dear Sir:

Enclosed please find a digest of my proposed speech February 23 at Cooper Union.

Very sincerely yours,
W. E. B. Du Bois

PROFIT AND CASTE

Independence is not being denied the Filipinos because they are incapable of it but rather because today, it is profitable to keep the colored races in subjection. This subjection varies from actual slavery up through serfdom and a low-wage system to a system of public monopolies. The best modern method of insuring this domination of dark labor is by spreading a propaganda which will hinder democratic development from crossing the color line. A vast propaganda of this sort is going on. It is not scientific because science is more and more denying the concept of race and the assumption of ingrained racial differences. But a cheap and pseudo-science is being sent broadcast through books, magazines, papers and lectures which makes the mass of people in civilized countries think that yellow people and brown people and black people are not human in the same sense that white people are human and cannot be allowed to develop or to rule themselves.

The money which supports this propaganda comes directly and indirectly from the profit accruing from the denial of political democracy and industrial democracy to the mass of colored laborers and this same vast profit it is which serves in cultured countries to keep the mass of workingmen from realizing industrial democracy and from using their political power to free themselves. Continually they are diverted by spectres of war with Japan, of competition with China, of intermarriage with Negroes. Meantime their taxes are squandered in armies and navies, the industrial process is made long and costly, and the competition of colored labor is made inevitable because colored labor is denied a voice of its own.

On the other hand, if by counter-propaganda we are able to put the real facts before the masses of the working people of the world, not only will the Filipinos be freed, but Asia and Africa will follow and the working people of Europe and America will finally achieve a real freedom, of which they have today but the shadow.

Rarely were the interchanges between Spingarn and Du Bois without significance. Early in 1925, letters were exchanged between the two men when Spingarn was still rather incapacitated, but Du Bois was in the splendid vigor of one of his most productive decades. The Amenia Conference, bringing together scores of Black and white people interested in overcoming racism, was Spingarn's idea; it was held in the summer of 1916 at his home, "Troutbeck," in the town of Amenia in upstate New York. Du Bois wrote the essay Spingarn requested; it was published in Amenia in 1925 as one of the "Troutbeck Leaflets": *The Amenia Conference: An Historic Negro Gathering.*

Amenia, New York, February 9, 1925

Dear Dr. Du Bois:

I wonder if you would be willing to become a permanent part of the history of Troutbeck by writing something for "Troutbeck Leaflets." You have seen one of them, The Whitman essay,[1] and several others are underway—all more or less devoted to a single spot of American earth and to those who have touched its life. A distinguished poet is writing an account of my predecessor there, Ingram Benton.[2]

I hardly know what to suggest as a subject, unless perhaps the memory of the Amenia Conference strikes your fancy—its shadowy lake and hills, its tents, its people, and what they hoped for and accomplished. Nothing that the war did to me (and I have hardly yet recovered from the crippling) has caused me half as many regrets as my inability to go on in full vigor with the fight we once waged together and my enforced subsidence into the side-lines among what you call the "philanthropists." That is why, perhaps, the Conference takes on such rosy colors of memory, and why I want your name associated with the place I love.

The Leaflets contain from 2000 to 4000 words, are intended solely for private distribution (you would of course have your share), and appear in from 40 to 200 copies. You could use your article later either for magazine or book publication; and think of the zest this "rare item" would give to your future bibliographers!

Ever yours,
J. E. Spingarn

February 14, 1925

My dear Mr. Spingarn:

I should be delighted to have the privilege of contributing to the "Troutbeck Leaflets" and especially would I like to write on the Amenia Conference. Just when do you want it? I imagine that the late Spring or early Fall would do but you can let me know about this.

I know just how you feel the disappointment of being withdrawn from activity and yet there are compensations in contemplative idleness. Just now I am being rushed about so by my friends and enemies that it is exceedingly difficult to get either breath or calm judgment.

I have had a splendid lecture trip in the Middle West—two thousand students at the University of Michigan; a lot of smug preachers at Indianapolis whom I addressed on the thesis: "Of all present forces of social uplift I have least faith in white Christian ministers." Some of them had apoplexy. Then there were women's clubs and forums. Now I am back, trying to attack my literary work again.

---

1. *Walt Whitman: A Criticism: An Unpublished Essay*, ed. J. E. Spingarn, Troutbeck Leaflet no. 2 (Amenia, New York: privately printed at Troutbeck Press, 1924).
2. Charles E. Benton wrote the essay on Spingarn's predecessor at Troutbeck, *Four Days on the Webutuck River* (1925).

I hope I may be permitted to call some time when you are well enough. With best regards to you and Mrs. Spingarn,

    Very sincerely yours,
    W. E. B. Du Bois

Du Bois's concern with the economics of racism was profound; during the 1920s, his concern led him to careful inquiry into, and warm advocacy of, cooperative production and distribution as of particular importance to his people. This direction in his thinking, as it developed, was to be important in subsequent difficulties with the board of the NAACP. Letters to and from Dr. James Peter Warbasse (1867–1957) reflect this aspect of Du Bois's interests. Warbasse, an eminent surgeon, became especially interested in the cooperative movement while pursuing postgraduate studies in Germany. The founder of the Cooperative League of the United States in 1915, he remained its president until 1941. He authored many books in medicine and surgery, and in the cooperative movement.

    February 13, 1925

My dear Dr. Warbasse:

I still have some faint hopes of starting cooperation among Negroes in Harlem. It seems to me there are unusual facilities there—a large group of like elements with wide demand of the same kind of goods, and living near together. I have a feeling that if somehow a start was made there, great things might come out of it. I am writing to ask if you have any thoughts or suggestions on the subject. Do you think it would be possible to interest the trustees of any fund in such a venture?

    Very sincerely yours,
    W. E. B. Du Bois

    New York, February 19, 1925

Dear Dr. Du Bois:

I think you are right. There are possibilities of co-operation among the Negroes in Harlem. Much education is needed, however, before entering upon a business undertaking. My own feeling is that the fields in which they would perhaps do best are housing and restaurants. It might be possible to undertake co-operative banking, insurance, bakeries or retail distributive stores. These latter are the less promising. A motion picture show or a theatre might be considered. In the field of recreation also are the possibilities of the dancehall and general recreational club.

Co-operative housing succeeds so well in New York and is so pressing a necessity among the Negroes, especially in the light of the exploitation which they suffer at the hands of landlords, that it should offer great possibilities. I think it might be possible to interest the trustees of some of our welfare funds in such a housing project. This should not be as a philanthropy in any sense. What is needed is an organization with funds that would make some money available for second mortgages at a reasonable rate of interest, let us say 8 per cent. It is possible for housing groups, even of working people, to get together the necessary preliminary money together with the first mortgage. But working people always need an additional amount which the security of the property renders difficult to raise. This must be gotten on second mortgage and for second mortgages people have to pay anywhere from 14 to 20 per cent. This makes the cost exorbitant. Money can be loaned upon second mortgage to a genuine co-operative housing society at 8 per cent and the investment made perfectly safe.

Should the Negroes of Harlem desire to get together and discuss this matter, we should be glad to give you the names of a number who have, from time to time, visited this office for the purpose of securing information. We are in touch with a number of Harlem Negroes who should be very useful in co-operative developments, since they have seen fit to inform themselves on this subject. If there is any further information or opinion I can give you, please call upon me.

With best wishes

Sincerely yours,
J. P. Warbasse

James W. Ford (1896–1957), born in Alabama, was a founder of the American Negro Labor Congress in 1925. He joined the Communist party in 1926 and in the 1930s and 1940s in particular was an outstanding leader of that party; he was its vice presidential candidate in 1932, 1936, and 1940. There was occasional correspondence between him and Du Bois; Ford, for instance, wrote early in 1925.

Chicago, Illinois, February 20, 1925.

My dear Dr. Du Bois:

I hope you have my letter of recent date concerning my position in the matter of Fisk University. Please find enclosed a money order for two dollars ($2.00) which I trust will be of some help towards publishing Fisk Herald. I also stated that I would write in detail concerning experiences which I had at Fisk, and with F. A. McKenzie.

I entered Fisk, from the High School in Birmingham, Ala., in 1913 finishing with the class of 1918. I volunteered for service in the U. S. Army in the latter part of my senior year; and saw eight months service in France with the Signal Corps.

Now that the exposure of conditions at Fisk has started we must not relent. Already reports have come out of Nashville. This is a fortunate omen—a warning that we must fight harder. It will be to your "eternal glory" that you have started this thing.

I recall, during my stay at Fisk, the abrogation of the fundamental principles of education; and the attempt at suppression of manhood and courage by Pres. McKenzie. Most of all, I recall a day in December of 1917 when seven of us fellows, four seniors and three juniors, volunteered for service in the U. S. Army. The day we left was a sort of holiday. We were given a send-off in Jubilee Hall. Dr. Morrow prayed; women teachers and girls wept and were eager; professors were sad; and men students were hesitant. It was a solemn affair—an adventure for Democracy!

I remember too those hellish days in Southern Camps, and those more vital days of hell in France. Upon my return, I found myself again at Fisk for a few days' visit. At Chapel service I was asked to talk by Pres. McKenzie.

I sensed that the students were eager for experience and something of the practical contacts of war. I told them something of these contacts; of hope for better conditions thru out the world; and most of all, of the contribution of black men, from all parts of the world to this war. This said, I took my seat, and to my surprise I was followed by the President who delayed chapel long enough to make, in a sarcastic manner, the statement that there was nothing to feel "chesty" about; that we had contributed no more than anybody else.

The next day I was asked to speak to a small class of students. I spoke. Again I found that the President's private secretary was in the rear of the room taking down everything I said—this same woman whom you spoke of in the Chicago meeting.

All of this happened following a great fight for Democracy—when the world was seeking self-knowledge and truth—at a Negro University with a white-president who had, previously, so willingly espoused the cause of democracy and urged Negro students to go to war. I trust this experience of mine will be of some service.

In the meantime, your statements of men and conditions at Birmingham, Ala., in your address at Nashville in June of 1924 are absolutely true. More could be said I am sure.

Yours in the Cause,
James W. Ford

In the spring of 1924, Du Bois lectured at Mounds, Illinois. In attendance were seniors of a recently built high school in the unincorporated, all-Black community of Sandusky in Alexander County. The students had earlier been asked to suggest an appropriate name for the school, and following Du Bois's talk, the class president, Almyra Randall, told the principal, Joseph C. Penn, that they wanted the school named for Du Bois. When the principal informed Du Bois, he agreed, asking only that its conduct be such as not to reflect badly upon his name.

This background explains a letter, written (on Du Bois's birthday) on the stationery of the Du Bois Community High School.

Sandusky, Illinois, February 23, 1925

Dear Sir,

Last spring we were very fortunate in securing the majority of votes for a new high school in this community; so now it stands by itself on a four acre lot in our little town as beautiful and as white as can be.

Without a doubt you will be interested in knowing that our school is the second largest colored high school in southern Illinois which we are very happy to call our own *Du Bois High*.

On the night of last spring when you gave a lecture at the A.M.E. church in Mounds, Ill., you also gave Mr. J. C. Penn, our prin., permission to name our school in honor of you. Sir, we feel highly honored and hope to do our part in making the school worthy of that name that we love so well.

We, the first graduating class (four girls), are writing to you for a favor. We feel that if you could see our beautiful, clean, white walls, that are bare of pictures, that you would not hesitate one minute to give to our class a picture of yourself for us, on our class night, to present to the school as a token of you and our class. A large picture of you will inspire us and all of our fellow students to go on and upward. Sir, as a token of love we wish to present this picture.

Trusting and believing that you will gladly grant us this favor.[1]

We are

Yours truly,
The First Senior Class of Du Bois Hi.
Almyra Randall
Pres. of Senior Class.

The Reverend Joseph B. Glenn, a Catholic priest in charge of Saint Joseph's Mission in Richmond, Virginia, in 1925 wrote Du Bois a rather ill-tempered letter that evoked a significant correspondence. The article to which Father Glenn referred appeared in the March 1925 *Crisis* (25:207); its author was Yolande Du Bois, Du Bois's daughter. It may well be that a defense of his daughter added something to the sharpness of Du Bois's reply. The subject of Miss Du Bois's piece was Lizzie A. Pingree, who had passed away early in 1925 in her Maine home; this white woman had served as a teacher for decades in Alabama and

---

1. Du Bois did send the photograph and it was placed on the wall of the school's assembly room. The school closed in 1933; the building now serves as an elementary school in the Tamms School District. The editor is grateful to Dr. Grace Duff of the Educational Service Region in Alexander County, and to Mr. Joseph C. Penn of Carbondale, Illinois—former Principal of Du Bois High School and now a Consultant for the Superintendent of Education of the state of Illinois—for their generous assistance.

Florida before becoming matron of South Hall at Atlanta University, where, according to Miss Du Bois, she was universally loved by the students.

Richmond, Va., Feb. 28, 1925

The Editor, *The Crisis*
Dear Sir:

Anent the article: "Thy people shall be my people," you may assure the author that she can dry up her tears—she weeps over the fact that the last of the "old guard of New England men and women who went South to teach black children" has just departed. Please assure the dear lady that there are probably nearly two hundred priests and brothers and sisters from New England and its environs laboring without pay in the South today and many of them are "old guards." We have several sisters here who are over forty years in the service; there are many more in Norfolk, throughout North Carolina, in Tennessee, etc. I do hope that the weeping lady will now dry up her tears and be comforted.

Respectfully yours,
Joseph B. Glenn

March 18, 1925

Dear Mr. Glenn:

The "old guard" of Catholic priests and sisters teaching in the colored South deserve all credit for their unselfish work. Of course they are not laboring "without pay" because they are assured of food and clothes and shelter for life which is more than most of us get; and especially they differ from teachers like Elizabeth Pingree in this fact; they are unable or unwilling to produce leaders for the black race. In over 400 years the Catholic Church has ordained less than a half dozen black Catholic priests either because they have sent us poor teachers or because American Catholics do not want to work beside black priests and sisters or because they think Negroes have neither brains nor morals enough to occupy positions open freely to Poles, Irishmen and Italians. Which is the real reason, dear Mr. Glenn—we pause in our tears for a reply and for a reply more humbly suitable to the great and glaring failure of the Catholic Church among American Negroes than your first flippant and sarcastic note.

Very sincerely yours,
W. E. B. Du Bois

Richmond, Va., March 20, 1925

Dear Dr. Du Bois:

I am much surprised that my note of the 28th of February should prompt you to send a reply so bitter. I beg of you as a personal favor that you kindly send me a copy of my letter to you.

My mind travels with your own up to a certain point in matters you touched on in your letter.

It is disgraceful that we have not provided more and better schools. I beg to assure you that nobody can remedy such defects more quickly than yourself. Give publicity to the defects as you observe them. The sluggishness to provide means is not due to any hostile feeling but to a condition peculiar to Catholic life. Up to and including the present time the church in America has been put to it to provide suitable housing for worship and education to accommodate the multitude of immigrants arriving on these shores yearly. To such an extent is this true that up to ten years ago Catholic America did not have one priest on the foreign missions; and in contributions to foreign missions she was several thousand dollars behind Canada or Ireland. However I do not mean to infer that nothing has been attempted. There are hundreds of Colored Catholic schools scattered throughout the country. The product of these schools will take the reins of leadership some day. The process of training may be slow but it is deep. These schools are becoming more numerous and are getting better year by year. They have already turned out several thousand Colored sisters. You should get acquainted with these sisters, they have lots of God's grace and marvellous zeal. These sisters stand in the first ranks of American life and we can all follow their leadership with perfect security. We have not been altogether bankrupt in putting Colored people into place in American life. Bishop Healey of Portland, Maine, the bishop of a powerful diocese was a Colored man.[1] I do not know of any other denomination which has raised a Colored man to be the spiritual ruler of many thousands of whites and yet to have but a mere handful of Colored followers. His brother, Father Healey, became the president of Georgetown University, one of the oldest in the country. A sister of the above became the head of the Ursuline Nuns in America. The Foundress of the Nuns of the Immaculate Heart of Mary was a Colored woman. There are of course minor celebrities. The number who will take the reins one day will be greater. You can well hasten the day by stirring up interest in these matters. Giving a good deal of publicity to the efforts now being made would help some. I don't recall having read a kindly word in the Crisis of anything Catholic. The Church has not tried and failed. She has not yet fittingly tried. We are on the eve of greater effort.

I beg to assure you in the kindest way possible that you could do much good by a more kindly attitude to the Catholic efforts. It is generally accepted as a fact that you are hostile to Catholics. Try to recollect any instance of a kindly word said by the Crisis in behalf of the many who have labored for years in this field. It is a pity that you have left such an impression of hostility; personally I am sure that it does not exist. Why should it?

1. James Augustine Healy (1830–1900): his father, an Irish immigrant, married a former slave. Healy graduated in 1849 from the College of the Holy Cross in Massachusetts, studied in seminaries in France, was ordained in 1854, and served the church for many years in Boston. In 1875, he became Bishop in Maine, where he died. See A. S. Foley, *Bishop Healy: Beloved Outcast* (New York, 1954).

By the way it occurs to me that there must be a great number of Colored priests and Colored Catholic leaders in South America.
Respectfully,
Joseph B. Glenn.

March 24, 1925

Dear Sir:

You miss the main point of my criticism. The Catholic Church in America stands for color separation and discrimination to a degree equalled by no other church in America, and that is saying a very great deal. In this it is false to the great tradition of Catholicism through the ages—in Europe, Asia and Africa, in South America and the West Indies. I am not blaming the church for so few Negro schools. I am blaming it because in its higher schools it has with few exceptions rigidly excluded Negroes and refused to educate black priests or even give high school training to black children until it could afford a complete and separate set of Negro schools from kindergarten to college and seminary. And today instead of even building a great "Jim Crow" system with a university at the top, it is multiplying primary schools of the lowest and most inefficient type with nearly all the teachers white. Meantime the white parochial schools even in the North, exclude colored children, the Catholic high schools will not admit them, the Catholic university at Washington invites them elsewhere and scarcely a Catholic seminary in the country will train a Negro priest. This is not then a case of blaming the Catholic Church for not doing all it might—it is blaming it for being absolutely and fundamentally wrong today and in the United States on the basic demands of human brotherhood across the color line.

The Crisis is no enemy of Catholicism. We admire and praise much of its mighty history. I have just written for the Knights of Columbus a volume in their admirably conceived series of monographs for inter-racial understanding of the making of America.[1] But because Catholicism has so much that is splendid in its past and fine in its present, it is the greater shame that "nigger" haters clothed in its episcopal robes should do to black Americans in exclusion, segregation and exclusion from opportunity all that the Ku Klux Klan ever asked.
Very sincerely yours,
W. E. B. Du Bois

Two very sensitive men were Du Bois and Carter G. Woodson. Mutual respect existed, but Dr. Woodson, especially, maintained a distance approaching hostility. It is thus all the more revealing that Du Bois pressed for some years the propriety of awarding the Spingarn Medal to Dr. Woodson, as the founder (in

---

1. *The Gift of Black Folk: The Negroes in the Making of America* (Boston: Stratford Co., 1924).

1915) of the Association for the Study of Negro Life and History. After 1915, the Spingarn Medal was awarded annually by the NAACP for "the highest and noblest achievement of an American Negro." The award committee consisted of Osward Garrison Villard; James H. Dillard, director of the Jeanes Foundation and a member of the Southern Education Board; Bishop John Hurst of the AME Church; John Hope; and ex-President Taft. Woodson was the Spingarn Medalist in 1926.

March 25, 1925.

My dear Mr. Hope:

I want to bring to your attention the claims of Carter G. Woodson as Spingarn Medalist for the year 1925.

Several times his name has been mentioned and always with appreciation; but it seems to me that on the 10th anniversary of the founding of The Journal of Negro History that Woodson becomes the one outstanding figure for honor at our hands.

Woodson is not a popular man. He is, to put it mildly, cantankerous. But he has done the most striking piece of scientific work for the Negro race in the last ten years of any man that I know. He has kept an historical journal going almost single-handed, founded a publishing association, and published a series of books with but limited popular appeal. At the same time he has maintained his integrity, his absolute independence of thought and action, and has been absolutely oblivious to either popular applause or bread and butter. It is a marvelous accomplishment. He ought to have a Spingarn medal.

Very sincerely yours,
W. E. B. Du Bois

A 1925 letter from a student, R. H. Athearn, brought a probably jolting, but characteristic, reply from Du Bois.

Nashville, Tenn., March 19, 1925

W. E. B. DuBoise
Dear Sir:

As a student in the Southern College of Young Men's Christian Associations, I am preparing to make a study of the contribution of the Y.M.C.A. to the negro race. The suggestion has been made to me by Dr. W. D. Weatherford that you in all likelihood possess much first hand information which is not available from any other source, and which would be very valuable to me in the research work I am now planning.

I would very much appreciate any literature and personal information or opinions that you should give me in regard to the contribution of the Association to the race as a whole.

Thanking you in advance for any courtesies which you may be able to extend me in this matter, I am

> Very truly yours,
> R. H. Athearn

April 2, 1925

My dear Sir:

I have no information as to the contribution which the Y.M.C.A. has made to the Negro race. I should imagine that the Negro race might teach the Southern College of the Y.M.C.A. a good deal about christianity.

> Very sincerely yours,
> W. E. B. Du Bois

William Christopher Handy (1873–1958) was the genius who fathered the "blues." His *Memphis Blues* appeared in 1912, the *St. Louis Blues* two years later, and the *Beale Street Blues* in 1917. In 1925, the Handy Brothers Music Company issued *Blues: An Anthology;* it is to this anthology that W. C. Handy refers here.

New York City, April 7, 1925

Dear Dr. Du Bois:

Please accept the autographed copy of the collection of *Blues* as a token of appreciation of your favorable mention of my humble efforts in the March edition of the "Graphic." [1]

The service you are rendering our Race in particular and the American people in general through such articles is incalculable.

With very best wishes, I am

> Respectfully yours,
> W. C. Handy

In May 1925, Du Bois wrote to the secretary of state requesting an authenticated copy of his appointment as envoy extraordinary representing President Coolidge at the 1924 inauguration of President King of Liberia. The reply from the secretary's assistant included enclosures of interest.

Washington, May 28, 1925

My dear Doctor Du Bois:

In accordance with your request contained in your letter of May 14, 1925, I

---

1. The reference is to Du Bois's article "The Black Man Brings His Gifts," *Survey Graphic* 53 (1 March 1925):655–57.

am transmitting herewith an authenticated copy of the letter of credence accrediting you as the Special Representative of President Coolidge with the rank of Envoy Extraordinary and Minister Plenipotentiary, upon the occasion of the inauguration of President King of Liberia in 1924.

The original of this letter of credence, as you are doubtless aware, is now in the possession of the Liberian Government and forms a part of the permanent records of that Republic.

I am, my dear Dr Du Bois,

Sincerely yours,
W. R. Castle, Jr.

The first enclosure was a certificate signed by Frank B. Kellogg, secretary of state, attesting that the document annexed to it—and published below—"is a true copy from the records of this Department"; the certificate is dated 26 May 1925. The second enclosure was the letter of credence from President Coolidge to President King.

To His Excellency
Charles D. B. King,
President of the Republic of Liberia
Great and Good Friend:

I have made choice of Doctor W. E. B. Du Bois as my Special Representative, with the rank of Envoy Extraordinary and Minister Plenipotentiary, on the occasion of your inauguration for another term as President of the Republic of Liberia.

I have entire confidence that he will render himself acceptable to Your Excellency in the distinguished duty with which I have invested him.

I therefore request Your Excellency to receive him favorably and to accept from him the assurance of the high regard and friendship entertained for Your Excellency and the Government and People of Liberia by the Government and People of the United States, and the sincere felicitations which they, and I in their name, tender to Your Excellency on this auspicious occasion.

May God have Your Excellency in His safe and Holy Keeping.

Your Good Friend,
Calvin Coolidge

By the President;
Charles E. Hughes
Secretary of State
Washington, December 26, 1923.

Agnes Smedley (1894–1950) was born in Missouri and educated at the University of California, New York University, and the University of Berlin. In Berlin, she was also a teacher and occasional contributor to German newspapers. In 1928, she went to China as correspondent for the *Frankfurter Zeitung*, thus beginning her prolonged relationship with the revolutionary struggles in that country, recorded in such widely read books as *Chinese Destinies* (1933) and *China's Red Army Marches* (1934).

Berlin, June 9, 1925

Dr. W. E. B. Du Bois
Dear Sir:

Permit me to introduce myself to you as a former member of the Civic Club, and an American woman who was actively engaged in the work connected with the movement for the independence of India. I met you in that connection some five years ago.

I am now living in Germany and among other work, am teaching in Berlin University. This summer semester I am teaching a class on problems in America. We are to take up the problem of the Negro American after two or three weeks, but although I have looked through all the libraries in Berlin, I have found very little material. Your books are to be had here, but I need the magazine which, I believe, you edit, and I need urgently facts and figures on lynchings of the Negro in America. It is needless to tell you that I have no prejudice against the Negro and that before I take up the study of this problem in America, I want to have all the facts and the figures which you can furnish me on this question, that I may place these in the hands of my students for study. I need statistics showing the number of lynchings and the reasons for the lynchings, for I wish to prove that rape is not the cause of the lynching madness.

It is impossible for me to pay for any publications from America, because I do not make enough money. I wish to ask you, therefore, to send me what free material you have at your disposal on this problem. I remember that your Association used to issue press bulletins of importance, giving just the information I need. I should like such material.

I need this information *at once*, for I am holding up the study of the Negro problem in America only until I can receive this material. Furthermore, I wish it because I also write occasion articles for the German press, and I have been asked for an article on the American Negro.[1]

With cordial greetings, believe me to be,

Respectfully yours,
Agnes Smedley

1. A notation on this letter shows that, in accordance with Du Bois's instructions, Miss Smedley was sent copies of the *Crisis* for 1924 and 1925, the NAACP pamphlet, *Thirty Years of Lynching*, and Du Bois's *Gift of Black Folk*.

Charles Waddell Chesnutt, the distinguished writer, served as one of the judges of short stories in the contests regularly run by Du Bois as editor of the *Crisis*. A letter offering his estimate of entries in one such contest is of interest.

Cleveland, Ohio, August 3, 1925

My dear Dr. Du Bois:

I have read the four stories which you have been good enough to send me, and am prepared to tell you what I think about them. In my opinion the quality of a story depends upon several elements: 1, the theme; 2, the plot and its working out; 3, the language, including the style; 4, the effect on the reader. The theme is important. A motive which in real life is improbable (except of course in fairy tales and others of that sort) does not make a good story. A plot which suffers from the same defect or is not well worked out does not make a good story. Good English or whatever the language may be, which is easily understood by the reader, is essential. But the most important of all is the effect upon the reader. However irreproachable your theme, however well developed your plot, however fine your style or however choice your language, if the story does not ring true and does not convince the reader, it is not a good story.

Applying these principles to the stories you sent me, and which I return herewith, I should say that the story "Three Dogs and a Rabbit" is well conceived, well written, but not convincing. The race motive is dragged into it unnecessarily. There was no dramatic necessity for this fine old woman to betray the secret of her origin, with the extremely probable effect of embarrassing her children and their future. The story would have been, from any standpoint but that of a colored reader, equally dramatic and effective without that disclosure. So the story is not convincing.

"Easy Pickin's" is merely a character sketch in dialect. I suspect this bum's condition was due to more than his wife's misconduct. He could not have been any good or he would have managed his wife better, nor would he have permitted his life to be ruined by a worthless woman. Speaking of dialect, in my view there is no such thing as Negro dialect. Dialect is a form of speech which has become to a certain extent fixed or at least conventionalized, like the Scotch dialect or perhaps the Pennsylvania Dutch speech. Negro dialect is largely if not entirely merely mispronunciation of English. Mr. Octavus Roy Cohen has either dug or created some forms of speech which savor of dialect, as for instance the phrase of which this would be an example, "Time is somethin' I ain't got nuthin' else but." But, generally speaking, Negro dialect is merely the local corruption of good English, except as it may here and there include some of the Elizabethan allocutions of which Mr. Mencken has collected so many in his "The American Language." A dialect which is so difficult that the reader has to stop to figure out what it means detracts from the interest of the story, in which respect this writer sins.

"High Yaller," the most ambitious of the four stories, is very well written. Of course an editor reading it with a view to publication could make certain suggestions as to the language and figures of speech here and there. The plot is well worked out, with a heroine and a hero and a villain, and its atmosphere may be a correct reflection of Negro life in Harlem, with which I am not very familiar. But to me at least the theme is not convincing. I have never yet met knowingly a fair colored girl who wanted to be darker. The almost universal desire is, as the advertising pages of the colored newspapers and periodicals bear witness, to get as much whiter as possible. So the story is not convincing.

"There Never Fell A Night so Dark" is in my opinion the best of the lot. The theme is human. It is a simple sketch, with some elements of improbability in the plot. For instance as I read her story, her son was killed in the war, and according to his story his son is in prison, innocent of course, though they turn out to be the man and the woman. But the little story touches the emotions and to that extent meets the essential requirement of a good story.

If I were grading the stories I should make "There Never Fell a Night So Dark" No. 1, "High Yaller" No. 2, "Three Dogs and a Rabbit" No. 3, and "Easy Pickin's."

I suspect you only wanted my opinion on the relative merit of the stories and that I have inflicted on you my reasons unnecessarily. If so you will pardon the superfluity.

Your letter found me and my family well, and we all join in sincere regards.[1]

Cordially yours,
Charles W. Chesnutt

P. B. Young, owner and editor of an influential Afro-American newspaper, the *Norfolk, Virginia, Journal and Guide*, wrote to James Weldon Johnson in 1925 asking for detailed information on the position of the NAACP *vis-à-vis* Marcus Garvey and his movement. For reasons that will be clear in the letter, Du Bois wrote the reply; it is one of his fullest statements on his relationship, and the NAACP's (as he saw it), to the Garvey effort.

August 8, 1925

Mr. P. B. Young
My dear Sir:

Mr. Johnson has asked me to answer your letter of August 1, which found him away on his vacation and was forwarded to him.

It is possible that the judge who tried Garvey had at some time contributed to the N.A.A.C.P. or cooperated with it. Most people of prominence have. The Chief Justice of the United States for a long time acted upon one of our committees.

---

1. This letter is in the Chesnutt Papers held by the Western Reserve Historical Society, Cleveland, Ohio.

It is absolutely untrue that the N.A.A.C.P. is a rival organization to the U.N.I.A. or instigated the charges against Garvey. The charges of misusing funds originated with the prosecuting attorney of New York City before The Crisis had ever mentioned Garvey and before the N.A.A.C.P. had known anything of his activities. When finally he was indicted the officers of the Department of Justice came to us for information. The only information which we furnished were copies of Garvey's own paper and copies of articles published in The Crisis. Outside of this the N.A.A.C.P. took absolutely no action of any sort against Mr. Garvey.

The articles in The Crisis were four in number. The first three were expository and on the whole friendly, and simply published information open to the public. The fourth article which was severely condemnatory was not published until after his conviction and because of the propaganda which he was sending out against our organization and against all Negroes in the United States who were standing up for their rights as American citizens.[1]

The charges against Garvey originated in two ways. First because of suits brought against him by members of his own organization who had invested in the Black Star Line under false representation, and secondly by the effort of the state and city of New York to make Garvey stop violating the law in his issuing and selling of stock. The prosecuting witnesses in every single case were former members of Garvey's organization or officers of the law. Not a single member or officer of the N.A.A.C.P. appeared as witness against Garvey.

When the Garvey organization asked to be admitted to Liberia they were told that Liberia wanted immigrants and that all immigrants would be allowed every facility that Liberia could furnish. Then Liberia discovered that the Garvey organization was practically setting up a government within a government. When they realized this, they issued a proclamation which was afterward enacted into law, saying that no immigrant would be allowed to enter Liberia who was a member of the Garvey organization. This action was taken not only in reasonable self-defence but also because of the questions which were being asked Liberia by England and France. That is, these countries asked if Liberia was going to allow her soil to be used as a center of agitation against the sovereignty of friendly nations.

I am rushing this letter to you and am sorry that it has been delayed. It just came to my hands this morning.

Very sincerely yours,
W. E. B. Du Bois

---

1. See the *Crisis* 21 (December 1920):58, 60; 21 (January 1921):112–15; 24 (September 1922):210–14; 28 (August 1924):154–55. See also Du Bois's article "Back to Africa," *Century* 105 (February 1923):539–48; and his contribution to "A Symposium on Garvey," *Messenger* 4 (December, 1922):551.

A. Philip Randolph (b. 1889) began in the 1920s, while editor of the radical magazine the *Messenger*, to organize into a union the Black men who served as porters on the nation's railroads. A very early announcement of this historic effort occurs in a letter from Randolph to Du Bois. Though in this instance Du Bois was not able to serve Randolph, he did in other cases, and his writings and voice consistently supported efforts to organize Black workers*

The goal of this organizational effort, as described by the brotherhood itself, was: "More wages; better hours; better working conditions; pay for overtime; pay for 'preparation' time; abolition of 'doubling out'; conductor's pay for conductor's work when in charge and manhood rights."

New York, September 10, 1925

My dear Dr. Du Bois:

Just a word to acquaint you of the fact that I have organized the Pullman porters into the Brotherhood of Sleeping Car Porters. This occurred on the 25th of August, in the Elks' Auditorium, 160 West 129th Street, New York City.

May I request you to address the men on either Tuesday or Wednesday evening, September 22nd or 23rd, at 8:30 P.M., at the above named address? I assure you that the men will appreciate it.

It may be interesting to you to know that the movement is getting the whole hearted support of white organized labor. Mr. W. J. Orr, special Organizer of the Locomotive Engineers and Ernest Bohm, representative of Mr. Hugh Frayne, have addressed the men. Mr. Hugh Frayne, Organizer of the A.F. of L. will speak on the 17th of September. We hold two meetings every week.

We hope to organize 51% of the men in the next 60 days, and the prospects are that we will get them.

Sincerely yours,
A. Philip Randolph
General Organizer

September 14, 1925

Mr. A. Philip Randolph
My dear Sir:

I regret to say that it will be impossible for me to address the Sleeping Car Porters this month as my engagements will not allow it. I very much regret my inability to serve them.

Very sincerely yours,
W. E. B. Du Bois

* Editorials by Du Bois urging support of the organizational work of Randolph appeared, for example, in the *Crisis* 33 (January 1927):131; and 34 (December 1927):348.

[320] Correspondence 1920–1929

Earlier letters have indicated the difficulties under which the poet Claude McKay labored. Another communication to Du Bois, late in 1925, reflects the persistence of difficulties and McKay's own determination as a creative person.

Paris, October 27, 1925

Dear Dr. Du Bois:

I was happy that someone sent me the October "Crisis" with its fine literary features that is to my mind the greatest work the "Crisis" has ever done yet! Although it may be that I am prejudiced in rating creative work too highly and above social work even as highly as I do rate the second, I say this despite the fact that in competitions, like examinations, I've never had any interest or faith even though they do produce fine results sometimes.

I am sending you a sheaf of poems (five) that you might be able to use and pay me something for them.[1] I had a set back and have been ill again. I am staying in a little town here in the Midi and am without any money. To help myself I have sent out a number of things to a couple of liberal New York magazines including yours and I am anxiously awaiting the result.

With kind regards I am

Yours Sincerely
Claude McKay

The poems are taken from a collection that I am making for another book but so far I have not enough *good* ones yet and publication in magazines may help me now as well as the hoped-for greater event.

CMcK

Du Bois's faith in the power of righteousness to move and the influence of reason to persuade is shown to a marked degree in the following communication to Harvey S. Firestone, of the Firestone Tire and Rubber Company. The reply came from W. D. Hines, who identified himself as being connected with the "Office of the President."

October 26, 1925

Personal
Mr. Harvey S. Firestone
My dear Sir:

Early in the year 1924 I was in Liberia as special representative of the President of the United States at the inauguration of President King with the rank of Minister Plenipotentiary and Envoy Extraordinary. During that time I accompanied the resident minister, Solomon Porter Hood, and the rubber expert of the Firestone Company to look over the rubber forest with a view to deciding whether

---

1. Poems by Claude McKay appeared in the *Crisis* 33 (February 1927):202; and 35 (June, 1928):196.

it would be worth while for the Firestone Company to invest in Liberia.

Since that time I have learned that arrangements have been made by the Firestone Plantations Company for raising rubber on a large scale in Liberia and making other industrial improvements. I am very much interested in this development because I have long followed the history of Liberia. I write to bring certain considerations to your attention.

It would be very easy for a great industry properly capitalized to enter Liberia and repeat there the same kind of industrial history which one finds in the Belgium, Portuguese and English colonies and to some extent in the French. There would be no doubt that such an enterprise could certainly for a time make money. But on the other hand with the awakening that is taking place in Africa and with the long struggle that the Liberians have made for independence and freedom, I do not think this method would be nearly as profitable in the long run as another method which I am venturing to bring to your attention and which I am sure would work.

I have seen parts of British and French colonial Africa and have come in close contact with those who know colonial conditions in other parts of Africa. In all these cases with the exception of the French, the procedure has been to enter the black country with an entirely white personnel; to use the natives as laborers with the lowest wage and to use imported whites as the personnel in control. This is, of course, justified by the fact that the natives are not acquainted with the modern industrial processes or industrial organization and that white persons who know them must be imported if the work is to be properly done. But the difficulty comes in the type of person who exercises this control. Usually Americans send whites used to "handling" colored labor. These get results by cruelty and brow-beating alternating with pandering to drunkenness, gambling and prostitution among the blacks. Usually no attempt is made to train the blacks for the higher positions and the result is a system of caste and of oppression and misrepresentation to the outside world leading to intense dissatisfaction on the part of the colored people. In French colonies there is the same system, mitigated only in that it is possible for black men to enter the ruling caste either through the civil service or in business and while comparatively few do this still there is the opening.

What I propose to you is that in this experiment in Liberia you give from the beginning unusual attention to the ruling industrial personnel who will conduct your venture. Of course you are in Liberia primarily to raise cheap rubber and not to reform the world; but I assume that if in raising rubber you could also in other ways help the world and particularly the black world forward a step, you would not be averse.

I suggest therefore that you choose your governing industrial personnel from the following groups:
1. White American rubber experts
2. Educated and trained Liberians

3. Colored Americans of education and experience

I am aware that this will bring protests; the white experts will not want colored colleagues and will not believe that capable ones can be found. They will want in Liberia to be like their fellows in neighboring English and French colonies, a close racial caste with all "niggers" beneath them.

If now this caste is based on fact, i.e. if it is impossible to put colored men in authority or find colored experts or train them, then there is no help for the resultant situation. But this is not entirely true. Certain it is that there are no colored men in Liberia or America who could completely man and conduct the business of a rubber plantation. But there are many who could gradually learn the profession if given the proper opportunity.

I suggest therefore that from the very beginning you seek to avoid a strict color line in your business. For instance, you will have to have a hospital and nurses. Why not take American Negroes for this work? They have proven themselves skilled in medicine and nursing, they would do a good job. Just as soon as there were properly trained colored nurses and physicians in Liberia they should, of course, be used.

But I suggest further that you do not stop there; that in addition you make it a point to give to educated black men, both African and American, a chance to work up in your industrial system. We have in America well trained young men who could do this. None of them know the rubber business. They could not expect to begin at the top, but they could begin at the bottom if allowed a chance for promotion. You would, of course, in any scheme of this kind meet at first a good deal of opposition from your white personnel, but if the proper Negroes were selected they would in the end prove their efficiency and gain the confidence of their white fellow workers. This is not merely a matter of philanthropy, it is an excellent policy. The Liberians have been trained in freedom. They are called bumptious and given a bad name by their English and French neighbors but this is merely because they have successfully resisted the encroachment of whites and have tried to rule their own land. When now a great industry dominated by white people comes into their country they are going to be sensitive. They are going to make unnecessary trouble unless they are satisfied from the first that they are going to be treated as men, without any imported color line. They themselves, because of lack of educational facilities cannot furnish much help in the higher parts of your organization, but they can furnish some persons and you can secure Negroes of the highest intelligence and training in the United States. There again you may meet some opposition from the Liberians themselves, but not much if the American Negroes prove themselves and act with discretion and sympathy toward the Liberians.

I believe that in this way you can inaugurate one of the greatest and far reaching reforms in the relations between white industrial countries like America and black, partly developed countries like Liberia if it can once be proven that industry can do the same thing in a black country like Liberia that it does in a white country like Australia: that is, invade it, reform it and uplift it by incorporating the native born into the imported industry and thus make the industry a part of the country. Only in this way can the relations between Europe and America on the one hand and Africa and Asia on the other hand be transformed and led toward mutual dependence and prosperity. If, on the other hand, you send to Africa and put in authority in your organization men who know about rubber but do not know about the aspirations of modern colored men and do not care about anything except the profit of the investment, then I do not doubt but what you may for many years carry on a successful enterprise; but in the long run, if the Negro develops as I think he is going to develop and if colored countries develop, then you and your enterprise are going to suffer just as white European enterprises are beginning to suffer in their relations with Africa and Asia.

I trust you will pardon my temerity in bringing this matter to your notice. My only excuse is my great interest in the development of the Negro race. I hope that you will perhaps let me further develop this plan if you are interested in it. I am, sir,

> Very respectfully yours,
> W. E. B. Du Bois

Akron, Ohio, November 10 1925

Dr. W. E. B. DuBois
Dear Sir:

Your letter of October 26 has just been called to Mr. Firestone's attention, due to his absence from the city during the past ten days. He was much interested in your outline of conditions and suggestions relative to our Liberian personnel and operation. Mr. Firestone is very glad at all times to receive suggestions and advice relative to his proposed rubber growing enterprise, and appreciates very much your recent communication.

We have felt all along that this enterprise is much greater than a purely commercial project, and have put it more in the light of a large movement with considerable patriotic and philanthropic aspects. Of course, in the first place, it is a business proposition, but we fully realize that its success is based upon mutual good will, co-operation and profit for Liberia, its people, and America and its people. We hope that it will bring both of them to a better understanding of each other, and feel quite sure that it will greatly strengthen Liberia from a national and international standpoint.

If you have any further ideas or suggestions relative to work in Liberia, we would be very glad to hear from you at any time.

Thanking you for your letter, I remain

> Yours sincerely,
> W. D. Hines
> Office of the President

Carl Van Vechten (1880–1964) was a leading music critic for the *New York Times* in the early years of the present century. In the 1920s, he turned to novel-writing, producing seven by 1930; thereafter, he devoted himself to photography and gained prominence in this area, also. He was an early white enthusiast of Black creative work, especially in music but also in fiction. His letter to Du Bois, and the reply, illuminate a significant problem that has yet to be resolved.

New York, October 29, 1925

To the Editor of "The Crisis"
Sir:

In your November issue I have read a review by Emmett J. Scott, Jr., of Haldane MacFall's novel, "The Wooings of Jezebel Pettyfer," in which the reviewer asserts, "A book less appealing to a colored man would be hard to find." I feel an inclination to make some reply to this review, since I am the critic Mr. Scott quotes as having hailed the book "as probably the best novel yet written about the Negro."

It is quite true that I made this recommendation, but when I made it I was thinking of "Jezebel" as a work of art. It is certainly written with more skill and inspiration than any other novel about the Negro that I have read. Whether or not it presents an accurate picture of Negro life in the Barbadoes I have no means of knowing; I have never been in the Barbadoes. I do know, however, that it presents a credible picture, that the characters and scenes awaken my interest and arouse my imagination.

There exists, it would appear, an explicable tendency on the part of the Negro to be sensitive concerning all that is written about him, particularly by a white man, to regard even the fiction in which he plays a role in the light of propaganda. Mr. Scott seems to be suffering from this prevalent sensitiveness. This will probably do no hurt to a work which has been as generally admired as "Jezebel," but it is an attitude of mind which may be utterly destructive when it is applied to the work of Negroes themselves. It is the kind of thing, indeed, which might be effective in preventing many excellent Negro writers from speaking any truth which might be considered unpleasant. There are plenty of unpleasant truths to be spoken about any race. The true artist speaks out fearlessly. The critic judges the artistic results; nor should he be concerned with anything else.

I do not believe it was Mr. MacFall's intention to be unpleasant. Nevertheless, apparently because the author of "Jezebel" writes of "slipshod Negresses" and "slattern gossips" Mr. Scott conveniently dubs him a "Negro hater," as if there were no "slipshod Negresses" (Mr. MacFall surely was unaware of the unreasonable prejudice existing against the use of this substantive. I myself, who can scarcely be called a "Negro hater," have often employed it, because all its synonyms are exceedingly clumsy).

It would be quite as just, after reading "The Fire in the Flint," to call Mr.

Walter White a white-man hater, but I am sure no good critic would think of doing so. Until novels about Negroes (by either white or colored writers) are regarded as dispassionately from the aesthetic standpoint as books about Chinese mandarins, I see little hope ahead for the new school of Negro authors. What, for example, will become of one of the most promising of the lot, Mr. Rudolph Fisher, if he be attacked from this angle? Would it have been possible, indeed, for a white man to write "High Yaller" without being called a "Negro hater"?

It will be recalled that Synge's poetic comedy, "The Playboy of the Western World," was hissed in Dublin, because the author, an Irishman himself, spoke of the heroine as appearing in her shift. This was construed by the mob as a direct insult aimed at Irish womanhood. This attitude may always be expected from the uncultured mob. When it is detected in a book review in an influential magazine, it may, however, be regarded with alarm. I am convinced, as a matter of fact, that such an attitude does more harm to a race in the eyes of its ready detractors than any amount of ridicule—and I persist hotly that "Jezebel" was never intended as ridicule—aimed from without.

Very truly yours,
Carl Van Vechten

November 5, 1925

My dear Mr. Van Vechten:

I should be very glad to use your letter if you would let me make it a part of an article which I am going to prepare on the problems of Negro art to be published in *The Crisis*[1] We receive as you know, continual criticism on things appearing in *The Crisis* and out of it, if it shows the Negro to any disadvantage. The reason for this is that this side of the Negro's life has been overdone and there is almost no corresponding work on the other side. I want to make a fight for art freedom in the work of Negroes and work about Negroes and at the same time show the basis of the ordinary, unintelligent criticism.

Very sincerely yours,
W. E. B. Du Bois

Late in 1925, it became known that an extension course for the benefit of schoolteachers given by Johns Hopkins University in Wilmington, Delaware, was open only to white persons. Du Bois wrote to the president of Johns Hopkins, Frank J. Goodnow, inquiring about its policy on race and raising the specific case in point. The president's reply evaded the issue involved; there appears to

---

1. See Du Bois, "Criteria of Negro Art," *Crisis* 34 (April 1927):70; and "Mencken," *Crisis* 34 (October 1927):276; see also his "Negro in American Literature," *Epworth Herald*, 28 January 1928.

have been no reply to a second letter from Du Bois to the Johns Hopkins president.* Goodnow (1859–1939) was educated at Amherst and Columbia Law School; was a professor and a dean at Columbia; served various governments (including the United States) as an adviser; and became president of Johns Hopkins in 1915. At his death he was president emeritus.

Baltimore, November 18, 1925

Dr. W. E. B. Du Bois
Dear Sir:

I have your letter of November 17th asking what is the policy of the Johns Hopkins University with regard to colored students.

This question has been raised a number of times already in the history of the University and we have felt that inasmuch as we are chartered by the State of Maryland and receive a considerable grant from the State, we should conform to the educational policy of the State with regard to the admission into the University of colored students.

The policy of the State as you probably know is the segregation of the races in all the schools of the State, including training schools for teachers.

These being the facts, I do not see that we have any alternative in the matter.
I am,

Yours very truly,
Frank J. Goodnow

November 21, 1925.

President Frank J. Goodnow
My dear Sir:

I have your letter of November eighteenth. I trust you will permit me an additional word.

It does not seem to me that the Wilmington case is a case of admitting students to Johns Hopkins University. This is an extension course given under the auspices of the university. Do you mean to say that the university so strictly interprets its obligations to the state of Maryland that if Johns Hopkins should offer courses in the District of Columbia or in Pennsylvania that it would feel that it must draw the color line which the local law does not draw, and that if in Wilmington, Delaware the education authorities do not draw a line among their teachers who are studying, is it nevertheless the policy of Johns Hopkins University to insist upon such a line?

I ask these questions because it seems to me a tremendous surrender to pro-

---

* Twenty-four of the teachers seeking to take the extension course were Black; when it was learned they were to be barred, the white teachers withdrew from the course.

vincialism and race discrimination for a great university like yours to take the stand which apparently you do.

Very sincerely yours,
W. E. B. Du Bois

Abram L. Harris, Jr. (1899–1963), whose training included a Ph.D. from Columbia in 1931, served as a research assistant for the National Urban League and later as a professor at West Virginia Collegiate Institute. At the time of his letter, he was executive secretary of the Minneapolis Urban League; later he headed Howard's Economics Department, and in his last years, he was a professor at the University of Chicago.

His letter to Du Bois, and the reply, reflect plans and hopes and discontents now nearly half a century old and never more intense than at present.

Minneapolis, Minn., November 21, 1925

My dear Dr. Du Bois:

I am writing you rather confidentially upon a subject which I wished to talk to you concerning when I was in New York last spring.

You recall perhaps, that after teaching economics at the West Va. Collegiate Institute for little over a year, I resigned to take the executive secretary-ship of the Minneapolis Urban League in July. While at Institute, your exposé of the Fisk University situation had just begun to arouse the Negro public from its stupor; and some of us younger members of the faculty at Institute felt that a general shake-up was needed not only at Fisk but thru out the entire realm of Negro education. You know the superstitions and orthodoxies by which even the so-called higher institutions among us are bound; and how skeptical administrators—white and black—view liberal thought among the faculty. A liberal on the faculty of the average Negro college usually succumbs to his orthodox environment or leaves the class in disgust. Were the liberal individual the only victim, the situation would not be worth such serious attention as some of us think necessary. The fact of the matter is that the cultural development of the Negro people is bound up inextricably with the life or death of liberalism in the various universities and colleges.

Dr. Sumner, professor of psychology at Institute and I have weighed the factors underlying the apathy which prevails in the average Negro college toward intellectual attainment and the need for broadening their sociological and biological courses. We have come to the conclusion that the best way to convey liberalism to the Negro is not by going into the present institutions as teachers. A new college similar to the New School of Social Research must be founded. What do you think of the idea? Utopian? We think the idea of a Newer Spirit College is worth consideration, particularly yours, since you may rightly be called the Father of the Negro intelligentsia.

I have already spoken to Dr. Francis Tyson, professor of economics at the University of Pittsburgh, about the proposition. He liked the notion but felt that financial backing was the greatest drawback. (I believe that there are lots of untouched philanthropies waiting for such a chance as this one!) He asked me to write you about it. I think Alain Locke should be interested, don't you?

The plans have not been worked out in any great detail, for we are desirous of creating a favorable sentiment among a small group and let it do the planning.

May I hear from you?

Sincerely yours,
Abram L. Harris

December 15, 1925.

My dear Mr. Harris:

Your letter of November twenty-first touches a very important question. I wish we could have somewhere in the north, an institution which would be a center of Negro culture and learning, and that would have in it an unshackled faculty of men of real education aand untrammeled ideals. The trouble is such an institution would cost money and I do not see or know any one whom I think would be willing to finance it even in a small way. But I should be very much interested in such a movement if it could be started. It is certainly true, as I am writing in an article to The Nation,[1] that Negro higher education even with Negro teachers for Negro students is not what it should be.

Very sincerely yours,
W. E. B. Du Bois

Roland Hayes (b. 1887), the great tenor, was born of poor Black parents in Curryville, Georgia. With great sacrifices, his musical education began at Fisk and continued in Boston and Europe. His experiences included being almost murdered in the South, but for many years, and before tens of thousands, his voice conveyed with astonishing quality the passion and fibre of his people.* Du Bois, for whom music was a source of great refreshment and inspiration, heard Hayes at every opportunity. Occasionally they met, and they sometimes exchanged letters.

November 30, 1925

My dear Mr. Hayes:

May I tell you what very deep and enduring pleasure I received from listening to you at Carnegie Hall last Friday night? I am under great obligations to you

---

1. Du Bois, "Negroes in College," *Nation* 122 (3 March 1926):228–30.

* See MacKinley Helm, *Angel Mo' and Her Son, Roland Hayes* (Boston: Little, Brown and Co., 1942).

for the opportunity and I hope that your health and strength will enable you to carry your great message further and further for an indefinite time.
Very sincerely yours,
W. E. B. Du Bois

Nashville, Tenn., December 16, 1925

My dear Dr. Du Bois:
What deep chords of infinite inspiration do the commendatory words, contained in your most kind letter, strike within my breast. Such understanding as here shown, helps to afford building stones to one foundation of a bridge which, when completed, will enable all to pass over into a fuller knowledge of the various benefits that each individual in *the race*, and, of *the races*, can derive from the other.
Yours, sincerely,
Roland Hayes

Du Bois sought to produce a national discussion—among white as well as Black writers and thinkers—of what was meant by Negro literature and of what that literature ought to be. One of those who participated in this effort was Sinclair Lewis; by the time of the writing of these letters, he had already published *Main Street* (1920), *Babbitt* (1922), and *Arrowsmith* (1925). In 1930, Lewis was to be the first American awarded the Nobel Prize in literature.
Miss Jessie Fauset, as assistant editor of the *Crisis*, had written Lewis late in 1925 apprising him of Du Bois's concern and inviting Lewis's reflections. This was the occasion for the correspondence published here in full.

New York, November 17, 1925

Dear Miss Fauset:
Your letter brings so many extremely complicated thoughts to my mind that I could not even begin to put them down on paper without taking a week to do it. And as I am off here in Bermuda (but only for two or three weeks more—I shall be back at the Hotel Shelton after that) writing a play, I can't at the moment take the time.
After reading your letter it suddenly occurred to me that just possibly *all* of the astounding and extraordinarily interesting flare of negro fiction which is now appearing may be entirely off on the wrong foot. All of you, or very nearly all of you, are primarily absorbed in the economic and social problems of the colored race. Complicated though these problems are in detail, yet inevitably they fall into a few general themes; so that there is the greatest danger that all of your novels will be fundamentally alike.
For example, this problem of going over and passing for white must be one

which will appeal to all of you. It must needs be much the same in your book or in Walter White's.

Ordinarily I hate committees, conferences and organizations like the very devil. But I wonder if there isn't a problem here which demands a real and serious conference? Suppose at some time in January we could get about twenty people together—yourself, Dr. DuBois, Jim Johnson, Walter [White], Countee Cullen, Carl Van Vechten, Joel Spingarn if he is feeling well enough, Roland Hayes, myself and so on—and really try (with a consciousness all the time that at best we could only suggest new points of view) to talk over some of these matters. Should American Negroes write as Americans or Negroes? Should they follow the pattern of an Edna Ferber who is quite as likely to write about Wisconsin Nordics as about her fellow Jews; or that of Zangwill, who is of the slightest importance only when he is writing about Jews? Should there be a Negro publishing house so that the Negro author can tell all of the ordinary publishing houses to go to the devil? Should there be a club—a comfortable small hotel in Paris to which the American Negroes can go and be more than welcome?

These and a thousand like topics suggest themselves to me as they have, of course, suggested themselves to Dr. DuBois and yourself. Their very complexity makes me feel that it is impossible to give any definite answer to them. Of this alone I am sure—you cannot, all of you, go on repeating the same story (however important, however poignant, however magnificently dramatic) of the well-bred, literate, and delightful Negro intellectual finding himself or herself blocked by the groundless and infuriating manner of superiority assumed by white men frequently less white than people technically known as Negroes.

So let's talk it all over when I come back to New York. Just when that will be I do not yet know, but you will be able to find out by calling up Harcourt, Brace.

My warmest greetings, and believe me
Yours sincerely,
Sinclair Lewis

Lewis wrote next in answer to Miss Fauset's request, in December 1925, for permission to publish his letter in the *Crisis*.

New York, January 28, 1926

My dear Miss Fauset:

I shall be glad to have you use my letter, but I should want to look it over again before it was published, as it was more or less hastily dictated for your eyes alone.

Do you want to send me a copy in care of Harcourt? As I am starting off for the Southwest for a couple of months of motoring, it may be some time in reaching me, as I shall only get mail every two weeks or so, but as soon as possible I will look it over and perhaps re-write it.

I am feeling enormously better than I did when I saw Mr. Spingarn, and hope to feel even better when I am through with my motoring trip.

Yours sincerely,
Sinclair Lewis

February 3, 1926

My dear Mr. Lewis:

Enclosed I am sending you a copy of part of the letter which you wrote Miss Fauset. I should be glad to have you correct and return it at your earliest convenience.

Very sincerely yours,
W. E. B. Du Bois

San Francisco, February 14, 1926

Dear Dr. Du Bois:

I think the changes I have made in the copy of my letter make it more suitable for publication. They are, you will note, mostly elisions of personalities.[1] The point in my last paragraph might be emphasized by an analysis of a good many different stories, which you know much better than myself, to show how fundamentally alike they are when a few superficialities are stripped away.

If my letter is of any value to you, I should be very happy indeed to have you use it.

Sincerely yours,
Sinclair Lewis

The first, but not the last, exchange between Du Bois and Nnamdi Azikiwe, later to be the first president of Nigeria,* occurred when Azikiwe was a twenty-two-year-old visitor, studying at Storer College in West Virginia.

Harpers Ferry, W. Va., February 24, 1926

The Crisis

I am a British West African author who is studying in this country.

Among my unpublished work are "Lays of Antique Onitsha and other poems," "The Founding of Onitsha" (Legend) "Follies of Friendship" (Drama) "Groundwall of Onitsha History."

---

1. Lewis's letter was published in the *Crisis* 32 (May 1926):36. Omitted were the sentence listing people to be invited to a conference and that discussing Jewish writers.

* For a recent examination of Azikiwe's life and thought, see Edward H. Schiller's essay in *Black Academy Review* 1, no. 3 (Fall 1970):11–25.

[332] Correspondence 1920–1929

I shall be greatly obliged to you if you let me know whether you publish books and if so, what are your terms please.

I shall be very interested to go into the matter further with you and you have my assurance that if agreeable, I shall try to do my best in this case.

Best wishes,

Yrs faithfully,
Ben N. Azikiwe

March 12, 1926

My dear Sir:

The *Crisis* does not undertake to publish books. We are always glad to examine single poems and articles.

Very sincerely yours,
W. E. B. Du Bois

For over fifty years, David Belasco (1853–1931), playwright, actor, and manager, was a leading name in the American theater. One of his great successes was *Lulu Belle*, first shown in 1926, starring Lenore Ulric. Letters from Belasco to Du Bois deal with that production.

New York, February 12, 1926

My dear Mr. Du Bois:

It has just come to my knowledge that you have not been invited to see my production of "Lulu Belle," which opened last Tuesday evening at the Belasco Theatre. As editor of The Crisis, I want you to see it.

Would it be convenient for you to come, as my guest, Thursday evening, February 25th? I wish I could have you in sooner but the advance sale has been so tremendous that I cannot provide seats for you before that date. We always throw our sale open to the public some weeks before the opening and the sale has been very heavy.

Please let me know if the evening designated is convenient and I will have two tickets sent to you.

With regards and good wishes.

Faithfully,
David Belasco

Du Bois did see the play and sent Belasco an advance copy of his review, to which Belasco replied with a letter.

March 23, 1926

My dear Mr. DuBois:

The advance copy of your review of "Lulu Belle" was given to me today and I hasten to thank you for it. I am glad you found so much about the play and production to your liking and it is especially satisfactory that you brought out the point that an opportunity is given a gifted people to show, to some slight degree, what they are capable of.[1]

Please accept thanks for your interest. I have autographed some books which deal with some of my productions and work and am sending them to you in the hope you may like to have them for your library.

With good wishes and regards,

Faithfully,
David Belasco

Sydney Strong (1860–1939), trained at Oberlin and Yale Divinity School, served as a pastor in Chicago for over twenty years and also briefly in Melbourne, Australia. Most of his life, however, was spent in Seattle. At the time he wrote Du Bois early in 1936, he was serving a church in that city and was also an associate editor of the important Chicago-based magazine, *Unity*. The daughter to whom he refers was Anna Louise Strong (1885–1970), later a world-famous journalist and author whose final years were spent in the Chinese People's Republic.

Seattle, March 5, 1926

Dear Doctor—

Enjoyed your article in Nation—on "Negro in Colleges"—Reminded me time I first got acquainted with you, in "Souls of Black Folks"—I gave away many copies.

Wonder if it isn't about time for you to write a story on the "Souls of All Folks"—with the spirit and sweep of your "Credo." Think it over. I mean, give us a description of the *Rainbow of Humanity*—all colors. Your wide experience will give you the right touch.

Cordially
Sydney Strong

Taking liberty of sending you a copy of my daughter's little book, "Children of Revolution."

1. Du Bois's review appeared in the *Crisis* 32 (May 1926):34; central to his evaluation were these comments: ". . it is a decisive step in the curious psychology of race relations in the United States. . . . for the first time on the American stage the Negro has emerged as a human being who is not a caricature and not a comedian . . . ninety-seven persons in the cast of one hundred and fourteen are really colored . . . never before in the history of the American theatre has a promoter dared to stage a play whose plot involves love-making between white and colored folk although that love-making has been going on for three hundred years. . . ."

[334] Correspondence 1920–1929

March 15th, 1926.

My dear Mr. Strong:

I thank you very much for your kind words concerning my article in the *"Nation"* and also for your suggestion concerning *"Souls of All Folks."*[1]

I shall be glad to see a copy of your daughter's book.[2]

With best regards.

Sincerely yours,
W. E. B. Du Bois

In the many-sided struggle of the Afro-American people, the militancy of women has been outstanding. One Black woman, Mrs. Kathryn M. Johnson, who made her home in Brooklyn, New York, for years carried on a nationwide campaign to disseminate the literature produced by her people. She worked as a roving salesperson for the Associated Publishers, the book-publishing firm of the Association for the Study of Negro Life and History, founded by Woodson in 1915 and located then, as now, in Washington. In particular, she toured the nation selling what she called her "Two-Foot Shelf of Negro Literature," consisting of fifteen books issued by the association. Her purpose was to offset "the silence of our educational system regarding twelve million American citizens"; reading these books, she added, "will increase your respect for the Negro race."

Something of her effort and spirit appears in this letter to Du Bois.

Birmingham, Ala., March 26, 1926

My dear Dr. Du Bois:

Very frequently I am in towns in which there seems no possible way to get the Crisis. One of these places is St. Petersburg, Fla. where I recently spent a couple of weeks.

As a result of this I am just now getting an opportunity to purchase a copy of the March issue, and I am writing to congratulate you on your article on Tuskegee & Hampton.[1]

On my way thru this section to Florida I spent about ten days at Tuskegee Institute, arriving there at the time of The Farmers and Teachers Conference. There were several white people there, and they were all entertained free of charge in Dorothy Hall, a building put up especially for white guests. In this

---

1. Years before, Du Bois had published a penetrating essay, "The Souls of White Folk," in the *Independent*, 18 August 1910, pp. 339–42.

2. Anna Louise Strong, *Children of the Revolution: A Story of the John Reed Children's Colony on the Volga, which is as well a story of the whole great structure of Russia* (Seattle: Pigott Publishing Co., 1925).

1. The editorial was "Five Million," in the March 1926 *Crisis* (31:216).

building the girls get their vocational training evidently with the idea of impressing white visitors of the effort put forth in that direction.

Colored visitors were placed about here and there. I stayed in Douglass Hall, and ate in the teacher's dining room, and paid for everything I got.

On the program, even at open forums, white people were always given preference. I tried to get an opportunity to speak, but failed. One white man was asked to speak—and prefaced his remarks by stating that he had spoken four times that day, and had about talked out. When the vice-president—who presided during Dr. Moton's illness—refused publicly to give me a hearing, these same white men came to me and expressed regret, saying that they would have given me their time gladly.

I feel that colored people need vocational training, along with all other races; but when it has to be gotten at the price of the continual flaunting of the white man's superiority into their faces—thus accentuating their own inferiority complex—I doubt whether the good that's done isn't entirely offset.

I saw the same thing happen here at the State Teachers Association, which closed its session yesterday. Always the platform was filled with white people—who were constantly giving the people soothing syrup, to make them feel that their school system was altogether wonderful.

But by some means the fact finally came out that only 2% of the teachers in the state are college graduates, only 12% normal graduates, and that there isn't a single accredited high school in the state, not even at Tuskegee.

So many white people had to be given a chance to speak that I gave up the idea of trying. On my way down I spoke at Fisk, Walden, Roger Williams, State Normal schools in Nashville, Montgomery, and Tallahassee, and a number of other places. All told I have had a very satisfactory hearing except as before mentioned.

I hope your article will do good. Heaven knows it is needed—and should be said over and over again.

Very truly yours,
Kathryn M. Johnson

A student at the University of Minnesota asked Du Bois a direct and significant question; as usual in such cases, he received a pithy and profound reply.

Minneapolis, March 30, 1926

Dear Sir:

I am on the negative team in a forthcoming debate in which the question is: Resolved that residential segregation if properly handled can be beneficial to the Negro. I am writing to you to get an expression of your view on the question, to be used as a means of support in the argument against the question.

[336] Correspondence 1920–1929

Thanking you for anything which you may care to say on the question, I am,
Sincerely yours,
Ferdinand Johnson

April 3, 1926

My dear Sir:
Residential segregation is the first step toward War. The intervening steps may, to be sure, be round about and long. Segregation, slums, crime, race and class hatred, national hatred, defense against enemies, offense against people whom you despise, economic discrimination, War. This is the history of the past. It will be the history of the future.
Very sincerely yours,
W. E. B. Du Bois

In 1926, the 150th anniversary of the Declaration of Independence was commemorated, with appropriate state exhibits, in Pennsylvania. At that time, the governorship was held by one of its more enlightened incumbents: Gifford Pinchot (1865–1946), the distinguished conservationist whose dismissal from the Forestry service by Taft in 1910 helped lay the groundwork for the historic 1912 split in the Republican party. Pinchot was, indeed, second only to Theodore Roosevelt in the launching of the Progressive party effort of that year. From 1923 to 1927 and again from 1931 to 1935, he was governor of Pennsylvania; Du Bois consulted with him in an effort to assure some special and dramatic presentation of the role of Black people in the state's history. Correspondence between Du Bois and Pinchot tells that story.

May 8, 1926.

My dear Governor Pinchot:
Following our conversation of last Tuesday, may I bring the following matters to your attention?
The connection of the Negro with the State of Pennsylvania has been extraordinary, close and important. I am enclosing a short survey of their history taken from Chapter 3 of my Philadelphia Negro. Perhaps I may note a few of the high points of this history.
The Dutch and the Swedes had planted slavery in Pennsylvania before Penn came. Penn, after his coming, recognized slavery "for a term of years." In 1688, came the protest of the Germans against slavery, followed by [George] Keith's attack upon the Quakers because of slavery. The Quaker Yearly Meetings of 1696, 1711, 1716 and 1719 wrestled with the problem of the slaves. By 1730, the slave trade was declared "disagreeable." Then [Benjamin] Lay, [John] Woolman and [Anthony] Benezet began their crusade, which resulted in the condemnation of slavery in 1758 and the exclusion of slave owners from the Society

of Friends in 1775. Side by side with this Quaker development went action in other fields; severe slave codes beginning in 1700, protests of the free white mechanics in 1708 and 1722. Finally, in 1780 came gradual Emancipation and thereafter a curious group fight on the part of the Negroes for real freedom. Between 1780 and 1820 the fight centered in the church and [Richard] Allen founded the great African A.M.E. Church which now has a half million members. In 1770, a Negro school was established; in 1799, a petition for freedom influenced from Haiti caused consternation. In 1794, there was the general conference of abolition societies. In 1814, Pennsylvania called for Negro troops to defend it against the British. In 1820 to 1840 Negro and foreign laborers rioted in the streets and the Negro was disfranchised. Then from 1840 to 1870 came the first great drive of black men in the celebrated success of the caterers; the enlisting of Negroes in the Civil War and the new freedom. From 1870 to 1896 the new freedmen from the outside began to pour in and again there was trouble, poverty, crime, political complications, and thus we come down to the last era of thirty years from 1896 to 1926.

Now I am aware that there is no really logical place where this story can be told in the Exposition. The pageant plan will give Pennsylvania's history from well known points of view. Here, however, is *special* history, peculiar to the State, really a part of State activity and at the same time not a part of governmental activity. If the state does not support a pageant of this sort it will not be supported. I am aware that as you frankly told me there is little chance that $10,000 can be found to promote this; but I want to emphasize the fact that if that amount can be found and such a pageant put on in the stadium of the Sesqui-Centennial, it will be, I guarantee, the most striking pageant of the whole Exposition.

I beg to remain, Dear Governor Pinchot

                        Very respectfully yours,
                        W. E. B. Du Bois

                        Harrisburg, May 13, 1926

Dear Mr. Du Bois:

I am very glad to receive your most interesting letter of May 8 and want to assure you that a Committee is at work to complete the plans already laid for appropriate presentation within the State Building at the Sesqui-Centennial of the progress and achievements of the Negro. It will be kept on the same high plane as that followed in the other State displays.

                        Sincerely yours,
                        Gifford Pinchot

But I see no chance, after investigation, for a pageant.[1]

---

1. These words were added in ink by the governor. Du Bois in the December 1926 *Crisis* mentioned the exposition and described it as a half-hearted celebration of freedom.

[338] Correspondence 1920-1929

In the first four decades of the twentieth century, probably the best-known member of the United States Senate was William Edgar Borah (1865–1940), a Republican from Idaho. He gained national prominence as the (unsuccessful) prosecutor in the 1907 murder trial of William (Big Bill) Haywood, the leader of Industrial Workers of The World. From 1907 until his death, he served continually in the Senate. At the time of the following correspondence with Du Bois, he was chairman of the Senate Foreign Relations Committee. The tendency of his views was anti-monopolistic and, in foreign policy, relatively enlightened (he opposed intervention in Latin America and favored disarmament and the recognition of the Soviet Union, for example); he was identified with the more liberal wing of the Republican party. All the more significant is the exchange with Du Bois and the revelation of the senator's regressive position on the Black people. Parts of the letters from Borah were printed in the August 1926 (32:165) and the January 1927 (33:132–33) *Crisis*.

June 17, 1926

My dear Senator Borah:

I had the pleasure of meeting you when you spoke in New York on the Haitian question and, should you wish, you can find out facts about me in "Who's Who in America."

I have been greatly disturbed by your attitude toward the 13th, 14th, and 15th amendments. I remember some years ago when you made a speech in the Senate against the 15th amendment, and recently I understand that in a speech before the National Law School at Washington you said that "the enfranchisement of the colored race at the time it was enfranchised was one of the greatest mistakes ever made in this country."

I write to ask, first, if you would kindly furnish me the exact statement that you made; and, secondly, I, and I think millions of colored people throughout the United States, would like to get a clearer idea of your attitude towards them and towards their rights. I am one who believes that the enfranchisement of the colored people by the 14th and 15th amendments was absolutely justifiable and that the result has proved its wisdom. I believe that any other action would have made real emancipation impossible.

I am the Editor of a magazine, *The Crisis*, which circulates largely among educated colored people. I know how busy you are and yet I wonder if you could not find time to make a short, clear statement of your attitude on the question of rights of Negroes to vote so that the doubts in our minds could be satisfied?

Personally, I am unable to conceive that a man of your breadth and knowledge of world events, and sympathy with the struggling classes can except from your sympathy the twelve million Negroes of the United States.

I hope I am not asking too much of you and that I may hear from you at your convenience.

I am, Sir,

Very respectfully yours,
W. E. B. Du Bois

Washington, D.C., June 18, 1926

My dear Mr. Du Bois

I have your letter of the 17th.

I have said nothing about the 13th Amendment. The news dispatch was wholly erroneous. Of course, I never said emancipation was a mistake. On the other hand, had I been speaking of it at all, I should have said it was altogether the right and noble thing to do. My view of the enfranchisement of the colored man is different.

If you will permit me a little later, Mr. Du Bois, I will write you fully. In the crowded hours of the closing of the session, I haven't the possible time to write you as the subject and the party to whom I am addressing this letter would require. But I promise you I shall do so a little later.

In the meantime, permit me to say that my views with reference to the enfranchisement of the colored people is that which Mr. Lincoln put forward. I think it would have been the greatest possible benefit to the colored man to have pursued that course. If the colored people could have been dealt with in accordance with the actualities and free from the manipulation of politics, they would have been infinitely better off today.

But I shall write you at length later.

Very respectfully,
Wm E Borah

Washington, D.C. July 15, 1926.

My dear Mr. DuBois:

Sometime ago you wrote me in regard to my statement concerning my views on the Thirteenth, Fourteenth, and Fifteenth Amendments.

I answered with reference to the Thirteenth that I had made no statement at any time to the effect that the emancipation of the negro[1] was a mistake, that upon the other hand, had I been discussing that subject I would have said it was the right and noble thing to do. I did not have time to reply as I desired to reply relative to the Fourteenth and Fifteenth Amendments. I promised you I would do so and I now keep that promise.

1. In reprinting this letter in part in the *Crisis,* "Negro" was capitalized; it is lowercase in the original.

During the discussion of the Woman Suffrage Amendment in 1914, I had this to say: "I am one of those who has never hesitated to say that the writing into the Constitution of the United States of the fifteenth amendment at the time it was written there was a mistake. It was a serious mistake. It came before the hot passions of the Civil War had cooled and judgment had time to resume its sway, while the engendered feelings which had been accumulating through years of strife and conflict still prevailed. It came in a large measure as a sort of retaliation and revenge. The idea of taking a people and lifting them out of a thousand years of savagery and barbarism, of three hundred years of slavery, and placing them in a position where they [are] required to perform all the duties and obligations of citizenship of a highly civilized republic! No race in the history of the world has ever been equal to such a thing and no race in the history of the world could do such a thing. And then, when they did not measure up to the task we either turned upon them or left them to their political fate. Men rise to the duties and responsibilities of citizenship in a great republic under years of stress and strain and under years of tutelage and education."

I have never changed my view as then expressed. By this I do not mean to say the negro should not have been enfranchised at all or that he should not have been given definite assurance that, upon measuring up to certain conditions, he would be enfranchised. The true policy was the policy pointed out by Mr. Lincoln when he declared in his last public utterances that the right to vote should be "conferred upon the very intelligent and those who served our cause as soldiers." His policy was that of educating and preparing the negro for his new duties and responsibilities in citizenship. Beginning with those who were more thoroughly equipped, the right of franchise should have been assured as others according to definite standards earned it. If the North had devoted its efforts to bettering the conditions of the negro, to educating him instead of confining its action to politics, it would have been better for all concerned, for the white and the black and for the whole country. The negro in my judgment would be infinitely better off today had such a rule been adopted.

But all this is a discussion of history. My views at the time first expressed were called out by reason of the pending Suffrage Amendment to the Constitution. The fact is, however, that the Fifteenth Amendment became and is a part of the Constitution, and every effort in good faith should be made to live up to it. The negro has made great progress, all things considered, during the last fifty years. He is particularly entitled to credit for, amid his adverse circumstances, he has shown little, or no, inclination to join with those political sects which rail at constitutional government. It is under these circumstances that we must deal with the Fifteenth Amendment at the present time.

I know of course you will not agree with me for I have read much after your views, but in my opinion the South is in good faith seeking to work out this problem under and in accordance with the Constitution. I do not find any spirit of nullification. It was an almost insuperable task imposed upon the South but, considering all things, I believe the South has acted quite as well with the negro as has the North. We have been just as intolerant when occasion seemed to call for intolerance as the South. We have employed the mob also. We have played politics with the negro from the time that Charles Sumner declared that to enfranchise this uneducated mass was foreign to his convictions and to his whole habit of thought, but that politics required it. We should seek to secure right and justice to the negro. But I would do so in recognition of the real facts rather than upon the basis of political expediency and at the expense of the physical and moral advancement of the negro. I would do so by cooperating with the South and not in distrust of the South. This is a problem of great national interest and can only be satisfactorily solved by complete cooperation between the North and the South. Such bills as the force bill and the Dyer Anti-lynching bill were and are founded upon a wholly false theory.

I do not claim, of course, that the South has fully and completely solved the problem nor established absolute equity between the two races. But I do unhesitatingly claim that, taking into consideration race and conditions and also the manner in which this problem was thrust upon a proud and brave people, the South is entitled to the confidence and cooperation of the North. I think that during the last ten years especially, there has been the most gratifying evidence of effort to work out this problem in harmony with the Constitution.

Very respectfully,
Wm. E Borah.

July 16, 1926.

My dear Senator Borah:

I thank you very much for the letter which you have sent me and would like your permission to use it in the *Crisis*.

Very sincerely yours,
W. E. B. Du Bois

Washington, July 17, 1926

My dear Mr. Du Bois:

I have no objection to your using the letter if you think it worth while.

Sometime when you are this way, Mr. Du Bois, I should like to talk with you about the history of the Dyer Anti-lynching bill and its progress through the Judiciary Committee of the Senate. It is one of the finest illustrations of how we played politics with the negro that I know of. I do not know whether you are familiar with it or not. But I take the liberty of saying that so far as the constitutionality of the measure was concerned, there was only one Senator on the Committee who had any doubt as to its unconstitutionality—and he was inclined to believe it was unconstitutional but thought probably it might be well to submit it to the Supreme Court.

I shall not go into detail at this time. But it may be interesting to you sometime to know the details.

Very respectfully,
Wm E Borah

Sherwood Anderson (1876–1941) was among the authors whose opinions Du Bois sought on problems connected with the creation of Afro-American literature. Anderson's reply, addressed to Miss Fauset, bears no date but was certainly written sometime in 1926. By this date, Anderson had published several books, including collections of short stories in *Winesburg, Ohio* (1919) and *The Triumph of the Egg* (1921), the novels *Poor White* (1920) and *Dark Laughter* (1925), and the autobiographical *A Story Teller's Story* (1924). Du Bois seems not to have published the letter.

New Orleans [1926]

My dear Jesse Fauset

Naturally I think it a great mistake for negroes to become too sensitive. If, as a race, you were the ideal people sentimentalists sometimes try to make you how uninteresting you would be.

Why not quit thinking of negro art. If the individual creating the art happens to be a negro and someone wants to call it negro art let them.

As to negroes always being painted at their worst I think it isn't true. Suppose I were to grow indignant every time a white man or woman were badly or cheaply done in the theatre as in books. I might spend my life being indignant.

I have lived a good deal in the south among common negro laborers. I have found them about the sweetest people of humor. I have said so sometimes in my books.

I do not believe the negroes have much more to complain of than the whites in this matter of their treatment in the arts.

Sincerely,
Sherwood Anderson

The conscientiousness of Charles W. Chesnutt in his role as a literary judge for the *Crisis* was marked; his commentary accompanying stories he thought especially notable always contained some matter of interest, as his remarks concerning 1926 entries indicate.

Cleveland, October 15, 1926

My dear Dr. Du Bois:

Replying to your letter of September 25th inclosing manuscripts which I return herewith, and to your follow-up letter of October 13th, would say that I have read the manuscripts submitted several times with mingled feelings. Almost without exception they are well enough written from the standpoint of construction and dramatic interest, but the theme and the story! Mr. Fischer's sketches[1] and Mr. Van Vechten's powerful and vivid delineation of certain tawdry if not sordid aspects of Harlem Negro life are Sunday school stuff compared with the scenes and subjects which these budding realists have selected. If they are writing about the things they know, as a writer ought to, they must have a wide knowledge of the more unsavory aspects of life among colored people.

I should grade the stories about as follows, although this is of course a mere guess:

1. "The Swamp Moccasin." A clean, simple, dramatic and convincing story, written in a snappy style. 2. "The Death Game." A rather ambitious and well constructed story. The descriptions of places are good, the characters vividly drawn and the story well built up to a dramatic climax. 3. "How Farmville Came to Jesus." Characters well drawn, story well constructed. 4. "The Flaming Flame." 5. "The Wall Between." 6. "The New Dawn." 7. "The House of Glass."[2]

Of course I realize that these are amateur efforts and as such they are promising. If or when the writers learn how to employ effectively the literary expedients of humor and pathos and apply their tragedy to subjects that appeal, some of them will make good writers. I can see the reason for your concern about themes for colored writers. It is not only a matter of editors and readers, but, if it can be considered separately, a matter of literary quality and human appeal.

It would be interesting to know from how many manuscripts these seven were selected, but I presume that will be announced in The Crisis. Hoping that I have not delayed the decision, and with best wishes for you and The Crisis, I remain

Cordially yours,
Chas. W. Chesnutt.

1. Rudolph Fisher (1897–1934) is meant here. Trained as a physician, he published stories in the *Atlantic* and the *Crisis;* in 1928 Knopf brought out his novel, *The Walls of Jericho*. His promise as a scientist and writer was great, but his life was tragically short.

2. Choices one and two were published: "Swamp Moccasin," by John F. Matheus, in the December 1926 *Crisis* (33:67–69); "The Death Game," by E. D. Sheen, in the January and February 1927 issues (33:34–37; 33:198–201).

[344] Correspondence 1920–1929

Louis F. Post (1849–1928) was an editor and attorney. In the early 1870s, at the beginning of his law career, Post participated in investigations of the KKK in South Carolina; for some years thereafter he practiced law in New York City. He was a follower of Henry George and an unsuccessful candidate for Congress on a Labor party ticket. He served as assistant secretary of labor during the two administrations of Wilson and distinguished himself as an opponent of the dominant anti-Communist hysteria. The letter from Du Bois mentioned below does not appear to be extant.

Washington, October 20, 1926

My dear Mr. Du Bois:

Thank you for your letter. The item I sent was only of passing importance. I shall be very much interested in seeing your European reports, especially for Russia.[1] One of my wonders is why the "blacks" of Italy are so popular among classes in this country to whom the "reds" of Russia are so objectionable.

Sincerely yours,
Louis F. Post

Indicative of the profound influence of Du Bois and the *Crisis* under his editorship on younger Black people, and especially on artists and writers among them, is correspondence between Du Bois and the then very young Arna Bontemps. Bontemps here tells something of himself up to the year 1926; it may be added that he had a most distinguished career as editor, poet, playwright, and novelist. Bontemps, born in 1902, was for many years the chief librarian at Fisk and more recently a professor of literature at Yale University.

The judges of the 1926 poetry contest for the *Crisis* were Babette Deutsch, James Weldon Johnson, and Langston Hughes. Second prize was won by Countee Cullen for his "Thoughts in a Zoo."

The correspondence begins, with a formal announcement, dated 23 October 1926, of the award to Bontemps.

The Crisis Magazine is happy to announce that Mr. Arna Bontemps has been awarded the First Prize of $100 for his poetry "A Nocturne at Bethesda." The prize will be given him Monday night, October 25th at International House if he can be present, and if not, will be mailed to his address.

Will you please send us by return mail a recent photograph and the main

---

1. Du Bois first visited the Soviet Union in 1926. His article "My Recent Journey" was printed in the *Crisis* in December 1926 (33:64–65), and "Judging Russia" appeared in the February 1927 issue (33:189–90). He mistakenly placed this journey in 1928 in *Dusk of Dawn* (pp. 285–87); the date is given correctly in his *Autobiography* (pp. 29–30). On the whole, all three accounts are quite similar.

facts of your biography? Please do not forget this and let us have these very soon for *The Crisis*.

Arna Bontemps sent two letters in response to this announcement. Both were dated 23 October 1926; one was addressed to Du Bois and the other to the *Crisis*.

New York, October 23, 1926

Dear Dr. Du Bois:

Of course I am overjoyed and very much excited over the good news of your letter. This is my second prize this year. But this is the only one I had courage enough to hope for. The reason was that I sort of liked the Nocturne myself—as compared with my other attempts. Indeed I shall be at the International House Monday night. Could I know the time? I shall try to find the place—I have never been there.

Many, many thanks to you and to the 'perfect' judges.

Very sincerely yours,
Arna Bontemps

Dear "Crisis":

You ask for a photograph and biographical facts. Here are the facts. The photo I can mail you within three days if that is not too late.

I am a Californian, born in Louisiana and living in New York City. I went to California schools until I had earned a B. A., stayed at home a year waiting for my twenty-first birthday, then came East. In New York I have been teaching and studying a bit on the side.

My first published poem appeared in the Crisis of August, 1924. This year has been a rather good one with me: two poetry prizes and a wife.[1]

This is all that I can think of. I have decided not to attempt an autobiography soon.

Very truly yours,
Arna Bontemps

Among the most distinguished poets, essayists, editors, and teachers has been Sterling A. Brown of Howard University. He was the senior editor of that still preeminent anthology *The Negro Caravan*, first published in 1941 by the Dryden Press in New York; his *The Negro in American Fiction* and *Negro Poetry and Drama*, both published in 1937 in Washington by the Associates in Negro Folk Education, remain vital. Among his earliest published works was a poem in the *Crisis* in 1927, and precisely how that publication occurred remains mysterious, as correspondence between Brown and Du Bois shows.

1. In addition to the *Crisis* prize in 1926, Bontemps won the Alexander Pushkin Prize in poetry that year; and in August 1926, he married Alberta Johnson.

[346] Correspondence 1920–1929

Jefferson City, Mo., March 28, 1927

My dear Mr. Du Bois:

I have at hand a copy of the April *Crisis* in which I see included a poem of mine, *After The Storm*. I am properly thankful that you thought it worth publishing, but I am in the dark as to how it got into your hands. I hope you will understand the spirit in which this is written. I did not expect to see it, and still do not quite understand the publishing of it. That bit of mystery I am writing you to clear up for me. Would you send me the source from which you got it?

The second reason for my writing you is to request entry blanks for your contest. I have for a long time wished to compete but the press of teaching, etc. has always kept me out. I intend submitting a number of articles for your next contest. I am enclosing a stamped envelope.

I have a number of—shall I call them poems—of more recent a writing than the one of mine you have published. I am wondering if any of these might interest you for your poetry page. Many are of a different type from the single sonnet of mine which you have mysteriously (?) seen. I have been teaching in the South, and have registered now and again my glimpses of 'Aunt Hagar's Chillen' and the 'Children of Miss Anne.' If you desire to see any of them, I wish you would let me know.

I have been a constant reader of The *Crisis* since my high school days. I think highly of the work you have done and the work you are doing. My subscription has run out and I buy from newsstands. I intend to subscribe with the May issue.

Three things then I wish. First, information as to how you procured the poem of mine you published unknown to me; second, entry blanks for your next contest, and third, word from you as to whether you would be interested in any others things of mine. I had intended sending you some poetic efforts (the one published however I had not expected to send).

Sincerely yours,
Sterling A. Brown

April 2, 1927

My dear Sir:

The only way that we get matter for publication in the *Crisis* is by having it sent to us. A number of your poems were received here sometime ago. I did not know who sent them, but I thought, of course, that you did. We will return those which we have not used. We are, of course, glad to see literary efforts.

I am enclosing an entry blank.

Very sincerely yours,
W. E. B. Du Bois

Havelock Ellis, the English physician, psychologist, and author, produced the monumental seven-volume *Studies in the Psychology of Sex* (1897–1928), which was banned at various times and in various places, but which was a historic effort and remains a basic work. The wife to whom he refers in this letter to Du Bois was Edith Lees; they were married in 1891 and she died in 1916. Du Bois's visit to the Ellises occurred in 1911 when he participated in the First Universal Races Congress.

London, England, April 25, 1927

Dear Mr. Burghart Du Bois,

I much appreciate your kind thought in sending me the pamphlet on the Amenia Conference,[1] which I have read with pleasure and sympathy. It must be an immense satisfaction to you to realize that the great work to which you have devoted your life is now producing such fine results of every kind.

Your visit to our cottage at West Drayton some fourteen years ago remains a vivid & cherished memory. I believe you met my wife again in New York a little later. Her death occurred only a few days after the Conference you write of. She was a wonderful personality & for me is still alive. Dr. Ettie Sayer died more recently.

With best regards

Sincerely yours
Havelock Ellis

George W. Forbes (1864–1927), born in Mississippi, educated at Wilberforce and Amherst, was closely associated with William Monroe Trotter for several years in bringing out the *Guardian* in Boston. Beginning in 1896, Forbes held the position of reference librarian at the West End branch of the Boston Public Library, then serving a largely Black population. Gradually, the Afro-American population moved to the South End and Jewish people moved into the West End. Forbes remained for thirty-two years as the reference librarian. Upon his death early in March 1927, there was an extraordinary showing of Black-Jewish unity in paying tribute to this remarkable man. It is within this context that one may appreciate an exchange between Fanny Goldstein, librarian of the West End Branch of the Boston Library, and Du Bois.

Boston, April 14, 1927

My dear Dr. Du Bois:

It has been brought to my attention that you were a personal friend of George Washington Forbes, for many years an employee of the Boston Public Library,

---

1. This is Du Bois's study published in 1925 as Troutbeck Leaflet no. 8, to which reference was made earlier.

who recently passed away. Mr. Forbes was associated with this Branch Library for thirty-two years serving in the capacity of Reference Librarian, which brought him in very close touch with the Public, especially with the children. He was ever modest and faithful, and always gave to this Institution the best that was in him.

At the time of his death all the Boston papers commented on his very faithful service rendered these many years. Of all these obituaries, however, I think that the Yiddish press was even more than the Colored newspaper deeply appreciative and sympathetic.

In view of the fact that you were his friend and are connected with The Crisis, it has been suggested to me that you would be particularly interested in the enclosed translation which I am sending you of the article that appeared in the Jewish Daily Forward of March the 26th. This article, you will agree, is a splendid eulogy and a glowing tribute to this "hidden servant" from one race to another.

If Mr. Forbes's life was simple, he was supremely happy in his work, and always gave of himself unstintingly. We may well say of him in closing "well done Thou good and faithful servant."

Very respectfully yours,
Fannie Goldstein

April 25, 1927

My dear Madam:

I thank you so much for the translation of the Jewish Forward article on the late Mr. Forbes. We are going to use it.[1]

Very sincerely yours,
W. E. B. Du Bois

In the May 1927 *Crisis* (34:93) was published a letter from M. Estello Montgomery, the daughter of Isaiah T. Montgomery; the letter came from the all-Black town of Mound Bayou, Mississippi, founded by Montgomery on land he managed to accumulate after the Civil War. Montgomery was one of two Black members of the 1886 state convention in Mississippi which began the legalization of disfranchisement and jim-crow; he had denounced the move in the convention.

Miss Montgomery told in her letter of efforts by white politicians to divest her of title to Mound Bayou and of her three-year struggle against those efforts; she noted that involved were not only her own rights but the very existence of a community founded and governed by Black people. In printing her letter, Du

1. It appears, with an introduction by Du Bois, under the title "George Forbes of Boston: A Servant of Jew and Gentile," in the *Crisis* 34 (July 1927):151–52.

Bois was helping conduct a campaign—finally successful—to protect the title and the all-Black character of Mound Bayou; he asked pointedly of *Crisis* readers: "What have others to say?" One of the replies came from Mississippi in printed script on a kind of business ledger.

> Hinds County, Miss. Hester Plantation
> April 26, 1927. In the evening.

Unto the N.A.A.C.P.
Kind Sirs:

This letter is mailed and sent under a camouflaged address, to avoid the consequences of racial hatred and mob violence. (Please reply to me at once to let me know whether you get this or not.) It is written to the N.A.A.C.P. in general and to Mr. DuBois in particular. But the outside address on the front of the envelope had to be camouflaged. So, please excuse the address. It is dangerous for the name of Mr. DuBois or the name of Mr. Spingarn to be seen in this section. I even fear that this letter will be opened and read before it reaches you; before it leaves Mississippi. The eternal danger is highly imminent. I am writing this sad letter to notify you all that my sister Mary C. Jones died suddenly on the 31st day of March, 1927 in this year and this spring season. My long persecuted father and mother died before she did. She finally broke down under the trials and cruelty of the reign of terror. She leaves me alone in the ceaseless toils of whitecap persecution. I am practically isolated and see nothing before me but despair. I am struggling against pitiless odds and shall continue to struggle until the end. So, we have lost a faithful, hard-working member from our N.A.A.C.P. Her deplorable loss can not be filled in Hinds County.

Last night, late, I read the May Crisis, which came in my mail yesterday morning. A cry of despair comes from Mound Bayou, Miss. This girl is in the very same trouble that has pounced upon me. She needs prompt aid. She needs unfaltering succor. Shall we turn deaf ears to her? I say, Brethren and Sisters, shall we turn deaf ears to this poor girl in her agony? There is no truce with the Southern white man. Nothing but the Negro's destruction or absolute slavery can satisfy him. Shall we stand back like rotten fence posts and see this outrage finished?

If they can gain this land-holding victory over this lady, they will speedily multiply such victories in every direction, and our black race will lose one of its life-legs. Let us all rush to the rescue like one man. Call up every ounce and every atom of our N.A.A.C.P. strength and hold her up. She needs all of our help and she needs it *now!* I am ready. I am always ready and eager for the affray. Let the United States Supreme Court have this case. Let no one stand back. I repeat, shall we stand back like rotten fence posts and see this outrage finished? I say never! Never Shirk! She needs us *now.*

I want every tract of land owned by the American Negroes or Negro to be fixed firmly under the guardianship and protection of the N.A.A.C.P. I want all of these Negro-owned lands to stay in the possession of the Negro race forever. Let us *now* take legal steps to end this danger.

Please reply at once and tell me whether or not you get this letter.

Yours respectfully and in earnest,
Tillman Jones.

In 1926, a letter to Du Bois from H. B. Hayden of New York City evoked a reply from Du Bois that dealt with several expressions of opinion still common among American white people.

May 6, 1927

My dear Sir:

In your letter of April 24th, I note the following statements:

(1) "The Negro in the past 6,000 years has not been known, as far as I can discover, to have given anything of any great value to the world of his own initiative.... There is but little use in denying the superiority of the whites as a race."

This statement is untrue. The Negro has given to the world the first steps in civilization, and especially the discovery of the use of iron. The village unit among African Negroes is one of the earliest and most unique and effective of human organizations. Art in sculpture and in music has been a peculiar African gift, and finally, the primitive religions of Egypt and of some other parts of the world have been based on African beliefs. That Negro peoples were the beginners of civilization among the Ganges, the Euphrates and the Nile is proven without a reasonable doubt. The white race is not a superior race. The Secretary of the First Races Congress held in London in 1911 said: "An impartial investigator would be inclined to look upon the various important peoples of the world as to all intents and purposes essentially equal in intellect, enterprise, morality and physique." You may follow this matter if you wish by reading the following books: *What Is Civilization?* (Chapter 2, Duffield and Company);[1] *The Negro*, W. E. B. Du Bois (Home University Library, Henry Holt and Company, 1915, Chapter 8), and also works by [Franz] Boas, [Friedrich] Ratzel, [William] Schneider, [Jean] Finot.

(2) "It is only natural that the white should want to preserve his own life and race without having it mixed with the black."

This is not true. It has been the white race which has demanded and practically compelled the colored races to submit to the intermingling of blood. This is the reason that we have in America some three or four millions of mulattos, and the same thing in Central and South America, in the West Indies, and in

---

1. The reference is to the essay "The Answer of Africa" in *What Is Civilization?* ed. Maurice Maeterlinck (New York, 1926), pp. 41–57.

West and South Africa, and there has been similar intermingling of blood in Asia and Australia.

(3) "The Negro is always trying to get in somewhere where whites don't want them. The whites won't have it. They prefer death."

This again is untrue. It is not the Negro or the darker races that are trying to get in with the whites. It is the whites who are continually interfering with and intruding upon the darker races. It was the whites that went to Africa and killed some 60 millions of people in order to transplant 15 millions of black people to America. It is the whites who are now intruding in China, India and elsewhere.

(4) "Why don't Negroes build up their own communities . . . separate and stay separated?"

Because white people do not want separation from Negroes or Chinese or Indians. Negroes had their own communities from the beginning of time until whites by force and brand destroyed them. If the Negroes went to the ends of the earth and built up new communities, white people would hasten there in order to steal what the Negroes had accumulated or to dominate their labor. This is what the United States is doing to Haiti, the Philippines, San Domingo and Nicaragua. This is the reason that Liberia has not been allowed to succeed.

(5) "Whites and blacks will never get along together."

If the white, black, brown and yellow people of the world cannot get along together then the world is doomed. The world is getting smaller and smaller. Commerce, culture and communication are making all people neighbors. If different races cannot get on together in America today they will not get on together in the world tomorrow. But all this is nonsense. Races can get on together if they treat each other as men. The Negro and other colored races, not only demand their rights as men, but gradually they are achieving this demand. Brought as slaves to the United States they are now citizens; they cast over 2 million votes; they own property; they are members of the legislatures of ten states and judges on the bench in two; they have sat in Congress and will again.

(6) "Association in a Pullman car or anywhere else with a black man or woman is objectionable to the vast majority of the whites."

This is untrue. The vast majority of whites are perfectly willing to associate in Pullman cars, homes and bedrooms with black people. Civilized white people are willing to associate with black people under those circumstances only as equals, and the number of civilized white people is increasing.

(7) "There is a strong race feeling among people of all races, right or wrong."

There is nothing of the sort. Without education or deliberate propaganda there is no race feeling at all. Children have no race prejudice. Race feeling and race repulsion only come because of persistent teaching and because scoundrels can profit by it.

I have tried to answer all of the chief allegations in your letter.

Very sincerely yours,
W. E. B. Du Bois

In the 1920s, student and faculty unrest in the colleges of the United States, and especially in colleges devoted to the education of Black youth, was marked. At Howard University the discontent of students and faculty merged; one of the results was the dismissal in 1927 of four members of the faculty, one of whom was Professor Alain Leroy Locke (1886–1954), the first Black Rhodes Scholar and one of the main inspirers of the Harlem Renaissance. The battle for the reinstatement of these professors was finally successful.

Dr. Jesse Edward Moorland (1864–1940), to whom Du Bois wrote in connection with Locke's dismissal, was trained as a minister and held pastorates briefly in Nashville and Cleveland; in 1891, he entered work with the YMCA and in 1924, succeeded William A. Hunton as director of Negro work for the association. Dr. Moorland was a founder, with Dr. Woodson, of the Association for the Study of Negro Life and History and for many years served as its treasurer. In 1907, he became a trustee of Howard University. He gathered one of the greatest collections of books and papers on the African and Afro-American, which he donated to Howard.

May 5, 1927

My dear Mr. Moorland:

I am interested in having Alain Locke reinstated at Howard University. My interest has nothing personal in it. While I have known Mr. Locke for some time, he is not a particularly close friend. I have not always agreed with him, and he knows nothing of this letter. On the other hand, there are two tremendous principles at stake as it seems to me in Mr. Locke's case. First, there is the privilege of free speech and independent thinking in all Negro colleges. We have got to establish that, and the time must go when only men who say the proper thing and walk the beaten track are allowed to teach our youth. Of course, there must be limits to this freedom, but the limits must be wide. In the second place, we must have cultured and well-trained men in our institutions. We have lamentably few. Locke is by long odds the best trained man among the younger American Negroes. His place in the world is as a teacher of youth and he ought to be at the largest Negro college, Howard. Nothing will discourage young men more from taking training which is not merely commercial and money-making, than the fact that a man like Locke is not permitted to hold a position at Howard. I am writing to you because I have been told by disinterested parties that the chief objection to Locke is from you. I do not know whether this is true or not, but in any case, I am sure that your advocacy of his reinstatement would go a long way. I write, therefore, to ask you that you will do all you can conscientiously to accomplish this end.

Very sincerely yours,
W. E. B. Du Bois

Brooklyn, N.Y., May 12, 1927

My dear Dr. Du Bois:

I thank you for your letter of May 5th regarding Dr. Locke—the full responsibility of the case rests with the President and the Board of Trustees—In as much as they have all the facts in hand I am sure they will act in accordance with the best interest of the University.

Very sincerely yours
J.E. Moorland.

The correspondence between Ralph J. Bunche (1904–71) and Du Bois began with a letter from Bunche, then a college student, written in May 1927. This is, of course, the man who was United Nations undersecretary from 1955 until his death in 1971, and winner of the Spingarn Medal in 1949 and the Nobel Peace Prize in 1950.

Los Angeles, Cal., May 11, 1927

Dear Dr. Du Bois

I am quite sure that you do not remember me though we did meet on more than one occasion when you have visited Los Angeles. However, I happened to be just another college student, which certainly is no cause for distinction. Nevertheless, I am taking the liberty of corresponding and trust that some consideration may be accorded my mission.

It happens that I am about to receive the A. B. degree in political science at the University of California this spring. I have made a rather creditable record during my college and high school days and have been accorded some recognition for it, including the pages of the Crisis. But I do not wish to dwell upon that. I may only say that my plans for the future are rather definitely formed. In recognition of my work Harvard University has granted me a scholarship, good for next year and I intend to take advantage of this opportunity.[1] Which brings me to the reason for this letter. Since I have been sufficiently old to think rationally and to appreciate that there was a "race problem" in America, in which I was necessarily involved, I have set as the goal of my ambition service to my group. To some extent I am even now fulfilling that ambition. I have been very active in Cosmopolitan clubs,[2] inter-racial discussion groups, and have often been sent from this University to other nearby colleges to speak on the question or

1. Harvard University awarded Bunche an Ozias Goodwin Fellowship; he received from Harvard an A.M. in 1928 and a Ph.D. in 1934.
2. The early history of the Cosmopolitan Club movement is described in a paper by Louis Lochner, one of its founders, presented at the 1911 First Universal Races Congress and published in its *Proceedings*, edited by Gustav Spiller (reprint ed., with an introduction by this editor, New York: Citadel Press, 1970), pp. 439–42.

to lead discussion groups, and I feel that a great deal of good has been done thereby.

But I have long felt the need of coming in closer contact with the leaders of our Race, so that I may better learn their methods of approach, their psychology, and benefit in my own development by their influence. That is why I am anxious to come east and anticipate enjoying the opportunity extremely. Now specifically, I would like to inquire if there is any way that I can be of service to my group this coming summer, either in the east or in the south? Admittedly my resources are limited, but I am willing to tackle any problem or proposition which will give sufficient return for bare living expenses. I feel that there must be some opportunity for me, either connected with the N.A.A.C.P. or as a teacher. I have had a liberal education, extensive experience in journalism, forensics and dramatics, as well as athletics, and am young and healthy. I can furnish the best of recommendations, both from the faculty of the University and from the Race leaders of the Pacific Coast.

I hope that you will not think me presumptuous in taking this liberty. I assure you that it is inspired by a sincere desire to serve my group.

Our local commencement exercises (at which I am to be valedictorian) will be over June 9, and I will be ready to depart on any mission the day following.

I might add that I can refer to Rev. Bradby of Detroit, my birthplace, for further recommendation.

Trusting that I may hear some word of encouragement from you in the near future, I am

Sincerely yours,
Ralph J. Bunche

June 7, 1927.

My dear Mr. Bunche:

I do not know of any opening for you just now, but I shall keep your case in mind. I would be very glad to help you in any way if I see a chance.

Very sincerely yours,
W. E. B. Du Bois

After the death of George Washington Forbes in March 1927, Du Bois wrote to his friend Clement G. Morgan, a Boston attorney, for his recollections of the deceased.* Morgan's reply is of historical interest, especially in terms of its references to the Forbes-Trotter relationship. Morgan was himself an old friend of

---

* Morgan was a classmate of Du Bois at Harvard; he was elected class orator at Harvard in 1890—an event that gained national attention; see Du Bois's *Autobiography*, pp. 139-40. When Morgan died in August 1929, Du Bois wrote of him in the *Crisis* 36 (August 1929):278.

Du Bois, an original member of both the Niagara Movement and the NAACP, and very active in the early years of the Boston branch of the latter.

Boston, May 31, 1927

My dear Du Bois:

Pardon my delay in sending on the information, concerning Forbes, about which you wrote me some days ago: Forbes, [William H.] Lewis, and [George H.] Jackson were all classmates at Amherst, where they graduated in 1892. I wonder whether you recall attending their graduating exercises that year, when Mrs. Ruffin chaperoned the young women, among them Fannie Bailey (Grant), Bessie Baker (Lewis), Tan Evans (Wilson), and Ella Smith (Elbert).

After graduation, Forbes came immediately to Boston, and took up the editorship of The Boston Courant, a weekly sheet, which he ran for ten years or more with great success, entering in the meantime the services of the Boston Public Library, in its West End Branch, established, 1896, in the old West Church, made famous by Charles Lowell, father of James Russell, and Cyrus Bartol, two of Boston's distinguished clergymen. In 1903, Forbes and Trotter started the Boston Guardian, the former furnishing the newspaper knowledge and literary ability, and the latter supplying the greater part of the funds to begin with, and putting his name in as proprietor, manager, and what not? The two separated over the Booker Washington controversy, Forbes saying that Trotter's bumptiousness and egotism, and eagerness for notoriety made a mess of a well-thought out scheme to nip in the bud Washington's "one-as-the-hand, separate-as-the fingers" doctrine, put forth in his Atlanta speech [of 1895], while Trotter claimed that Forbes lacked the boldness, daring, and risk-all-to-win courage for so subtle and cunning a wizard as the Tuskegeean.

How this difference lasted through the years, cutting into almost every thing here, that was worth while, I need not repeat, beyond reminding you of our determination to try to keep it out of the Niagara Movement, and of Trotter's sulking and going off to start his Equal Right's League. Some papers have already been sent you, telling of Forbes's work here. I enclose another.

Sincerely yours,
Clement G. Morgan.

One of the veteran United States Colored Infantry units was the Twenty-Fifth Infantry Regiment. The Reverend Louis A. Carter, its Chaplain, wrote Du Bois a sharply critical letter in the summer of 1927; the reply is equally forthright and the exchange illuminates significant and persistent points of view.

Nogales, Arizona, July 15, 1927

My dear Dr. Du Bois:

I have been a reader of your magazine for many years—a warm admirer of your manly stand for the advancement of the members of the Negro race.

Your magazine has and does yet receive staunch support from the members of the Twenty-Fifth Infantry and I myself have had something to do with the support it receives.

You will, I am sure, permit me to invite your attention to some of the statements in your issue of July, 1927—a front page editorial under the caption: "As the crow flies," especially the following:

> "Meantime, we need not less but more funds for *health,* for *education,* for *social uplift.* We ought to get this by taxing the rich and by spending less for silly and dangerous battle ships and for the salaries of impudent army officers."

As citizens of the United States and as members of the Twenty-Fifth Infantry, an organization which, in our opinion, is doing as much for the advancement of the Negro race as any University in the country—we take serious exceptions to the justice of that statement.

We do not feel that our battleship program is silly and from my experience of many years in the military service my observation is that army officers are not generally impudent—certainly they are less impudent than any other similar body of citizens.

The defenders of the rights—life—liberties and free institutions of the American people are too often, I fear, misunderstood, under-rated and unappreciated.

Langley should not have been laughed at but he should have been encouraged —helped.[1]

The tax system may be all wrong as to method of collection and distribution— American justice may be blind and group courage (subjective and objective) might put an end to lynching; but there is nothing "Red," nothing "impudent" about the officers whose appropriate and designed function is to defend their nation's honor and their country's flag.

It is believed that in permitting yourself and your magazine to sponsor such pacifist–bolshevic doctrines you are lessening your influence in your chosen field of endeavor in which you have done so much good.

Very respectfully yours,
Louis A. Carter,
Chaplain, 25th Infantry.

---

1. Samuel P. Langley (1836–1906), the astronomer-physicist, headed the Smithsonian Institute from 1887 until his death. He pioneered in developing flying machines; with a fifty thousand dollar grant from the War Department, Langley, assisted by Charles Manly, tried unsuccessfully for a flight in 1903. In later years, the same plane, with slight modifications, did fly, but the 1903 failure brought him ridicule. Du Bois in commenting upon the exploits of Lindbergh in the July 1927 *Crisis* (34:147), recalled Langley's failure: "The world laughed, but Langley made flying possible."

July 27, 1927.

My dear Sir:

In your letter of July 15th you take exception to my statement that (1) battleships are "silly and dangerous." (2) that there are "impudent army officers" and (3) you fear that I hold "Pacifist-Bolshevic doctrines."

In answer to that, may I say that the very fact that great nations of the world are today trying to limit the number of warships shows that the whole program of spending on one instrument of murder enough money to endow a great university, is in the opinion of the best minds of the world, "silly and dangerous." (2) I do not mean to say that all army officers are impudent. How could I when I knew Colonel Young and General Barnum? But I do insist that a large number of them are, and this was proven by their attitude toward colored officers during the World War. Large numbers of white army officers at that time were more anxious to insult Negroes than to fight Germans. (3) I am a Pacifist. So was Jesus Christ. I am not sure as to what you mean by the word "Bolshevic." If you mean everything that is contemptible, cruel and wrong, I do not think that I deserve the name; but if you mean to apply the word to those people who are striving with partial success to organize industry for public service rather than for private profit, then I also am a Bolshevic and proud of it.

I trust that even with this knowledge of my personal aims and attitudes we may continue to have your sympathy and the support of your great regiment for the *Crisis* and the N.A.A.C.P.

Very sincerely yours,
W. E. B. Du Bois

In May 1925, Superintendent Ulysses S. Baskin, of Okolona Institute, a school for Black students run by the Episcopal Church in Mississippi, was shot eight times and killed by two white men. The attack was a reprisal for Baskin's killing of a dog that attacked sheep belonging to the school. The founder of this school, and principal for 25 years, was Wallace Battle, who hitherto had taken as mild and conservative a position as possible. This cold-blooded murder on the grounds of his school, however, was too much; Battle seized a rifle and started after the murderers until his wife and students restrained him.

Battle served a short time thereafter at the school, but, failing to get any real support from what he had thought influential white "friends" and getting no help from the church, he left in 1926 and resigned in 1927. By that year, the full truth became publishable and the entire story was told by Du Bois in the October 1927 *Crisis* (34:261 ff.).

When Battle went North, he turned for help to J. Max Barber, Du Bois's friend of years, a former editor of the *Voice of the Negro* in Atlanta, and at this time a dentist in Philadelphia. It is in this connection that one may understand the letter from Barber to Du Bois.

[358] Correspondence 1920–1929

Philadelphia August 8, 1927.

My dear Du Bois:

There are some things connected with the murder on the campus of Battle's school which he does not want given to the public yet. This much I may say: A sheep-killing dog belonging to a white man just over the fence from his school farm was killing the sheep and goats belonging to the school. Battle's superintendent caught the dog eating a goat. He shot the dog. The white man and his son came over on the campus with guns and shot the superintendent. He died game. He had been in the army, so he got his army revolver and attempted to shoot back, but the thing had not been oiled recently and jammed. The men who killed him were never arrested. Battle got his rifle and started for the white man but was prevented by students and his wife from going. When that fact became known his trustees voted him a year's absence from the school to travel until things cooled down. He has just resigned as head of the school, but did not go back to Mississippi. His wife ran the school all winter. I would advise that you write him before you give any facts to the public. He only recently gave me permission to allow the public to know where he is. I have attended to his mail, etc. for the winter. These are some of the facts. I am just getting away this morning for my vacation. Will motor as far as Riviere Du Loup, 120 miles above Quebec. Back Labor Day. Best regards.

Sincerely yours,
J. Max Barber

The concept of an all-Black state in the United States had rudimentary beginnings going back to Thomas Jefferson's suggestion of settlement of freed slaves west of the Mississippi, and to more serious efforts in the 1890s at making of the Indian Territory (later Oklahoma) a Black state. In the 1930s a Forty-Ninth State Movement had some following, especially in and around Chicago; variations of the idea appear again in the present period. An expression of this concept occurs in a letter written in 1927 by a graduate student to Du Bois; his reply, while expressing grave doubts as to the plan's possibilities, does not rule out the idea altogether.

Washington, D.C., August 15, 1927

My dear Sir:

I am a nephew of Miss Anna H. Jones of Monrovia, Calif., and lived at Ann Arbor while you were at our home and [I was] attending the Univ. of Michigan. It is with a good deal of hesitation that I write this letter but I have been troubled with a matter for a number of years and I would like to get your mature judgement in the matter.

While attending a constitutional history class at Howard Univ. some three years ago I received the suggestion of the "peaceful penetration" of a propitious

State (commonwealth in the Union) as a solution of our race problem in the U. S.

Last year while attending the U. of So. Calif. I heard a professor from the U. of Washington express similar ideas. He pointed out that the problem occurred only where there were a large number of Negroes living in a white community. The centralization of Negroes in one state would mean political control of that State. There would be only a few Negroes in other States hence no Negro problems in those States. It is a question however if the Negroes could maintain themselves economically. There might also be a second "bleeding Kansas" in the attempt to control the State but it could be done I think.

So far as I can see race troubles are by no means diminishing and education does not seem to help a bit. In an attempt to get a driver's permit here a few weeks ago I was forced to impersonate an influential doctor here over the telephone in a talk with the director. He assured me if [I] would send the Negro down in the morning at 8 A.M. he would have no trouble. Altho I had gone half a dozen times and been held up, this time I received the permit.

I wonder if my efforts when I have received my J. D. degree from the Univ. of Mich. will be as void of results as were my first attempts to get a permit from those ignorant white clerks. Yet perhaps the best thing to do is to let things alone and continue to study as best I can with the vacillating hope of success. My experiences as president of the Les Belles Lettres Club of the U. of So. Calif. last year show me some of the difficulties involved in working with people and I am consequently less anxious to depart on new enterprises for the benefit of others at my own risk. Please advise me.

Most sincerely yours,
James M. Jones

P.S. Enclosed is a letter I just received from the Dean of the School of Speech at So. Calif. Please return it in stamped envelope enclosed.

September 2, 1927.

Mr. James M. Jones
My dear Sir:

I am returning the letter which you sent me. With regard to the plan that you mentioned, I may say that this has been proposed several times. It is, of course, feasible but it has certain difficulties and differences. Probably if Negroes started to take possession of one state they might meet mob violence from the residents of that state while there would be every tendency in other states to drive away Negroes and segregate them in the new state. Such eventual segregation of twelve million people would make it the most thickly populated state in the United States. New York has only ten million and that is by far the richest, the next being Illinois with six million. Then there would be, as you have said, difficulties of self support and guidance. American Negroes have had only some experience in politics. They would have to go through a difficult time of appren-

ticeship and adjustment, and every mistake would be held up to criticism and ridicule. I suppose if anything of this kind is seriously adopted it would have to be done very gradually so that the whole movement would be spread over ten, twenty, or thirty years. It is quite possible that something like this may happen.
Very sincerely yours,
W. E. B. Du Bois

In the second week of October 1927, a student strike hit Hampton Institute in Virginia, the very center of conservative thought and conduct in the South. The two letters that follow describe the historic event; one is from an anonymous student, the other from a young and newly appointed teacher, Louise A. Thompson. The latter was published in part—unsigned—in the December 1927 *Crisis* (34:345). Miss Thompson did meet with Du Bois, as she suggested in the postscript. The next year she terminated her association with Hampton and began a militant career that has continued to the present.

Hampton Institute, Va., Oct. 10, 1927

Dear Sir:

Just a word of a very serious matter here at Hampton. The school is in a very critical situation.

We the students have been wronged, wronged. Yesterday we struck. No inspection, no church, no grace at dinner. At chapel we refused to show off before some Governor from Europe.

The whites are bewildered at the sudden actions of these "Southern Negroes." They know not how to act toward the situation. No classes whatsoever today. We have a strong committee of twenty bold, honest upright men pleading for just—Justice, Justice. Ah, if you only knew half. The future of the Negro youth depends upon the results of this serious uprising. Would like for you to help us before we 900 are sent away out in the world.

Strike began after the refusal to turn out lights in Ogden Hall at a movie Saturday night.

We must stick. The officials praying that such will not leak out but please let our mothers, fathers and our race know.
Sincerely,
A loyal Hamptonian.

Hampton Institute, Va., Oct. 17, 1927

My dear Dr. Du Bois

I feel now that I have enough data at hand to lay before you the causes which brought about the student strike and the condition in which it has left Hampton. I shall not mention any of the details of the uprising as I am sure you will get this information from other sources. I want to explain to you the attitude a few of us have taken in this matter who are not afraid to think for ourselves even at the risk of personal security.

Dr. Du Bois, I believe in the motives which actuated the student strike; but unfortunately for the students, their petition did not get to the root of the situation. I talked with some of them about this matter and they said they did not know how to frame in words what really actuated them to such a manly sacrifice as they have made. So that now that the strike is over, the task seems to be to explain to the outside world what caused the greatest upheaval in Hampton's history.

I am a very recent comer here; but through my own observations and experience, and what I have learned from others in position to know what they are talking about, I have become keenly aware of the state of hypocrisy, racial prejudice, and backwardness into which Hampton has fallen. Within my one month's residence here I have suffered keenly and racial antipathy has grown within me.

Rumors of the general unrest among the students and of the prospects of an uprising had reached me a week or two before the incident occurred which kindled the flame. Consequently, at the moment of its incipiency, some of us realized the seriousness of the situation, but we were in a sad minority. Others laughed and scorned the childish actions of the students, calling them fools.

The administration forced the issue which resulted in practically seven hundred students leaving the campus last Friday and Saturday by the very domineering and unsympathetic manner in which they handled the situation from beginning to end. Dr. Gregg publicly acknowledged to the students that he was somewhat hasty and derogatory in his first ultimatum of last Monday. The sad part of the situation, was, however, that they did not profit by their first mistakes and continued on with the same threatening, non-conciliatory policy which precipitated the disaster. Even now they do not realize that Hampton has been dealt a serious blow, and are carrying on in the same high-handed manner, not realizing if every student should return, the Administrative Board failed in ever forcing them to leave.

Very much depends on public opinion in this affair. The authorities are crediting this strike as the work of disobedient boys and girls who were led on to do what they did. On the other hand, each student I have talked with has impressed me with the serious attitude he has taken in the matter—with each one of them it became a holy cause. The strike to them was not a prank, in fact it was partly forced on them; but when they found themselves too deeply involved to back out, they went straight ahead with great religious fervor. Previous petitions have always been ignored; their student council has six faculty members, and they felt drastic action was necessary if they were to be heard this time. Many are arguing that the students went about their strike in the wrong manner; but be that as it may, they carried it through in an orderly and manly fashion that brought commendation on every side.

The next thing is, of course, what is to come of it? Classes began informally this morning to occupy some students that are on the grounds. The formal opening is scheduled for October 25. The authorities are optimistic and feel that all will go on as before. Others of us do not feel as confident. Last night there were 300 students here, today, others have come in so that there are possibly 400. Many are here because of parental order and others, because they have no other alternative. It has been a terrible ordeal to witness the struggle some of them have gone through, feeling that they cannot stay, yet cannot go. Many may return, but I fear that a feeling of dissatisfaction and unrest will be present in them in a greater degree than ever. Some have found that other schools have closed their doors to them; others away from the crowd have lost their enthusiasm. But there are others who will never return, and they are the best of the school. Dr. Gregg acknowledged that the leaders in the strike were the foremost men on the campus and those who had been some years in the institution. The wholesale slaughter that has come about of the school's best is too great for no good to come of it and the Negro world should be made to see the justice in the students' stand.

As I stated in the beginning, I have not attempted to give you a detailed account of this affair. I shall await your observations on what I have said and what you have learned through other sources. I have gathered together a number of incidents which are interesting sidelights on the situation. The conciliatory steps taken by some of the white teachers have been most amusing. They threw aside the protecting garment of the Massenberg Bill and the wife of the most prejudiced leader on the campus, whose home is never open to any but the white teachers, sponsored auto parties to take the girls to Yorktown, some thirty miles away. Other white-haired ladies wandered around with checker boards, organized sewing bees, gave teas in their rooms, pop-corn parties, and other rather silly amusements as a sop. They cannot realize that there has been a fundamental upheaval which cannot be appeased by simple pastimes. Many pled with tears in their eyes to no avail, for the girls laughed in their faces. They cannot understand that these students for whom they have sacrificed their lives to civilize, in the meantime receiving very comfortable salaries and living quarters which they might have difficulty in securing elsewhere, could feel anything but the deepest respect and gratitude toward them. The teachers as a body do not understand these Negro students, the Administrative Board does not understand them, Dr. Gregg does not understand them—and the tragedy is that they never will. I have found a few, a very few white people who believe in the ideal for which Hampton is supposed to stand, but whose faith has been deeply shaken by this whole affair. As a friend said to me the other day: "I believe that interracial experiments will always fail, not because of the impossibility to effect them, but because we cannot be careful enough in the selection of representatives of each side." Especially in the Trade School, I learn that there are many inferior white men, some members of the Ku-Klux, who are steeped in southern prejudices. On the other hand, I have witnessed the action of some of the Negro teachers and workers who are just as deadly enemies.

My position in this situation has been a trying one. My first impulse was to resign at once, but those whose opinions I value have urged me not to be hasty in taking this step. They pointed out that that inarticulate thing which really motivated this student outburst is not known but to a very few of us, and that it would be taken that I was acting on the issues raised by the students which are not big enough to warrant a teacher's participation. Again, being a new comer, many would not think I could know enough about Hampton to register such disapproval of the administration, and that I should not only aid the students, but injure the cause of young Negro teachers at Hampton. Dr. Gregg at a workers' meeting last evening issued an ultimatum to workers as well. He told us that he had been made aware that there were those among us who were student sympathizers and such persons as these were not wanted at Hampton under the regime of the present Administration. Loyalty on the part of the teachers in the present administration is just as necessary as the loyalty of students, and those who felt that they cannot back up the present policies were politely asked to get out.

Our minority group had a very heated discussion later in the evening as to what action we should take. To remain means to live a lie, for Dr. Gregg said that loyalty would be assumed on the part of those who remain in the institution. Some voiced the opinion that Dr. Gregg could not autocratically define loyalty and that there is a loyalty higher than loyalty to an administration to consider. With those who hide behind southern legislature and prejudice, we can best serve Hampton by remaining and fighting from the inside. To resign would be to play into their hands for that is what they wish us to do.

I am not yet convinced as to what I should best do. I should like very much to talk with you on this whole matter, but I do not feel I can afford to come to New York just now. Being so much a part of the affair, I fear I lack vision concerning it, and I should like to talk with some one who is able to look at it more objectively. There is much I can add to all that I have told you—in fact, I began a more detailed dissertation, but cast it aside for the present until I might hear from you.

I hope that I have given you a view of the matter which is not too biased. I have talked with those on all sides and tried to give credit where credit is due.

Very sincerely yours,
Louise A. Thompson

P.S.: Since writing this letter I have decided to come to New York this coming weekend if you consider it worthwhile.

Questions posed in a letter from a white college student to Du Bois almost half a century ago not only were "discussed warmly" then, as the writer states, but remain still in the minds of many whites. Du Bois's answers are characteristically pithy and unambiguous.

San Diego, Calif., November 1, 1927

Dear Sir:

A week or so ago I had the opportunity of glancing thru an issue of "The Crisis" for the first time. Apparently you are decidedly in favor of Negro equality with the white race in every respect. I am very much interested in the so called "race problem" just at present; especially as I have chosen the Negro problem as the theme of a term paper I am preparing in connection with one of my courses here at college.

Considering you an authority in your field, I am making the following queries in hope that you may find time to answer them. I should like to incorporate your statements in the above mentioned term paper, if possible.

First, do you consider the white and black races to be naturally on an equal footing intellectually & morally? (Disregarding the possibly artificial color discrimination prevalent in the South.)

Second, is the segregation of one race from another an incorrect and harmful custom? Do you advocate race amalgamation, or do you think the negro has enough pride and confidence in his own race to wish to keep it distinct?

Third, I have heard it said that unless the white man keeps the upper hand on the negro, the negro will insist upon domineering as tho a superior. They can not remain on an equal footing, in other words. One must always have the upper hand. Do you agree with this view point?

Fourth, do you advocate the return of negros to Africa for the purpose of permanent colonization? Why or why not?

Fifth, should the Negro race as a whole "dig in" and work its way to the top as other races have done, or should it be accepted in all society because of the eminence of a few negro celebrities at the present time?

Sixth, does race amalgamation bring out inferior tendencies in either or both uniting peoples?

These perhaps sound meandering and not to the point, but they are questions which are discussed warmly and at length every week in our class rooms.

Thanking you for the favor of a reply to these queries, I am
                                Sincerely,
                                (Miss) Bernice E. Brand

November 16, 1927

My dear Madam:

Answering your questions, I beg to say:

(1) I consider the white and black races "potentially equal." Of course, this leaves untouched the question as to what you mean by "white" and "black" races and what anybody would mean by "potentially equal."

(2) I consider attempted race segregation harmful because it is increasingly impossible under the present organization of the civilized world. I neither advocate nor oppose race amalgamation. I accept it as a fact as old as humanity. It

is none of my business and none of yours if two people wish to get married who are sane, healthy and of full age. If we try to stop such marriages because they do not please us the result is more harmful than the marriage could possibly be. Whatever pride or self-confidence the Negro race has or may have in America, he has found it impossible to protect his women from the lust of your fathers, brothers, husbands and sons. The only way to make a race self-protecting in its pride is not to degrade it, disfranchise it and insult it.

(3) I do not believe that the only relations between men or groups of men are the relation of master and serf, ruler and ruled.

(4) I do not advocate the return of Negroes to Africa nor the return of white people to Europe. I believe that the world belongs to its inhabitants and that if an Englishman wishes to migrate to America or a Negro wishes to migrate to Africa both should have the right to do so under such general rules of physical health and economic opportunity as could be laid down by fair and just men.

(5) I believe that all men, white and black, should be accepted and rated according to their individual accomplishment.

(6) Race amalgamation "brings out" nothing. Everything depends upon the social environment of the offspring and the parents.

Very sincerely yours,
W. E. B. Du Bois

One of the few projects upon which Du Bois expended much labor that never reached fruition was a history of Black troops in the First World War. His effort is described at some length in a letter to Raymond Blaine Fosdick (1883–1972), who had been civilian aide to General Pershing in France and, before going to the Rockefeller Foundation, undersecretary-general of the League of Nations. The James Hardy Dillard (1856–1940) Du Bois mentions was at this time president of the Jeanes Foundation for Negro Rural Schools and president of the John F. Slater Fund.

The reply came, not from Fosdick, but from the personal secretary of John D. Rockefeller, Jr.; it indicates what that gentleman's principles did not encompass.

November 18, 1927

Mr. Raymond B. Fosdick
Dear Sir:

I am writing you at the suggestion of Mr. J. H. Dillard with whom I have discussed the history of the Negro in the World War which I have been writing since 1919.

In the fall of 1918, on motion of Mr. Oswald Garrison Villard, the Board of Directors of the N.A.A.C.P. sent me to Europe to collect facts and documents concerning Negro soldiers. The idea was that this matter would eventually form the basis of a history of the participation of Negroes in the World War. I arrived in Paris in December 1918 on the press boat, the Orizaba, and began the collection of books, documents, personal narrations, etc., concerning this subject. This collection of material continued for several years after my return in March, 1919.

I began on the basis of this material to write a history, but I soon found the task much larger than I anticipated. I therefore sought cooperation. I negotiated first with representatives of Harper & Brothers who in cooperation with Mr. Emmett D. Scott, war-time assistant to the Secretary of War on Negro matters, were planning a history of Negro troops. They, however, wanted a popular subscription book written to sell and edited by an expert on such volumes. I declined cooperating as my material could not be ready so soon, nor was it suited to this kind of a project.

I next sought cooperation with Mr. Carter G. Woodson, whose excellent work in Negro history is widely known. We came to a tentative agreement to issue a history under our joint names. Afterward Mr. Woodson demurred. I think he was afraid that he might be called upon to do most of the work and get the smaller part of the credit. This was not at all my idea and I was certainly prepared to be most generous in any distributions of work and responsibility that Mr. Woodson would consent to and was very sorry when the scheme failed.

I continued my study and writing until I finished a history which at present contains more than 781 typewritten pages, letter size. With notes and final corrections this would expand to over 1500 pages and probably make from three to five printed octavo volumes.

This, of course, greatly exceeds my original plan and puts me face to face with two difficulties: *first*, the final correction of so long a manuscript with the verifications of authorities and a new search of the most recent war literature calls for expert clerical and scientific assistance in this country, England and France; *second;* I realize that the publication of this work cannot be a commercial proposition, for it is too long and its sale too problematical.

Up to this point I have had very little financial assistance. The N.A.A.C.P. paid my fare to France in 1918–19. *The Crisis Magazine*, which I edit, has given me clerical assistance and Mr. E. C. Williams of Howard University library has helped me classify my documents during two summer vacations.

I realize now that I have undertaken a larger job than I can finish unaided. I hate to give it up and I do not relish the idea of surrendering my material or conclusions entirely to other hands. What I need to finish the work properly is this:

1. Expert clerical aid to go over the manuscript and authorities.
2. Collaboration of two or more graduate students in history to check up on literature and reports.
3. Some work in England, France and Belgium on books and official reports.
4. Enough cash to induce a publisher to issue the completed work.
5. Enough leisure from my main work to superintend my helpers and see the manuscript through the press.

I have not yet tried to estimate carefully what these costs would amount to altogether. I have thought of a maximum of $5000 for all items except No. 4, but I should have to make a more careful estimate than I have had time to yet.

This brings, of course, the question: what is the design and scope of the history?

It is a survey of "the Black Man and the Wounded World"—a study of the effect of the great war on Negroes chiefly in the United States but also in the French, German, Belgian and British colonies; it tries to trace not simply their action as troops and laborers but their reaction to their treatment and environment and the effect of all this on modern culture.

It goes without saying that anything I write is pro-Negro. Naturally it is going to defend the poor black and ignorant against prejudice and power. At the same time, in the past, my work in history and social science has, I think, stood up well under severe criticism. My "Suppression of the Slave Trade," the first volume of the Harvard Historical Series, is still the last word on the subject. My Atlanta University studies of the Negro problem, covering 1896 to 1912, form the largest body of fact for studying the Negro collected in America up to that time. My "Philadelphia Negro" and volume on the Negro race in the Home University Library have been regarded by many as authoritative. I have done several monographs for the United States Bureau of Labor and one for the United States Census.

I hope in this history of the black troops to be absolutely honest and thorough in my examination of the truth and to spare neither white England and America nor the darker world in an endeavor to write a history which will paint war as the greatest of human catastrophes and race prejudice as its worthy coadjutor.

I trust you will pardon this long explanation. If you are interested and think there is any chance of my securing aid for this work, I shall be glad to go into the matter further with you.

Very sincerely yours,
W. E. B. Du Bois

New York, N.Y.
November 28, 1927

My dear Mr. Du Bois:

Mr. Fosdick has referred your letter of November 18th addressed to him in care of the Rockefeller Foundation, directly to Mr. Rockefeller, Jr.'s office, since the matter is one which could not be considered by the Foundation, limited by charter, as it is, to other fields.

As far as Mr. Rockefeller is concerned, although the considerations which you raise are appreciated, it is regretted that he is not inclined to contribute in accordance with your suggestion. Mr. Rockefeller is necessarily limited by principles which experience has shown him to be wise. Certainly, there is no lack of

[368]   Correspondence 1920–1929

sympathy with the objects which you have in mind. On the other hand, it is regretted that the project represents one in which Mr. Rockefeller, in accordance with his principles, does not feel that he can participate.

I am sorry, particularly in the circumstances, for the necessity of an unfavorable reply.

Sincerely yours,
Thomas B. Appleget

The following correspondence between Du Bois and H. L. Mencken has intrinsic interest enhanced by Du Bois's specifics on the realities and the impact of disfranchisement of Black people in the United States.

December 19, 1927

My dear Mr. Mencken:

I have another proposal.[1] I have just been trying to figure out some facts about *voting* in the South. I have taken the figures from eleven states of the Far South for each presidential election from 1856–1924. I have compared these figures with the growth of population in each of these states during this time. The *discrepancy* is *astonishing*.

In practically all cases the population has increased largely. In some cases the vote cast has increased slowly and in other cases it has remained at a standstill or actually decreased.

I then went further and tried to calculate the number of people disfranchised voluntarily or involuntarily. As a result it is possible to figure that for every Negro disfranchised in the South one or more white people have been disfranchised. For instance, there are more than a million white people, twenty-one years of age and more in Texas, who do not vote!

From Louisiana I have exact data of voting by parishes and color in 1924; the total registered voters in the state are:

white   274,592
colored   828

There were in the state in 1920, 924,184 persons 21 years of age or more!

These facts, added to the well-known figures of Southern over-representation

---

1. Du Bois had written Mencken on 14 April 1927, proposing he do an article on Black political efforts in Chicago; on 9 November 1927, he wrote suggesting an article on economic conflicts between African cocoa producers and outside financiers. Mencken rejected both ideas.

in Congress and the controversy between Mr. Borah and Mr. Glass,[2] might possibly make an article which would not be too hackneyed.
>Very sincerely yours,
>W. E. B. Du Bois

New York, December 20, 1927

Dear Dr. Du Bois:

Thanks very much for your note. Unfortunately, I have a fear that the current discussion of representation in the South stands in the way of the article you propose. The matter is apt to be talked of at immense length during the next few months, and I believe that this would discount the effects of the article. We have to work, at the shortest, seven weeks in advance and so I always hesitate to undertake a subject that is under public discussion. My very best thanks again.
>Sincerely yours,
>H. L. Mencken

Note was earlier taken of Du Bois's friendly relations with the family of Mr. and Mrs. M. V. Boutté in New York City. As February 1928 approached, bringing Du Bois's sixtieth birthday, a movement developed for a public celebration. Those making the plans hoped that one result would be a financial gift to Du Bois to assure his economic independence and thus enhance his productivity. His detailed and frank reply is of consequence.

December 27, 1927

My dear Mrs. Boutté:

I have thought over your proposal all Christmas Eve and all day Christmas and I am writing you to ask you not to attempt it. You surely know how deeply I appreciate your offer and the kindness of other friends.

If there should come to me a spontaneous outburst of applause and good-will in the shape of a gift that would give me more leisure, I would receive it with deep gratitude. But you do not realize my friend—no one realizes as I do—how unlikely, how impossible any such manifestation of approval of me and my work is from either black folk or white today. It is possible that in some far off day much praise will come to my memory; although even that is not certain, for history plays curious tricks. Today, at any rate, I have a few fine and loyal friends; I have a small audience which, while it does not particularly like me per-

---

2. As part of the pre-1928 election campaigning, there was some discussion of the over-representation of the (white) South in the Congress; it is to remarks in that connection by William E. Borah, R., Idaho, and Carter Glass, D., Va., that Du Bois refers.

sonally, approves and applauds my work; but there is a company of Negroes entirely ignorant of my work and quite indifferent to it; there are very many of the envious and jealous; and there is an appalling number of those who actively dislike and hate me.

Any attempt then at a nation-wide Jubilee gift could only succeed on the crest of a great popular wave, worked up by every method of publicity and so powerful as to sweep along the fools, the indifferent and all those who fear to be absent from any band-wagon. The experience of my office with the splendid dinner given me in 1923 convinced me of this. I swore then—"never again"!

Even such a popular movement worked up by long and intensive effort could only accomplish tangible success by the contributions of rich whites. Our people have little surplus money. Especially those few to whom this would really appeal can ill afford any large sums. The white people would have to furnish the bulk of the contribution.

Now it happens that the whites have borne the brunt of my attacks for thirty years. They are a group sore and sensitive over my activity. They believe that I hate white folks. Even my nearest white friends shrink from me. Under such circumstances to ask white America to help finance the balance of my life and work would seem to most men presuming if not actually impudent.

The price that I must pay for speaking plainly is at least silence of word and deed on the part of white America. At best you could only hope that a few broad souls who have already responded to other calls in which I have been interested, would now offer to be taxed again and further for an object they would not of their own volition have chosen.

Success then in this enterprise, if it came, would involve humiliation; and failure would be heart-breaking. I cannot then consent for you and any one else to undertake this plan, as lovely and thoughtful as it is. Indeed, your thinking of it at all is reward enough for my work.

Finally, the deed is not necessary. I am still well and strong. The chances are that for 10 years I can easily earn a living. After that, if I am compelled to pass the hat, well and good. We'll pass that bridge when we come to it. But today there is no necessity and it must not be done. I know you will respect my strongly felt and carefully considered wish and at the same time, you will know how deeply and utterly I appreciate your kind thought and the wish of the others willing to work with you.

Very sincerely yours,
W. E. B. Du Bois

Though often discouraged by the racism that permeated much of the United States trade-union movement, Du Bois strongly favored such organization as a matter of principle and especially favored it for Black workers, as not only a matter of principle but also one of survival. It is not surprising, therefore, that he did all he could, personally and through the *Crisis*, to assist the organization of the Pullman porters. A very warm letter from A. Philip Randolph, the general organizer of the Brotherhood of Sleeping Car Porters, acknowledged Du Bois's service.

New York, December 28, 1927

Dear Dr. Du Bois:

Permit me in behalf of the members and officials of the Brotherhood of Sleeping Car Porters to express our sincere appreciation for your interest in and cooperation with our Movement.

Your able and brilliant editorials on our fight have been constructive and helpful.[1]

May we wish for you a happy and long life of service for the cause of Negro freedom in particular and the freedom of all mankind in general to which you have dedicated your great ability and fine soul. Kindly accept our best wishes for the season's greetings and felicitations.

Very sincerely yours,
A. Philip Randolph

Amy Spingarn (Mrs. Joel E. Spingarn) provided the funds for the annual Spingarn Award offered by the *Crisis* in the 1920s for prize-winning poems, plays, and short stories. This exchange followed a letter from Du Bois that asked if she wished to continue the awards for the year 1928. The result of the correspondence was a fund from which the *Crisis* was enabled to pay authors whose efforts were published in its pages.

New York, January 17, 1928

Dear Dr. Du Bois:

I have received your letter, but have delayed answering it as I have been thinking the matter over very carefully. I think the experiment has been well worthwhile, but I am inclined to believe it has already accomplished the purpose for which it was intended. You will recall that when I first offered these prizes there was no recognition or outlet for the young Negro writer . . . Since then both the Harmon and Opportunity prizes have been established and the "Literary Renaissance" is in full swing.

I wonder if you agree with me that the multiplicity of these prizes has a tendency to be harmful rather than helpful. I feel this experiment has been thor-

---

1. See, for instance, "Pullman Porters," *Crisis* 34 (December 1927):348.

oughly successful, and if you could suggest an equally interesting plan to which I would be sympathetic I should be glad to consider it.

With best wishes

> Very sincerely yours,
> Amy Spingarn

January 19, 1928.

My dear Mrs. Spingarn:

I have your letter of January 17th. I agree with you that it is a little difficult to know just what the best procedure would be to help further the development of literature and art among young Negroes.

The opening for young Negro writers is greater than ever before and the number who are writing is encouraging. Some difficulties, however, still remain: if the young colored writer writes naturally, expressing his own life and his own reaction to the environment about him, it is still hard for him to get his work published. He is therefore tempted in order to get an audience and to get adequate pay, to follow the lead of Carl Van Vechten and Knopf and Boni and Liveright and cater to what white America thinks that it wants to hear from Negroes.

How can we build up a counterpoise to this? I want to suggest three ways for your consideration:

1. Instead of offering prizes to be given at the end of a year for articles written especially for the prizes offered, we might ask for contributions to *The Crisis* Magazine; and then once a month, for twelve months, distribute among the signed contributions sent to *The Crisis* Magazine by persons not connected with the staff, the sum of Fifty Dollars or Six Hundred Dollars for the year.

This would change a little the object of writing. The person would write primarily to express his ideas. His contribution would be received and published with no promise expressed or implied that he would receive anything for it. A month later we could say to him: "This piece of work is well done and in order to encourage more work of this sort, we are giving you this honorarium."

I would suggest that no set sum be given, except that the average should be Fifty Dollars for each month and that for the whole year the limit should be Six Hundred Dollars. It might be that one month we would feel that one poem should receive the whole Fifty Dollars; another month five articles might receive Ten Dollars each; still another month a cover receive Twenty-Five Dollars, while the other Twenty-five Dollars would go over to a succeeding month.

This would be a variation of the payment by space which is made by most magazines, and I think a variation worth trying. It should be limited, of course, to the kind of things that can be published: covers, illustrations, articles, essays, fiction and poetry.

2. Perhaps you have heard of the colored author, Anne Spencer. She is a teacher in Lynchburg, Virginia. She has not written much but what she has done is very beautiful. I wrote her recently for something to publish in *The Crisis*. In promising me to send something she said:

"But why, for the sake of little Negro children don't you have Effie Lee Newsome put some of her lovely stories, bits of charming information and verse, into slender books, say, Vol. I. II. III. IV., etc., for our grade children—primary and elementary. I work here in the library and know at first hand the dearth of such material. We use Miss Ovington's "The Upward Path" freely, but that is too advanced for primary children. Last spring when the librarians met at Hampton this need was discussed at length, and its remedy, but nothing was done, of course, about it."

I wrote to Mrs. Newsome and she is enthusiastic about it and says "Why not call them the 'Brown Thrush' books?" It might be that with a small fund to start these publications we could make an experiment that would be nearly if not entirely self-supporting after a year or so.

3. Both of the above plans really hark back to a fundamental difficulty. American Negroes are not buying books and supporting literature in the way that they ought. Even when they would be willing to buy books they do not know what books they should buy or where they can get them. If a Book-of-the-Month Club is needed for whites, it is especially needed among colored people.

I have talked over this matter with Mr. Johnson and with persons connected with the Literary Guild. We have been advised to try to get from two to five thousand subscribers who would take, say three or four books a year. The question is, however, whether that number of subscribers could be gotten. With two thousand subscribers it would pay to start; with five thousand it would be an assured success. But the campaign of getting these subscribers would call for funds. And there would, of course, be the uncertainty of how many persons we could get and how faithful they would be to their obligations.

I am more doubtful of this plan than of any of the others and yet there is a possibility of its succeeding; and if it did succeed it would carry the other plans and many other things with it.

I put these matters before you for your consideration at your leisure and would be glad to hear from you.

> Very sincerely yours,
> W. E. B. Du Bois

Langston Hughes (1902–67) was at the beginning of his distinguished literary career, and still a student at Lincoln University, when he offered an estimate of some of his own poetry in a letter sent to Du Bois early in 1928.

[374] Correspondence 1920–1929

Lincoln University, Pa.
February 11, 1928

Dear Dr. Du Bois:

Please, if you have any old poems of mine in your office, do not print them in *The Crisis* as I'm afraid they're not up to the things I'm doing now. When I have some new poetry finished I shall be pleased to submit some of it to you. I'm always proud of *The Crisis* and proud when you print me there, that's why I want it to be my best poetry in your pages and not old things written years ago. Some months ago I asked for my old manuscripts in your office, but they couldn't be found. I was hoping they were really lost, but lately some of the poems have been in *The Crisis*, and I don't think they are quite good enough to be there so please throw them in your waste basket if there are any more left.[1]

Sincerely,
Langston Hughes

Du Bois reviewed Claude McKay's novel *Home to Harlem* (New York: Harper and Bros., 1928) in the June 1928 *Crisis* (35:202). He did not like the book: some of the writing was "beautiful and fascinating," some of the sections "have all the materials of a great piece of fiction"; but, "for the most part," he wrote, the book "nauseates me." He went on to suggest that perhaps McKay had "set out to cater for the prurient demand on the part of white folk." Du Bois thought that "a number of New York publishers" were encouraging such fiction, marked by an "utter absence of restraint." Few people are more furious than authors whose books have not been kindly reviewed; a letter from McKay to Du Bois is indicative. The latter's reply is marked by great restraint, and ensuing correspondence was much calmer.

Barcelona, Spain, June 18, 1928

Dear Mr. Du Bois:

I think I beseeched you over a year ago *not* to publish those poems I sent to the "Crisis" towards the end of 1925.

I must remind you again that those poems were sent to the "Crisis" for a special purpose. I was ill. I had no money. I wrote to a number of New York publications, including the "Crisis," frankly stating my situation and asking them to help me by buying a poem or more. I received prompt replies and help from some of the publications. Others that did not accept had the courtesy, with one

---

1. The Hughes poems which appeared in the *Crisis* in the period suggested by the above letter were: "The Childhood of Jimmy" and "Song for a Dark Girl" (May 1927); "Ma Lord" (June 1927); "Tapestry" (July 1927); "Freedom Seeker" and "Being Old" (October 1927); "Montmartre Beggar Woman" (November 1927); "Johannesburg Mines" (February 1928). By this time, two of his books had appeared: *Weary Blues* (1926) and *Fine Clothes to the Jew* (1927).

exception, to return my poems. The exception was the "Crisis" (the only Negro publication I wrote to) which neither replied nor returned the poems. About a year and a half later, when I saw two of the poems in the "Crisis" I was surprised, because, as I said then in a letter to you (the duplicate unfortunately is in Paris) I thought the poems had gone astray in the mails. You replied with a cheque for the published ones and stating that Miss Fauset was in charge when I wrote and she, I suppose, had no time to waste on a non-influential and down-and-out fellow-writer!

I had expected you, after receiving my letter, to return and not make use of the remaining poems. I wrote to my agent in New York to call in all the prose and verse that I had sent out to various magazines. These were all returned and if I did not list the "Crisis" it was because I had already written to the Editor and I took it as a matter of course that a Negro publication of a recognized high standard would not fail to conform to the common rules of journalistic ethics.

My reasons for not wanting any of the things out long ago published now are private and tactical, and I particularly resent the publication of my poem in the same number of the "Crisis" in which, in criticizing my novel, the Editor steps outside the limits of criticism to become personal. I should think that a publication so holy-clean and righteous-pure as the "Crisis" should hesitate about printing anything from the pen of a writer who wallows so much in "dirt," "filth," "drunkenness," "fighting," and "lascivious sexual promiscuity."

But I have no objection to the quoted phrases as criticism, if you did not also choose (to employ Coolidgism) to question my motive in writing my book and bring it down to the level of the fish market. Now this is personal and you have been an editor long enough to know that it has nothing to do with criticism. And so I will reply personally to you Mr. DuBois by retorting that nowhere in your writings do you reveal any comprehension of esthetics and therefore you are not competent nor qualified to pass judgement upon any work of art.

My motive for writing is simply that I began in my boyhood to be an artist in words and I have stuck to that in spite of the contrary forces and colors of life that I have had to contend against through various adventures, mistakes, successes, strength and weakness of body that the artist-soul, more or less, has to pass through. Certainly I sympathize with and even pity you for not understanding my motive, because you have been forced from a normal career to enter a special field of racial propaganda and, honorable though that field may be, it has precluded you from contact with real life, for propaganda is fundamentally but a one-sided idea of life. Therefore I should not be surprised when you mistake the art of life for nonsense and try to pass off propaganda as life in art!

Finally, deep-sunk in depravity though he may be, the author of "Home to Harlem" prefers to remain unrepentant and unregenerate and he "distinctly" is not grateful for any free baptism of grace in the cleansing pages of the "Crisis."

Yours for more "utter absence of restraint"

Claude McKay

August 2, 1928

My dear Mr. McKay:

I presume that I must have misunderstood your former letters and assumed that you did not mind the publication of poems which you voluntarily placed in my hands, so long as you received some compensation. I shall, of course, publish no more, and I am returning three that I have left.

I trust this will find you in good health and that you are planning to return sometime to the United States.

Very sincerely yours,
W. E. B. Du Bois

Barcelona, Spain, August 26, 1928

Dear Dr. Du Bois:

I beg to acknowledge receipt of your letter and the poems. But I did not receive the compensation you mention for the poem, "The International Spirit" published in the June number of the "Crisis." You might send it direct to me or to my representative, W. A. Bradley, 5 Rue Saint-Louis-en-l'Isle, Paris, France.

Yours sincerely
Claude McKay

Richmond Barthé (b.1901), one of the distinguished sculptors of the twentieth century, was born in Mississippi; as a young man he went to Chicago and, from 1924 to 1928, studied first painting and then sculpture at the Chicago Art Institute, under Charles Schroeder. At that time, he made an unsuccessful application for a Guggenheim Fellowship, concerning which he wrote Du Bois; in 1931 and 1932, he was awarded Rosenwald Fellowships and in 1940 and 1941, Guggenheim. His work is now in permanent collections at the Whitney and Metropolitan museums in New York City and at other leading museums and galleries throughout the world.

Chicago, Ill., August 5, 1928

My Dear Dr. Du Bois:

I have completed my fourth year, here at the Chicago Art Institute, and expect to study in New York this fall. After that I would like to continue my studies abroad. I am specializing in Sculpture.

I am sending in an application for a Guggenheim Scholarship, and I wondered if you would help me out by allowing me to give your name as reference.

Mr. Schroeder my instructor here, suggested that I had enough of the class room, and that I just do a lot of research work and work alone, and only have some one to give me criticisms.

He suggested that I go to France or Italy to do this research work, but it will be impossible, unless I get help from some one.

I have hope of finishing my studies so that I will be able to teach my people something about Art. I already have an offer from Fisk University to teach modeling when I am through my studies.

Hoping that you will grant me this favor,
I am hopefully—
Richmond Barthé

P.S. Some of my work was recently exhibited at Fisk University.

August 13, 1928

My dear Mr. Barthé:

I should be glad to recommend you for a Guggenheim Fellowship if they write me. You ought to give a great deal of attention to your general education as well as your art.

Very sincerely yours,
W. E. B. Du Bois

Victor F. Calverton (pseudonym for George Goetz, 1900–1940) was educated at Johns Hopkins and contributed frequently to the *Nation* and the *New Republic* and for a time wrote regularly for *Current History*. He was a founder and editor of the *Modern Quarterly*, a monthly magazine published in Baltimore with some influence in the 1920s, and wrote several books, especially in literary theory and criticism, of which perhaps *The Liberation of American Literature* (New York: Charles Scribner's Sons, 1932) was best known. He had been introduced to Du Bois by Abram Harris.

Baltimore, September 15, 1928

Dear Du Bois:

It will interest you to know, I am sure, that I am editing a volume entitled Representative American Negro Literature for The Modern Library.[1] I am very anxious indeed to have your cooperation in the compilation of this volume, because I want to make it the most wonderfully comprehensive and inclusive volume of this type that has hitherto been published.

The volume will be divided into several classifications. First let me note that it will begin with Phyllis Wheatly and extend to our active contemporaries, [Rudolph] Fisher, [Eric] Walrond, Countee Cullen, etc. There will first be a section devoted to the short story, another to the novel (selections from various novels by Negro writers will be chosen); a section to poetry, a section to essays, and a final section to autobiography.

Before asking you any other advice I should like to have you tell me first what essay of yours do you think would be most representative and would prefer

1. *Anthology of American Negro Literature* (New York: Modern Library, 1929).

having me include in this anthology. I like in particular your essay, included in the New Negro, entitled The Negro Mind Reaches Out. Secondly I am anxious to make several selections of your novels—a chapter from each perhaps—and I should like to have your aid in doing this. Will you suggest for me a few chapters which you think include your best writing in fiction, chapters which as far as possible can stand alone. Of course, I know how mischievously difficult it is to do this but since I wish to include selections from novels, we must do the best we can with the difficulty.

If you have any suggestions of particular chapters from novels such as The Sport of the Gods, There is Confusion, etc., I should appreciate your recommending one to me.[2]

Another request—will you list for me what you consider the ten best short stories by Negro authors—by different authors I mean—one for instance of Dunbar, one of Chestnutt, one of Walrond, one of Fisher, etc.

I shall appreciate also any other suggestions that you would like to make in reference to this whole project.

Because so many communications will be necessary in connection with this volume before it is completed I shall appreciate it deeply if you will let me have a very prompt response to this.

Yours very sincerely,
V. F. Calverton

September 18, 1928.

My dear Mr. Calverton:

Answering your letter of September 15th, I beg to say:

1. I like the essay that you mentioned, or any of the following: Essay 1 and 2 in "Darkwater." Chapter 11 in "Souls of Black Folk."

2. I have written only 2 novels: "The Quest of the Silver Fleece," 1911, and "Dark Princess," Harcourt Brace and Company, 1928. I have also written two short stories, Chapter 13 in "The Souls of Black Folk" and Chapter 10 in "Darkwater." I should suggest that you might include any of the following: Part 1, Chapter 6, of "Dark Princess"; either of the short stories, Chapter 19, of "The Quest of the Silver Fleece." Of the best short stories there is, of course, "The Wife of His Youth" by Chesnutt. (And for Heaven Sakes do not spell his name wrong.)

I do not have any other suggestions.

Very sincerely yours,
W. E. B. Du Bois

---

2. Paul L. Dunbar wrote *The Sport of the Gods* (New York: Dodd, Mead and Co., 1902), and Jessie Fauset, *There Is Confusion* (New York: Boni and Liveright, 1924).

An early, explicitly anti-fascist publication in the United States was the *Lantern;* it was published monthly and began in 1927 in Boston, with the subtitle "Focusing Upon Fascism and Other Dark Disorders of the Present Day." On its advisory board were Powers Hapgood and Gardner Jackson, among others. Its last number was dated August 1929. A young man who worked for the publication, L. C. Cartwright, wrote a very revealing letter to Du Bois late in 1928; the response is certainly not less illuminating.

Boston, Mass., September 27, 1928

Mr. W. E. B. Du Bois
Dear Sir:

I come of Nordic, 100% American stock and my family has been in America for nearly three hundred years, but I am neither proud nor ashamed of that, for ancestry matters little. Born on a Missouri farm, tenth child of a poor family, I lived there for thirteen years. Then with my mother and father and one brother I moved to Miami, Florida, where my parents still live. Four years in high school at Miami, four years studying chemical engineering at the University of Florida, with my family unable to help me with expenses, as a result of which my indebtedness grew steadily, and you have my history to a year ago. Add to that the fact that in college I began to turn sharply away from the fundamentalist Baptist doctrines instilled into me in my earlier days, and began to question the perfection of the existing order of society and government in our great America. In other words, I became an atheist and a radical in the eyes of my family and friends. Such action is unpardonable at the University of Florida, which is referred to by its few radical students and professors as "a good old Baptist prep school." But my high scholastic standing gained for me partial forgiveness from some.

Then I received appointment as an Austin Teaching Fellow in Chemistry at Harvard, where I arrived the first of last October. Here, I thought, at "the oasis in the great American desert," is intellectual freedom. My position required that I register for half-time graduate work in chemistry, which I was glad enough to do, thinking that I would eventually receive the doctorate in chemistry.

I joined the Harvard Student Liberal Club, thinking there to find the best and most liberal minds in Harvard. By the middle of the school year I found myself disappointed in Harvard and disappointed even in the Liberal Club. Perhaps I had expected too much. I felt an increasing interest in literature, philosophy, and sociology, and my so-called radicalism became more pronounced. I was even considered a radical in the Liberal Club, particularly upon the race question.

I first became actively interested in the race question through the Harvard Liberal Club–Lincoln University debate last March, as a result of which I made many friends among the Negroes of Boston. Then the Liberal Club sponsored the production of Porgy in Boston, and I met and liked the Porgy cast. Since that time I have greatly enlarged my circle of Negro friends. I have also read a great deal of literature by and about the Negro race. I have friends of almost every race and nationality, but I come in more direct contact with the American Negro.

More recently I have joined the staff of The Lantern, because I believe it has a great field in the development of liberal and intelligent thought. It started a year ago as an anti-Fascist paper, but it is rapidly broadening its field to cover all dark disorders of the present day.

I am sending you copies of The Lantern, and of two circular letters which will help to explain its present position. I feel that you could help us a great deal through your own connections with liberal thinkers, through The Crisis, and through the N.A.A.C.P. I am very much interested in your work and wish to learn more about it and to help you if possible. I feel that all who are working in the interests of humanity and the advancement of liberty, truth and freedom have a common cause and should work together.

At my suggestion, The Lantern is going to take up the race question as one of the most important problems in America and the World today. Our next issue will contain an article by Eugene Gordon entitled "A New Religion for the Negro."[1] It will also contain a letter from me in the nature of an appreciation of your novel, *Dark Princess*. I am planning an article on Police Brutality practiced on the Negroes of Boston. We are asking for further articles on the Negro, and perhaps you would like to write some for us. We only ask our contributors to speak the truth, boldly and unafraid.

I have shown your article in The Crisis on "The Possibility of Democracy in America" to members of the Editorial Board of The Lantern.[2] They praised it and said they would like to quote from it in The Lantern, with your permission.

I wish to devote myself wholly to writing, speaking and working for the advancement of liberalism, truth and justice, and for the freedom and happiness of human beings. How I am going to make a living I don't know or care. I have definitely given up chemistry as a career; in fact I don't want a career other than the one mentioned above. I am absolutely broke, three thousand dollars in debt, almost an outcast from my family and former friends in the South, but I will not recant or turn back from the work I have chosen. It is my life. At present, the Editors of the Lantern are paying me, out of their own pockets, just enough money to live on, while I try to increase the circulation of The Lantern and put it on its feet financially. It is hard to get publicity for such a publication without

---

1. Eugene Gordon (born in South Carolina and now living in New York City) wrote editorials and articles appearing regularly in the Boston Black newspaper of this period, *Plain Talk;* he was simultaneously on the editorial staff of the *Boston Post*. He contributed to such magazines as *Scribner's* and Mencken's *Mercury*. After World War II, he was an editor of the *National Guardian* in New York.

2. Du Bois's article appeared in the September 1928 *Crisis* (25:336, 353–55).

money, but I am doing what I can. I want the co-operation of every honest liberal and liberal organization.

Perhaps I can do some writing for The Crisis. I should like to. And I should like to know more about the N.A.A.C.P. and its work. Perhaps I could help in that, too. I hope to be in New York on business for The Lantern for a few days some time soon, and I should like to meet you then, and have a long talk with you, if you will grant me that favor.

I am enclosing the first rough draft from which I wrote my letter to The Lantern about your novel. It will indicate to you how much I was impressed by your *Dark Princess*. I have just read the review of Dark Princess in the October issue of The Crisis, but I had not read it when I wrote the letter to The Lantern.

I hope that I may hear from you very soon and that I may have the pleasure of meeting you ere long. Write to me at the address at the bottom of this page.

Very sincerely yours,
L. C. Cartwright[3]

October 4, 1928.

My dear Mr. Cartwright:

I have read your letter of September 27th with much interest. I have also received copies of *The Lantern* which I shall look over. I am glad you liked *Dark Princess*, and if at any time I can be of service to you, it will give me pleasure.

There is one thing that you must remember. The world will not give a decent living to the persons who are out to reform it. From one point of view this is [missing word]. Those persons who control income are not going to yield any part of that income to the people who propose to disturb their power. Reformers, therefore, have to take the vow of poverty and they are in for a hard time. Most of them are compelled by starvation to compromise in some degree: by silence, by not saying all they think, at all times, or by finding some niche where they can be fairly free to talk within certain limits. This means usually that they must be satisfied with a small and precarious income. This is what you are going to face. *The Crisis*, for instance, has no capital and just barely pays expenses, which means that most of the people who write for us, write for nothing. Only now and then can we pay them small sums. *The Crisis* does earn the salary of its Editor and Business Manager, and of our six clerks, beside helping in the support of 400 or 500 agents distributed through the country. Outside of this, we are not able to be of much help to the radical course.

What you have got to face frankly is this: how long can you get the necessary bread and butter by speaking out frankly and plainly? When you can no longer

3. Leonard Carl Cartwright, a well known chemist and engineer, now living in New York City.

do this, what compromises can you make in unessentials that will allow you to save your soul? Beyond that, is oblivion. The oblivion of complete surrender or of complete silence. The object of life is to avoid either of these.

Very sincerely yours,
W. E. B. Du Bois

George S. Schuyler, born in Providence, Rhode Island, in 1895, is best known as a journalist. He was on the editorial staff of the *Messenger* in the 1920s and in that same period began his column in the *Pittsburgh Courier* that continued for some thirty years. In the 1930s he worked on publicity for the NAACP and, from 1937 to 1944, was business manager of the *Crisis* after Du Bois left it. His novel, *Black No More* (1931), was widely read. In recent years, he has taken an increasingly conservative position; he authored *Black and Conservative* (1966). Late in 1928, he was editor of an illustrated feature section put out by Middle Class Group, Inc. and taken by eighteen Black newspapers. He wrote Du Bois late in 1928.

Chicago, October 11, 1928

Dear Sir:

The other day I received a copy of your latest book, "Dark Princess," from the publisher for review. Although I have only reached Page 127, I couldn't resist the temptation to write and tell you what a masterful piece of work it is. It has gripped me as no other book has since Knut Hamsun's "Hunger." It has reduced me to tears more than once.

You are the master! Beside you other contemporary writers hailed as "great" pale into insignificance. Not only do I think "Dark Princess" is a fine work from a literature standpoint, but it is also great as a portrayal of the soul of our people. No one has done this near as well as you have, and I think every Negro should be grateful to you.

Sincerely yours,
George S. Schuyler

Mrs. Margaret Wade Deland (1857–1945) was a very popular short-story writer and novelist for some forty years after her first success, *John Ward, Preacher*, was published in 1888; her novel *The Iron Woman* (1911) was a best-seller. Her autobiography, *Golden Yesterdays*, appeared in 1941. The exchange she had with Du Bois in 1928 raises an important question.

Kennebunkport, Maine, Dec. 3, 1928

My dear Dr. Du Bois:

I remember with great pleasure meeting you very many years ago at the house of my friend, Mrs. Evans,[1] in Boston. I recall that William James was there also, and that we four had a delightful time. As I have always been profoundly interested in the political, industrial and spiritual welfare of the people who were so deeply wronged some three hundred years ago, I am keenly alive to the advancement of Negro Americans to-day.

So, remembering your good nature in answering the questions I asked that day at Mrs. Evans', I am venturing to send you the enclosed clipping in regard to the election to Congress of Oscar De Priest. I have a feeling that few things would be so impressive to persons who desire not only justice, but spiritual advancement, for the colored people, as to have a colored man of your eminence protest against the political advancement of any person of his race who does not display intellectual and moral integrity. Of course, the same protest should be made to the political advancement of any unethical white man—and, as we both know well, there have been many opportunities for such protest! But political indignation expressed against white scoundrels, in papers conducted by white men—desirable as such expression of opinion is—can not draw forth the same approval, as that same indignation expressed against an unethical colored man, in a magazine such as The Crisis.

I am sure that you will see my point in this, and I most earnestly hope that The Crisis will repudiate this man in no uncertain terms.

Sincerely yours,
Margaret Deland

December 12, 1928

My dear Miss Deland:

I have your letter of December 3rd. The point which you bring up is most difficult. I have always said something about it in *The Crisis*, and I am going to say more.

In New York a fine type of colored man ran for Congress, and received forty-four thousand out of one hundred thousand votes.[2] If the better class of white

---

1. Mrs. Elizabeth Glendower Evans was the widow of a Boston attorney and was prominently involved in anti-colonial and pro-labor cases and in the struggle around Sacco-Vanzetti. Alfred Lief referred to Mrs. Evans as the "dearest friend of the Brandeises." *Brandeis: The Personal History of an American Ideal* (New York, 1936), p. 469.

2. He refers to the 1924 congressional campaign by Dr. Eugene P. Roberts, a physician; in 1917, he had been appointed by Mayor John P. Mitchel a member of the

people had voted for him, he would have been elected, but they did not. No 100% American will vote for a Negro candidate under ordinary circumstances, no matter what his qualifications. The only way in which the Negro can secure representation in local, state and national government, is by co-operating with a corrupt political machine, like the Vare machine in Philadelphia, the Tammany machine in New York, and the Thompson machine in Chicago. What now is the ordinary Negro voter going to do? He knows the political organization back of Mr. De Priest. I have described it faithfully in my novel, "Dark Princess," published in 1928. On the other hand, if I had been voting in Chicago, I would have voted for De Priest. I know that he will stand against lynching, against color discrimination, against Negro disfranchisement, and for the enforcement of the 13th, 14th and 15th Amendments. I know of very few white Congressmen who will stand for any of these things. For this reason, I have supported corrupt machines by my vote in many cases.

When I first came to New York in 1910, we did not have a single colored Policeman. We have dozens of them now, and we got them through Tammany. And the colored policemen in Harlem have reduced crime and made life more bearable. The same thing happens in other cities. The race prejudice which keeps white people from voting for Negroes or for their interests, not only hurts them, but also makes it impossible for Negroes to vote on the merits of the great problems confronting us. Our voting is a matter of survival: of sheer life and death. *The Crisis*, therefore, is not going to repudiate Mr. De Priest.[3] We are sorry for what he stands for in many respects, but as long as men like Borah, Hoover and Smith stand for color caste and disfranchisement, we will vote for Thompson and Vare.[4]

Very sincerely yours,
W. E. B. Du Bois

Positive hostility to Black people was not absent from the public role of Herbert Hoover, both while he was in Coolidge's cabinet and while he was president; his stand was of some consequence in the massive switch of allegiance among Black voters that was to mark the election of 1932. One act of hostility was the appoint-

---

board of education. He had also served as an inspector for the department of health and earlier had been a leading member of the Committee for Improving the Industrial Conditions of Negroes in New York. The white Tammany candidate, Royal Weller, defeated him in 1924.

3. Du Bois dealt with the question in an editorial, "De Priest," in the *Crisis* 36 (February 1929):57.

4. William H. Thompson was "boss" of Chicago and its mayor, 1915 to 1923 and 1927 to 1931. William S. Vare was "boss" of Philadelphia and eventually of all Pennsylvania. He served in the House of Representatives from 1912 to 1927; elected to the United States Senate in 1926, he was barred from his seat because of financial scandal.

ment by Hoover of William N. Doak (1882–1933) of Virginia—for many years an official of the lily-white Brotherhood of Railroad Trainmen—as his secretary of labor. Reactions to rumors concerning this appointment appear in an exchange between Du Bois and Robert Page Sims (1872–1944), president of what was then called Bluefield Institute, now Bluefield State College, in West Virginia.

Bluefield, W. Va., January 9, 1929

Dear Dr. Du Bois:

The morning paper is carrying a statement which is said to be copied from the press reports out of New York City that Wm. Doak, Vice President of the Brotherhood of Railroad Trainmen, is to be asked to serve in the Hoover Cabinet as Secretary of Labor.

Mr. Doak was for a long time an employee of the railroad yards in the City of Bluefield and in his official capacity while here there was no man more active and more determined to remove Negro employees from the railroad than Mr. Doak. Since leaving here and going to Roanoke, Virginia Mr. Doak has maintained this attitude of hostility. For this reason those of us who know Mr. Doak feel that no greater calamity could come to Negro Labor than to have [a] man of this type in the position of responsibility and influence as that of Secretary of Labor in the President's Cabinet.

Very sincerely,
R. P. Sims

January 15, 1929

My dear Mr. Sims:

I have brought your letter of January 9th to the attention of the Executive Office. They will do what they can. I shall mention the matter in *The Crisis*.[1] I would advise you also strongly to write to Moton.[2]

With best regards

Very sincerely yours,
W. E. B. Du Bois

Du Bois's interest in the struggles of the peoples of India was intense and of long standing. A leader in such struggles, Lajpat Rai, was a personal friend of Du Bois who had himself shown keen concern about the struggles of Afro-American people. In November 1928, Lajpat Rai was killed by police while leading a boycott demonstration against British rule. In February 1929, a committee of the

1. Du Bois denounced Doak and his appointment in the *Crisis* 36 (March 1929):93. Doak died in office in 1933.
2. This was Robert R. Moton, then head of Tuskegee and of some influence in Republican party politics.

Legislative Assembly in India was appointed to investigate; but the investigation was ineffective. Du Bois sent a letter to the editor of a radical Indian journal, the *People*, published in Lahore (now in Pakistan).*

January 10, 1929

My dear Sir:

It was my good fortune to know Lala Lajpat Rai while he was in exile in America during the great War. He was at my home and in my office and we were members of the same club. I especially admired his restraint and sweet temper. When a man of his sort can be called a Revolutionist and beaten to death by a great civilized government, then indeed revolution becomes a duty to all right thinking men. As a matter of fact, the people of India, like the American Negroes, are demanding today things, not in the least revolutionary, but things which every civilized white man has so long taken for granted, that he wishes to refuse to believe that there are people who are denied these rights.

I hope that the memory of Lala Lajpat Rai will be kept green in India, and that out of the blood of his martyrdom very soon a free colored nation will arise.

Very sincerely yours,
W. E. B. Du Bois

As editor of the *Crisis*, Du Bois frequently wrote to people of accomplishment inviting them to contribute to its pages. Among those to whom he wrote, probably late in 1928 (the letter has not been found), was the distinguished jurist, Louis D. Brandeis, then associate justice of the United States Supreme Court. Justice Brandeis replied in a letter handwritten on the stationery of the Court.

Washington, D.C.,
January 10, 1929

My dear Mr. du Bois:

To my regret, judicial duties preclude compliance with your courteous request.

I recall with pleasure our meeting at Mrs Glendower Evans' house many years ago and have watched ever since your work on behalf of your people.

Cordially
Louis D Brandeis

---

* He also wrote about Lajpat Rai in the May 1929 *Crisis* (36:151); see too the *New York Times*, 16 February 1929, p. 2.

Oswald Garrison Villard, editor of the *Nation*, wrote early in January 1929 to Herbert Putnam, chief of the Library of Congress,* that he "was very much bothered" by reports that "deliberate and illegal discrimination is being practiced by the cafeteria of the Congressional Library against colored people." Putnam replied that "it was difficult to deal with general allegations" and asked for specifics. Villard turned to Du Bois; in this connection Du Bois sent two letters —one to Putnam and the other to Villard.

January 17, 1929

Mr. Herbert Putnam
My dear Sir: (Personal)

Mr. Oswald Garrison Villard has brought to my attention the correspondence between him and you concerning color discrimination in the dining room connected with the Library of Congress.

It is a fact that for at least ten years colored visitors to this dining room have either been refused, several outright, or segregated in separate rooms or behind screens, so much so, the only colored people who go there now are strangers who do not know the conditions. This fact of discrimination is perfectly well-known to every colored person of intelligence in Washington, and it must be well-known to all the members of your staff. The proof of it is perfectly easy for you to find if you so wish. The fact that the cafeteria is run by a concessionaire is almost no excuse. The Government has no right to permit a concessionaire to do what is prohibited by law from doing themselves. I know that if any colored person had had the slightest idea that you had any interest in this matter or dreamed that you did not know of it, that complaint would have been made to you long since.

Very sincerely yours,
W. E. B. Du Bois

January 22, 1929

My dear Mr. Villard:

I am returning Mr. Putnam's letter. It is a ludicrous evasion.[1] I did not know anything about the incident of which he speaks, but I will venture to say there has not been a single week in the last ten years when colored people who have tried to dine in the cafeteria of the Library of Congress have not been either

* Herbert Putnam (1861–1955), born in New York City, was a graduate of Harvard and of Columbia Law School. He practiced law briefly and then became a librarian, heading the Minneapolis and Boston public libraries in the late nineteenth century and, from 1899 to 1939, the Library of Congress. If Mr. Putnam replied to Du Bois, no record of such a letter has been found.

1. Mr. Putnam had written Villard that he had known of a specific case "of some years ago, which we had supposed disposed of."

refused or segregated or insulted in some way. It is impossible to think that Mr. Putnam did not know of this. If he wishes information on the subject, he can obtain it by writing to any of the following persons: Judge James Cobb, of the Municipal Court, Washington, D.C. 609 "P" Street, N. W., Mrs. Mary C. Terrell, widow of a former Municipal Judge, and herself formerly a member of the Board of Education, 609 "F" Street, N. W., Principal of the Dunbar School, Washington, D. C., Principal of the Armstrong School, Washington, D. C., and Mordecai Johnson, President of Howard University, Washington, D. C.

As Mr. Putnam well knows, the United States Government cannot delegate to a concessionaire the right to break the law. Charles Sumner's Civil Rights Law is in full force in the District of Columbia, and the Library of Congress has repeatedly broken this law.

Very sincerely yours,
W. E. B. Du Bois

On 2 February 1929, Du Bois addressed the Current Events Forum at the Rand School in New York City on the relationship between the Socialist party and Black people. In it he referred critically, and accurately, to the chauvinism that marked the practice of that party and urged its termination as a matter of mutual interest: "The appeal for justice which the black workingman is making today is not simply an appeal for charity; it is an appeal to white laborers to stop cutting off their own noses to spite their faces, for denial of economic justice to Negroes by white labor is beginning to make justice for the white workingman impossible." *

Algernon Lee (1874–1954), who chaired the meeting, raised rather heated objections to Du Bois's remarks. Lee had edited Socialist publications, including the *Daily Call,* and was president of the Rand School. He also was chairman of the New York State Socialist party and, from 1918 to 1921, a member of the New York City Board of Aldermen. Later Lee moved to the Right and in 1936, became chairman of the Social Democratic Federation. This February event at the Rand School produced an exchange between Lee and Du Bois.

February 15, 1929

My dear Mr. Lee:

In thinking further of the question of the relation of Negroes to the Socialist Party, it seems to me that the debate of February 2nd ought not to be allowed to rest. I suggest that you encourage some of your students to take up in further

---

* Substantial parts of Du Bois's speech were published in the *New York Times,* 3 February 1929, p. 1, and in the *New Leader,* 9 February 1929.

detail the relation of the Socialist Party, in particular, and also the various other labor parties to the Negro problem. I think a search ought to be made of resolutions, debates, and party decisions. I can see no harm that would come, for instance, of airing that question of separate locals in the South and the resolutions on race differences that were tabled in 1900 or 1904.[1]

I am convinced that the importance of the Negro as a laboring group is going to advance by leaps and bounds in the next twenty-five years, partly on account of increasing intelligence, partly on account of the restrictions of emigration, and for other reasons. If the Negro does not embrace the doctrines of socialism his advance will increase difficulties of the labor movement.

The first step toward understanding will be to clear up the past relations of socialism and the Negro so as to form a firm foundation on which we may build for the future.

Very sincerely yours,
W. E. B. Du Bois

New York City, February 19, 1929

Dear Dr. Du Bois:

I have read with great interest your letter of February 15, and welcome the suggestion that we should get some of our students to give special attention to the attitude of the Socialist Party and also of our labor organizations toward the special problems of the Negroes in the United States.

It is possible that in the discussion which followed your lecture here I expressed myself a little too strongly—or rather, that I failed to say all that I should. Certainly, I am not too glad to deny that our Party and its press might and should have done more in this matter than we have ever done. The important thing is that we should find how to do better in future and of course, that is your purpose in commenting upon the past.

I have it in mind to try to arrange in the near future a little informal and altogether unofficial conference where we could talk over the situation and the possibilities more effectively than in a public meeting. You could, I am sure, give us a great deal of helpful information and advice. I know that there are a number of our white comrades who are interested and would like to see something done.

With best regards, I am

Fraternally yours,
Algernon Lee

1. For very recent studies of the Socialist party and the Afro-American people, with citations to the literature, see R. Moore, "Flawed Fraternity: American Socialist Response to the Negro, 1901–1912," *Historian* 32, no. 1 (November 1969):1–18; and H. Meredith, "Agrarian Socialism and the Negro in Oklahoma, 1900–1918," *Labor History* 11 (Summer 1970):277–84.

Late in the 1920s, plans were begun for the fourteenth edition of the *Encyclopedia Britannica*. Mrs. Worth T. Hedden, a friend of Du Bois associated with its production, helped arrange for several Black scholars in the United States, including Du Bois, to contribute. Early in 1929, however, Franklin Henry Hooper, the American editor,* began to edit Du Bois's contribution in ways unsatisfactory to the author. A very long correspondence developed, parts of which are published below; the upshot was that Du Bois withdrew his essay (as did, in support, James Weldon Johnson, George E. Haynes, Alain Locke, and William S. Braithwaite).

February 14, 1929

My dear Sir:[1]

I received the Galley Proof of my article on "The Negro in the United States" this morning. I am very much dissatisfied with it.

You perhaps know that I undertook this article after personal interviews with Mrs. Hedden and a long correspondence. The article as it now stands, even with the additions and restorations which I suggest, comes well within the limit of length which was decided upon at that time.

First of all, the word "Negro" which was capitalized in my manuscript and which is always capitalized in everything I write, has been changed to a small letter. I feel very strongly on this point. I regard the use of a small letter for the name of twelve million Americans and two hundred million human beings, as a personal insult, and under no circumstances will I allow this article to be published unless the word "Negro" is capitalized in this article. Of course, elsewhere in the Encyclopedia you will follow your own rule.

With regard to the other changes that I have indicated, there are two classes: one set involves changes in my meaning. For instance, on Page 2, I have said: "The legislation of the South at the time showed a determination to re-establish Negro slavery in everything but in name." Your Editor has changed it so as to say: "Seemed to show an inclination." On the same page, I have explained the curious fact that there were 3,777 free Negro owners of slaves. Your Editor took out the explanation, although it was very short. At the bottom of the page, I do not like the changes which he has made with regard to my statement as to intermarriage, and I have changed it back to the original, except making it shorter. On Page 3, at the bottom of the page, I see no reason why the number of Negroes lynched should not be plainly stated; and on Page 4, at the top of the page, a part of my statement has been cut out in spite of its well-known truth. On Page 5, I have restored three statements which in my opinion are essential to the text.

---

* Franklin Henry Hooper (1862–1940) was a Harvard graduate who devoted most of his life to editorial work; his association with the *Britannica* began in 1899.

1. This letter was actually addressed to L. P. Dudley, an assistant to Hooper.

In addition to these changes, there are some others where I do not feel as strongly and I am willing to yield to editorial opinion if necessary; that is particularly true of the statements concerning the slave trade and Reconstruction on Page 2. It would be illogical to say nothing about the reason for the beginning of the slave trade; and the explanation of Reconstruction which your Editor has cut down to "Negroes were gradually forced from the Ballot Box by one means or another" is in my opinion inadequate and misleading.

The additions and restorations which I have made will not add more than twenty or thirty lines to the manuscript. On the other hand, they will add a great deal to my peace of mind. I do not wish to appear captious in this matter or over-sensitive, but when I am asked to write an article I think that in all essential particulars the article should represent my own thought and conviction.

I shall be glad at your convenience to have your judgment as to these matters, and I hope that nothing further will be done toward the printing of this article until I have seen a revised proof and consented to its publication.

Very sincerely yours,
W. E. B. Du Bois

New York City, February 19, 1929

Dear Mr. Du Bois:

I have your letter of February 14th and am sorry to learn that you are dissatisfied with the changes made in the manuscript of your article. Most of them were made simply to save space, and a few of them because I felt that they were written, shall I say in vindication of the colored people, and that, it seems to me, is quite unnecessary. In one or two cases the statements were excessive and contradicted information given in other articles. As an instance of this latter, I struck out the figures "5,000,000" as the number of colored people who have migrated from Africa to America. If by "America" you mean the whole Western Hemisphere, my comment would be that this article deals only with the Negro in the United States and not with the Negro in the whole Western Hemisphere. If you mean by "America," "United States," I can only say that in my judgment the figure is much too large and in any case is certainly at variance with other articles in the New Edition of the Encyclopaedia Britannica.

Your manuscript also contains the statement "After the Civil War it was Negro loyalty and the Negro vote alone that restored the South to the Union, established a new democracy, both for white people and black...." This statement, in my judgement, is largely a matter of opinion and as such should find no place in an encyclopaedia. Had any statement as broad as this and as questionable, on which scholars differ, appeared in any other article, I should have struck it out, as I did in this.

The greater number of changes that you propose do not seem to me essential to the article, and I feel that I must leave them out if only because the space that I have given to the subject is all that we can possibly spare. I will insert the sentence "Most of the slaves being members of their own families whom they have thus emancipated from whites," but to do so I shall have to change the wording somewhat in the paragraph where this occurs, for this change is in the middle of a long paragraph and I do not wish the entire paragraph to be overrun. I shall also put back the words "on plantations in the country districts or if in towns in the" as this unquestionably is an improvement. The other changes that you have made do not seem to me necessary.

There only remains that I should speak of the capitalization of the word "Negro." As far as I personally am concerned, it seems to me that to capitalize Negro when we do not capitalize "whites" is a mistake. I will, however, if you feel very strongly in the matter make the change so that throughout the article the word will be spelled with a capital letter.

May I ask if you will let me hear from you by return mail as to whether the arrangement as stated above is satisfactory to you. If I do not hear from you by return mail, I shall go on the principle that the arrangement is satisfactory. It is very necessary that I have this immediate decision, we are are now paging in *M* and I cannot hold up the paging for one article.

       Yours very truly,
       F. H. Hooper

      February 20, 1929.

Mr. F. H. Hooper
My dear Sir:

I thank you for acceding to my request that the word "Negro" be capitalized.

My statement concerning the Slave Trade applied to the whole of America and not simply to United States. The omission of the figures, therefore, is understandable.

I am still unwilling to have certain statements included over my signature, particularly:

A. Concerning Reconstruction. I want the privilege of working out with you to our mutual satisfaction a statement to which I can honestly subscribe.

B. Also, the statement under Number 9 of "Disabilities of the South" as cut down, is not at all clear. Something more definite should be said.

C. It is unfair not to make some reference to Negro explorers. This could be done without increasing the length of the article.

You say that these other changes "do not seem to me to be necessary"; but the point is that I am the author of the article and to me some change does seem necessary. I do not ask you to consent to a change which contradicts authority or seems exaggerated, but on the other hand, you have no right to ask me to subscribe to a wording which I deem false or misleading.

I trust I may have your consent to these three changes.

       Very sincerely yours,
       W. E. B. Du Bois

February 25, 1929.

Dear Mr. Du Bois:

I have your letter of February 20th. I have not, of course, the slightest right to print over your signature any statement that you do not yourself agree to. That is fundamental and I have no wish to induce you to say anything that you do not approve. On the other hand, the Editor must decide ultimately as to whether or not an article shall be inserted in the Britannica. In the many years that I have been connected with the Encyclopedia Britannica, stretching over four editions, I have not hesitated to strike out certain statements which it seems to me were irrelevant, not needed for the clarity of the article, at variance with other articles, or not in accord with the facts. I do not question in the slightest your right to include any statement you wish in a book which you publish, but I do reserve the right, whoever the writer may be, to leave out certain statements when in my judgement they render the article unfit for the Britannica or at variance with the facts.

Of the three passages which you wish me to put back, the first, marked in your letter "A," stating "that negroes helped to restore order, institute a public school system, open the ballot box to the mass of white men, and abolish cruel and unusual punishments etc.", I cannot conscientiously allow to pass, and if you insist on its being inserted, I shall be forced, greatly to my regret, to leave out your article altogether.

The second paragraph which you wish inserted is one that gives certain details which I deleted simply and solely because they seemed to me unnecessary. I do not think they add to the value of the article, and as I have to save lines wherever I can, I took them out.

As regards the third point you raise, namely the explorers, I will by all means insert this as you ask, for I am anxious to meet your wishes as far as I can.

I do not wish, and I know you do not wish, to prolong this correspondence, and as we have already paged *N*, I must ask that the matter be settled at once. As I have said above, if you insist on the restoration of the first two points, I shall be compelled to leave your article out. This I am reluctant to do, and I hope, therefore, that you will not insist. I ought perhaps to add that I have not done anything in the case of your article that I have not done in the case of scores of others. I simply must use my discretion as Editor in all cases alike. May I ask if you will kindly let me have your final decision by return mail?

Sincerely yours,
F. H. Hooper

February 27, 1929

My dear Sir:

Answering your letter of February 25th, I beg to say that I understand perfectly your right as an Editor to reject an article or to suggest that sentences be

Yolande Du Bois: Fisk University graduation portrait.
Courtesy of Mrs. Alice Burghardt Crawford.

Tuskegee Institute postcard: portrait of W. E. B. Du Bois. From the collection of Milton Meltzer.

Members of the Third Pan-African Congress, Lisbon, Portugal, May 1923. Du Bois is seated center.

1924 sketch of Du Bois by H. J. Turner

Dr. and Mrs. Du Bois with James Weldon Johnson, late 1920s. Courtesy of Mrs. Alice Burghardt Crawford.

W. E. B. Du Bois, late 1920s

left out or changed. What I have maintained and still maintain, is, that you have no right to write a sentence yourself and insert it and then require that I sign the article as mine. That I absolutely refuse to do, and I am, as you acknowledge, quite within my rights.

As the matter stands now, I am not at all clear as to what my article is going to say, and I will not consent to its publication until I am clear and until the article says, not necessarily all that I would like to say, but certainly nothing that I do not believe.

Take, for instance, the paragraph marked (A) in my letter of February 20th: "Concerning Reconstruction. I want the privilege of working out with you to our mutual satisfaction a statement to which I can honestly subscribe." You say in your answer of February 25th that the particular statement on Reconstruction which I have made does not suit you. Very well. I am perfectly willing to suggest another statement or statements on which I trust we will agree. If, therefore, you will kindly send me another copy of the proof, I should be glad to go to work on the matter.

You will, of course, understand that I recognize your desire to hurry this matter. At the same time, the reason for the present haste is yours, not mine, since my article has been in your hands for several months. I cannot think that the cause for hurry is so great that there is not time for a just and decent settlement of the matter.

Very sincerely yours,
W. E. B. Du Bois

March 2, 1929

My dear Mr. Du Bois:

Your favor of February 27th reached this office in due course and would have been answered immediately except that I have been under the weather and not at the office for a day or two.

I send you enclosed herewith proof of your article on the *Negro in the United States* for the New Edition of the Encyclopaedia Britannica. It seems to me that I have met the points you considered the most fundamental in your first letter to me and I hope therefore, you will pass the article as it is. It is in my judgment, and in the judgment of others in the office, an excellent one and one with which, it seems to me, we may all be well satisfied.

Will you kindly let me know whether or not you will pass it as it is? I hope you will for I should greatly regret if the New Edition of the Encyclopaedia Britannica appears without an article by you.

Sincerely yours,
F. H. Hooper

March 4, 1929.

Mr. F. H. Hooper
My dear Sir:

Answering your letter of March 2nd, I beg to say that I am suggesting one change in the article as printed. If you will consent to this, the article may be published. If not, you may omit it.

Very sincerely yours,
W. E. B. Du Bois

Enclosure:

(Text of proposed statement on "Reconstruction" to be inserted)

White historians have ascribed the faults and failures of Reconstruction to Negro ignorance and corruption. But the Negro insists that it was Negro loyalty and the Negro vote alone that restored the South to the Union; established the new Democracy, both for white and black, and instituted the public schools.

March 8, 1929.

My dear Mr. Du Bois:

I am in receipt of your letter of the 4th stating that you desire that the article *Negro* as written by yourself for the New Edition of the Encyclopaedia Britannica go in with the new paragraph or else be deleted altogether. I regret to say that I cannot pass the article with this new paragraph and I am therefore deleting it altogether. I am very sorry to be compelled to do this, but I don't see what other course there is open to me. I am very sorry also for all the time and thought that you have given to this article.

Sincerely yours,
F. H. Hooper

There have never been lacking Southern white people who have opposed racism; one who deserves to be better known was the Reverend Quincy Ewing (1867–1939), an Episcopal clergyman who was born in Louisiana and educated at the University of the South in Tennessee. He served one year in Cleveland, Ohio, but most of his life was devoted to church work in Louisiana and Mississippi. From 1929 until 1935, however, he served a church in California; retiring in 1935, he returned to live in Mississippi and died in 1939 at the home of a daughter in New Orleans.* Mr. Ewing and Du Bois exchanged letters in 1929.

* See the excellent essay by Charles E. Wynes, "The Reverend Quincy Ewing: Southern Racial Heretic in the 'Cajun' Country," *Louisiana History* 7 (Summer 1966):221–28.

Napoleonville, La., March 6, 1929

Dear Doctor Du Bois:[1]

You may possibly recall that, a good many years ago, I preached a sermon against the lynching of Negroes, in Greenville, Miss., which was widely copied and commented on; and you may remember that I once delivered the Commencement Address at Atlanta University. Also you may have seen an article by me in the March 1909 *Atlantic* on the *Heart of the Race Problem*.[2] Therefore my name may not be altogether unfamiliar to you.

I have recently written an article called, *The Truth about the Southern Negroes, A Word in Defence*, and I am wondering what to do with it. The magazines to-day are so commercialized, that I do not know where to look for an editor who would not be likely to shy away from an article in defence of a people whom it is to the interest of the dominant race to condemn. I should like for you to see this article, and to get your advice concerning it. The facts I have set forth I think ought to be broadcast in the interest of truth and justice; but, as to that, I should defer to your judgment.

Let me add that I am the descendant of several generations of slave-owners, and have lived in the South for over fifty years, face-to-face with the black people. I think I know them pretty well, and I think it would puzzle the most astute psychologist to account for any motive on my part to over-state their virtues.

Please let me know if you would be willing to read the article and advise me. With best regards

Sincerely yours,
Rev. Quincy Ewing.

March 26, 1929

My dear Mr. Ewing:

I remember you very well and I shall certainly hope that your article may find publication. It is, as you say, extremely difficult to get anything in the popular magazines today that is at all controversial no matter what its merit. You might try "Current History," published by the *New York Times*, and the *North American Review*. If the article could be made very short there would be a chance in *The Nation* and the *New Republic*. If you cannot get it published

---

1. This letter was addressed to Du Bois at his Brooklyn home, not to his office at the *Crisis* or to the NAACP. How Ewing obtained that address is uncertain, although Du Bois was listed in *Who's Who*. Perhaps also, when posting a letter in rural Louisiana, it was wiser to address it to a street in Brooklyn than to the magazine or the NAACP.

2. *Atlantic Monthly* (103:389–97). The article is an incisive one, rejecting conventional stereotypes and insisting that rationalization for exploitation was at the heart of the so-called "race problem."

anywhere else and if it is not too long, perhaps we could print it in *The Crisis*.
I am very glad to hear from you and to know that you are still in the field.

                          Very sincerely yours,
                          W. E. B. Du Bois

A leading figure in post-World War I real-estate and housing in New York City was Alexander M. Bing; in the 1920s, he was president of the City Housing Corporation, which described itself as "A Limited Dividend Company Organized to Build Better Homes and Communities." * Two of its notable ventures were Sunnyside Gardens in New York City and in Radburn, New Jersey. Both were deliberately lily-white, despite the presence of Felix Adler, William Sloane Coffin, and Eleanor Roosevelt, among others, on the board of directors of the corporation. Correspondence between Bing and Du Bois discussed this segregation.

                          New York, April 23, 1929

My dear Mr. Dubois:
Our effort at Sunnyside to improve housing conditions has been sufficiently successful to warrant a much more ambitious undertaking. We are accordingly proceeding with a 1200 acre development of a new planned town at Radburn, New Jersey.

Will you take a few minutes to read the accompanying circular explaining the program of City Housing Corporation and its financial structure?

We need your interest and active support to enable us to continue. We are glad at any time to answer any inquiries.

                          Very sincerely yours,
                          Alexander M. Bing

                          April 24, 1929

My dear Sir:
I have your circular letter of April 23rd concerning the new development in Radburn, New Jersey. May I bring to your attention the fact that if a proposition of this sort is carried through and persons of Negro descent are refused any chance for residence in this new town just because they are Negroes, as was the case at Sunnyside, then the result of your effort is not merely negative, it is a positive drawing of race and color lines, which is going in the future to have tremendous effect upon American civilization. A separate Negro community

---

* See Alexander M. Bing, "A Possible Billion Dollars for Better Housing," *American City* 41 (October 1929):160. During World War I, Bing was a "dollar-a-year-man" in charge of the Housing Department of the United States Shipping Board.

would not settle the problem thus brought up—it would only aggravate and emphasize it. If an enterprise of your sort lays it down as an incontrovertible proposition that American Negroes cannot be allowed to live near decent people, you are making a decision which affects the relations of white and colored peoples throughout the civilized world. Have you thought of this? Are you going to do anything about it?

Very sincerely yours,
W. E. B. Du Bois

April 29, 1929

My dear Mr. Du Bois:

In reply to your letter of the 24th, I realize the seriousness of the problem to which you refer and have given a good deal of thought to it. I must confess, however, that I do not see any solution so far as our new development at Radburn is concerned. We have in mind embarking shortly on a separate negro community. While I realize that this does not meet with your approval and see the force of the arguments on the other side, I do not see any other way of handling the matter.

Sincerely yours,
Alexander M. Bing

The correspondence between Gandhi and Du Bois speaks for itself. The message from Gandhi was published, in slightly altered form, in the July 1929 *Crisis*, (36:225); it, together with the covering note to Du Bois, bears Gandhi's signature.

February 19, 1929

Mr. Mahatma Gandhi
Sir:

I have just had the pleasure of meeting two of your friends, Madame Naidu and Mr. C. F. Andrews.[1] The inspiration received from them has emboldened me to make a personal request of you.

I am the Editor of a small magazine, the *Crisis*, which has a circulation of about thirty thousand copies among educated American Negroes. I very much want a message from you to these twelve million people who are the grandchildren of slaves, and who amid great difficulties are forging forward in America. Can you grant this request?

1. Mrs. Sarjini Naidu was very close to Gandhi; she succeeded him in December 1925 as president of the Indian National Congress; at the time of his murder she was governor of the United Provinces. Charles Freer Andrews was a beloved British disciple of Gandhi.

I know how busy you are with your own problems, but the race and color problems are world-wide, and we need your help here.

> Very sincerely yours,
> W. E. B. Du Bois

> As at the Ashram, May 1, 1929

Dear Friend,

I was delighted to receive your letter with a footnote by Mr. Andrews. It is useless for me even to attempt to send you an article for your magazine. I therefore send you herewith a little love message.

> Yours sincerely,
> M K Gandhi

Enclosure:

Let not the 12 million Negroes be ashamed of the fact that they are the grandchildren of the slaves. There is no dishonour in being slaves. There is dishonour in being slave-owners. But let us not think of honour or dishonour in connection with the past. Let us realize that the future is with those who would be truthful, pure and loving. For, as the old wise men have said, truth ever is, untruth never was. Love alone binds and truth and love accrue only to the truly humble.

> M K Gandhi

Sabarmati,
1st May, 1929.

Raymond Leslie Buell (1896–1946), despite a relatively short life, produced a vast literature and held many distinguished positions in international affairs; he is perhaps best known for his two-volume study *The Native Problem in Africa* (1928). He taught at Harvard, Princeton, and Columbia; from 1927 to 1933, he was research director for the Foreign Policy Association in New York City. In that capacity he and Du Bois exchanged letters in the spring of 1929.

> New York, May 25, 1929

My dear Dr. Du Bois:

We are planning to publish a report on Haiti within the next several months, similar to our reports on Porto Rico and Cuba. I am writing to inquire if you have any sources of information which have kept you up with the situation in Haiti, and whether you have any definite proposals as to what the next step in Haiti should be. I should certainly welcome any information, and especially any suggestions as to people who have recently visited the island.

With best wishes, I am

> Sincerely yours,
> Raymond L. Buell

May 28, 1929

My dear Mr. Buell:

There are two persons who have been in close touch with Haiti, whom I think you ought to consult. One is Ulysses G. Bassett, 1505-12th Street, N. W., Washington, D. C. His father [Ebenezer D.] was United States Minister to Haiti, and he has since kept in touch with the best class of Haitians. He receives a good many confidential documents, and has much information. The second person is Napoleon B. Marshall, 229 West 135th Street, N. Y. You probably know him. Harding started to appoint him United States Minister, but finding that the banking interests did not want this, he compromised and sent Marshall to Haiti, as a sort of clerk with indefinite duties. Marshall has stayed there many years and knows much of the inside workings of the American Occupation. He has recently resigned and is now in New York. I feel very strongly and in accord with the conclusions of the report edited by Emily Greene Balch.[1] I think we ought to make a definite promise of withdrawal at a certain time; then we ought to withdraw the marines immediately, and then we ought to send to Haiti civilian helpers in every line of education and social uplift. Especially, we ought to stop the beginning of land monopoly and exploitation and restore to their rightful leadership the educated class of Haiti with every effort to induce them through example and advice to lead a movement for the uplift of the masses.

Very sincerely yours,
W. E. B. Du Bois

Rabindranath Tagore (1861–1941), perhaps the best known of Indian authors, was awarded the Nobel Prize in literature in 1913. He visited the United States in 1916 and again early in 1929; the latter trip he cut short because of the prevailing racism, some of which was aimed directly at him. Through the good offices of Gandhi's friend, Charles F. Andrews, Du Bois was able to get to the poet a letter which does not seem to have survived; ensuing correspondence came first from the poet's private secretary and then from Tagore himself.

July 12, 1929

Dear Sir:

Dr. Tagore has just returned from Canada to Sastraikebar where he finds your

1. *Occupied Haiti* (New York: Writers' Publishing Co., 1927). A committee of six visited Haiti in 1926 and urged the withdrawal of marines and the restoration of full Haitian independence; in addition to Miss Balch, the committee included: Charlotte Atwood, a teacher at Dunbar High School in Washington; Zonia Baber, a retired professor from the University of Chicago; Paul H. Douglas, then a professor at the University of Chicago, representing the Quakers; Mrs. Addie W. Hunton, president of the International Council of Women of the Darker Races; and Mrs. J. Harold Wilson of Pennsylvania, representing the Fellowship of Reconciliation.

letter awaiting him. He is extremely sorry that he could not send you a message earlier, but he hopes that the few lines which he offers to you now may still be some use to you and your friends.

The writing I may add is in the Poet's own hand.

With regards

Yours truly
Amiya C. Chakravartz

What is the great fact of this age? It is that the messenger has knocked at our gate and all the bars have given way. Our doors have burst open. The human races have come out of their enclosures. They have gathered together.

We have been engaged in cultivating each his own individual life, and within the fenced seclusion of our racial tradition. We had neither the wisdom nor the opportunity to harmonize our growth with world tendencies. But there are no longer walls to hide us. We have at length to prove our worth to the whole world, not merely to admiring groups of our own people. We must justify our own existence. We must show, each in our own civilization, that which is universal in the heart of the unique.[1]

Rabindranath Tagore.

In the late 1920s, mounting discontent with the two-party system brought into being a movement resulting in 1929 in the League for Independent Political Action.* Prominent in this effort were John Dewey; James Maurer, president of the Pennsylvania Federation of Labor; Zona Gale, the author; Paul H. Douglas; Howard Y. Williams, a clergyman; Devere Allen; and Du Bois. In the league's formative stages, Allen served as chairman of the executive committee. Devere Allen (1891–1955) was educated at Oberlin. From 1921 to 1933, he was one of the editors of the *World Tomorrow;* he was also an associate editor of the *Nation* in 1931–32. He ran for various political offices in Connecticut, as a Socialist, in the later 1930s. He retained his socialist and anti-war views until the end of his life.

June 24, 1929.

My dear Mr. Allen:

In accordance with the vote of our last meeting, I am proposing for adoption by the League for Independent Political Action the following plank:

To insure democratic control on the broadest basis and with the highest in-

---

1. Tagore's message was published in the *Crisis* 36 (October 1929):333.

* Under the title "A New Party," Du Bois published a positive estimate of the league in the *Crisis* for August 1930 (37:282). There is a rather full page-one story on the league in the *New York Times,* 9 September 1929; see also the letter by Howard Y. Williams in that paper, 17 September 1929, p. 7.

telligence, the right to vote must not be artificially narrowed by consideration of sex, race or color. Today, we are allowing widespread prejudice against Negroes and foreigners to put a premium upon disfranchisement and thus to distort the possibility of making an intelligent appeal to the electorate. When any part of the country without loss of political power, can by law or custom disfranchise a large proportion of its voters, harm is done, not simply to the disfranchised voter, but to all other voters, and the temptation to graft and manipulation, is almost irresistible and difficult to deal with.

In the United States today it has been calculated that in the regular presidential election of 1924, a million voters in the Northwest sent 12 representatives to Congress; a million voters in the Middle West sent 13; a million voters in the Border States sent 14; a million voters in the Southwest sent 18 representatives; and a million voters in the South sent 47 representatives. It does not make any difference what the reasons for such discrepancy are, the fact of such striking inequality makes real democratic government in the United States impossible and makes the chance of success for any third party movement highly improbable. And yet, without the corrective of the Third Party, party government degenerates into plutocracy.

Very sincerely yours,
W. E. B. Du Bois

New York City, July 25, 1929.

Dear Dr. Du Bois:

I should have written you before to acknowledge your plank regarding the disfranchisement of the Negro voter, etc., for the League for Independent Political Action. However, I have been struggling against an accumulation of work which has kept me jumping and only now am I beginning to emerge to the surface.

As I have tentatively worked out our preliminary statement of principles, it has seemed to me wise to boil things down rather crisply and I shall try to incorporate into that statement the essence of your suggestions. Later, there will come a time when we will have room to spread ourselves, in the formulation of a real platform under which to wage a campaign, and there, it seems to me, your two paragraphs would be fine and I am keeping the letter for our committee meeting with that purpose in mind. Of course you will understand that my draft of the statement of principles is only preliminary to a final statement which we will work out in the fall at our first meeting.

By the way, I thought it wise to stiffen our interracial attitude a bit by adding a statement to the effect that we welcomed to membership all those who shared our aims, irrespective of sex, creed, color or previous political affiliation. I feel only shame, personally, that I had paid so little attention to the preliminary work of the L.I.P.A. that I was not able to insist, myself, that we make our position in this issue absolutely clear. If we have to compromise on that for the sake of votes, we might as well go out of business before we start.

While I am writing let me express the hope that you liked the article by Jessie Fauset in our August issue.[1] All of us here thought it excellent. Under separate cover I am sending five copies of that issue. When you have the time, will you, at your convenience, look the article over with care and send me any changes you feel ought to be made before the article is published in book form along with the other biographical sketches in the series? If I could have any corrections any time between now and New Year's, it will be in plenty of time.

Sincerely yours,
Devere Allen

August 5, 1929

My dear Sir:

Answering your letter of July 25th, let me first thank you very much for the article in "The World Tomorrow," I shall try to live up to it.

With regard to the plank on disfranchisement of Negro voters: You can not condense it too much to suit me. You can say with my approval:

The disenfranchisement of the American Negro, especially in the southern states, not only hurts him but threatens the very foundations of democracy.

I should think it would be well to welcome all people to membership of every creed and color. But, that will be useless so far as the colored people are concerned unless you make a clear definite statement about disfranchisement.

Very sincerely yours,
W. E. B. Du Bois

[undated]

Dear Friend:[2]

At the meeting of the Executive and National Committees of the L.I.P.A., I was asked to revise the general statement of purpose in the light of suggestions made at the meeting and others to be sent to me subsequently by certain individuals.

You are asked to examine the attached revision thoughtfully and in as much detail as possible, then to send me your criticisms and further suggestions. Once more I shall revise the statement in view of your comments, and ultimately,

---

1. "'Wings for God's Chillun': The Story of Burghardt Du Bois," published anonymously in the *World Tomorrow* 12 (August 1929):333–36.

2. This was a mimeographed form letter, undated, but sent out around 15 August 1929; enclosed was a three-page statement setting forth the league's functions, its general principles, and its prospect of eventually uniting opponents of the two-party system into a new, nationwide, challenging party, somewhat along the lines of the British Labor party. Number seven of its eight "general principles" was that proposed in the Du Bois letter dated 24 June 1929.

this second revision will be worked over by the Executive Committee and submitted to the National Committee.

While you are writing, will you kindly also send the name of anyone who might make a good Treasurer for the L.I.P.A.?

Finally, may I urge upon you the great value of having your personal reaction to the statement?

Sincerely,
Devere Allen

August 21, 1929

My dear Sir:

I have received your circular on the League for Independent Political Action. It has my complete adherence.

Very sincerely yours,
W. E. B. Du Bois

Clarence Darrow (1857–1938) was the most famous American lawyer of his time; he was the defense attorney for Eugene V. Debs in the 1890s; for "Big Bill" Haywood early in the twentieth century; for Scopes in the "Monkey" trial in Tennessee; in the Sweet case in Detroit and in the Leopold-Loeb murder case in Chicago in the 1920s. His association with the NAACP was long standing. In the fall of 1929, Du Bois asked him to contribute his opinions on organized religion to the *Crisis*.*

October 8, 1929

My dear Du Bois:

I suppose you might as well go at the question of religion. I imagine that the preachers do nothing of any consequence for our organization and probably never will. They and their churches are a terrible load on the poor workers. Of course sooner or later the preachers will be shaken off but it is a hard job. I am going west for about two weeks. I will try to figure out something for you on my journey.

With best wishes always

Your friend
Clarence Darrow

The *New York Times* (17 November 1929, p. 21) reported that President Hoover had approved the appointment of twenty-two members of an Advisory Committee on National Illiteracy, to be chaired by the secretary of the interior, Ray Lyman Wilbur (1875–1949); twenty-one names were listed, all white. Du Bois wrote the federal Bureau of Education requesting explanation. In re-

---

* Clarence Darrow, "The Religion of the Negro," *Crisis* 38 (June 1931):190.

sponse came a letter from William John Cooper, commissioner of the bureau; Du Bois replied on 18 December. The secretary of the advisory committee wrote Du Bois that same day, and the next day, Dr. Wilbur himself did so; the day after that, Cooper again wrote Du Bois. Du Bois commented on this somewhat frantic letter-writing in a letter to Mrs. Florence Kelley (1859–1932), secretary of the Educational Committee of the NAACP when Du Bois was its chairman, and general secretary of the National Consumers' League. She was the original translator of Engels's *Condition of the Working Class in England*.

Washington, December 4, 1929

My dear Mr. Du Bois:

Your letter of November 29 to Doctor Barnard has been forwarded to this office.

The conference called by the Secretary of the Interior on Saturday next consists very largely of individuals who have been engaged in illiteracy crusades more or less as a private venture. Doubtless all aspects of the problem will be brought out in the discussions with this group. It will be possible also for this office to learn what aspects of the problem are now adequately cared for and what aspects of it are of little or no interest to already existing agencies.

The Secretary's future action will doubtless grow out of what he learns next Saturday and I can assure you that should a program go forward under his direction all interested groups will be consulted.

Very truly yours,
Wm. John Cooper

December 18, 1929

My dear Sir:

Referring to your letter of December 4, you say "the Conference called by the Secretary of the Interior on Saturday next consists very largely of individuals who have been engaged in illiteracy crusades more or less as a private venture." Will you permit me to say by way of commentary that if there are any people in the United States who have been more consistently and continuously, both as individuals and as a group, engaged in "illiteracy crusades" than American Negroes, I should be very much interested to know their names and race. It seems to me little less than outrageous that a Conference on illiteracy will omit representatives of the most illiterate group in the United States; the group for whom illiteracy was for two centuries compulsory, and a group which by its own efforts, as well as the efforts of friends, has done more to reduce its illiteracy than any similar group in the world in the same length of time.

I trust you will permit me to say that this seems to me a most inauspicious beginning of your leadership of the Bureau of Education.

Very sincerely yours,
W. E. B. Du Bois

Washington, December 18, 1929

My dear Mr. Du Bois:

Your inquiry of November 29 as to whether there are any negro members of the Advisory Committee on National Illiteracy which has been appointed by Secretary Wilbur with the approval of President Hoover, has been referred to me as secretary of this committee.

Unfortunately the newspapers did not publish complete lists of the members. Dr. Benjamin F. Hubert, President of the Georgia Industrial College, Savannah, Ga., is also a member of this committee.

We thank you very much for the interest you have shown and hope we may count on your cooperation in this worthy endeavor.

Sincerely yours,
Rufus W. Weaver

Washington, December 19, 1929

Dear Mr. Du Bois:

Your recent letter enclosing copy of one to Commissioner Cooper, has just reached me. At the first meeting of the Executive Committee of the National Advisory Committee on Illiteracy, I, as chairman, was empowered to send an invitation to Mr. Benjamin F. Hubert, President, Georgia State Industrial College, Savannah, Georgia, who, from all that we hear, will be a capable representative. So far, I have not yet received Mr. Hubert's acceptance. Thank you for writing me.

Sincerely yours,
Ray Lyman Wilbur

Washington, December 20, 1929

My dear Mr. Du Bois:

Your letter of December 18 was received by me with amazement. I feel that only lack of knowledge on your part of what the present Administration has done and is planning for the advancement of educational opportunities for colored people would have led you to express yourself as you did.

If you are ever in Washington I trust you will call upon us.

Cordially yours,
Wm. John Cooper

December 21, 1929

My dear Mrs. Kelley:

I had hardly received Commissioner Cooper's intelligent answer [dated 4 December 1929], when I saw in the Associated Press dispatch that a colored man named Hubert, the head of the Colored State College at Savannah, Georgia, had been appointed to the Board. I, nevertheless, sent off the enclosed letter [of 18 December 1929] in spite of this information. Apparently, the Hoover Administration never realizes that there are any Negroes in the United States until after they have appointed some Commission.[1]

                        Very sincerely yours,
                        W. E. B. DuBois

Anna J. Cooper, who died in her 106th year in 1964, graduated from Oberlin in 1884 and forty years later, at the age of 66, received a doctorate from the Sorbonne. She taught modern languages and was an administrator in what was then the M Street High School in Washington (later the Dunbar High School); her home was for generations a center of learning and culture.

No reply to this letter from her to Du Bois seems to have survived; his true answer was the monumental study *Black Reconstruction*, published less than six years after this letter was received.

                        Washington, December 31, 1929

My dear Doctor Du Bois:

It seems to me that the *Tragic Era* should be answered [2]—adequately, fully, ably, finally & again it seems to me *Thou* art the Man! Take it up seriously thro the Crisis & let us buy up 10,000 copies to be distributed broadcast thro the land.

Will you do it?

Answer.

                        Faithfully,
                        Anna J. Cooper

1. The commission faded away after a report in the *New York Times* (27 January 1930, p. 3) that a campaign to reduce illiteracy was to begin in about two weeks.

2. Claude G. Bowers, *The Tragic Era: The Revolution After Lincoln* (Boston: Houghton Mifflin Co., 1929), was a Literary Guild selection and was reprinted in 1930 in a popular edition by Blue Ribbon Books; it is still in print in cloth and paper. It is a kind of "scholarly" version of *The Birth of a Nation* and is among the works specifically and effectively attacked in Du Bois's *Black Reconstruction*.

NATIONAL AND

INTERNATIONAL LEADER

THE DEPRESSION AND RESIGNATION

FROM THE NAACP

1930–1934

IN THE late 1920s, Du Bois and the NAACP as a whole were actively opposing United States interventionist and colonialist activities in Haiti and Cuba. Mrs. Lillian A. Alexander, of Harlem, an ardent supporter of the NAACP and a close friend of Du Bois, asked him to speak in this connection to a group of friends at her home. Du Bois agreed; Mrs. Alexander apparently also raised questions about an idea Du Bois had for a people's college, and this matter is also briefly mentioned in his letter.

January 10, 1930

My dear Mrs. Alexander:

I think I can get to your home January 18 and talk very sketchily about Haiti and Cuba. With regard to the Peoples' College that I have in mind, it will, of course, be opened to students of every color and race. At the same time, its object would be to realize democracy in the United States by the education of human beings in liberal lines, but I am proposing to do the educating, with such help that I can get, and there is not much chance that many white students would apply. If they did, they would be welcomed just as white persons with the proper point of view would be welcomed on the faculty.

Very sincerely yours,
W. E. B. Du Bois

While a student at Lincoln University in Pennsylvania, the future founding president of the Republic of Nigeria had his first article published in the *Crisis* 37 (May 1930):164, 178. It was entitled "Murdering Women in Nigeria" and was occasioned by the slaughter of about thirty women in Opobo who were among thousands protesting a new British tax policy. In submitting his article, Azikiwe wrote to Du Bois.

Lincoln University, January 16, 1930

Dear Dr. Du Bois:

Apropos to the recent massacre of Opobo women by British commanded soldiers, I am submitting the attached article on this brutality for consideration in the Crisis.

It is not news in that part of the world when defenceless women are shot down by whites. Of course if white women are shot down by African natives, the entire British Navy would be on the scene.

The African native is being educated to the machine gun methods of Western culture and within few decades he will prove equal to the task.

                        Very sincerely yours,
                        Ben N. Azikiwe

Du Bois's struggle against discrimination was unending and was conducted privately as well as publicly. In the late 1920s, he set himself the task of helping break down the discriminatory character of library employment in New York City; by the early years of the next decade, a beginning had been made. Part of the effort is recorded in Du Bois's letter to Ferdinand Q. Morton (1882–1949). Morton, after studying at Harvard, received his law degree from Boston University and was in 1910 admitted to the New York bar. In 1915, the Tammany boss, Charles F. Murphy, designated Morton as the leader of the "United Colored Democracy," in acknowledgment of the growing political significance of the Black voter in Harlem. From 1916 to 1922, Morton was an assistant district attorney for New York county; in 1922, he was appointed first Afro-American member of the New York Municipal Civil Service Commission (of which he was elected president in 1946). He was a close and enduring friend of Du Bois and was one of Du Bois's sources of political influence.

                    February 18, 1930

(Personal)

My dear Morton:

Before the smoke of the battle of Harlem Hospital has cleared away (and I hasten to congratulate you upon it)[1] I want to bring another matter to your attention which has been simmering a long time, and that is the matter of Negroes in the service of the New York Public Library. I presume you know the main facts.

For a long time no Negroes were admitted at all and the library branches, even in colored districts, paid just as little attention as possible to the colored constituency. Then, a few colored Assistants were appointed but their promotion has been very slow.

Mrs. Regina Andrews entered the system several years ago, coming from

---

[1]. It had taken a struggle of many years to accomplish the appointment of Black physicians as interns and residents at Harlem Hospital. The distinguished physician and surgeon Dr. Louis T. Wright, a close friend of Du Bois, was appointed as a physician for the female outpatient department of Harlem Hospital in 1919 and, in 1921, for the male outpatient department. Some years later, he was appointed "provisional adjunct surgeon" and, in 1926, "permanent adjunct surgeon." By 1929, in at least a formal sense, the non-Black character of professional staffing at Harlem Hospital was overcome.

library work in Chicago. According to the statement of Mr. Franklin F. Hopper, Chief of the Circulation Department, her record has been excellent and he was "sorry" for the delay in her promotion and did not blame her for being "impatient." He assured me that the promotion of many candidates had been just as slow, but this, I believe, is the case only with candidates who have not done their work or passed their tests. Mrs. Andrews has done her work well, and yet she has had to fight every inch of the way. She has continually been doing, as she is now, the work of a higher grade, while being paid for a lower grade. She has been promised promotion repeatedly and the promises just as repeatedly broken. The objection to her promotion comes from white branch librarians, and also, I have been told, from a certain Trustee, Mr. Anderson, with offices at the 42nd Street Library.

At any rate, this is the present situation. For several months, Mrs. Andrews has been eligible for appointment as First Assistant Librarian. After much hesitation and dilly-dalling, Miss [Ernestine] Rose of the 135th Street Branch recommended her without promising to receive her as her own Assistant. However, the Librarian of the 115th Street Branch not only recommended Mrs. Andrews, but expressed her willingness and desire to have her as Assistant there. After much delay and hesitation, it was proposed that Mrs. Andrews be made a Second First Assistant at the 135th Street Branch, which meant that she would do the First Assistant's work, without having the grade or without occupying a position for which there was any precedent. She was finally certified as eligible to be First Assistant but still the appointment has not come. There has been, I am told, a vacancy in the 124th Street Branch of the Library, which is near or in a Negro district, but it is said that the Librarian there refused to have a colored Assistant, and a girl was appointed First Assistant who had not passed her test. Meantime, Mrs. Andrews is doing the work of First Assistant at the 135th Street Library, but not receiving the pay, and the only explanation that I can see is that the Library does not wish to appoint a Jew as Branch Librarian, or a colored woman as First Assistant Librarian. The First Assistant at the 135th Street Branch is waiting for an appointment as Librarian, but her thesis, I am told, has been mysteriously mislaid, and her appointment is held up. Only once, I believe, in the history of the present Public Library has a Jew been appointed Branch Librarian.

It seems to me that it is high time for an investigation into this situation to be made with the purpose of bringing the appointment of a library staff under the Civil Service laws of the City of New York. I should like to have you consider this matter and arrange if possible to allow me and others to lay the facts before the Mayor of the city at his convenience. Later, I propose to approach the Aldermen, starting with the Aldermen of Harlem, and finally, it is my plan to give the facts to the public press.

I shall be very glad to hear from you at your convenience.

Very sincerely yours,
W. E. B. Du Bois

[418] Correspondence 1930–1934

One of the forty-nine members of the executive committee of the Socialist party early in 1930 was a printer named Edward P. Clarke. In renewing his subscription to the *Crisis* that year, he added thoughts about the trade-union movement that evoked significant comments in Du Bois's reply.

New York, February 8, 1930

Dear Friend:

Although working but two days a week at the printing business and have to make every penny count, I am sending in my renewal to The Crisis which I have taken for some time.

As a member of Typographical Union #6, I am sorry that the union label no longer appears in The Crisis nor does it adorn any of your printed matter. Knowing your sympathy for the workers, organized and unorganized, I do feel disappointed. Of the many publications I take, yours is one of the few minus the label.

I trust it will reappear in The Crisis. I naturally like to spend my union wages on the products of union labor where possible.

Very truly yours,
Edward P. Clarke.

February 18, 1930

My dear Sir:

I appreciate what you said concerning The Crisis magazine and the Union Label. I regret to say that I have entirely lost faith in the American Federation of Labor and its attitude toward Negroes. For years, I have in The Crisis and on the platform advocated the trade union movement. While I deplored the excluding of Negroes by trade unions, I tried to explain it. The course of [William] Green, however, is indefensible, and until the trade-union movement stands heartily and unequivocally at the side of the Negro workers, I am through with it. I know that this attitude is unfair to some unions which do admit the Negro, but the attitude of most unions is such that I think I am justified. We print The Crisis in a union shop, but it is almost impossible to get a black man into the Typographical Union; a few have been admitted but a very few.

I trust you will understand this frank expression of opinion.

Very sincerely yours,
W. E. B. Du Bois

Early in 1930, the League for Independent Political Action published in New York City a pamphlet by Professor Paul H. Douglas of the University of Chicago, entitled *Why A Political Realignment?* In 1929 correspondence with Devere Allen of that league, Du Bois had voiced the need for the sharpest attention to the disfranchisement of the Black voter and he had, apparently, convinced the leadership of the league. Yet the pamphlet by Professor Douglas ignored the question—again; and again Du Bois wrote about it; Douglas replied with the lame response published below.

February 21, 1930

My dear Mr. Douglas:

I have just been looking over your pamphlet "Why a Political Realignment?" published by the League for Independent Political Action. I have the same criticism with regard to it that I voiced in the meeting of the Executive Committee at the International House last spring. Namely: nowhere in this pamphlet, and more particularly in the program for the new party, is any mention made of political rights for Negroes or for other disfranchised classes. When I mentioned this before, I think you said that in the former statements the matter had simply been forgotten. I am wondering what the difficulty is now [since] in the alignment of parties I find absolutely no reference to the South. Yet, with the South as the center of a new industrialism, and with the rotten borough vote system there, I can not see how that situation can be ignored.

I shall be glad to know from you just what your attitude is on this matter. The tendency to forget or ignore the place of the Negro in American democracy puts me in an extraordinarily difficult position.

Very sincerely yours,
W. E. B. Du Bois

Chicago, Ill., February 28, 1930

My dear Mr. Du Bois

I quite agree with you in the tone of your letter and I had not realized that we had omitted the Negro from our program. We declared, you may remember, in the tentative statement of principles that we were opposed to representation which was based upon the disfranchisement of any class in the population. This, we pointed out, applied to the disfranchisement of the Negro in the South and the migratory laborers in the Northwest. I am sure that our group will stand for complete civil rights and adequate economic protection for the Negro by every proper means. All this is certainly stated in the tentative leaflet on principles issued by the League in, I believe, November, and while explicit recognition of it may be missing in my pamphlet (although I called attention to the rottenness of the Democratic machine in the South) that does not mean that we do not have the issue at heart. It is not necessary to stress every issue all the time!

Faithfully yours,
Paul H. Douglas

Rayford W. Logan (b. 1897)—for many years chairman of the history department at Howard University and now professor emeritus there—was early in his distinguished career a teacher at Virginia Union University. From there he wrote to Du Bois about the persistent effort to make uniform the capitalization of the word "Negro."

Richmond, Virginia, March 3, 1930

Dear Dr. Du Bois:

I was very happy to see your statement in the current issue of The Crisis concerning the policy of certain publishers in refusing to capitalize Negro.[1] There was, however, one notable error which I hope you will see fit to correct. Unless the Macmillan Company has recently changed its policy, it uses the form negro. In your review of [Raymond L.] Buell's *Native Problem in Africa* you will recall that you criticized him for spelling negro. That book was published by Macmillan and I felt at the time that it was the company rather than the writer who should have been attacked. On page 784 of [Carlton J. H.] Hayes, *Political and Social History of Europe*, Vol. II, published by Macmillan I find, e.g., "Russians, Koreans, negroes, Jews, Irishmen, Abyssinians, etc." Incidentally, the Foreign Policy Association immediately began spelling Negro as soon as I wrote them about it. You undoubtedly observed this in Dr. Buell's bulletin on *The American Occupation of Haiti*. Why not suggest in an early issue that all colored teachers in colleges and universities agree not to buy from publishers who refuse to capitalize Negro?

Very sincerely yours,
Rayford W. Logan

Early in 1930, the trustees of Howard University voted to bestow an honorary doctorate upon Du Bois. In announcing the decision to him, the new president, Mordecai Johnson, suggested that Du Bois deliver the commencement address on 6 June of that year; Du Bois accepted, in a letter that illuminates his thinking at a moment of deepening economic depression.

March 4, 1930

My dear President Johnson:

I have been thinking over the subject of a possible Commencement oration at Howard University. I suggest this subject:

"Education and Work."[2] My thesis would be: "How can the higher training of the Negro professional be so arranged as to settle his present economic difficulties?"

It has been assumed in the past by many thoughtful people that college and university training was an attempt to divorce its recipients from the necessary

---

1. The reference is to the editorial "The Courtesy List," *Crisis* 37 (March 1930):102.
2. See Du Bois's "Education and Work," *Crisis* 37 (August 1930):280. The address itself was published in Howard University *Bulletin* 9 (January 1931):17–20.

work of earning a living and to make them particularly despise manual toil. Repeated attempts have been made within and without the race to so change the contents and object of education as to produce trained workers. On the other hand, the defenders of higher training have insisted that while it was not the object of our education to make men carpenters, it was the object of all true education to make carpenters men, and that the vocations of educated people as captains, leaders, human beings, as well as workers, called for an education that transcended and went far beyond technical training for manual labor. It must be confessed that both sides of this controversy have had a degree of failure. Industrial education has not produced any great number of farmers and artisans among American Negroes, and, on the other hand, college training is sending a disproportionate number of our trained men into the learned professions, and into the white-collar proletariat. The time has come, therefore, for us to orient ourselves concerning the future problem of Negro education, and this task is not simply a Negro problem, it is a problem world-wide and has to do with the whole problem of work and income in the modern world. There is the psychological problem of making all necessary work honorable, whether it be digging ditches or defending law cases. The practical way of accomplishing this is through great equality of income. So long as a lawyer is paid $100,000 a year and a maid servant $1,000 a year, it is idle to talk about the equality of their service. On the other hand, in a world where manual and mental work are distributed among all men, we will have manual workers who are intelligent thinkers, and leaders of thought who get helpful exercise out of artificial sports. And when we have this, there will follow a far greater equality of income.

Next, there is the physical and technical problem of doing the world's necessary work competently with trained and intelligent workers, and with not the greatest but with little expenditure of human toil and discomfort. Out of this arrangement, there should come a larger and larger surplus of time for all human beings, which they could devote to art and literature, education, religion and recreation. To make the object of education the training simply for manual labor, and not for these other admittedly higher things, is a curious perversion of the objects of human training. But, on the other hand, to train men for art, literature and thought, and to leave the necessary technicality of manual toil to be done by ignorant people, is to undermine the basis of civilization and to work straight toward caste and slavery.

There is, finally, a human side to the problem. After all, what is the object of life but human happiness and how far can and ought education to increase the sum of this happiness? An institution, like Howard University, is called upon frankly to face and settle these problems for the American Negro, and by that same process for America and for the world.

I will be very glad to have your criticism of this very tentative outline.

Very sincerely yours,
W. E. B. Du Bois

Lady Kathleen (Harvey) Simon was the wife of Lord John A. Simon, who had entered the House of Commons in 1906, served as solicitor general in 1910, and was Asquith's attorney general in 1913. He was home secretary for a time during the First World War; at the time of his wife's letter to Du Bois, he was chairman (1927–1930) of a commission studying aspects of British rule in India. Lady Simon was the author of *Slavery* (London: Hodder & Stroughton, 1929), which dealt with conditions that prevailed in much of the colonial world. Du Bois reviewed it in the *Crisis* 37 (April 1930):129; while finding value in it, he thought it seriously weakened by over-dependence upon, and uncritical acceptance of, British official reports. This correspondence began a friendship that lasted for several years.

Banbury, England, April 22, 1930

Dear Mr. Du Bois:

I have received the copy of The Crisis with your review of my book on Slavery. My only complaint is that you call me an English woman. I am an *Irish woman*. I have travelled up & down this country denouncing England's treatment of my country & helped thereby to get it changed. By law, on account of my marriage I am an English woman but [by] my heart & my nature I am Irish & I shall ever be. I am married to the greatest & finest Englishman & he is really Welsh!! For that reason I am often more reticent than my nature desires.

I have been denounced loudly for my remark, "Let us clean up our own home before criticizing others." Ceylon hates me because I called their child adoption Slavery so while *you* at one side of the world condemn me for being pro British they at the other condemn me for being Anti British.

Dear Mr Du Bois if you knew me you would realize that the call of oppressed humanity comes to me from all quarters. Nature has made of one blood all nations of men & *all* oppressors receive my condemnation. Hong Kong, as well as Ceylon shrieks against me. "Lady Simon has brought our colony into disrepute." I shall do it wherever I find Slavery & under whatever name.

Your review is very clever & I feel very just. No one can know better than you how often we are misunderstood! Anyway, whatever you think of me & my efforts, your efforts move me to admiration & your writings give me perpetual joy! I am visiting the States in August as the Bar Association is inviting us. Where shall I find you to make your acquaintance?

Yours sincerely
(Lady) Kathleen Simon

May 12, 1930

My dear Lady Simon:

I have no doubt at all of the sincerity of your desire to put down the crying wrong of slavery. I do doubt the testimony of the English official class. I shall certainly hope to see you when you come to America in August.

Very sincerely yours,
W. E. B. Du Bois

Du Bois persisted in giving special attention to "bread and butter" where his people were concerned; as the depression continued, his thought and activity in this direction intensified. Illustrative are the letters he wrote in 1930 to T. P. Sylvan, then vice president of the New York Telephone Company, and to the "President or General Manager" of the A & P grocery chain; similar letters went to the Butler and the Reeves grocery chains. The results at this point were only formal replies, but continued effort and altered circumstances were to bring, in time, different results.

May 8, 1930

Mr. T. P. Sylvan
Sir:

I have been a subscriber to a telephone in New York City for twenty years and before that to telephones in other parts of the country for nearly twenty years more. I have never seen or heard of a colored person being employed by any telephone company in America above the grade of common labor, except in a telephone exchange at Boley, Oklahoma. In New York City, I think no person of Negro descent has been so employed. With the increasing interlocking of industry and service, if the Negro is going to pay his way, he must be given decent employment. If he is not given employment, he will swell the ranks of the paupers and criminals.

I write to ask if you will not consider the employment of colored girls in your telephone exchanges and of colored men in the skilled and semi-skilled work of your organization?

Very sincerely yours,
W. E. B. Du Bois

May 10, 1930.

The Great Atlantic and Pacific Tea Company
Attention of President or General Manager
Gentlemen:

It seems to me that it would be in accordance with the dictates of ordinary good business for you to employ at least some colored persons as clerks and managers in your Harlem stores. If retail business is going into the hands of chain stores and chain stores are going to discriminate against the groups of people who are their customers, how are those customers going to earn decent wages which they could spend at your stores? Certainly, their first effort will be to patronize stores in their community which give them employment.

I trust you will change your present policy at your earliest convenience.

Very sincerely yours,
W. E. B. Du Bois

Though the letter answered by Du Bois below has not been found and the references remain obscure, aspects of Du Bois's thinking revealed in the reply warrant its inclusion here. The addressee, the Reverend E. Mdolomba, was during his career in South Africa president of the Cape Africa Congress and secretary-general of the African National Congress.

May 13, 1930

The Reverend E. Mdolomba
P.O. Confimvaba, South Africa
My dear Sir:

I have your letter of April 4th. I am afraid my answer may be too late but I hasten to say that the great note of encouragement in the South African situation is the organization and regular meetings of the natives. Only in this way can you accomplish your freedom. I hope you will speak out frankly and fearlessly. Send the facts concerning your situation to the newspapers of England, America and the Continent. Let the whole truth be known. Do not be too timid or conservative. Remember that if you ask little you will get little. The time has come for the black man in Africa to assert himself to have a voice in his government and to receive a modern education. Above all, he must seek and maintain a place in industry with the wages and safeguards that workingmen today are demanding.

I wish you all success in this meeting.

Very sincerely yours,
W. E. B. Du Bois

One of the worst episodes in the history of racism in the United States was the Hoover administration's order directing that Negro Gold Star Mothers, voyaging to Europe to view the graves of their sons, were to be jim-crowed. William E. King, who corresponded with Du Bois on the matter, was born in Louisiana in 1885 and educated at Howard and at John Marshall Law School in Chicago. He was an assistant corporation counsel for Chicago in 1919 and assistant state's attorney from Cook County in 1923; thereafter, through much of the 1920s and 1930s, he was a member of the Illinois legislature and played an important role in limiting the activity of the KKK in that state.

Chicago, May 9, 1930

Dear Sir:

As a member of the Illinois Legislature, I am contemplating introducing a resolution in the Lower House, memorializing the Secretary of War to countermand the order whereby colored Gold Star Mothers will be sent to Europe on a separate boat. I am therefore asking that you submit to me at your earliest convenience, an expression of your views on the matter, hoping thereby to get material which I may use in the presentation of an argument in favor of such proposed resolution.

I hope you will do this at your very earliest convenience, and oblige,

Yours very truly,
William E. King.

May 13, 1930

My dear Sir:

The segregation based mainly and specifically on race and color which the United States Government carries on is despicable, illogical and uncivilized. To perpetuate it in the case of Gold Star mothers who are visiting great cemeteries where the putrid remains of their dead sons were buried very largely by Negro soldiers, is the last word in this national disgrace.

Very sincerely yours,
W. E. B. Du Bois

Kirby Page (1890–1957), an influential editor and author of the 1920s and 1930s, was a pacifist with socialist leanings. As editor of the *World Tomorrow*, he asked Du Bois in June 1930 to comment on questions of war and war guilt.*

June 24, 1930

My dear Mr. Page:

I think your questionnaire on war guilt is important for two reasons: first; it shows that intelligent human beings change their minds. I know this is true in my case. I knew something of German militarism and greatly feared it. I did not know as much then as I do now about the manipulations of the English and French in international intrigue, and with millions of others I was swept off my feet during the world war by the emotional response of America to what seemed to be a great call to duty. The thing that I did not understand is how easy and inevitable it is for an appeal to blood and force to smash to utter negation any ideal for which it is used. Instead of a war to end war, or a war to save democracy, we found ourselves during and after the war descending to the meanest

---

* See "Symposium on War Responsibility," *World Tomorrow* 13 (October 1930): 399–403.

and most sordid of selfish actions, and we find ourselves today nearer moral bankruptcy than we were in 1914.

I am ashamed of my own lack of foresight, and yet war is so tremendous and terrible a thing that only those who actually experience it can know its real meaning. Even today the camouflage of military glamour is being drawn over the nasty mess again but the gathering of honest and well-founded opinions, such as you have made, must give hope to the future.

Very sincerely yours,
W. E. B. Du Bois

Roy Wilkins, the present executive director of the NAACP, was born in St. Louis in 1901. After graduating from the University of Minnesota, he became managing editor, in 1923, of the *Kansas City Call*, a position he held until 1931. In August of that year, he became assistant secretary of the NAACP, and succeeded Du Bois as editor of the *Crisis* (1934–1949). Early in 1930, Wilkins wrote to Du Bois in reply to his offer of employment with the *Crisis*.

Kansas City, Mo., July 9, 1930

Dear Sir:

I am sorry it is not possible for me to accept definitely at this time your offer of the business managership of The Crisis. As I have stated in previous letters, your offer comes at a time when affairs on this publication are in a state of transition with more than an even chance that, as far as I am concerned, the new order will be much better than the old.

Added to this is the fact that the salary offer of The Crisis, as good as it is considering the magazine's finances and earning power, is some less than I am drawing at present on The Call. When the difference in living conditions and the expenses of moving be considered, it will be seen that a downward difference in salary is of some consequence.

Further than all this, I am here in my special field—news writing and editing. There is no strain here of having at once to learn a new angle to the business, of having to produce revenue or die, of having to adjust oneself to a new environment and new people. Do you see? Could I carry my little specialty under my arm I would ask nothing of any man or any city. Bereft of my tools in a strange city and with the business destiny of a publication on my hesitant shoulders, I would be something like an expert motor launch engineer adrift in a sailboat.

But may I suggest, Dr. DuBois, that whether the magazine secures a business manager at once or not, that especially during this business depression it make an effort only to hold its present circulation, to keep its accounts collected as near as possible to date, to scrutinize new business carefully and tighten up on the old accounts gradually, but effectively; in short, not to lose any money and if possible to accumulate a surplus so that a manager will have some money to begin the promotion program which will be necessary to the securing of more circulation and thereafter of more advertising.

The big advertising agencies will be absolutely deaf to proposals from a class magazine, and especially a Negro class magazine which cannot talk at least 100,000 audited and certified circulation. You can see that 50,000 would command no attention for the average man knows that there are approximately that number of Negro families in the Greater New York area; therefore a magazine claiming a national, even international circulation and having only 50,000 would receive hardly an interview.

Getting circulation costs money and it would be better, in my judgment, for The Crisis to hire a man and call him "assistant business manager," that is, assistant to you in your capacity of business manager, pay him a moderate salary, and lay aside the difference in his salary and that of a good business manager for use as a promotion fund when a good man becomes available. This may not be feasible, but you can be the best judge of that.

I do not know that I shall stay in Kansas City forever. I hope not. But my wife and I will stick it out for another year, at least. We are both employed and we can save against the day when the right chance comes along. I am not unaware of the prestige of a connection with The Crisis and the N.A.A.C.P. and I am grateful to you for considering me as a member of the staff. Of course I have no right to expect that this particular offer will be available then, but in another year, perhaps, I can see more clearly whether the rewards on this paper are going to compensate for the lack of freedom in this city.

Very sincerely yours,
Roy Wilkins

Paul Robeson, born in 1898 in Princeton, New Jersey, graduated from Rutgers, where he was elected a member of Phi Beta Kappa and was an outstanding athlete, and completed Columbia University's school of law in 1923. Soon after, he embarked upon a professional theatrical career, playing the lead in Eugene O'Neill's *Emperor Jones* and conquering the musical world with his remarkable baritone voice. He then triumphed in *Showboat* and in the 1930 London production of *Othello*. It is in connection with that production that Du Bois wrote to Mrs. Paul (Eslanda Goode) Robeson and received her reply.

July 10, 1930

My dear Mrs. Robeson:

I want very much some pictures of your husband for The Crisis. For instance, the enclosed was reproduced in one London paper. There must be some other pictures and pictures of the other actors or a group or a scene? Won't you please let me have some such original photographs for The Crisis?

I need not say how thrilled we are by Mr. Robeson's success.

Very sincerely yours,
W. E. B. Du Bois

London, July 22, 1930

My dear Mr. Du Bois:

Odd that you should have written me when you did. I was just about to write you.

Last week I had tea with Mrs. [Sidney] Ponsonby, and there met the first Ránee of Sarrarek.[1] We had a delightful talk, and I have already seen them both since, and we are beginning to be friends. Both the Ránee and Mrs. Ponsonby asked after you, and told me all about a dinner the Ránee gave for you, where you made them all weep over the conditions of the Negro in America.[2]
They asked me to convey their greetings and good wishes to you.

I know you could not have forgotten the Ránee, but you may have forgotten Mrs. Ponsonby. She is tall and slender, white haired, a great friend of the Queen, and her husband is Equerry to King George. One of her daughters is the present Duchess of Westminster I think. They are all charming, intelligent and delightful people.

Now, as to your letter. I am forwarding you, under separate cover, the pictures you asked for.[3] They are all original and new. When you have finished with them, will you please return them to me, as I need them to keep my files complete.

Paul joins me in sending you greetings. Our small son has been dreadfully ill, and is only now recovering. It was a ghastly business, because he is, of course, the only baby there is—for us.

Very sincerely
Eslanda Goode Robeson

(John Gibbs) St. Clair Drake, the distinguished social anthropologist and professor at Roosevelt and Stanford universities, was born in Virginia in 1911 and received his bachelor's degree from Hampton Institute in 1931, before going on to graduate work and to his career as teacher and author. His first published work appeared in the October 1930 issue of the *Crisis* (37:337); the correspondence below concerns this work.

1. "Sarrarek" is an error for "Sarawak."
2. This dinner was given in connection with Du Bois's participation in the 1911 Universal Races Congress; see this volume I, 173–74.
3. A photograph of Paul Robeson, as Othello, appears in the October 1930 *Crisis* (37:322).

Hampton Institute, Va., Aug. 10, 1930

Dear Sir:

As a senior in the College of Education at Hampton, and a student in the advanced English courses I was very interested in the article by Mr. Arthur P. Davis, for it showed that teachers are meeting the same problems in the liberal arts colleges that Hampton faces in her more or less vocational atmosphere.[1] While Mr. Davis undoubtedly drew upon his experiences as a student and resident of Hampton Institute, I think that the greater part of his experiences has been with [Virginia] Union students. Students of the two schools studied together, and in conjunction with the summer attendants give an excellent cross-section of Negro student types.

Mr. Davis, I realize, was attempting to typify the Negro college student without analyzing him, and such a criticism has its limitations. The judgment was entirely from the standpoint of a well trained graduate of a northern school, who seems to have had but little intimate relationship with individual students.

Much of what he said was absolutely true, and we ourselves often give up in despair at the insincerity of our fellow students. But, through it all we see reasons that are beyond the control of the students themselves and for which they should not be blamed. If it were a case of sheer laziness and indolence we should attempt no explanation, but the Negro student is caught in an endless chain of circumstances that can only be broken by patient endeavor on the part of Northern Negroes and a superhuman effort on the part of their southern brothers. We don't want sympathy, but we want understanding. We want the best; we want it thrown around us everywhere and we will respond. Someday there may be a grand mutation in this evolutionary scheme, and if not, the species will gradually vary. Either method will take time.

I have briefly recorded a few of my observations and a general view of my impressions. If it is of sufficient merit I submit it for publication.

I am enclosing the return postage.

Sincerely yours,
J. G. St. Clair Drake.

August 14, 1930

My dear Mr. Drake:

I shall be glad to use in The Crisis a part of the article in answer to Mr. Davis which you sent us.

Very sincerely yours,
W. E. B. Du Bois

Tension in the relationship between Du Bois and other leaders of the NAACP appeared early and never disappeared. With the continuation of the depression,

1. Arthur P. Davis, "The Negro College Student," *Crisis* 37 (August 1930):270-71.

however, the relationship grew even more strained, basically because Du Bois's interests in economic and mass activity within the United States, and his growing concern with thwarting colonialism abroad, were counter to the legalistic and rather provincial orientation of most board members. There were also subjective reasons—personality clashes with Villard, White, and Ovington, for example—but these were not at the root of the dissensions which culminated in Du Bois's resignation from the NAACP in 1934. A 1930 exchange between Miss Ovington and Du Bois is to be read in this context.

New York City, December 20, 1930

Dear Dr. Du Bois:

Since our talk of yesterday I have thought a great deal about the situation at the office as it is and as it is likely to be, and I have wondered whether you could ever again occupy the position that you have held. What controversies there may have been in the past have been around the matter of your personal liberty in handling the magazine. We have had many a bout on that matter in old times and generally you won. But when you won the Crisis was more important than the Association. In the early days the magazine amounted to more than the organization.

As time has gone on the organization has become increasingly important, and the Crisis less important, not just in relation to the Association but in relation to the Negro world. It is not unique as it once was. Much of its news is of the character of the news carried by the weekly papers. It is doing a useful, interesting work, but it is not as essential to Negro progress and to radical Negro thought as it once was.

Since that is the case, the magazine is bound increasingly to become an adjunct to the Association rather than an important magazine of itself. Only if it had a large gift of money, such capital as a white weekly would have, could it expect to have its old prestige. Such an endowment does not seem to be anywhere on the horizon.

If I am right in this, I cannot but think that, whoever may be secretary, the Crisis will not give you the position that you have formerly held. You will have less and less control of it and it cannot belong to you as it has in the past. You won't enjoy it in the way you have.

What I am writing now is entirely my own suggestion, one on which I have no one else's opinion. It is quite confidential. Would you wish to be a member of the staff with the rest, doing two definite things? Writing occasionally or regularly for the Crisis, and lecturing at stated times for the N.A.A.C.P.? Such a position to carry with it a salary on the basis of the amount of work done, a definite sum for each lecture and for each piece of writing? This would be a part-time job and would pay less than now, but it would not be likely to clash with other executives and it would bring you before our branches more than has been the case for some years.

This is just something I have thought of since we talked together. It looks to me as though the Crisis would either disappear or become distinctly an N.A.A.C.P. organ, and that means it must be under the secretary. I am not speaking of the immediate future but of what I see a year or so ahead.

If there is anything at all in this, we can have a talk together. If not, just tear the letter up. I am not making a copy. It is meant for you alone.

Very sincerely,
Mary W. Ovington

December 24, 1930

My dear Miss Ovington:

I have your letter and appreciate its intent. Nevertheless, I hasten to say that I would not be at all interested in the work which you outline nor would I consider it for a moment if it were offered me.

Either The Crisis is necessary to the work of the N.A.A.C.P. or it is not.

If it is not, I should be given the opportunity of conducting it independent of the Association. If it is necessary, then I have earned the right to conduct it under just and reasonable control.

I will consider no other proposition nor will I work with the N.A.A.C.P. under any other conditions.

Very sincerely yours,
W. E. B. Du Bois

That there were differences of opinion within top levels of the NAACP became an open secret by the latter part of 1930. In 1929, Moorfield Storey died and the presidency was assumed the next year by Joel E. Spingarn; at the same time, James Weldon Johnson decided to accept a professorship at Fisk University and he was succeeded as executive secretary by Walter White in 1931. These actual and pending events induced a late-1930 exchange between Robert L. Vann, owner and editor of the powerful *Pittsburgh Courier*, and Du Bois.

Pittsburgh, Pa., December 26, 1930

My Dear Doctor:

The contents of this letter may mean absolutely nothing, but I am prompted to write because of a telegram which has just come to my notice.

Telegraphic opinion brings the report that there is dissension among the officers of the N.A.A.C.P., because of the recent election to the presidency of Mr. Spingarn, a white man. This telegram appearing in a newspaper would be a happy morsel for Negroes who delight in disorganization; and before I go to press with it, I want to hear from you at length, if possible, on this whole matter. Our information is that Mr. Johnson is to take a chair of history at some southern school; that Mr. White is to be made executive secretary, and that other resignations are in the offing, etc., all tending to show that the officers of the association have reached a disagreement.

The Pittsburgh Courier has supported the N.A.A.C.P., without stint, and with the exception of the unpleasantness which occurred a few years ago, the attitude of this writer toward the association has been favorable and persistently so.

My personal feelings, however, are frequently in conflict with editorial policy, and very frequently I destroy my personal feelings entirely in order to preserve a healthy editorial policy. As to the presidency of the association, it seems to me to be most unfortunate that a white man had to be elected. You may say that the first president was a white man, and I will answer you that this is no reason in the world why all the other presidents should be white men. You have preached Negro leadership and I have been guilty of the very same thing, and it certainly does appear inconsistent for us to preach Negro leadership one day and elect white leadership the next. In other words, how can we expect Negroes ever to learn to follow Negro leadership if Du Bois is going to follow white leadership? Personally, I think the election of a white president will destroy some of the confidence we have labored to build up, because by so doing you have said to the Negroes of the country, in so many words, "We are not able to lead ourselves."

I appreciate certain circumstances surrounding the organization. I appreciate the financial help Mr. Spingarn has been to the association, but I can't appreciate his desire to be president as a reward for his financial help. Personally, I like the man; I like his attitude; but in dealing with cold facts, you must admit that the Christian world as we know it does not react too favorably to non-Christian leadership. Of course Mr. Spingarn cannot help that he is a Jew, but his leadership will offer all the excuse certain white elements desire to justify their withdrawal of moral and financial support.

I hope you will write me fully and set me right because I do not want to give the public any impressions that will retard the progress of the association, but I cannot swallow my own convictions on Negro leadership when it comes to editorial comment. We are either right in trying to assert Negro leadership or we are wrong. We cannot be both.

If you will be kind enough to give me your observations on this whole matter before we go to press next Tuesday, I shall be very happy to receive them.

Yours very truly,
R. L. Vann

December 29, 1930.

My dear Mr. Vann:

There has been in the N.A.A.C.P. absolutely no dissension or difference of opinion over the election of Mr. J. E. Spingarn as President. This is because the office of President is a purely honorary position. His only duty is, if he so wishes, to preside at the annual mass meeting. The real executive power of the Association is vested in the Executive Secretary and the Chairman of the Board. Both Mr. Johnson and myself were heartily in favor of Mr. Spingarn's election. The resignation of Mr. Johnson had nothing to do with this election. His health last year did not permit him to keep up his work and he was given a year's leave of absence without pay. He has decided now to devote himself to literary work and he will probably lecture for a term or more at some Southern college.

The above is an exact statement of the facts. At the same time, there are many questions concerning the future of the Association that are under consideration, and sometime when you are in the city, I shall be glad indeed to go over the situation.

Very sincerely yours,
W. E. B. Du Bois

Du Bois remained interested in the idea of a people's college—a concept he no doubt related to that of a college to be owned and conducted by Black people, as discussed in earlier correspondence with Abram L. Harris. Early in 1931, he wrote to Soren A. Mathiasen, director of both the Pocono People's College in Pennsylvania and the Pocono Study Tours in New York City. Only Mathiasen's reply is extant.

New York, N.Y., January 6, 1931

My dear Dr. Du Bois:

I was exceedingly interested in your letter of January 2nd regarding your ideas of the value of the people's college for the American Negro. I am sending a little booklet about Pocono People's College under separate cover. We found at Pocono that one isolated experiment could with difficulty withstand the many attacks from powerful conservative forces. Dr. [John] Dewey formed a group that has been working for a year or more on a plan to form a group of people's colleges which united would be strong enough to withstand the opposition.[1]

1. An American People's College was organized also in Europe, at Oetz-in-Tyrol, in 1930. Soren A. Mathiasen was its director, and its advisory committee included John Dewey, George S. Counts, Harry A. Overstreet, and Robert S. Lovett. At the same time there appeared, quite independently, an International People's College at Elsinore, Denmark, and on its United States committee were Jane Addams and Eduard C. Lindemann. Both colleges were not only international, but also interracial, with Black and white Americans participating. Contemporary descriptions may be found in *Progressive Education* 11 (April–May 1934):307-10; *Journal of Adult Education* 5 (April 1933):174-76; and *School and Society* 37 (28 January 1933):115-16. After Du Bois returned to Atlanta University, it began to operate (in 1942) what was called a people's college, where tuition was free, teachers were not paid, and there were no scholastic requirements or examinations. Over four hundred working people of the community participated. Du Bois was decisive in this effort. See *Journal of Negro Education* 14 (Summer 1945):308.

In view of this experience it interested me particularly that you were thinking in terms of several. I will send you a "Presentation for a Chain of Peoples Colleges" which is the result of some months work on the part of Dr. Dewey's committee.

I hope you will start an experiment along this line yourself. I should do everything in my power to assist you. Please feel free to command my services.

Sincerely yours,
S. A. Mathiasen

Quite common were letters to Du Bois from aspiring students asking for help in one form or another. Early in 1931, a Harvard student named Robert C. Weaver—who was to be, from 1966 to 1968, the first Black cabinet member and, in 1969–70, president of Bernard Baruch College in New York City—wrote such a letter.

Cambridge, Mass., January 29, 1931

Dear Dr. Du Bois:

I doubt if you remember all of those who took part in your daughter's wedding.[1] If, however, you do recall the ushers, it may be that you can place me. Be that as it may, this letter has little to do with the memory; it is a request for advice.

I am at the present time in the extremely unpleasant stage of my education that befalls all graduate students. I [am] soon to present myself for my general examination for the PhD degree. As you may well deduce from my location, I am at Harvard. My field is Economics. Among the many problems that present themselves at this time that of a thesis subject is, of course, one of the most important. It is in reference to this that I write you.

Since my particular interest is in Labor Problems, and since I am a Negro (and most of my future work will concern Negroes), I plan to work on something in the field of Negro Labor. Indeed, I cannot see how a person interested in the economic life of the Black American could hope to escape treating of the Negro worker. At the present I am considering the possibilities of a study of the present industrial (and perhaps business) education of the Negro in light of his economic opportunities. Such a piece of work would, I believe, involve a consideration of the economic theory of the time and the individuals that produced it. I would like you to express your opinion of the value and the possibilities of the project. In connection to the latter I might say that I shall probably be in the South teaching after this year.

My training up to this point has been as follows: primary and secondary edu-

---

1. In the spring of 1928, Du Bois's daughter Yolande was married to Countee Cullen in New York City at the Salem Baptist Church, whose minister was the groom's father.

cation in Washington Public Schools, B. S., cum laude, Harvard, 1929. At the present time I am a second year graduate student. Not only am I asking you to comment on the subject that I have suggested, but I would appreciate any further suggestions as to a subject that your vast experience in the subject matter may prompt.

I earnestly hope that this request will not take too much of your time, and I trust that my future work will compensate you for any inconvenience.

Sincerely yours,
Robert Weaver.

New York City, February 10, 1931

My dear Mr. Weaver:

I presume you are familiar with Spero and Harris' recent study of "The Negro Worker".[1] I should think your proposed subject would be a very interesting continuation of this line of research. I am sending you herewith a copy of my Howard speech, last Commencement, which touches the subject. I should think that your thesis should confine itself pretty carefully to the theory of Negro industrial education as enunciated from 1894 down to the present day, and that this should be supplemented by a study of the curricula of Negro industrial schools, and finally, a study of results. It is this latter phase where you are going to find your greatest difficulty. What, for instance, are the graduates of Hampton and Tuskegee actually doing? How far have they entered industry by reason of their industrial training? And what industries have they entered? I should think that a thesis along these lines would be of very great interest.[2]

W. E. B. Du Bois

Buell G. Gallagher was born in Illinois in 1904 and educated at Carlton College, Union Theological Seminary, and the London School of Economics. In 1929, he became an ordained Congregationalist minister and in 1930-31 was field secretary of the Interseminary Movement, located in New York City and having on its committee Reinhold Niebuhr, Henry P. Van Dusen, and Jerome Davis. It was as field secretary that he wrote to Du Bois. Later Gallagher was to be president of Talledega College from 1933 to 1943 and president of the City College of New York throughout the 1950s and 1960s. He is today vice-president of the NAACP.

1. Sterling D. Spero and Abram L. Harris, *The Black Worker: The Negro and the Labor Movement* (New York: Columbia University Press, 1931); Weaver's first book was *Negro Labor: A National Problem* (New York: Harcourt, Brace, 1946).

2. Weaver's 1934 Ph.D. thesis at Harvard was "The High Wage Theory of Prosperity"; it has never been published.

New York City, January 30, 1931

Dear Mr. Du Bois:

I am writing to get your help in advising a young white boy as to where he can best invest his next fifteen years in some form of interracial work.

He graduates from theological seminary this spring, having had good college work and having finished his theological work at a high standard. He has an intense interest in interracial matters and wants to put his life where it will count most. Could you give me your best opinion as to what form of work he should undertake and what organizations, if any, he ought to consult before finally locating himself?

It is a matter of supreme importance to this man, and I think his ability is such that if we can help him get located strategically his influence will count greatly in the next two decades.

Yours cordially
Buell G. Gallagher

February 9, 1931.

Mr. Buell G. Gallagher
My dear Sir:

Answering your letter of January 30, I must say that I do not know where the young man in question could best pursue his inter-racial work. There is the inter-racial movement centering at Atlanta, and there is inter-racial development of the Federal Churches of Christ in America at New York. Either of these might have some opening for a young worker. The addresses are: 409 Palmer Building, Atlanta, Georgia and 612 United Charities Building, 105 East 22nd Street, N.Y.

I imagine, however, that most of the real inter-racial work is going to be done in the future outside of organizations especially designed for such work. I should think, for instance, that a man with a church in a small town, who could bring into that church white and black, natives and foreigners, employers and employees, would in the end be doing an inter-racial job far beyond any organization. I regret to say, however, with the present attitude of white Christians, I do not anticipate that the young man would find such a job easy.

I am sorry not to be able to give you more specific advice.

Very sincerely yours,
W. E. B. Du Bois

Oliver La Farge (1901–63), anthropologist and novelist, is best known as the author of *Laughing Boy*, which won a Pulitzer Prize in 1929. In the late 1920s, he directed archeological expeditions in Mexico and Guatemala for Tulane University, and in Arizona for Harvard. In 1930 he served as director of the

Eastern Association in Indian Affairs, and in the 1930s and 1940s was a leading official of the American Association on Indian Affairs.* The occasion of this exchange with Du Bois was La Farge's role as a judge for a literary prize to be created and awarded to the author of the best novel on Afro-American life.

New York City, February 10, 1931

Dear Dr. Du Bois:

With some shame at my delay, I send you a revised version of the Law and the Prophets. It is, of course, a document for discussion, not a finished product. I wish you would look it over, cogitate, and then give me an appointment or make some date at your convenience, for us two to talk it over.

As I understand it, Mrs. Mathews wants this prize revocable and changeable. Personally, I think that we should work out a set of rules for publication which will be merely a statement of the manner in which the thing shall work. When we get them to suit, and have our nominating committee made up, is the time to publish them. At that time I think I should write you a chatty little letter telling you a lot of things which you know already to be published with the prize rules—or better still, you should have an informal explanation prepared. However, all that is for discussion.

Things have been an unpleasantly mad whirl recently, and the cool, connected thoughts of solitude and meditation have been sadly missing from my life. I'm getting to the point where, as they say, "I want to get away from it all." Meantime I'm getting so *damn* mad over some of the things that are being done in the course of using the Indian as a political football, that I see little ahead of me save bloody war and lots of it. I am slowly coming to the conclusion that artistically, morally, and spiritually a sensitive man will find a better life in Mexico than here. However, I didn't mean to start pouring out my woes, all I intended was to set forth my alibi for having let so much time pass by. It's in here somewhere.

Wanden hasn't been very well, but is now better, and in good spirits. Please give my best regards to Mrs. DuBois.

Yours sincerely,
Oliver La Farge.

February 13, 1931

My dear Mr. La Farge:

I have your letter of February 10. You need never apologize to me for delays. I sometimes think I am all Delay.

I know you have been having a warm fight in Washington. I hope things have gone well.

---

* See D'Arcy McNickle, *Indian Man: A Life of Oliver La Farge* (Bloomington: Indiana University Press, 1972).

I am returning your set of suggestions with a few possible modifications. My best regards to Mrs. La Farge.

Very sincerely yours,
W. E. B. Du Bois

Edwin R. Embree (1883–1950) had considerable influence in the 1920s and 1930s as president of the Julius Rosenwald Fund. In addition to his educational and administrative work, he wrote several books dealing with aspects of race relations; the first of these was *Brown America: The Story of a New Race*. (New York: Viking Press, 1931). The exchange given here concerns that book, then nearing completion.

Chicago, Illinois, April 25, 1931

My dear Dr. Du Bois:

You will remember that I spoke to you some weeks ago about the book I am working on about the Negro. It is beginning to take fairly definite shape. You were good enough to say that you would help me in such ways as you could. I am enclosing the present suggested table of contents. I should like your comments and opinions about the general scope, and also your frank criticism of one or two of the chapters.

You will remember that my general thesis is that a new race is growing up in America—new, biologically and culturally—and that it has accomplished, at least in part, in a hundred years what many races spent millenniums in achieving. The new race has had the benefit of direct association with a people that have a highly developed material culture, and it has also had the handicaps of bitter discrimination by that people—of being relegated only to certain specified positions in the strategy of western industrial civilization.

The thing I hope to do in the book is to reach a wide circle of reasonably intelligent white readers—to give them some idea of the present position of the Negroes as a whole, their place in the nation, and their contributions both in folk art and folk music and the achievements of an increasing number of individuals. I am appalled as I go about the country to find abysmal ignorance, as well as indifference, on the part of white people who should be taking an intellectual interest in this new race growing up in the nation.

It is essentially to this white audience that I am writing. I want to point out the terrific handicaps of the new race and also its distinctive gifts. I think the danger is likely to be that I will state the case too sympathetically. I think I must make sure that my record is not only fair but that it will appear so to the disinterested reader.

I am particularly anxious to have you read and criticize two chapters: one on discrimination, and the other on public and political influence. The first of these I am enclosing herewith. The second, I hope to have ready, at least in first draft, within a week or two. The discrimination chapter I have entitled "Odds against the Nigger." This seems to me exactly to fit the case. I have used the offensive noun in the title because that is part of the odds. In fact, the connotations that go with "nigger" represent a very large part of the odds. The whole thing is psychological—in so far as it is not economic.

In this chapter, I have only given passing references to disfranchisement, as I have also to health and education, because these subjects are treated extensively in other chapters. I have included the references here simply to make this particular picture complete.

I hope I am not asking too much of you. I want to make the book as effective as possible. To this end, I shall value highly your criticism and suggestions.

      Very truly yours,
      Edwin R. Embree

      May 12, 1931

My dear Mr. Embree:

I am so sorry to have been so long reading your manuscript but as I wrote you before, I was away having my tonsils out when it came. I am returning the chapter which you sent. I like it very much and have very few criticisms.

 1. I suggest that when you entitle the chapter, "Odds Against the Nigger," you put "Nigger" in quotation marks.[1] That will avoid much criticism and be just as effective.

 2. I think possibly you are not quite severe enough upon the Southern aristocrats and a little too severe on the poor whites. I know that your thesis is a popular one but it always seems to me that the aristocracy of a group is much more responsible for the delinquencies of the mob than they are willing to admit. The mob often does vicariously that which the aristocrats want done but do not soil their hands with.

 3. In the matter of Negro crime, I have usually made the same statements that you are making. But the reading of one article has led me lately to modify that. Please glance at the book "The American Negro," published by the American Academy of Political and Social Science, November, 1928. It has on Page 52 a note on the Negro criminal by Sellin which is illuminating.[2]

---

 1. This suggestion was not adopted by Embree in the first edition; however, in 1943, Embree published, through Viking, a substantially revised edition entitled *Brown Americans: The Story of a Tenth of the Nation*, and there followed Du Bois's advice.

 2. Thorstein Sellin, "The Negro Criminal: A Statistical Note," in *The American Negro*, ed. Donald Young (Philadelphia: American Academy of Political and Social Science, *Annals* 140, 1928), pp. 52–64. Sellin's point was "to indicate some of the ways by which the differential treatment to which the Negro is subjected by our agencies of criminal justice artificially increases his *apparent* criminality," as contrasted with the white, so that "comparisons between the two become exceedingly hazardous. . . ." Embree did not refer to this source.

I should be glad to read the other chapter promptly when you send it to me.
                              Very sincerely yours,
                              W. E. B. Du Bois

Early in 1931, Du Bois, as editor of the *Crisis*, wrote to several United States senators asking their views on the political role and future of the Afro-American people; while senators Pat Harrison of Mississippi, Robert La Follette of Wisconsin, and Dwight Morrow of New Jersey did not respond, some others did. One, Simeon D. Fess (1861–1936) of Ohio, had been a president of Antioch College, a member of the House from 1913 to 1923, and after 1923 a senator. Fess was, at the time of Du Bois's query, chairman of the National Committee of the Republican Party. George W. Norris of Nebraska, a leading figure among "progressive" Republicans and at this time chairman of the Judiciary Committee of the Senate, was another respondent. Parts of their replies were published in the September 1931 *Crisis* (38:297–98), where Du Bois changed nothing except the word "negro," which he rendered with a capital *N*. The letters of Fess and Norris are given below.

                              Washington, May 23, 1931

My dear Mr. Du Bois:
  Complying with your request for a statement concerning the future of the negro in politics, I am submitting the following:

> The effectiveness of the negro in politics will depend upon his adherence to the fundamental principles of the government, in which he has not only become a prominent part as a citizen, but has, through a wise leadership, been given a voice at the ballot box.
>
> Thus far he has represented a fine type of stability, unresponsive to radical proposals which would ultimately undermine American institutions. By this course he is rendering not only a great service to the nation at large, but is serving his own best interests.

                              Yours very truly,
                              Simeon D. Fess

                              McCook, Nebraska, May 26, 1931

Dear Mr. Du Bois:
  Your letter of May sixteenth, directed to me at Washington, has been forwarded and has reached me here at McCook, Nebraska, my home.
  In your letter you say that you have not been able to find anything I have said or done on the negro question. My record in Congress is an open book and during that time I have always done what seemed to me to be just and proper on every occasion where the interest of the colored race was a subject for action

by the National Legislature. I think my record shows I have always had a deep interest in the advancement and the welfare of the colored race.

To my mind, the colored race has made wonderful advancement since its emancipation. A people who were liberated from bondage after years of servitude cannot be expected to at once reach the highest type. It is a question of educational development, sometimes a slow and tedious development. In such cases the danger is that the leaders of a liberated race are misled by various promises made for partisan political purposes by leaders who are not always moved by the highest and the best of motives and I think it has often happened that the colored race has been misled in this way.

The best friend of the colored people, it seems to me, is one who does not try to make of them a political machine or to cause them to exercise the elective franchise through rank partisanship. The best leadership is the leadership which causes them to study and to think, so that action can be had upon deliberate judgment rather than partisan bias. Instead of being led by the politicians who have an ulterior motive, they should be taught control, so far as possible, by honest political convictions and to work out their own advancement through intellectual and political improvement.

Very truly yours,
G. W. Norris

John W. Davis, born in Georgia in 1888 and now living in New Jersey, was president of West Virginia State College from 1919 to 1953. As a member of President Hoover's Organization on Unemployment Relief, he sent a telegram late in 1931 to Du Bois at the *Crisis* office.

Institute, W. Va., Sept. 19, 1931

I beg your cooperation as follows Send me in letter to be received Tuesday September 22 factual information covering first names of national or local organizations operating in your community for any purposes of relief of distress Second indicate the degree of relief needed among Negroes Third state clearly whether or not Negroes experience difficulty in getting aid and relief from local organizations Fourth make suggestions for temporary or permanent relief in connection with Negro unemployment or general unemployment Let your answers to these four propositions be made in a letter of not more than three pages

John W. Davis

New York, N.Y., September 21, 1931

My dear Mr. Davis:

I am not in a position to answer your telegram of September 19 except in a very general way.

1. There are a large number of organizations operating in New York for relieving distress. Negroes are in great need of help. They were displaced from their regular positions early in the depression. Many have gone down to lower grades of jobs and even there find themselves in competition with white workers and very often the white workers are preferred over them for no reason other than color.

2. The difficulty always with Negro labor is that even in prosperous times it is not distributed according to ability or desert and in times of depression some of the best workers find themselves in needless competition with the worst of all races.

3. It is always more difficult for a Negro to prove his social needs than for a white man. If the relief agencies are localized, the Negro sections get things a little later and get a little less and with poorer quality. I do not think the discrimination in New York is nearly as great as it is in many cities but there is discrimination.

4. The United States government ought to make appropriations for relief. There ought to be a national dole distributed without reference to the color line, and wherever there are considerable numbers of Negroes they ought to be represented on the Executive Boards of the distributing agency. In the past, it is well-known that the Red Cross has in some cases discriminated outrageously against Negroes. In other cases, they have not. The difficulty is that the Negro has no adequate representation in the Red Cross organization. They are deliberately kept out on account of color.

Very sincerely yours,
W. E. B. Du Bois

In August 1931, the Black press reported that the Julius Rosenwald Fund had made a grant to Du Bois to help him prepare a history of the Reconstruction period. Alfred Harcourt (1881–1954), who had joined the Henry Holt publishing house in 1904, after his graduation from Columbia, had associated with Du Bois professionally since the 1915 publication, by Holt, of Du Bois's book *The Negro*. In 1919, Harcourt and Donald C. Brace founded Harcourt, Brace & Co.; one of its earliest books was Du Bois's *Darkwater* (1920). Hence, when Harcourt learned of Du Bois's work on Reconstruction, he wrote to Du Bois; the result was the 1935 publication by Harcourt, Brace of Du Bois's *Black Reconstruction: An Essay Toward A History of the Part which Black Folk Played in the Attempt to Reconstruct Democracy in America, 1860–1880*. Though the *American Historical Review* never reviewed the book, the historical profession has never been the same since its appearance.

New York City, September 11, 1931

Dear Dr. Du Bois:

My spies tell me the very interesting news that you are at work on a history of the Reconstruction period. If you have not arranged for the publication of this, I do hope you will discuss the matter with me.

Looking forward to hearing from you, I am

Sincerely yours,
Alfred Harcourt

September 23, 1931

My dear Mr. Harcourt:

I thank you very much for your letter of September 11. I am, as you have heard, attempting a history of "The Black Man in the Reconstruction of Freedom in America, from 1860–1876." My thesis is that the real hero and center of human interest in this period is the slave who is being emancipated, and that forgetting this most writers of reconstruction have thought of the influence of war and emancipation on the white business men of the South and the Southern slave holders, and that what the Negro did and what the Negro thought has been glossed over and forgotten.

I am going, therefore, to write a history from this point of view and then to that I am going to add next year as a second volume "The Black Man in the Wounded World"; that is, the part which Negro troops took in the World War and its significance for the world today.[1]

I am very glad to know of your interest and I shall be delighted to talk over this work with you at any time that you have leisure.

Very sincerely yours,
W. E. B. Du Bois

New York City, October 6, 1931.

Dear Dr. DuBois:

I have had a little spell of illness, and so have delayed replying to your favor of September 23rd. What you say about your history of "The Black Man in the Reconstruction" promises a really interesting book. I should like to hear more about it at your convenience. I am in the office pretty regularly these days, and I should be glad to see you any time that it would be convenient for you to drop in. You might just telephone in advance to be sure that I am free. If it should, for any reason, be inconvenient for you to come to this part of town, I should be glad to come to see you.

Sincerely yours,
Alfred Harcourt

---

1. Du Bois, in the years immediately after the First World War, worked on a massive study of this subject that was never completed.

New York City, October 22, 1931

Dear Dr. DuBois:
Thanks for your note of the 21st and the outline of the proposed volume.[1]
I have read the outline, and it sounds splendid. It's a book that you probably can do better than anyone else. I look forward to hearing from you next Tuesday.
Sincerely yours,
Alfred Harcourt

In October 1931, Du Bois wrote to Albert Einstein, then in Germany, asking that he send some appropriate message to be published in the *Crisis*. Einstein's response appeared in the February 1932 *Crisis* (39:45), both in German and in an English translation made by Du Bois. In introducing this message, Du Bois noted that Einstein had won the Nobel Prize in physics as well as the Copley Medal in 1895. He added that "Einstein is a genius in higher physics and ranks with Copernicus, Newton and Kepler. . . . But Professor Einstein is not a mere mathematical mind. He is a living being, sympathetic with all human advance. He is a brilliant advocate of disarmament and World Peace and he hates race prejudice because as a Jew he knows what it is."

October 14, 1931

Mr. Albert Einstein
Sir:
I am taking the liberty of sending you herewith some copies of *The Crisis* magazine. *The Crisis* is published by American Negroes and in defense of the citizenship rights of 12 million people descended from the former slaves of this country. We have just reached our 21st birthday. I am writing to ask if in the midst of your busy life you could find time to write us a word about the evil of race prejudice in the world. A short statement from you of 500 to 1,000 words on this subject would help us greatly in our continuing fight for freedom.

With regard to myself, you will find something about me in "Who's Who in America." I was formerly a student of Wagner and Schmoller in the University of Berlin.

I should greatly appreciate word from you.
Very sincerely yours,
W. E. B. Du Bois

Berlin, October 29, 1931

Very honored Sir:
Herewith I send you a short contribution for your publication. Since I am overburdened with work it is not possible for me to send you a fuller statement.
With distinguished respect
A. Einstein

1. The outline forms a substantial manuscript; it is in skeleton form what Du Bois developed in his volume of almost 750 pages.

1 Enclosure

[Du Bois translated the enclosure.]

It seems to be a universal fact that minorities, especially when their individuals are recognizable because of physical differences, are treated by the majorities among whom they live as an inferior class. The tragic part of such a fate, however, lies not only in the automatically realized disadvantages suffered by these minorities in economic and social relations, but also in the fact that those who meet such treatment themselves for the most part acquiesce in this prejudiced estimate because of the suggestive influence of the majority, and come to regard people like themselves as inferior. This second and more important aspect of the evil can be met through closer union and conscious educational enlightenment among the minority, and so an emancipation of the soul of the minority can be attained.

The determined effort of the American Negroes in this direction deserves every recognition and assistance.

Indicative of Du Bois's mounting concern about the impact of the depression upon the Afro-American people was a questionnaire that he mailed in October 1931 to the mayors of several of the leading cities in the United States. Most did not reply, or replied in so formal and abrupt a manner as to render their answers worthless; among the exceptions was John D. Marshall, the mayor of Cleveland.

October 19, 1931

My dear Sir:

The Crisis magazine is the oldest monthly periodical published in the general interest of American Negroes. It has been successfully published by the National Association for the Advancement of Colored People for twenty-one years.

With all American citizens, we are interested in the present unemployment and depression. As you know, this crisis bears with special weight upon Negroes. *The Crisis* is, therefore, seeking to collect data from the leading American cities on the following points:

1. What did your city do last year, especially for unemployment and relief among your Negro citizens?

2. What special plans have you for this class of citizens during the coming year?

May I beg a frank statement in as much detail as will not take too much of your available time on the above questions or matters germane to them.

I should deeply appreciate a reply at your earliest convenience.

Very sincerely yours,
W. E. B. Du Bois

Cleveland, Ohio, October 22, 1931.

My dear Dr. DuBois:

In reply to your letter of the 19th, in which you ask what the city did last year especially for unemployment and relief among negro citizens and what special plans we have for this class during the coming year, wish to advise that as far as I know there was no distinction made in any program during the last year, nor will there be any during the coming year, based upon color or in any other way.

It is true that a great many of the colored citizens of Cleveland are out of employment and are in need. While I have no statistics on the matter, from general information I would say that the percent of unemployment and of need is perhaps greater among certain sections of the colored population than among the rest of the population generally. To the extent that the need is greater, to that extent the proportionate relief has been greater. However, as I pointed out in the beginning, our effort has been to deal impartially and to relieve distress wherever found, & to give employment to every worthy person wherever possible.

A year ago the city spent $875,000 in providing work on the streets and in the parks because at that time we were advised by the best authorities that the situation would probably improve in the spring and at that time the plan was to give work rather than charity. We conducted a registration at which about 17,000 people were registered and I know from my personal contact with the situation that a very considerable portion of these were colored people. All people registered were given some employment and the most needy as shown by the records of the charitable organizations were given extra work. These funds, however, were exhausted by spring and the conditions not having improved since the spring, we have been concentrating on the problem of direct relief as no further funds were available for employment beyond our usual construction operations. The city has spent $1,000,000 and the county $1,450,000, and the Community Fund about $1,400,000 in direct relief so far this year. These funds will be completely exhausted about November tenth. The County Commissioners have placed on the ballot a one mill levy on which there is a very intensive campaign being waged, which is designed to furnish public funds to supplement the Community Fund resources for the balance of this year and as far as possible next year. Unless conditions improve very much by spring, in all probability these sums will be insufficient and some new source of revenue will have to be found at that time.

Public funds are expended by the charitable organizations who have trained workers and I believe the plan has met with general satisfaction. It is true that Communistic agitators have stated that there has been discrimination in the application of these funds, but the best informed opinion is that such is not the case and that as a matter of fact the situation is as I have indicated above.

I am writing you at such length because I know of your sincere interest in these matters and having met you personally several times on your visits, I want you to know just the situation as I understand it.

With kindest personal regards, I am

Very truly yours,
John D. Marshall

As we have seen, Du Bois projected the concept of an encyclopedia of the Negro prior to World War I, but the necessary resources were never forthcoming. Then, in 1931, Du Bois heard that the Phelps-Stokes Fund, with the active participation of Thomas Jesse Jones and T. J. Woofter, Jr.—leading white "consultants" on the "Negro problem" for various philanthropic agencies and government bureaus—was taking steps to produce such an encyclopedia. Neither Du Bois nor the leading Black historian of the period, Dr. Carter G. Woodson, was invited to the initial meeting; when Du Bois did receive notice of the second meeting, an exchange with James H. Dillard (1856–1940) resulted. Born in Virginia and educated at Washington & Lee University, Dillard was founder of the Jeanes Fund for the training of Black teachers and of the Southern University Race Commission. His association with the Phelps-Stokes Fund began in 1914 and lasted until his death. Dillard University in New Orleans was named in his honor.

November 30, 1931

My dear Mr. Dillard:

I am a little puzzled about the matter of the Negro encyclopedia proposed by the Phelps Stokes Fund and others. As you know, I was not invited to the first meeting, but since then, an invitation has come to the second meeting.

I do not want to be over-modest or over-sensitive, but I initiated the scientific study of the American Negro in the United States and contributed something to it. To be left out of the original invitation to consider a Negro encyclopedia came pretty near being a personal insult and a petty one at that. On the other hand, it is a great project. If properly carried out, it would mark an epoch, and I have no right to let any personal feelings stand between me and the best accomplishment of this work. On the other hand, if I should come in to help in this project, I should have to criticize what seems to me now to be its tendency, and under the circumstances, I rather doubt how far I should be justified in criticizing even the beginnings already made. On the other hand, I cannot sit in on a proposition of this sort as a figurehead.

As, of course, you realize, I could not for a moment contemplate a Negro encyclopedia dominated and controlled by Thomas Jesse Jones and Mr. Woofter. I do not, of course, want to exclude them or what they represent, but a Negro encyclopedia that was not in the main edited and written by Negroes would be as inconceivable as a Catholic encyclopedia projected by Protestants.

As it is, through the initiative taken and though the Executive Board which has been appointed, the Phelps Stokes Fund is in full control of the project. Frankly, now what would you advise me to do? To attend the next meeting and state my ideas fully, or to keep out of the whole thing on the ground that evidently I was not wanted by those who started it?

I should be glad to have your advice and to give it great weight.

Sincerely yours,
W. E. B. Du Bois

Charlottesville, Va., Dec. 2, 1931

Dear Dr. Du Bois:

I do not think there is yet certainty about Dr. Stoke's encyclopedia. I see, by the way, that in a letter to Dr. [Benjamin] Brawley, Dr. Woodson speaks of the intention of his for a 10-vol. work. He should know, it seems, about the cost of such an undertaking! By all means you should come to the meeting, and meantime it would be a good idea for you to write a *"nice"* letter to Dr. Stokes, presenting your views, but naming no names.

Yours sincerely,
J. H. Dillard

Du Bois knew Carter G. Woodson to be a man of fierce pride, but he attempted —as this exchange indicates—to persuade Woodson to participate in the plans for an encyclopedia of the Negro even though he had not been invited to participate in their original formulation. Du Bois clearly feared the negative response he was to receive. Unfortunately, neither man lived to see the completion of this project, and its realization, as they had envisioned it, is yet to appear.

January 29, 1932

My dear Sir:

I was asked to act as a Committee by the Conference on Negro Encyclopedia to induce you to join us. I had hoped to see you personally but had to rush back from Washington. When I am there again, I shall talk with you. Meantime, as time is passing, I am venturing to write.

I do not doubt but what you have made up your mind on this matter and that nothing I can say will change it. However, perhaps I ought to bring to your attention the motives that influenced me.

I was omitted from the first call, as you were, and for similar reasons. My first impulse on receiving the invitation to attend the second meeting was to refuse, as you did. Then I learned that this invitation did not come from the Phelps Stokes Fund, but was the unanimous wish of the conferees, and that if I refused to heed it, I would be affronting them, even more than Stokes and Jones. Then, in the second place, I had to remember, as both of us from time to time are compelled to, that the enemy has the money and they are going to use it. Our choice then is not how that money could be used best from our point of view, but how far without great sacrifice of principle, we can keep it from being misused. By the curious combination of accident and good will, we appointed at the last meeting a Board of Directors and Incorporators which leave out the more impossible members of the Conference. A place on that Board was left for you. If you do not accept it, that will leave us so much the weaker.

I hope you will see your way open to join us.

Very sincerely yours,
W. E. B. Du Bois

Washington, D.C., February 11, 1932

My dear Dr. Du Bois:

I should have answered your confidential letter before I left the city for a long stay. I have nothing to say, however, except that I am not interested. I never accept the gifts of the Greeks.

I should add that the Associated Publishers, drawing upon data collected for this purpose since 1922 by the Association for the Study of Negro Life and History, will bring out its Encyclopaedia Africana by the end of 1933. We welcome competition, because it is the spice of life.

Respectfully yours,
C. G. Woodson

Letters exchanged between Du Bois and Mrs. Mildred Scott Olmsted in 1932 reflect his remarkable prophetic powers and his mounting concern, not only with the immediate economic needs of his people, but also with the international ramifications of racism. Mrs. Olmsted, a renowned social worker and opponent of war, graduated from Smith College in 1912 and continued her studies at the School of Social Work of the University of Pennsylvania. When these letters were exchanged, Mrs. Olmsted was executive secretary of the Women's International League for Peace and Freedom.

January 20, 1932

My dear Mrs. Olmsted:

I know that you are interested in *The Crisis* magazine and the development of the American Negro. I have certain work for *The Crisis* in mind concerning which I am venturing to ask your advice. The difficulty in a problem like that of the Negro is that the problem itself gets to be provincial; that is, people do not think of it in connection with other problems, but set it entirely apart and the result is that it does not become a part of the general liberal movement and this makes it possible for people to be liberal concerning Negroes and reactionary on other advanced projects, and vice versa, advanced and progressive upon everything except the race problem.

I want, therefore, to inaugurate in *The Crisis* a series of articles from time to time designed to tie up liberal and radical thought with the problem of the Negro. For instance, here is the problem of peace and disarmament.[1] Most Negroes would not be interested in it at all. We would not think of it as having anything in particular to do with their status. On the other hand, the mass of people who are intensely interested in the peace movement, either know little or are but faintly interested in the racial problem of the American Negro.

I should like to get out a number of *The Crisis* which would show to both these classes that they are making a grave mistake. That peace is today and always has been very largely a racial problem, and that, on the other hand, the race problem cannot be satisfactorily settled if this continues to be a warlike work.

Now to get out a number of *The Crisis* which would illustrate this and be properly arranged to appeal to both classes, would mean an extra expenditure of money. Do you think that any peace organization could be appealed to contribute, say $500 to such a piece of propaganda? I think it would be of tremendous importance and perhaps later we could in the same way tie up the Negro problem with other racial movements.

I should be very glad to have your advice and thought on this matter.

Very sincerely yours,
W. E. B. Du Bois

Philadelphia, Pa. February 18, 1932

My dear Dr. Du Bois:

I have been much interested in your letter telling of the plan you have in mind to get out a number of The Crisis devoted to the racial question and peace. I think it is badly needed. My experience, which is of course more limited than yours, brought me some time ago to precisely the same conclusions which you have reached, that is that neither Negroes nor whites see the connection between these two problems, and that there is apparently not much material on this subject available.

I have laid your letter before both our executive committee and our Board. They are all interested in it and would like to help, but our own treasury has grown so slim that we do not yet know where or how we shall secure the funds to complete our year. Five hundred dollars looks like an impossible sum for us at the present time. Under these circumstances we have been casting about to see what other sources of money would be possible. Of course the various Foundations were proposed, but I imagine you have already approached them,

---

1. Du Bois devoted part of his "Postscript" column in the *Crisis* 39 (March 1932):93 to "Disarmament," linking its achievement to the advancement of the colored peoples of the earth.

also other peace groups. I found that I did not have enough information when it came to discussing definite plans with our Board. It was left that we shall be glad to be one of a number of peace organizations each of which would appropriate twenty-five dollars or more toward the expenses of such an issue, and that we should be glad to work with you in approaching other peace groups if you desire it. Mrs. Ruth Verlenden Poley was appointed as our special representative on this matter, but as Mrs. Poley was not present I have not heard whether she was able to accept. Let me know what you think is the next step.

     Sincerely yours,
     Mildred Scott Olmsted

     March 5, 1932

My dear Miss Olmsted:

I have delayed my answer to your letter of February 18 because my practical plans are indefinite, but the point I want to make is perfectly clear. For instance, the Japanese Exclusion Act of the United States and the refusal of the League of Nations to take a stand on race equality, together with the cavalier treatment of Japan by America and Europe from the days of Perry down to the present Far Eastern propaganda, are vivid illustrations of the way in which race prejudice encourages war and bedevils the discussion of peace. Or again, at the very time that the world is discussing universal peace, they are saying absolutely nothing of the native oppression and revolt in the French Congo and the Belgian Congo, in Portuguese Angola, and in various other parts of Africa. Yet, these happenings are the seeds of future wars, as sure as the world moves. What I want to do is to get out an edition of *The Crisis* and distribute it widely, and publish therein, articles and statements which will show that race prejudice and war are two sides of the same thing, and that no movement for universal peace and disarmament can ignore this connection. That the peace forces must resolutely face race prejudice as a dangerous incentive to an excuse for war, and that persons interested in the problems of race relations must learn that the most usual and natural contact of separate and distinct races is a contact for the murder and theft, which we call war.

Of course, such an edition of *The Crisis* would have to be gotten out carefully and with consultation between the editors and peace societies, as to just what should be included and how the number be planned. This is, as I say, still a bit vague in my mind, but perhaps will convey to you more clearly than my former letter just what I plan. I want to do the same thing with the advocates of birth control, with the health movements, with the Red Cross, and with the promoters of a third political party.

I shall hope to hear from you at your convenience.

     Very sincerely yours,
     W. E. B. Du Bois

The perennial question of racism in education is illuminated in letters between Du Bois and Miss Elizabeth Nutting, secretary of the Character Building Division of the Council of Social Agencies of Dayton, Ohio.

Dayton, Ohio, March 15, 1932

Dear Dr. Du Bois

As the leader of a discussion group of influential white women which has chosen to concern itself with the plans and policies connected with a new junior high school which is being built in the center of Dayton's Negro section, I am writing to ask you for some of the information which we seem to lack, especially with regard to what Negroes themselves think about the relative values of an all-colored as over against a mixed school.

The significant factors in our situation seem to be as follows:

Dayton has a population of 200,000—10% of which is colored; we are situated near enough to Kentucky to have some distinctly southern attitudes on the part of many of our citizens; Negroes and whites ride together on street cars, but Negroes are not admitted to down-town moving picture shows or restaurants. Up to the present time we have had no all-colored schools, though Negro children have been restricted in the use of swimming pools, and segregated in gymnasium classes. One grade school has a main building with both white and Negro children under white teachers, and a temporary building for colored children under colored teachers. There seems to be an unwritten law that white children should not be placed under Negro teachers.

The new school is so located as to insure a large majority of Negro children in attendance. The whites on the West Side are bringing heavy pressure to bear on the superintendent of schools to have an all-Negro school, both faculty and children. Others interested in this situation fear that the practice of segregation will be much more firmly established in the community if this is done, and would like to see at least two or three white teachers and if possible a few white children to keep the Paul Laurence Dunbar School from being, to all intents and purposes, a segregated school.

May I ask what you yourself would consider wise in such a situation, and what you would think the main trends of Negro thinking would be? We are very anxious to see this school started right—whatever that may be—and will deeply appreciate your viewpoint on this matter. I might add that the time element is important—what is done must be done quickly—so a prompt reply will be much appreciated.

Sincerely,
Elizabeth Nutting

March 22, 1932

My dear Miss Nutting:

Your letter of March 15 has just reached me as I have been away from my office in order to lecture at Atlanta University. I am afraid my answer will be too late for any specific use you may have had in mind but I venture to express my opinion as follows:

It is always unfortunate and against the fundamental idea of free popular education to separate the pupils on any artificial basis. As far as possible public school children should not be segregated according to the income of their parents, according to their home culture and surroundings, according to their national race or color. The public school should be a great democracy where all elements of the population come to realize the essential humanity of each.

This ideal cannot always be reached. We find continually in modern cities that the arrangements of the community into exclusive sections and slums segregate the rich from the poor. There are schools mainly attended by Italian workers and schools initiated and designed for old American families. Nevertheless usually there is no open and advertised segregation according to wealth and nationality; but there is an attempt in the United States to educate colored and white children separately.

Where public opinion is as fixed and immovable as in this city where I write, Atlanta, Georgia, separate schools are inevitable and at present best for the purposes of education. On the other hand it would be a calamity if in New York or Boston there were similar segregation. In a border city like Dayton the problem is such that no outsider can bring much wisdom. Public opinion among thoughtful colored people, and I think among most far-seeing white people, would think it would be most unfortunate if the new Dunbar High School were made exclusively a Negro school. On the other hand if Negro children in the mixed schools are not receiving proper attention and training, if they do not enlist the interest and the friendliness of the teachers, if the teachers must inevitably and always be white, then colored children cannot receive in such schools the education that is their due and some separation is almost inevitable.

Even in such case, however, it may be possible to save some remnants among the debris and as you suggest in your fourth paragraph, keep in the school some white pupils and insist upon a mixed staff of teachers. But whether Dayton is civilized enough for this procedure, I do not know.

If there is any further information that I can give you I shall be very glad to do so.

Very sincerely yours
W. E. B. Du Bois

On 5 April 1932, Du Bois received a telegram signed by the political prisoner Tom Mooney.

IN FALL OF YEAR NINETEEN EIGHTEEN WHILE IN SAN QUENTIN IN DEATH CELL I READ IN CRISIS STORY OF LYNCHING OF PREGNANT WOMAN IN GEORGIA WHICH WAS SO REVOLTING THAT UNITED STATES PRESIDENT MADE STATEMENT ON CASE WOULD PROFOUNDLY APPRECIATE HAVING ENTIRE ARTICLE CONTAINING STORY COPIED FROM FILES OF CRISIS FORWARDED IMMEDIATELY AIR MAIL TO MOONEY DEFENSE COMMITTEE POSTOFFICE BOX FOURTEEN SEVENTY FIVE SAN FRANCISCO

TOM MOONEY

The case Mooney had in mind was the lynching of Mary Turner on 17 May, 1918, in Georgia; she was one of several Black people slaughtered by a lynch mob on that day for being "uppity." She was in her eighth month of pregnancy when she was killed because she had remonstrated with the lynchers, threatening to expose their identities. In June 1918, Robert Moton of Tuskegee warned the president of intensifying Black unrest and pleaded that he speak out against lynching; Wilson did so in a public statement for the press, issued 25 July 1918. Mooney's letter incorrectly states that this was the first time a president had denounced lynching: Benjamin Harrison did so in a message to Congress on 6 December 1892; William McKinley several times denounced the lynchings in the United States of Italian and Mexican citizens; and Theodore Roosevelt spoke out against lynching in a message to Congress, 3 December 1906.

After receiving the above telegram, Du Bois sent the September 1918 issue of the *Crisis* which contained the account requested. In response he received a letter on behalf of the Tom Mooney Molders' Defense Committee, signed by Anna Mooney, his wife.

San Francisco, Cal.
April 8, 1932

Dear Sir:

We want to express our profound appreciation for your prompt action in complying with our request made in a telegram sent April 4th.

We received copy of *Crisis,* September, 1918, and it was just what we were looking for.

Enclosed is a check for 55¢ which, we believe, covers cost of pamphlets and postage.

Thanking you for this favor, with best wishes and fraternal greetings, we remain,

Very sincerely yours,
Anna Mooney

On 5 April, from his cell in San Quentin, Tom Mooney wrote to Du Bois a letter "so delayed" as not to be mailed until 16 April.

California State Prison
San Quentin, Cal., April 5, 1932

Dear Mr. Du Bois:

During the Fall of 1918, in my condemned cell awaiting execution I read a story in some paper—which one, I am not sure—it may have been the New York Call— it may have been some other paper, but it stamped its self upon my mind so deeply that nothing this side of the grave will ever erase it.

This story, if my memory serves me right as to some of its details was an editorial comment upon an article or editorial by, I think a man by the name of White—it appeared in "The Crisis" and it was about that terrible cruel attack upon members of your race, in Georgia, if I am not mistaken.[1] This particular "Lynching," so the article I have in mind relates, was the only one that ever caused a President of these United States to remonstrate against this barbarous Southern institution. President Wilson urged the people put a stop to it.

There were a number of persons "Lynched" and Killed on both sides and the point that I am mostly interested in, is the final act of the Lynchers in the methods they used to so cruelly and barbarously torture an eight months pregnant Mother to death.

I am sure this description will refresh your memory sufficiently to help locate in your files the details of this monstrous outrage against members of your race. I should certainly appreciate it if you would make me a copy of all of the essentials—the facts of this crime, its consequences, and penalties if any were inflicted upon any one on either side and send same to my Defense Committee. *(Tom Mooney Molders Defense Committee 675 Minna St. San Francisco California)* via Air Mail *Special Delivery,* at your earliest possible convenience.

I want you to know, that all my adult life, I have been keenly, warmly and sympathetically interested in the problems that confront your race and that I hate the hundreds of wrongs they have suffered with all of my being. I have one purpose only in asking for this information at this time—to help in the general direction of betterment for your race struggle for real freedom and equality.

Thanking you very kindly in advance for your early compliance with this request, I am

Very sincerely yours,
Tom Mooney
31921

A reflection of the long and ongoing effort to eliminate the chauvinism infecting textbooks used in the United States appears in correspondence of the spring of

---

1. Walter F. White, "The Work of a Mob," *Crisis* 16 (September 1918):221–23.

1932. S. L. Smith was at this time director for southern schools of the Julius Rosenwald Fund.

Nashville, Tenn., May 7, 1932

Dear Mr. Du Bois

At a meeting of a Joint Committee of the National Education Association and National Association of Teachers in Colored Schools held in Washington last February, I was appointed Chairman of a Sub-Committee on Negro history with a view (1) to working out some means of having the American histories (particularly those used as textbooks) record notable achievements of Negroes just as is done now for other races, and (2) to arranging for a moving picture showing the achievements of the race from early days to the present. The Committee is composed of Doctor Arthur D. Wright, President of the Jeanes and Slater Funds, Washington, Doctor W. T. B. Williams, Dean of Education at Tuskegee Institute, and myself.

It seems that something ought to be done to encourage the historians to include notable achievements by Negroes. I do not believe including events about Negroes that are worthy to go into history would prejudice superintendents and school officials of the nation against adopting such books as texts to be studied by children of all races. There seem to be great hopes of better race relations in the next generation than at the present, and I think it would improve conditions if children of other races could have opportunity in their regular textbooks to learn more of the achievements of the Negro race and to see the important part the race has played in the development of our country.

For information and guidance in this important undertaking we naturally turn to you, because of your unusual contributions to Negro literature and journalism as well as to all phases of Negro life. Many things you advocated a decade ago, which were thought utterly impossible by even your close friends, you have seen come true wholly or in part. The changes seem to be gaining in momentum.

You will be interested to know that Mr. Will Hays, President of the Motion Picture Producers and Distributors of America, has shown great interest in helping the Committee to get in touch with the leading producers and distributors to see whether some one of the group might be willing to undertake the stupendous task of preparing a moving picture of national import to be shown in theaters throughout the country. The talking picture would necessarily have to include entertainment as well as instructive features. I can think of no picture more thrillingly fascinating than a picture portraying Negro life and history from the early days up to the present. There would be woven into this great talking picture history, literature, music, education, art, dramatics, business and religion. Leading characters of the race would be brought into the picture representing the various phases of life.

Please think over these two problems and write us your frank reactions. The task of either of these undertakings will be difficult, but I do not believe that either will be impossible, and if they are worth while thinking about and working on, now seems to be an opportune time when, I believe, the Committee will have the full cooperation of both the National Education Association and the National Association of Teachers in Colored Schools, as well as other organizations.

Trusting to hear from you at your convenience, I am,
Sincerely yours,
S. L. Smith

May 10, 1932.

My dear Mr. Smith:

I was very much interested in your letter of May 7. For many years, I have tried to do something toward both the efforts which your sub-committee has in mind.

I have continually sought to sift out the well-known and verifiable facts concerning the part which the Negro has taken in American history. I'm sending you herewith one of my last attempts, which is a pageant on "George Washington and the Negro." There are others mentioned in my "Gift of Black Folk." Some of these historic data will be in dispute because it has so long been assumed that the Negro has made no contribution. The first reaction, even of trained historians, is to doubt many facts. But there is a large body of easily provable fact which should find place in textbooks.

The dramatic possibilities of the Negro's story have always fascinated me. In 1912, I wrote a pageant of the Negro in American History which I offered to the National Association for the Advancement of Colored People. But they hesitated because of the cost to stage it and the uncertainty of the return. In 1913, when I was made one of the commissioners of the State of New York to celebrate Emancipation, I succeeded in getting a part of the appropriation set aside to put on this pageant, which I called "The Star of Ethiopia," and made it upon the whole history of the Negro race. It was very successful. Every night that the pageant was given it simply jammed the armory where we were, and received considerable notice. This encouraged me, so that in 1914, I took the pageant to Washington. Money was raised by subscription and we gave it in the baseball park, with costumes and outdoor scenery painted by the late, young, colored artist Richard Brown. There are over one thousand persons in the cast, and the artistic success was tremendous. We gave it three nights: Monday, Wednesday and Friday, and every night the audience doubled, so that the last night we had some ten thousand people there. But the cost was tremendous and I had to pay part of the deficit out of my own pocket.

I think you will find many people now in Washington who remember the occasion. In 1915, I gave the pageant again in the Conference Hall, Phila. to celebrate the 100th Anniversary of the African M. E. Church, and finally, in 1925, in Los Angeles in the Hollywood Bowl.

But pageantry is, of course, too costly and too limited in its appeal to be a popular success, and I have always hoped that something could be done in the theatre and in the moving pictures to popularize this story. I have a volume of plays on similar but less historic themes which publishers have been considering, and at which some playwrights have looked, but always hesitate because of the subject.

So much for my own attitude. I was sure that a moving picture manager, with the right amount of imagination, could evolve a stirring and interesting picture, and after all, there are twelve million Negroes in the United States who would be eager to see something beside the kind of Negro picture that has been filmed hitherto. I think, therefore, that your project is an excellent one, and I shall be only too glad to do anything I can to forward it.

Very sincerely yours,
W. E. B. Du Bois

Basic and lasting questions relative to the tactics and strategy of Afro-American liberation were considered incisively in an exchange in the summer of 1932 between L. F. Strittmater of New Jersey and Du Bois.

Bloomfield, N.J., July 28, 1932

Dear Sir:

I read the Crisis regularly, especially the half-page "As The Crow Flies." I have read your books "Darkwater" and "The Souls of Black Folk" repeatedly, among other books by Booker T. Washington. The chapter on Washington in "The Souls of Black Folk" has so constrained me to express my views of the divergence of your respective policies with regard to conciliation, that with your indulgence I will presume upon a few moments of your valuable time and address myself to you candidly and as briefly as possible.

Quoting: "While it is a great truth to say the Negro must strive and strive mightily to help himself, it is equally true that unless his striving be not simply seconded but rather aroused and encouraged by the initiative of the richer and wiser environing group, he cannot hope for success."

Granted. But how can you expect to elicit encouragement from the richer and wiser environing group without softening at least their harshest prejudices? without conciliation?

For the present, it devolves upon Negroes as a subject class, to forge their advancement along two divergent avenues of approach, namely, education and conciliation. Both of these must progress abreast; they are mutually important. Education has no function or value if those educated are restrained from using or materially profiting by their acquirements. And certainly they will be, just so long as the master class are hostile to them or their education. Education must be sustained by conciliation. Each, individually, is impotent and powerless without support from the other, in the present status of the Negro.

Security for the Negro race depends upon acquisition of, and opportunity to exploit, means of a competent livelihood; of inner growth and expansion, moral and spiritual; and of equal protection of the law. How can any of these vital and fundamental factors of the Negroes' development advance appreciably or normally in the fact of the unconciliated prejudices of the master class? There cannot be a maximum of progress for Negroes until at least the harshest hostilities of the power in control are allayed and their aspiration for a greater measure of assimilation into American society is viewed with more tolerance, kindliness and understanding.

Thorough and well-ballasted development of Negro men and women to their full capacity as human beings irrespective of sex or color, and willing acceptance by their white neighbors of the Negroes' best contributions to American life, broadly speaking, are the two essentials of the Negro problem. Education strikes directly and effectively at the former of these and conciliation is an indispensable element in any feasible progress that aims at the latter. Legislation may be simultaneously desirable, but certain it is, that amenable legislation will not precede conciliation of the law makers, but rather follow it. And this cannot be abnormally spurred and quickened but very easily it can be delayed and deflected.

Washington secured that difficultly acquired encouragement and sponsorship from the best white people for which you plead. He did not bring the race to its ultimate maximation; he could not, nor can any other individual. The race cannot be established in one person's lifetime. But among other things, he did gain much of what you would have, by methods which you disapprove, preferring for your own part, truculence and bitterness to conciliation.

Your aim, if I interpret it correctly, is not paramountly justice for the Negro, but rather vindication of the Negro, as such. In this aspiration, if I make so bold, you are reaching for the moon, centuries over the times in which you live, and oblivious to the possibilities inherent in the conditions in which both races stand today. For the present, practical men with not too long-ranged vision, for the service of the race must apply themselves to doing first things first, however unpleasant. That is, they must attend to the initial step of establishing the race in the best status obtainable as an accepted and recognized, integral part of the American commonwealth, however humble, in which position they can ensconce and entrench themselves, and as opportunity allows, peaceably and permanently extend and widen their status' horizon into eventual full citizenship. Such men are vastly more adapted to advance the well-being of the race at this early and chaotic day of its nominal independence than are they who aim to establish and direct by the tenets of promiscuous censure, blind defiance and tactless aggressiveness towards the governing class. That, in my opinion, is mistaken zeal. You cannot bully evolution, nor sentiment.

All nature, and human nature is no exception, is predatory. To expect a people who have had their slaves filched from them not by inner consent to suddenly adopt those ex-slaves and their descendants as normal, accepted members of their community and civilization, is Utopianism. Negroes, at the present time, do not receive, and cannot reasonably expect to receive, extensive understudying from the white race. If that understudying comes, and I have no doubt it will, it must be secured at a price; it must be bought and paid for, like everything else; and the coin for its purchase, in the absence of power, is conciliation.

A minority cannot, at best, vaunt its power; it must substitute for it with diplomacy. You cannot hope to secure that sponsorship and encouragement from the richer and wiser environing group which you strongly desire with such malapropos stimulus as deliberate provocativeness and vindictiveness. Nor can your followers. If you are able to transmit to any large number of your race that virulent bitterness which you radiate in all your writings, especially in The Crisis, I cannot help but feel you will be doing them a lasting disservice. Heat and vindictiveness are no substitutes for light, and as to their possibilities as a solution to the race problem, they are worthless. A constructive, discreet, long-ranged, unswervingly conciliative spirit must supplant it. This may be difficult—noblesse oblige.

Hatred and prejudice are just as inimical to adjustment and understanding between the races when entertained by members of your own race as when held by the other. Hatred must not be rooted in new places, but destroyed in the old ones, or nothing is accomplished. The desire for peace and adjustment between the races must be reciprocal; good-will must be mutual; hatred must be quenched in black hearts as well as in white; education of the dominant and admittedly prejudiced master class to a more kindly and tolerant attitude towards the subject class must be essayed with supreme deftness by the subject class, else friction and fallacy will not be obliterated but doubled; and the day of the actual freedom of the Negro thrust merely still further into the future.

If, as you maintain in the passage from your book which I quoted, the development of Negroes is so largely referred to the disposition of the richer and wiser environing group, I need hardly indicate that conciliation of that group is obviously a sine qua non of their development.

I should be pleased to receive a note of rebuttal.

Respectfully,
L. F. Strittmater

August 3, 1932.

Mr. L. F. Strittmater
My dear Sir:

The chapter which you have read concerning Booker T. Washington in my "Souls of Black Folk" was written nearly thirty years ago. Since then, I have written a good deal to explain and expand my philosophy, although I do not think that there has been any essential change in it. You might be interested in another book of essays, "Darkwater," published in 1920, and in my novel, "Dark Princess."

Briefly, of course, conciliation must be in any social worker's program, but, on the other hand, fawning and stupid yielding to the vagaries of a master class not only secures nothing from them, but helps to submerge one's own self-respect. In the last quarter century, the colored people of the United States, following very largely my advice and the advice of others, based upon it, have made notable strides in advance, and by standing up as men instead of crawling like animals, they have forced you and your friends to yield much which you never would have yielded to the Washington program alone. Minority must always "vaunt its powers," otherwise, it will lose what little power it has, and while I should hate to be justly accused of bitterness and vindictiveness, nevertheless, if what I am writing in *The Crisis* comes under that head, you will, I regret to say, see as much of it in the future as you have in the past.

Very sincerely yours,
W. E. B. Du Bois

Clarence Senior, born in Missouri in 1903, was national executive secretary of the Socialist party from 1929 to 1936, and in 1932 was the party's campaign director when it ran Norman Thomas and James H. Maurer on its presidential ticket. From the 1940s, Senior's interests turned to Latin-American questions and to teaching; since 1961, he has been a member of the New York City Board of Education.

In his position as campaign director of the Socialist party, in 1932, Senior was struck by a sentence Du Bois wrote in the *Crisis*; the question he raises and Du Bois's reply have lasting importance.

Chicago, Illinois, August 8, 1932

Dear Mr. Du Bois:

Just as a matter of my own personal information, I would appreciate it if you could elaborate upon the statement you made in "Postcript" in this month's *Crisis* as follows:[1] "Contrary to many philanthropists and Socialists, he included among the laboring classes, the yellow coolies of Asia and the black slaves of Africa."

I don't know any Socialists, particularly the American Socialists, against whom this charge might be levied.

In order to identify myself, I have been a member of the N.A.A.C.P. some time and was on the executive board of the local organization in Cleveland while I

---

1. The sentence is from a paragraph on Albert Thomas, who died in May 1932, and had been director general of the International Labor Office under the League of Nations; it appears in the August 1932 *Crisis* (39:266). Du Bois had met Thomas in 1921.

lived there. I am also an honorary member of the Brotherhood of Sleeping Car Porters. This, by way of identifying myself with the problem with which we are both concerned.

Yours sincerely,
Clarence Senior

September 15, 1932

Mr. Clarence Senior
My dear Sir:

I regret very much that your letter of August 8 got misplaced in my letter-box and has just turned up.

The question of the attitude of the Socialists toward the colored peoples has been long a matter of debate. The German Socialists, back in the Nineties, frankly declared that their program did not include Asiatic laborers. In the United States, the Socialists at first tried to ignore the Color Line, but at last when they went into the South, early in the 20th Century, there seemed to be a chance to get hold of the white workers, but it could only be done on condition that there be separate white and Negro locals. This, they carried out. At last, just before the World War, it seemed necessary to make a statement concerning the attitude of Socialists on race relations. A committee was appointed, under the Chairmanship of, I think, Robert Hunter, and an elaborate statement prepared which recognized pretty clearly race differences, and consequently some segregation and difference of treatment. This report was laid on the table, and then the war came, and it has never been brought up. Finally, the Labor Government of England made some very fine statements concerning black African labor, but when they came to power, they did not attempt in any way to really approach the problem of exploitation in Africa.

The statement to which you allude is based upon the above facts.

Very sincerely yours,
W. E. B. Du Bois

Henry Hugh Proctor was born in Tennessee in the same year as Du Bois (1868) and received his bachelor's degree from Fisk, as did Du Bois, in 1891. In 1894, he received a Bachelor of Divinity degree from Yale and, ten years later, his D.D. from Clark University in Atlanta. Meanwhile, he had been ordained a Congregational minister and was the pastor of the First Congregational Church in Atlanta (1894–1920) during much of the time Du Bois was there. In 1920, Proctor moved North and became the pastor of the Nazarene Church in Brooklyn; he also authored books on religious themes. He died in 1933.*

Proctor wrote Du Bois in 1932—in a letter that seems to be lost—asking for his

---

* There is an obituary on Proctor by Du Bois in the *Crisis* 40 (September 1933):212.

views about President Hoover, then standing for re-election against Franklin Delano Roosevelt.

September 28, 1932

My dear Proctor:

The chief points against President Hoover, so far as the colored people are concerned, are as follows:

1. His support of the Lily-White movement in the South.
2. His practical refusal to appoint any Negro to any important office.
3. His appointment of white men, who have been known enemies of the Negro race to office, illustrated by the appointment of Doak as Secretary of Labor, and his nomination of Parker to the Supreme Court.
4. His refusal to interfere in the case of known injustices to the Negro, as in the unfair distribution of relief after the Mississippi flood in 1927, and the treatment of Negro workers on the Mississippi levees under government supervision this year.
5. His segregation of the Gold Star mothers in their trips to France. His treatment of Haiti and Liberia. In Haiti, he took several forward steps, but he is today insisting on keeping financial control of Haiti independently, and is reaching out for the same kind of domination in Liberia.
6. His failure to speak out on lynching, segregation, peonage or disfranchisement.

I think this about covers the count that you have in mind.

Very sincerely yours,
W. E. B. Du Bois

Earl Burrus Dickerson, an attorney, was born in Mississippi in 1891. He was educated at the University of Illinois and pursued his graduate studies at the University of Chicago, earning a Doctorate in Jurisprudence in 1920. From 1923 to 1927, he was assistant corporation counsel of Chicago; he was later assistant attorney general of Illinois and a member of the Chicago City Council. In 1928, he was a regional director for the Democratic party's national campaign. His leadership in that party led Du Bois to ask him to prepare for the *Crisis* an article explaining why the 1932 vote of Black people should go for Roosevelt.

Chicago, Illinois, October 1, 1932

My dear Dr. Du Bois:

Ever since I received your letter of September 12th, asking that I furnish you with a short article of 1000 to 1200 words, setting forth why the colored people should support Roosevelt and the Democrats, I have been trying to make up my mind definitely to prepare such an article and have the same ready for you by October 1st. To this day, however, I have not been able to do so.

Perhaps I owe you an apology for not giving you this information sooner, but all along I had hoped that I could make myself believe that an article written by me in favor of Roosevelt and the Democrats would not only be fair to myself but to the colored people themselves. Personally, I think Roosevelt, because of his progressive views, is much more acceptable to the masses of the people in this country, among whom our group constitutes a large part, than is Hoover, and I think it is easy to select Roosevelt as our candidate as between the two of them.

On the other hand, I doubt if Roosevelt, in the event of his election, will be able to carry through any of his progressive views, largely because of the fact that the reactionary, bourbon South would be in control of both the Senate and the House of Representatives—and we could expect certainly no more, if as much, under Roosevelt in such circumstances, than under Hoover.

In the light of the above, I do not see how I could conscientiously go on record asking the colored people to vote for Roosevelt and the Democrats, although I may personally do so myself. In my judgment, it would be the thing of wisdom if a large part of our vote were cast for Norman Thomas, or [William Z.] Foster, for certainly the economic program of these two minority parties would be much more beneficial to us than anything thus far suggested by either the Republicans or Democrats.

I trust my failure to send the article is excused and that you are not thereby inconvenienced in any way.

Very sincerely yours,
Earl B. Dickerson

Ben N. Azikiwe, future founding president of the Republic of Nigeria, wrote Du Bois in 1932 to question his relationship to Liberia's rejection of the Garvey movement; Du Bois's reply definitively and clearly answered the question raised, yet innuendoes persist to this day.

Lincoln University, Pa., Nov. 6, 1932

Dear Dr. Du Bois:

With reference to my dissertational work on the Republic of Liberia, I desire your version on an important topic, and I trust that you will be kind enough to enlighten me.

I note that during the inauguration of former President King in 1924, you were appointed Ambassador Extraordinary and Minister Plenipotentiary to Liberia. This has been interpreted in certain quarters to imply the alienation of the friendship which had hitherto existed between Liberia and the Universal Negro Improvement Association.

For my authorities, I may cite the following: Amy Jacques-Garvey, Philosophy and Opinions of Marcus Garvey, vol. II; R. L. Buell, The Native Problem in Africa, vol. II, pp. 731-33; Cuthbert Christy, "Liberia in 1930," Geographical Journal (London), June 1931, vol. 77, pp. 515-40. Consequently, Garvey's colonization scheme was rejected by the republic; cf. Legislative Acts 1924-25, p. 22.

From these citations there is nothing definite to prove the part the American Ambassador played in urging the Republic to reject the Garveyites. Even Mr. Buell did not clarify the innuendoes of Mr. Garvey and I am glad he did not attempt to interpret same one-sidedly. Any statement from you in this regard will be sincerely welcomed and will enable me to strengthen or refute the theories of Mr. Garvey.

Believe me to be,

Sincerely yours,
Ben N. Azikiwe

November 11, 1932

My dear Sir:

Answering your letter of November 6, I beg to say that I had nothing to do at all with the relations of Garvey and the Republic of Liberia. Garvey's colonization scheme had already been rejected by Liberia before I went there and before there was the slightest intimation of my appointment. Compare *The Crisis* for February, 1924 and June, 1924. My relations to Liberia were purely formal and I did not mention Garvey to Mr. King or to any Liberian official during my stay there.

Very sincerely yours,
W. E. B. Du Bois

As the depression continued, Du Bois became increasingly convinced of the validity and relevancy of the Marxian analysis; believing that Marx had "put his finger squarely upon our difficulties," he wrote in *Dusk of Dawn*, "this conviction I had to express or spiritually die" (p. 303). In mid-1933, he taught a seminar on "Marx and the Negro" at Atlanta University; while working on his *Black Reconstruction*, he found the Marxian insight more and more helpful. This line of thought began to penetrate the *Crisis*, so that in the March 1933 issue appeared an unsigned paragraph from Du Bois entitled "Karl Marx and the Negro" (40: 55-56); in May 1933, a signed essay, "Marxism and the Negro Problem," was published (40:103-4, 118).

The latter article resulted in correspondence with David de Sola Pool. Born in London in 1885 and educated there and in Germany, Pool was the rabbi at the Spanish and Portuguese Synagogue Shearith Israel in New York City after 1907; for many years, he was president of Young Judea of America and the Synagogue Council of America. He died in December 1970.

[466] Correspondence 1930-1934

In a letter to Du Bois, written 10 May 1933, Rabbi de Sola Pool quoted from the essay this sentence: "The shrill cry of a few communists is not even listened to, because and solely because it seeks to break down barriers between black and white." He thought that Du Bois was in error in suggesting this as the only reason for the prevalent hysterical anti-communism and wondered if, on second thought, Du Bois might agree.* Du Bois replied:

Atlanta, Georgia, May 19, 1933

My dear Sir:

As I review my statement concerning the Communist, I think it is true, as you remark, that there are plenty of other American reasons for their unpopularity. Still, I am certain that the race equality business ranks very high.

Very sincerely yours,
W. E. B. Du Bois

One of the pioneering and foremost scholars in African history and civilization was Mississippi-born William Leo Hansberry (1894-1965). He taught at Howard for two generations. It was not until the last five or six years of his life that appropriate recognition of his work began to appear, largely from leaders of independent African states. His inspirer, as he states in this letter, was Du Bois. Despite Du Bois's urging, Hansberry did not publish any of his work. An obituary appears in the *New York Times*, 4 November 1965; a penetrating account of his work appears in *Africa Report* (November 1965), pp. 28-29.

Washington, D.C., July 13, 1933

My dear Dr. Du Bois:

I am forwarding you today *via* insured parcel post, a selected assortment of the slides promised some weeks ago. To save cost, in making up the slides, I omitted titles in most instances; but to facilitate your use of these, I have drawn up a descriptive list of the ones I am forwarding you. This little effort, together with numbering and packing, accounts for the delay in getting off the assortment to you.

Thanks for your advice concerning the publication of a book. I am spending this summer in an effort in that direction—an historical essay (of book length) under the title, "*Egypt Under the Ethiopians: A Study in Ancient Negro Imperialism and Statesmanship.*" I hope to have this ready for the Press by October of this year. If it is not asking too much, I would be very happy to have you read the finished manuscript for your suggestions and criticism.

The next time you are in Washington I hope it will be convenient for you to

---

* Rabbi de Sola Pool's letter has been summarized since permission to publish was not given by Mrs. de Sola Pool.

come out to the University and look over my complete collection of slides, prints and reprints. I should also like to discuss with you, for your advice, certain projected plans for the future development of my work.

As I told you some years ago, I consider myself a kind of spiritual son of yours, for it was your book *The Negro*, more than anything else, which was largely responsible for my determination to "carry on" along my present lines of endeavor. I hope eventual accomplishments will prove me worthy of the self-appointed adoption.

Yours very sincerely
William Leo Hansberry.

Atlanta, Ga., July 17, 1933

My dear Mr. Hansberry:

Thank you very much indeed for the trouble that you have taken to send me the slides. I shall use them this week and get them started back to you before the end of the week.

I hope you will keep at that historical essay no matter how long it takes you. I shall be very glad to help in any way I can.

Very sincerely yours,
W. E. B. Du Bois

William Nesbit Jones, born in South Carolina in 1882, graduated from Benedict College in Columbia in 1907. As a working journalist in the 1930s, he became managing editor of the *Baltimore Afro-American*; it was in this capacity that he visited Africa late in 1933. At the beginning of this assignment, while in London, he wrote a long and illuminating letter to Du Bois; the reply was short but revealing.

London, England, October 14, 1933

My dear Dr. Du Bois:

For several reasons I had hoped that I would get in touch with you before leaving on this mission to Africa. First of all I wanted to pick up, through you, some threads of the Pan-African movement and those connected with it. While I am going to Liberia on a newspaper mission or assignment, I have some practical objectives in mind. Hence the desire to make every contact possible. I am going, not as exponent of any faction or group, but merely to study what can be done to save Liberia as matters now stand.

Another reason which is prompting me to write you now was something told me by Mrs. Elizabeth Meijer, a white woman entering upon an interracial work in Baltimore and who had a conference with you on the matter during a recent visit in New York. I was very much surprised when she came back to Baltimore frantically telling me that you had advised her that in an interracial program in Baltimore, I would be more of a hindrance than a help because of my connection with the Communist party.

There were many reasons why her information as to your attitude struck a vital spot in my consideration. First of all, practically every fundamental policy on racial matters I have acquired, I have imbibed under your leadership. I am not a member of the Communist Party; not even a member of the International Labor Defense. I did support openly their policy on the race question and their effective Euel Lee fight in Maryland.[1] But strange to say, I supported this policy because it corresponded with the policy I had pledged myself, as a student, to support as a result of your teachings.

You may recall that many years ago you were invited to Benedict College to speak on Abraham Lincoln. It was I, as a student, who headed the organization which invited you—and in doing so I brought down upon myself a frown from a goodly portion of the faculty. With this same impulse, and guided by your leadership, I insisted, even to the point of relinquishing promise of a place on the faculty there, of selecting the subject of "John Brown" as my commencement oration. Another ironic twist to this matter is the fact that I faced serious opposition in a Memphis, Tennessee Municipal Board, and finally broke with it, because I insisted on becoming a member of the Memphis branch of the N.A.A.C.P., in a time when that organization under you and [John R.] Shillady was regarded much more radical than communism is regarded in Baltimore today.

I have no brief for communism. In fact there are things about it which I have argued against violently. But on the race question—the policy of complete social, political, and economic equality—is one which I have consistently adhered to since first reading "The Souls of Black Folk" and discussing your leadership with my old schoolmate, Jesse Max Barber, years ago.

In Baltimore, strange to say, I am not regarded as unduly radical. Even with my outspoken views on the communist policy on the race question—and even tho I felt that some colored person should speak out in behalf of the jury fight they made in Maryland, I am the Vice-President of the Baltimore Urban League, a member of the Executive Board of the N.A.A.C.P., Scout Commissioner for

---

1. Euel Lee, an elderly Black man, was charged with killing a family of four white persons in Worcester County, Maryland, in October 1931. Through the energetic actions of a young attorney, Bernard Ades—acting for the International Labor Defense—the execution of Lee was blocked with two appeals; a third failed, and he was executed in 1933. In this case, important precedents were established on such matters as the need to change venue where local prejudice is established, the right of the accused to a lawyer of his own choice, and the illegality of excluding Black people from juries. Disbarment proceedings were brought against young Ades, but he was successfully defended by Charles H. Houston and Thurgood Marshall. Mr. Ades kindly supplied the editor with the record of the judge's opinion in rejecting his disbarment. See also W. M. Beaney, *The Right to Counsel in American Courts* (Ann Arbor, Michigan: University of Michigan Press, 1955), p. 31; and J. North, *Robert Minor* (New York: International Publishers, 1956), pp. 205-8.

Colored Boy Scouts, a member of Public School Recreation Advisory Commission, a member of the Vocational Education advisory committee and a member of the local Interracial Commission. In addition I am the Big Brother of and helped to organize and develop the City Wide Young People's Forum here. I mention these connections only to indicate to you that my views on the Communist policy are not new—but the result of a long standing attitude. The only difference is that I am not afraid of the word "Communism," if it agrees with any attitude I have. In the same manner I was not afraid of the name N.A.A.C.P.

It is therefore in the same open and honest spirit that I acquaint you with my reaction when Mrs. Meijer told me of what you said. So profoundly have you projected yourself into and motivated my life attitudes, that I could not pass over as I would an ordinary criticism—your advice to her in this matter. The fact is, I almost had a sensation of having the very foundation of my objectives shattered.

I am expecting to be in Liberia until November 25. I expect to be back in the States December 22. I am sure you will understand the spirit of this letter. On my way back I shall stop in Hamburg, Germany, London and Paris. If you are so disposed I would be glad to have the names of any persons to whom I might talk in these towns. My Liberian address will be the Executive Mansion.

Very truly,
William N. Jones

Atlanta, Georgia, December 21, 1933

My dear Mr. Jones:

I am sorry that I did not have a chance to see you and co-operate with you with regard to your Washington trip. I think that my advice with regard to inter-racial work in Baltimore was misinterpreted and that, of course, was easy under the circumstances.

What I was trying to say was this: In order to get the races to work together effectively for any particular end in Washington, you have got to select persons who are acceptable to each other, and my opinion was that a Communist or even a Socialist would stand absolutely no chance of being listened to at all by the average white Baltimorian. This, of course, was no criticism of the Communist or Socialist point of view. Quite the contrary. I have long been a Socialist myself and have great sympathy with the Communist idea. The thing that we have got to face is that when for the sake of principle we take a radical position, we have got to pay for it. There is no use of either you or I expecting any position in an inter-racial movement until, of course, such a movement moves much further toward the Left than it has yet. I think the various positions which you have taken and outlined in your letter from London are quite right and the sort of position which I would have taken myself. On the other hand, if I were living in Baltimore, I know that I would not be successful in an inter-racial movement.

I am sorry indeed that I could not have had a long talk with you before you went to Liberia but I should certainly enjoy a word with you when you are back.

Very sincerely yours,
W. E. B. Du Bois

The forces and considerations moving Du Bois more and more to the Left were having similar impact upon many others. These included a considerable number of rather young Afro-American professionals and intellectuals, outstanding among whom was Abram L. Harris, then teaching at Howard University. From him came the proposal, late in 1933, for the creation of a Black lectureship bureau whose members would tour college campuses and bring radical social and economic concepts to the fore. Correspondence between Harris and Du Bois relates this proposal and the ideas behind it. The "recent events" in New York, mentioned at the end of Harris's letter, were Du Bois's increasingly sharp challenges to the traditional line and tactic of the NAACP board.

Atlanta, Georgia, January 3, 1934[1]

My dear Harris:

Your proposal of December 26 is interesting and valuable, but it will take some thought to get it properly started and there is no reason to rush. If we can get it planned for the fall of 1934, we will be doing very well indeed. Meantime, there ought to be a conference on the matter as you suggest, and a good deal depends on the personnel. I should say by all means; Franklin Frazier, Ernest Just, Allison Davis, Sterling Brown, Charles Wesley, Valvarez Spratlin and Rayford Logan.[2] I should be personally very much inclined to add [Robert C.] Weaver to this. An evening's conversation with him has impressed me greatly. I am not so sure about [William H.] Hastie and [Ralph] Bunche. I do not remember Dunham. I am a bit leary about [Alain] Locke and Charles Johnson, but I have no final attitude toward any of these.

Of course there is a fundamental difference between you and me on the present status of Negro learning. You are assuming scholarship and talking from the point of view of what a free and independent mind should seek in the matter of truth. I am conceding all that when we get a free and independent mind in such quantity, but at present our talent is being strangled to death and there is

1. In the original, the letter is inaccurately dated 1933.
2. Among those named here, perhaps only Valvarez B. Spratlin needs identification. He was educated at the University of Denver, taught at Wiley and West Virginia colleges, and in 1932, was associate professor of romance languages and head of his department at Howard. His doctoral dissertation—on Juan Latino— is discussed in the *Crisis* 39 (September 1932):281-83, 300.

no more tremendous proof of the Marxian dogma than the fact that our fundamental economic situation today is making science, art and literature among us almost impossible. Therefore it is that economic problem that we have got to attack and we cannot wait until somebody attacks it for us. While, therefore, I have no doubt that a group of Negro scholars could form an institute for intercollegiate lectures, the chief object of this in my mind would not be the information which they can impart, but the action toward economic salvation that they can induce.

All this, however, is not an argument against your scheme. A plan by which Negro students in the best colleges could hear and see Ernest Just and could have Karl Marx interpreted to them by you and have a dozen others who have something to say say it beyond the walls of one institution, that would be a great step forward no matter what its ultimate object was.

I shall be coming up late in January or early in February and before then we will correspond and at that time perhaps we can have a preliminary conference.

My best regards to Mrs. Harris and you and a Happy New Year!
Very sincerely yours,
W. E. B. Du Bois

Washington, D.C., January 6, 1934

My dear Dr. Du Bois:

I am very pleased with your reactions to my proposal of December 26th. I agree with you that there is a fundamental difference between us. But the difference I fear is not the one that you stated. I agree with you that at present there is hardly a handful of Negro scholars among us and almost no independent thinking. I contend, however, that no program of economic welfare that is planned for the Negro is going to succeed until his socalled intelligentsia is emancipated so that it can furnish guidance. We can't wait for minds and scholars to spring up out of the earth. We have got to develop them ourselves. Even if you would start a fool proof program of Negro economic advancement I am sure that it would soon collapse for want of determined intellectual guidance and support. Now I am going to take your time to tell you what is back of my suggestion so that when we meet we will know where each of us stands. Let me first of all state that the inclusion of some of the names in my letter was due to my belief that you might suggest them yourself.

I am as much concerned about the present economic status of the Negro as you are. But I do not see how very much can be done behind the back of present social changes. These changes are taking place rapidly in our industrial life and I feel that if they continue in the direction they are now going we are going to have industry permanently cartelised. If this takes place small industry whether individualistic or based upon racial self-help is going to have hard sledding. If therefore we decided to launch a co-operative movement among the Negro as a means of economic self-help we must be prepared to see it wiped out of existence by these changes. On the other hand, it is possible that a cartelised industry which will restrict output, maintain high prices, and subject the industrial life of the country to increasing control will, at the same time, so enrage the American consumers that they will subject it to greater and greater control. Given sufficient provocation this control might lead into the establishment of guilds through which the present ownership and management of industry will be eliminated. There is considerable talk about this eventuality around Washington these days, I mean in responsible government circles. This of course would amount to guild socialism which I am beginning to believe is the only kind we are going to see established in our life time, if at all, in this country. If present tendencies culminate into guild socialism I can see that a cooperative movement among Negroes might prove very valuable. Whatever happens it is going to take independent Negro intellectuals to furnish guidance both indirectly and directly. If these intellectuals' thinking is done in the same grooves in which present leadership does its thinking nothing will be accomplished, I am sure. They will merely capture the movement for their individual advantage. Because of this it seems to me that this generation ought to be prepared to give us a leadership which will galvanize, at least conceptually, the Negro's demands for specific changes with the general demand for Change. If organizing certain definitely Negro movements, say the Negro co-operative movement, is the means to facilitate that purpose I am all for it. If not I am against it. From the standpoint of social direction and intellectual perspective there should be no *Negro* movements.

All this may sound as so much day dreaming to you who have seen the world longer than I and have been engaged in practical reforms all your life. It is my conviction, however, that nothing is going to be done with the Negro and about his special problems until we are willing to throw over board certain political and social values that govern our thinking. The whites have begun to do this on a small scale. The Negro must follow suit. I know that I am criticized for constantly demanding that the Negro intellectual think of the race problem in terms of general economic and social changes. But the more I study the economic life of this country the more I am convinced that if the Negro intellectual does not begin to think in this fashion he will effect no permanent or fundamental change in the conditions of the Negro masses. This is going to take a lot of internal purging which we ourselves have got to do. Take for example the power of certain conservative white interests in the realm of education and race politics. The only opposition that you can muster against these interests is a cheap personal one, or perhaps, a racial one. There is hardly a Negro of national prominence with the exception of yourself who would attack these interests on grounds of broad social and economic policy. The reason for this is that the Negro leaders want the Negro masses to emulate the values which these interests represent. And we have got to give the Negro masses a new set of values if anything is to be accomplished. That's why I want these inter-collegiate lectures. With them we can at least open up a new world of ideas to the Negro student and thus lay the basis for the necessary leadership of tomorrow. You are not going to get hold of the Negro masses until you begin to liquidate the influence of certain Negroes and whites who are now assuming leadership. I do not propose that these persons be attacked on personal grounds. What I want and what I think necessary is a persistent drive against the ideals they hold up to the Negro masses for emulation and against the unreality of those ideals. You can't rely upon the James Weldon Johnsons and the Walter Whites for any new program, for they represent just those values that I think stand in the way of clear thinking on the present relation of the Negro to world forces. As long as they, the Brawleys and others I might name are supported by the Phelps-Stokes and the Embrees and the Negro masses are taught to accept them and the things that they represent, you, or perhaps I should say we,* will find that any thing we plan will have to have their moral support or approval if we want it to succeed. Thus as important as a practical economic program is, we must have people behind us who are sick of the old intellectual rubbish whether in literature or some other phase of life. This means that we have got to start digging a new intellectual foundation.

I am more convinced of the logic of my position by recent events that I understand are taking place in New York. I think you know what I have in mind when I say that when I first heard of these moves I started to resign from the National Association's Board of Directors. Upon second thought I decided that I'd better wait to see you. Now if this thing leads into a fight that brings into existence a new movement there is no one to lead it but yourself. Should this come to pass I feel that you are going to [have] a much harder fight on your hands than you did against Booker T. Washington. The issues in that fight were drawn upon fairly simple lines of disagreement. The issues in the fight which might now be brewing are cut across by a thousand and one different interests. It will therefore take a most discriminating mind to cast his lot with you. That discrimination is almost wholly lacking among us and it is the thing I want created.

Let me know when you are coming through so that I will have everything out of the way for a long talk. This meeting I think should be confined to the two of us, and, of course, Callie.[1]

Our best love to you.

Always
Harris.

* I say "we" because you ought to be sure by now of how much I feel myself a part of you; that in spite of fundamental disagreement there is hardly a single living man for whom I have greater affection and genuine admiration.

1. Mrs. Harris.

Harry E. Davis, a Cleveland attorney, was a long-time friend of Du Bois. Prominent in Republican politics, he was a member of the Ohio legislature in the 1920s for four terms, was for many years on Cleveland's civil service commission, and was very prominent in the efforts of the NAACP. Early in 1934, his letter to Du Bois about rumors of the latter's impending resignation from the *Crisis* brought an important response.

> Cleveland, Ohio, January 8, 1934
>
> Dear Dr. Du Bois:
>
> I have today received a letter from a group in New York hinting that there is a movement under way to oust you from the N.A.A.C.P. and presumably from the editorship of the Crisis. The letter is rather vague as to real facts and mentions only common rumor as the basis for the great concern of this group, some of whom I know and others whose acquaintance I do not recall.
>
> However, there may be something to the letter, and I am therefore asking you to write me frankly as to the situation.
>
> With best wishes and kindest regards in which Mrs. Davis joins, I am
>
> Sincerely,
> Harry E. Davis.

> Atlanta, Ga.
> January 16, 1934
>
> My dear Davis:
>
> I did not know of the letter which the New York group was sending out and did not advise it although it was done in good faith and based on the truth.
>
> The outline of the facts is that when the N.A.A.C.P. and *The Crisis* got in financial difficulties last year, I offered to ease the burden by teaching a part of the year at Atlanta University at half salary, and then again for this year I offered to reduce my salary further so that we could hire a business manager. I think we have got a good one in George Streator. But somehow while this legislation was being put through by the Board, I found to my surprise that they had put "sole and complete control" of *The Crisis* in the hands of the Business Manager and Wilkins. I talked the matter over frankly with the Spingarns, who seemed to have engineered the move, and refused to accept the arrangement and offered my resignation. They demurred and persuaded me to outline an acceptable vote by the Board. I did so and the Board passed it, so that I am still carrying on. Nevertheless, it has left a bitter taste, both in their mouths and in mine. It all goes back to the fact that I have believed for two or three years that Walter White is not the proper person to head the Association. I have told the Board frankly this in his presence.
>
> Meantime, I am having a very pleasant year teaching here and have just finished a book on Reconstruction. When it comes out next fall, you'll have to lay aside everything and read it, and believe me it's thick. My best regards to you

and Mrs. Davis. I may be passing through Cleveland in March on a lecture tour somewhere about the middle of the month. If you know of any opening in Cleveland, let me know, but don't for heaven sakes try and work anything up. I could stop there probably sometime late in the week of March 11.

A Happy New Year to you both in which Mrs. Du Bois would join me if she were here.

Very sincerely yours,
W. E. B. Du Bois

As part of Du Bois's concern with the basic needs of his people, he devoted much attention to economic questions, including cooperatives, socialism, and self-sustaining efforts. In this connection, he insisted that unity among the Black people, and the development of their own forms and institutions, was vital for their very survival. Reflecting this emphasis was Du Bois's editorial, "Segregation," in the January 1934 *Crisis* (41:20), which began, "The thinking colored people in the United States must stop being stampeded by the word segregation." He went on to insist that the point was to fight *discrimination* and that this might best be done through Black unity. An exchange in this connection ensued between Walter White and Du Bois.

On 15 January 1934, White wrote to Du Bois at some length, indicating his belief that the editorial was contrary to NAACP policy, and that it had been and would be highly embarrassing to the association in its efforts to persuade the Roosevelt administration toward positive action in regard to the Black people of the nation. In particular, White wished to know in what way Du Bois felt his —White's—position was wrong; White concluded by affirming his wish to express his understanding of association policy in the *Crisis*.

To this, Du Bois replied:

Atlanta, Ga., January 17, 1934

My dear Mr. White:

I am glad to answer your letter of January 15. I have long recognized that the matter of segregation has got to be threshed out very carefully by the Association and in the columns of *The Crisis*, and in the February number I am formally opening the columns for a prolonged discussion of this sort, and I am re-stating from an examination of the Annual Reports of the N.A.A.C.P. some of the actions which the N.A.A.C.P. has taken in the past, and I am saying that our attitude, while clear and unmistakable on certain specific points, has never been complete and logical.[1]

1. In the February 1934 *Crisis* (41:52), Du Bois published three paragraphs announcing "A Free Forum" in the magazine "to discuss Segregation and seek not dogma but enlightenment." Two pages on "The N.A.A.C.P. and Race Segregation" followed, in which

[476] Correspondence 1930–1934

At this point you send me an article on segregation which says among other things: "It is fitting and proper that the statement of the Association's position should first appear in *The Crisis*, the official organ of the Association." This, at the very beginning, assumes by inference that your article is the official statement of the Association's position. You go on to say: "I merely wish to call attention to the fact that the N.A.A.C.P. has never officially budged in its opposition to segregation." This, as I intimated in my telegram, is untrue. We advocated and strongly advocated a segregated Negro officer's camp after we found that we were not allowed to enter the regular officer's camp during the war. And in other cases where the opposition has been strong and the need for united segregated effort apparent, we have not hesitated. Of course, this does not for a moment say that the Association wanted race separation. It did, however, in many cases accept it. Throughout your article the assumption is that the N.A.A.C.P. in the past has taken the extreme stand which you take and that your personal opinion is that the Association should not change this position. This is what I called in my telegram unfair and untrue. On the other hand, I should be very glad to have you or any other officer of the Association in future numbers of *The Crisis* do either one or both of two things:

1. Show by the record of the Association just what its stand on segregation has been.
2. Express their own personal opinion as to what it should be in the future.

For this purpose most of the enclosed article, except the parts which I am marking, are quite admissible, and I should be glad to publish it in March.

Of course in my editorial and in your letter, it is manifest that we are not both speaking always of the same thing. I am using segregation in the broader sense of separate racial effort caused by outer social repulsions, whether those repulsions are a matter of law or custom or mere desire. You are using the word segregation simply as applying to compulsory separations. Evidently the matter of difference here will require thought and explanation.

I am enclosing your article marked.

Very sincerely yours,
W. E. B. Du Bois

---

he summarized the historical data and concluded: "It would be idiotic simply to sit on the side lines and yell: 'No segregation' in an increasingly segregated world. On the other hand, the danger of easily and eagerly yielding to suggested racial segregation without reason or pressure stares us ever in the face." Du Bois published discussions of this question from March to June 1934. He resigned in a letter dated 26 June and as of the end of that month was no longer editor of the *Crisis*. In the March issue, contributions appeared from a number of sources, including Joel E. Spingarn, Walter White, Leslie P. Hill, Clark Foreman, and Clarence Pickett.

George Vaughan (1873–1945) was born in Arkansas and spent his entire life there. An attorney, he obtained an LL.D. from the University of Arkansas in 1926. He was a member of the state senate (1919–21) and from 1929, served as professor of law at the University of Arkansas. In that capacity, he wrote to Du Bois, receiving a characteristically cogent answer.

Fayetteville, Ark., February 9, 1934

Dear Sir:

The distinguished world missionary, Dr. E. Stanley Jones, in the opening passage of his "Christ of Every Road" (1930), said, as you may recall: "The world-ground, I am persuaded, is being prepared for a spiritual awakening on a very extensive scale."

A similar belief has been recorded by Dr. Albert Buckner Coe, and by other competent observers of divergent faiths. On the other hand, there are those whose current messages sound the opposite note, as of a voice "crying in the wilderness." I am wondering how the present spiritual outlook reads to you.

For my part, I have been an optimist; but the later years of contact with the world, especially with my own (the legal) profession, have revealed symptoms of a discouraging indifference to the things of the spirit. In fact, there looms on my horizon an almost irrepressible drift to lower ideals. And sometimes I feel that this *moral lapse* is the "depression" that besets the world today.

"Watchman, what of the night" is a question not for preachers and missionaries alone. The opinion of the secular mind, it seems to me, is quite an important factor in a fair appraisal of our moral and spiritual status.

Hence it is that I am addressing you and a number of other laymen of selected groups in an attitude not of idle curiosity but of earnest and friendly inquiry.

Just what is your general reaction?

While hesitating to trespass on your time, I should really appreciate a frank expression, brief if necessary, in response to the hungering desire which this letter but faintly conveys.

Yours very truly,
George Vaughan

Atlanta, Ga., February 23, 1934

My dear Sir:

Answering your letter of February 9, I may say frankly that I am unable to follow the reasoning of people who use the word "spirit" and "spiritual" in a technical religious sense. It is true that after any great world calamity, when people have suffered widely, there is a tendency to relapse into superstition, obscurantism, and the formal religion of creeds in a vague attempt to reassure humanity, because reason and logic seemed to have failed. This instead of being a spiritual "awakening," is to my mind, an evidence of ignorance and discouragement.

On the other hand, among some people, there comes in time of stress and depression, an increase of determination to plan and work for better conditions. This is not usually called a "spiritual" awakening, but it is apt to be condemned by the ignorant as "radicalism" and an "attack" upon the established order. It is, however, a manifestation of the spirit in the highest sense and something of this I seem to see beginning today.

Very sincerely yours,
W. E. B. Du Bois

Two communications from Du Bois to the board of the NAACP were sent in May and June 1934. One, announcing his resignation, was an open letter widely published at the time.

Atlanta, Georgia, May 21, 1934

To the Board of Directors of the
N.A.A.C.P.

At the May meeting of the Board, the following action was taken:

On motion of Dr. [Louis T.] Wright, duly seconded, it was *voted*, That The *Crisis* is the organ of the Association and no salaried officer of the Association shall criticize the policy, work, or officers of the Association in the pages of The *Crisis;* that any such criticism should be brought directly to the Board of Directors and its publication approved or disapproved.

I did not know of this action until a week after the June editorials had been written.

I regret to say that I am unable to comply with this vote. I do not for a moment question the right of the Board to take this action or its duty to do so whenever differences of opinion among its officers become so wide as to threaten the organization. On the other hand, I seriously question the wisdom or right of any distinction between the opinions of salaried and unsalaried officials.

In thirty-five years of public service my contribution to the settlement of the Negro problems has been mainly candid criticism based on a careful effort to know the facts. I have not always been right, but I have been sincere, and I am unwilling at this late day to be limited in the expression of my honest opinions in the way in which the Board proposes. In fact, *The Crisis* never was and never was intended to be an organ of the Association in the sense of simply reflecting its official opinion. I could point to a dozen actions of the Board confirming this. My ideal for *The Crisis* has always been that anyone's opinion, no matter how antagonistic to mine, or to the Association, could to a reasonable extent, find there free and uncensored expression. I will not edit *The Crisis* unless this policy can be continued.

I am, therefore, resigning from my position as Director of Publications and Research, Editor of *The Crisis,* member of the Board of Directors of the

N.A.A.C.P., and member of the Spingarn Medal Committee—this resignation to take effect immediately.

I am grateful for the opportunity of service which this organization has given me for twenty-four years, and for many marks of its confidence.

Very respectfully yours,
W. E. B. Du Bois

Atlanta, Georgia, June 26, 1934

To the Board of Directors of the
N.A.A.C.P.

In deference to your desire to postpone action on my resignation of June 11, I have allowed my nominal connection with *The Crisis* to extend to July 1, and have meantime entered into communication with the Chairman of the Board, and with your Committee of Reconciliation.

I appreciate the good will and genuine desire to bridge an awkward break which your action indicated, and yet it is clear to me, and I think to the majority of the Board that under the circumstances my resignation must stand. I owe it, however, to the Board and to the public to make clear at this time the deeper reasons for my action, lest the apparent causes of my resignation seem inadequate.

Many friends have truthfully asserted that the segregation argument was not the main reason for my wishing to leave this organization. It was an occasion and an important occasion, but it could have been adjusted. In fact, no matter what the Board of the National Association for the Advancement of Colored People says, its action toward segregation has got to approximate, in the future as in the past, the pattern which it followed in the case of the separate camp for Negro officers during the World War and in the case of the Tuskegee Veterans' Hospital. In both instances, we protested vigorously and to the limit of our ability the segregation policy. Then, when we had failed and knew we had failed, we bent every effort toward making the colored camp at Des Moines the best officers' camp possible, and the Tuskegee Hospital, with its Negro personnel, one of the most efficient in the land. This is shown by the 8th and 14th Annual Reports of the National Association for the Advancement of Colored People.

The only thing, therefore, that remains for us is to decide whether we are openly to recognize this procedure as inevitable, or be silent about it and still pursue it. Under these circumstances, the argument must be more or less academic, but there is no essential reason that those who see different sides of this same shield should not be able to agree to live together in the same house.

The whole matter assumed, however, a serious aspect when the Board peremptorily forbade all criticism of the officers and policies in *The Crisis*. I had planned to continue constructive criticism of the National Association for the Advancement of Colored People in *The Crisis* because I firmly believe that the National Association for the Advancement of Colored People faces the most gruelling of tests which come to an old organization: founded in a day when a negative program of protest was imperative and effective; it succeeded so well that the program seemed perfect and unlimited. Suddenly, by World War and chaos, we are called to formulate a positive program of construction and inspiration. We have been thus far unable to comply.

Today this organization, which has been great and effective for nearly a quarter of a century, finds itself in a time of crisis and change, without a program, without effective organization, without executive officers who have either the ability or disposition to guide the National Association for the Advancement of Colored People in the right direction.

These are harsh and arresting charges. I make them deliberately, and after long thought, earnest effort, and with infinite writhing of spirit. To the very best of my ability, and every ounce of my strength, I have since the beginning of the Great Depression, tried to work inside the organization for its realignment and readjustment to new duties. I have been almost absolutely unsuccessful. My program for economic readjustment has been totally ignored. My demand for a change in personnel has been considered as mere petty jealousy, and my protest against our mistakes and blunders has been looked upon as disloyalty to the organization.

So long as I sit by silently consenting, I share responsibility. If I criticize within, my words fall on deaf ears. If I criticize openly, I seem to be washing dirty linen in public. There is but one recourse, complete and final withdrawal, not because all is hopeless nor because there are no signs of realization of the possibilities of reform and of the imperative demand for men and vision, but because evidently I personally can do nothing more.

I leave behind me in the organization many who have long thought with me, and yet hesitated at action; many persons of large ideals who see no agents at hand to realize them, and who fear that the dearth of ability and will to sacrifice within this organization, indicates a similar lack within the whole race. I know that both sets of friends are wrong, and while I desert them with deep reluctance, it is distinctly in the hope that the fact of my going may arouse to action and bring a great and gifted race to the rescue, with a rebirth of that fine idealism and devotion that founded the National Association for the Advancement of Colored People.

Under those circumstances, there is but one thing for me to do, and that is to make the supreme sacrifice of taking myself absolutely and unequivocally out of the picture, so hereafter the leaders of the National Association for the Advancement of Colored People, without the distraction of personalities and accumulated animosities, can give their whole thought and attention to the rescuing of the greatest organization for the emancipation of Negroes that America has ever had.

I am, therefore, insisting upon my resignation, and on July 1st, whether the

Board of Directors acts or does not act, I automatically cease to have any connection whatsoever in any shape or form with the National Association for the Advancement of Colored People. I do not, however, cease to wish it well, to follow it with personal and palpitating interest, and to applaud it when it is able to rescue itself from the present impossible position and reorganize itself according to the demands of the present crisis.

Very respectfully yours,
W. E. B. Du Bois

Owen Reed Lovejoy (1866–1961) was born in Michigan and educated at Albion College. He served as a minister of Protestant churches in Michigan and in New York City until 1904 and, thereafter, devoted himself largely to children's welfare work; from 1927 through 1935, he was the secretary of the Children's Aid Society in New York City. His letter to Du Bois was written shortly before the latter's final resignation from the NAACP.

New York City, June 18, 1934

My dear Dr. Du Bois:

I was glad to notice in the Amsterdam News this morning that the Board of Directors of the N.A.A.C.P. did not take action on your resignation from the Editorship of the Crisis and your other connections.

For many years I have been a reader of the Crisis greatly to my profit and I should consider it a distinct loss not only to the welfare of the American Negro but to the educational and cultural interests of all of us if the paper were to be deprived of your leadership.

Earnestly as I have advocated for years the abolition of segregation in railroad stations, transportation vehicles, schools and other public facilities, I see no practical answer to the position you have taken. A perfectionist ideal on any great public question has tremendous educational value, but after all, I think we must face this great question not as a unit but as a congeries of quite disparate elements to be approached with pragmatic realism.

In my own case, for instance, I have been sharply criticized for attempting to provide through this Society for particular groups of Negro children, on the ground that they were being treated as a special group. But we face the choice of either doing that or nothing, and I cannot feel that neglected and dependent children should be compelled to wait for some distant millenium before having anything done in their behalf.

If I understand the position you have taken it is in no sense a reversing of the principles you have held for years but only an attempt to discriminate between principle and strategy. Let me express the hope that the differences which now seem so sharp may be resolved so that the needs of neglected Negroes—especially children—may receive the united service of all who wish them well.

With great respect and personal regards, I am

Sincerely yours,
Owen R. Lovejoy

Atlanta, Georgia, July 19, 1934

My dear Mr. Lovejoy:

I appreciate very much your kind letter of June 18. It is extremely difficult to make an organization grow and change in accordance with the times. Most organizations get accumulations of directors and friends, who think entirely in the past. I have been very sorry to give up the N.A.A.C.P. and *The Crisis*, but I saw no way to orientate the objects of the Association in accordance with the definite economic needs of the Negro today, and it seems to me a good deal better to do my talking unattached, than to fight within the organization.

I am glad to have a word from you in appreciation of the difficulties of my position.

Very sincerely yours,
W. E. B. Du Bois

From a young Black woman in a small town in Indiana, on vacation from Oberlin College and just about to embark upon a career of distinction in drama, music, and literature, came a deeply felt letter on Du Bois's parting from the N.A.A.C.P.

Kokomo, Indiana, June 23, 1934

My dear Dr. Du Bois:

To you, who have lived a thousand years of thinking, of study, of working and striving, to you, whose face has turned ever towards a far distant horizon, I, whose foot is barely lifted to begin that endless climb up a path which some folks call Achievement, but others know is Calvary, I dare to hail and bring greetings.

All great men have lived years ahead of their time—Socrates, Plato, Galileo, John Locke, Descartes. They have all lived surrounded by that consuming fire of loneliness. They have been born with the curse of work upon them, "born to work and to love it." Critics may not consider Michelangelo's last works his best, but for me certainly one of the most powerful and truly the most poignant work of the renaissance is the group in which beneath the monk's cowl he has carved his own face—that face which had looked out upon life for nearly ninety years. Pain, disappointment, disillusion show in this face, fatigue, such as fell upon it during those years he spent upon his back painting the Sistine ceiling, heartbreak over thwarted hopes and broken dreams. But his head is bowed over the burden which he bears in his arms—the dying Christ—and in his eyes and over his face transfiguring age and pain glows his belief in the importance of his Mission.

Who has ever understood you—the youth in school, sure of the manhood which lifted his head, certain that Right makes Might, leaping over bars with careless indifference, developing every faculty, laughing at boundaries; the young teacher, anxious to impart knowledge, bewildered by the stupidity, the bigotry and shortsightedness of his "superiors"; the man, heart torn with grief, raising his hands to high heaven and calling down the wrath of God upon the hordes of a maddened city?

You have gone on.

The years have passed and you have seen the things "you gave your life for broken, twisted by knaves to make a trap for fools." Discrimination, hate, segregation, misunderstanding would seem to be increasing rather than decreasing. Our churches have fallen into disrepute, our best schools air their grievances through the newspapers, our "leaders" are either ignorantly quarrelsome or wrapped in gloomy silence.

Monroe Trotter is dead.

We build monuments for our great men when they are dead. I like the German word better—*denkmal*. It is well that we should set up a thinking mark for them. After all, only in so far as any man has made us think is he great. It is therefore only fitting that at this time, when the outward appearance of things is so discouraging, you should know that there is a group in America in whose heart has been set up for you a "denkmal." I bring you this word from the students who are today going forth from every college and university of the land. You have said that education would bring solutions and we, white and black students, believe that it is true. You know how in the leading colleges of the country the Negro and his contribution is being studied as never before. Dr. Herbert A. Miller will again this summer conduct classes at Swarthmore. No doubt you also will speak there. You know the attitude of the men who gather there, but even more important is the attitude of the college youth who will in a few years control the affairs of this country.

The increasing number of Negro students in the colleges, universities, conservatories and art schools, the honors which they are receiving are having their effect upon the increasing numbers of white students. There is the incident of the conservatory in which a black violinist was not only the acknowledged best musician but was also socially the most popular student. A girl from Georgia in begging him to assist her on her senior recital and share honors with her at the reception emphasized her request by saying that her father and mother "might as well learn." At Western Reserve this spring the college magazine printed a bitter editorial of indictment against the national debating fraternity which would not admit John Cobb simply because "he is a Negro." At another university a marriage between the two races has been carefully concealed from the authorities. The groom, who is white, is one of the most brilliant graduate students in the country. His student friends seem to heartily approve of his marriage. You know of the reaction of the students in several southern colleges when asked whether or not Negroes should be admitted.

We firmly believe that the discrimination which seems to be increasing in America represents the last stand of the "old guard" who see the end of the day of racial hatred fast approaching. Many parents are being "shown" by their children. They are appalled and they are doing everything in their power to hold the Negro back. It is too late. You and Monroe Trotter have led us too far. And with us are thousands of other young folks who see no reason why we should be held back. It is true that some of them will weaken when they come in contact with certain issues, but we ourselves are gaining strength and enough of us will hold on to make real that progress.

I think we have fewer illusions than our parents had. We do not expect miracles, we have no faith in the white man's religion. We know that "social equality" and "amalgamation" are but by-products of a natural process. We are not particularly interested in either. We do not expect the white man to give us anything. We are preparing ourselves to take our places in the sun as other men have taken theirs.

For all that you have done for us, we thank you.

We, who are about to live, salute you, our Chief.

Sincerely yours,
Shirley Graham

Atlanta, Georgia
June 27, 1934

My dear Miss Graham:

I appreciate very deeply indeed your kind and flattering letter of June 23. Words like these make effort worthwhile.

Very sincerely yours,
W. E. B. Du Bois

INDEX

to and *from* indicate letters to and from

Abbott, Lyman, 46 n
Abbott, Robert S., 261, 271
   from: 262
Achimoto College (Ghana), 182
Adair, James F., 258
Adams, Charles Francis, 142
   to: 142–43, 144
   from: 143
Adams, Ephraim Douglass, 231, 231 n
   from: 231
Adams, Herbert B., 17 n
Adams, John, 142
Adams, John Quincy, 142
Addams, Jane, 56, 169 n, 175, 186, 302, 433 n
Ades, Bernard, 468 n
Adler, Felix, 76, 173, 401
Advisory Committee on National Illiteracy, 408–10
Africa, 15, 115, 124, 181–84, 222, 250 n, 253–54, 260–61, 290, 291, 292, 303, 311, 391, 451, 461–62, 467; development, 320–23
African Development Company, 260
African history, 466
African Methodist Episcopal Zion (AMEZ) Church, 92
African national independence movements, 75
Africa Report, 466
Aggrey, J. E. Kwegyir, 181
   from: 181–84
Agricultural Adjustment Administration, 292
agriculture, study of, 26–27, 175
Aitkins, M., 5
Aitkins, S. G., 93
Alabama, 56, 123, 151, 306
Albion College, 481
Alcorn Agricultural and Mechanical College, 37
Alexander, Lillian A., 415
   to: 415
Allen, Devere, 405–8, 418
   to: 405–6; 407; 408
   from: 406–7; 407–8
Allen, Richard, 337
Allied Expeditionary Force, 230
Amenia Conference, 303–4, 347
American Academy of Political and Social Science, 439
American Association for the Advancement of Science, 215
American Association for Indian Affairs, 437
American Bar Association, 136
American Church Institute for Negroes, 130
American City, 401 n
American Crisis Biographies, 60–61
American Colonization Society, 123
American Economics Association, 122
American Federation of Labor, 319, 418
American Historical Association, 10, 16, 150
American Historical Review, 150 n, 171, 442
American Journal of Sociology, 131
American Labor party, 267
American Magazine, 128 n, 132 n
American Mercury, 292, 296, 298, 380 n
American Missionary Association, 47
American Museum of Natural History, 115
American Negro Academy, 91
American Negro Labor Congress, 306
American Peace Commission (1918), 250
American People's College, 433 n
American Social Science Association, 75 n
Amherst College, 226, 277, 326, 347, 355
Amsterdam News, 481
Anderson, Charles W., 258
Anderson, Jeremiah, 154, 156, 159
Anderson, John, 155
Anderson, Matthew, 93
Anderson, Osborne Perry, 168
Anderson, Sherwood, 342
   from: 342
Andrews, Charles Freer, 402, 402 n, 403, 404

Andrews, Regina, 416-17
Andrews, R. McCants, 267
anthropology, 115, 130, 132, 350, 436
Anti-Imperialist League, 136-37
Anti-Lynching League, 55
Antioch College, 440
anti-Semitism, 23, 417, 432
Anti-Slavery Society, 204
Appleget, Thomas B.
  from: 367-78
Aptheker, Herbert, 39 n, 44 n, 104 n, 112 n, 173 n
Argonne, Battle of, 255
Arkansas, 151; University of, 477
Arlington National Cemetery, 223
Armistice (1918), 230, 254
Armstrong Association, 119
Armstrong, Samuel, 216
Armstrong School (Washington, D. C.), 388
Arthur, Chester A., 185
Arwood, W. B., 45
Asia, 303, 311, 461
Asquith, Herbert Henry, 184, 422
Associated Negro Press, 101, 299
Associated Press, 290
Associated Publishers, 334, 449
Associates in Negro Folk Education, 345
Association for the Study of Negro Life and History, 140, 150, 312, 334, 352, 499
Athearn, R. H., 312
  to: 313
  from: 312-13
Atkinson, Margaretta, 83
  to: 84
  from: 83-84
Atlanta, 39, 42, 45, 56, 58, 60, 67, 95, 103, 141, 167, 436; 1906 riots, 123
Atlanta University, 43, 44, 46 n, 47, 49, 52, 67, 69 n, 80, 83, 92, 100, 103, 107, 108, 110, 111, 112, 115, 118, 139, 145, 175, 203-4, 226, 309, 400, 433 n, 453, 465; 474; Conferences, 81, 121-22, 131, 133 n, 140, 146 n; Publications, 78, 136, 204 n, 367
Atlantic Monthly, 46 n, 47, 48, 113, 128, 155, 400, 400 n
Atwood, Charlotte, 404 n
Azikiwe, (Ben) Nnamdi, 331, 464

  to: 332; 465
  from: 331-32; 415-16; 464-65

Babar, Zonia, 404 n
Badley, J. H., 187 n, 188
Bagnall, Robert W., 271, 288
Bailey, H. L., 144
Baker, Newton D., 223, 236, 278 n
  to: 224; 236
  from: 224-25; 236-37
Baker, Ray Stannard, 128 n, 132
Baker, T. Nelson, 117, 118
  to: 117
Balch, Emily Greene, 404
Baldwin, William H., Jr., 52, 76
Baltimore, Md., 125, 257, 267, 377, 467-69
Baltimore Afro-American, 467
Baltimore Sun, 290
Baltimore Urban League, 468
Barber, Jesse Max, 95, 145, 176, 357, 468
  from: 176-77; 358
Bar Harbor, Maine, 108, 109
Barnett, Ferdinard L., 55
Barthé, Richmond, 376
  to: 377
  from: 376-77
Bartol, Cyrus, 355
Baskin, Ulysses S., 357
Bassett, Ebenezer D., 404
Bassett, Ulysses G., 404
Battle, Wallace, 357-58
Beaney, W. M., 468 n
Bedales School (England), 187-88, 207
Belasco, David, 332-33
  from: 332; 333
Belgium, 278 n, 305-7
Benedict College, 467
Bennett, Arnold, 220
Bentley, C. E., 93, 248
Bentley, Charles, T., 53
Benton, Charles E., 304 n
Benton, Ingram, 304
Berger, Victor, 253
Berkshire Courier, 19
Berlin, University of, 18, 22-23, 26, 28, 314, 315, 444; Social Political Club, 23
Bernard Baruch College, 434
Bing, Alexander, 401
  to: 401-2
  from: 401; 402

Birmingham, Ala., 306, 307
birth control, 301-2
Bishop, H. C., 258
Bishop, Samuel H., 130
  to: 131
  from: 130-31
Black Academy Review, 331 n
Black Laws, 64
Black Lectureship Bureau (proposed), 470-73
Black Star Line, 261, 271, 318
Black State (United States), 358-60
Blatch, Harriot Stanton, 209
  to: 210
  from: 209-10
Bluefield Institute (Bluefield State College), 385
Blyden, Edward Wilmot, 145, 184, 185 n
  to: 146
Board of Missions of the Protestant Episcopal Church, 130
Boas, Franz, 77, 114, 131, 132 n, 350
Bohm, Ernest, 319
Boissevain, Inez Milholland, 132 n
Bolles, Frank, 11
Bontemps, Arna, 344-45
  from: 345
Booker, H. Arthur, 258
Booklover's Magazine, 57 n
Borah, William Edgar, 338, 369, 369 n, 384
  to: 338-39; 341
  from: 339; 339-41; 341-42
Boston, Mass., 48, 49, 83 n, 91, 137, 138, 156, 168 n, 169, 300, 354-55, 453; Zion Church disturbance, 67
Boston Colored Citizen, 96, 99, 103
Boston Courant, 355
Boston Guardian, 49, 67, 68, 82, 100, 347
Boston Herald, 10, 194
Boston Literary Association, 132
Boston Negroes, 379-80
Boston Post, 380 n
Boston Public Library, 347-48, 355, 387 n
Boston Transcript, 110, 180
Boston University, 416
Bourne, Edward G., 17 n
Boutté, M. V., 297 n, 298
Boutté, Mrs. M. V., 369
  to: 369-70
Bowen, J. W. E., 54, 93

Bowers, Claude G., 411
Bowers, L. A., 8
  from: 8-9
Boyd, R. A., 93
Boy Scouts, Negro, 469
Brace, Donald C., 442
Bradley, W. A., 376
Braithwaite, William S., 176
Brand, Bernice E., 363
  to: 364-65
  from: 364
Brandeis, Louis D., 175, 386
  from: 386
Brascher, N. B., 299
  to: 299-300
Brawley, Benjamin, 448
Brewster, William T., 177
  to: 178
  from: 177-78
Briggs, Cyril, 251
Brooks, Van Wyck, 291
Brooks, W. H., 118, 148, 258
Brotherhood of Railroad Trainmen, 385
Brotherhood of Sleeping Car Porters, 267, 319, 371, 462
Browne, Hugh M., 105
Brown, John, 60, 61, 64-65, 113
Brown, Owen, 156
Brown, Peter, 155
Brown, Sterling A., 345, 470
  to: 346
  from: 346
Brown University, 109, 171
Brown, William Wells, 184, 185 n, 258
Brownies' Book, 235
Brownsville (Texas) Incident, 134-35
Bruce, B. K., 64
Bruce, John E., 258
Brumbaugh, M. G., 77
Brussels, 250-51
Bryn Mawr College, 195
Buell, Raymond Leslie, 403, 420, 464-65
  to: 404
  from: 403
Bulkley, William L., 118, 119, 120
Bumstead, D. Horace, 47, 67
  from: 47-48; 69-70
Bunche, Ralph J., 353, 470
  to: 354
  from: 353-54

Burghardt, Jack, 15
Burghardt, Mary S., 15
  to: 3
Burghardt, Othello, 15
Burghardt, Sarah Lampman, 3
  to: 3
Burghardt, Thomas, 15
Butcher, Philip, 7 n
Butler, Nicholas Murray, 130

Cable, George Washington, 6, 7 n
  to: 7
Cable, James A., 49
  to: 52
  from: 51
Cabot, Charles M., 186
Calhoun, John C., 61
California, 399; University of, 195, 314, 335
Call, 270
Calloway, Thomas J., 37
Calverton, Victor F., 377
  to: 378
  from: 377-78
Cambridge, Mass., 213; City Council, 277
Capacity of Black people, 13-14, 74, 75, 350-51, 364-65
Carlton College, 435
Carnegie, Andrew, 52, 121, 165
  to: 121-22
Carnegie Foundation, 284
Carnegie Institution, 122, 171
Carter, Louis A.
  to: 357
  from: 355-56
Cartwright, Leonard C.
  to: 381-82
  from: 379-81
Casement, Sir Roger, 173
Cashin, Lillian E., 299
caste in America, 82
Castle, W. R., Jr., 277 n, 278 n
  from: 313-14
Catholic Church: and American Negroes, 308-11
Catholic encyclopedia, 447
Century, 144, 200, 318 n
Chakravartz, Amiya C., 404
  from: 404-5
Chamberlain, Joseph, 183
Chambers, Clarke A., 186 n
Channing, Edward, 9

Charities Publication Committee, 186
Charity Organization Society (New York City), 119, 175
Charlotte Observer, 182
Chase, F. A., 11
Chatham Convention, 154
Chesnutt, Charles Waddell, 56, 57 n, 62 n, 316, 342, 378
  from: 56-57; 316-17; 343
Chicago, 53, 93, 151 n, 176, 248, 257, 267, 333, 358; Art Institute, 376; City Council, 463; University of, 71, 140, 171, 195, 327, 404 n, 418, 463
Chicago Conservator, 96, 98, 100
Chicago Defender, 261
Child, Francis, 9
child labor, 135-36
Children's Aid Society (New York City), 481
China, 303, 315
Chinese People's Republic, 333
Chipman, Miner, 213
  from: 213-14
Christy, Cuthbert, 465
City College of New York, 435
City Housing Corporation (New York), 401
Civic Club (New York City), 255, 315
Civil Rights Law, 388
Civil Service: and Negroes, 274
Civil War, 61, 129 n, 142, 151 n, 208, 283, 337, 340, 348, 391
Clarke, Edward, 418
  to: 418
  from: 418
Clark, Novella, 236
  from: 236
Clark University, 92, 462
Clemenceau, Georges, 233
Clement, Edward Henry, 180
  from: 180
Cleveland, Grover, 91
Cleveland Journal, 103
Cleveland, Ohio, 223, 257, 352, 395, 445
Clifford, Carrie W. (Mrs. W. H.), 220
  to: 221
  from: 221
Clifford, J. R., 93
Cobb, Irwin, 259
Cobb, James, 388
Cobb, John, 483
Coe, Albert Backner, 477

Index [489]

Coffin, William Sloane, 401
Cohen, Octavus Roy, 258–60, 316
Coigney, Virginia, 301 n
Cole, Bob, 115
College of the Holy Cross, 310 n
college, proposed Black, 327, 433–34
colleges, unrest in, 352–53
Collier, John, 175
Collier, Robert T., 72
　to: 73
　from: 72–73; 73; 73–74
Collier's Weekly, 72–74, 131
colonization of Black people, 123–25, 364–65
Colored American Magazine, 96, 104
Colored Catholic schools, 310–11
Colored Methodist Episcopal Church, 233
Colta, Frau Vroula, 19
Columbia University, 77, 115, 122, 130, 150, 175, 182, 189 n, 327, 403; Law School, 326, 387 n, 427
Columbus, Christopher, 19
Comings, Samuel Huntington, 78, 79
　to: 80–81
　from: 79–80
Committee for Consideration of a National Budget, 252
Committee for Improving Industrial Conditions of Negroes in New York City, 118
Committee of One Hundred, 170, 220
Committee of Twelve, 104–6
Committee on Industrial Relations, 175, 176
Committee on Social Investigations, 77
Committee on Urban Conditions among Negroes, 118
Communist party, 306, 468–69
Communists, 253, 267, 344, 465–66, 468–70
Congregationalist, 16, 17 n
Congregationalist and Christian World, 117
　to: 118
Constitution League, 132, 145, 150
Cooke, Jay, 61
Coolidge, Calvin, 271, 277–78, 297, 313, 384; "Coolidgism", 375
　from: 314
Cools, G. Victor, 292
　to: 294
　from: 293–94

Cooper, Anna J., 411
　from: 411
Cooperative League of the United States, 305
co-operatives, 305–6, 471
Cooperative Settlement Society of New York, 77
Cooper, E. E., 98, 101, 102
Cooper, Joseph, 184, 185 n
Coopers' International Union of North America, 49, 51
Cooper Union (New York City), 302
Cooper, William John, 409–10
　to: 409
　from: 409
Copley Medal, 444
Cornell University, 65–66, 74, 125, 126, 290
Cosmopolitan Club Movement, 353, 353 n
Cotton Exposition (1895), 39
Counts, George S., 433 n
Cravath, Erastus Milo, 6 n, 11, 37 n
Creel, George, 232
crime, Negro, 121, 439
Crisis, 57 n, 66, 76 n, 144, 147 n, 174–80, 188–97, 203–7, 209, 214, 219–20, 223, 225–30, 232, 234–37, 245–46, 247 n, 251–52, 254, 260, 263, 267–70, 273–76, 278, 281, 283–84, 290, 292, 294–97, 308–11, 316, 318–20, 324–25, 329–34, 337–38, 339 n, 341–46, 348–49, 353, 354 n, 355–57, 360, 364, 366, 370–76, 380–83, 385–86, 400 n, 401–2, 405 n, 408, 411, 415, 418, 420, 422, 426–31, 440–41, 444, 449–51, 454–55, 458, 460–61, 463, 465, 470 n, 474, 478–79, 480–81, 482
Crogman, W. H., 92
Cromwell, John W., 100, 151, 184
Cromwell, Mary, 117
Crosswaith, Frank R., 266
　to: 270–71
　from: 266–70
Cruikshank, Brodie, 183 n, 184, 185 n
Cuba, 212, 403–4, 415
Cullen, Countee, 330, 344, 377, 434 n
Current History, 377, 400
Curtis Publishing Company, 258

Dana, Richard, 142
Daniel, Pete, 273
Daniels, John, 132

Darrow, Clarence, 169 n, 408
  from: 408
Dartmouth College, 264
Davidson, E., 45
Davis, Allison, 470
Davis, Arthur P., 429
Davis, D. R., 50
Davis, Harry E., 474
  to: 474-75
  from: 474
Davis, Jefferson, 61
Davis, Jerome, 435
Davis, John P., 255 n
Davis, John W., 241
  to: 441-42
  from: 441
Dayton, Ohio, 452-53; Council of Social Agencies, 452-53; Paul Lawrence Dunbar School, 452-53
Debs, Eugene V., 408
Declaration of Independence, 150th anniversary of, in Pennsylvania, 336-37
DeFrantz, F. E., 249
  to: 249-50
  from: 249
Dei-Arrang, Michael, 183 n
Deland, Margaret Wade, 382
  to: 383-84
  from: 383
democracy, 114, 250, 406-7, 415
Democratic National Committee, 67
Democratic party, 267-71, 463
Demker, Joseph, 115
Denver, University of, 470 n
depression, economic, 441-42, 445-47
DePriest, Oscar, 383-84
Des Moines, Iowa, 105, 221, 222
Deutsch, Babette, 344
Devine, Edward T., 77, 175, 186
  from: 176
Dewey, John, 79 n, 169 n, 405, 433-34
Dexter, Carolina, 180
  to: 180
dialect, 316
Dickerson, Earl Burrus, 463
  from: 463-64
Diggs, J. R. L., 150
  to: 152
  from: 150-51
Dillard, James H., 312, 365, 447
  to: 447-48
  from: 448

Dillard University (New Orleans), 447
Dill, Augustus G., 178, 204, 204 n, 205, 226, 235, 296
Dingle, A. E., 259, 259 n
Dixon, Thomas, 114
Doak, William N., 385, 463
Dole, Charles Fletcher, 195
domestic workers, 42
Domingo, William A., 263
  to: 263-64
  from: 263
Douglas, Paul H., 404 n, 405, 418
  to: 419
  from: 419
Douglass, Frederick, 55, 60-63, 157 n, 168, 210 n
Dowd, Jerome, 185, 185 n
Drake, J. G. St. Clair, 428
  to: 429
  from: 429
Dreiser, Theodore ("Dreiser Protest"), 220
Du Bois, Alexander, 3, 15
Du Bois, Alfred, 15
Du Bois, Burghardt (son), 127
Du Bois clubs, 125
Du Bois Community High School (Sandusky, Ill.), 308
Du Bois, Nina Gomer (Mrs. W. E. B.), 38, 48, 67, 92, 121, 127, 132, 187, 292, 437
Du Bois, W. E. B., *Autobiography*, 3, 13 n, 15 n, 37, 38, 225, 334 n, 354 n; *Black Reconstruction*, 150, 190 n, 411, 442, 465, 474-75; *Black Folk: Then and Now: An Essay in the History and Sociology of the Negro Race*, 210 n; "Credo," 78, 82, 91, 95, 333; *Dark Princess*, 378, 380-82, 384, 461; *Darkwater*, 190 n, 378, 442, 458, 461; *Dusk of Dawn*, 13 n, 15 n, 39 n, 67 n, 108 n, 190 n, 223, 277 n, 334 n, 465; *Gift of Black Folk*, 315 n; *John Brown*, 153-64, 168-69, 197; *The Negro*, 114 n, 177, 210-11, 350, 367, 442, 467; *The Philadelphia Negro: A Social Study*, 40, 42 n, 43, 122, 123, 177, 336, 367; *The Quest of the Silver Fleece*, 113, 197, 378; *Souls of Black Folk*, 47, 54, 55 n, 56-57, 60, 66, 76, 79, 83, 106, 116, 122, 124, 125-26, 134, 141, 152, 159, 182, 196, 198-99, 213,

Index [491]

300, 332–33, 378, 458–61, 468; *Suppression of the African Slave Trade*, 17 n, 123, 177, 367
Du Bois, Yolande, 92, 121, 127, 132, 187–88, 207, 255, 308, 434 n
  to: 127–28; 207–8; 255–56
Dudley, L. P., 390
  to: 390
Duff, Grace, 308 n
Duffield, Mrs. E. A., 275
  to: 276
Dunbar High School (Washington, D.C.), 388, 404 n, 411
Dunbar, Paul Lawrence, 259–60, 378
Dunning, William A., 150
Duster, Alfreda, 55 n
Dyer (anti-lynching) Bill, 262, 341

East and West, 74
Eastern Association in Indian Affairs, 437
Eaton, Isabel, 40 n, 42 n
Eatonville, Florida, 137–38
Eddie High School (Milledgeville, Ga.), 233
education, 46–48, 58–59, 78–80, 93, 110, 135, 137, 166–67, 187, 208, 215–16, 249–50, 266–67, 272–73, 326, 327–28, 335, 420–21, 429, 433, 452–53
Edwards, H. J., 258
Eikson, J. A., 45
Einstein, Albert, 444
  to: 444
  from: 444–45
Elbert, Ella Smith, 355
Ellis, Alfred B., 183, 184, 185 n
Ellis, Havelock, 347
  from: 347
Ellis, Mrs. Havelock, 173. See also Lees, Edith
Emancipation Proclamation, 50th anniversary celebration of, 14, 168 n, 185–86
Embree, Edwin R., 438, 439 n, 473
  to: 439–40
  from: 438–39
emigration, of Black people, 113–15
Encyclopedia Britannica, 390–93, 398–99
Encyclopedia of the Negro, plans for, 145–47, 152, 447–49
Encyclopedia of the Social Sciences, 122
Enfield, O. E., 183 n

England, 20, 116, 124, 134, 173–74, 177, 220, 301, 302, 318, 365–67
Enright, Richard E., 257
  to: 264
  from: 257–58
Episcopal Church, 357
Epworth Herald, 325 n
Equal Rights League, 355
Essien-Udom, E. U., 271 n
Ethical Culture Society, 125, 173; School, 265
Europe, 18, 250 n, 311, 328
Evans, Elizabeth Glendower, 383, 386
Ewing, Quincy, 399
  to: 400–401
  from: 400

Farmer-Labor party, 267–71
Farnum, Henry W., 175
Farrand, Livingston, 77
fascism, 379
Fauset, Jessie, 65–66, 74, 94, 255–56, 295, 329, 375, 378 n, 407
  to: 330–31; 331–32; 342
  from: 66; 94–95
Featherstonhaugh, Thomas, 156–57
Federal Church of Christ in America, 436
Fellowship of Reconciliation, 302, 404 n
Fels, Joseph, 79 n
Ferber, Edna, 330
Ferris Institute (Ferris State College), 213
Ferris, Woodbridge N., 213
Fess, Simeon D., 440
  from: 440
Finot, Jean, 350
Firestone, Harvey S., 320
  to: 320–23
Firestone Rubber Tire Company, 281, 320–23
First International, 268
First Universal Races Congress, 173, 347, 350, 353 n, 428 n
Fisher, Dorothy Canfield, 246
  from: 246–47
Fisher, Herbert, 177
Fisher, Rudolph, 325, 343, 377–78
Fisk Herald, 6, 306
Fisk News, 299
Fisk University, 5, 6, 8, 11, 12, 14, 15, 37, 47, 71, 94, 103, 118, 255, 292, 296, 298,

Fisk University *(Cont.)*
  299–300, 306–7, 335, 344–45, 377, 431, 462; student strike at, 327–28
Flexner, Eleanor, 210 n
Florida, 91, 115, 151, University of, 79
Foley, A. S., 310 n
Foraker, Joseph B., 134
  to: 135
  from: 135
Forbes, George Washington, 48, 67 n, 68, 347–48, 354–55
Ford, James W., 306
  from: 306–7
Foreign Policy Association, 403–4, 420
Foreman, Clark, 476 n
Fortune, T. Thomas, 53, 54, 101, 102
Fort Valley High and Industrial School, 130, 246
Forty-Ninth State Movement, 358
Forum, 113
Fosdick, Raymond Blaine, 365
  to: 365–67
Foster, William Z., 464
France, 224, 230, 232, 234–35, 260–61, 306–7, 318, 365–67, 376
Frayne, Hugh, 319
Frazier, E. Franklin, 283–84, 470
Freedman's Aid and Southern Education Society, 47
Freedomways, 235 n
Freund, Ernst, 175
Fugitive Slave Law, 62

Gallagher, Buell G., 435
  to: 436
  from: 436
Gandhi, Mahatma, 284, 402
  to: 402–3
  from: 403
Garfield, James A., 185
Garnett Distributing Company, 223
  to: 223
  from: 223
Garrison, William Lloyd, Jr., 47, 96
Garvey, Amy Jacques, 271 n, 464–65
Garvey, Marcus, 214, 245, 261, 263–64, 271–72, 318–19, 464–65
  to: 215; 245–46
  from: 214–15; 245
Garvey movement, 251, 263–64
General Education Board, 189, 215
General Electric Company, 96

General Theological Seminary, 268 n
George, Henry, 344
Georgetown University, 310
Georgia, 45, 124, 141, 151, 164, 180, 233–34, 441, 454; University of, 152
Georgia Normal School, 233
Georgia State Industrial College, 410
Germany, 17, 18–29, 195, 234–35, 305, 315, 425–26, 444, 462
Ghana, 181–82
Gibson, Truman K., 110
Giddings, Franklin H., 77, 175
Gilman, Daniel Coit, 10, 17, 20, 37, 38
  to: 18; 20–21; 21–22; 26–27; 28–29; 38
  from: 18; 25; 29
Gladden, Washington, 175
Gladstone, William E., 80, 106
Glass, Carter, 369, 369 n
Glenn, Joseph B., 308
  to: 309; 311
  from: 309; 309–11
Goetz, George. *See* V. F. Calverton
Gold Coast, 182, 183; Aborigines Rights Protection Society, 184
Gold Star Mothers, 463
Goldstein, Fanny, 347
  to: 348
  from: 347–48
Gomer, Nina. *See* Nina Gomer Du Bois
Goode, J. Paul, 71
Goodnow, Frank J., 325
  to: 326–27
  from: 326
Gordon, Eugene, 380, 380 n
Grady, Henry W., 6
Graham, Shirley, 482
  to: 484
  from: 482–84
Grant, Abraham, 53, 93
Grant, Fannie Bailey, 355
Great Atlantic and Pacific Tea Company, 423
  to: 423–24
Great Barrington, Mass., 12, 15, 19, 37, 225; High School, 4, 5, 6 n
Great Britain, 113, 145, 185, 260–61. *See also* England
Greener, Richard T., 168
  to: 169
  from: 168–69
Greenpoint Settlement (Brooklyn), 77
Green, Shields, 156, 168

Greenwich House, 77
Green, William, 418
Greer, David H., 130
Gresham, N. G., 93
Grimké, Angelina, 91
Grimké, Archibald H., 91, 93, 100, 104, 112, 149, 217, 229
  to: 105–6; 112–13
Grimké, Francis J., 54, 91
  from: 91–92
Grimké, Mrs. Francis J., 92
Grimké, Sarah, 91
Gruening, Ernest H., 194
  from: 195
Gruening, Martha, 194
Guggenheim Fellowship, 376–77
Guggenheim, William, 186
Gunner, Byron, 93, 228
  to: 228
  from: 228

Hagan, John A., 93
Haiti, 15 n, 211–13, 221, 403–4, 415, 463; revolt, 263
Hall, G. Stanley, 122
Hallowell, Emily, 130
Hampton Institute, 69 n, 80, 120, 146, 189 n, 208, 215–16, 267, 334, 360–63, 373, 428, 429, 435
Hamsun, Knut, 382
Handy, William Christopher, 313
  from: 313
Hansberry, William Leo, 466
  to: 467
  from: 466–67
Hanus, Paul H., 215
  to: 216
  from: 215
Hapgood, Powers, 379
Harcourt, Alfred, 177, 178, 442
  to: 443
  from: 442–43; 443; 444
Harding, Warren G., 273, 404
Hardwick, S. H., 45
  to: 45
Harlan, Louis R., 37 n, 39 n, 141 n, 189 n
Harlem, 214, 257, 269, 271, 276, 284, 305–6, 317, 343, 415, 417, 423; Fair-Play League, 258, 264; Hospital, 416; Renaissance, 295, 352
Harmon Prize, 371

Harper's Ferry, Virginia, 65, 154–55, 166, 168 n
Harper's Magazine, 157
Harris, Abram L., 327, 377, 433, 435, 435 n, 470
  to: 328; 470–71
  from: 327–28; 471–73
Harris, Callie (Mrs. Abram L.), 471, 473
Harrison, Benjamin, 185, 454
Harrison, C. C., 39–40
  from: 40
Harrison, Pat, 440
Hart, Albert Bushnell, 9–13, 25, 65, 110
  to: 111
  from: 110
Harvard University, 5, 11, 37, 39, 46, 48, 103, 111, 122, 142, 168, 215, 264, 268 n, 290, 379, 387 n, 403, 416, 434, 435 n; 1890 commencement, 8; Division of Education, 256; Historical Series, 17 n, 367; Law School, 277; Student Liberal Club, 379. *See also* scholarships
  to: 6; 7
Hastie, William H., 470
Hawkins, W. Ashbie, 93, 144
Hayden, H. B., 350
  to: 350–51
Hayden, Lewis, 155
Hayes, Carleton J. H., 420
Hayes, Roland, 328, 330
  to: 328–29
  from: 329
Hayes, Rutherford B., 10, 11, 16, 17, 22
  to: 10–14; 16–17
Hayes, W. H., 258
Hayford, Casely, 75, 145, 183, 185, 185 n
  from: 76
Haygood, Atticus G., 14
Hay, John C. D., 184, 185 n
Hays, Will, 456
Haywood, William "Big Bill," 338, 408
Healy, James Augustine, 310, 310 n
Hedden, Mrs. Worth T., 390
Helm, MacKinley, 328 n
Hendrick, Burton J., 300
  to: 300–301
Hershaw, Lafayette M., 131, 144, 228
  to: 229
  from: 228–29
Hewlett, William A., 234
  from: 233–34

Hill, Frederick Trevor, 157
Hill, Leslie P., 476 n
Hines, W. D., 323
  from: 323
Historian, 270 n, 389 n
Hixson, William B., 136 n
Holden, Edith, 145
Hollander, Sidney, 254
  to: 254-55
Holland, Frederick M., 62 n
Holmes, John Haynes, 175, 302
Holt, Henry, 177-78
Home University of Modern Knowledge, 177
Hood, Solomon Porter, 320
Hooper, Franklin Henry, 390
  to: 392; 393; 398; 399
  from: 391-92; 393; 398; 399
Hooper, William Davis, 152
  to: 153
  from: 152-53
Hoover, Herbert, 384, 385, 408-10, 424, 441, 462-63; 1932 campaign, 463-64
Hope, John, 164, 210, 297, 312
  to: 167; 312
  from: 165-67; 210-11; 297-99
Hopkins, Mark, 5
Hopper, Franklin, 417
Horizon, 57 n, 131, 144, 147, 229 n
Horton, James Africanus B., 184, 185 n
Hosmer, Frank A., 5, 6 n, 11, 225
  to: 226
  from: 225-26
Hosmer, Mrs. Frank A., 225-26
House, Edward M., 250
housing, 401-2
Housing Authority (New York City), 267
Houston, Charles H., 468 n
Howard, Oliver O., 169
Howard, Perry W., 278, 278 n
Howard University, 52, 91, 92, 268 n, 327, 345, 352-53, 358, 366, 388, 419-21, 424, 435, 466, 470; law school, 168
Howe, Annie H. (Mrs. John K.), 273
  to: 274-75
  from: 273-74
Hubert, Benjamin F., 410
Hughes, Charles Evans, 217, 250, 260, 314
  to: 250-51; 260-61
  from: 251

Hughes, Langston, 198 n, 275, 276, 344, 373
  from: 374
Hull House (Chicago), 56
Humphreys, A. B., 150
Hunter, Robert, 462
Hunt, H. A., 247
Hunton, Addie W., 404 n
Hunton, W. A., 184, 352
Hunton, Mrs. W. A., 184, 288
Hurst, John, 312

Illinois, 358, 435; legislature of, 424-25; University of, 297 n, 463
imperialism, opposition to, 136, 180, 211-12, 303
Independent, 16, 17 n, 45 n, 78 n, 82, 83, 91, 95, 110, 123 n, 140, 147, 154 n, 334 n
Independent Liberal Church (Chicago), 55 n
India, 262, 315, 385-86, 422
Indiana, 249, 482
Indianapolis, 257, 304
Indianapolis Freeman, 96, 99, 100, 103
Indian National Congress, 402
Indian Rights Association, 37 n
Indians, American, 71-72
Indian School (Carlisle, Pa.), 208
Industrial Workers of the World, 338
insurrections, by slaves, 64-65
intelligentsia, Black, 327, 470
International Convention of Negroes (1920), 245
International Council of Women of the Darker Races, 404 n
International House, 419
International Journal of Ethics, 121 n
International Labor Defense, 468, 468 n
International Labor Office, 250 n, 461 n
International Ladies' Garment Workers' Union, 267
International People's College at Elsinore, Denmark, 433 n
Interseminary Movement, 435
Interstate Commerce Commission, 45
Iowa, 155, 156
Ireland, 116, 309-10
Irish Agricultural Organization Society, 116
Irvine, Alexander, 133

Italy, 26, 128, 309, 344, 376

Jackson, Gardner, 379
Jackson, George H., 93, 355
Jackson, James C., 289
  from: 288–89
Jacksonville, Fla., 60, 93
Jacobs, George W., 60, 61
Jaffé, Albert, 106
Jaffé, Elizabeth von Richthofen, 106
Jamaica, 212 n, 214–15, 271
James, Henry, 133–34
  from: 134
Jameson, J. Franklin, 171
  to: 171; 172; 172
  from: 171–72
James, William, 9, 133, 383
  to: 133–34
  from: 10; 11; 133
Japanese Exclusion Act, 451
Jeanes Foundation for Negro Rural
  Schools, 312, 365, 447, 456
Jefferson, Thomas, 358
Jesup, M. K., 25
Jewish Daily Forward, 348
jim-crow, struggle against, 45, 93, 117, 194,
  348–50. *See also* segregation
job discrimination, 416, 416–17, 423–24
Johns Hopkins University, 10, 11, 14, 38,
  171, 325, 377; segregation at, 325–26
Johnson, Alberta, 345 n
Johnson, Alvin S., 175
Johnson, Charles, 470
Johnson, Ferdinand, 336
  to: 336
  from: 335–36
Johnson, H. T., 93
Johnson, James Weldon, 115, 219, 265,
  285, 296, 318, 344, 373, 431, 433, 473
  to: 219–20; 285–87
  from: 115–16; 287–89
Johnson, Jim, 330
Johnson, John, 258
Johnson, Kathryn M., 334
  from: 334–35
Johnson, Mordecai, 388, 420
  to: 420–21
Johnson, Rosamond, 115
Johnson, Tom L., 223
Johnston, Henry Halco, 172 n
Johnston, Sir Harry H., 172, 178

Jones, Anna H., 358
Jones, E. Stanley, 477
Jones, James M., 358
  to: 359–60
  from: 358–59
Jones, Jenkin Lloyd, 55 n
Jones, Mary C., 349
Jones, Rufus, 302
Jones, Thomas Jesse, 447
Jones, Tillman, 350
  from: 349–50
Jones, William Nesbit, 467
  to: 469–70
  from: 467–69
Journal of Adult Education, 433 n
Journal of Negro Education, 433 n
Journal of Negro History, 140, 312
Journal of Southern History, 273
Just, Ernest, 470, 471

Kansas, 65, 154
Kansas City, 427
Kansas City Call, 426
Keelan, Mrs. Mottie, 53
Kelley, Florence, 175, 409
  to: 410–11
Kellogg, Charles F., 169 n, 219 n
Kellogg, Francis B., 119
Kellogg, Frank B., 314
Kellogg, Paul U., 186, 206 n
  from: 186–87
Kemp, Dennis, 183, 184, 185 n
Kentucky, 258, 452
Kidder, C. G., 194
  to: 194
  from: 194
King, Charles D. B., 277–83, 313–14, 320,
  464–65
  to: 279–80; 282–83
  from: 280–82
King, William E., 424
  to: 425
  from: 425
Kingsbury, John A., 175
Kingsley, Mary Henrietta, 183, 185
Knights of Columbus, 311
Knox, George L., 101, 102
Kuhn, Loeb and Company, 108
Ku Klux Klan, 249, 268, 275, 293, 311,
  362, 424; in South Carolina, 344
Kumasi, Ashanti, 182

labor, "labor question," 21, 388-89, 434, 461-62
Labor History, 389 n
labor, organized, 42. *See also* trade unions
Labor party (United States), 344
Labour Government (England), 462
Labour party (England), 188, 250, 376, 407 n
La Farge, Oliver, 436
  to: 437-38
  from: 437
La Farge, Wanden (Mrs. Oliver), 437, 438
La Follette, Robert M., 107, 292-94, 297-98, 440
  to: 107
  from: 107-8
Lajpat Rai, Lala, 385-86
Lake Mohawk Conference, 226
Lampman, Sally, 15
Landon, Letitia Elizabeth ("L. E. L."), 183
Langley, Samuel P., 356
Lantern, 379-81
Laski, Harold J., 277 n
Latin America, United States intervention in, 211-13, 250 n, 338. *See also* South America
Latino, Juan, 470 n
League for Independent Political Action, 405-8, 418-19
League for Industrial Democracy, 267
League of Nations, 250 n, 365, 451, 461 n
Lee, Algernon, 388
  to: 388-89
  from: 389
Lee, Euel, 468
Lee, Robert E., 61
Lees, Edith (Mrs. Havelock Ellis), 344
Lewis, Franklin C., 264
  to: 265
  from: 265
Lewis, Morris, 267
Lewis, Silba M., 110 n
Lewis, Sinclair, 329
  to: 331
  from: 329-30; 330-31; 331
Lewis, William H., 54, 68, 277, 355
  from: 277-78; 278-79
Liberia, 24, 145, 221, 260, 313, 318, 320-23, 351, 463-65, 467, 469; proposed United States loan to, 277-83
libraries, 347-48, 387-88, 416-17
Library of Congress, 122, 171; segregation in, 387-88
Lief, Alfred, 383 n
life, its meaning, 382
Lincoln, Abraham, 142, 185, 186, 339, 340, 468
Lincoln, C. Eric, 198 n
Lincoln, Robert Todd, 185
  from: 186
Lincoln Settlement (Brooklyn), 120 n
Lincoln University, 37, 373-74, 415
Lindbergh, Charles, 355 n
Lindemann, Edward C., 433 n
Link, Arthur S., 217 n
Lippmann, Walter, 214, 233
  from: 214; 233
Literary Digest, 82
Literary Guild, 373, 411
literature, Black people and, 324-25, 329-31, 342, 343, 372-73, 377-78
Livingstone College, 182, 184
Livingstone, David, 184, 185 n
Lochner, Louis, 353 n
Locke, Alain Leroy, 328, 352-53, 470
Locomotive Engineers Union, 319
Loeb, Jacques, 195, 196 n
  from: 195-96
Loeb, William Jr., 112
  from: 112
Logan, Rayford, 419, 470
  from: 420
London (England), 24, 37, 92, 134, 173-74, 214, 250, 276, 465, 467
London, Jack, 198
London School of Economics, 435
Long Island Railroad, 52
Lorimer, George H., 258
  to: 259
  from: 259-60
Louisiana, 151, 368, 399, 424
Louisiana History, 399 n
Lovejoy, Owen Reed, 481
  to: 482
  from: 481-82
Lovett, Robert S., 433 n
Lowell, Charles, 355
Lowndes County, Ala., study of Negro farmer in, 132 n
Luther, Martin, 19, 20

Lyceum Club, 173
Lynch, Hollis R., 145
Lynch, John R., 151
lynching, 217, 226–27, 233, 262, 274, 315, 340, 400, 454–55, 463
Lyons, J. W., 53

McClure's, 128, 129 n
McClure, S. S., 128
  to: 128, 129
  from: 129, 129
McDonald, George, 183, 185
MacDonald, J. Ramsay, 173, 187, 276
  to: 187–88
  from: 188; 276; 277
McFall, Haldane, 324
McGhee, F. L., 53
Mack, Julian W., 271–72
McKay, Claude, 234, 251, 252, 289, 320, 374
  to: 376
  from: 374–75; 376
McKenzie, Fayette A., 70–71, 292 n 299–300, 306–7
  to: 72
  from: 71–72
McKinley, Whitfield, 93
McKinley, William, 111, 134, 454
Maclea, Captain George, 183 n
Maclean, Mary Dunlop, 147, 147 n, 148, 176, 211
McMaster, John Bach, 61, 65
Macmillan Company, 420
McNickle, D'Arcy, 437 n
Macon Telegraph, 233
Magazine of the Arts, 302
Mahan, Alfred T., 130
Manchester Guardian, 122
Manhattan Trade School for Girls, 120
Manly, Alexander, 101
Manly, Charles, 356 n
Manning, Joseph C., 150
Maran, René, 290 n
Marshall, John D., 445
  to: 445
  from: 446–47
Marshall, John, Law School, 424
Marshall, Napoleon B., 404
Marshall, Thurgood, 468 n
Marston, M. B., 127
  to: 127

Martin, James Arthur, 233
  from: 233–34
Marx, Karl, 268, 405, 471
Marxism, 251
Maryland, educational policy of, 326–27
Massachusetts, 180; Historical Society, 142; legislature, 277; militia, 236
Massenberg Bill, 362
Matheus, John F., 343 n
Mathiasen, Soren A., 433
  from: 433–34
Maurer, James H., 450, 461
May, Samuel J., 137
May, Samuel Jr., 137
  to: 138; 139–40
  from: 138–39
Mdolomba, E., 424
  to: 424
Meharry College, 297 n
Meier, August, 98 n
Meijer, Mrs. Elizabeth, 467–69
Melish, John Howard, 175
Meltzer, Milton, 198 n
Memphis Free Press, 54
Memphis, Tenn., 54, 109, 178
Mencken, H. L., 220, 317, 325 n, 368
  to: 368–69
  from: 220; 369
Meredith, H., 389 n
Messenger, 203, 318 n, 319, 382
Mexico, 124, 212, 221, 436, 437
Michigan, 481; University of, 119, 304, 358–59
migration from South, 262
Milholland, John E., 132, 145, 148, 173–74
Miller, George Frazer, 268–69
Miller, Herbert A., 483
Miller, Kelly, 52, 57 n, 92, 93, 100, 104, 143, 148, 149, 176, 196–97
  to: 53; 105–6; 112–13
  from: 93
Minneapolis, Minn., 93; Public Library, 387 n; Urban League, 327
Minnesota, University of, 335, 426
Mississippi, 151, 358, 376, 399, 440; flood of 1927, 463
Missouri, 129 n, 314, 379, 461
Mitchel, John P., 383 n
Modern Language Quarterly, 183 n
Modern Quarterly, 377
Montgomery, Isaiah T., 348
Montgomery, M. Estello, 348

Moody, Dwight L., 5
Moon, 57 n, 108, 120, 131, 178
Mooney, Anna, 454
  from: 454
Mooney, Tom, 453
  from: 454; 455
Moore, E. W., 149
Moore, Petruchio E., 235
  from: 235
Moore, R. L., 270 n, 389 n
Moorland, Jessie E., 184, 256, 352
  to: 352
  from: 353
Moorland-Spingarn Collection, 105 n, 112 n
Morehouse College, 164, 210, 297–98
More, Paul Elmer, 154–64
  to: 154; 154–55; 157; 158
  from: 155–57; 158
Morgan, Clement G., 53, 54, 354
  from: 355
Morgan College for Negroes (Morgan State College), 247
Morgenthau, Henry, 175
Morris, Edward H., 53, 57 n
Morris, Robert, 61
Morris, W. M., 93
Morrow, Dwight, 440
Morton, Ferdinand Q., 258, 416
  to: 416-17
Morton, Franklin Wheeler, 184
Morton-Jones, Verina, 120, 184
Motion Picture Producers and Distributors of America, 456
motion pictures, 456–57
Moton, Robert R., 232, 273, 298, 335, 385, 454
Moscow, 289–90
Mound Bayou, Miss., 348–50
Mount Holyoke College, 148 n
Murgrave, George C., 185
music of the Afro-American, 130, 313, 328, 438
Murphy, Charles F., 416
Murray, Freeman H. M., 131, 144
Murray, Gilbert, 177
Murray, Margaret, 37 n
Muste, A. J., 302

NAACP (National Association for the Advancement of Colored People), 65–66, 76, 91, 96, 107–8, 112, 115, 120 n, 122, 132 n, 136, 144, 150 n, 169–70, 172–74, 176–77, 181, 184, 186–95, 197, 203–7, 217, 219–20, 223, 227, 232–33, 247–48, 253–54, 262, 265, 268–71, 274–75, 278, 283–84, 286, 349, 354–55, 357, 365, 380–82, 400 n, 408–9, 415, 426–32, 435, 445, 447, 461, 468–69, 474–76, 478–82; Chicago branch of, 249; founding of, 147 ff.; and the Garvey movement, 317–18; 1914 annual meeting of, 195–96; 1924 annual meeting of, 286–88, 291–92, 294, 305, 312, 315
NAACP "Board of Directors," 200 ff., 227, 229, 288, 292, 432–33, 470, 473
  to: 227; 478–79; 479–81
Naida, Mrs. Sarjini, 402
Nail, John E., 271
Nash, Royal F., 219
Nashville, Tenn., 58, 352
Nation, 122, 153–64, 194, 260, 290, 292 n, 328, 333, 334, 377, 387, 400, 405
National Association of Colored Women, 220
National Association of Teachers in Colored Schools, 456–57
National Consumers' League, 409
National Education Association, 456–57
National Equal Rights League, 228 n, 268 n
National Guard, segregation in, 236–37
National Guardian, 380 n
National Law School, Washington, D.C., 338
National League for the Protection of Colored Women, 118
National Negro Board, 159
National Negro Committee, 173
National Negro Conference, 1909, 148 n, 168 n; 1910, 147
national Negro journal, proposed, 56–57, 108–10
National Negro Political League, 148 n
National Urban League, 118, 327
Negro American Political League, 149
Negro Bureau, La Follette-for-President Committee, 392–94
Negro, capitalization of, 171–2, 214, 390, 394, 420
Negro encyclopedia. *See* encyclopedia of the Negro
Negro Gold Star Mothers, 424–25

Index [499]

Nelson, John M., 294
Nerney, May Childs, 186, 188 n, 201, 205, 206
New Bedford, Massachusetts, 3, 15
New Horizon, 144–45
New Jersey, 180, 440, 441
New Leader, 388 n
New National Era, 168
New Orleans, La., 58, 60, 399
New Republic, 214, 233, 260, 377, 400
New Review, 270 n
New School of Social Research, 327
Newsome, Effie Lee, 373
"New South," 6
New York Age, 96, 99, 103
New York Call, 454
New York City, 18, 37, 52, 76, 104, 113, 116, 123, 129, 145, 147, 153, 156, 166, 168, 169, 180, 182, 185, 257, 263, 280, 423, 427, 435, 453, 467, 481; Association of Neighborhood Workers, 148; Board of Aldermen, 388; Board of Education, 401; Bureau of Social Statistics, 81; Park Department, 264; Police Department, 258, 265
New York Evening Post, 96–7, 154 n, 159, 164, 169, 216
New York Public Library, 284–85, 416–17
New York School of Philanthropy, 77, 175
New York State, 280, 359; Civil Service Commission, 416–17; National Guard, 236
New York State Socialist party, 388
New York Telephone Company, 423
New York Times, 147 n, 324, 386 n, 388 n, 400, 405 n, 408, 411 n, 466
New York Times Magazine, 46 n, 77
New York University, 268 n, 314
Niagara Movement, 59, 92, 112, 115, 116, 134–35, 137, 142, 144, 148 n, 150–51, 166, 176, 220, 228, 228 n, 229, 355
Nigeria, 331, 415, 464; British atrocities in, 415–16
Nineteenth Century and After, 172 n
Nobel Prize, 329, 404, 444; for Peace, 353
Norfolk, Virginia, Journal and Guide, 318
Norris, George W., 440
  from: 440–41
North American Review, 400
North Carolina, 113, 151, 309

North, J., 468 n
Norton, Charles Eliot, 9
novels, writing of, 324–25
Nuns of the Immaculate Heart of Mary, 310
Nutting, Elizabeth, 452
  to: 453
  from: 452

Oahu College, Honolulu, 11, 225–26
Oberholtzer, Ellis Paxson, 60
  to: 62; 64
  from: 61–62; 62–63; 63–64; 65
Oberlin College, 333, 405, 411, 482
Ogden, Robert C., 76, 105, 120, 193–94
"Ogden Movement," 189
Ohio, 134, 220, 440
Okolona Institute (Miss.), 357
Olmsted, Mildred Scott, 449
  to: 449–50; 451
  from: 450–51
O'Neill, Eugene, 294, 427
  from: 294–95
Opportunity prize, 371
Orr, W. J., 319
Outlook, 46, 95, 122–23, 172, 273, 273 n, 274–75
Overstreet, Harry A., 433 n
Ovington, Mary White, 76, 77, 118, 131, 147, 148, 188, 205–7, 227, 287–89, 291, 373, 430
  to: 78; 188–91; 431
  from: 76–77; 78; 118–21; 131–32; 191–93; 430–31
Owens, John R., 252
  from: 252–54

Pace, Harry H., 108, 178–79
  to: 179–80
Page, Kirby, 425
  to: 425–26
Page, Thomas Nelson, 106, 107 n, 128, 129
Page, Walter Hines, 113, 300–301
  to: 113–14
  from: 113; 114
Paine College, 233
Painter, C. C., 5, 12, 37
Palmer, George, 9
Pan-African Conference, 1900, 92
Pan-African Congress, 231, 233, 250–51, 251 n, 260, 276–77

Pan-African movement, 232, 467
Paris, 37, 250, 276, 330
Paris Exposition, 45
Parish, C. H., 93
Paris School of Economics, 22, 24
Patten, Simon N., 71
Peabody, Francis G., 9–12
   from: 12
Peabody, George Foster, 52, 66, 69, 70, 76, 101, 130, 175
   to: 67–68
   from: 69
Peace Jubilee (Atlanta, 1899), 111
Pearce View State College, 292
Penn, Joseph C., 307, 308
Pennsylvania Federation of Labor, 405
Pennsylvania: Historical Society of, 440; history of Negroes in, 336–37; sesquicentennial celebration in, 336–37; University of, 39–40, 43, 44, 46, 60, 71, 125; School of Social Work, 449
Pennsylvania Magazine, 44 n
peonage, 51, 56, 133, 266, 463
People (Lahore, India),
   to: 386
"People's College" proposal, 415
Perry, Bliss, 47
   from: 47
Pershing, John, 212 n, 221, 224, 365
Pestovsky, Stanislav, 289
Phelps-Stokes Educational Commissions, 182
Phelps-Stokes Fund, 447, 448
Phelps-Stokes, J. G., 52
Phi Beta Kappa, 427
Philadelphia, 40, 83, 125, 156, 168, 176, 257, 357, 457
Philippines, 125 n, 136, 262–63; independence of, 302–3
Phillips, Wendell, 226
Phillips, William, 278, 278 n
Phipps tenement, 118
physicians, Black, 416
Pickens, William, 247, 271, 288
   to: 247–48
   from: 248–49
Pickett, Clarence, 476 n
Pickett, William P., 123
   to: 123–25
Pinchot, Gifford, 336
   to: 336–37
   from: 337

Pingree, Lizzie A., 308–9
Pittsburgh Courier, 165, 382, 431–32
Pittsburgh, Pa., 257; University of, 328
Plain Talk, 380 n
Plunkett, Sir Horace Curzon, 116
   to: 116–17
   from: 116
Pocono People's College, 433–34
poetry: by Black people, 276–77, 310, 344–45, 346, 374–75
pogroms, 123, 176, 233
Poley, Ruth Verlenden, 451
police activities, 257
Political Science Quarterly, 122
Ponsonby, Mrs. Sidney, 428
Pool, David de Sola, 465–66
   to: 466
Pool, Mrs. David de Sola, 466 n
Populist-Republican Fusion (Ala.), 150 n
Porter, Dorothy B., 146 n
Post, Louis Freeland, 344
   from: 344
Pott, James, Company, 56
Pratt, Richard Henry, 208
   from: 209
presidential campaign of 1924, 267–71, 292–94
press, Black, 57, 95–104, 261
Prest, S. T. Mitchell, 38
   from: 38
Price, J. C., 14
Princeton University, 154 n, 403
prisoners, 452–55
prison reform, 132 n
Proctor, Henry Hugh, 462
   to: 463
Progressive Education, 433 n
Progressive party (1912), 336
Prohibition, 293
Providence, R.I., 4, 164, 382
publishing, as a business, 114
Puerto Rico, 403–4
Pulitzer Prize, 148 n, 294, 300, 437
Pushkin, Alexander, Prize, 345 n
Putnam, Herbert, 387–88
   to: 387

Queen, Hallie E., 125
   from: 125–26

racism, 262–63, 303, 351
Radburn, N. J., 401–2

Raleigh, Va., 42, 113
Randall, Almyra, 307
  from: 308
Randolph, A. Philip, 251, 269, 319
  to: 319
  from: 319; 371
Rand School, 267; currents events forum of, 388
Ratzel, Friedrich, 115, 350
Reconstruction era in U. S. history, 49, 64, 129 n, 150–52, 171, 197–98, 391–93, 398–99, 411, 442–44, 474
Red Cross, 226, 442, 451
Reform Club (London), 227
Republican party, 142, 267–71, 336, 338; National Committee, 440
resistance, militant, 233–34, 283–84, 349–50
revolution, 386
Revolution, Bolshevik, 251, 289–90
Reynolds, Ira May, 271
  to: 272
  from: 271–72
Rhodes Scholar, Black, 353
Robert Hungerford Industrial School, 137–39
Roberts, Eugene P., 383 n
Robeson, Eslanda Goode, 427
  to: 427–28
  from: 428
Robeson, Paul, 294, 427–28
Robinson, John W., 258
Rockefeller Foundation, 365–68
Rockefeller Institute for Medical Research, 195
Roosevelt, Eleanor (Mrs. F. D. R.), 401
Roosevelt, Franklin Delano, 67, 462; 1932 election of, 463–64, 474
Roosevelt, Theodore, 92, 104, 111, 134, 136 n, 143 n, 200, 277, 336, 454
  to: 111–12
Roosevelt University, 428
Rose, Ernestine, 284, 417
  from: 285
Rosenwald Fellowships, 376
Rosenwald, Julius, 186
Rosenwald (Julius) Fund, 233, 438, 442, 456
Ross, B. Joyce, 190 n
Royce, Josiah, 9, 121
Rubinow, Isaac Max
  to: 82
  from: 81–82

Ruffin, Mrs. George, 355
Russell, Charles Edward, 148, 149, 176, 262
  from: 262–63
Russell, James, 355
Rutgers University, 427

Sage (Russell) Foundation, 133, 186
Sage, Henry W., 126
Saint Augustine's Church (Brooklyn), 268 n
Saint Augustine's College, 130, 292
St. Louis, Mo., 71, 105, 257, 426
Saint Mark's Episcopal Church (New York City), 148 n
Sampson, M. J., 76 n
Sanborn, F. B., 65
Sanger, Margaret, 301
  to: 302
  from: 301
San Quentin, Calif., 454–55
Santayana, George, 9
Santo Domingo, 91, 253
Saturday Evening Post, 258–60
Sayer, Ettie, 173, 347
  to: 173–75
Schieffelin, William J., 118, 119, 120
Schiff, Jacob Henry, 52, 108–10
  to: 108–9; 109–10
  from: 109
Schiller, Edward H., 331 n
Schmoller, Gustav, 21, 22, 23, 24, 25, 26, 27, 444
  from: 28
Schneider, Pauline, 196
  to: 196–97
  from: 196
Schneider, William, 350
Schomburg, Arthur, 284
School and Society, 433 n
Schoonmaker, F. P., 232
  from: 232
Schroeder, Charles, 376
Schurz, Carl, 121, 129, 129 n
Schuyler, George S., 290 n, 382
  from: 382
Science and Society, 52 n
scholarships, Harvard University, 6 n, 7, 10, 11, 12, 13, 15, 16, 110, 353, 354 n
Scott, Emmett J., Jr., 324, 366
Scottron, Samuel R., 120

Scribner's, 128, 380 n
Scudder, Rev., 5
  to: 5
Seager, Henry B., 77
Searchlight, 208
Seattle, J. T., 93
Seaver, Edwin, 302
  to: 302-3
  from: 302
segregation, 138, 249-50, 272-73, 311, 326, 335-36, 350-51, 359, 364-65, 387, 401, 424-25, 452-53, 463, 475-76, 479
Seligman, Edwin R. A., 77, 122
  from: 123
Seligman, Isaac, 120
Sellin, Thorstein, 439 n
Seneca Falls Convention (1848), 209, 210 n
Senior, Clarence
  to: 462
  from: 461-62
Sexton, S. M., 49
  from: 50
Shaler, Nathaniel S., 9, 10 n, 11, 12
Shapiro, Herbert, 132 n
Sheen, E. D., 343 n
Shillady, John R., 219, 468
short-story writing, 316, 343
Shoshoni Agency, 70
Siebert, W. H., 62
Silcox, Harry C., 44 n
Simkhovitch, Mrs. Mary Kingsbury, 77
Simkhovitch, Vladimir G., 77
Simon, E. L., 108
Simon, John A., 422
Simon, Kathleen Harvey, 422
  to: 422-23
  from: 422
Sims, Robert Page, 385
  to: 385
  from: 385
Sinclair, Upton, 198
  to: 199-200
  from: 198; 198-99; 199
Sinclair, William A., 148-49
Sinnette, Elinor D., 235 n
Sixth International Neo-Malthusian and Birth Control Conference, 301
Slater (John S.) Fund, 15-17, 20, 25, 26, 29, 37, 38, 365, 456
  to: 15-16; 22; 23-25; 26

slavery and slave trade, 16, 62, 124, 336-37, 390-91, 422
Slemp, Campbell B., 278, 279
Smalls, Robert, 151
Smart Set, 220
Smedley, Agnes, 314
  from: 315
Smith, Alfred E., 67, 384
Smith College, 449
Smith, H. C., 14
Smith, S. L., 456
  to: 457-58
  from: 456-57
Smithsonian Institute, 356 n
Snelson, F. G., 258
social equality, 128, 186
Socialism and Socialists, 23, 76, 81-82, 133, 147, 148 n, 180, 192, 198, 251-54, 267-71, 388-89, 405, 418, 425, 461-62, 469
Socialist party, 82, 180, 198, 267-71, 418, 461; and Negroes, 388-89
social work, 76-77, 118-20, 175
Society for Ethnic Culture, 122
Society for Organic Education, 79 n
soldiers, Black, 134, 209 n, 221, 224-25, 230, 232, 234-35, 236-37, 254-55, 355-56, 365, 425
Sorbah, John Mensah, 184, 185 n
Sorbonne University, 411
South America, 212, 310, 311. *See also* Latin America
Southern Ballot Rights League, 150 n
Southern California, University of, 359
Southern Education Board, 189, 312
Southern Railway, 45
Southern Sociological Congress, 184
Southern University Race Commission, 447
South, University of, 399
Spanish-American War, 125 n, 151 n
Spectator, 122
Spencer, Ann, 373
Spero, Sterling D., 435, 435 n
Spiller, Gustav, 173, 353 n
Spingarn, Amy (Mrs. Joel E.), 292, 305, 371
  to: 372-73
  from: 371-72
Spingarn, Arthur B., 190 n, 286
Spingarn, Joel E., 146 n, 181, 189, 200, 217, 219, 227, 229, 230, 291, 303, 304 n,

Index [503]

330–31, 349, 431–33, 476 n
  to: 203–7; 291–92; 304–5
  from: 200–202; 230–31; 303–4
Spingarn Medal, 91, 189 n, 311, 312, 353, 371
Spratlin, Valvarez, 470
Springfield, Ill., riots (1908), 147
Stanford University, 428; history department, 231
Stanley, Robert H., 273
Stanton, Elizabeth Cady, 209; centennial, 209–10
Starr, Frederick, 283
Stead, William T., 132
Stevens, Lionel, 183 n
Steward, Theophilus G., 151
Stone, Alfred Holt, 75 n, 143
Storer College, 332
Storey, Moorfield, 136, 147, 229, 431
  to: 136–37
  from: 137
Straker, D. A., 93
Streator, George, 474
Stribling, Thomas S., 256
  to: 257
  from: 256–57
Strittmater, L. F., 458
  to: 460–61
  from: 458–60
Strong, Anna Louise, 333, 334 n
Strong, Sydney, 333
  to: 334
  from: 333
students, 125, 352, 360–63, 429
Student Volunteer Movement Convention, 117, 118
Studin, Charles H., 189, 190 n
suffrage, for Black people, 45, 56, 141, 142, 194, 252, 338–41, 368–69, 505–7, 419, 463
Summer School of Philanthropy (New York City), 76
Sumner, Charles, 136, 198, 341, 388
Sunnyside Gardens, New York City, 401–2
Supreme Liberty Life Insurance Company (Chicago), 110 n
Survey, 175, 205–6; National Council of, 186
Survey Graphic, 313
Swanson, Dorothy, 180 n

Swem, C. L., 218
Synagogue Council of America, 465
Sylvan, T. P., 423
  to: 423

Taft, William Howard, 68, 136 n, 277, 312, 336
Tagore, Rabindranath, 404, 405 n
  from: 405
Talledega College, 80, 435
Tammany, political machine, 384, 416
Tanner, Henry O., 57 n
Taussig, Frank, 9
Taussig, T. W., 11
Taylor, Booker, 45
Taylor, Graham, 186
Taylor, Thomas E., 258
Tebbel, John, 258 n
Tennessee, 256, 309, 462
Terrell, Mary C., 388
Terrell, Robert H., 151 n
Terry, Lambert Maxim, 296
  from: 296–97
Texas, 151, 368
textbooks, Negroes in, 455–57
theatre, Black people and the, 333, 427–28
Third party (1924), 292–94
Thirkield, W. P., 47
  from: 48
Thomas, Albert, 461 n
Thomas, Norman, 302, 461, 464
Thompson, Louise A., 360
  from: 360–63
Thompson, Richard W., 102
Thompson, William, 155
Thompson, William H., political machine of, 384
Thomson, J. Arthur, 177
Tillinghast, Joseph A., 75, 75 n, 185
Tillman, Benjamin R., 132 n, 197
  from: 197–98
Times, The, of London, 122
Toombs, Robert, 61
Toomer, Jean, 295
  to: 295
  from: 295–96
Torrence, Ridgely, 165, 297 n
Trachtenberg, A., 175 n
trade unions. *See* unions, trade
travels, by Du Bois, 3–4, 19–21, 23, 26, 37, 113–14, 276–77, 291–92, 304, 344

Trotter, Geraldine (Mrs. William Monroe), 67, 82, 148
  to: 83
  from: 82–83
Trotter, William Monroe, 48, 49, 67–68, 70, 92, 93, 97, 98, 101, 103, 110, 147, 228 n, 347, 354–55, 483–84
  to: 97–98
  from: 49; 98
Troutbeck Leaflets, 303–4
Trower, John, 53
Tucker, Charlotte Maria, 184, 185 n
Tulane University, 436
Tumulty, Joseph P., 217, 219, 232
  to: 218
  from: 218–19; 232
Turner, Henry M., 54
Turner, Mary, 454
Turner, Nat, 61, 64–65
Tuskegee Institute, 37, 38, 46, 52, 53, 58, 69 n, 80, 82, 92, 96, 99, 102, 108, 121, 133, 139, 189 n, 232, 267, 298, 334–35, 435, 454, 456; press bureau, 102
Tuskegee "machine," 57, 95–105, 112
Tuskegee Veterans' Hospital, 273–75, 479
Typographical Union #6 (New York City), 418
Tyson, Francis, 328

Ulric, Lenore, 332
underground railroads, 58, 62
Union of Soviet Socialist Republics, 289–90, 338, 344, 344 n
unions, trade, 49–52, 80, 256, 319, 370–71, 418
Union Theological Seminary, 189 n, 435
United Mine Workers, 49, 50
United Nations, 353
United States, 37, 124, 260–61, 262, 302–3
United States Army, 103, 208–9, 221, 224–25, 254–55, 297, 306, 307, 355–56; General Staff, 227, 229; Military Intelligence Bureau, proposed commission in, 227, 229, 232
United States Bureau of Education, 408–10
United States Bureau of Labor, 40, 367
United States Census, 367
United States Census Bureau, 65, 74
United States Congress, 175–76, 277, 278 n, 383

United States Constitution: 13th Amendment, 338–41, 14th Amendment, 338–41; 15th Amendment, 93, 338–41; Interstate Commerce Clause, 93
United States Detective Service Bureau, 257
United States Department of the Interior, 229 n
United States Department of Justice, 318
United States Department of Labor, 122, 227
United States Department of State, 260, 261, 278
United States Department of War, 221, 226–27, 229, 236–37, 254–55, 356 n
United States Forestry Service, 336
United States government, 135, 275, 282, 388, 424–25, 442
United States Indian Bureau, 12
United States Marines, 211
United States Military Academy (West Point), 221
United States Post Office Department: and *Crisis* ban, 254
United States Senate, 262; Foreign Relations Committee, 338; Judiciary Committee, 341, 440
United States Supreme Court, 93, 342, 349, 386
United States Treasury Department, 151 n
United States Veterans' Bureau, 274–75
Universal Negro Improvement Association and African Communities League, 245, 263 n, 318
Universal Negro Improvement Association of Jamaica, 214
Unity, 55 n, 333
Urban League, 262
Ursuline Nuns, 310

Van Dusen, Henry P., 435
Vanguard, 292
Van Lennep, Edward, 5, 18–19
  to: 18–19
van Loon, Gerard Willem, 290 n
van Loon, Hendrik Willem, 290
  to: 290; 291
  from: 290–91; 291
Van Norden Magazine, 132

Vann, Robert L., 431
　to: 432–33
　from: 431–32
Van Vechten, Carl, 324, 330, 343, 372
　to: 325
　from: 324–25
Vare (William S.) political machine, Philadelphia, 384
Vaughan, George, 477
　to: 477–78
　from: 477
Vaux (Robert) Consolidated School, Philadelphia, 43
Vera Cruz (Mexico) bombardment of, 212 n
Verez slave insurrection, 91
Vermont, 246–47
Victoria, Queen, of England, 182
Villa, Pancho, 212 n
Villard, Henry, 96
Villard, Oswald Garrison, 96–98, 118, 147–48, 152–54, 168, 176, 181, 186, 189–90, 192, 195–96, 201, 204, 205–6, 217, 302, 312, 365, 387, 430
　to: 97; 98–102; 103–4; 164; 169; 181; 387–88
　from: 97; 102–3; 153; 158–59; 164; 219
Virginia, 151, 428
Virginia Constitutional Convention, 151
Viginia Military Institute, 278 n
Virginia Theological Seminary and College, 150
Virginia Union University, 420, 429
Virgin Islands, 267
Voice of the Negro, 95, 98, 102, 145, 176, 357
Vollum, Alfred, 135
　to: 135–36
Von Holst, Hermann Edward, 65
Voorhees Normal and Industrial School, 130

Wagner, Adolf, 21, 23, 24, 26, 27, 28, 444
　from: 27–28
Wagner, Charles, 78
Wagner, Robert: *Tannhauser*, 20
Walden, J. A., 272
　to: 273
　from: 272
Wald, Lillian D., 169 n, 175
Waldron, J. Milton, 144, 148, 149

Wallace, David R., 142
　from: 142
Waller, O. M., 93
Walling, William English, 147, 169
　to: 170–71
　from: 147–50; 169–70
Walrond, Eric, 377–78
Walters, Alexander, 69, 92, 93, 213
　to: 93
　from: 93
Warbasse, James Peter, 305
　to: 305
　from: 305–6
Warburg, Paul, 186
Ward, William Hayes, 69, 95
　to: 96; 141
　from: 96; 141
Ware, Edward T., 67
Warlich, Reinhold von, 193
war, opposition to, 293, 302, 357, 425–26, 449–51
Washington and Lee University, 447
Washington, Booker T., 37, 39, 44, 46, 46 n, 48, 49, 52, 53, 55–56, 57 n, 63, 67–68, 70, 73, 79, 82, 92, 96, 100, 101, 102, 103, 105, 106, 110, 111, 111 n, 112–13, 133, 141 n, 143, 165–67, 172–74, 193, 214, 232, 266–67, 278 n, 296, 355, 458–61, 473
　to: 37; 39; 54; 58; 59; 61
　from: 38; 44; 46; 53–54
Washington Colored American, 96, 99, 100
Washington, D. C., 44, 91, 151, 156, 168, 171, 209, 220, 257, 334, 387–88, 437, 456; Board of Education, 388
Washington, George, 20
Washington Post, 81
Washington Record, 98, 100
Washington, University of, 359
Wartburg Castle, 19–20
Watson, Thomas, 197
Weatherford, W. D., 312
Weaver, Robert C., 434, 435 n, 470
　to: 435
　from: 434–35
Weber, Max, 106
　from: 106–7
Weisbord, Robert G., 251 n
Weiss, Nancy J., 219 n
Weld, Theodore, 91

Index

Wells-Barnett, Ida B., 54 147, 148, 149
    from: 55–56
Wells, H. G., 173, 220, 276
    from: 277
Wendell, Barnett, 9
Wesley, Charles, 470
West Church (Boston), 355
West Indies, 12, 15, 124, 262, 311
West Virginia Collegiate Institute, 327
West Virginia State College, 441, 470 n
Wetmore, J. Douglas, 93
    from: 60
Wheatley, Phyllis, 377
Wheeler, Kittridge, 58
    from: 58–59
Wheeler, Lloyd, 55
White, Andrew D., 126
White House, 231–32, 278
White, Jacob C., Jr., 43
    to: 43–44
White, Poppy Cannon (Mrs. Walter Francis), 266 n
White, Walter Francis, 205, 286–89, 296, 325, 330, 430, 431, 455 n, 473, 474, 475, 476 n
    to: 266–67; 475–76
Whitney Museum (New York City), 376
Wilberforce University, 37, 38, 39, 147, 221, 292, 347
Wilbur, Ray Lyman, 408
    from: 410
Wiley College, 247, 470 n
Wilkins, D. R., 98
Wilkins, Roy, 426
    from: 426–27
Willcox, Walter F., 65, 66, 74, 106, 107 n, 122, 126, 175
    to: 75
    from: 74–75
Williams, Daniel H., 57 n
Williams, E. G., 366
Williams, Howard Y., 405, 405 n
Williams, Talcott, 122
Williams, W. T. B., 146, 456
Wilson, Mrs. J. Harold, 404 n
Wilson, Tan Evans, 355
Wilson, Woodrow, 67, 128, 180, 198, 211, 212 n, 222, 223, 226, 231, 232, 245, 344, 454–55
    to: 211–13; 216–18
    from: 218

Winslow, Irving, 137
    from: 137
Winsor, Ellen, 283
    to: 284
    from: 283–84
Winsor, Justin, 9
Wisconsin, State Historical Society of, 144 n
"Wisconsin Idea," 107
Wise, Stephen S., 169 n, 175
Wissler, Clark, 114
    from: 115
Wolgemuth, Kathleen, 219 n
Woman Suffrage Amendment, 340
women, Black, 117–18, 120, 125, 194, 220–21, 226, 334, 482
Women's International League for Peace and Freedom, 449
Women's Political Union, 209
women's rights, 126–27, 132 n, 209–10
Wood, Clement, 198, 199 n
Wood, Leonard, 137
Woods, Granville T., 57 n
Woodson, Carter G., 140, 140 n, 311, 312, 334, 352, 366, 447–48
    to: 448–49
    from: 140; 449
Wooley, Mary E., 148
Woolley, Celia Parker, 55, 55 n
Work, Monroe, 55, 130
World's Work, 113, 131, 133 n
World Today, 81
World Tomorrow, 273 n, 405, 407, 408 n, 425, 425 n
World War I, 79 n, 80, 175, 187, 209 n, 223, 226, 231, 233, 234, 237, 247, 251, 256, 261, 273, 278 n, 284, 290, 298, 299, 351, 422, 424–25, 447, 479; Black men and, 254–55, 306–7, 365–67, 443–44
World War II, 267
Wright, Arthur D., 456
Wright, Carroll Davidson, 40, 122
    to: 41–43
Wright, Louis T., 416 n, 478
Wynes, Charles E., 399 n

Yale Review, 107
Yale University, 111, 115, 344, 462
Young, Charles, 221, 223 n, 357
    from: 222–23
Young, Donald, 439 n

Young Judea of America, 465
Young Men's Christian Association, 262, 352; in New York, 256; Colored Men's Branch, Indianapolis, 249; Southern College of, 313

Young, P. N., 318
  to: 318–19
Young Women's Christian Association, 262